THE

Peter Collier

with DAVID HOROWITZ

S I M O N   &   S C H U S T E R

New York   London   Toronto   Sydney   Tokyo   Singapore

ROOSEVELTS

An American Saga

SIMON & SCHUSTER
Rockefeller Center
1230 Avenue of the Americas
New York, New York 10020

Designed by Karolina Harris
Picture sections designed by Liney Li

Manufactured in the United States of America

2   3   4   5   6   7   8   9   10

Library of Congress Cataloging-in-Publication Data
Collier, Peter.
The Roosevelts : an American saga / Peter Collier with David Horowitz.
p.   cm.
Includes bibliographical references (p.) and index.
1. Roosevelt family.   II. Title.
E747.C66   1994
94-5729
929.7'0973—dc20   CIP

ISBN: 0-671-65225-7

To my son
Nicholas Tyrie Collier,
with love and admiration

CONTENTS

OYSTER BAY ROOSEVELTS

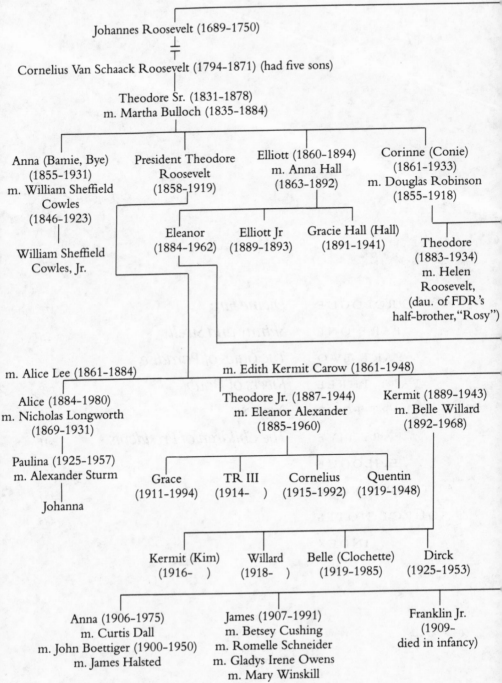

Johannes Roosevelt (1689-1750)

Cornelius Van Schaack Roosevelt (1794-1871) (had five sons)

Theodore Sr. (1831-1878)
m. Martha Bulloch (1835-1884)

Anna (Bamie, Bye)
(1855-1931)
m. William Sheffield
Cowles
(1846-1923)

President Theodore
Roosevelt
(1858-1919)

Elliott (1860-1894)
m. Anna Hall
(1863-1892)

Corinne (Conie)
(1861-1933)
m. Douglas Robinson
(1855-1918)

William Sheffield
Cowles, Jr.

Eleanor
(1884-1962)

Elliott Jr
(1889-1893)

Gracie Hall (Hall)
(1891-1941)

Theodore
(1883-1934)
m. Helen
Roosevelt,
(dau. of FDR's
half-brother, "Rosy")

m. Alice Lee (1861-1884)

m. Edith Kermit Carow (1861-1948)

Alice (1884-1980)
m. Nicholas Longworth
(1869-1931)

Theodore Jr. (1887-1944)
m. Eleanor Alexander
(1885-1960)

Kermit (1889-1943)
m. Belle Willard
(1892-1968)

Paulina (1925-1957)
m. Alexander Sturm

Grace
(1911-1994)

TR III
(1914-   )

Cornelius
(1915-1992)

Quentin
(1919-1948)

Johanna

Kermit (Kim)
(1916-   )

Willard
(1918-   )

Belle (Clochette)
(1919-1985)

Dirck
(1925-1953)

Anna (1906-1975)
m. Curtis Dall
m. John Boettiger (1900-1950)
m. James Halsted

James (1907-1991)
m. Betsey Cushing
m. Romelle Schneider
m. Gladys Irene Owens
m. Mary Winskill

Franklin Jr.
(1909-
died in infancy)

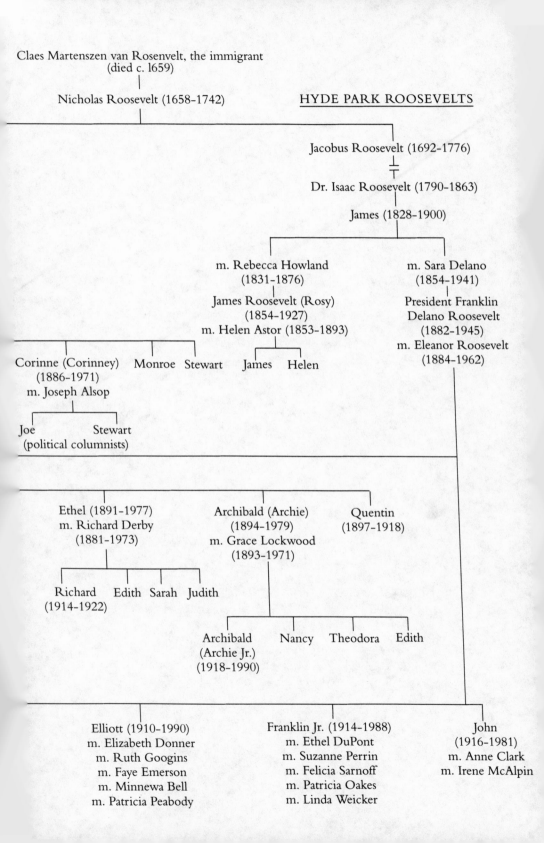

Claes Martenszen van Rosenvelt, the immigrant
(died c. 1659)

Nicholas Roosevelt (1658–1742)

HYDE PARK ROOSEVELTS

Jacobus Roosevelt (1692–1776)

Dr. Isaac Roosevelt (1790–1863)

James (1828–1900)

m. Rebecca Howland
(1831–1876)

James Roosevelt (Rosy)
(1854–1927)
m. Helen Astor (1853–1893)

m. Sara Delano
(1854–1941)

President Franklin
Delano Roosevelt
(1882–1945)
m. Eleanor Roosevelt
(1884–1962)

Corinne (Corinney)   Monroe   Stewart   James   Helen
(1886–1971)
m. Joseph Alsop

Joe   Stewart
(political columnists)

Ethel (1891–1977)   Archibald (Archie)   Quentin
m. Richard Derby   (1894–1979)   (1897–1918)
(1881–1973)   m. Grace Lockwood
                           (1893–1971)

Richard   Edith   Sarah   Judith
(1914–1922)

Archibald   Nancy   Theodora   Edith
(Archie Jr.)
(1918–1990)

Elliott (1910–1990)   Franklin Jr. (1914–1988)   John
m. Elizabeth Donner   m. Ethel DuPont   (1916–1981)
m. Ruth Googins   m. Suzanne Perrin   m. Anne Clark
m. Faye Emerson   m. Felicia Sarnoff   m. Irene McAlpin
m. Minnewa Bell   m. Patricia Oakes
m. Patricia Peabody   m. Linda Weicker

"I don't care for the Henry James kind of ghosts. I want real sepulchral ghosts, the kind that knock you over and eat fire; ghosts which are ghosts and none of your weak shallow apparitions."

—THEODORE ROOSEVELT

Divine Fire

ST. PATRICK'S DAY, 1905

*I*t was after the big parade had ended and the spectators, many of them still carrying the little Irish flags they had spent the morning waving at the line of march, had begun to disperse throughout the city, when another crowd began to form outside the stately townhouse on East 76th Street where a wedding was about to take place. Police had cordoned off Fifth Avenue and Madison Avenue and were checking the credentials of the people asking to be let through. Carriages came through the checkpoints to deposit well-dressed guests at the front steps and hurry off. The appearance of an occasional horseless carriage caused a surge of excitement.

Fugitive sounds of fiddles and sweet tenor voices coming from private parties throughout the city could be heard in the background. This event did not have anything to do with the wearing of the green, but it had its own ethnic implications. Although it was not possible to tell by their appearance, many of the guests at the wedding were descendants of the Dutch colonists who had arrived in the New World two hundred and fifty years earlier. Their material and social success since then might stand in stark contrast to the experience of the Irish, whose travails were the subtext of this St. Patrick's Day celebration, yet these Knickerbockers had retained a clannish sense of identity all their own. Indeed, the man and woman about to be married, Franklin and Eleanor Roosevelt, were cousins with the same last name. They were distinguished from each other by coming from different branches of the family tree, whose places of origin were Hyde Park and Oyster Bay, but united by larger affinities of kinship that one outsider tried to define when he said that "whenever two Roosevelts met, each talked vociferously and ceaselessly to the other, paying no attention to what anyone else had to say."

In time, when these two branches had fallen out and were engaged in one of most celebrated feuds of American politics, self-defined experts, exaggerating the differences, would claim that the Oyster Bay branch were REW-sevelts and the Hyde Park clan were ROSE-velts. In fact, the name was the same for both of them. It came from the Dutch "field of roses," and many of the household items owned by both branches of the family—christening gowns, book plates, linens—were embroidered and printed and embossed with cascades of buds and petals.

For most of their time in America, the Roosevelts had been too busy to look back, too busy making money and becoming part of the civic life of the emerging nation. But recently they had arrived at a summit that allowed family elders to employ genealogists to examine the past that had resulted in such a flowering.

Rather than noble antecedents the researches led to a shadowy figure named Claes Martenszen van Rosenvelt—"our *very* common ancestor," in Theodore Roosevelt's phrase—who had left his Dutch homeland for the New World in the mid-1600s. Claes settled in New Amsterdam, where his name first appears in civic records as *Cleyn Claesie,* "little Claes," and he died sometime before 1660, when these records began to refer to his children as orphans whose name was changed to Roosevelt by an orphanmaster.

His only son, Nicholas, was a boy when New Amsterdam was transformed into New York. As a young man he disappeared into the upstate wilderness as a fur trapper. By the time he was middle-aged, Nicholas Roosevelt was back in New York, married and with eight children of his own. He opened a mill near the waterfront and was elected alderman in 1700. The first Roosevelt to hold public office in America, he was also the first to be removed—for making "very violent and passionate expressions" against the mayor.

The Dutch had come to the New World neither as adventurers nor religious zealots but as merchants whose first act, after erecting a fort, was to build a counting house. Two of Nicholas's children, Johannes and Jacobus, born in 1689 and 1692, were the first Roosevelts to begin the journey toward wealth and power. They would become the Romulus and Remus of the family.

Johannes became a merchant who was granted a monopoly to manufacture linseed oil and who also supervised some of the construction projects that began to define Manhattan in the early 1700s. He served on dozens of municipal committees. He imported paintings and furnishings from Holland and his house was regarded by his fellow citizens as a "wonderland." Meanwhile, his brother Jacobus invested his money in real estate, including the Beekman Swamp, adjacent to the land where City Hall sat by the time of the marriage of Franklin and Eleanor.

Between them, the brothers (who had Anglicized their names to John and James by the end of their lives) sired twenty-two children, most of whom survived the plagues and pestilences of New York to found prolific families of their own.

A dominant line of Johannes's heirs had moved within Manhattan toward destinations like Greenwich Village where they could re-create the small-village identity they'd enjoyed upon first arriving at Manhattan, far from the teeming immigrants who continued to pour into the city after they themselves were established. Eventually they went to Long Island to rent summer homes and then established substantial country residences. This line produced Eleanor. Meanwhile, some of Jacobus's heirs wandered north and picked up a life of bucolic ease as gentlemen farmers along the Hudson. This line produced Franklin.

After five generations, the founding brothers were now joined together once again on this St. Patrick's Day.

Writing a few years before this wedding, the Roosevelts' fellow Knickerbocker Mrs. Schuyler van Rensalaer noted patronizingly in her *History of New York in the Seventeenth Century* that "at no pre-Revolutionary period was the Roosevelt family conspicuous nor did any member of it attain distinction." Technically she was right, but the Hyde Park branch might have pointed out that Franklin's great-grandfather Isaac ("Isaac the Patriot") had been a friend of Alexander Hamilton and an important enough figure in the independence movement to have attended the Constitutional Convention in New York and get his portrait painted by Gilbert Stuart. But by 1905 the point was moot, since one man had remedied whatever deficit of notoriety had existed among the Roosevelts by making the name world-famous and initiating that half century of power and glory which would become the Roosevelt time in America's national life. It was this man the crowd outside the brownstone had gathered to see.

As the time of the ceremony drew closer and people inside the townhouse began to look around nervously, Theodore Roosevelt, the President of the United States, made his usual dramatic appearance when his open landau pulled up and he jumped out energetically still wearing the limp shamrock on his lapel that had already served him through two speeches that morning. Giving a choppy wave to the crowd and flashing the famous clenched smile, he took the steps of the brownstone two at a time. His irreverent daughter Alice said that he was the sort of man who wanted to be the corpse at every funeral he attended and the groom at every wedding, but today his role was circumscribed—to give away the bride, his niece.

The townhouse on East 76th Street, owned by one of Eleanor's cousins on her mother's side, had a drawing room that could accommodate two hundred guests. On this day it was perfumed by a sea of white lilac and clematis. Pink roses intertwined with palm leaves formed a bower where the vows would be exchanged. Standing near the altar was Franklin, tall and strikingly handsome at twenty-three and the one Roosevelt present who really looked like a patrician. He had already thrown the schedule slightly off by gossiping too long with the Reverend Endicott Peabody, his old headmaster at Groton and educator of his entire Roosevelt generation.

As the small orchestra played background music to subtly drown out the ghostly sounds of Irish jigs and drinking songs wafting into the house, Franklin rushed to get into his place. Then there was an elongated pause before the service began. Momentarily frozen, the wedding party looked for an instant like one of those tableaux vivants that were all the rage at New York society functions.

As the guests evaluated the main figures, their eyes naturally went to the President himself. He was a man who had worked hard to make himself larger than life and had succeeded, although some of those present must have noted that while his barrel chest and bull neck gave the impression of robust size when he stood alone, he was actually shorter than his niece Eleanor, and his feet, a dainty size seven, were a little smaller than hers.

TR believed that the ideal life was lived equally in the active and contemplative realms. As the Hero of San Juan Hill, he was well known as a figure of adventure and action. But he was also author of a handful of books, some of which like *The Winning of the West* were already acknowledged as classics. He was a great talker and reader whose intelligence was dominated by a prodigious memory. When a journalist who was once watching him reading an abstruse volume on genetics in the middle of a multitude of distractions commented that he couldn't possibly be retaining anything, Roosevelt had immediately handed him the volume and demanded to be examined. The journalist, shocked to find that the President recalled whole pages almost verbatim, later called it "one of the most extraordinary mental feats I ever saw."

The novelist Henry James once called Roosevelt "a wonderful little machine" running almost on perpetual motion. (Roosevelt's assessment of James was less subtle and less flattering: "His polished, pointless, uninteresting stories about the upper social classes of England make one blush to admit that he was once an American.") But if TR was a machine, he was more than the sum of the parts that made him go. He had infused an ardor into his life that spilled over into the lives of those close to him. People talked constantly of his "electric quality," perhaps, as one Roosevelt watcher noted, because being near him made them tingle.

If TR was the commanding figure, one of the subtly controlling figures slightly in the background of the wedding scene was Franklin's mother, Sara. When the Roosevelts talked among themselves of little Claes and Johannes and Jacobus and all the other Dutchmen in their past, she was apt to note dryly that one of her ancestors on her mother's side, Isaac Allerton by name, had come over on the *Mayflower*. She also liked to talk about her own family, the Delanos, and how they had made two fortunes in the China trade—one lost and the other saved—although she never mentioned that opium had been one of their chief commodities.

Somewhat stout now, although still "handsome" in the parlance of the day, Sara had been a great beauty when she was a girl, and had, in fact, been wooed by Stanford White—fortunately for her reputation, unsuccessfully, since the debauched architect was later killed by Harry Thaw, one of his cuckolds. While still young, Sara had married James Roosevelt of Hyde Park, a descendant of the Jacobus line who was almost twice her age. She had devoted herself to him and especially to their only child, Franklin. Even before the death of James, Sara had dominated her son remorselessly. Since his engagement to Eleanor she had made it clear that she did not regard Franklin's marriage as a development that would change the extent of her involvement in his life.

If Sara had an opposite number among the Oyster Bay Roosevelts, it was the President's monumentally composed wife, Edith. Her widely spaced eyes took in everything; but her face rarely showed more than a ripple of emotion. She had been TR's neighbor and close friend when they were growing up and had married him after the tragic death of his first wife. She was perhaps less obvious than Sara in attaining her ends, but no less successful. She was the only person who, simply by saying the President's first name in a certain intonation, could make him stop talking and blush defensively.

By rights, all eyes should have been on the bride, but Eleanor seemed of secondary importance even on this her day of days. She wore the wedding gown of her mother, Anna Hall—long-sleeved heavy satin with tulle at the neck—along with a dog collar of pearls from her future mother-in-law and a gold watch from Franklin. But she also wore an air of patient suffering that was uniquely her own. At twenty years of age, Eleanor had come to accept the fact that nothing belonged to her, not even the tragedy of her growing up. Everyone in the room knew the story—how her mother had died young, a bitter and humiliated woman abandoned by her husband, Elliott, a once-promising man who had himself died a drunk and profligate after languishing half a lifetime in the Olympian shadow of his brother Theodore. They knew that Eleanor had been raised a demi-orphan dependent on the kindness of relatives who had provided her with places to live but never with a home. She was neither fully a part of her father's family nor of her mother's. "Little Nell," the pet name her father gave her, captured perfectly the Dickensian pathos of her situation.

In addition to other woes, Eleanor was betrayed by her appearance. The velvety gray eyes were appealingly vulnerable, but for the rest, the President's wife, Edith, had captured it years earlier in a letter to a relative: "Poor little soul, she is very plain. Her mouth and teeth seem to have no future." Eleanor had first met Franklin when she was two years old and had seen him intermittently at gatherings of the extended Roosevelt clan since then. She was even more surprised than the rest of the family when he began to court her. After accepting his proposal, she had experienced one of her frequent crises of confidence. "I shall never be able to hold him," she had sobbed to the President's daughter Ethel at one point in the engagement. "He is too attractive."

Her deep compassion was one aspect of her appeal for him, the ability to focus an intense care and concern on those with whom she sympathized. But another one of her attractions was her closeness to the President. Franklin was proud of the traditions of his own branch of the family, and had in fact designed diamond stickpins with the three-feathered family crest of the Hyde Park Roosevelts for his ushers matching plumed headdresses for Eleanor's ladies-in-waiting. Yet me even than other young men of his generation his imagination had bee. galvanized by the President. He had lost his own father early in his life and TR had become a shadowy surrogate. After the stirring victory in Cuba, Franklin had adopted a gold pince-nez exactly like the one his cousin had worn in the charge up San Juan Hill, and for a long time afterward, things that were good he termed "Bully."

After what she regarded as altogether too much talk about the Roosevelts, his mother once snapped, "He is a Delano, he is not a Roosevelt at all." But Franklin felt differently. His engagement to Eleanor had brought him closer to the charmed circle of the TR family. The President himself was enthusiastic about the union. He had written Franklin effusive letters and invited the couple to attend the ceremonies marking the beginning of his second term. This event had taken place just two weeks ago, and Franklin was gratified to have felt part of the excitement surrounding the First Family.

Yet even though at times they had grown tantalizingly close to the TR clan, since their decision to marry, Eleanor and Franklin remained outsiders. Indeed, the power of the President and his immediate family was such that it almost made the two of them secondary figures at their own wedding. Onlookers couldn't help, for instance, but compare Eleanor with her bridesmaid and cousin, the President's striking daughter Alice. There was a certain congruence of circumstance between the two young women. Alice's mother, TR's first wife, Alice Lee, had died shortly after she was born. Alice too had been raised by aunts and grandparents; and she and Eleanor had, in fact, spent long periods of time together as children. Yet while Eleanor lapsed into a limbo of uncertainty and self-denial, Alice had grown up with petulant good looks, a biting wit, and a saucy personality whose arabesques the American people followed with a cultlike fascination. Popular songs were named after her; a certain shade of blue had become wildly popular because it was associated with her. She was "Princess Alice," the most eligible young woman in the country," and her name was linked romantically with European princes and American patricians.

Some said, in fact, that there had been a flirtation between Alice and Franklin. But it was actually she who had first forced him to notice her wallflower cousin Eleanor, years earlier when they were all teenagers at a dance. Now that they were getting married, one malicious observer had noted, it would be economical for Alice since she could condescend ɔth at once instead of separately. Eleanor's histrionic self-doubts she ɩnd tiresome. And Franklin was not only too much under the thumb ᴑf his imperious mother, Sara, whom Alice termed a "domineering tartar," but he was also a little *too* handsome, too much like the stylized figures used for advertising purposes on men's handkerchief boxes. Behind his back she called him "Miss Nancy" because he "pranced and fluttered." (It was a cruel cut, but after all, his own friends at Harvard had called him "Rosey Roosevelt, Lily of the Valley" for the same reason.) Always looking to draw a sharp line between her branch of the family and his, Alice pointed out that *her* Roosevelts liked to *row,* even in the hottest weather; and Franklin did nothing but *sail.*

The distinction would have made sense to the President's sons, who were also at the wedding, and who, knowing that Franklin had a tendency to refer to himself as F. D. Roosevelt, sometimes joked among themselves that the initials must actually stand for "Feather Duster." Young Ted, TR's eldest boy, was the groom's opposite, six years younger, but at eighteen already an apostle of his father's vision of the Strenuous Life. He was small but sinewy, his face featuring a nose flattened in football and fistfights at Groton and Harvard, activities in which Franklin would later claim also to have engaged, although he hadn't. Moreover, Ted would succeed socially, like his father, by being invited to join Harvard's exclusive Porcellian Club, whose members had already rejected Franklin, causing him perhaps the greatest unhappiness of his life.

Ted and his brothers and sisters had not only come of age in the public eye; they were, in a sense, America's family. Everyone in the country, it seemed, had read about the first hunting trip of TR's second son, Kermit; laughed at Ethel's energetic tomboy qualities; agonized over Archie when diphtheria had him at death's doorstep; and followed the exploits of little Quentin, the impish Tom Sawyer of the White House, who walked through the living quarters on stilts and pelted Secret Service men with snowballs.

The unique "bee-line" hikes on which the President led his children at their Sagamore Hill estate on Long Island's Oyster Bay were a sort of metaphor for his view of life. On these hikes, the object was to follow TR in walking, climbing, crawling, or swimming over, but never going around, what lay directly ahead. (As they hiked, they often chanted, "Over, under, through, but never around!") The children went exactly where he led them, seeing themselves as a small tribe whose laws were an outgrowth of the meaning he had extracted from his experience.

TR's friend Rudyard Kipling, who had sat at their dinner table many times, might well have had their worldview in mind when he wrote in *The Jungle Book,* "For the strength of the pack is the wolf/And the strength of the wolf is the pack."

This family, the First Family, was an outgrowth of the family TR had been born into along with Eleanor's father, Elliott. Many who knew *that* family had regarded its members as destined for greatness, "so uniquely gifted [in the words of one young woman] as to seem . . . touched by 'divine fire.' " That fire was still burning brightly in TR. The question for Franklin and Ted and all the other young Roosevelts at the wedding was clear. What was in this famous name? Who would be ignited by the sparks TR threw off? How did one seize and extend the heritage this President had established?

Ultimately, finding an answer to these questions would break the Roosevelts into warring factions and cause a family civil war with almost Homeric overtones that would dominate and define American politics for a generation. But for the time being such vexing issues of identity and succession were held in check by the overwhelming presence of the President himself. Indeed, the minute the orchestra finally began the wedding march, TR set the scene in motion again, briskly descending the staircase with Eleanor on his arm, exuding energy and purpose and looking as though he would have liked to walk faster than the ceremony allowed. When they reached the altar and the Reverend Peabody asked, "Who giveth this woman?" he boomed, *"I* do!" Then, after the vows had been exchanged, he clapped the groom on the back with a force that made him wince and said, "Well, Franklin, there's nothing like keeping the name in the family!" Then he headed off to the dining room—one observer used the word "galloped" to describe his movement—where his loud laugh and high-pitched voice could be heard as all the guests, even Franklin's mother, followed and surrounded him there.

The bride and groom were left standing almost alone. Later on when they opened their presents they found that their gift from their "noble kinsman," as Sara Delano Roosevelt was wont to call the President, was a Dutch genre painting. What they did not know was that someone had given it to TR when he was governor of New York in the belief that it might call up for him the rich heritage running in his veins. But Theodore, always more interested in deeds than in bloodlines, had pronounced the painting boring, and the thrifty Edith, not wanting to waste the gift, decided that they might as well pass it on to the newlyweds, who probably wouldn't realize that it was a hand-me-down.

PART ONE

Skinny and Swelly

"Thee is so able and no mistake—shrewd and clever,
by no means behind the age. What I have often smiled at
in the Old Boy are I am now sure some of his best
points—a practical carrying out in action of what I,
for example, am convinced of in theory but fail to
put into practice."

—ELLIOTT ROOSEVELT

$\mathcal{A}$ remarkable photograph in the Theodore Roosevelt collection at Harvard's Houghton Library shows Abraham Lincoln's funeral procession passing through New York on the way to the train that would complete the long journey home to Illinois. The shot, taken as the procession moved through the Union Square area, captures both the formal solemnity of the occasion and the life of the street. The caisson carrying the coffin has not yet come into view, but an honor guard of infantry in blocky formation follows a straggling line of riders up ahead. People dressed in black line both sides of the street four or five deep. A few of the spectators, hoping to secure a better vantage, have climbed up onto ledges beneath the recessed windows of a commercial building.

There were probably other shots of this scene taken at about the same moment. But in this one the anonymous photographer also captured an arresting accidental detail: two tiny heads poking out of the second-story window of an elegant brownstone. They are six-year-old Theodore Roosevelt and his younger brother, Elliott, four, looking down at the scene below. Their faces are framed by the shutters of the window in a way that suggests a depth of field, thus inviting the eye to enter the dark room behind them, the private world of the Roosevelts.

The brownstone belonged to the boys' grandfather, Cornelius Van Schaack Roosevelt, a great-grandson of Johannes, one of the two founding brothers of the Roosevelt clan, and at the time of Lincoln's death the most prominent member of the family. He was a short man with reddish hair and a large head. (One acquaintance had said of him, "His appearance suggested to me a Hindoo idol roughly carved in red porphyry.") His eyes magnified by thick spectacles, C.V.S., as he was known, was a man of few words whose face wore the stern and inquiring look of a bookkeeper with power. The look was one that had settled on him as a result of a life devoted to the art of the bottom line, but it was probably also congenital. The one moment of frivolity anyone recalled from his childhood occurred one Sunday in his youth when C.V.S. was going home after attending his second church service of the day. He came upon a party of pigs, which ran free in the streets of New York in those days, and on a whim he mounted a huge boar that promptly turned and bolted, carrying him back at full tilt directly into the outraged members of the congregation gathered outside the Dutch Reformed Church he had just left. Those who did not move quickly were bowled over.

Afterward, C.V.S. moved steadily through life establishing a record as a conservative man, thrifty and enterprising. As far as anyone knew, his only other unusual act was becoming the first Roosevelt of his line to marry a non-Dutch woman, a Quaker named Margaret Barnhill. When they were first engaged, he wrote her, "Economy is my doctrine at all times, at all events till I become, if it is to be so, *a man of fortune.*" It was couched as a caveat emptor, but it became a prophecy, the underlined words indicating the emphatic nature of the wish. C.V.S. took the family investment firm, Roosevelt and Son, which had been founded by his grandfather, into new areas of enterprise, making it the largest importer of plate glass in the city. He also bought up land all over Manhattan during the Panic of 1837. Five years later he was worth $250,000, and three years after that his net worth had doubled. In 1868 when a newspaper listed the names of Manhattan's handful of millionaires, the name Cornelius Van Schaack Roosevelt was among them.

Although a man of the new age, C.V.S. tried to maintain the old ways where his family was concerned, bringing his five boys into his business and reminding them of their heritage. (When TR, nearly fifty, visited Africa in 1909 and recited a Dutch rhyme for a contingent of Boers he met there, it was a fragment he had retained from Sunday afternoons with his grandfather.) He was, in a sense, the last Dutch Roosevelt.

The sons of C.V.S. were such energetic youngsters that family and friends began referring to their mother as "that lovely Mrs. Roosevelt with those five horrid boys." They spoke a language all their own. As Silas, the oldest of the boys, said later on, "A Stranger must be somewhat scandalized by the sudden fits we take of irony, cordiality . . . sense and nonsense, which succeed each other without apparent connection or warning approach."

All of the sons of C.V.S. had acquired their father's gravity by the time they went forth into the world. All had significant achievements as lawyers and businessmen, directors of banks and railroads. One of them, Robert Barnwell Roosevelt, was a writer, newspaper editor, and politician, who changed his middle name from Barnhill to escape jokes about manure when he ran for and was elected to the U.S. House of Representatives. He fought Boss Tweed and became a pioneering conservationist. But it was Theodore, youngest of the boys (and later called the *first* Theodore Roosevelt to distinguish him from his more famous son), who strayed furthest from his father's expectations.

Like his brothers, Theodore stopped off to see his mother every morning on his way to work and joined his father for dinner every Saturday evening. If he was different from the others, it was because he was less adept at making money and less interested in extending the reach of the family business. As the youngest, he had more latitude to explore personal values. He traveled widely at home and abroad. Unwilling to look at the world through plate glass, he began while still young to do volunteer work in New York charities, which provided him with a clear view of the social disorganization caused by the sudden glut of immigrants and the pell-mell urbanization remaking the city. Without knowing it at the time, he had stumbled on what became his life's calling.

Perhaps influenced by the "inner light" of his mother's Quaker background, Theodore had a "troublesome conscience" of his own that not only drew him to social problems but also made him more anxious to give money away than make it. Made wealthy by the hard work of C.V.S., Theodore made the transition from business to philanthropy while still in his thirties, becoming one of a small group of men who founded the American Museum of Natural History, the Metropolitan Museum of Art, and other cultural institutions. But his primary interest was in relieving human misery. He helped begin the Newsboys' Lodging House to benefit thousands of urchins who survived by selling papers, and was deeply involved in such organizations as Miss Sattery's Night School for Little Italians.

He wanted to do good, but he was also drawn to the compelling human interest of the netherworld of human suffering he discovered, a world that, if not for his "social work," would have remained as invisible to him as it was to most in his class. "My boys at the Lodging Home were very interesting tonight," he once wrote his son Elliott after spending an evening with the newsboys. "One little fellow eight years old was particularly so, as he had neither father nor mother and felt perfectly able to care for himself. He described how a policeman had 'bringed' him to the Station House once but seemed not quite sure which particular crime it was for."

He was a handsome man, powerfully built with a big head and shaggy beard inevitably described as "leonine." (When still a boy, his son and namesake Teddy, punning on the metaphor, called the first Theodore "a handsome and good natured lion.") He was filled with such charismatic energy that one contemporary referred to him as "a force of nature." There was such an obsessive quality to his philanthropy that a family friend called it a "maniacal benevolence."

The first Theodore would never know the extent to which he had altered individual lives, but almost a quarter century after his death, when his son, then governor of New York, joined some of his colleagues at a conference, Joseph Brady, the governor of Alaska Territory, made a point of seeking him out. While others might greet him as the head of a great state, Brady said, he wanted to shake TR's hand because he was the son of the first Theodore Roosevelt. He went on to describe how as a boy he had been picked up off the streets of New York by TR's father, who placed him in a home in the West, paying for his travel there and periodically checking on his progress as he grew up. The first Theodore Roosevelt, Governor Brady said, had made him who he was.

All the five boys of C.V.S. relied on the women they married for emotional subtlety. Theodore's brother and next-door neighbor Robert (C.V.S. had bought them connected houses at 20th Street and Broadway to keep the family together) had a wife who was a full-fledged eccentric. Elizabeth, or Aunt Lizzy, as the first Theodore's children knew her, kept a menagerie of animals in her enclosed yard, including a cow that had to be carried there in a sling through her living room. There was also a monkey named Topsy that she dressed in brocaded shirts, gold studs, and trousers. Theodore's oldest child, Anna, would remember Topsy as having a "violent temperament," and indeed she once suffered an attack by the monkey while carrying a message through the passageway linking the two houses. Hearing her screams, Aunt

Lizzy came running, but was less worried by the teeth marks on the girl's arm than by the emotional trauma possibly suffered by her pet. "Poor Topsy," she cooed, as the monkey stood on top of a dresser chittering angrily and tearing off all the miniature clothes except for the pants, which caught on his tail, thus driving him to even greater rage.

The woman Theodore married would, in time, become almost as peculiar as Aunt Lizzy. She was Martha Bulloch, a Southern belle from Roswell, Georgia. Called Mittie, she was a captivating beauty whose bisque skin nested in thick dark hair. ("Sweet little Dresden China Mother," her son Elliott would call her.) The Bulloch heritage exhaled the antebellum scent of Southern gentility and was exemplified by a Greek Revival plantation home, Bulloch Hall, which some claimed was one of the models for Tara in Margaret Mitchell's *Gone with the Wind*.

Mittie's forebears on her father's side included a representative to the Continental Congress as well as an assortment of duelists and desperate men. On her mother's side one particularly notable figure was Archibald Stobo, a minister who had migrated to Panama late in the seventeenth century with other Scottish religious dissidents to found the utopian community they intended to call New Caledonia. Eventually the colonists were driven out by the Spanish. Trying to get back to Scotland, they anchored outside Charleston, South Carolina, to take on supplies. Because he was an ordained minister, Stobo was asked to come ashore to perform a marriage. While he was there a violent storm arose, sinking his ship and drowning the other colonists and leaving him beached in a different part of the New World than the one he had set out for. His daughter married one James Bulloch, another Scot newly arrived in America, and they went off to Savannah to live, establishing a family that had, by Mittie's time, become prominent in Georgia's civic life.

In 1850, the first Theodore, then nineteen, traveled to the South and met the Bullochs through an introduction provided by an in-law of his elder brother Silas. Mittie, then fifteen, thought him stuffy; and for his part, Theodore was bothered by the fact that the first face he saw at Bulloch Hall was that of "Toy," the slave about Mittie's age who had slept at the foot of her bed since she was a little girl. After this cool introduction, he saw Mittie again three years later when she was touring the North. In a more hospitable environment, Theodore wooed and won her. When they were married at Bulloch Hall in 1855, Mittie's mother sold four slaves to pay for the wedding.

Returning to New York with her husband, Mittie brought with her a feel for the mythic and grandiose, an imaginative dimension that was not otherwise part of the Roosevelt mentality. It was expressed in the stories she told her children, tales filled with sentimentality and Southern gothic, as well as the derring-do of high adventure.

Her moods oscillated between deep melancholy and febrile gaiety, yet her Roosevelt in-laws quickly learned that it did Mittie an injustice to regard her merely as a vaporish daughter of the South. On one well-remembered occasion the horses pulling her carriage were spooked and bolted, unseating the driver. As the vehicle careened wildly through the streets of New York, bystanders stepped up to try to stop the team but were thrown back. Finally, after a terrifying ride, the horses reached the Roosevelt home, dashed into their stable and ran into a wall in a crash that killed one of the team. By the time servants caught up, Mittie was out of the carriage dusting herself off. "Will you hand me my card case, James?" she coolly asked one of them, as if she had just arrived by plan.

She and Theodore had four children in quick succession, each with nicknames serving almost as clan designations. Anna, who was not only "Bye" but "Bamie" (from *bambina*), was born in 1855 with the physical deformity of a curved spine but what everyone agreed was a "large soul" that would eventually make her one of the most respected women of the age. Three years later came the future President, Theodore, who was called "Teedie" and sometimes "Thee." Elliott, whom everyone agreed was the sweetest one in the family and who would move through his life with his brother in an odd and tragic *pas de deux* that defined them both, was "Ellie." In 1861, a year after his birth, came Corinne, or "Conie," the baby of the family, who was both the most sensitive of the Roosevelt children and also the most sentimental.

Friends remarked on how the first Theodore had to baby Mittie almost as much as his children. His uxoriousness, which might otherwise have been just an amusing eccentricity, took on a tragic aspect with the coming of the Civil War. He was caught in the tension between Mittie and his own abolitionist-minded parents. (Mittie's eldest child, Bamie, later said of her mother: "I shudder to think of what she must have suffered . . . [because] the Roosevelts think they are just but they are hard.") The pleasurable Sunday dinners at the home of C.V.S. became ordeals of silence. On many evenings when Mittie was expected to help entertain her husband's friends and associates, she instead stayed upstairs and ate with the children in the nursery to avoid having to defend once again her Southern sympathies.

Mittie did not simply pine, however. She had brought her mother and sister to live with her in New York, where circumstances forced on them the identity of conspirators. When Theodore was gone, the Bulloch women rolled bandages and packed supplies under a surreptitiously unfurled Confederate flag while whispering about the real and imagined victories of The Cause.

Hoping to head off the conflict inside his family, Theodore had joined other prominent New Yorkers in petitioning Congress against the war at its onset. He did not enlist because of what he referred to as his "peculiar circumstances": Mittie had brothers fighting for the Confederacy and it was a remote but terrifying possibility that Theodore might kill or be killed by one of them if he went into battle. Instead, he hired a substitute to serve in the army in his place. Others of his class did the same thing, but this act, although necessary, was deeply at odds with Theodore's sense of principle. As his daughter Bamie said later, "He always afterward felt that he had done a very great wrong in not having put every other feeling aside and joined the fighting forces."

Theodore tried to serve the Union by bringing his philanthropic concerns to the war. Designing a program that would encourage soldiers to send their pay home and thus ease the privations of their families, he spent months in Washington, frequently meeting with Lincoln himself. (Although much shorter, he was, in fact, more than once mistaken for the President in walking down the street with White House secretary John Hay.) Theodore became such a favorite of the peculiar Mrs. Lincoln that she sometimes wrote him a note (spelling his name "Rosevalt") asking him to escort her when she went to town to buy bonnets.

"I know you will not regret having me do what is right," Theodore wrote Mittie in one rather plaintive letter, "and I don't believe you will love me any the less for it." But back home there was tense ambiguity. The war that had divided the nation was dividing the consciousness of his family. The consequences were especially apparent in little Teedie, who seemed to have caught faint echoes of his father's dilemma. Once during the war the women in the household dressed him in a miniature Zouave outfit for a photographer and while posing the precocious four-year-old asked, "Are me a soldier laddie, too?" His mother's sister, Aunt Anna, told him that he was indeed a little soldier and he promptly saluted her. But he wasn't sure which army he served in. He collaborated in the hushed melodrama of provisioning the Confederates that took place during his father's absences. Yet when he and his brother and sisters went to Central Park to play "Blockade Runner," a game he made up, Teedie insisted always on being the government captain who intercepted the rebels. Later, when he watched the funeral cortege of his hero Lincoln, it was probably not the Great Emancipator that he mourned, but the Commander in Chief of the Armies of the Republic.

As the war ended, it was clear that the wounds the Roosevelts suffered, while perhaps invisible, were deep. Mittie's mother died just as Sherman's men were nearing Bulloch Hall. Mittie herself was still gay and charming, but her behavior was often odd. Increasingly obsessive about cleanliness, she now bathed twice a day and insisted that each bath have two washes and rinses. It was almost as if a part of her was washed away by all this water, for she now drifted off into periods of remoteness. It was now that her children began to use diminutives to refer to her in their letters: "Darling Little Mother" or "Motherkins."

For his part, the first Theodore was left with a guilt for not having fought that would become part of the psychological heritage he passed on to his eldest son, in whom it would become the irritant that eventually produced a pearl.

No mere paper saint, the first Theodore Roosevelt was a man of power as well as compassion. Moving easily in the upper echelons of Knickerbocker society as part of his birthright, he used his charities to join the emerging elite that would define the culture of New York and eventually the entire country in the postwar period. He was a man who gave generously, but also took for granted fine things and good living. When he moved the family from the place at 4th Street and Broadway where Teedie and the others were born to a new house he had built on West 57th Street, it was at immense cost. Yet, there was more than enough money for such indulgences. The first Theodore would spend a fortune on homes and horses, cutting a dandy figure on the bridal paths of Central Park, and yet also have enough left of the inheritance he received from C.V.S. when the old man died in 1871 that he himself would be able to will each of his own children the equivalent of more than $1 million in contemporary dollars upon his own death.

As his children got older, much of that intensity contemporaries noted in Theodore's personality focused on them. He held a daily Bible reading at which they scrambled to get the prized seat on the sofa beside him, the "cubbyhole," as they called it. One of the enduring images of the Roosevelt family was of Theodore's four children lined up on their stomachs on the raised deck of the summer house he rented each year on Long Island as he came by and slipped peach slices into their mouths so adroitly that no juice dripped on their chins. Each one of them looked forward to their birthdays because their father "gave" himself completely for an entire afternoon, doing whatever the child wished.

The Roosevelt children grew up as a little tribe that got all it needed from within. But instead of making them insular and obtuse, this intensity made them appealing for members of the outer world, who envied their charmed circle. In time people who knew them individually would regard each of the first Theodore's children as the most extraordinary person they had ever met. Together they possessed something almost undefinable that seemed from the onset to set them aside from others—a divine fire.

The leader was Bamie. Large-headed and heavy-lidded, misshaped in body and with what one acquaintance regarded as a curiously dark complexion, she had none of Mittie's fragile beauty, but had a power that transcended her defects. She believed that the spinal deformity that her father tried to remedy with torturous back braces and manipulation resulted from having been dropped by some servant in her bath as a baby, but it was probably caused by tuberculosis of the spine. Less because of her disability than because of her courageous response to it, she became her father's favorite. Because of her, he helped found the New York Orthopedic Hospital. One of the few times Teedie could remember being punished by his father was at the age of four when he bit Bamie on the arm and then hid under the kitchen table in an attempt to escape Theodore's wrath. She had a special status with her parents. The other children sometimes called themselves "We Three."

Bamie inserted herself into the vacuum created by Mittie's emotional withdrawal and became the strong feminine figure in the Roosevelt family. Her brother Teedie would later compare Bamie to "a little feminine Atlas" taking the world's problems on her deformed shoulders. She herself was more matter-of-fact, saying simply that she was the family's "odd job man." (In time she would help raise two of the family's semi-orphans—Teddy's first child, Alice, and Elliott's daughter Eleanor.)

But if she inherited her father's "capacity for compassion," she also had an incisive mind that was developed when she went abroad in 1870 to board at a school outside of Paris run by a famous educator named Madame Souvestre who would give her a thought just before each day's rest period and return after two hours to examine her on the different ways she had translated this thought into French. As the other side of her nature, Bamie developed what one family member called a "caustic disapproval" that made people careful with her.

Corinne was less "granitic" than her sister, more volatile and with the youngest child's desire to please. The author of a large body of sentimental poetry that she began as a youngster, Conie was particularly alive to nuance and soon became the most purely social of the children. Later on the family would joke gently about how at dinner parties whoever was sitting next to her got the "elbow in the soup" treatment as she appeared to hang on their every word. One such moment occurred late in her life at Buckingham Palace where she had been invited for dinner. Queen Mary was telling about a recent camping expedition in India and had gotten to the point in her story where she was describing a strange noise she'd heard outside the royal tent. "What was it, ma'am?" Conie blurted out. Annoyed at having her denouement anticipated, the Queen stood up and said huffily, "It could have been a wolf," and then swept out of the room.

Bamie and Conie would eventually rank among the most accomplished women of their time. Yet from childhood, they would accept a position in the shadows of their brothers, Theodore and Elliott, fretting over them, urging them on, basking in the reflected glory of their accomplishments, and suffering with them in their defeats. It was clear to them and to everyone else that the Roosevelt boys would write the next chapter in the family story.

Mittie said that Teedie looked like a "terrapin" when he was born. Ellie, on the other hand, she pronounced "decidedly pretty" as a baby. While Theodore was off on his travels during the Civil War, Mittie wrote to say that Teedie had become "miserably jealous" to find her in bed with his little brother stroking his ears. Teedie had insisted on getting in bed with them. When the baby allowed him to stroke his ears too, four-year-old Teedie said haughtily, "Oh, do look, Mama, how he do obey me." The question of power would always lurk just below the surface of their relationship.

If Teedie was the most imaginative, Ellie was the most lovable of all the children, learning early on that there was power in his charm, a quality he would rely on too heavily later in life. He inherited his mother's high spirits and his father's compassion for the less fortunate. One of the stories the family always told about Ellie—an epiphany of his character when it was still innocent—was how at the age of seven he had gone off in an overcoat on a cold morning and returned later on bareshouldered, having given the coat to a shivering urchin he saw during his walk.

Elliot was lithe and active, exploring his world with a confidence that

sometimes made him seem older than his older brother. He felt protective of Teedie and when he was six wrote their father in alarm that he
had just watched his brother have "a small attack of _____ (I don't
know how to spell it)." The word was "asthma," and throughout his
boyhood it threatened to close up Teedie's lungs and suffocate him. The
attacks came on without warning and terrorized the family, although
the boy himself settled into them with resignation. Each recovery left
him frail and battered. Each new attack brought new intimations of his
mortality. Never voiced, the thought was always there in the minds of
his parents: Teedie might die.

What the worried family—and the sufferer himself—did not see were
the subtle compensations. Young Theodore's acceptance of his plight
allowed him to show his brave endurance; his recoveries allowed him to
show his resourcefulness. His illness became the play within their play
with Teedie taking on the role of director as well as star. It was he who
made his mother stay up all night beside his bed telling him stories with
chivalry and adventure. It was he who caused his father to order up the
carriage in the middle of the night and command the driver to speed
through the darkened streets of New York in an effort to force air into
his failing lungs.

Ellie assaulted the outer world, becoming for Teedie the exemplar of
physical daring. He was the "captain of games," his small dark face alive
to what was happening and what it took to succeed. Teedie watched
him carefully as he was forced to retreat to the world within, temporarily finding himself in thought rather than action.

Reading became his prowess. He also developed a maguslike ability as
a storyteller, using this talent to draw his brothers and sisters and any
other children who happened to be around from their robust outdoor
play into his secondary realm inside the house.

He was curious about how things worked. He captured insects, rodents, and other specimens and took them apart on makeshift dissecting
tables, almost as if by opening them up for examination he might better
understand what was wrong with his own machinery. He drew, cata-
logued, and described what he saw. At the age of eight, when his
mother threw out the corpses of two mice he had stored in the icebox
for future autopsy, he accused her, in a tiny indignant voice, of "defeating the ends of science."

While Ellie was outside with handmade swords and spears, Teedie
often played with his sister Conie and her dolls. One of Conie's friends
who often joined them was their neighbor Edith Carow, a composed

and bookish girl who went to Miss Comstock's School. Edith Carow's own family had gone into a slow decline when her father's business losses sent him into genteel alcoholism and her mother into hypochondria. Yet she had a spirited intelligence that kept her on even footing with the Roosevelt children. The only friend who penetrated their tight circle, she became something like a member of the family. At the age of three, in fact, she had stood for a moment with Ellie and Teedie at the window as Lincoln's funeral procession passed by below, but then the melancholy of the occasion (and the grotesquerie of veterans with all sorts of amputations and deformities) made her cry, and Teedie locked her in a closet so that he and Ellie could concentrate on the mournful spectacle.

When young, the children were tutored by Mittie's sister Anna. In 1869, Theodore decided to give their education another dimension by taking the family to Europe for a year's Grand Tour. They docked in Liverpool and were met by Mittie's brother James, a former Confederate officer still living in proud exile. Ten-year-old Teedie wrote home to Edith: "Conie and I want you very much to play with. The day after we landed we saw our cousins. . . . I do not think you would like them so much because they kiss so much."

Theodore had hoped that a new environment would help Teedie's health. But the asthma flared up suddenly when the family least expected it, causing hurried trips to spas and ascents high into the mountains in search of easier air. The doctors of the Continent were as authoritative as their American counterparts and equally ineffective. In addition to asthma, Teedie continued to suffer from grim bouts of dysentery, a malady referred to within the family by the coded term, "cholera morbus."

Mittie worried to see Teedie sitting alone reading while the other children played. But the journal he kept of his trip showed how rich an experience play was for him when he felt well enough to join in. While they were in Rome, for instance, his imagination transformed a game with sticks that he and Ellie and a boy named Charles played into an intense experience out of one of the epics he read so avidly: "Ellie was on me with his sword and had me on my knees but I hurled him on Charles. I saw, however, that I would be beaten in another battle and I rushed down a steep hill but when we fought again I defeated them and rushed up to another position and again encountered and beat them."

Also clear from the journal was the tendency to dramatize himself and the desire to be at the center of any spectacle. On another afternoon in Rome, the Roosevelts happened to be in the path of the Pope when he appeared in his sedan chair. Teedie hissed to Conie that he didn't "believe in" the Pope, yet when the procession passed by and the Pontiff reached out his hand, Teedie impulsively grabbed and kissed it.

He recorded odd moments in his journal, events that someone else might have regarded as contradictions in his parents, but which to a child's eye were part of an unquestioned continuity. When they were passing through Italy, for instance, his father, who might have been a philanthropist but was no pacifist, violently attacked a monk whom he believed had roughly elbowed Teedie out of the way on the street. Later on in this trip, the first Theodore bought cakes for hungry Italian peasants and then he and his family "fed them like chickens," in Teedie's words, forcing them to give "three cheers for the USA" before they were allowed to gobble up the bits of food.

The chauvinism was infectious. Nine-year-old Elliott, who, along with Teedie and Conie, stayed with a German family to enhance his education while Theodore and Mittie traveled for a while by themselves, wrote his father: "Don't you think that America is the best country in the world? Please when you write tell me if we have not got as good Musick and Arts as the Germans have at the *present* time?"

"New York!!! Hip! Horray!" Teedie wrote when the boat carrying them home docked after their year abroad. But he brought home with him what Mittie called "wheezy miserable nights," and over the next year he wore out remedies the doctors prescribed: coffee and cigars, cups and clysters.

The illness was painful and frightening; the physical weakness it caused was a humiliation. One event he remembered for the rest of his life occurred when he was fourteen and traveling home on a stagecoach from the countryside where he had been sent for pure air. Running afoul of two boys about his age who began to tease him, he tried to stand up to them, but each handled him easily, emphasizing the humiliation by not even bothering to hurt him. Teedie knew that his brother, Ellie, would have been able to give a good account of himself in similar circumstances and he wrote his father a shamed account of the incident.

It was clear that a crisis point had been reached. His father sat him down for a formal discussion: "Theodore, you have the mind but you have not the body, and without the help of the body the mind cannot go as far as it should." He asked Teedie if he would be willing to try to remake himself. The boy promised manfully that he would.

Theodore installed a gymnasium on the second-floor "piazza" of the family home. Because of her disability, Bamie was an observer. But the other three children worked at the swinging bars, weight pulleys, dumbbells, medicine balls. Ellie excelled effortlessly at what became known as the "piazza games." Teedie attacked the exercise equipment with a desperate frenzy. Conie watched with amazement over the months as he slowly transformed his thin chest, broadening it by regular monotonous training.

Slowly he began to change. He was far from robust, but he was no longer pure mind. With his father's approval, he also took boxing lessons from a man named John Long, who saw his natural competitiveness and set up matches with other boys with a pewter mug Teedie coveted as the prize for the championship that he eventually won.

Ellie was his training partner. They rowed and ran; wrestled and boxed. Elliott wrote, "Boxing is one of Teedie's and my favorite amusements; it is such a novelty to see the stars when it is not night." Teedie was still second best but he was becoming competitive. The brothers kept elaborate records of their competitions, referring to themselves in their journals as "Skinny" and "Swelly," names taken from Teedie's thin body and Ellie's easy charm.

After their father introduced them to the outdoors on a trip to the Adirondacks in 1871, they often went tramping together in the woods. Ellie was interested in feats of endurance—long hikes, difficult climbs. Teedie was interested in observation. He became an accomplished ornithologist, able to identify birds by call as well as sight and maintaining elaborate records in which he dissected birdsong into vowels and consonants just as he was dissecting rodents and insects in his makeshift lab at home.

Nature would always have a Wordsworthian quality for him: a place to recreate (and re-*create*) his spirit. But it was also Darwinian. From the moment his father bought him his first firearm, a French double-barreled shotgun, Teedie began to kill things in great numbers, especially after he was fitted for glasses, which brought the world into true focus for the first time. In 1872, when the family went on another leg of its Grand Tour, this time to the Holy Land, Teedie kept meticulous account of the death he caused, winding up with a tally of over two hundred birds. The killing was an act of mastery, and perhaps an odd way of celebrating the power of his own life, which until recently had been in doubt. He also became an accomplished taxidermist, and this allowed him to turn death into transfiguration.

For Ellie, the elder Theodore Roosevelt was discipline and direction, a shining example. For Teedie their father was all this and something more. Later on he would say, in effect, that his father had been responsible for a double act of patrimony, not only giving him life but saving his life as well: "My father—he got me breath. He got me lungs, strength, life." He had in mind all the things that the first Theodore had done for him—the desperate midnight rides, the hurried visits to doctors all over the world, and construction of the home gymnasium—but none more than this stern command to remake his body into a life-bearing vessel capable of holding the luminous intelligence. When TR wrote his *Autobiography* he saw as a completed act the process that unfolded gradually and often with great difficulty throughout his adolescence: "I had to train myself painfully and laboriously, not merely as regards my body but as regards my soul and spirit."

A characteristic letter from teenaged Teedie to Bamie says: "At present I am writing in a rather smelly room, as the fresh skins of six night herons are reposing on the table beside me. . . ." His days were "full of ornithological enjoyment and reptilian rapture." The odor of preserving substances clung to him like an aura. (One well-meaning family maid took a toothbrush with which he applied arsenic to specimens out of his taxidermy kit, rinsed it off, and put it in a drawer for personal use.) He had enough of the absentminded professor about him that Ellie lampooned his unkempt appearance in a limerick:

> There was an old fellow named Teedie
> Whose clothes at best looked so seedy
> That his friends in dismay
> Hollered out, "Oh! I say!"
> At the dirty old fellow named Teedie.

This thrust hurt less than it might have before because the balance of power between the brothers was shifting. They were still Skinny and Swelly—the one far from robust, however much his outlook had improved, and the other still characterized by an abundance of good nature. But Teedie was not only remaking his body but also moving ahead quickly intellectually, excelling in the Greek and Latin lessons given by the tutor his father had hired as well as in the informal but equally demanding regimen he had designed for himself in natural history. Almost as if riding on the opposite end of a seesaw from his brother, Ellie fell a little as Teedie rose. Not only was he unable to keep up with his brother's prodigious intellectual accomplishments, but, more disturbing, now it was *his* health that was declining.

In 1875, when Teedie was beginning to prepare for Harvard, Elliott began to experience fainting spells, "blood rushes to the head," blackouts, and a sudden pain that filled his skull. With odd detachment, he wrote Teedie, "My body is getting so thin I can get a handful of skin right off my stomach, and my arms as well as legs look like I have the strength of a baby. I jump involuntarily at the smallest sound and have a perpetual headache. . . ."

Suspecting that these problems might have something to do with Teedie's new dominance, Theodore decided to send Ellie South to stay awhile with his Bulloch relatives. But even with the boys separated, he continued unconsciously to double-knot the invisible string binding them together. He wrote Elliott to remind him that Teedie was someone worthy of his support, at the same time that he was sending letters to Teedie enjoining him to take care of his younger brother at all costs.

On his fifteenth birthday, Elliott wrote home to his mother feeling lonely and forgotten, although cloaking these emotions with the bravado that was becoming his defense: "Lately I have been feeling rather hurt for I always answer a letter as quickly as received and if you all did this I would get a letter nearly every day. . . . I have received no birthday letter from 6 West 57th Street so I think they must have forgotten me."

He sent his father a letter lightly referring to him as "Governor" and attempting to be jocular while actually revealing the anxiety he felt about the competition with his brother: "Oh father will you ever think *me* a 'noble boy,' you are right about Tede he is one & no mistake a boy I would give a good deal to be like in many respects. . . ."

As his younger son's problems concentrating and applying himself worsened, Theodore, thinking some individual attention might help, took the boy with him on a business trip to London. But while there he wrote back despairingly to Mittie that Ellie, once so fearless and confident, now could not sleep unless it was in his bed with him.

Because of his deteriorating condition, it was decided that Ellie should not follow Teedie to college. Missing a higher education did not seem to the parents a decisive issue: Theodore himself had not gone to college and was still considered an interesting enough person that Matthew Arnold had gladly accepted a dinner invitation from him while traveling in America. But Elliott saw the question in different terms—not whether he would get a college degree, but whether he could keep up with Teedie. He pleaded with his father to be allowed to go away to school, and in the fall of 1875, he was enrolled as a boarding student at St. Paul's. Within weeks, he had a rush of blood and headache in the middle of Latin class and became unconscious.

"I can't remember what happened," he wrote home with a forced offhandedness. "I believe I screamed out. . . . It had left me rather nervous, therefore homesick and unhappy. . . . I would not bother you with this but you want to know all about me, don't you?"

Other boys in the Roosevelt social circle suffering from complaints ranging from consumption to neurasthenia had been sent out West for toughening up, and this was the solution Theodore decided on for Elliott. He arranged for the boy to go to Fort McKavett in Texas for several months in 1876.

Elliott's stay at this frontier outpost came as the West was entering the American imagination with particular drama. It was the year that George Armstrong Custer made his last stand; the last year that the great buffalo herds roamed the prairie. The experience in the lone prairies of Texas played to Elliott's strengths—a zest for adventure, an ability to achieve easy camaraderie with his fellows. Yet he must have wondered why he was always having to leave his home and wrote sentimentally to his father, "Oh dear splendid old pater I wish I could tell you how much I love you but I can't you know, so there's no use wishing."

He soon adapted to life with cowboys and Indian fighters and a bravura tone entered his letters: "I have gone through some regular roughing since I last wrote you at Weatherford. After we left there we came slowly camping at night and shooting all that we wanted to eat. . . ." In another letter, he wrote that he was sleeping out under the stars in a bedroll and using a mongrel dog for a pillow, "partly for warmth and partly to drown out the smell of my bed partner."

Elliott tried to spend time preparing for another try at school, but was too taken with the distracting excitement of frontier life to succeed and wrote home apologetically, "I feel well enough to study and instead here I am spending all your money down here as if I were ill. . . . Altogether I feel like a general fraud. . . ." He also noted, somewhat ominously given what was to follow, that there was a good deal of drinking that took place at the fort and that while he had so far avoided temptation it had not been easy.

Meanwhile, the "noble boy" Teedie was continuing to come into himself. He was not handsome. His face had a dominating square jaw, which, combined with the way his eyes got lost behind the reflective discs of his glasses, sometimes gave him a severe look. His teeth were strikingly regular and white, but sometimes seemed out of control, chopping at his wounds and amputating the ends of his sentences. In a candid self-inventory, he said that his well-formed ears were his only good feature.

He knew from the tone of his brother's letters that Ellie was having success with frontier girls, who were captivated by his urbane charm. He himself was looking with new eyes at Edith Carow, who as usual visited his family when they went to Oyster Bay for the summer. One of her schoolmates at Miss Comstock's had said of her: "I believe you could live in the same house with Edith for 50 years and never really get to know her." But Teedie felt that he knew her as well as his own past. He rowed her across Oyster Bay every day of her stay and she read to him. When he went off to Harvard that fall, it was assumed that they were pledged to each other.

It was a sentimental leave-taking from his father. The two Theodores had grown closer in the time of Elliott's troubles, collaborating in concern over him. They had talked of Ellie's problems and also of young Theodore's own future. If he really wanted to be the next Audubon, as he said he did, then Thee (he had now graduated from "Teedie") must realize that he was in effect taking a vow of poverty, his father said, although there would always be enough money to help support him in this poorly paid occupation.

His departure for Cambridge was seen by the first Theodore as a rite of passage: "As I saw the last of the train bearing you away the other day I realized what a luxury it was to have a boy in whom I could place perfect trust and confidence who was leaving me to take his first important position in the world." A few weeks later came a more emotional letter on the occasion of Thee's eighteenth birthday: "I have worked pretty hard all my life and anticipate passing over to you many of my responsibilities as soon as your shoulders are broad enough to bear them."

Teddy wrote back to his father a letter pledging that this trust was not misplaced. While he was out of the cloister of the family for the first time in his life, he was still to be counted on: "I do not think there is a fellow in College who has a family that loves him as much as you all do me, and I am *sure* that there is no one who has a father who is also his best and most intimate friend, as you are mine. I have kept the first letter you wrote me and shall do my best to deserve your trust."

Meanwhile, he had already begun to establish his own legend at school. Dr. Johnson's definition of the salient feature of metaphysical poetry, picked up by a later Harvard man, T. S. Eliot, could have been made with young Theodore in mind: heterogeneous concepts yoked together with violence. One woman who met him in his freshman year recalled him as "a campus freak with stuffed snakes and lizards in his room, with a peculiar violent vehemence of speech and manner, and an overriding interest in everything." Friends went to his rooms for boxing and wrestling contests, which were followed by recitations of "The Raven" and then long discussions of the metaphysical significance of Tennyson's "In Memoriam." Becoming agitated over some abstruse point in class, he would sometimes jump up and talk so long and intensely that the professor would finally have to remind him he was the student, not the teacher.

He was stepping into a larger social world at Harvard. He wrote home that he had been on a hay ride with a group of friends and said that one of the girls "looked quite like Edith—only not nearly so pretty as her Ladyship: who when she dresses well and don't frizzle her hair is a very pretty girl." The girls he met found him eccentric. One of them said to his sister Conie, "If I were writing to Theodore I would have to say something of this kind, 'I have enjoyed Plutarch's last essay on the philosophy of Diogenes excessively.' " Yet she added that he had such high spirits and good humor that she feared being seated next to him at dinner parties lest he trigger a laughing fit that would embarrass her in front of the other guests. Unlike Ellie, however, who was already beginning to make amatory conquests, Teddy was obsessed with personal virtue. The moralistic views he was beginning to apply to others he applied with equal stringency to himself. "Thank Heaven I am pure!" he wrote in his journal.

He returned for his second year at Harvard near the top of his class. But something important was happening back home that took precedence over his own success. His father had become involved in politics. It seemed an odd development to some of the first Theodore's friends, but after all his brother Robert had been a congressman and it was actually a short step from trying to mitigate suffering to trying to change the institutions that produced it.

When he went to the 1876 Republican presidential convention as the head of a reform delegation dedicated to blocking the candidacy of New York's egregious Senator Roscoe Conkling, Theodore came to the attention of the party's eventual nominee, Rutherford B. Hayes. After becoming President, Hayes nominated him as collector of the Port of New York, one of the biggest and hitherto most corrupt patronage positions in the country. It was another challenge to the Republican machine controlled by Conkling.

The collectorship was of such potential prestige that it would have vaulted Theodore, just forty-six and apparently full of vigor, into a position of immense political power. But the vindictive Conkling succeeded in blocking the nomination and worked hard to blacken Theodore's reputation. After being the target of unremitting attack for several weeks, Theodore sent a letter to Teddy at Harvard admitting that he had been defeated: "The machine politicians have shown their colors. . . . I fear for your future. We cannot stand so corrupt a government for any length of time."

Soon afterward Theodore began to experience terrible stomach pain. Word of his illness reached Cambridge and Teddy worriedly wrote Bamie shortly before Christmas: "I am very uneasy about Father. Does the Doctor think it anything serious?" But the thought seemed impossible and he dismissed it: "The trouble is the dear old fellow never does think of himself in anything."

Miraculously, Theodore Sr.'s pain abated enough for the family to make it through the holidays. But shortly after the New Year it returned. Having recently come home from Texas, Elliott took charge of the situation, giving his brother censored reports of the seriousness of the illness to keep him from worrying. But soon what had been thought to be a simple inflammation of the bowel was diagnosed as an inoperable cancer.

Over the next few weeks, Elliott showed his strength of character by becoming his father's chief caretaker and the midwife of his death. His sister Corinne watched Ellie at their father's bedside and compared his tenderness to that of a woman, especially in the last stage of the illness, when "his young strength was poured out to help his father's condition." Elliott left his own account of the horror of the first Theodore's last days: "He never said anything but 'Oh! My!' but the agony in his face was awful. Ether and sedatives were of no avail. . . . Pretty soon Father began to vomit after which with face fearful with pain he would clasp me tight in his arms. . . ." Feeling himself failing, Theodore issued an injunction: Elliott must now take care of Mittie.

Finally, on the morning of February 9, 1878, with some of the newsboys and orphans his father had spent much of his life helping huddled
together in a death watch on the steps of 6 West 57th Street, Elliott at
last heard "the gurgling breathing of death. . . . [Then] his eyelids fluttered, he gave three breaths. It is finished." Mittie cried out, "I expect
he is safe in the arms of Jesus now!"

Elliott tried to sleep knowing that he would have to explain to his
brother why he had not called him: "I promised if there was danger to
have him there. May God forgive me as the old boy did. . . ."

When Teddy got home the next day flags throughout New York City
were lowered to half mast. The *New York World* headline for the next
day read: FUNERAL OF HIM WHO WAS EYES TO THE BLIND, FEET TO THE
LAME, GOOD TO ALL. Teddy came into the parlor and kissed his dead
father's face.

Elliott was devastated. The props had been kicked out from under his
future just as he seemed ready to pick up his life again. For Teddy—he
was the only Theodore Roosevelt now—the death was tragedy but also
a call to responsibility. There was a swirling series of imperatives. He
was now head of the family. He had to make his own way and yet lead
the rest of them too. But he was weighed down with guilt for having
failed the man who twice gave him life in his time of need.

He tried to rise to the occasion, writing Bamie soon after the death
when he was trying to pick up the pieces back at Harvard: "I really feel
badly when I think how much you overrate my abilities; but I shall try
my best to reflect credit on father's name." The same day he wrote
Conie that his vision of their father was still so real that "it seems as if
I could see him and hear his voice." Indeed, the memory was almost like
the ghost of Hamlet's father—steering him in the direction of duty,
inspiring him to action. Teddy told Conie that he would always keep his
father's letters close by, "if merely as talismans against evil."

Years later TR would say that he never made an important decision as
President without asking himself what his father would have thought.
He always kept the first Theodore's portrait on the wall of his study so
that the beloved face looked down on him at his desk. Whenever asked
about his father, TR said simply, "He was the best man I ever knew."

*A*fter his death," Bamie later said of her father, "we all had to work out our own solutions." Her solution was to become more than ever the anchor of the family, not only fulfilling the role of elder sister but taking on more of her mother's duties as well. Mittie's increasing eccentricity was apparent in the way she reacted to Conie's debutante season. She waited up for her daughter when she came in late from dances but was afraid of opening the door lest an intruder get in, so she made Conie stand on the porch and prove her identity by reciting a password phrase: "How doth the busy bee improve each shining hour."

Bamie made no attempt to hide her scorn for such foolishness. The tension between her and Mittie was such that TR wrote in his diary, "How I wish Mother and Bamie would not quarrel among themselves." Yet Bamie needed her mother's advice in another matter. It was an unexpected courtship from James Roosevelt, a fourth cousin descended from the line of Jacobus who lived a leisurely life on an estate in the Hyde Park region of the Hudson River Valley.

Already in his fifties, James Roosevelt was old enough to be Bamie's father. In fact, he even looked a little like the first Theodore, enough so that people had mistaken the two men for each other on the streets of

New York. Yet James was a very different sort of man—the sort of man who would have regarded the first Theodore's emotional spontaneity and charitable work with some incredulousness. He'd had one moment of romance in his own life. It came when he was touring Switzerland as a twenty-year-old in 1848, the year of revolutions, and crossed over into Italy on a whim to drill with Garibaldi's soldiers for a couple of weeks, prudently moving on just before they went into battle.* Otherwise James Roosevelt pursued a sober and calculating life, coming back home from his European fling to attend law school and go to work to build the family fortune.

He married a distant relative named Rebecca Howland in 1853, and a year later they'd had a son, also named James Roosevelt Roosevelt and called "Rosy." (The middle "Roosevelt" was an attempt to imitate the old Dutch form, "son of.") Like the first Theodore, James Roosevelt had chosen not to serve in the Civil War, but he was not afflicted by a guilty conscience. He had the wealth and good name to travel extensively in Europe during and after the war, hobnobbing there with fellow Americans such as General George McClellan. Like the general, James Roosevelt was a Democrat; he may have shared McClellan's bitter hatred of Abraham Lincoln and of blacks.

Having migrated from New York to the Hudson Valley generations earlier, James's branch of the Roosevelts became significant landowners. He had inherited an estate called Mt. Hope from his father, a man so convinced of the superiority of the country to the city that when James announced that he was going to New York University, he had moaned that his son would now become "a corrupted Dandy and will walk Broadway with a cane."

After Mt. Hope burned to the ground in 1865, James bought another place a few miles away called Springwood, which sat on one hundred acres with a long sloping view of the Hudson. (In time he would add other tracts until the estate comprised over nine hundred acres.)

James's branch of the family did not see the first Theodore's branch very often, but when they did meet there was a shared feeling of family identity. James, Rebecca, and Rosy happened to be in Europe when Theodore took his children on their Grand Tour in 1869 and the two

---

* In the years to come, this brief encounter would be magnified into something larger. In 1965, Franklin Roosevelt, Jr., dedicating a plaque on the Verrazano Narrows Bridge, told his audience, "I feel a close affinity to all Italians here because my grandfather, James Roosevelt, fought as a member of Garibaldi's army in the fight for unification and independence of Italy."

families staged a rendezvous in Rome. Only a little bit older than Bamie, James's son Rosy became her companion during the trip, and they were both watching with amusement when ten-year-old Teedie impulsively reached out and kissed the Pope's hand near St. Peter's Square. The two families had sailed home together in a passage so turbulent that it was impossible to remain below, and above the deck chairs had to be lashed to the ship's mast.

A dignified-looking man with a high brow, deep-set eyes and rusty-colored muttonchops, James Roosevelt had made a large sum in his business dealings and had invested shrewdly during his early retirement. His great dream had been to put together a monopoly in coal or railroads like those Carnegie, Gould, and others had created. His maneuvers always made money, but never quite put him on a par with the robber barons. His last great chance was a large stake in the Maritime Canal Company, which proposed to build an interocean canal through Nicaragua, a dream that persisted until Panama was chosen as the site for the isthmian canal.

As he grew older, James gradually turned his attention from making money to enjoying Springwood, his estate at Hyde Park. He adopted the identity of "Squire James," importing tweed suits from England and spending his time supervising the grounds of his estate, indulging a passion for horses, and striding around the grounds with a quirt in his hand. He was acknowledged as a leader in the civic affairs of Hyde Park, and when he went into the city of New York it was to attend sumptuous evenings with wealthy friends such as the Astors. His son Rosy became engaged to the immensely wealthy Helen Astor, whose mother, Caroline, had appointed herself the social arbiter of New York high society. When they married, Helen brought a dowry of a $400,000 trust fund and a mansion on Fifth Avenue.

James's wife, Rebecca Roosevelt, died of a heart attack not long before the passing of the first Theodore. After a brief period of mourning, James began to think about remarriage. It was logical that he should become interested in Bamie, who had proved herself a young woman of spirit and intelligence when her family visited him at his Hyde Park estate. In the days after the death of her father, he gingerly pressed his suit, meeting her at her home and then trying to carry on a decorous epistolary romance from France, where he had gone for an extended visit. Given her deformity, spinsterhood was a possibility for Bamie, but her family, particularly her brothers, provided so rich a life that she was far from desperate. She responded to James Roosevelt with courteous sympathy but gave him no encouragement.

Teddy was only remotely aware of his sister's romantic possibilities. Coping with his father's death was a full-time task for him. He was encompassed by fears and self-doubt, which he tried to exorcise by grueling physical activity that first summer of mourning at Oyster Bay. He rowed like a demon, as much as twenty-five miles a day. He engaged in punishing boxing and wrestling matches with Elliott. He took long horse rides, pushing his mount and himself to the limit.

Gradually he began to emerge from his grief. Edith Carow visited at Oyster Bay, ostensibly as Conie's friend, but actually to see him. Their courtship appeared to be on the verge of commitment, but then there was a moment of dark misunderstanding when they were alone in the summerhouse—perhaps an inept advance or a wounding word. Neither of them ever said what happened, but it caused a coolness between them. When he returned to Harvard that fall Teddy wrote his sister about Edith, "Tell her that I hope when I see her at Xmas, it will not be on what you might call one of her off days."

He had dropped his idea of becoming a natural scientist, claiming that the Harvard science curriculum produced mere "microscopists," and soon plunged into the social waters by accepting an invitation to join the exclusive Porcellian Club, which meant meeting Brahmins like the Saltonstalls, who were Boston's equivalent of the Knickerbockers. Through the Saltonstalls he was introduced to a striking young woman named Alice Lee, whose family lived in nearby Chestnut Hill.

She was just seventeen in the fall of 1878, blonde, blue-eyed and willowy—a perfect composite of the images of purity and innocence from Victorian novels. Theodore courted Alice Lee obsessively in the early months of 1879, getting up early to study for six hours or so each morning and then riding to her house to escort her on long walks, which gave him an opportunity to recite from his prodigious storehouse of memorized poetry and show off his knowledge of ornithology. He wooed her with ghost stories and invited her to watch him in the finals of the lightweight boxing championship of Harvard, a match in which he finished second best, his face badly bloodied.

She responded to his furious courtship with coquetries, not understanding the desperation of his need and urged by her parents to be noncommittal. In the late spring of 1879, he precipitously proposed. She declined without wholly discouraging him. He continued to think about her over the summer and resumed his pursuit in the fall. A friend remembered his intensity at a party that took place at the beginning of his senior year where Alice Lee was also present. "See that girl?" Theodore pointed her out in a crowd. "I'm going to marry her. She won't have me, but I'm going to have *her!*"

It was a trying period for him, but he could still count on the fellowship of his family. In December he and Elliott went on a memorable duck hunting trip on Long Island Sound. In the account Teddy wrote of the adventure later on, it was his brother who once again took charge of a dangerous situation and saved them from disaster.

After breaking through the shore ice, the twenty-one-foot sloop commanded by Elliott hit open water. The brothers began to shoot the flock of ducks, hitting so many that the feathers left floating made it appear that someone had burst pillows on the water. The sport was so good that they forgot about the louring weather. Then the sky suddenly became dark and threatening. They headed for shore into a freezing wind. At the prow, Teddy was able to shield himself by turning his head, but Elliott, keeping a grim hold on the tiller, looked straight ahead despite the cold that formed icicles on his beard.

Without warning a large boat loomed up out of the gloom and cut across their path, but Elliott kept his course and they avoided a collision, finally making it to shore so cold and tired that they almost lacked the energy to let down the sails. Seeing a reminder of that heroic quality his brother had demonstrated as a boy, TR later wrote of him in his account of the episode: "He kept his eyes steadily ahead, not flinching for an instant although the cold was terribly bitter."

Their old companionship and competition was renewed that spring. Taking time off from the job he had taken in a bank, Elliott came up to Harvard for a visit. As in earlier days, Skinny measured himself against Swelly by plunging into a day-long Olympiad and then entered the results in his journal: "As athletes we are about equal; he runs best, I row best. He can beat me sailing or swimming; I can beat him wrestling and boxing. I am best with the rifle, he with the shotgun, etc., etc."

The competition had a subtext because of Elliott's acknowledged appeal for young women in a time when TR was suffering rejection. But his persistence finally paid off and Alice Lee said yes to his renewed proposal. They kept their engagement secret for a while and then finally told the family. His possessive sisters had taken the girl's measure during her visits to New York and agreed on a verdict: "Attractive without great depth." Alice Lee was as openhearted and innocent as she looked and would not only share their beloved brother with them but would probably let them dominate her.

While his sisters evaluated Alice, Teddy gloried in her. His father had made him conscious of the perils of the double standard, an issue that concerned Elliott far less. ("He made us understand that the same standard of clean living was demanded for the boys as for the girls.") In fact, TR took the issue of the rights of women seriously enough that he made it the subject of his senior thesis, "The Practicality of Equalizing Men and Women before the Law." But now he was the archetypal lovesick swain. "I am all the time thinking of you and wishing to be with you," he wrote Alice. "You pretty little witch! I wonder what makes me love you so! Darling, I care more for you than for everything else in the world."

The great literary abilities incubating in him were not on display in his letters to her. She was the Victorian ingenue, he the lovelorn Victorian suitor. What does shine through the conventional language, however, is the spell Alice has cast on him: "My own sunny faced queen, I don't think you are ever ten minutes from my thoughts; I know every one of your saucy, bewitching little ways, and every expression of your sweet, bright pretty face. . . . I can really almost see as I write your slender, graceful figure, the pretty poise of your head, and your pure, innocent little face. Sweetest, I love you with my whole heart."

At the same time that Teddy's romance was winding up, Bamie's was winding down. James Roosevelt had returned from his sojourn in France and asked her to marry him. Bamie graciously declined his offer, but, because James was a Roosevelt, immediately began to look among her acquaintance's for someone else who might interest him. She picked out a handsome but haughty young woman named Sara Delano and then she and Mittie invited James Roosevelt to dinner so he could meet her.

Sara Delano, as she made perfectly clear at this first meeting, considered herself quite the equal of any Roosevelt. She had lived in Hong Kong as a girl when her father, Warren Delano, returned to China as a trader at the age of fifty to remake the fortune he had earned as a younger man and lost on Wall Street. After several years her family had returned to America to take up residence once again at the Hyde Park estate they called Algonac, which they filled with Buddhist temple bells, teakwood screens, and other chinoiserie. The Delano women were legendary for their good looks and also for their eccentricity. (When she was in her seventies, Franklin's aunt Laura—by then known as "Aunt Polly"—came down from the Roosevelt summer home on Campobello Island the morning of a solar eclipse dressed to the teeth and carrying her jewels with her. When FDR asked what she was doing, she answered, "Despite what you have said, Franklin, this is clearly the end of the world. I have dressed for the occasion. I have my jewels and I am ready to go to heaven.")

The Delanos were as rich as the Roosevelts, Sara made quite clear to James, and had bloodlines that were even better. Instead of putting him off, however, her pride attracted him. Mittie noted after the dinner that the fifty-two-year-old widower had been unable to take his eyes off the young woman the entire evening. A few weeks later she and Bamie were called upon to chaperone the girl on a visit to James Roosevelt's estate at Hyde Park, after which it was a short time until he proposed and then asked her father for permission. The gruff Warren Delano was impressed in spite of himself, saying of James, "He is the first person who has made me realize that a Democrat can be a gentleman."

The servants at Algonac had cried at the thought of Sara marrying such an old man, but she herself was happy. As Sara later told their son, Franklin, if it had not been for Bamie she might have wound up "old Miss Delano with a rather sad life."

Realizing that he had one last chance to spend time with his brother before his marriage to Alice, Teddy planned a trip tramping out West with Elliott the summer of 1880. As they traveled through Ohio by train, he wrote in his diary, "It is great fun to be with old Nell. He and I can do about anything together." He was disappointed that they were only in the "Middle" West of Illinois and Iowa and not the "Far" West, which was synonymous with the Wild West in his imagination and which he envied Elliott for having experienced in his Texas days. But it was good to be Skinny and Swelly one last time, even if Elliott outshot him every day.

They were going into an area where his brother's frontier experiences a few years earlier gave him superiority. Elliott knew how to handle the rough types they encountered; he also saw that Teddy's arduous pursuit of Alice had left him physically depleted, and so, as in the old days, he had to take charge. "I try to keep him at something all the time," Elliott wrote Bamie, "and certainly he looks a hundred percent better than when he came out." He added that he was glad that "we two brothers have been able at last to be together. All the happier we are solely dependent on each other for companionship."

During the trip. TR wrote uxorious letters to Alice: "Get plenty of sleep, and as much exercise and lawn tennis as you want, and remember that the more good times you have—dancing, visiting or doing anything you like, the happier I am. . . . I do love you so, and I have such complete trust in your love for me; I know you love me, so that you will *like* to get married to me—for you will always be your own mistress, and mine too."

She, in return, sent him childlike and self-deprecatory answers: "Don't you think I am pretty good to write you every day? I suppose you laugh and say, these funny letters, they sound just like Alice."

But as the deadline for marriage drew closer, a note of sexual anxiety entered her correspondence. "How I wish it was three weeks from today our wedding day," she wrote him in early October. "I *perfectly remember* my promise not to have the faintest alarm Teddy and I *know* that I shall not, as I just long to be with you all the time. . . . Teddy, I am going to try and be a good wife for you." A few days later, with the endgame to their courtship that much closer in sight, she returned to these same themes: "I just long for our wedding. I know I shall be very happy then, being all your own, and you must never think that I have the slightest fear of giving myself to you."

But he was as tumescent as she was demure, replying the next day: "I worship you so that it seems almost a desecration to touch you; and yet when I am with you I can hardly let you a moment out of my arms."

When the brothers returned from their expedition, it was clear to both of them that a part of their life together was ending. Theodore would now be taking up his role as man of the family. Elliott decided to give him the right-of-way by planning a trip around the world. When TR insisted that he stay for the wedding, saying that he would have him as his best man or not have a best man, Elliott postponed his departure long enough to be present at the ceremony which took place on October 27, 1880, Theodore's twenty-second birthday.

Edith Carow was the only non-Roosevelt New Yorker invited to the Lee home in Brookline for the marriage. A relative later theorized that this was Teddy's way of paying homage to the girl who had been in his life all those years and whom he was now leaving forever. At the reception, the normally staid Edith was unusually vivacious, dancing "the soles off her shoes."

*   *   *

The newlyweds postponed a longer trip they had planned to Europe because Theodore had decided to enter law school and went instead to Oyster Bay for a brief honeymoon. The area was saturated with memories of his father and of family vacations. TR purchased 155 acres at the top of a rise and in his mind began to design the family manse he intended to name, in Alice's honor, Leeholm.

Back in New York, the couple moved in with Bamie and Mittie. It was a time of new domestic arrangements for the Roosevelts. Corinne had married a wealthy man named Douglas Robinson, whom one relative described as "a large man with a large voice." Robinson had an active wit and quick laughter, although he was perhaps too proud of his virtue, on display when he personally conducted Sunday services for his employees. He was older than Conie, who had sobbed steadily during their six-month engagement, wanting to break it off—after knowing her father and brothers any other man would seem inadequate—but afraid of the blow to her reputation if she did. Her loyalties would always be divided. In time she would come to admire Robinson, but, as her daughter later said, "maddened him by her cool and dutiful approach to the worship he felt for her." It was Douglas Robinson who acutely observed what others would feel upon marrying a Roosevelt—that one risked being "hung on the family like a tail to a kite."

The rapidly extending family looked forward to letters from Elliott, who was now the Roosevelt argonaut. On the first leg of his around-the-world adventure, he had inadvertently tightened the connection between his family and the Hyde Park cousins when he found that James and Sara Delano Roosevelt, just married and on their honeymoon, were also passengers on his ship bound for England. The threesome became so close during the voyage that James and Sara insisted that Elliott use the flat they had taken as his own headquarters in the weeks he planned to be in London before going on to the Far East, and extracted a promise from him to be godfather to the child they were already expecting.

Elliott found himself in demand in London high society in part because of the celebrity still attached to his father's good name. When he left for India he carried with him letters of introduction that would make him welcome at officers' clubs and colonial headquarters all over the country. After getting settled in Bombay, he hunted by day and at night listened to the officers' stories in an experience reminiscent of the time he had spent in Texas as a teenager. He wrote with bravado that his days were filled with "glorious freedom and the greatest excitement." But to his mother, he noted revealingly that this lotus land he had entered had certain perils: "I would not trust myself to live here. There is no temptation to do anything but what you please and so many ways of doing it that no one never tires." Being in this exotic environment was pleasure, but it also had the feel of exile.

For TR, however, what his brother was experiencing set the standard for adventure: it was dangerous and demanding. After killing an immense tiger, Elliott moved on to hunt elephants in Ceylon and ibex in the Himalayas. Few white men had set foot in the areas where he was now traveling. At one point in the wilds of Kashmir he became so ill with tropical fever that he had to be carried by bearers in a litter and subsisted for fifteen days on rice and milk.

During his year-long absence Elliott frequently reassured Mittie that he intended to look after her, as his father had charged him on his deathbed: "I have good broad shoulders and am myself amply strong. When I come back dear I come to you alone. Not to leave you again until you tell me, and that will be never." In writing to his brother, however, he allowed himself to be vulnerable and admonished TR to play the role that their father once had: "I shall need you often in your old strong way to give a chap a lift or for that matter if I am on the wrong road a blow to knock me back again."

For the time being, Teddy was having enough problems getting himself on the right road. Desultorily studying the law, he worked also on what would be his first book, *The Naval War of 1812,* and paid attention to the wife he sometimes referred to as his "darling, pretty, pink baby." That she jealously distracted him from other pursuits was clear from a letter he wrote her when she was visiting her family: "I am going to bed, and sit down at my desk to talk to you for a minute. How I have missed my little, teasing, laughing, pretty witch! My little sweet, pure queen, I have had no one to jog my arm and make me blot the papers while I was writing; it always made me feel rather bad tempered, but I loved it all the same. I feel dreadfully lonely going to bed without you."

That summer when they went to Europe on their delayed honeymoon, a picture of an unsophisticated young woman emerges from his letters home to his sisters: "I don't think I ever saw anyone enjoy herself so much; and indeed, I myself have never had a better time. It is perfectly ideal. We had a compartment to ourselves in the train; and Baby buzzed from one end to the other like a bee in her efforts to see out of both windows at once." Perhaps comparing them in his mind's eye to his willowy bride—now his standard for female beauty—he wrote home an art critique after seeing Rubens's fleshy female figures: "I don't like a chubby Minerva, a corpulent Venus and a Diana who is so fat that I know she would never overtake a cow, let alone a deer."

In the fall of 1881, his book was published and immediately acknowledged as a minor classic. TR thought of pursuing a literary career. But something else was beginning to seize his attention. He had begun prowling around politics, showing up at the Republican club late at night so that he could talk to the tough Irish characters who controlled the local machine. It was a world that pulled at his father in the last years of his life—and perhaps helped pull him down. In this sense, politics involved unfinished family business. But it also involved what Teddy called the "rough-and-tumble," a place where a young man might prove himself. He began making appearances in behalf of "good government" and positioning himself to run for the state assembly.

TR himself said later on that he had to use a "jimmy" to pry open the door that led to a political career. There was some resistance from the bosses, but far more from members of his own class. Before 1830 political office would have been regarded as the birthright of someone from a good family with a history of civic involvement. Since then, however, it had become something like a stigmatized profession for a patrician. It was assumed that anyone who entered politics was either serving the business class or blackmailing it. Henry Adams, scion of the leading political dynasty in the United States, told his class at Harvard, "I have never known a young man to go into politics who was not the worse for it." Members of TR's own immediate circle let him know that they believed politics to be a world peopled by "saloon keepers, horsecar conductors and the like." All this opposition only whetted his appetite and made him campaign hard to get himself elected New York's assemblyman from the 21st District.

Arriving in Albany in 1882, he wore his pomaded hair parted in the middle and a pince-nez perched superciliously on his nose. Sometimes he affected a single eyeglass with a gold chain over his ear and carried a gold-headed cane in one hand and a silk top hat in the other. A Democratic assemblyman took one look at Teddy and said that the Republicans now had sixty and one half members.

He was regarded not just as a fop but also as an eccentric. The sharp and rasping voice shot out words like projectiles. There was also the eye-catching Roosevelt dentition. One newspaperman compared his teeth to dominoes; another wrote about "the castanet-like ecstasy of his snapping teeth." No one considered the possibility that TR was aware of the image he presented and that he manipulated it for his own ends.

Politics as practiced in New York was indeed the rough-and-tumble— the "arena," as TR would later call it, where a man must engage in trial by combat. Under attack from the moment he arrived at the legislature, he made it a point of giving back as good as he got, bearing down with special vehemence on the Tammany Democrats, whom he said were "totally unable to speak with an approximation of good grammar; not even one of them can string three intelligible sentences together to save his neck." It was an atmosphere where words might always lead to violence. When one of his opponents let it be known that he thought Teddy a good candidate for a blanket toss, Teddy went right up to him: "By God, if you try anything like that, I'll kick you, I'll bite you, I'll kick you in the balls, I'll do anything to you. . . ."

Elliott kept tabs on his brother during his time abroad, a little jealous but also admiring of such audacity. Others might consider the new assemblyman as being somewhat unfinished—obviously talented but still callow; all surface with his depths unexplored—but to his brother he was everything a Roosevelt ought to be. Elliott wrote to Bamie from India: "His plans for occupying the position he should as father's son and namesake seem [to be] going so splendidly smoothly—all success to him." He probably would have been surprised to know that when Mittie read aloud his letters about hunting and exploring, Theodore was not only attentive but paced nervously "like a caged lynx."

But if TR was envious of the experiences Elliott was having, he was also worried that he might appear to be trying to outdo his brother. He had a heartfelt conversation with his Aunt Anna Bulloch, which she promptly paraphrased in a letter to Elliott. Teddy had told her, she wrote, that while normally "he would wish to surpass other men, he could never hold in his heart a jealous feeling toward you." In their conversation, TR had gone out of his way to downplay his own pre-cocious literary and political accomplishments, saying that neither would "bring him advancement . . . so that you will *both* in point of fact start your careers together, he having gained this immediate experience while you gain yours in a different way during your travels."

At Albany, however, there was no pretense of humility. TR regarded his political foes with chilling hauteur, writing Alice on one occasion: "All the small curs—whether on the floor of the House or in the newspapers—are now howling at me; and the harder thing to stand is the *shallow* demagogues who delight to see a better man than themselves stumble or seem to stumble. I would not care a snap of my finger if they would attack me where I could hit back. Not a man has dared to say anything to my face that I have not repaid him for with interest."

But if he often struck attitudes, he also worked hard, both in the chambers and out of them. But his curiosity and iconoclasm allowed him to take many positions that were wholly unexpected from someone of his youth and upbringing. There was a bill before the assembly, for instance, to ban the manufacture of cigars in workers' houses, on the grounds that the teeming tenements were breeding grounds for disease. Union leader Samuel Gompers lobbied Roosevelt strenuously but without hope of successs to tour these tenements. Teddy finally agreed and was so struck by the wretched conditions—a number of women, men, and children living in one filthy room where they worked and slept—that he not only backed the bill but did so with passionate vehemence, even going before Governor Grover Cleveland to urge him to sign it after passage.

Politics allowed him the same kind of opportunities for self-dramatization that illness had when he was a child. He saw himself as having entered the lists against the "black horse cavalry." These were the ones who had spurned his father, the "curs" who blocked reform; they were the "wealthy criminal class," as he described those who wanted to back the notorious Jay Gould's effort to raise the fare on the Manhattan elevated train system from five to ten cents. Once when he found himself calculating whether taking a principled position would hurt his personal advancement, he became disgusted with himself. "I then made up my mind," he wrote later on, "that I would proceed on the assumption that each office I held would be the last I should hold."

For all his combative bravado, however, he was still not well. When the Assembly recessed for the summer of 1882, doctors told him that his long ordeal with asthma had left him with a chronically weak heart. In the summer of 1883, even though his "pretty pink baby" was now in the first stages of pregnancy, he decided to go on a hunting trip, this time to the *real* West, not that in-between state he and Elliott had visited a couple of years earlier. An acquaintance had been telling him about Dakota Territory, so he took a train to the tiny town of Medora, on the edge of the Little Missouri River, in the middle of the Badlands.

Arriving as the typical lightfoot, TR hired a guide, provisioned a buckboard, and set off. He was awed by the geological jumble of coulees and dry riverbeds gouged out of the land; and the turrets, spires, and minarets cut by the forces of wind and weathering into the sandstone buttes. The problem was that the dramatic landscape didn't appear to contain any buffalo. Bands of local Sioux had slaughtered the herd the previous year in response to federal regulations they regarded as unjust, and buffalo hunters had finished off what they left.

It took TR two weeks of privation, which he endured with gusto, before he finally got his sights on a bull. When he finally brought the animal down, he astonished his guide by breaking into an improvised war dance and whooping like a banshee before settling down to saw off the head for a trophy.

He was so galvanized by his brief experience in the Badlands that by the time he left for New York a few days after getting his buffalo, he had agreed with a couple of local cattlemen, Sylvane Ferris and Bill Merrifield, who owned the Maltese Cross Ranch, to put up $14,000 to become a partner with them in the cattle business.

That fall, Elliott returned home after nearly a year and a half abroad, bringing as *his* trophy a stunning rug for Mittie made of the skin of the tiger he had shot. Except for TR's glasses and an inch or so difference in height, the brothers looked alike—hair precisely parted slightly off center as if by caliper, faces elongated by thick mustaches angling down the sides of their mouths. But the similarities were only skin-deep. Elliott lacked the confidence Teddy had in such abundance, although his doubts were in their own way as appealing as TR's certainty. Conie captured one crucial difference between the young men when she wrote of Theodore: "If I were to do something he thought very weak or wrong, he would never forgive me, whereas Elliott no matter how much he might despise the sin would forgive the sinner."

Elliott tried to work up the notes he had taken during his exotic trip into a book the way his brother had done with his researches on the War of 1812. But he couldn't summon the concentration. He also tried to follow his brother's footsteps by joining the local Republican club, but TR was so much a presence there that he felt little room for maneuver and dropped out. His inheritance made it unnecessary for him to work and he didn't.

Soon Elliott drifted into the occupation at which he had come to excel—looking for boon companions and good times. He had taken up polo in India and now played constantly, distinguishing himself as a fearless rider. He joined the Knickerbocker Club. Always charming, he now cultivated the aura of those dashing English grenadiers he had met abroad.

As part of Elliott's "rambles" through high society, he met a belle named Anna Hall and wooed her through an unbroken round of midnight suppers and champagne breakfasts. Coming from a family with a Hudson River country home (named Tivoli) about twenty miles from James and Sara Roosevelt's Springwood, Anna was so beautiful that the poet Robert Browning once asked merely to be allowed to gaze at her while she was sitting for a portrait, but she was not particularly well educated and, in TR's opinion, somewhat frivolous. Nonetheless Elliott wanted to make the commitment that he, like his mother and sisters, hoped would set him on the path to success. He announced his engagement to Anna during a party at the home of Laura Delano, younger sister of Sara. Their marriage, which took place on December 1, 1882, with Theodore as best man, was described by the *Herald* as "one of the most brilliant social events of the season."

Elliott and Anna quickly became part of a lively set of young New Yorkers referred to as "swells" in local papers. The first year of their life together was a nonstop round of teas and cotillions and polo matches. Anna's beauty made her a trophy for any man. Elliott's urbanity and his ability vividly to describe the interesting experiences he'd had abroad made him much sought after. As one acquaintance said, "If personal popularity could have bestowed public honors in any man, there was nothing beyond the reach of Elliott Roosevelt."

By the beginning of the new year of 1884, Elliott's Anna was in the early stages of her pregnancy while Teddy's Alice was in the last stages of hers. TR left her in New York during the week when he went to Albany because he found the capital cold and inhospitable and wanted her to be as comfortable as possible. After the first of the year, as her term neared, he had her move from their rented flat into the family home at 6 West 57th Street so that his mother and sisters could look after her.

Alice treasured his weekend visits home and found it increasingly difficult to let him return to Albany. On February 11, a Sunday evening, with the baby due any moment, she wrote a shaky pencil note to tell him that she was feeling poorly but that it was his mother he should worry about: "I hated so to leave you this afternoon. I don't think you need feel worried about my being sick. . . . I am feeling well tonight, but am worried over your little mother. Her fever is still very high and the doctor afraid. . . . I do love my dear Thee so much. I wish I could have my little new baby."

The infant, a girl, was born the next evening at 8:30. Mittie's sister Anna took her from the doctor and said, "You should have been a boy." Alice murmured dissent from her bed: "I *love* a little *girl*." When the baby sneezed, Alice said, "Doctor, don't let my baby take cold." When it sneezed again, she repeated, "Doctor, you must attend to my baby." The doctor replied that he always attended to the mother first. Anna washed and dressed and weighed the baby at just under nine pounds and then took her in to the depleted mother, who took the child in her arms and kissed her. The baby would be a second Alice, named after her.

Theodore spent the next day at Albany receiving the congratulations of his colleagues and handing out cigars. Then came an urgent telegram telling him to hurry home. By the time he arrived, a death sentence had already been pronounced by Elliott: "There is a curse on this house! Mother is dying, and Alice is dying too!" Teddy found Mittie upstairs in the last stages of typhoid fever and Alice downstairs nearly comatose from Bright's disease. He gathered his wife into his arms and began the death watch that would last the next several hours, leaving her only briefly to go up and see his mother one final time as she took her last breaths. The next afternoon Alice too was gone.

TR made a brief anguished entry in his diary—thoughts that would be translated into a heartfelt threnody later on: "She was beautiful in face and form, and lovelier still in spirit; as a flower she grew, and as a fair young flower she died. . . . Fair, pure and joyous as a maiden; loving, tender, and happy as a young wife; when she had just become a mother, when her life seemed to be but just begun, and when the years seemed so bright before her—then, by a strange and terrible fate, death came to her. . . . And when my heart's dearest died, the light went out of my life forever."

She represented youth and he pressed her into the album of his past, a memory so truly preserved that it could never be examined without causing pain. After writing her memorial, TR rarely mentioned her name again.

The life he had known was over. The symbolism of its passing was everywhere. The family house was sold. He gave up the apartment where he had lived with Alice. He had a daughter but could scarcely bring himself to hold her in his arms because of the heartrending associations she called up. Referring to her as "Baby Lee," as if unable to pronounce her given name, he put her in the care of the indefatigable Bamie, who was always ready for someone else to love.

TR returned to Albany and to the cause of political reform, but despite his determination not to be an object of pity he gave the impression, in the words of one colleague, of someone "working bravely in the darkness." It was as if there had actually been three deaths: in addition to his mother and his wife, "Teddy" (as Alice had always called him) had died too. After watching him try to cope in the weeks following the tragedy, his sister Conie wrote to Elliott, "He feels the awful loneliness more and more and I fear he sleeps little for he walks a great deal in the night and his eyes have that stained red look."

Ironically, just at this moment, when he was thinking about giving up politics, he was becoming most effective as a politician. In April, he went to Chicago where the national Republican presidential convention was taking place. He made a name for himself there as a spokesman for reform and an opponent of the machine backing the candidacy of James Blaine, a stance that allowed him also to attack his father's old enemy Roscoe Conkling, head of a rival and equally corrupt, although less powerful, machine. (When he would tell about how he had confronted Conkling, TR would become agitated, doubling his fist and punching the air.) His performance made him lifelong allies like Henry Cabot Lodge, the young Boston aristocrat with a voice like "the tearing of a sheet" who shared TR's love for literature and for a new kind of Republican Party. It also increased his standing among a large number of people who had come to regard him as one of the most promising young politicians in the country, one of those men who might possibly redeem politics from sordid corruption.

After his performance at Chicago he might have had higher office. But TR had no heart for it. He made a decision to give up his assembly seat and accept no other offers. He was empty and sensed that he needed to throw his fate to the winds in order to discover it. He decided to go back to Dakota Territory.

"The romance of my life," he later said of the Badlands, "began here." That is exactly what the West became for him: a theater for romantic solitude and exile, for romantic melancholy and visions of romantic self-transformation. Later in his life TR told a young man who wanted to write a book about him that he should concentrate on his experiences in the West if he wanted to know him "when he had his bark on." After researching his years in the Badlands, the writer came to TR and said that it was "an idyll." Roosevelt nodded and said, "That's it exactly."

Yet all this was to come. Stepping off the train in the summer of 1884, he was a devastated twenty-five-year-old widower with wife just buried and a child left behind. He had gone West not thinking to recover from his loss, but merely to live what was left of his life in its afterglow.

On his previous brief trip he had found the geography merely exotic. But now he saw something in the grim and desolate environment that resonated with his inner state. The nineteenth century, inclined to make moral judgments about nature, regarded an area such as the Badlands as a deathscape. Indeed, the ground over which TR rode in his first lonely days in Dakota Territory was strewn with bones and buffalo skulls. The maze of connected gullies below the tabled-off buttes had bogs and quicksand where animals and sometimes men and horses got caught. The lignite coal seams running through the area smoldered from subterranean fires, and where their heat came in contact with ground water a mephitic mist of steam might hiss up ominously.

The first whites to explore the area, French explorers down from Canada, had called it *mauvaises terres à traverser*, bad lands to travel through. For the American cowboys who came to Dakota Territory a generation later to work cattle on one of the great open ranges of North America, it was just Bad Lands. Yet for TR, gripped by heartbreak, it was something else. He said later that the Badlands looked like Poe sounded. He was not referring to the Poe who had written macabre horror stories, but to the author of a body of verse filled with the elegiac music of loss. It is possible that in his solitary explorations during his first few weeks in the Badlands, lines from "Annabel Lee" ran through TR's mind. It was a morbid coincidence that the name of the tragic heroine in Poe's most compelling poem was so close to that of Alice Lee, whose early death also left a lover distraught.

The landscape of the Badlands had a mournful beauty that drew out his inner torment like a poultice. For weeks TR explored the "jagged buttes [which] throw the most curious shadows, under the cloudless, glaring sky." It was, he later wrote, "as grim and desolate and forbidding as any place on earth could be." Signs of the constant assault of natural forces—sandblasting, eroding, freezing, and scorching—were everywhere. Yet he gradually realized that this might be as easily considered evidence of endurance as of breakdown. And within this devastated grandeur he glimpsed the possibility for the kind of deep mourning that might, in time, lead to respite and even reconciliation.

But he had not come West simply to experience the pathetic fallacy. He had already bought into a cattle herd and now he set up headquarters with his partners at the Maltese Cross Ranch, a cabin about seven miles outside of Medora. He added another $26,000 to the money he had put up the previous summer to expand the herd. But while the Maltese Cross would do as a working ranch for the cattle enterprise, he needed to have a more remote spot to be alone. In his explorations he found a building site thirty-five miles farther away from Medora on a rise looking at the Little Missouri. He decided to build a "lodge" he called Elkhorn.

He would spend much of his time at Elkhorn reading and writing and just sitting on the porch watching the light on the buttes dissolve into a purple shade and the line of cottonwoods across the way from him go dark. But he also threw himself into his new occupation of rancher. On most days, he was set up before dawn, working the cattle, and he didn't stop until dusk. He was attracted by the world of the cowboy—an elemental world of laconic humor and occasional violence—and he wanted to succeed on the cowboy's terms. With the steely determination of the asthmatic teenager who had *made* his body, he now pushed himself to the limit, proving that he could survive in a rugged society of men, a world away from his petticoat upbringing. "I have just come in from spending *thirteen* hours in the saddle," he breathlessly wrote Bamie shortly after arriving in the Badlands, and then went on to detail his exploits.

It would be several years until historian Frederick Jackson Turner pronounced the official closing of the West, but it was already almost an accomplished fact. The buffalo TR killed on his trip to Dakota Territory the previous summer was perhaps one of the last in the area. The Sioux Indians had been for the most part corraled on reservations, although TR would have an edgy confrontation or two during his time in the Dakotas. The dime novelists were already beginning to practice colorful taxidermy on the still warm corpse of the Western experience. Yet something of its authenticity still remained. Locking his grief away in a secret chamber of his heart, TR plunged into the dusky *fin de siècle* atmosphere with enthusiasm.

Soon he was being transformed, and he watched, almost from the outside, as it happened. In a letter to a New York newspaperman he wrote: "It would electrify some of my friends who have accused me of representing the kid gloved element in politics if they could see me galloping over the plains. . . ."

He was viewed as an oddity by his cowhands, but he gradually won respect by his hard work, forthrightness, and courage. One incident that became locally famous occurred when he went into the tiny town of Mingusville—named after its founding couple of Minnie and Gus—after a day spent looking for strays. Overtaken by darkness, he went to the town's ramshackle hotel to get out of the cold. Going into the bar for a cup of coffee, he saw a dangerous situation—a man drunkenly waving a pair of revolvers and talking with "strident profanity" while a frightened group of onlookers cowered. TR could tell that the drunk had been firing his guns by the three bullet holes in the clock.

"Four Eyes is going to treat," the man said when he saw TR. Roosevelt joined in the laugh and sat down at a table, ignoring the threat. The drunk came over and stood above him, a gun in each hand, using foul language as he again commanded him to buy drinks. "Well, if I've got to, I've got to," Roosevelt shrugged. Standing up quickly, he suddenly struck the man in the face with both fists. Both guns discharged as the drunk went down, unconscious, but no one was hit. TR disarmed him and the others dragged him out to a shed to sleep it off until morning when he was put aboard the first train out of town.

There were thieves and sinister figures all around him, mixing with the hardworking men and women sculpting their lives out of the grudging Badlands environment. TR made himself part of this drama, which he would later celebrate with lyrical prose in *The Winning of the West*. He had no doubt read Ned Buntline's saga of Buffalo Bill as a teenager and knew that the West was a theater where life could imitate art. (It was *after* Buntline's books about him were published that William Cody killed the Cheyenne chief Yellow Hand, thus finally inhabiting the legend the author had already created.) It no doubt occurred to TR that he might be his own Buntline, creating a fantasy self that would become real.

He took pains to outfit himself for his role. Thus, as he made ready to go on a hunting expedition into the Big Horn mountains, he wrote Bamie: "I wear a sombrero, silk neckerchief, fringed buckskin shirt, sealskin chaparajos or riding trousers; alligator hide boots; and with my pearl hilted revolvers and beautifully finished Winchester rifle I shall be able to face anything." He didn't even mention the silver-mounted Bowie knife by Tiffany, the silver belt buckle shaped like a bear head, or the silver spurs embossed with his initials.

If he was different from other dudes who came to the West to act out their fantasies, it was because he understood that he was engaging in behavior a later age might have called existential. As he later wrote in his *Autobiography*, "There were all kinds of things of which I was afraid at first. . . . But by acting as if I was not afraid, I gradually ceased to be afraid."

Opportunities to *act as if* came frequently. After TR returned from a hunting trip to the Big Horn where he shot a charging grizzly bear ("The bullet hole in his skull was as exactly between his eyes as if I had measured the distance with a carpenter's rule."), he found that a local bully named Paddock had stopped by the Elkhorn Ranch with several of his henchmen to say that he owned the rights to the range on which TR was running his cattle and that if TR did not pay grazing fees he would take the money out of his hide. Roosevelt immediately rode to Paddock's house. Rapping on his door, he looked the man in the eye: "I understand you have threatened to kill me on sight. I have come over to see when you want to begin the killing and to let you know that if you have anything to say against me, now is the time to say it." Taken aback by that "foolish grit" in TR that Elliott had once noted with admiration, Paddock replied weakly that he must have been misunderstood.

Men might still refer to him as "Four Eyes," but if so it was only after following the famous injunction in the classic western *The Virginian* written by TR's Harvard friend Owen Wister: "Smile when you say that, stranger."

TR would talk about his days in the Badlands later on as if they constituted a single piece of time. And they did in an imaginative sense, the same way that Thoreau's time at Walden Pond composed itself imaginatively into a single season of solitude. But just as Thoreau had actually walked into Concord every now and then, so TR periodically left his ranch during his time in the Dakotas to travel back to New York to get photographed in his frontier getup, keep his hand in politics, check on "Baby Lee" (it was still hard to say that first name), and indulge his gregarious side, which was unrequited by taciturn ranch hands and shopkeepers.

He was pleased to hear that Elliott was the father of a new baby girl named Eleanor who had been born and christened at the Hudson River home of Anna's parents. His brother had been very much on TR's mind during the Western sojourn. He had always envied the ease with which

Elliott rode and shot, abilities perfected in his early experiences in Texas, and now he was acquiring by dint of hard effort what came naturally to his brother. He would dedicate *Hunting Trip of a Ranchman,* the book he was writing about his adventures even as they were unfolding, to "that keenest of sportsmen and truest of friends, Elliott Roosevelt." Yet even so, the long competition still smoldered, and TR could not resist asserting, when telling the story of his bear, that a grizzly's size and ferocity would certainly enable it to make short work even of the largest tiger.

On one of his trips home in the fall of 1885, he ran into Edith Carow on the doorstep of Bamie's house. It was their first meeting in nearly two years. Edith must have seen immediately that the remnants of "Teddy" had been bleached out of TR by the harsh alkaline environment of the Badlands. The sickliness that had stayed with him since his boyhood was gone; he was bronzed and toughened. It was clear that somewhere in the hundreds of dusty miles he had ridden, the excitable prodigy she once knew had gotten lost and the steady young man had been found.

As for Edith herself, TR must have seen that while she was still proud and self-contained, she was also perhaps a little chastened by the possibility of spinsterhood that lay ahead. Although not a beauty like the dead Alice, she had matured into a handsome woman with a strong face and widely spaced eyes that took on a look of dreamy sensuality in repose. In her own way she had become as seasoned during their years apart as he had been.

When they separated this time, it was after having reestablished the strong feelings they once had for each other. Returning to the Elkhorn Ranch, TR began a correspondence with Edith. Soon there was an understanding: at some time in the near future, they would pick up their life together. In retrospect, there seemed an element of fate in their rediscovery of each other. As Edith wrote him: "I do care about being pretty for you & every girl I see I think, 'I wonder if I am as pretty as she is.' . . . You know I love you very much & would do anything in the world to please you. . . . You know all about me darling. I never could have loved anyone else & love you with all the passion of a girl who has never loved before."

Theodore Roosevelt's Wild West Show, as one critic later termed his days in the Badlands, was almost over. In the spring of 1886 Edith sailed for England for an extended visit with her mother and sister and TR decided to meet and marry her there. But there was one final adventure that took place in late March. TR and his hands had been holed up in his cabin through the deep of winter—they playing cards and he reading books such as his friend Henry Cabot Lodge's *Studies in Literature*. Outside, as the thaw began, the Little Missouri was a jagged thoroughfare of ice chunks roaring and crunching as they worked their way down the channel. The only way to hunt the game on the other side of the river was to cross in a small boat TR kept staked to the shore. One day he went out to find that the tether was cut and the boat gone.

It was clear who had taken it—a gang of three horse thieves headed by a notorious character named Redhead Finnegan who was trying to get out of the territory to avoid a lynching. Roosevelt ordered his men to quickly build another boat and then they took off after the thieves. The weather was so cold that ice formed on the handles of the oars his two men used to navigate the flow while TR sat in the stern reading Matthew Arnold's essays.

After three days' journey down the Little Missouri, he finally saw his boat tied up at the shore. He and his men landed and sneaked up on the thieves' camp and got the drop on them in a tense confrontation. TR was contemptuous of the outlaws, particularly after he discovered that among their cache of reading material there was nothing more elevated than a few dime novels like *The History of the James Brothers* and worn copies of the *Police Gazette*.

After several days keeping Finnegan and his henchmen under the gun while waiting for the weather to break—he would later say that this duty combined the functions of "sheriff and arctic explorer"—TR finally found a cowboy who loaned him a horse. Riding fifteen miles through the snow to a ranch in the Killdeer Mountains, he hired a prairie schooner driven by a "rugged old plainsman." After sending his men on with the boats, Roosevelt packed the outlaws into the wagon and followed on foot with his Winchester cocked and ready. It took two days to get to the small town of Dickinson, during which time TR could not allow himself to sleep or relax his guard on the men. When he completed his mission, he was delighted to find that he would get a fee as deputy sheriff that amounted to fifty dollars. In a letter to his sister Conie he said that now he felt "equal to anything." Pursuing the osmotic exchange between myth and reality in the West one last time, TR had a picture of himself taken standing guard over his outlaw captives. It would be accepted as authentic for about a hundred years, until a descendant of one of the "bad men" noted that he was actually her grandfather, one of TR's ranch hands, who had gone on the chase.

With the onset of summer, TR put his affairs at the ranch in order. He knew he would probably take a loss on the cattle when they were eventually sold, but he had found something during his two years in the West that was priceless—a serviceable self that would last him the rest of his life. He had found a voice too—not that of a partisan politician, although he knew he would probably play that role again in the future, but of a public man. As a valedictory to the experience, he agreed to give a July 4th oration in the small town of Dickinson:

"I do not undervalue for a moment our material prosperity," he began. "Like all Americans, I like big things; big prairies, big forest and mountains, big wheat fields, railroads—and herds of cattle too—big factories and steamboats and everything else. But we must keep steadily in mind that no people were ever yet benefited by riches if their prosperity corrupted their virtue. It is of more importance that we should show ourselves honest, brave, truthful and intelligent than we should own all the railways and grain elevators in the world. We have fallen heirs to the most glorious heritage a people ever received and each of us must do his part if we wish to show that this nation is worthy of its good fortune."

After the speech he had a conversation with Arthur Packard, editor of the local paper of record, *The Badlands Cowboy*. Packard had known something about TR's past when he arrived in Dakota and had always suspected that his time there would turn out to be only an interlude in a larger drama. Now he asked Roosevelt what he planned to do and TR replied that he had decided to return to the East and pick up his work in public life.

"You will be President of the United States," Packard said after thinking for a moment.

"If your prophecy comes true," Roosevelt replied, making no effort to disagree with the proposition, "I will do my part to make a good one."

*L*ate in her life, as Edith sat one afternoon in the yard at Sagamore Hill talking to one of her granddaughters about her marriage to TR, she suddenly looked off in the middle distance and then said, almost to herself, "I always knew he'd come back to me! I knew it!"

In reality, however, the path to their reunion was strewn with obstacles, most of them the result of TR's guilt and the Victorian morality from which it sprang. In the first days after he had rediscovered Edith, when he was back at the Elkhorn Ranch, some of the hands who worked for him were surprised to see him pacing back and forth in the ranch house, pounding a fist into his palm and muttering disconsolately to himself about "constancy." He felt he had committed a double infidelity—to Edith, whom he had betrayed by first marrying someone else; and to Alice Lee, whom he was betraying now by his moral weakness in falling in love again. Almost as if fearing censure, he had kept the news of his engagement secret from his family as long as possible, admitting it only after a New York paper published the rumor.

"You could not reproach me one-half as bitterly for my inconstancy and unfaithfulness as I reproach myself," he finally wrote in a grimly self-lacerating letter informing Bamie of his plans. "Were I sure there were a heaven my one prayer would be I might never go there, lest I met those I loved on earth who are dead."

Yet his anxiety began to diminish when he and Edith were finally married in a small private ceremony in London in December 1886. The guilt would evaporate over time, as Edith filled up his life. It was more than a marriage or even what a later age would call a partnership; the two of them were mates in a relationship that completed them both.

TR's daughter Alice later described her stepmother as being characterized by a "rather parched quality," attributing this to her frayed-cuff upbringing, and said also that she "had a gift for making her own people uncomfortable." But a Roosevelt cousin interpreted some of the same qualities in a different way and wrote to congratulate TR for having chosen "a girl whose main characteristic is truth."

As might be expected of someone descended from Puritan divine Jonathan Edwards, Edith stood for the virtues of duty and discipline. She was formidable enough that a niece later said, "She was the only person I ever knew Auntie Bye to be a little bit afraid of." She would occasionally function as a censor for TR's sudden enthusiasms and a governor of his appetites, yet she also nurtured what his friend Owen Wister called "the boy eternal" that lived within him. Her cool exterior hid a passionate heart, and the bond between her and TR was based on satisfactions of the flesh quite as much as those of the spirit. Her keen intelligence and high standards made her a soulmate in a way that her predecessor never could have been. ("She would have bored him to death," was Edith's summary judgment on the dead Alice.)

Each of them molded to the other's contours. Edith later wrote her eldest son, Ted, that TR had drawn her out, keeping her from giving in to the selfish temptation to "live to oneself." TR also wrote Ted about the relationship, saying that he had entered marriage "thoughtless and selfish" but that Edith had reformed him: "Had she not done this, I would in the end have made her life much harder, and mine much less happy."

When the newlyweds returned to America in March 1887, after a honeymoon on the Continent, TR moved them into the big house he had designed at Oyster Bay. Instead of Leeholm, it was now called Sagamore Hill, after the Indian chief who had once ruled this part of Long Island. Built to his specifications during his years in Dakota Territory, it was austere and somewhat gloomy, and Edith moved quickly to civilize the savage frontier look given by the hides on the floors and heads on the wall. She was pregnant, which gave a new meaning to the Roosevelt family motto carved onto the facade of the house—*Qui Plantavit Curabit,* "He who has planted will preserve." Supervising the landscaping around Sagamore, TR planted a variety of trees in orderly confusion, including the weeping elm at the corner of the house where all his children in turn would watch from upstairs bedrooms as orioles built their purselike nests each spring.

There was one immediate problem—what to do about his golden-haired daughter, "Baby Lee," who had acquired something of the ambiguous status of a love child. Bamie had mothered the girl since the tragedy three years earlier. She wanted to keep Alice, and surprisingly, TR was willing, but Edith refused. In part she may have wanted to break the hold the sisters had always had on her husband, but she also wanted to embrace his past and make it her own.

Little Alice had lived with Bamie on Madison Avenue (a few blocks up from Conie's house). She always remembered the exact moment when she entered her new family. She wore a dress trimmed in elaborate lace and carried a bouquet of pink tea roses as an offering for her stepmother. (She also wore leg braces which Bamie, especially sensitive to physical defects, had prescribed to correct pronated ankles.) Bamie had said to her before the meeting, "If you are unhappy you can always come back to me." But there was a sense of finality to the arrangement, and after Alice entered her new home, Bamie tried to remove herself as far as possible to make things easier for both of them, eventually accepting an offer from Sara and James Roosevelt to go with them and two-year-old Franklin, Elliott's godson, to Mexico in a private rail car where she spent her time fearful of being attacked by bandidos and worrying about her "blue eyed darling."

Within days Alice was coming downstairs every morning on TR's shoulders, commanding him imperiously, "Now, pig!" Yet, she would always be her father's most difficult child, a sophisticated connoisseur of his faults even if she was always ready to jump to his defense when he was criticized by anyone other than herself. The relationship between her and Edith was even more complex, requiring a constant adjustment that, despite the touchy love that eventually developed between them, they never quite got right. For Edith, the girl would be a headstrong reminder of a time when she had not been in the picture. For Alice, Edith could be kind (she always remembered the gentle way her stepmother had massaged her ankles after the braces were off for the day) but she had a sharp tongue that intimidated even TR, although, as Alice later said, "He'd stop her if she was being *very* disagreeable." In addition to possessing her father, Edith collaborated with him in allowing her real mother to disappear down a memory hole. Even when she visited her doting Lee grandparents twice a year the subject of the dead woman hardly came up, although they otherwise indulged Alice's every whim, showering her with elaborate gifts such as her own pony and cart. The only mention of Alice Lee came from the little girl's new nurse, who demanded a prayer "for your little mother in heaven" each night.

Alice's sense of the ambivalence of her position was accented by the birth of a brother a few months after she came to live at Sagamore. She characterized Theodore Jr. as a "howling polly parrot" and said, after watching him at Edith's breast, "he eats Mama." Ted was the beginning of a new family that grew up around her over the next few years. Alice was in it but not fully *of* it, forming strong bonds with her brothers and sister, but always remaining a little distant from the unity they had among themselves. "Sister," the title they gave her, indicated her slightly distant relationship to the children who soon surrounded her. Irony, a sensibility of distance, would become Alice's defense. Her aunts and cousins might occasionally whisper sentimentally about the beautiful ghost whose pictures were on her dresser, for instance, but as Alice learned to read and was quickly exposed to the classics by her stepmother, she came to think of her absent mother, ironically, as Little Dora, the Child Bride.

For the first year of his marriage to Edith TR worked on *The Winning of the West*. His other books had been successful, and so while he had lost much of his inheritance on the cattle business (the herd had been decimated in the violent winter of 1887, which virtually ended open-range ranching in the Dakotas), he felt that he could support the family as a writer. But he was also maneuvering to get back into the political arena, which he now saw as a sort of analogue for the West—a place that rewarded resourcefulness and strength of character and offered personal power commensurate with personal risk. In 1888, as the first two volumes of his work were receiving rave reviews in England as well as the United States, his friend Henry Cabot Lodge, now a senator from Massachusetts, convinced the Harrison administration to offer TR an appointment on the Civil Service Commission. The pay was low and the job was in Washington, but civil service reform (a matter no doubt connected in TR's mind with his father's fate) was one of the burning issues of the day and would thus place him at the center of things.

Roosevelt immediately created a stir. Partly it was his pugnacious commitment to reform that drew attention. But there was also the *spectacle* of him. Enemies might deride him as "that damned cowboy," but the persona he had created was closer to that of the archetypal Victorian intellectual. There was the same commitment to knowledge, the same effort always to extract a general truth from his learning and experience, the same inclination to argue for victory, and the same fondness for the telling phrase. Speaking of the phlegmatic son of Ulysses S. Grant, for instance, TR said, "He is one of the most interesting studies that I know of from the point of view of atavism. I am sure his brain must reproduce that of some long lost arboreal ancestor." About another opponent encountered in his days on the Civil Service Commission he merely said, "Every time he opens his mouth, he subtracts from the sum total of human wisdom."

A coterie of Roosevelt-watchers soon formed. One of them, and by no means the least critical, was Henry Adams, whose exclusive salon TR and Edith were invited to join. Endpoint of the most famous dynasty of American politics (and as such a precursor of the comparable one that would flow from TR himself), Adams particularly liked Edith, who typically appeared at his afternoons cool and collected in a white muslin dress with balloon sleeves and a sailor hat riding the waves of her chestnut hair. He was a little more ambivalent about TR, both fascinated but also faintly repelled by his inexhaustible energy and finding in him "that quality that medieval theology assigned to God—he is pure act."

Others besides Adams would see TR as chewing his way through his future like a buzzsaw, always busy and fully engaged, exploiting his chief quality, which was the ability to live intensely every action and feel intensely every thought. This was the self he offered them. It was so overpowering that they often missed the private family man who was being created along with the public figure. Yet until the end of his life, TR always made it clear that he believed his children were his best piece of work, the thing he had done that would best stand the test of time.

His second son, Kermit, was born in 1889, and soon TR's letters to his sister were filled with delighted observations about how the baby was regarded by two-year-old Ted, who called him "little brother in a blanket" and accused him of "miaowing." Then a year later came his daughter Ethel, a sturdy and good-natured child he called "Elephant Johnny" because of her stout frame and healthy constitution.

The appearance of three children in three years led one of Edith's friends to comment acidly, "When I think of their very moderate income, and the recklessness with which she brings children into the world without the means either to educate them or provide for them I am quite worked up." Yet TR was delighted. A practicing Social Darwinist, he believed that people with a bloodline such as his own should not be reluctant to do battle with the immigrant classes in "the warfare of the cradle."

While he was eminently Victorian in some ways, TR was no remote Victorian father when it came to the children. They were dear to him and he felt their joys and sorrows keenly. When three-year-old Ted became seriously ill in the spring of 1890, TR wrote Bamie: "It was just heart breaking to have the darling little fellow sick; and the first forty-eight hours I look back on with a shudder. When he would rally at times and come out of his stupor and begin to say the cunning things he always says, in his changed, sick voice, it was about as much as Edith and I could stand."

Thinking of his son, moreover, always reminded TR of the deep love that had produced him. In the summer of 1892, when he was back in the Badlands for a last farewell to the Elkhorn Ranch, Roosevelt wrote to "My Own Darling Ted-Boy": "Your father thinks of you all the time; almost as much as he does of your mother. Put your soft chubby arms around her neck and kiss her many many times for me because I love you both so dearly."

A crucial figure in the growing Roosevelt household was the Irish nurse "Mame," Mary Ledwith, who had come over from Ireland over thirty years earlier to take care of Edith at her birth and had easily transferred her affections to the next generation. A woman with an austere Irish face and a warm heart, she figured in their earliest memories. Kermit, for instance, the Roosevelt child who would ultimately inherit his father's wanderlust, never forgot Mame's story of leaving her homeland during the Potato Famine and sailing across the Atlantic, in her telling a tale of adventure, not tragedy.

The one who gave Mame the most trouble and the most pleasure was Ted. Slightly cross-eyed and with a mild speech defect, the boy was scrawny and energetic. He focused on his father, once looking in the mirror and howling, "Ted got no mufstache, Ted got nothin' but a mouf." He liked to put on TR's shoes and clomp around the house, a premonitory acceptance of the thankless task that would fall to him in life. One of his earliest memories was playing hide-and-seek with TR in the dark upper rooms of Sagamore. He and the other children would seek their father—that was the object of their lives as well as their games—and when they found him TR would rush out of the shadows with a savage ursine roar and they would scatter in terror.

Closer to Alice than the rest of the children, Ted nonetheless tormented her when they were little. Mishearing the story of how she had been given out to a nurse after her mother's sudden death, he ran around the house shouting "Sissy had a sweat nurse! Sissy had a sweat nurse!" Knowing that any child who became ill got a "sickness present," he spent a day embracing Alice warmly when she got the chicken pox in hopes of getting the disease too.

As Ted got older he and Kermit became pals, developing odd games such as drinking as much water as possible and then showing their distended stomachs to their mother, causing her to gasp in alarm. TR got the two boys a tutor and was interested that Ted was strong in history, particularly when it was about warfare, while Kermit, described by his sister Ethel later on as "pale and yellow-haired, dreamy, detached and timid," showed a natural aptitude for languages.

But TR and Edith were always the real schoolmasters in the household. Edith read Maria Edgeworth and Sir Walter Scott to the children. She also gave moral instruction and when challenged to give sources for her pronouncements, she would cite "that military gentleman, General Information." TR seemed to personify this figure. He recited *The Song of Roland* in French and identified the species of elephant used by Hannibal by the shape of the ears on the animals portrayed on Carthaginian coins. The children sometimes tried to argue with him, for instance, about the spelling of "chaps," but when they went to check they found that their father was not only correct but cited as an authority by the dictionary.

TR recited ballads and sang Civil War songs and chanted epic poems such as the *Nibelungenlied*. All the children were expected to memorize poetry and recite it on command. When Rudyard Kipling came to visit Sagamore, Ted stood up and manfully recited "The Ballad of East and West," persevering, as Alice later recalled, despite the fact that the poet "glowered and raised his tremendous eyebrows."

During TR's years in the Civil Service Commission, the family made annual summer pilgrimages from Washington to Sagamore. TR joined them there whenever his work permitted. When he could not, he wrote the children daily from his office, often "picture letters" filled with hand-drawn animals illustrating some moral fable. One such letter to

Ted began, "A cow, a calf, a pony and a big dog all lived happily in a barnyard in Texas. . . ." The drawings showed the cow and calf being attacked by a wolf, which the cow tries to hold off while the pony runs back and gets the dog, who rushes to aid them.

Another picture letter showed some beavers, an elk, and a bull moose. It began: "A beaver had built himself a nice mud house in which his wife and children lived; it was beside a pool, with big trees near by, which the beaver gnawed on. He had lovely fur and a flat, scaly tail, and he swam in the pool with the kitten beavers. . . ." The moose and elk begin to fight and the beaver rushes out to gnaw down a tree, whose fall separates the combatants and frightens them away, restoring peace to the pool. As always the fable is concluded with a personal message: "Darling Ted, I love you very much and I shall be home Saturday, and we'll all go and climb trees Sunday."

These picture letters became the quintessence of Father, one of the few things that could mitigate his absence. The children would continue to demand them, sometimes with chagrin, when they were adolescents and the author was in the White House. Almost sixteen, for instance, Kermit, then attending Groton, begged for one and, when he got it, wrote back to TR: "I loved the picture letter, and I, for one, think that you are *most* decidedly wrong in saying that your pictures were limited to seven year olds. *Decidedly wrong.*"

When his first son and namesake, Elliott Jr., was born in 1889, Elliott wrote Bamie: "I know you will like him when you see him; he is such a funny, sturdy little chap and really don't look so ugly."

He had tried to be as much the paterfamilias as TR was, but in this endeavor too he seemed to fall behind his brother. For the world at large, Elliott was still one of the most pleasant fellows around. There was no more daring polo player or better huntsman; no more convivial drinking partner. But his wife and children acquired a different view of him as moody and sidetracked. He had no job and lived as other of his friends among the idle rich did, off his inheritance. Instead of anchoring him in a domestic life, his wife, Anna, exaggerated his self-indulgent traits by her own frivolity.

Everyone who knew him searched for causes to explain Elliott's inability to achieve a foothold. Perhaps the blackouts he had suffered since adolescence were actually epileptic seizures or even the result of a tumor. Perhaps his heavy drinking was actually a way of keeping the symptoms

under control. Nobody considered the possibility that Elliott's problems were in any way related to his brother. Yet he seemed to have
timed many of the critical moves of his life with TR in mind. During
TR's Badlands interlude, Elliott had functioned fairly well as a stand-in.
But then, in 1887, a few weeks after TR married Edith and returned to
New York, Elliott had left again with his own family for an extended
trip to Europe. The ship he took was rammed in the fog shortly after
leaving port and several passengers were killed. His baby daughter,
Eleanor, always remembered her father standing in a lifeboat below
gesturing for a crewman to drop her down to him. The three-year-old
was terrified, crooning afterward, "Baby does not want to go in the
water. Not in a boat." When Elliott booked another passage, Eleanor
was so disturbed that she had to be left at home with Aunt Anna.

After six months abroad, Elliott returned to make another of his new
starts. He took a position in the brokerage firm of an uncle. But he was
bored and aimless, unable to commit himself to a career. He built an
elaborate house at Hempstead, Long Island, where he reestablished himself as one of the most reckless figures in weekend polo matches.

He no longer looked like his brother. While TR was now heavily
muscled from his cowboy days, Elliott was slim and elegant, typically
attired in a Panama suit and straw hat, nonchalantly puffing on a che-
root. He no longer seemed to crave TR's company either. Hempstead
was only twenty miles from Sagamore, but Elliott made it a world
away.

Wounded by the fact that his brother visited so rarely, TR wrote
bitterly to Bamie that he guessed Elliott found Sagamore "insufferably
dull," which indeed was probably the case. TR tried to keep up the
relationship by visiting at Hempstead. He took up polo too to have
something in common with his brother but once again found himself in
competition. Corinne described one game in which Theodore rushed
after Elliott at terrific speed as he took the ball downfield. "There was
a thump of horseflesh as brother tried to ride brother out. Suddenly—no
one saw how—Theodore was thrown, and knocked unconscious."

Ultimately, TR retreated from Elliott, noting sadly to Bamie that the
life their brother led was "very unhealthy and it leads to nothing." As
if to prove this theorem, Elliott broke his ankle while practicing for an
amateur circus that summer and when the bone did not knit properly
began to use, in addition to increasing volumes of alcohol, a new drug,
laudanum, to kill the pain. Out of TR's sight, he was often out of
control as well.

Elliott's domestic arrangements seemed almost calculated to confuse his children. He was emotionally expansive and yet morally off course; Anna was morally correct, although emotionally remote. Their five-year-old daughter, Eleanor, particularly was whiplashed between their extremes. She received a maudlin, often self-pitying love from her father, who promised her a never-never land of perfect attention; and a cold shoulder from her mother, who seemed affronted by the fact that the girl had inherited none of her beauty. ("Eleanor, I hardly know what's going to happen to you," Anna once sighed. "You're so plain that you really have nothing to do except *be good.*") As a result, the little girl was overly earnest, censorious, needy. Taking a cue from her mother, she called herself "an ugly little thing." When Anna called her "Granny" in front of strangers," Eleanor later said, it made her want to "sink through the floor in shame."

She would retain some good memories of growing up—in particular a time when she was two and went with her parents to Hyde Park to stay with James and Sara Roosevelt. While there, she met her father's godson, Franklin, then four, for the first time. A gentle and overprotected boy with a large imagination, he watched her for a moment standing in the doorway with her fingers in her mouth. Then he asked if she wanted to play "horsey" and then took her to the nursery and began a game that required her to ride on his back.

But for the most part, Eleanor was unhappy. Without doing anything—just by her awkward looks and presence—she felt that she was "always disgracing my mother." The only moments of closeness between them came when Anna was incapacitated by blinding headaches and little Eleanor was called on to massage her temples. "Feeling that I was useful," she said later on, "was perhaps the greatest joy I experienced."

Elliott was blind to the growing misery of his daughter. He seemed unable to get off the emotional seesaw that rode him down as TR rose. Each new reminder of his responsibilities—responsibilities that his brother handled so well—caused Elliott to tumble deeper into the hole he dug for himself. In addition to drinking heavily, he began to keep company with other women. Soon the relationship between him and Anna had become the archetypal Victorian melodrama involving the long-suffering wife and the profligate husband careening between debauchery and remorse.

In early 1890, attempting to save his marriage, Elliott sold his Long Island estate and his brownstone in Manhattan and once again took the

family on an extended trip abroad. The announced purpose of the move
was to break with his life of aimlessness and dissipation. But some
wondered if he was only trying to get out of the sight of his brother and
sisters so that he could do what he wanted without fear of censure. After
alluding to his situation, he said in a letter to Bamie, "But I am not
going to speak of this all again even to you. I am too sad & need no
friends."

But for a while it seemed that he had found his old charismatic self in
Europe. He had a memorable meeting with Buffalo Bill in Germany
where the Wild West Show was on tour, and sang with the gondoliers
during the family's prolonged stay in Venice. He was pleased when
Anna told him that she was pregnant again. He seemed so reformed that
Anna added a note to a letter to Bamie, "Ask Theodore to write praising
him for keeping straight and pulling himself together." But then, as the
birth of the child neared, he began drinking heavily again, and Anna
became so fearful of his erratic behavior that she asked Bamie to come
to Switzerland to stay with them. About this time, a servant girl back in
New York named Katy Mann who had worked for Elliott threatened to
publicize the fact that he had seduced and abandoned her, leaving her
with a child.

While fighting for civil service reform in Washington, TR also began
to fight with his brother in an accusatory transatlantic correspondence.
His prudish morality made the offense with the servant girl particularly
hideous to him. He urged Bamie, who was about to sail for Europe, to
get their brother into a Swiss sanatorium, but when she arrived Elliott
had already committed himself.

TR wanted to believe the letters Elliott sent denying the relationship
with Katy Mann and at first he refused to pay the blackmail the woman
asked for. But when her baby was born with what he had to agree were
"Rooseveltian features," he felt betrayed anew.

The next thing TR heard, Elliott had left his Switzerland sanatorium
for Paris, taking Bamie and the rest of his family with him. His son Hall
was born there, and Eleanor was placed in a convent school. Her most
memorable moment there came when she saw all the attention another
girl got from swallowing a coin and claimed that she had swallowed one
too. The nuns didn't believe her and under questioning Eleanor had to
admit that she had lied just so that someone would notice her.

When Bamie informed TR that Elliott had now taken up with an
American woman living in Paris, it was the last straw. He wrote back:
"Anna must be made to understand that it is both maudlin and crim-

inal—I am choosing my words with scientific exactness—to continue
living with Elliott." Soon afterward, Elliott became violent and suicidal, and Bamie put him in an asylum and brought his family back to
America.

The issue of the Roosevelts' early years had been whether or not
Theodore would survive. Now Elliott was the leading character in what
had become the family's ongoing melodrama. He and Anna and their
pitiful children were talked about endlessly in the letters that other
family members passed back and forth between themselves. As Anna
took up residence alone, Corinne was the only one who supported
Elliott, Bamie and Theodore having both hardened their hearts against
him. TR, in fact, had gone so far as to petition the court for a "writ of
lunacy" that would secure his brother's assets for his wife and children.
This led to a shocking headline in the *Tribune: "Elliott Roosevelt De-
mented by Excess."* Elliott wrote an indignant letter of coverup to the
editor: "I wish emphatically to state that my brother Theodore is taking
no steps to have a commission pass on my sanity with or without my
wife's approval. I am in Paris taking the cure at an établissement hy-
drothérapeutique, which my nerves shaken by several severe accidents
in the hunting field, made necessary."

TR went to Paris to reason with Elliott one last time, agreeing to drop
the court proceeding if his brother would agree to settle two thirds of his
property on his family and to refrain from seeing them until he had
proved his "worthiness" by taking a "cure" and then gradually showing
himself capable of leading a normal life.

Slinking back to America, Elliott agreed to try to rehabilitate himself,
saying that he wanted Anna to see him "not as she last saw me, flushed
with wine, reckless and unworthy but [as] an earnest, repentant self
respecting gentle-man." He put himself under a doctor's care in Illinois
and took a cure based on bichloride of gold. After staying away from
drink for several months, he went to Virginia to manage the land and
timber holdings of his sister Corinne's husband, Douglas Robinson.

Anna tried to work her way through her situation. Should she continue to behave as a married woman? Was it appropriate to go to a social
function with a gentleman if she was chaperoned? In the fall of 1892, she
underwent surgery for an unknown malady and just as she was going
under the ether cried out about her unbearable life. Hearing about Anna's anguish, Elliott wrote a guilt-ridden letter to her mother: "Did she
say she wanted to die, that I had made her so utterly miserable that she
did not care to live anymore? . . . Know, Mrs. Hall, that for all the

suffering I have caused I have suffered ten fold more myself. For it was *I* who sinned and I know it, and I had none of the Divine comfort of being able to *grant forgiveness."*

Anna recovered from surgery, but soon after contracted diphtheria. As she sank deep into the sickness, Elliott asked to be allowed to visit her and she refused. He appealed to Anna's mother: "It is most horrible and full of *awe* to me that my *wife* not only does not want me near her in sickness or trouble but *fears* me." Before Mrs. Hall could send an answer, Anna died on December 7, 1892. A few months later his son and namesake, little Elliott Jr., died of scarlet fever.

As his brother faced tragedy, TR was experiencing triumph. His exploits on the Civil Service Commission had made him one of the most discussed figures in the Harrison administration. His family, so different from Elliott's, was happy in the sleepy town of Washington, D.C. A headstrong tomboy (or "guttersnipe," as Edith once called her), Alice was now the head of a gang of boys who formed a secret society in which they dressed like girls and held meetings in the loft of a stable. ("She always had a string of a dozen boys at her heels," Edith wrote disapprovingly, "and being a large and handsome girl was very conspicuous.") Along with Ted and Kermit, Alice liked to coast her bicycle down Connecticut Avenue to Farragut Square to meet TR when he got off the streetcar every day and then walk back home with him. He often bought some little trinket for them. Among the favorites were small farm animals covered in felt, which they branded using a hairpin shaped into a tiny iron with the Maltese cross or the locked horns of the Elkhorn Ranch and then heated over a match.

There were also the lazy days at Sagamore where an expanding menagerie of pets included flying squirrels, guinea pigs, mice, dogs, horses, a bad-tempered badger named Josiah, and an equally bad-tempered bear named Jonathan Edwards in honor of Edith's Puritan forebear. Because of their name, Kermit had tried to eat the firecrackers during one Fourth of July celebration, TR wrote Bamie. And Alice had cut her hair short like a boy's and decided she wanted to give birth to a monkey instead of to twins, her previous ambition. Ted had been given his first gun late one night and because it was too dark to go outside and shoot it, TR took the boy upstairs and, after making him promise not to tell his mother, shot off a round into the ceiling. Kermit, who was still emotionally dependent on Edith, had his leg in a brace because of his

"Roosevelt bones" and, during a fight with Ethel, managed to kick her with the device. When TR began to punish him, Ethel dissolved into tears and tried to interpose herself between them: "Shake *me*, father!"

Edith gathered them together on evenings to read Milton's *L'Allegro* and *Il Penseroso* with classical dictionary at hand to understand the allusions. TR was master of the revels, telling stories and making up games. He was a figure of fun to them because he was so exaggerated. Once when they had a friend to dinner he immediately asked her if she liked the *Nibelungenlied*. Terrified, the girl said yes, although, as Ted said later, this could have been anything from a vegetable to a board game as far as she knew. TR was about to expound on the epic when the children interrupted him: "Father! Don't talk to Isabelle about the *Nibelungenlied*. She doesn't know it. She's just trying to be polite."

Ted was the first to go to school, beginning at the local Cove Neck public school. On good days he and Kermit rode bicycles two miles over the road paved with oyster shells, and on rainy days they were driven by a servant in a yellow-wheeled buggy with a rubber top. The schoolhouse was heated by a potbellied stove and outside there was a bell that summoned the students. Their schoolmates were children from the village, the sons and daughters of laborers and shopkeepers. (When Ted fought with a boy named Gallagher, it was taken as a sign that the resident Knickerbockers did not think themselves too good to mix it up with the local Irish working class.) Inside the one-room schoolhouse, there was always a fresh verse from the Bible copied out on the blackboard every morning in neat Spenserian script by the teacher. Each Christmas every child in school wrote down a gift he or she particularly wanted and TR and Edith got it for them.

TR's family occasionally saw Elliott's pathetic children. Eleanor and her brother, Hall, lived with Anna's mother, Grandmother Hall, in what even the usually optimistic Conie called "grim circumstances" among their mother's grown but still dependent brothers and sisters. Because of her grandmother's repressive nature, Eleanor learned to say she didn't want things as a way of avoiding the disappointment of being told that she couldn't have them, denial thus becoming one of her survival skills. Her Oyster Bay elders felt guilty about her unhappiness but unable to help her, Grandmother Hall having decided to keep the girl from visiting them very often.

Bamie, as always, took in the semi-orphans when she was allowed to. And they sometimes visited Sagamore where TR, unhappy at being unable to approve of their father, showered them with compensatory attention, once hugging Eleanor so hard that he popped the buttons on her frock.

The waiflike girl was close to Alice in age and there were superficial resemblances between their situations. Yet Alice was strong and supple while Eleanor, with her protruding teeth and recessive chin, gave off a downtrodden air. Her behavior was calculated to win sympathy, yet there was something in Eleanor—a combination of smugness, vulnerability, obtuseness, not to speak of an ability to absorb emotional pain—that made an individual like Alice want to punish her. She was a gifted mimic and could "do" her buck-toothed cousin exactly. But for the most part, her assault was more subtle. Knowing that Eleanor was shy about sex, for instance, Alice once got her so upset by talking about the "begats" in the Bible while they were staying at Bamie's house that Eleanor tried to sit on her head with a pillow to stop the prurient talk.

In their ambivalent relationship there were ongoing revelations of character. Once TR was teaching the two of them to dive off a float in Oyster Bay. "Dive, Alicy, dive," he beckoned his daughter from the water. Regarding him as a sort of "sea monster" with his wet mustache and squinting eyes, Alice angrily conquered her fears and dived. Then TR turned to Eleanor. Despite her early near-fatal experience with the ocean, she too dutifully followed his command. After sinking like a rock, she finally rose gasping to the surface, rigid with old fears of shipwreck and drowning. Alice swam by and pushed her under again. It is no wonder that Eleanor later said of their relationship, "While I always admired Alice, I was afraid of her."

In April 1894, TR's fourth child, Archibald, was born, "a cunning little polyp," as he described him in the birth announcement to Bamie. Kermit said that he liked his "dushtpan," a toy cleaning tool, better than the new brother. But the rest of the children were happy. TR reported that "Ted worships the baby . . . [and] Ethel loves 'that Archibald baby,' as she calls him . . . [and] Alice has such a humorous way of looking as she speaks of the small boy."

While TR's life was brimming over, Elliott's was emptying out. Working for his brother-in-law, he wrote Eleanor, now ten, bittersweet letters from his Virginia exile about how he planned someday to reassemble what was left of the family: "Maybe soon I'll come back well and we'll have such good times together, like we used to have." Eleanor was too ready to believe him. Her mother's death, as she later said, had meant nothing to her. In her fantasies, her father had been the only one who ever cared for her, a perfect gentle knight who could rescue her from her austere grandmother. She was pathetically eager to live in the utopia he painted. "Somehow it was always he and I," she wrote later on. "I did not understand whether my brothers were to be our children or whether they would be at school and college. . . ."

Not realizing that it meant the end of his program of rehabilitation, Eleanor was pleased when Elliott left Virginia to return to New York. Disturbed that her Grandmother Hall allowed him to come for her so rarely, she looked forward to those times when he was given permission to pick her up. They would spend the day walking around Central Park, spinning out fantasies of the ideal life they would have together when he finally got a house of his own and was able to bring her and her brother, Hall, to live with him. Once he took her to the Knickerbocker Club and asked her to wait outside for a moment while he went inside to get something. Six hours later, when he had still not come out, the door-man took her home.

He became evasive about his whereabouts and then cut off contact even with Corinne, the family member closest to him. He disappeared into the netherworld of New York, surfacing now and then under his pseudonym, "Mr. Eliot," living with a mistress and periodically drinking himself into unconsciousness. Bamie, Conie, and TR tried to find him, but he eluded them in his furtive descent into the lower depths.

Elliott must have been "feeling the awful night closing in . . . [and] wandering like some stricken, hunted creature," TR later said. He wanted to reach out for him, but he was repelled by the degeneracy. Elliott wanted to reach out too but could not stand to be near the brother he could never hope to match. Drinking anisette and brandy and champagne at the rate of a half dozen bottles a morning, he wrote TR at the Civil Service Commission in Washington two and three times a day, yet would not agree to meet with him.

Elliott became gripped by delusions. At one point he was convinced he was showing dogs to his dead son, Elliott Jr. He began randomly knocking on the doors of strangers, asking them, "Is Miss Eleanor Roosevelt at home?" and then running off in agitation when they didn't understand what he was talking about.

Finally, on August 14, 1894, Elliott had a seizure and fell off some steps at his rooming house, and died while moaning for his family. The *World* wrote his obituary as if describing the sad ending of a Whartonesque social tragedy: "There was a time when there were not many more popular young persons in society than Mr. and Mrs. Elliott Roosevelt. . . ."

Skinny came to Swelly one last time at the mortuary, sitting for a long while beside his body. As Conie wrote Bamie of their brother Theodore, "he cried like a child for a long time." Yet TR said that death seemed to have composed the facial features of "dear old brother" and taken away all his pain. In his last look at Elliott, Theodore convinced himself that he saw once again the person he had grown up with and defined himself against, the "old, generous gallant self of fifteen years ago."

It was the end of a chapter, but not the end of the story. Elliott was gone, making his brother the victor in a contest TR had never really wanted to have. But he had left behind a daughter and godson who would carry on the struggle between the Roosevelts in the next generation.

PART TWO

The Gates of Paradise

"God save you from the werewolf and from your
heart's desire."

—THEODORE ROOSEVELT

*W*hen the 1st Volunteer Cavalry reached camp after marching all day in the tropical rain, it was late in the evening of June 30, 1898. Darkness prevented them from clearly seeing their surroundings, but they knew that the next day would bring the climactic battle they had been hoping for since landing in Cuba eight days earlier. The Rough Riders, as the unit was also known, ate a quick meal and were bedding down when they experienced what one literary sergeant called "a little touch of Teddy in the night." It was Theodore Roosevelt passing among them, clapping a few of the younger men on the back, calming those who looked apprehensive, and speaking at length to particular friends like "Bucky" O'Neil, the "wild reckless lawman" of Arizona Territory who was equally comfortable discussing the novels of Balzac and the desperadoes of the border. As one soldier later recalled, "Roosevelt was talking about two things—duty and glory."

General Leonard Wood, who had won a reputation—and a Congressional Medal of Honor—for his actions in the campaign against the Apache leader Geronimo, was technically in charge of the 1st Volunteers, but the unit had borne TR's stamp from the beginning. Since his days in the Badlands he had fantasized about "wild rough riders" form-

ing a "cowboy cavalry" that would be as quintessentially American a
mounted unit as the Cossacks were Russian. The ethos of the West was,
in fact, embedded in the 1st Volunteers. Buffalo Bill Cody had been
asked to join the Cuban expedition as head of scouts. (An episode of his
Wild West Show of six years earlier had been entitled "The Rough
Riders of the World.") His show business partners wouldn't give Cody
permission to leave for the Cuban campaign, but some of his cowboys
had joined Roosevelt's unit, and after the expedition was over, many
Rough Riders would join the Wild West Show to re-create their battle
in nightly performances, thus completing the flow from myth to reality
and back again.

In addition to cowboys and Indians, Texas Rangers and lumberjacks,
the 1st Volunteer Cavalry included an odd collection of Harvard scholars and the idle rich from the Knickerbocker and Somerset clubs, men
like John Jacob Astor's cousin Woodbury Kane, William Tiffany, and
Hamilton Fish, grandson of President Grant's secretary of state. All of
its diverse human elements made the Rough Riders, in the words of one
journalist, "an elaborate photograph of the character of its founder." TR
had built their élan and given them a sense of their uniqueness. He knew
almost all of the 486 volunteers by name and he understood precisely his
relationship to them. As he wrote his son Ted later on: "Nine tenths of
the men were better horsemen than I was and probably two thirds of
them better shots than I was, while on the average they were certainly
hardier and more enduring. Yet after I had them a very short time they
all knew, and I knew too, that nobody else could command them as I
could."

Some of the men thought the Cuban campaign would be a lark.
Roosevelt never minimized the dangers they faced. When they had
passed through Alabama and Georgia on the train from their San Antonio training camp and saw Confederate veterans standing at the stations waving tiny flags, he described the battles fought on this bloody
ground thirty-five years earlier. It became a cautionary tale. The day
before they shipped out from Florida, he had a grim moment with the
men: "Nobody can tell how many of us will get back, and I don't
suppose that there is much glory ahead, but I hope and believe we shall
do our duty, and the home coming will be very pleasant for those that
do get home." But on board the transport steaming for Cuba, when
orders for battle had been dispersed among the convoy and the fact that
they would soon see combat began to sink in, he had rallied them—and
himself—in a speech that culminated in a macabre war dance adapted

from similar ones he had done around the carcasses of big game he had killed.

When the regiment disembarked from their troop ships on June 22 at the fishing village of Daiquiri in seas so high that several men and their mounts were drowned during the landing, Roosevelt's shrill voice could be heard above the chaos, cursing the elements and commanding the bugler to sound recall in hopes of getting back the disoriented horses that had begun swimming out to sea in panic. He had proved himself to the men repeatedly since then, insisting on walking on the march into the interior, although as an officer he had the right to ride his horse, Little Texas; and showing his disdain for Spanish snipers during a deadly ambush the second day out that killed Hamilton Fish and others by nearsightedly collecting spent shells as souvenirs for his sons while bullets whizzed around him. He had strong-armed quartermasters when the rations ran low demanding that they give his men cans of beans they were holding for the officers of the Regular Army.

He knew, of course, that his exploits were being closely followed at home, and that all of America was hanging on the newspaper accounts of the Rough Riders' progress into the interior. He had entered a sort of partnership in self-promotion with journalists like the celebrated *Tribune* correspondent Richard Harding Davis, who ultimately found himself trading his notebook for a rifle at a critical moment in the campaign. ("The enemy were hidden in the shade of the jungle," Davis had written breathlessly of one of the first engagements, while the [Rough Riders] had to fight in the open for every thicket they gained, crawling through grass which was as hot as a steam bath, and with their flesh and clothing torn by thorns and the sword-like blade of the Spanish 'bayonet.' The glare of the sun was full in their eyes and as fierce as a limelight.")

Around eight o'clock, as the moon rose up into the heavy tropical night, Roosevelt left the men and walked over to the derelict sugar factory where General Leonard Wood had established a field headquarters. Although older than TR, the quietly professional Wood was almost as much under his spell as the men were. He and Roosevelt had talked about the possibility of a conflict with Spain throughout the early spring during hikes around Rock Creek in Washington. Wood had come to understand TR's enthusiasm for the war and indulged the mutual attraction between him and the journalists. They had such a perfect understanding that they did not need to talk very long. After briefly discussing the next day's likely battle plan—pushing up over the fortifications on San Juan Ridge—they both got into their bedrolls, spreading their yellow ponchos over them in case it began to rain.

Looking up at the shadowed heights of San Juan, Roosevelt wondered (as he later wrote) what the next day would bring. Would he falter when the call came? Would he survive the battle? He had seen violent death in the first skirmish a few days earlier when bullets from enemy Mausers "humming like telephone wires" began to strike the unit. Unable to tell where the Spanish were because they were using smokeless gunpowder, the Rough Riders had taken serious losses. Almost immediately after the men fell, huge land crabs attacked the bodies, beginning their demolition work by tearing out the eyes and lips. Watching them, Bucky O'Neil had said, "Colonel, isn't it Whitman who says, 'They pluck the eyes of princes and tear the flesh of kings'?"

With his usual precision TR had calculated that his chances were one in three of getting killed. Preparing for the worst, he had written home to Edith that if he didn't return she should give his sword and revolver to his sons, Ted and Kermit. (When Edith read the letter to the boys, she reported, "They put their heads in my lap and sobbed bitterly.") Yet he had also come to believe in what Henry Adams somewhat dyspeptically referred to as his "luck"—that sense of inevitability and personal momentum he had acquired over the last few years. He was filled with a kind of expectancy, as if some breakthrough moment was waiting for him. What had at first seemed a series of random choices in his career had now taken on the feel of a related sequence of events leading up to this time and this place, and to a possible apotheosis.

It was only four years earlier, in 1894, depleted by his brother Elliott's tragedy, that TR had been unsure about the future. He had wanted to leave the Civil Service Commission and run for mayor of New York, but Edith, worried about supporting the growing family, was opposed. TR gave in to her wishes, although, as he told his friend Henry Cabot Lodge, he "would have given his right arm" to make the race. (And Edith, in one of the few times anyone could recall, lost her composure and wrote Bamie a letter filled with near hysterical self-accusations of having failed her husband.)

The man who was ultimately elected mayor, Republican William Strong, had offered TR the position of president of the Board of Police Commissioners. Buoyed by the prospect of a new set of conflicts that would act as a whetstone for his fate, TR had accepted, writing Bamie: "I shall speedily assail some of the ablest, shrewdest men in the city, who will be fighting for their lives. . . ."

He had quickly become a household name in his new position by associating himself strongly on the side of change, which put him in opposition to New York's police chief and also many of the cops on the beat, some of whom he found asleep or occasionally in the embrace of ladies of the night during his celebrated "rambles," which began at 2 A.M., usually in the company of one or more of the city's journalists, who quickly came to relish the copy TR provided them, and continued until 7 A.M., when he went straight to his desk to begin his day's work.

He had guessed correctly that the Police Commission job, apparently so local in emphasis, could have national implications. People around the country who had heard of his cowboy exploits or read some of his books now began to associate him with the growing movement for municipal reform. Although thirty-five, he was still regarded as a "boy wonder" destined for great things. He became almost superstitious about discussing his future. One of his new fans, journalist Jacob Riis, was in TR's office one day with his muckraking colleague Lincoln Steffens and happened to ask Roosevelt if he wanted to be President. TR jumped up from his desk, his voice rising into an octave of agitation: "Never, never, you must never . . . remind a man at work on a political job that he might be President. It almost always kills him politically. He loses his nerve; he can't do his work; he gives up the very traits that are making him a possibility. . . . I won't let myself think of it; I must not, because if I do, I will begin to work for it. I'll be careful, calculating, cautious in word and act—and so I'll beat myself. See?"

He loved the drama of the job—midnight invasions of vice dens and conflict from decisions like the one to enforce the Sunday closure law for saloons, a maneuver that also allowed him to strike a blow at Tammany Hall, which organized in barrooms. But after a year he felt bogged down in the details of the Police Commission job—the bureaucratic inertia and recrimination. Once again, he was restless for movement, for some defining event. "If it wasn't wrong," he wrote Bamie, "I should say that personally I would rather welcome a foreign war."

Looking to win a job where he could make national policy, he had crisscrossed the country for the Republican nominee McKinley in 1896, spending most of his time in the West because the Badlands experiences that were now part of his growing legend allowed him to campaign effectively on the heels of the Democrats' candidate, William Jennings Bryan.

After McKinley's election, TR had immediately launched another campaign—this one for himself. He knew exactly the position he wanted in the new administration, assistant secretary of the navy, and he worked hard to get it. It took longer than he anticipated for Henry Cabot Lodge and his other sponsors to wear down the resistance of those who were wary of his well-known desire to command. Among the doubters was Navy Secretary John Long, who would be TR's superior and who warned that if Roosevelt was appointed, he would "dominate the department in six months."

And this, of course, was exactly what happened. Sitting at his desk in the Navy Department in front of a window that exactly framed the White House, TR helped spread the virus of expansionism he had caught when he was in Washington serving on the Civil Service Commission and listening to the debate over the annexation of Hawaii. Claiming that the U.S. Navy had not only fallen behind the British, but behind the Russians and Japanese as well, he worked tirelessly for a buildup that bore the stamp of his particular philosophy: "It is only through strife, or the readiness for strife, that a nation must win greatness."

The most likely opponent for such strife was Spain, which TR saw as manhandling "plucky little Cuba." He became a one-man drum corps beating constantly for war. In the fall of 1897 he wrote a memo whose emphasis was telling: "When war comes, *it should come fully on our initiative,* and after we have had time to prepare." It was not *if* war came, but *when.*

The growing public crisis regarding Spain had blended into TR's private affairs. In November, as his sixth child, Quentin, was born (causing friends like Lodge to criticize him for being "anti-Malthusian"), TR was trying to persuade McKinley to act against the Spanish. As the new year of 1898 dawned, war was a near certainty, but his eldest son, Ted, had begun to experience horrible headaches that recalled the fate of his dead brother, Elliott. Then Edith fell ill with a lingering fever that wasted her strength.

As the situation in the Caribbean deteriorated, Ted's condition improved, but doctors were unable to diagnose the exact nature of Edith's illness, which was alarming enough that TR had prepared for war and death at the same time, parceling out the kids as Edith became unable to look after them—Alice and Ted to Bamie in New York; Ethel, Archie, and infant Quentin to the Lodges. Shortly after the *Maine* exploded, he got the famous Canadian doctor Sir William Osler to examine her and finally found what was wrong—an abdominal tumor. With war fever spiking, Edith underwent an operation. "For two weeks we could not tell whether she would live or die," TR wrote his sister Corinne. "Sometimes one seemed likely, sometimes the other. . . ." Then she began to gain strength, and by April was "crawling slowly back to life." One afternoon she felt well enough to drive in a coach to the Metropolitan Club where TR was having a war strategy meeting. He came out on the front steps and saw her waiting for him, thin and wan in billowing dress, and he ran to embrace her.

Released by his wife's recovery to concentrate on Spain, he fulminated against the "peace at any price men" and groused that his own President had "no more backbone than a chocolate eclair." Finally, on April 11, largely as a result of TR's prodding, McKinley finally agreed reluctantly to loose the dogs of war and sent his declaration to Congress.

TR immediately got permission, along with Leonard Wood, to raise a regiment of volunteers. After three months' training in San Antonio— the locale charged his imagination because of the proximity of the Alamo—he went up to Bamie's house in New York to say goodbye to Alice, who was staying there. His daughter never forgot the surge of apprehension—a physical sensation located at a precise spot in the stomach—she experienced at the thought of him going off to battle. Four-year-old Archie was confused, asking, "And is my father going to war? And will he bring back a bear?" After TR left for Texas, Kermit knocked down a classmate who'd said that his father was going to be killed.

Why did he go? When people asked him TR replied that he had helped inspire the war and didn't want to be labeled a "parlor jingo." There were other factors—the desire posthumously to redeem his father who had not served when his call had come, the only blemish in an otherwise exemplary life, which TR, by this act of fealty, could remove. And of course there was the sense of adventure, the excitement of an opportunity to be blooded in battle he knew came only once in a generation. Edith's timely recovery had spared him an agonizing decision, but later on in a moment of surprising candor he said to a friend: "You know what my wife and children mean to me; and yet I made up my mind that I would not allow even a death to stand in my way; that it was my one chance to do something for my country and my family and my one chance to cut my little notch on the stick that stands as a measuring rod in every family. I know now that I would have turned from my wife's death bed to have answered that call."

The morning of July 1, a day TR would always remember as his "crowded hour," dawned hot and humid in the Cuban interior. Having pitched camp after dark the previous evening, the Rough Riders were now able to see their situation clearly for the first time. They were in a valley with hills rising up on three sides. TR described it as an "amphitheatre for the battle." The figure of speech was apt: he understood that this was the stage on which he would play out a personal drama.

By the time he had finished shaving and washed down some hardtack with campfire coffee, the American guns behind him had begun a deafening artillery barrage. When the Spaniards answered from their vantage point above, the shrapnel immediately downed four Rough Riders near TR. Sticking a pistol into his belt that someone had salvaged from the *Maine* and given to him as a good-luck charm, he took cover.

After the big guns fell silent about half an hour later, Roosevelt and his men received orders to advance. Their mission was to support the regular army troops up ahead who had been pinned down at a crossing of the San Juan River. Upon arriving they saw that the regulars had already taken losses from sniper fire. After "an hour of hell," TR got his men across the ford. The column moved along slowly in the high grass until it came to a clearing where he got his first good view of two hills up above. To the right was San Juan Ridge, where the Spanish were visible in their trenches and behind their fortifications. To the left was Kettle Hill, so named for a giant kettle at its crest once used for boiling sugar.

The men were now falling from the enemy's withering fire, some of it raining down from Spanish sharpshooters invisible in the trees. Some of the shells exploded in the air. Cocky Bucky O'Neil, who had made a career out of subduing outlaws in Arizona Territory, was strolling up and down in front of his men nonchalantly smoking a cigarette. One of the sergeants yelled at him to get down: "Captain, a bullet is sure to hit you!" O'Neil exhaled a wreath of smoke and laughed, "The Spanish bullet isn't made that can kill me." As he turned, a bullet hit him in the mouth and blew out the back of his head.

Finally an order arrived for the Rough Riders to support a general advance. TR vaulted onto Little Texas, the horse whose courage he had come to depend on, and formed the men, yelling at those who were still flattened to the ground, "Are you afraid to stand up when I am on horseback?" Falling in behind him, the Rough Riders began to move forward until they ran up the backs of a contingent of army regulars that had taken cover in front of them.

The captain in charge of this unit said he was awaiting orders from a senior officer before moving. TR replied, "I am the ranking officer here and I give the order to charge!" When the captain looked at the volunteers' insignia and hesitated, Roosevelt bellowed, "If you don't wish to go forward, then let my men through, please." The regulars' line opened and he went through with his men. Seeing daylight ahead, he stood up in the stirrups, his shrill voice rising into an incoherent yell, and waved the men forward. Roweling Little Texas hard with his spurs, he bent low in the saddle and was off.

At first the men were beside him. But then he had outrun them and was alone. An enemy soldier loomed up in front of him and TR pulled out the pistol from the *Maine* and shot him. (After the battle he showed the weapon to reporters and said, "I made a vow to kill at least one Spaniard with it.") He had an exhilarating moment at the crest of the hill, alone in his conquest. When his men caught up with him bullets were still ricocheting off the giant kettle. As Richard Harding Davis wrote in his dispatch to the *Herald*, "No one who saw Roosevelt take that ride expected he would finish it alive."

TR looked off to the left and saw that the regulars were trying to work their way up San Juan Hill. He ordered his men to open fire on the Spanish gunners dug into their trenches. Then he ordered another charge against the next line of entrenchments. Passing through another hail of bullets, he reached the summit of San Juan Ridge with the enemy retreating in disorder. The Americans took prisoners and began to feast on captured wine and tins of canned flying fish.

Still astride his pirouetting horse, TR looked down at the bodies in the trenches with the clinical dissecting eye learned from his childhood science and noted that relatively few of the enemy had been wounded in the body because they were protected from the neck down by the trenches. In most cases, the dead had been killed by surprisingly neat bullet holes in the skull out of which their brains were now "oozing." Roosevelt vaunted over the enemy: "Look at all these damned Spanish dead!"

He began to get reports of casualties. (In all, eighty-nine Rough Riders would die, the largest number proportionately of any of the units involved in the battle.) A few Spanish artillery rounds whistled in, hitting close enough to spray him with dirt. But he refused to take cover. Observers later reported that he seemed to feel he was invulnerable, transcendent, protected by an invisible armor.

It was a feeling that abated in the weeks following the battle, when TR was still working to get his troops out of Cuba, a process that would prove much more difficult than getting them in and involve him in abrasive negotiations with the War Department that would rob him of the Congressional Medal of Honor he and others believed he deserved. Yet he was compensated by news that he was a national hero. At the end of July, a letter came from his brother-in-law, Douglas Robinson, congratulating him on the political career that would now surely be his. TR replied that he would "rather have led the charge and earned my colonelcy than served three terms in the Senate," adding that at any rate he doubted that it would happen.

He was being disingenuous, of course, for he knew that he had been on the front page of newspapers all over the country for weeks and that the Republicans were already talking him up as a candidate for governor of New York. He understood, moreover, that the Cuban campaign would allow him to vault over the slow years of caution and compromise that marked most political careers. In the past, Roosevelt-watchers, sensing the weight of his inevitability, had often compared his inexorable move forward to a locomotive. ("Silent and awful like the Chicago Express," said Henry Adams.) Before Cuba, however, TR had been forced to lay his own track as he went along; now it stretched out before him as far as the eye could see.

After returning home, he announced his candidacy for governor. He kept his crowded hour in Cuba in the public mind by making campaign appearances with a company of Rough Riders and a bugler who signaled the beginning of his campaign speeches by sounding a cavalry charge.

He would see the Rough Riders at reunions and special events for the rest of his life. They would always be something like a private honor guard, sharing with him what he always called "the great day of my life." It was the day he squared his father's accounts and proved himself; the day that he "rose above those regular army officers like a balloon"; the day he became a mythic figure. It was also the day, as his son Ted said later on, that TR approached "the gates of paradise" and saw clearly all those things—notably the presidency itself—that might someday be his.

After Cuba, magazine articles began to appear proposing TR as a brashly American version of the Renaissance man—writer, soldier, scholar, man of adventure, and man of affairs. Because he so clearly represented indomitability, rugged individuality, and other virtues of the day, TR became one of those inspirational figures that dominated contemporary literature for young people. (Edward Stratemeyer, who

later gained fame for his Tom Swift books, written under the pseudonym Victor Appleton, was one of those who wrote about him in this
vein.) One young man who scrutinized the text of TR's life with particular interest, hoping to find clues about how to lead his own, was his
cousin Franklin.

The year Franklin was born, 1882, TR was elected to the New York
legislature. By rights, the boy should have been named Isaac, this name
having alternated with James for males in his father's line for generations. But his mother put her foot down. She wanted to name the child
for her father, but her brother had already done that with his son, so she
took the name of an uncle.

Franklin's own father, James, had also begun to feel political stirrings
at about the time of the boy's birth, although he was less interested in
reform than in family advancement. A Democratic Roosevelt, he had
made large contributions to Grover Cleveland's gubernatorial and presidential campaigns, and could have had a diplomatic appointment after
his man got to the White House in 1884. But while declining any post
for himself, James did press Cleveland to consider his first son, "Rosy,"
now in his thirties and using what amounted to a dowry from his Astor
in-laws to live the life of the idle rich. The President gave Rosy a
diplomatic position in Vienna.

Franklin always remembered going to Washington at the age of five
with his mother and father to see the immense Cleveland, who ended
their brief conversation by engulfing the boy's fingers with a meaty
hand and making the odd comment, "My little man, I am making a
strange wish for you. It is that you may never be President of the United
States."

Franklin grew up healthy, never suffering a major illness until he
contracted a case of typhoid at the age of seven. The only real trauma
occurred when he was three and his parents took him on the first of
many trips to Europe. After a difficult passage, their ship foundered in
high seas and heavy weather; and as water streamed into their cabin, his
mother, Sara, wrapped him in her fur coat and said, "Poor little boy. If
he must go down, he's going down warm!" But the ship eventually
rode out the storm and the Roosevelts arrived safely in London.

The Delanos provided an extended family for Franklin. He went there
to be pampered and to enjoy the interplay between his grandparents and
his mother's sisters and brothers. They regarded him as a prodigy,
passing his sayings around as epiphanies of his precociousness. (One
favorite came when he was four and one of his aunts congratulated him

on having a lot of tact for a boy his age, to which he replied, "Oh, yes, I'm chock full of tacks.") By comparison to the constant activity at Algonac, the Delanos' estate, life at Springwood was subdued. There he was the only son. Franklin called his father "Popsy" and James tried to live up to the jaunty name by taking him sledding and horseback riding and by arranging trips on the family yacht to the property he owned on Campobello Island off the coast of Maine. A conspiracy arose between them to circumvent the formidable Sara. On rare occasions when she would order her husband to punish Franklin, James would take the boy out of her sight, give him a significant look and then say, "Consider yourself spanked."

James was a man of affairs and power. He sometimes took Franklin and Sara with him when he went on inspection tours of the railroads in which he had invested, always commanding a private car with lavishly furnished sleeping quarters and his own private cook and porter. But after suffering a heart attack in 1890, James became a different man—a valetudinarian whose search for renewed health involved eight major trips to Europe in Franklin's first fourteen years for extended stays at spas in Germany and elsewhere. As James sank slowly into invalidism, his son was left more vulnerable to his mother's domineering love.

While she was affectionate to her sickly husband (although the two of them apparently had no physical relations after Franklin's birth), Sara poured her passion into the upbringing of their son. One of his earliest memories was of her reading sentimental literature to him that she believed would create a feeling person. She would become so affected by the stories that she would begin to cry, and Franklin, sitting on the floor playing with toys, would ask, "What's the matter, Mummy? Why do you speak like that?"

Dosing him with Castoria at the least sign of illness and smothering him with attention at all times, Sara became the overwhelming fact of his life. When she and his father went to the wedding of his godfather, Elliott, Franklin, left at Algonac with his grandparents, had wandered disconsolately through the house until he found one of his mother's jackets and then buried his face in it sobbing, "Mama! Mama!" Sara did not allow his golden hair to be cut until he was four, and then embalmed the braid in a satin-lined box. She kept Franklin in dresses until he was six, when he was allowed to graduate to kilts. It was not until nine that he was able to write his father with triumph, "Mama has left this morning and I am going to take my bathe alone." It was the first time that this had happened to him.

Sara sometimes asked the "good" boys of Hyde Park to come and play with Franklin, warning them that her son would bang his head on the wall if they refused. ("Please don't make Franklin do that," she would plead.) On the relatively rare occasions when there were playmates, Franklin behaved imperiously, and when she told him not to order the other boys around, he replied, "Mummie, if I did not give them orders nothing would get done." But for the most part, Sara was glad to be virtually her son's only companion. At the ages of eleven and twelve, playing by himself, he sometimes wrote her letters from his part of the immense house to hers and had the servants deliver them. He sometimes addressed her by her nickname "Sallie," but for the most part it was "Mummie," "Mommy, "Mama," "Mumpsy" and "Mumpy"—almost as many names for the chief element in his environment, someone pointed out later on, as the Eskimo had words for snow. Struggling against his mother's possessiveness, Franklin became uneasy when he did win a small measure of independence. His need for love was equaled only by a paradoxical unease with intimacy.

Sara helped him get interested in stamps, which she had saved herself since she was a little girl receiving letters from her father in the Orient. As part of his Delano heritage, Franklin also collected nautical prints and books, particularly those having to do with the great clipper ships that had sailed to China. When he was given a rifle, he began to shoot birds around the estate and announced that he wanted to stuff them himself as he had heard his cousin Teddy did as a boy. But Sara insisted on sending his specimens to a professional taxidermist.

When he traveled with his father in the carriage through the village at Hyde Park, people tipped their hats and hailed him as "Master" Franklin. He allowed Springwood to define him. Nearly fifty years later, in a ceremony donating the presidential library in front of the house he had grown up in to the government, Franklin would look back and see "a small boy [who] took special delight in climbing in an old tree, now unhappily gone, to pick and eat ripe sechel pears. . . . And he used to lie flat between the strawberry rows and eat sun-warmed strawberries, the best in the world. In the spring of the year, in rubber hip boots, he sailed his first toy boats in the surface water formed by the melting snow. In the summer with his dog he dug into woodchuck holes in this same field." The estate would always have the evocative power for Franklin that Rosebud did for Citizen Kane.

The deterioration of Franklin's godfather, Elliott, was an uncomfortable subject for Sara and James, but the bonds between the Oyster Bay and Hyde Park families remained strong and Franklin occasionally visited his cousins at Sagamore Hill. He enjoyed the noise and activity and "democracy" (as he later called it) of the place, although it was impossible for him to keep up with TR's children, younger but more fit, in their nonstop activities and in the "bee-line" hikes led by TR that went over any obstacle laying ahead. He probably did not realize the extent to which he was a figure of ridicule for them. But sharp-tongued Alice, two years younger than he, once summarized their attitude during a discussion of *Little Lord Fauntleroy* by saying that cousin Franklin probably not only read the maudlin book (which was forbidden from entering the Sagamore house) but also dressed like the hero. As it worked out, she was right on both counts.

Relations between the two Roosevelt branches grew even closer in 1893 when Rosy's wife, the former Helen Astor, died and the indefatigable Bamie traveled to London, where Rosy was now first secretary at the embassy, to help look after his two young children and preside at social functions. She had her admirers, particularly a coterie of younger men that family members called her "Joe-Bobs" (because two of them were Joseph Alsop, Sr., and Bob Ferguson). But while she captivated them intellectually, they were not romantic prospects. Bamie may have undertaken this mission to London thinking that a romance might develop between her and Rosy, an odd reprise of the moment some twenty-five years earlier when she had rejected the courtship of his father, at that time also a recent widower. She discovered that Rosy already had a mistress he wanted someday to marry. During her two-year stay in London, however, Bamie met a divorced naval captain named William Sheffield Cowles. "Shef" was "not a ball of fire, by any means," in the words of Rosy's daughter, Helen. But he was a kind and loyal man who, a mutual acquaintance later said, had the "sense" to see the *real* Bamie. Cowles proposed, and she accepted. As in the case of her sister, Conie, and her husband, Douglas Robinson, it was not a passionate relationship (Bamie forced Cowles to call her by her given name, Anna, instead of by the nicknames TR and other family members used), but it matured into a strong affection and she bore him a son at the age of forty, two years after they wed.

Franklin regarded TR, Bamie, and the other Oyster Bay Roosevelts as among his few social assets when he finally left the claustral atmosphere at Hyde Park for Groton in 1896 at the age of fourteen. He was a gangly teenager, slender and slope-shouldered. His long face was distinguished by a nose narrowing at the bridge in a way that suggested patrician hauteur and by gray eyes in which he tried to make sure that people saw what he imagined they wanted to see. Feeling miserably alone in his first days away from home, he got equally melancholy letters from his mother. ("It makes me miserable to go to your room and look at your clothes and things.") On one occasion he wrote her that he was recovering from a cold and hoped that he would get pink eye because then he would be sent home. He spent a good deal of time photographing himself—either from a desire to experiment with the self-timer on the camera or out of vanity.

Later on in his life Franklin would romanticize his relationship with Endicott Peabody, but the best that the Groton headmaster could say about him was that he had been "a quiet, satisfactory boy" during his years at the school. He had fantasies of being well liked at Groton and after he had been there for a while he began writing home letters to "Mommerr and Popperr" filled with accounts of imagined camaraderie. But he was unable to hold his own in the rough-and-tumble sports that were the key to popularity there and was always something of an outsider.

He confessed his failures obliquely, triumphing over painful situations by rich hyperbole. His second year at Groton, for instance, he wrote to his parents, "I have been playing baseball all day, and I am on a new team which is called the BBBB or Bum Base Ball Boys. It has no captain, but it is a republic and is made up of about the worst players." Then he wrote a few days later about the team's first game: "The only ball I received, I nobly missed, and it landed biff! on my stomach to the great annoyance of that intricate organ, and to the great delight of all present. The walls of my tummy caved in and a great panic ensued inside, similar to the Paris bonfire, only that a Thunderbolt caused my catastrophe." Language became for him something like the squid's ink—a medium that covered his retreats.

The one thing that did give him standing was his relationship to TR, who was a friend of Headmaster Endicott Peabody (who was himself a relative of Alice Lee) and was frequently invited to give chapel speeches. After one such appearance in 1897, Franklin wrote home in rapture, struck less by the "splendid talk" itself than by the fact that his increasingly famous cousin had singled him out for attention afterward.

Franklin treasured the infrequent invitations to Sagamore Hill, even though he knew that once there he would be hazed by the active TR children. The desire to be close to the Oyster Bay cousins, in fact, led to a rare contretemps with his mother during his second term at Groton. The problem began when he discovered that she had declined an invitation for him to the annual July 4th celebration at Sagamore, a notable event because TR himself procured and shot off elaborate fireworks. Franklin wrote his mother to insist that he would attend the party and closed his letter coldly, "Please don't make any arrangements for my future happiness."

The Christmas of 1898—the year of San Juan Hill—he was invited to a party at the home of TR's sister Corinne. In a house crowded with relatives, Franklin was most struck by the two female cousins closest to him in age. One was TR's daughter Alice, grown into a saucy, golden-haired girl with a pouting mouth; the other was his godfather Elliott's orphaned daughter, Eleanor, at fourteen the same age as Alice, but otherwise her opposite. Still living with her Grandmother Hall, who also took care of her grown sons and daughters, she was just beginning to emerge from what one relative called "the grimmest childhood I ever saw." Eleanor always seemed to look ill-kept despite a generous trust left by her dead father. (Once when a schoolmate asked her why she wore a frock she'd gotten dirty the previous day, she replied pathetically, "My other dress is in the wash.") On this particular evening she was dressed childishly in a short dress while the other girls her age at the party wore fashionable gowns, and she stood miserably alone in a corner until Alice, having danced with Franklin twice, whispered in his ear that he should pay attention to the wallflower, after which he came over to Eleanor and asked her to dance with him in an act of gallantry she never forgot.

Like everyone else, Franklin's imagination had been galvanized by TR's exploits in Cuba. He'd stood in the streets of New York with his mother and father cheering the Rough Riders' victory parade. Going one step further, he had begun to tell people that he himself had been on his way to Florida to volunteer until illness forced him to return home. The fact was that he had never left Groton, and spent the early part of the war in the school infirmary suffering from scarlet fever and dealing with his mother, who, desperate to see him but fearful that close contact might spread the illness to her ailing husband, had visited Franklin from a rickety ladder placed outside his window, climbing up to hand-feed him delicacies and read him newspaper articles about the exploits of the Rough Riders.

Fantasizing about imagined achievements, part of his personality since he was a child, was becoming one of Franklin's hallmarks. Later in life, he would claim that his persistent sinus trouble came from having broken his nose twice in football when in fact he had not made the Groton team. He would allow people to believe that he had been "quite a boxer," while in fact he always shied away from conflict. A more representative incident had occurred once when he had been hurrying through a New York neighborhood on his way to catch a train for school and had accidentally knocked a small Italian boy into the gutter with his suitcase. He took out a dollar bill and tried to hand it over to the boy as he started to move on, but this only made the child angrier. The boy's screams brought adults to the tenement windows. As Franklin started to walk off, they came outside to follow him. Dropping the dollar bill, he began to run, the people pursuing him. He managed to catch the train as it was pulling out of the station and stood at a window watching the Italians shaking their fists at him and cursing in their native tongue as he made his escape.

In his final year at Groton, Franklin watched from afar as TR campaigned for governor of New York. He participated vicariously in his cousin's early successes at Albany, keeping track of the bills he introduced and trying to understand the emerging issues of the Roosevelt administration—how to regulate the growing power of corporations; how to get a civil service law; how to control sweatshops and better working conditions for women and children. He defended TR to some Grotonians whose wealthy parents regarded him as a traitor to his class because of his "radical" opinions.

Going on to Harvard in the fall, Franklin tried out for football and made the lowest of the eight freshman teams. He angled unsuccessfully for a spot on the school paper, the *Harvard Crimson*. The following year he followed the controversy over whether TR should accept the vice presidential nomination in 1900 or wait for four years to seek the presidency itself. He was thrilled when his cousin stampeded the convention by entering in a broad-brimmed hat reminiscent of his Rough Rider days, outflanking his chief enemy, Senator Mark Hanna, who had already warned incumbent President William McKinley not to let such a "madman" be only one life away from the presidency. He followed accounts of TR's campaign against the Democratic candidate, William Jennings Bryan, in the West where he was sometimes introduced by Buffalo Bill: "A cyclone from the West has come; no wonder the rats hunted their cellar!" Some classmates felt that FDR was making rather too much of his association with TR, what with the spectacles perched on his nose and repeated exclamations of "Bully!," and they derisively called him "Kermit."

Franklin broke ranks with his father's Democratic affiliation to join the Harvard Republican Club to campaign for TR. (In fact, James broke ranks too, voting for TR in 1898 and 1900.) The night of the election he gathered with other Harvard undergrads in a torchlight march celebrating the victory of McKinley and Roosevelt, while his own father was entering the final phase of his long illness. Sara wrote every day with an update. She did not spare Franklin the details of James's last days. (After one harrowing bout of nausea, she wrote, "He has had this time more flatulency than I ever knew him to have, and also much bowel trouble which causes weakness. . . .") Franklin was sent for just before Christmas when the "beloved invalid" died. He was nineteen, about the same age, he noted, as TR had been when *his* father died.

Now Sara, who had split her love between her husband and her son, concentrated her attention even more forcefully than before on Franklin. She moved temporarily to Cambridge to be near him. She participated in his defeats—chief among them not being chosen for the exclusive Porcellian Club—and in his triumphs, such as finally making the editorial staff of the *Crimson* in 1901, although even she may not have appreciated the six-hour days and constant politicking it had taken for someone who was not a particularly gifted writer to make the cut. She hectored him when he expressed opinions contrary to hers, such as supporting the Boers of South Africa. This was "not a race to do good in the world," she wrote, telling how as a little girl traveling on a ship with her family she had gotten "a horror of the common Dutch men with their native and half native families." But after giving him her party line she added the perfunctory postscript: "Still I like you to form your own opinions and to look at things more deeply than Mummy does."

The mistaken assumption strangers had sometimes made that Franklin was TR's son took on new implications now that he was fatherless. While reading Jacob Riis's book on TR, Sara discovered that *his* father's last words to him had been, "Be a good man." She rushed to inform Franklin of this fact while reminding him that James's last words to her had been, "Only tell Franklin to be a good man." She wrote: "Is this not a coincidence?" almost as if to suggest that there was something more to it than that, some profound—if temporarily unclear—relationship that provided a special link between her boy and the man she called his "noble kinsman."

* * *

In one of his appearances at Groton after he been elected governor, TR said to Franklin and his classmates, "If a man has courage, goodness, and brains, no limit can be placed on the greatness of the work he may accomplish. He is the man needed in politics today." Afterward he took his young cousin aside, as usual, and expanded on the message. It was people like the Roosevelts who needed to get involved in the "arena" to keep it from being dominated by unscrupulous men. It was not only an obligation but also an opportunity for self-definition.

But it wasn't that simple in practice and the relationship between compromise and principle had been a vexing question for TR at Albany. He knew he had been chosen to run for governor in 1898 by Republican boss Thomas Platt only because the machine was desperate for a candidate who could win. Platt, moreover, had gotten his nickname as the "Easy Boss" because his demeanor was a pleasant change from the harsh personality of the man who had anointed him as his successor, Senator Roscoe Conkling. TR was aware of the irony in the fact that he had been elevated to the governorship by the protégé of the man who had destroyed his own father's fledgling political career. The question of using the machine more than it used him was a problem he and Henry Cabot Lodge discussed frequently, referring to it as "sailing between Scylla and Charybdis."

TR gained exposure in administration while governor, and began to discover some of the issues that could not help but become more pressing in the years ahead, especially the need to regulate the trusts that appeared to be in the saddle—in Emerson's conceit—riding mankind. Wary of the pitfalls of William Jennings Bryan's "demagoguery" on the matter of the trusts, TR nonetheless agreed that these malicious institutions caused "misery and injustice." His economic policy during his one term at Albany made Platt refer to him as "a perfect bull in a china shop."

The big question during his governorship was always what his next step would be, how he could step through the gates of paradise into the presidency. He worried that his hold on the voters was "entirely ephemeral." He could run for another two-year term as governor in 1900, but because of the opposition stirred up by the economic reforms he had launched and the powerful enemies he had made, reelection was not certain and even if he won he would still have a two-year hiatus before the 1904 elections. Trying to get appointed secretary of war had been another possibility, but then he would have to arrange another war to make the post interesting. The governor-generalship of the Philippines was the position most favored by his children—the boys because the role suited TR's heroic dimensions; Alice because she could imagine herself surrounded by handsome young officers in dress whites under the palm trees.

When he finally decided to go for the vice presidency it was over the opposition of Edith as well as Mark Hanna, senator from Ohio and from Standard Oil. Edith feared that all he could win was the right to languish in obscurity. Hanna feared quite the opposite—that Roosevelt's "luck" would somehow make the vice presidency a stepping-stone to the White House where he would implement a vendetta against the trusts.

Almost immediately after he and McKinley were elected, TR had experienced a moment of remorse, telling reporters gathered at Sagamore to watch the returns come in, "This election means my political death." With bitter self-mockery, he set about mending fences with the Republican money men who controlled the President, and a few weeks after the election wrote mordantly to a friend about a dinner he was hosting in honor of J. P. Morgan: "You see, it represents an effort on my part to become a conservative man in touch with the influential classes and I think I deserve encouragement."

As the inauguration neared, though, TR began to rise to the occasion and so did the rest of the family. Ted came by train from Groton where he had just enrolled. Edith had told him to wear his best clothes and so he had put on the best trousers from one suit; the best vest from another, and the best jacket from a third. She spent two hundred dollars renting Madam Payne's Manicure Shop, a second-story room along the parade route, so that the children could see their father. When TR came into view, Archie and Quentin became so excited she had to grab them to keep them from falling out of the open window. Alice, who had just been introduced to the concept of insurance, appraised the difference in appearance between her bronzed father and the pasty-faced McKinley and calculated the President's actuarial probabilities. After the parade the family all packed into the Senate to hear TR's speech. When he said, "A great work lies ready to the hand of this generation," it was clear to them and everyone else that the generation he was referring to was not William McKinley's.

TR presided over the Senate only from March 4 until March 8 when Congress was adjourned until the following December. This long recess gave him a chance to think about what he would do in his new and "useless" job. He considered going back to school part-time to finish his law degree, or perhaps teaching history somewhere. He went out West on a hunting trip, spent time at Sagamore, and made the ceremonial appearances expected of one in his position.

He had stopped in Vermont on September 6 for a speaking engagement when word came that an anarchist named Leon Czolgosz had shot the President in Buffalo. TR rushed to McKinley's bedside and then, when the President seemed to have rallied, left to meet his family in the Adirondacks for a long-planned hiking expedition. They all set out on a hike on the morning of September 13. Around noon, TR had reached a summit where he could eat lunch and look out over the vast panorama of the state when a runner brought word that the President had suffered a sudden relapse. By the time TR got to Buffalo, McKinley was dead. He saw the body and then took the oath of office.

He and Edith attended McKinley's funeral and gave his widow time to move her belongings out of the White House. On their own first night there, September 23, Bamie and Corinne joined them for a somber celebration. The two women were sitting with TR at a table in the living quarters when he suddenly looked up at them: "Do you realize that this is the birthday of our father? I have realized it as I signed various papers all day long, and I feel that it is a good omen that I begin my duties in this house on this day. I feel as if my father's hand were on my shoulder. . . ."

As soon as he finished the sentence, White House butlers served coffee, and according to a custom of the place, boutonnieres for each gentleman present. TR picked up one of the roses and noted that it was a saffronia, which had been the first Theodore's favorite. As he put it in his buttonhole he said, "I think there is a blessing connected with this."

It was a dramatic punctuation point in the rise of a man and also of a family.

*W*hen he took office, TR, aware that he was an "accidental" President, moved to reassure those like powerful Republican Senator Mark Hanna who had feared his position on the ticket in the first place. After an initial talk at the White House, Hanna grudgingly said that he was convinced that Roosevelt "had now acquired all that is needed to round out his character—equipoise and conservatism." Yet TR knew that Hanna's support was as insincere as his own reassurances. He believed that he had now reached a point where, if he played his cards right over the next few years, he would never have to compromise again with party bosses. As Lincoln Steffens noted after a visit to Washington in his first days in office, "He laughed at the rage of Boss Platt and at the tragic disappointment of Mark Hanna."

In the first months of his presidency, as he consolidated his power, Roosevelt showed himself to be an adroit politician, not the vindictive radical Hanna and other representatives of the vested interests feared. His controversial 1901 invitation to Booker T. Washington to dine with him at the White House, for instance, was not merely a symbolic social occasion or even an attempt to preach racial amity, but also part of an attempt by TR to build a Republican organization loyal to him in the

South, an effort in which he thought the Negro educator could be helpful.

But he had to build a national constituency as well as a Republican one. An extremist in self-presentation, he was a moderate in politics. He thought figures like Bryan and Progressive Party leader Robert La Follette were demagogues. Yet he was sympathetic to most of the Progressives' objectives—controlling the trusts, breaking the corrupt connections between the government and the corporations, establishing a more "direct" democracy through state primaries and municipal reform—even if he was mistrustful of the more radical "socialistic" demands for a methodical economic and social restructuring of the country. He saw himself as a common man, albeit a rather exceptional one. (Earlier in his career, he had been at a party next to a wealthy Knickerbocker lady who, after railing against the assault on privilege, said to him, "What are we going to do, Mr. Roosevelt?" His straight-faced response was, "What do you mean *we*?") His hatred of plutocracy was real, reiterated repeatedly in public statements and in his private correspondence with his children: "Of all forms of tyranny the least attractive and most vulgar is the tyranny of mere wealth. . . ."

On the great issue of the day, that of restraining monopoly and taming the trusts, he saw his task—as he phrased it in a letter to English historian George Macaulay Trevelyan, as "controlling the big companies without paralyzing the business community." Stating that he intended to move "cautiously but steadily," he chose his ground carefully.

Early in 1902, after six months as President, he was presented by a challenge from the business community in the form of the Northern Securities Company. The enterprise was the outgrowth of a struggle between the Union Pacific's E. H. Harriman and James J. Hill of the Great Northern to gain control over rail routes from the Pacific Northwest into Chicago. The fight, which ultimately involved the Rockefellers and other robber barons, caused such panic on Wall Street that J. P. Morgan had entered the fray as a mediator. He made peace by making profit, bringing Harriman and Hill and their railroads into a huge new holding company, the Northern Securities Company, capitalized at $400 million.

The public revulsion against Northern Securities inspired TR to act and he secretly ordered Attorney General Philander C. Knox to prepare a suit to dissolve the company. It was a dramatic step: the McKinley administration had not filed one suit under the 1890 Sherman Antitrust Act. Morgan immediately asked to meet TR in the White House. The banker, known as Jupiter because of his fiery glare and his Olympian financial power, had worked with the first Theodore on charitable boards in New York years earlier. He bluntly addressed the young President: "If we have done anything wrong, send your man [meaning Attorney General Knox] to my man and they can fix it up." TR responded that he was not inclined to "fix it up" but to "stop it." It would take two years for the issue to be resolved, but after long legal maneuvering the Supreme Court affirmed Roosevelt's position and an era of trust-busting was installed in the White House.

The other symbolic issue of the first term was the labor dispute in the anthracite coal fields, which had the potential to explode into a bloody labor war. Years later, when he came to write his *Autobiography*, TR would articulate the idea of worker rights with eloquence, restating the right to life, liberty, and the pursuit of happiness as "the right of the worker to a living wage, to reasonable hours of labor, to decent working conditions, and to freedom of thought and speech and industrial representation." Yet in 1902 it was not so clear. The miners were perhaps the most oppressed of the country's workers, laboring for five hundred dollars a year, most of which they were forced to spend at company stores that held them in a kind of debt servitude. But the mine operators represented the higher rights of property ownership.

Represented by the United Mine Workers, 150,000 miners walked out of the coal fields in mid-1902. Standing firm against demands for a higher wage and for representation, the mine operators assumed that as winter approached panic would force the government's hand. As the strike persisted through the summer and into the fall, coal prices did shoot up, as people worried about going cold. It was assumed that if TR acted at all he would call out the troops on the side of the operators. Instead, he called both sides together at the White House for a conference, the first time a President had attempted to mediate a labor dispute.

In the discussions, UMN President John Mitchell was courtly and polite. George Baer, President of the Reading Railroad and spokesman for the operators, was so arrogant and unpleasant that TR said after negotiations had broken down that he wished he had taken Baer "by the seat of the breeches and the nape of the neck and chucked him out of the window."

TR got the miners to agree to go back to work pending the arbitration of an investigating commission. When the mine owners balked, he threatened to call out the troops to take over the operation of the mines and they capitulated. The commission's findings were a compromise between the two sides—a 10 percent wage increase for the miners but no official recognition of the UMW. It was not a solution that pleased everyone. (Young Franklin wrote his mother from Harvard, for instance, that despite TR's success in resolving the issue, he himself considered it a bad precedent: "His tendency to make the executive power stronger than the Houses of Congress is bound to be a bad thing. . . .") But it was clearly a personal victory for the President.

TR reversed the normal course in which the party in the White House could expect losses in the off-year election. In 1902, largely because of his personal popularity, the Republicans increased their majority in Congress. He would continue to chip away at the power of the trusts, taking on the hated rebates and drawbacks on freight shipments by which the railroads made combination with large corporations like Standard Oil to the detriment of smaller companies. He would continue to define what he called the Square Deal for the working man and begin to define the emerging field of conservation. But it was foreign affairs—particularly the symbolic issue of Panama—that offered a strikingly attractive opportunity to define himself and mobilize popular sentiment.

Although he had spoken out with fervor on matters involving the Monroe Doctrine from the moment he took office, TR had actually remained aloof from the issue of a canal until the Byzantine question of whether it would go through Nicaragua or Panama was resolved in Panama's favor. But then he got intensely involved in what he would later call "the great bit of work of my administration," participating in the odd combination of intrigue and bombast that made the project a reality.

Colombia had argued strenuously for the isthmian canal, but once its territory had been chosen for the Panama route, its government officials had second thoughts. The $10 million in gold and $250,000 yearly payment was not enough, particularly since the French promoters who had agitated for the Panama route would be receiving several times that amount. As the standoff developed, the question of Panama's secession from Colombia, a possibility for years, was raised again. Philippe Bunau-Varilla, representative of the French interests, had a conference with TR in which the subject of Panamanian revolution came up. "A revolution?" Roosevelt murmured with a dreamy look on his face. "Do you think it would be possible?"

A few weeks later a ragtag army of railroad hands, ordinary citizens, and a few opportunistic Colombian soldiers staged a coup whose only casualties were a Chinese laborer and his dog. Under the protective eye of American marines, a treaty was negotiated between the United States and the self-appointed representatives of the new country that in effect made Panama a protectorate and gave America control of the ten-mile-wide Canal Zone in perpetuity. As ground was being broken on the great engineering project in time for his reelection campaign of 1904, TR predicted that the Panama Canal would rank with the Louisiana Purchase in defining the character of America. At the time it seemed a victory of U.S. policy; later on TR would personalize it. "If I had followed conventional, conservative methods," he wrote, "I should have submitted a dignified state paper to the Congress and the debate would have been going on yet, but I took the canal zone and let the Congress debate, and while the debate goes on, the canal does also."

After watching TR's early days in the White House, an admiring Grover Cleveland said that he was "the most perfectly equipped and most effective politician thus far seen in the Presidency." Something like this might just as easily have been said about his family. Corinne was frequently at the White House. Bamie lived in Washington (TR would use her N Street house for private get-togethers with his friends) and was often glimpsed driving down city streets in an open surrey with the Chinese ambassador, his pigtail trailing in the wind behind. But it was his children who galvanized public interest. His was the first family with so many young children to occupy the White House. The details of their domestic life obsessed the Sunday supplements. Soon after he took office, Edith wrote TR: "You can't believe how much anxiety pervades the country about the children's education. I receive letters from schools and teachers every day."

Close and cohesive, the Roosevelts were seen as a model for the nuclear family just beginning to distinguish itself from the extended family of the country's rural past. The Roosevelt children quickly became household names—Princess Alice, stalwart Ted, mischievous Quentin—whose doings were followed by the public with the same kind of attention that in a few years would be given to film stars.

They tried to be like other people. The boys, for instance, were as impatient with Secret Service men as TR himself was, and ranged all over Washington on their own, often not noticing, or pretending not to, the anonymous-looking figure with a bulge in his pocket who stood at intersections pretending to read a paper while they played or slipping into the rear of streetcars behind them. While they enjoyed their celebrity, they knew they paid a price for it. (When he was a teenager, Kermit, who had joined a cavalry unit for a week's trek through Kansas, awoke from a nap in his tent to find a woman "petting" him and crooning about his father.)

But if they were, as one newspaperman said, "America's family," they remained TR's children, and he often seemed to worry about them as much as he worried about matters of state during his presidency, sometimes writing several letters a day to them as they became dispersed in boarding schools and trying from afar to kindle in them the divine fire that had occurred in his own life by spontaneous combustion.

Shortly after they moved into the White House, Edith sent a thumbnail sketch of the children to a friend: "Alice is exceedingly pretty and has a remarkably steady head, though in some ways is very child like. Ted is a good boy and stands well at school. Kermit is odd and independent as always, and Ethel is just a handful. . . . Archie we call 'the beautiful idiot' and Quentin is the cleverest of the six."

The words on Alice were particularly perceptive. During TR's governorship, when Edith had decided to send her to Miss Spence's School for Girls, Alice, claiming to be "shriveled" by the idea of uniformed students obediently walking two abreast down Fifth Avenue, had refused: "If you send me I will humiliate you. I will do something that will shame you. I tell you I will." She had won the right to stay home and educate herself, subject to TR's review, which gave her license to browse through his extensive library, studying Darwin, white magic, and whatever else caught her imagination. As a consequence, while intuitively bright she was also undisciplined, her intelligence often held hostage by her impetuousness.

Deemed too young to dance at the inauguration ceremonies of 1901, she had sat on the arm of President McKinley's chair during the party waiting expectantly in hopes that his wife would have one of her epileptic seizures, which he would try to conceal by putting a handkerchief over her face. Alice was fascinated by politics and seemed almost as interested in her father's future as he himself was. During the family's hiking trip to the Adirondacks when word came that McKinley had been shot, for instance, she pulled a long face for observers and then went outside with her brother Ted and did a little jig.

Four months after her father became President, Alice had her coming out, the first presidential daughter to do so since Nellie Grant. She felt it was a disaster, largely because Edith had not allowed champagne at the party. The parquet in the East Room was being replaced, so the floor had to be covered with coarse fabric called "crash," which in her mind was a piece with the rest of the hideous White House decor of dark wood, oilcloth frescoes, and massive horsehair furniture she character- ized as "late General Grant and early Pullman." Her cousin Franklin came to the party with some of his friends but when they asked her to dance Alice said she preferred older men like the Rough Riders.

Pert-faced, with blue eyes one writer described as "phosphorescent," she always held her chin up to maintain a look of impassive coolness, having made up her mind after seeing how cartoonists caricatured her father that she would never let them see anything in her features they could exaggerate. Unlike her younger sister, Ethel, who enthusiastically joined Edith on receiving lines, Alice cultivated an identity as White House rebel. She took up smoking, furtively exhaling up chimneys when her father was around. She carried around a blue macaw named Eli Yale, and a garter snake named Emily Spinach that got its name from Edith's very thin spinster sister, Emily, and the fact that it was as green as the vegetable. In fact, Alice was wearing Emily Spinach coiled around an arm when she came into her father's office one day in the middle of a chat he was having with the novelist Owen Wister. After she left, Wister asked his friend why he didn't control his daughter, and TR gave his famous response: "I can do one of two things. I can be President of the United States or I can control Alice. I can't possibly do both."

There was an uncomfortable truth in the witticism. Alice was trying to get TR's attention, as she had since first meeting him at the age of almost three, the only child of his ghost family. But now, with a nose for publicity that rivaled his own, she could continue her quest for attention from the platform of the White House. In addition to smoking in public, she brought actress Ethel Barrymore for a visit, gambled on horse races, smuggled small flasks of liquor into gatherings that were supposed to be dry, and in the middle of one sedate party pulled a cap pistol out of her purse and started shooting. Her most daring act was to drive unchaperoned with another girl in an automobile from Newport to Boston, covering the distance in a record six hours.

The press loved it. As "Princess Alice," she was one of the first national figures of gossip, with reporters avidly writing about her whereabouts, her friends, clothes, and beaux. They might call her Alice Blue Gown, but what gave her image particular piquancy was that she was also Alice Blue Stocking. Doing what no man dared to—twitting Theodore Roosevelt—she harbored fantasies of a feminist rebellion against the prevailing order (of which he, of course, was kingpin) in which the men drove their carriages and kept their women locked away. "What effect would it have if the screen doors flew open and the ladies of the harem tumbled out in a giggle?" she once speculated. And when, in one of his more inflammatory statements, TR said that "race suicide" would occur if the average American woman had fewer than four children, Alice founded with her friends a secret organization dedicated to birth control they called the Race Suicide Club.

TR wrote Ted, always closest to Alice of all the children, to complain about how she made her daily appearance "well after noon—having been up until all hours during the night before." He added sourly a few days later, "Sister continues to lead the life of social exhibitionist. . . . I wish she had some pronounced serious taste."

The real problem for him was not Alice's sloth, however, but her new friends. She had decided to socialize with members of the amorphous group being called the Four Hundred, a concept created by an unctuous social climber named Ward McAlister, who had been hired by the Astors to design extravagant balls and said that it was appropriate that their Fifth Avenue mansion only held four hundred people for that was about how many "truly fashionable" individuals there were in New York.

TR regarded these socialites as parasitic snobs. (One of them, Mrs. Stuyvesant Fish, had insulted Edith by noting, "The wife of the President, it is said, dresses on $300 a year and she looks it.") Even worse, many of them were also exactly those "malefactors of great wealth" against whom he was struggling in his presidency. Alice's new friend Mary Harriman, for instance, was the daughter of E. H. Harriman, one of the principals in the Northern Securities Company. Alice's eager socializing with the Harrimans was obliquely rebuked by Bamie, who, after Harriman came to call on her in Washington and brought with him an elaborate model train for her son, Sheffield Jr., realized that she might be putting TR in a conflict of interest and boxed up the train and sent it back to the Union Pacific offices the next day. Alice had no such compunctions.

"Alice has been at home very little," TR wrote his other sister, Conie, in frustration as he read of his daughter's extended stays with the Harrimans and Vanderbilts. "[She is] spending most of her time in Newport and elsewhere associating with the Four Hundred—individuals with whom other members of the family have exceedingly few affiliations." As usual, he could not help contrasting her with his other daughter, and reported that Ethel had "entirely of her own accord undertaken the summer education of Archie in music and Quentin in everything. She is a little trump."

Given independence by money she received from her doting Lee grandparents, Alice was beyond his control. One journalist kept track during a period of just less than two years and estimated that she had attended 407 dances, 350 balls, and 680 teas, while also making 1,706 calls. She perfected the art of stringing along her many admirers, correctly assuming that most of them hoped to use her either to punish or seek a reward from her father. With her encouragement, for instance, James Hazen Hyde, the head of Equitable Life Assurance Company, spent $100,000 on a costume ball to honor Alice and her friend Margaret Cassini. He got the ballet corps of the Metropolitan Opera to agree to appear, along with the best musicians in New York and opera stars from the Continent. On the day of the ball, Alice got a better offer and sent Hyde a telegram regretting the fact that she would be unable to attend his function.

Edith tried to reel her in with a curt letter: "As you truly say the money is your own and my 'scolding' now would be both silly and useless. If you have debts they must be paid. I can only remind you that it is neither honest nor wise to incur them." She followed this with something more conciliatory, imploring Alice to write when she got to her next stop at Newport and "to try not to buy fifty hats at twenty dollars apiece, and two dozen stockings at five dollars a piece and thirty veils and ten pairs of shoes at fifteen dollars apiece as soon as you get there. How would you like to cause Archie to give up college to pay your debts?"

TR became so exasperated by his daughter's antics that he wrote her a scorching letter of criticism, which she angrily tore up. But there was a note of despair in her defiance. "Father doesn't care for me, that is to say one eighth as much as he does for the other children," she wrote in her diary. "It is perfectly true that he doesn't and Lord, why *should* he? We are not in the least congenial and I don't care overmuch for him and don't take an interest in the things he likes. Why *should* he pay any attention to me and the things that I live for except to look on them with disapproval?"

Within the extended family she was compared not only to her younger sister, Ethel, but also to her cousin Eleanor, recently returned from Allenwood, an all-girls boarding school in London run by the famous Madame Souvestre. (She had taught Bamie twenty years earlier when her school was located outside Paris.) Eleanor's stay there had been the equivalent of her father's trip West when he was a young man suffering from headaches. She later called it the beginning of "the second period of my life," a period marked by liberation from the misery of her childhood. Conie's daughter and namesake, Corinne (sometimes called Corinney, to differentiate her from her mother), attended Allenwood at the same time as Eleanor and later said that her cousin's distinguishing characteristic at the time was that "she did not seem to have any sense of humor." But she also noted that Eleanor was loved and appreciated by Souvestre, who taught her that she could achieve a sense of meaning in her life by concentrating on others rather than herself. Now, while Alice was flitting from one party to another, Eleanor, home for good from England, was working with settlement house children. While Alice toyed with many suitors, Eleanor had begun an unlikely romance with her cousin Franklin after becoming reacquainted with him when he was going to Tivoli by train and he happened to saunter through her compartment and took her back to see his mother, who was traveling in a private car.

The relationship became serious in 1903 when Franklin, in his last year at Harvard, was rejected by a Brahmin beauty named Alice Sohier, who had been put off when he confided to her that he wanted six children, the exact number TR had sired. On the rebound, he had begun to look at Eleanor with new eyes. She was tall and imposing, and, except for the protruding teeth and weak chin, her face was pleasing, although she herself was morbidly aware that she was the first girl on her mother's side not to be considered a belle and had left the coming-out party given by her Grandmother Hall as soon as she could.

"Cousin Eleanor has a very good mind," Franklin wrote in an observation that probably would have increased her insecurity. He himself had grown into a very handsome young man with hair parted in the middle and his face composed into a debonair mask. He was not actually effeminate, as "Feather Duster" and some of the other nicknames the Oyster Bay children had for him implied, but delicate. (Later on, when the two Roosevelt branches had fallen out, someone asked his mother what had caused the conflict and Sara replied without hesitation, "I can't imagine, unless it's because we're better looking.")

He felt somewhat sorry for Eleanor, but he was also appreciative of her ability to love selflessly. (Not knowing how she had been wounded as a child when her mother called her "Granny," he joked with her about her "grandmotherly concern" for him.) It was the kind of affection—focused and seemingly unconditional—to which his mother had accustomed him. Yet it actually came freighted with other qualities he didn't immediately see—particularly Eleanor's tendency to idealize self-discipline and to try too strenuously to exert control over her circumstances to keep from being victimized, as she had been as a child.

Franklin began referring to Eleanor in coded diary entries as an "angel." He wrote love letters to her beginning with the salutation, "My own Dearest Nell." His use of the pet name her father had coined for her seemed an omen: this was Elliott's godson, who wore a watch fob Elliott had given him, using Elliott's own language of love in addressing her! Franklin seemed a fulfillment of her childhood hopes. He was her father come again, the man who would gather her up into the perfect life she had been dreaming about like some sleeping princess since her father's death.

It was not considered particularly noteworthy within the family that the cousins should become engaged. Roosevelts were special, a breed apart; it was natural that they should seek each other out. There was also a recent precedent. In 1904 Corinne's son Theodore Robinson had married Helen Roosevelt, daughter of Franklin's half-brother, Rosy.

TR was enthusiastic about the engagement, writing Franklin, "I am as fond of Eleanor as if she were my daughter; and I like you, and trust you, and believe in you." But there was one person who was disturbed by the development. It was Sara, who called Franklin's news that he had proposed a "startling announcement." She was disturbed in part by the fact that she felt Eleanor was unsuited to Franklin, but even more by the fact that he had managed to hide an emotion from her so successfully.

Characteristically, Eleanor sympathized with her future mother-in-law's disappointment in her: "I know just how you feel and how hard it must be, but I do so want you to learn to love me a little. . . ." Sara convinced Franklin to test his newly discovered love for his cousin by accompanying her on a five-week cruise to the Caribbean. When they returned, in a last-ditch effort to sidetrack the engagement, she tried unsuccessfully to get him a post in England as a secretary to the U.S. ambassador.

Now that she was to become a wife, Eleanor took on matronly airs, joining Alice's own family in opposing her "feminism" and her "scandalous" behavior. ("Alice is looking well but crazier than ever," she wrote Franklin after one encounter. "I saw her this morning in Bobbie Goelet's auto quite alone with three other men.") The two young women met at Oldgate, Bamie's estate in Connecticut, and went row-ing. Eleanor, who was handling the oars, lectured Alice on what was proper to receive from a gentleman—flowers, books, cards—and what was improper—jewelry of any kind. Alice nodded agreeably while secretly fingering a string of pearls given her by an admirer earlier in the week.

There would always be a tension between the two women, just as there would always be a chemistry between Alice and Franklin, whom she recognized to have secret qualities that made him something more than a "good little mother's boy" (as she once called him). After his marriage to Eleanor, Alice ran into him in the hotel where they were all staying and sat with him in an alcove outside her room sipping mint liqueur and gossiping with the wickedness they both enjoyed. Discovering them together, Eleanor issued an ultimatum to her new husband: "No one would know that you were her cousin. I think it would be a good idea if you and Alice didn't see each other for some time."

What TR didn't realize was that Alice's rebellion had always been calculated to get into the family rather than get out. She was regarded as something of a spectacle by the rest of the children, the *real* family, who never experienced the ambiguity that drove her to extremes. This was especially true with Ethel, who was the "asset child" (in her father's phrase), just as Alice was a "liability child." As a girl Ethel had joyously ridden on her pony around Sagamore with apples stuffed into her bloomers. As a sturdy, Dutch-looking teenager, she became the dependable family loyalist. While Alice made news with the Four Hundred, Ethel taught Bible classes at St. Mary's Chapel for Colored Children and played football with her students in a vacant lot after class was over. She mothered her older brothers, especially Kermit, as a typical letter sent to him at Groton suggests: "I am sending you and Ted your rackets, and I am also sending you and Ted some chocolate and some ginger snaps, divide it evenly between yourselves."

While in the abstract a strong defender of women's rights, TR had been so unnerved by Alice's rebelliousness that he was glad to see his younger daughter adopt a more traditional stance. Throughout his presidency, he wrote Ethel tender and humorous letters that often contained stories he thought might amuse her. In one he told about going for a walk—as usual without his Secret Service man—and seeing two terriers chase a kitten. He scared off the dogs and got the kitten: "It was a friendly, helpless little thing evidently too well accustomed to being taken care of to know how to shift for itself. I inquired of all the bystanders and of people on the neighborhood porches to see if they owned it. . . . Then I saw a very nice colored woman and a little colored girl looking out of the window of a small home with on the door a dressmaker's advertisement and I turned and walked up the steps and asked if they did not want the kitten. They said they did and the little girl welcomed it lovingly."

Ethel made shifting alliances with all her brothers. Archie and Quentin ("the little boys") were treated as one unit, and Ted and Kermit as another. TR saw to it that his two eldest boys had outdoor experiences similar to his own. He had read both of them hunting literature and introduced them to men he regarded as great hunters. Too busy now to take them on extended trips into the wilderness, he sent both boys to the Black Hills for a hunting expedition headed by famous Dakota Territory lawman Seth Bullock. TR inducted them both into the Boone and Crockett Club (which he had helped found) after they had fulfilled the entry requirements of bringing down in fair chase three species of American big game.

Ted and Kermit were both students of their father's youth and saw it as a pattern to be followed. Just as he had put together a "Roosevelt Museum of Science" as a boy (he later donated this stuffed collection of birds and small mammals to the American Museum of Natural History), so they had their own natural science collection that they eventually donated to the Groton Science Department after going on to Harvard. Both became expert taxidermists, Kermit so much surpassing his father that in his later travels he was once observed, while on safari in Africa, skinning an exotic species of jungle mouse while riding on the back of an elephant.

Despairing of ever realizing what they saw as their father's protean complexity, the Roosevelt sons each seemed to pick an aspect of his personality to emulate. From the time he was a boy, for instance, Ted had TR's taste for battles and heroism and for public life. When the family first lived in Washington during the Civil Service years, a boy threw apples at Ethel and TR told Ted he must fight him, which Ted dutifully did, despite the fact that he was inferior in size and age and secretly sympathized with anyone who would assault the sister who pestered him. A couple of years later, when he was nine and TR was off campaigning against Bryan, Ted had stood on the porch at Sagamore and emulated his father in giving lectures on free silver to the other children, the gardeners, and anyone else who would listen. He illustrated one talk with a loaf of bread, a prop TR had used on the stump, which he ate after finishing, causing Kermit, who had hoped for a piece, to cry.

In the spring of 1898, when TR was preparing for war against Spain and Edith was fighting her illness, Ted had begun to suffer blinding headaches. Worried that he might have inherited the affliction from his dead brother, Elliott, TR had sent him to a series of specialists. Their consensus view was that he was pushing his son too hard. The diagnosis caused TR to look into himself. "Hereafter I shall never press Ted in body or mind," he resolved. "The fact is that the little fellow, who is peculiarly dear to me, has bidden fair to be all the things I would like to have been and it has been a great temptation to push him."

Yet just as Ted couldn't help idolizing his father, so TR could not help trying to make the boy complicit in his heroism. Just after assuming the vice presidency, for instance, he went to Colorado and wrote Ted an account of a cougar hunt. After describing how the dogs had treed their quarry several times only to have it get away, TR told about finally cornering the animal. "He bit or clawed four of [the dogs], and for fear he might kill one I ran in and stabbed him behind the shoulder, thrusting the knife you loaned me right into his heart."

With his wide face and high forehead and one lazy eye, which, as his father said, tended to "converge" on the other, Ted was far from handsome. In addition, he was small in stature. But he had a "bantamcock aggressiveness," in the words of one friend, and flung himself into activities with abandon. Soon after enrolling at Groton in 1900, he punched a schoolmate who called him "First Boy" and then got into a series of other scrapes. When questioned about Ted's pugnacity, TR admitted that he had probably instilled some of these "fighting proclivities" in his son, but said that some "came naturally." For his part, Ted wrote home from Groton of his exploits with the same keen sense of competition that had characterized his father's letters at the same age: "In boxing I have been beaten this morning. . . . The fellow was about eight pounds heavier than I and he fought left handed which puzzled me extremely. . . . I also came third out of about twenty in the hop skip and jump. There are from 20-30 in each class so third is not so bad as it seems."

In a truculent moment when the children were still young, TR had said that he would "disinherit" any son who refused to play organized sports. But now that Ted was actually competing on the Groton football team against older and heavier boys and there was a possibility of injury, he withdrew from that position in a letter mixing advice and instruction: "Athletic proficiency is a mighty good servant, and like so many other servants, a singularly bad master. Did you ever read Pliny's letter to Trajan in which he speaks of it being advisable to keep the Greeks absorbed in athletics because it distracted their minds from all serious pursuits, including soldiering, and prevented them from being dangerous to the Romans? . . . A man must develop his physical prowess up to a certain point; but after he has reached that point there are other things that count more. . . ."

In his second year at Groton Ted got pneumonia. Edith went there to be with him, and as his condition worsened, TR left the White House to join them. The press made the illness into a national concern. (The first *New York Times* headline read: *Double Pneumonia!* Then, as the crisis passed: *Better!* And finally, as the illness began to recede: *Safe!*) The net effect of the scare was to bring TR even closer to Edith as well as Ted. Once the boy was out of danger, he returned to the White House and wrote her: "My darling, I love you and prize and appreciate you more year by year; your sweet soul and your sweet body. I am so glad to have been with Ted while he was sick and as glad that you and I were together then."

Ted's imagination had been stirred by war since he was a boy, when he had walked to work with his father, then assistant secretary of the navy, and TR had described famous military campaigns, sometimes squatting down to draw them out with a finger in the dust. Ted had been old enough to follow the Cuban campaign closely. (At one point, when word came that a Spanish bullet had grazed one of TR's boots, Ted, thinking of relics, had said, "Save the boot!") Not long after recovering from his sickness at Groton he wrote a poem called "The Norman Baron's Prayer," which he submitted to *Harper's* under a pseudonym:

> Would God I might die my sword in my hand
> My gilded spur on my heel
> With my crested helmet on my head
> And my body closed in steel. . . .
> Would God when the morning broke
> I might by my friends be found
> Stiff in my war worn harness
> Ringed by dead foes all around.

It was natural that Ted should think of applying for West Point or Annapolis. TR tried to dissuade him without actually refusing: "I be-

lieve you have the ability and above all the energy, the perseverance and
the common sense to win out in civil life. . . . In the Army and the
Navy the chance for a man to show great ability and rise above his
fellows does not occur on the average more than once in a generation.
When I was down in Santiago [Cuba] it was melancholy for me to see
how fossilized and lacking in ambition and generally useless were most
of the men my age and over who had served their lives in the Army."

While talking down the army, TR indirectly talked up statecraft by
sharing his experiences in the White House. "I have had a most interesting time about Panama and Colombia," he wrote during negotiations
over the canal. "My experiences in all these matters gives me an idea of
the fearful time Lincoln must have had in dealing with the great crises he
had to face."

One of Ted's chief functions in the family, as Edith perceptively
noted, was to act as a sort of heat shield protecting the other children
from TR's dynastic ambitions. He particularly sheltered Kermit, who as
a result was able to grow up pacific, remote, not inclined to define
himself by physical prowess. "Very few outsiders care for him," Edith
said of her second son. "But if they care for him at all, they like him very
much." While Ted had a scrappy, battle-scarred quality, Kermit was
thin and wistful, aristocratic-looking and with a premonition of hand-
someness in his boyish face.

Everyone noted how close Kermit was to his mother. As Alice noted,
Edith was a keen taskmaster for everyone in the family but Kermit.
Something in him—perhaps his contemplative nature, perhaps the mere
fact that he was named after her own brother who had died in infancy—
particularly touched her. She allowed him to be possessive with her in
a way none of the other children would have dared. (One of TR's
friends observed that whenever he came into a room where Edith was
present he immediately went up to her and put an arm around her
waist.) When he went away to school, Kermit wrote home ordering her
to open all correspondence with good news of his dog Jack so that he
would not worry that something had happened to him. She indulged
this and other whims, and entered a conspiracy to try to run the blockade on certain home goods set up by Groton authorities. "I got the
water pistol it came through without getting caught," Kermit wrote her
after one shipment, "but all the chocolate and guava jelly got caught."

The two of them shared a love of poetry and a tolerance for silence that distinguished them from the rest of the family. They also shared a love of "snooping" around junk stores for interesting objects. "Snoopers are born, not made," Edith told a family friend. "No amount of training would make the President a snooper. . . . Alice is better, but of all my children Kermit is the ideal snooper. He has the nose of a perfectly bred snooper."

Confident of his mother's love, Kermit worked to find common ground with his father. He was not particularly interested in football, but became coxswain on the Groton crew team, and did some running, once writing home to TR about having just completed a thirteen-mile run in which he had "made use of all you had told me" by pacing himself while others went out too fast and did not manage to finish the race.

Letting Kermit too know that there were things he considered more important than sports, TR wrote him with oddments of information: Buffalo Bill's appearance at a White House lunch; the progress of a nest of birds near his office window; his decision to study jujitsu with a pair of Japanese wrestlers. ("I am not the age and build, one would think, to be whirled lightly over an opponent's head and batted down on a mattress without damage, but they are so skilled that I have not been hurt at all.") He probably inadvertently caused Kermit a bout of homesickness with letters describing romps with his younger brothers: "The last two or three nights I have had terrific pillow fights with Archie and Quentin. . . . Quentin's idea is to get as many pillows as possible in a heap and then lie on them, apparently on the theory that he is protecting them from me. This enrages Archie who addresses him with lofty contempt as 'kid,' and adjures him to stand up manfully and 'fight the bear!' "

Just as Ted shared TR's combative streak, so Kermit inherited his father's love of words. During the family's first tour of duty in Washington, he and Alice spent time in the city's gypsy encampments and he picked up the rudiments of Romany. Later, after he had gone off to Groton, Kermit wrote his father literary criticism: "The more I read, the more I come to the conclusion that when I read a novel or a story which is not true I like to have the nice people come out all right in the end, and to have the vallan [sic] either reform or be killed. . . ." TR agreed with these sentiments exactly.

As part of his "snooping," Kermit discovered a volume of poetry called *Children of the Night* by a little known writer named Edwin Arlington Robinson and brought it to his father's attention. Confessing

that he was not entirely sure he understood the work, TR was nonetheless enthusiastic and agreed to collaborate with Kermit in advancing
Robinson's career. He relaxed his vigilance about the spoils system
enough to get the needy poet a clerical job in the Customs House, then
convinced his own publisher, Scribner's, to take him on, and finally
wrote a review of *Children of the Night* for the influential magazine *The
Outlook*. Robinson became a friend of Kermit's for the rest of his life,
writing him, "I do not like to think of where I should be now if it had
not been for your astonishing father. He fished me out of hell by the hair
of the head. . . ."

As with Ted, TR let Kermit participate vicariously in great events he
was dealing with in the presidency. Some of the issues he chose to write
the boy about allowed him to comment obliquely on the issue of patrimony. After initiating some controls over the meat industry in response to *The Jungle*,, for instance, he wrote: "The packers have been
perfectly crazy. . . . I think the trouble is partly due to the fact that they
are not the original makers of the big fortune, but their sons. The
makers of the big fortune were themselves disagreeable men, hard,
selfish, grasping, but with tremendous energy and a great deal of clear
sightedness. Their sons have been brought up in great luxury; they are
self indulgent. . . ."

On the eve of the 1904 vote, after a grueling campaign for reelection,
TR wrote Kermit a letter whose words seemed meant primarily for
himself: "If things go wrong remember that we are very, very fortunate
to have had three years in the White House, and that I have had a chance
to accomplish work such as comes to very, very few men in any generation; and that I have no business to feel downcast or querulous merely
because when so much has been given me I have not had more."

It was a quirk in his personality—preparing for the worst and reassuring himself that he would be able to deal with tragedy with equanimity. (Alice called it "vaccinating himself against what might
happen.") But his family was sure that he would beat the colorless
Democratic candidate, Judge Alton Parker. Kermit canvassed schoolmates at Groton in an unscientific poll of how their families would vote
and said that victory was assured. Remembering the fate of McKinley,
Ted decided to become an informal bodyguard for his father, and stood
beside him at campaign appearances scrutinizing crowds for suspicious-
looking characters who might be assassins.

Even seven-year-old Quentin, who was attending a public school in
Washington, played a role. Demonstrating that he had TR's pugnacity

as well as his literary instincts, he got into a fight with a schoolmate who happened to come to class wearing a Parker campaign button. As he tattooed his opponent with punches, Quentin recited a limerick:

> There was a young lady of Clare
> Who was sadly pursued by a bear
> When she found she was tired
> She promptly expired
> That unfortunate lady of Clare.

Then, with a final punch, he added: "And so will you if you don't give me that button!"

It was a landslide. As the results came in, TR, vastly relieved not to have to practice the stoicism in defeat he had been recommending to the children, said to Edith, "My dear, I am no longer a political accident." Then, in front of the reporters, he said something that made her flinch: "Under no circumstances will I be a candidate for or accept another nomination." It was a rash move they would all regret, but for now the possible consequences of the impulsive gesture were secondary to the four years that lay ahead of them.

At the time of TR's swearing in, Secretary of State John Hay gave him a ring with a locket of hair that he himself, then a young presidential secretary, had taken from the head of Lincoln after his death. It was a sign that the boy who had stood with his brother, Elliott, four decades earlier watching the casket of the Great Emancipator roll through the streets of New York was now about to set foot in the pantheon of American heroes. But long before his reelection TR had already begun hand-marking certain of his private correspondence as "posterity letters" to make sure that the recipients saved them for the scholars who he knew would someday evaluate his place in history.

CHAPTER 6

A few weeks after TR's inauguration, Franklin and Eleanor were in London on their honeymoon. The passage had been difficult, less because of heavy weather than because of psychological turbulence. Eleanor was discovering, as she later told her daughter, that "sex was an ordeal to be borne." Franklin was perhaps beginning to realize that he was now yoked to a woman whose needs were much greater than he had imagined and who could create emotional demands more constraining than his mother's. During the voyage to England he suffered from bad dreams, broken sleep, and somnambulism. On one occasion he had begun babbling in the middle of the night about driving a car. Unable to wake him, Eleanor had wound up cooperating with the night terror. As he sat up in bed "at the wheel," she had gone to the foot of the bed to "crank" the starter.

Yet by day Franklin's unruffled surface was intact and the couple moved through London high society basking in the reflected glory of TR. They were given special suites at their hotel. They had a meeting with famous British socialists Sidney and Beatrice Webb at which Franklin discussed his views on Harvard College and Eleanor described "the servant problem" faced by good families in America. In Paris they went to a "clairvoyant lady," who told them that Eleanor would inherit a fortune and Franklin would be President of the United States. One of the treasures Franklin found in an antique store was a silverpoint drawing of the President, which he purchased and sent home. "Everyone is talking about Cousin Theodore," he wrote his mother in one of his daily letters. "[They are] saying that he is the most prominent figure of present day history, and adopting toward our country a most respectful and almost loving tone. What a change has come over English opinion in the last few years!"

Indeed, if TR could be said to have brought the United States into the twentieth century, it was also true that he did the same for the office of the presidency, increasing its scope and power and making it a post with international implications. This was shown dramatically in his brokering of an end to the Russo-Japanese War during the beginning of his second term.

He had been as surprised as everyone else by the devastating attack by the Japanese on the Russian fleet at Port Arthur in 1904. In the war that ensued, TR initially felt sympathy for the Japanese. They were underdogs, at least in the racist European view, and he was disgusted by the despotism of the Czar's regime, particularly as expressed in vicious pogroms against Jews. As he wrote his son Ted at the onset of hostilities: "For several years Russia has behaved very badly in the Far East; her attitude toward all parties, including us, but especially toward Japan, being gravely overbearing. We had no sufficient cause for war with her. Yet I was apprehensive lest if she at the very outset whipped Japan on the sea she might assume a position well nigh intolerable toward us. . . . Between ourselves—for you must not breathe it to anybody—I was thoroughly well pleased with the Japanese victory, for Japan is playing our game."

But as the Japanese quickly achieved the upper hand in the conflict, he became concerned about the possibility of a future clash with U.S. interests in the Pacific, especially the Philippines, and set about to negotiate a peace that would restore a balance of power. When his efforts to involve the Kaiser and other European heads of state failed he seized the initiative himself.

International diplomacy was tedious and frustrating. At one point TR grumbled to Lodge, "The more I see of the Czar, the Kaiser and the Mikado, the better I am content with democracy. . . ." Yet by August 1905 a meeting of the belligerents was scheduled to take place at the Portsmouth naval yard in New Hampshire. A few days before that, he entertained members of the peace delegation aboard the presidential yacht *Mayflower* anchored in Oyster Bay in view of his excited children and their friends and playmates.

When negotiations were threatened by a stalemate over the issue of reparations and the disposition of Sakhalin Island, he himself architected a compromise, as he had in the coal strike of a few years earlier. The Russians would not be forced to pay reparations, but they would cede half of Sakhalin to the Japanese. After the peace agreement was finally made, TR crowed, "It's a mighty good thing for Russia and a mighty good thing for Japan. And a mighty good thing for *me* too!" As a result of his role, he became the first American ever to be awarded the Nobel Prize. Yet while he reveled in the identity of peacemaker, he didn't want the Japanese to get the wrong idea and sent the American fleet to show the flag in an impressive around-the-world mission in 1907.

In the second term he would have other notable successes. He would further trim the power of the trusts (although Rockefeller's lieutenant at Standard Oil, John Archbold, was histrionically overstating the case when he said, "Darkest Abyssinia never saw anything like the course of treatment we received at the hand of the administration following Mr. Roosevelt's election in 1904"). He would bully Congress into passing pure food and drug and meat inspection laws. And, working with Chief Forester Gifford Pinchot, he would begin a revolution in conservation that would add 150 million acres to the country's public lands, including five new national parks and fifty-one wildlife refuges.

There would be failures too. The Brownsville Incident, in which he dishonorably discharged three companies of black soldiers, some of whom had fought with distinction alongside him in Cuba, for allegedly shooting up the town of Brownsville in Texas marked a capitulation to racist pressure. And his ineffectual reaction to the stock market crisis of 1907 caused him to lose some of the ground he had gained against the malefactors of great wealth.

During some moments of his presidency, as he himself remarked, TR was a progressive conservative, while during others he was a conservative progressive. He would alternate between these two identities for the rest of his political life. But he was always seen, almost without willing it, as a representative American. (In 1906, when he and Edith were returning from a trip to see his handiwork in Panama aboard the *Louisiana,* the sailors gave a cheer for "Theodore Roosevelt, the typical American citizen.") Henry James's philosopher brother, William, spoke for the majority of his countrymen when he said that he "rejoiced" in

Roosevelt. But it was Kansas newspaperman William Allen White who best expressed the effect he had on close admirers: "Roosevelt bit me and I went mad."

Some of his specific actions might cause qualms even among his most dedicated fans. Yet the person always excited his countrymen even when the politician left them cold. TR was the first President (with the exception of George Washington and possibly Andrew Jackson) to become a national icon. The increasingly powerful medium of advertising used his image, without permission, to sell everything from baby powder to cigars. Because of new techniques for mass manufacturing, his likeness was used on a variety of household items ranging from salt shakers to shaving mugs. His youngest son, Quentin, had a mechanical bank in which a bear came out of a tree to take a coin put into Teddy's hand. All his other children would play a Teddy Roosevelt board game put out by Parker Brothers whose object was to get "malefactors of great wealth" into Sing-Sing prison.

TR was far from being a spectator in the merchandising of his image. After all, he had been *making* himself since he was a frail youngster trying to survive. He had worked all through adulthood to create a marketable persona. That he knew it was a persona was clear from an episode that occurred during his Bull Moose candidacy in 1912. Reporters covering the campaign were killing time during a train trip from one city to another by engaging in a lighthearted contest to see who could do the best Roosevelt imitation. TR happened to enter the railcar in the middle of the competition and stood unseen for a while in the background watching. When the reporters had finished, he stepped forward and, in a performance that showed how well he knew himself and his effects, did by far the best Roosevelt imitation of all, replete with choppy gestures, the clicking teeth, crackling high-pitched voice, and even a parody of his stump speech with hilarious talk about how it was necessary to take care of "all the little bull mooses." It was Teddy doing "Teddy" to perfection.

He realized that he was good copy for the national press, which was beginning to play an increasingly important role in American life. Starting at the time when he was on the police commission of New York, TR had always had reporters around, good ones like Jacob Riis and Lincoln Steffens, who allowed him to go over the head of politicians to the people. That experience showed him the benefits that could be generated from the alliance with journalists. During the Cuban campaign, he had received some of the greatest battlefield publicity in the history of warfare from friendly correspondents like Richard Harding Davis and even from more critical ones like Stephen Crane. (Ever on the lookout for new technology to spread the image, TR had found a spot for two operators of the revolutionary new Vitagraph motion picture process on the boat to Cuba, although the press section was technically filled.) And there was, of course, his complicity in the birth of the Teddy Bear.

This courtship ritual had intensified in Albany, where TR had daily informal chats with newspapermen and delivered enticing off-the-record opinions while sitting on the corner of his desk. And now in the White House he continued to dramatize himself for the press in a way that made the cartoonists' job easy for them in creating "Teddy"—eyes blindly optimistic behind opaque discs and teeth clenched in a grin; a figure who tore through events riding his big stick with childlike glee.

He was the first to hold "backgrounders," briefings at which he would present his ideas not for attribution except as an "informed source." He was the first President to give out press releases on a Sunday so that he would have Monday morning's headlines to himself; the first to drive an opponent he knew was about to make news off the front page by purposely doing something newsworthy himself.

The coverage he got was often far from reverential. Some editors crusaded against what they saw as TR's overweening ego and thirst for power. They lampooned him for schemes like his intention to simplify spelling ("though," "through," and "thorough," for instance, would become "tho," "thru," and "thoro") and for the torrent of opinions on everything from literature to natural science that he delivered *ex cathedra*. He was also condemned by the papers for such departures from convention as the dinner invitation to Booker T. Washington, an event that drew an avalanche of racist cartoons showing him in blackface with ever present spectacles and gleaming teeth. (Press opposition in this case only strengthened TR's resolve: "The very fact that I felt a moment's qualm on inviting him because of his color, made me ashamed of myself and made me hasten to send the invitation.")

But whether obsequious or hostile, the coverage was always there—when he was in the White House and afterward. Until the day TR died, the major newspapers and wire services kept a reporter in Oyster Bay to make sure they could capture the opinions and actions that issued forth from Sagamore Hill. For his era he defined the term "newsworthy."

*   *   *

If there was one person in the country who generated an interest rivaling his own it was Alice. Songs ("Alice Blue Gown" and "Alice, Where Art Thou?") were written for her. Because of her more baby girls were now called Alice than any other name. There was constant talk of her making a match with some foreign monarch, and when Kaiser Wilhelm's brother Prince Henry had her christen his yacht, the *Meteor,* the fact that he was already married did not stop the newspapers from speculating that he and Alice would have a royal wedding.

As much as he had been annoyed by some of her antics, TR recognized that Bamie may have been right in saying that Alice was the child of his most like him. They were kindred in their impatience with dullness and hypocrisy as well as in their love of attention. And TR had to admit that she was a political asset. He had begun his reelection drive in the spring of 1904 fearful that the moneyed interests with whom he had been in constant conflict the previous three years might come to the Republican convention and try to deny him the nomination in favor of one of their own, Senator Mark Hanna. When he heard that Hanna's daughter Ruth was getting married, he dispatched Alice to go to the wedding and befriend the bride. A few months later, when Hanna suddenly died, he once again dispatched her to the Ohio household, this time to comfort the survivors and keep the Hanna family friendly to him.

In 1905, when Alice decided to join Secretary of War William Howard Taft and an assortment of other dignitaries in a trip to the Far East, TR took advantage of her celebrity by giving her some informal ambassadorial duties. It was a diplomatic tour that bore Alice's distinctive stamp. On the first stop in Hawaii she made a stir when she was shown an expurgated variety of the hula and demanded "a less *jeune fille* version." In Japan, she encouraged the Emperor to fuss over her by flattering his hopes of getting the lion's share of the spoils in the negotiations TR was conducting just then to end the Russo-Japanese War. In Korea, Alice got off a train to meet a delegation of missionaries in her father's behalf with her small dog under her arm, cigarettes spilling out of their case, and reeking of gin that someone had dropped from a cocktail on her coat.

The centerpiece of the trip was a stop in China. Alice met the Empress Dowager, a woman of ruthlessness and cunning who had already done away with a pair of rivals to retain her place on the Dragon Throne, one of the victims being her own son. The Empress asked her to stay in the Summer Palace while the rest of the delegation was housed in Peking. At one dinner, her interpreter was a man named Wu Ting Fang, whom

Alice had known in Washington when he was attached to the Chinese embassy there. They were all chatting amiably when the Empress suddenly said something to the interpreter "in a small savage voice" and Wu dropped to all fours, forehead touching the ground. He continued to cower that way for the rest of the conversation, only raising his head slightly to translate. TR's reaction, after reading Alice's detailed report of the episode, was to suggest that the Empress had been trying "to show us that this man, whom we accepted as an equal was to her nothing more than something to put her foot on."

There was a subtext to the trip. One of the other members of the junket was Nicholas Longworth, Republican congressman from Cincinnati, with whom Alice was madly in love. Short and balding, charming but somewhat vulgar and, save for a love of the violin, impatient with any art except the art of politics, the thirty-four-year-old Longworth had been the subject of a warning by Edith: "You know, your friend from Ohio is a heavy drinker." She could have added that he was also a heavy womanizer. But Alice already knew that: she had dueled several other women, notably her friend, the fortune hunter Margaret Cassini, for him for almost a year, at times feeling so unequal in the battle that she once wrote plaintively in her diary, "Oh, why am I such a desperate pill?"

Alice pretended to be more sophisticated about sex than she actually was. (She had once opened a closet at Bamie's house to find two male cousins groping each other and only much later understood what precisely they were doing.) Thus the relationship with the more experienced Longworth took on overtones of drawing room farce. Once when she was coming down from her room in the White House to meet Nick and Maggie Cassini, who were waiting below, so that the three of them could go to the theater, her brothers Archie and Quentin rigged the elevator so that it got stuck in between floors. Alice yelled for the hour it took to get her out, not so much fearful as frustrated because she knew that her rival had Longworth to herself all that time.

Her love letters became charged with passionate intensity: "_____ has told me all sorts of things about you this evening that have made me fearfully unhappy. He says that Katherine Elkins [another rival] means to have you before the winter is over. That she will marry you and that you really want to marry her. You are a cur and a cad if this is so. . . . I am afraid that I wish you should die rather than marry anyone else but me." Then come the postscripts: "Nick, think of me. I love you so very much. I am so jealous my darling please." And then another hastily scribbled addendum: "No matter what happens I have been happier than I ever imagined any one could be my darling."

During the trip to the Far East, Mrs. Taft called her husband's attention to the fact that Alice and Longworth spent too much time alone and indulged "in conversation on subjects that are ordinarily tabooed between men and women much older than they are and indeed are usually confined to husband and wife." The good-natured Taft finally took Alice aside and said, "I think I ought to know if you are engaged to Nick." She looked coyly at the three-hundred-pound secretary of war and replied, "More or less, Mr. Secretary. More or less."

Such flippancy would not work with her family. When Alice came home from the trip she decided to tell Edith about the engagement while her stepmother was brushing her teeth so that she would have to take a moment before responding. At the same time this conversation was taking place, Nick was downstairs formally asking the President for her hand. TR had heard stories about Longworth's wild bachelor life, but he was nonetheless pleased by the match. He had always been annoyed by the idea that Alice might marry a foreigner, particularly a member of royalty, and after all, Longworth was a fellow Republican and, more important, also a member of Harvard's elite Porcellian Club. These associations allowed TR to overlook the multitude of sins commonly laid at Longworth's door and welcome him to the family.

Some noted the irony in the fact that Alice had chosen to marry a man as much under the thumb of a domineering mother as her cousin Franklin was. (Longworth's mother had also been widowed young in life; like Sara Roosevelt she had taken an apartment in Cambridge to be near her son when he attended Harvard.) Susan Longworth and Alice disliked each other on sight, and Alice was appalled at the prospect of spending time in Cincinnati, although the Longworth estate, Rookwood, sat in the middle of 220 beautifully forested acres. Not only was the mother oppressive, but the feeling of inherited wealth—from the pottery business—was stultifying.

In her visits to Rookwood, Alice was struck by the feeling of unreality in which her future in-laws were enveloped. She told her friends that despite the fact that Nick was a powerful politician, they knew little about current events. And despite the fact that one of his sisters claimed to be a writer, they knew little about literature. Their idea of culture was to stage musical evenings, at which Nick sometimes played the violin. Although she was told that conversation was strictly forbidden at these events, Alice impishly turned to a man sitting next to her during one of them and chirped, "Isn't it extraordinary to think that Mozart never composed anything exclusively for the viola?" Only later on would she find the analogue that helped her define the Longworths: they were the Magnificent Ambersons.

Her wedding occasioned a final orgy of attention from the press. The story was on front pages for days before the ceremony. Then came the marriage, which was covered from every angle. There were long reports about her dress—white satin trimmed with lace from Alice Lee's wedding gown and trailing a long train of white and silver brocade. And about the gorgeous wedding cake they almost couldn't cut because they had forgotten a knife until a dashing young military attaché named Douglas MacArthur gallantly stepped up and offered his sword.

Alice's love-hate cousin Eleanor was forced to stay home, indisposed by her first pregnancy, but Franklin was there with his mother. He was not part of the wedding party and indeed became mortified when TR called Nick and other Porcellian members into another room for a secret toast, but he made himself useful by disentangling the train on Alice's dress at a critical moment in the ceremony.

England's King Edward sent Alice an enameled snuff box bearing a tiny portrait of himself. The Kaiser sent a bracelet with his miniature in diamonds. The Cuban government appropriated $25,000 for a string of pearls after Alice made it clear that she wasn't interested in its initial suggestion for a present—furniture carved from native woods. There were so many gifts, in fact, that upon her death seventy-five years later some were still unopened.

She chose Cuba for her honeymoon. After she forced Nick to recapitulate the trail of the Rough Riders in what became an ordeal of dust and mosquitoes, they had their first spat in Santiago. "Though I have not the faintest recollection what it was about," she wrote later on, "I remember feeling that I held my own and was successfully obnoxious."

The marriage would have rocky moments. But one thing it did accomplish was to bring Alice back into the family fold. Once she had to add Longworth to her name, she realized how much a Roosevelt she was. Having spent the previous five years testing the boundaries of independence, she now made her peace. She was still salty with her father. (Once she was present when he was discussing the Civil War and she asked him how he felt about the way his hero Lincoln had gotten his son Robert assigned to the staff of General Grant so he could "see a little war.") Yet they had found a common language in politics and after she campaigned for Nick in 1906 and helped him to a huge victory, TR wrote a letter that showed he appreciated her political instincts: "Let me congratulate you and Nick with all my heart upon the successful way in which both of you have run your campaign. . . ."

Almost every day from her marriage until the end of TR's presidency, Alice's little electric car could be seen parked outside the White House gates between tea and dinnertime.

While Alice reveled in the publicity she received as First Daughter, Ted continued to be uncomfortable in the attention focused on him. In the fall of 1905, having given up on the idea of attending a military academy, he entered Harvard where he was dogged by reporters from the moment of his arrival in Cambridge. TR tried to help him get through it: "The thing to do is to get on just as you have evidently been doing, attract as little attention as possible, do not make a fuss about newspapermen. . . . Whenever you go [to football practice] you will have to make up your mind that they will make it exceedingly unpleasant for you once or twice, and you will just have to bear it; for you can never in the world afford to let them drive you away from anything you intend to do." But it became an ongoing ordeal.

Playing in his first Yale game, Ted held his own, although the opposition tried to take advantage of the fact that he was not only the lightest player on the field but also the President's son by slanting the interference at him on every play. He suffered a broken nose and had to have it rebroken and reset, leaving it permanently flattened. To compensate for this assault on the boy's features, TR decided it was time to have his crossed eye surgically repaired, a procedure that forced him to inform Kermit and other members of the family that Ted's face was temporarily "a gruesome sight."

As his father's namesake, Ted had constantly to try to be diplomatic. But caution was alien to his reckless nature. During his second year at Cambridge, he and a friend became involved in a fracas with a couple of men after a "rag" on Boston Common. The friend got away; Ted was caught by the police. The arresting officer tried to get him to give the other boy's name and he refused. The policeman said that his father would no doubt advise him to do so. Ted replied, "I don't think he would." When he heard about the incident, TR told Ted that he had acted correctly and that in any case he shouldn't worry because most policemen were Democrats.

For the remainder of Ted's college career, TR continued to get notes such as this one from the Harvard deans: "Dear Mr. President, You may know where Ted is but we do not." Told that he had cut thirty-eight classes in the first term of his senior year, TR angrily referred to him as "Pendennis Ted" (after Thackeray's improvident character) in a letter to Kermit: "We are often defeated under circumstances which all our courage and ability do not enable us to cope, either with some adversary who is naturally more formidable or with a combination of enemies from which it is not humanly possible to wrest success. Therefore we are sure to have a sufficient number of defeats anyhow. The only way to come out ahead is not wantonly to court defeats where by exercise of ordinary prudence and foresight and skill and resolution it is possible to be sure of victory. . . . I am not only much irritated but I also seem apprehensive as to how Ted will do in after life."

TR gradually got Ted under control and made him bear down for his last year at Harvard and he graduated in good standing, although he often had to resort to stratagems his father didn't know about. In his last term, for instance, faced with a crucial Latin exam for which he had not studied, Ted drew on all the poetry read and memorized at the family dinner table to write the translation in blank verse, appending a note to the instructor saying that of course it must be understood that he had been unable to translate with literal exactness because of the requirements of meter. He got an A.

As TR's second term was drawing to a close, the older boys were inching into the world as public figures, making news on their own. When Ted went up in a balloon, the *New York Times* wrote of him: "He bids fair to be as strenuous as his father. Already he has hunted big game in the West, been battered up at football, and will ride anything that will let him." At about the same time, eighteen-year-old Kermit made the front page of the *Times* when he happened to be riding one day at Oyster Bay and saw a horse pulling a woman and her two young sons in a surrey suddenly bolt. Kermit spurred his mount and after a long and dangerous chase managed to overtake the runaway horse and get it under control. The spectators that had gathered congratulated him on saving three lives. When the hysterical woman tried to hug him, the *Times*'s reporter wrote, "the young man's face was flooded with blushes."

Feeling that his first two sons were "launched," TR took time to focus on Archie and Quentin. In his first term, the "little boys" staged roller skate races in the upper floors of the White House, and walked on stilts. Archie and his cousin and close companion, Nicholas Roosevelt, expected TR to play with them and once when they felt neglected they presented him with a verse:

Good morning Mr President
How are you today
We have obeyed your orders
We're very glad to say.
We went around the White House
Araisin up a row
And if you want to know about it
Then we'll tell you how
We want to have a pillow fight
With you this very night
And if you do not play with us
We'll squeeze you very tight!

TR had a soft spot for Archie, whom Edith had called, in a strangely insensitive remark that continued to hurt him for the rest of his life, "a beautiful idiot."* TR admitted that the boy might not be quite as quick as the others, but felt that he was the most stubbornly honorable and best-natured of all the children. The presidency almost shut down in March 1907 when Archie got diphtheria and hovered near death. Then he began to improve and TR knew that he was safe when he asked to see his friends, "Big Turkey" and "Little Turkey," sons of the Turkish ambassador. The highlight of the illness came when nine-year-old Quentin smuggled his brother's pony, Algonquin, onto the White House elevator and brought the animal into Archie's sickroom.

"Quenty-quee," as TR sometimes called Quentin, was the last child at home. He looked like TR—chunky body, features marked by open-faced candor. While all of the boys had inherited a slice of TR's personality, Quentin, as Edith noted, had it all in microcosm—the shrewdness and generosity, the romantic bravery and nagging sense of principle. And like his father as a boy, he was in love with language. After being badly sunburned, he amazed everyone by saying that his legs looked like "a Turner Sunset." Calling his elder brother "Kermit the Hermit," he added by way of explanation, "Of course, he isn't at all; only the name is so ap-pree-po."

*Many decades later, according to his daughter, Archie would often say after a few drinks, "I'm stupid, I'm just stupid."

Quentin was both the quintessential White House child and also an early example of that evolving concept, the All American Boy. The only Roosevelt son to become a baseball fanatic, Quentin struck up an acquaintance with onetime Chicago White Sox player Ping Bodie and went to games with him. His love of baseball puzzled TR, who unaccountably didn't have a feel for the American pastime, although he sometimes watched out of his office window as Quentin and his friends played on the makeshift diamond they carved onto the White House lawn.

In Edith's words, her last born was "a *fine* bad little boy." She and her husband smiled at behavior in him that they probably would have punished in one of the older boys. TR liked to tell how Quentin threw a snowball at a carriage during a snowstorm and then ran when a Washington policeman tried to grab him. With the policeman hot on his heels, he ran to the British embassy and then turned to yell: "This is English ground! You cannot come here!"

He attended Force School, a public elementary on Massachusetts Avenue. He roller-skated there, rode his pony, or sometimes walked, stopping at a firehouse along the way to slide down the pole. He quickly distinguished himself among his classmates. On one well-remembered occasion, a girl who had been called to the blackboard to do an arithmetic problem stood there not knowing that her dress was plastered to her backside. The class began to titter, bringing the uncomprehending student close to tears until Quentin jumped up with a red face and jerked the dress back into place.

The school had a vicious maintenance man of whom all the children were afraid. On one afternoon Quentin saw him grab a child in the hallway for some trivial offense and begin to shake him violently. "Stop that!" he yelled at the janitor. "You! You should be *smashed* for that!" The man reached for him and Quentin astonished them both by slapping him hard across the mouth.

TR indulged the boy, but didn't hesitate to apply object lessons when he was in the wrong. When Quentin insulted a teacher at Force School and made what TR regarded as only a halfhearted apology, the President himself appeared at the school the next day to apologize to the teacher for him in front of the entire class.

Unlike his older brothers, who had watched their father become an epic figure, Quentin was casual, even a little irreverent, about TR's stature. Once he and his friends were in the basement when the President came by to see what they were doing. When they gave a noncommittal response suggesting mischief, he asked, "Guy Fawkes?"

"Guy Fawkes?" Quentin was intrigued by the name. "Who is he?"

TR launched into an elaborate extemporaneous explanation about the Gunpowder Plot of 1604 and the attempt to blow up the King and House of Lords. He concluded by giving the boys some homework: "Find out what king reigned in England at the time and why it was that Fawkes said part of his plan was to 'blow the Scots back into Scotland.' . . . And please let me know if you discover—as you will—other interesting matters relating to Guy Fawkes."

As the President walked away, Quentin said to his friends with a mixture of irony and appreciation, "Father is simply a *mine* of information."

Another time he and Charlie Taft, son of the secretary of war, were playing a game they called "Spaniard and American." Quentin ran into his father's office where TR kept the sword that had kept getting tangled in his legs during the battle of San Juan Hill. Quentin pulled it out of its scabbard as if it were Excalibur. "Step up and see the i-d-e-n-t-i-c-a-l sword carried by Colonel Thee-a-dore Roos-a-velt in the capture of San Juan Hill. See it! See it!" Brandishing the weapon heroically, he opened a cut on his friend's cheek.

He and Charlie Taft had a gang in the White House that included several other boys from Force School. Boisterous and always on the verge of mischief, they were sometimes a trial for TR. When he found the presidential portraits covered with spitballs late at night he forced them to get out of bed and clean them. When they got on the White House roof and rolled snowballs onto policemen guarding the entrance, he lectured them on their responsibility to others, especially those they might be tempted to consider socially inferior.

But Quentin and his friends also gave TR a pure enjoyment he hadn't had with his older boys because of his anxieties about their development. Occasionally he would spy on the White House Gang, as they called themselves. Sometimes it was with trepidation, as when Quentin contrived a manhood ritual that involved putting some of Edith's knitting needles upright on the floor and then suspending his rigid body over them with his feet on a windowsill and his hands grasping the arm of a chair. More often it was with fond concern, as when the gang was playing in the attic and trapped one of its members in a chest and sat on it so he could not get out. As the boy began to make muffled sounds of terror, TR suddenly materialized from the shadows where he had been watching unnoticed. Chastising the others, he quickly freed the imprisoned boy, saving face for him by wiping away his tears and saying, "See, the moth balls have gotten into his eyes and made them water."

He wrote Edith's sister, Emily: "I love all these children and have great fun with them and I am touched by the way in which they feel that I am their special friend, champion and companion."

When he took the gang out on the presidential sloop for voyages along the Potomac, he played pirate with the boys. But the games always stopped when they sailed past Mt. Vernon. TR stood at attention and removed his hat and made sure that the ship's bell sounded. "That bell's tolling for the soul of a great man," he explained to Quentin and his friends. "We're now passing his house, and the things he loved; his body, too, which he had to leave behind him. Wouldn't it be fine if you and I grew up to be thus respected. Of course, you may not be able to get thousands to respect you, as Washington did; but you can begin by getting two or three—maybe six or a dozen—and *that's* fine too."

Unlike the older children, who had gone off to their boarding schools reluctantly, suffering from homesickness in advance, Quentin asked to go away when he graduated from Force and was enrolled at Episcopal High School in Alexandria. After a few weeks, Quentin was sent home by the rector to become a day student because of violent hazing (being forced to smoke until deathly ill by older students and to box a boy twice his size), which he had not told his parents about. But even his return did not change the melancholy mood that had settled on the White House. They were all getting older; their stay inside the gates of paradise was drawing to a close.

Early in 1908, TR wrote Archie a bittersweet letter in which he mentioned that Quentin recently had invited two friends from his new school to spend the night: "They played hard and it made me realize how old I had grown and how very busy I had been these last four years, to find they had grown so that I was not needed in the play. Do you recollect how we all of us used to play hide and go seek in the White House? And have obstacle races down the hill when you brought in your friends?"

As the end of TR's presidency drew near, the whole family regretted his rash pledge on the night of his 1904 victory not to seek another term. It seemed as though the White House belonged to them; it was certainly impossible to imagine the family of William Howard Taft, the man TR had designated his political heir and successor, taking their place. His family did not pressure TR to go back on his word and run again, as did others bothered by what some commentators were calling "the great refusal," although they wondered what would come next.

Roosevelt would leave the White House at the age of fifty, still vigorous and capable. Speculations about his future became a national activity. Some said that he should run for the Senate. Others said that he should become the mayor of New York. President Charles W. Eliot of Harvard was retiring and TR, already an overseer, was mentioned as a possible replacement. But Eliot was an opponent who believed the President was an undignified man and he never failed to tell colleagues with distaste of the time TR had come to visit the university in 1905, been shown to his room, and, after taking off his coat, had plunked a pistol he was carrying on the dresser. In any case, TR knew the university was not the right environment for him, telling his friend and fellow Harvard graduate Owen Wister that when he attended overseers' meetings he "felt like a bull-dog who had strayed into a symposium of perfectly clean, white Persian cats."

TR decided that after leaving office he would comment on national affairs by writing a monthly column for the influential magazine *The Outlook*. And for the first year, at least, he would be out of the country on a hunting trip to Africa followed by a leisurely tour of the European capitals, which would give his successor time to establish himself.

The spring of 1908, the family's last in the White House, was glorious. TR followed the progress of a yellow-throated vireo that was nesting in the tree outside his office and of the cardinal that was raising its young among nearby catalpa blossoms. He tried to reassure all the children with letters like the one he wrote Kermit: "I have had a great run for my money and I should have liked to stay in as President if I had thought it was the right thing to do. . . . Mother and I are in the envious position of having enjoyed the White House more than any other President and his wife whom I recall and yet being entirely willing to leave it. . . ." Yet behind these words could be heard the sound of whistling in the dark. Quentin spoke for the whole family when he said, "There is a little hole in my stomach when I think of leaving the White House."

As the campaign began the process of picking TR's successor, Nick Longworth worked hard for his fellow Ohioan Taft. Alice feigned enthusiasm, but secretly tried to work some of the white magic she had studied as an adolescent. "No one will ever know how much I wanted, in the black depth of my heart, that 'something would happen,' " she later said, "and that Father would be renominated." After the Republicans made their choice, she realized that all the good times were coming to an end. One afternoon when going out of the White House gates she rearranged her features to resemble Mrs. Taft's "hippopotamus look" and said to the guards, "This, my darlings, is what is coming after us."

That last Christmas in the White House, after Taft's election, was bittersweet. All the cousins, including Franklin and Eleanor, were invited for a last visit. (Franklin had surprised fellow law clerks in the firm where he was working whose consensus opinion was that he had a "sanguine temperament almost adolescent in its buoyancy" by announcing that he had decided on a career in politics and planned on taking the same route as his cousin—state legislature, assistant secretary of the navy, governor, and then President.) Soon after the first of the year Ethel had her coming out, and then in late February, the Great White Fleet TR had sent on an around-the-world cruise several months earlier to remind the Japanese that the United States was an international naval power made its triumphant return home. Reviewing the ships from the presidential yacht *Mayflower* anchored outside the Potomac, TR listened to the twenty-one-gun salute with misty eyes, remarking, "I could not ask for a finer concluding scene to my administration."

A newspaperman watching the gleaming white ships steam by also felt the recessional spirit: "It is as if America is docking after a long and splendid voyage under a great admiral."

It was more than one man's administration that was ending. The black and white world TR had grown up in and whose clear-cut imperatives he so well expressed was also drawing to a close. In just a few years, the gleaming white battleships would have to be repainted the color of gunmetal to serve in a gray and ambiguous cause.

Alice was pleased when the morning of Taft's inauguration dawned in a blizzard and plummeting temperatures insured a scanty turnout for the inaugural parade and forced the new President to take the Oath of Office out of view in the Senate instead of on the Capitol steps. After Taft finished his address, TR congratulated him and then immediately left without further ceremony to meet Edith at the train station for the ride back to Oyster Bay. Just before the train pulled out, someone passed a tureen of terrapin soup, TR's favorite, into his compartment. Lines of people, many crying, watched him go.

After saying goodbye to her parents, Alice went home to get ready for the inaugural ball, seeing herself as a Roosevelt agent in place who would take careful note of all the absurdities and gaucheries of the next four years. As she thought about how they had all left the White House for the last time, there was only one way to explain the feeling: it was like being expelled from the Garden of Eden.

PART THREE

Rivers of Doubt

"Normally I care for a novel if the ending is good,
and I quite agree with you that if the hero has to die he
ought to die worthily and nobly, so that our sorrow
at the tragedy shall be tempered with the joy and pride
one always feels when a man does his duty well
and bravely."

—TR TO KERMIT

*T*heodore Roosevelt's voice echoed sharply off the canyons up above as he stood on the banks of Brazil's Rio da Divuda slapping at the mosquitoes boiling up off the eddies of the river. He was anxious to be off on what he was already calling the "great adventure," although he knew it was actually only the next chapter of this unfolding saga. In the five years' time since he had left the presidency there had already been adventures aplenty—hunting big game in Africa and a Grand Tour of Europe; then a homecoming to America to reenter the political arena, precipitate a split in the Republican Party, form the insurgent Progressive Party, get shot by a would-be assassin, and suffer a crushing defeat in his 1912 run for the presidency.

Now, on the morning of February 27, 1914, he was ready once again to test his fate, this time by attempting to navigate the River of Doubt, as the Divuda was known in English. It was a calculated venture into the unknown: the waterway existed on no map; no white man had ever run its course. Like life itself, TR had noted more than once since deciding to make the trip, the river now stretching out before him had a beginning, but its end was a mystery.

His party included his son Kermit, the American naturalist George

Cherrie, and three Brazilians—Colonel Candido da Silva Enrique Rondon; the surveyor Lieutenant Juan Lyra; and a doctor named Antonio Cazjazeira. In addition there were also sixteen *camaradas*, native boatmen of the rain forest. It was Colonel Rondon who had discovered the Divuda in 1908 when he was on a mission to extend telegraph lines into the Brazilian wilderness. Waiting since then for an opportunity to trace its course, he had finally found in Theodore Roosevelt someone with the energy and power to help drive the quest to a conclusion.

It had taken over two months for the Roosevelt party to reach the heart of this Brazilian darkness. Early in December they had boarded the gunboat-yacht of the President of Paraguay and begun steaming up the Paraguay River. They crossed the Tropic of Capricorn on their third day out. Their gunboat flew the American flag, the first one ever seen on the Upper Paraguay, as TR proudly noted. This part of the trip had been leisurely, marked by stops along the way to collect plants and small animals for the Museum of Natural History, which was helping to underwrite the expedition. But always they were aware that they were heading upriver, deeper into the interior and farther from civilization.

On December 17, they detoured to the *fazenda* of a wealthy Brazilian for several days of jaguar hunting. Then on Christmas Day they took off once again in a riverboat called the *Nyoac*, passing into the narrower Cuyaba River, an area teeming with great kingfishers, crimson flamingos, ibises, black skinners, and other exotic birds, including communal nests swarming with parakeets. There was a stop at the settlement of San João for a ceremony with the governor of the state of Mato Grosso that involved a joint raising of the flags of the United States and Brazil and the playing of both countries' national anthems to the tinny accompaniment of a frontier band.

The more primitive conditions became, the happier Theodore Roosevelt seemed to be. A bulky figure outfitted in khaki bush clothes and a pith helmet, he was intrigued by the animal life—vicious piranha fish, strange rodents, and tropical birds with garish plumage that stunned his ornithologist's eye. He paused at one point to study a colony of fire ants. Examining the teeming insects with the intense attention he had given nature during his youth, he ignored the fact that his curiosity caused him to be stung repeatedly. "Capital!" he had called this prologue to the great adventure. "Bully!"

After going as far as possible by water his party had climbed aboard a pack train of mules on January 21 for an overland trip across the high tableland of the Brazilian wilderness. There was one disquieting sight:

bones of dead pack animals and abandoned crates from other expeditions and the graves of the men who had preceded them. Even naturalist George Cherrie, who had spent twenty-two years collecting and exploring in the American tropics and who was, in Roosevelt's estimation, "efficient and fearless," was stabbed by a sense of forboding. But by the time they reached the headwaters of the Divuda this scene was forgotten. All the members of the party had been infected by TR's enthusiasm. They were anxious to get out onto the river and begin discovering the undiscovered country ahead.

TR frankly admitted the appeal of the South America trip for him when he called it his "last chance to be a boy." But it was not simply a matter of turning back the clock or grasping one last handful of pure action. What he wanted was more elusive—a sense of clarity the claustral world of affairs no longer held for him. What this adventure offered was an opportunity to confront obstacles that he could defeat rather than those—age, diminution of his physical powers, the vagaries of the intractable world of politics—that he could not. In navigating this mysterious river he would perhaps find a part of himself that he seemed to have misplaced over the last few years.

When he left the White House, of course, it had seemed impossible that Theodore Roosevelt could ever become mired in indecisive outcomes. Some of his countrymen might have wondered how he would defy the maxim, whose truth was already felt even though its exact wording would not be articulated for another quarter century, that there were no second acts in American lives. But TR himself had seemed certain that a way would open up for him. It always had.

His first answer to the question of what came next was simple: Africa. He had planned his safari meticulously in his last days at the White House, focusing on the details to keep his mind off his expulsion from the garden of the presidency. He had gotten the Smithsonian to help sponsor the Africa expedition. (In return he would bring back the skins and bones of large animals of the Dark Continent to be reassembled by taxidermists for museum display.) And *Scribner's* magazine had guaranteed him $50,000 for articles about his experiences.

The Africa trip was to take a year and was his precious last chance to be a boy. The only troubling aspect of the experience was that he would be away from Edith for so long. (She later said there was only one thing worse in her life to that point: the experience of almost losing Archie to diphtheria two years earlier.) To keep from being wholly cut off from the family, TR decided to take a piece of it with him. The logical candidate was Ted, but his eldest son was determined to succeed in business and had taken a job in a Connecticut carpet company after graduating from Harvard. Archie and Quentin were too young. Kermit needed special attention so TR settled on him as his companion. After it was announced that he would be going, the second Roosevelt son, just turned nineteen, became something of a celebrity and the *New York Times* profiled him drawing pensively on a snub-nosed pipe with a Panama hat pushed back on his forehead: "Kermit shows a pair of rather high cheekbones, a fairly good brow, and eyes that are clear and free from any traces of dissipation."

TR had left America with a flourish in April 1909. J. P. Morgan was speaking for the malefactors of great wealth when he grumbled, "We hope that every lion will do his duty," but the country as a whole had collaborated in the grand exit. Bands played patriotic songs at the dock; a fleet of private boats had pulled up alongside the liner *Hamburg* as it was being towed out to sea to ring their bells and blow their whistles in a tumultuous send-off. People in the skyscrapers beginning to poke up on the Manhattan skyline had watched the spectacle and dropped confetti from their windows.

Not wanting to be reduced to ceremonial status of "Mr. President," TR decided that he wanted to be called simply "Colonel Roosevelt" in his out-of-office years. The identity was that of old soldier still in reserve, always ready to raise a regiment or take any enemy position if he was needed. Or, for that matter, to go up against man-eating lions and other dangerous beasts of Africa.

He threw himself into the romance of this new experience with gusto from the moment he landed in British East Africa. An enduring image for those in his party was of Theodore Roosevelt sitting in a kitchen chair he'd ordered strapped to the cowcatcher of the locomotive chugging out of Mombasa, squinting out at the passing countryside with a determination to take it all in.

The party the Colonel had assembled was like a small army. He and Kermit led the way on horses. Behind them were native gun bearers in white knickerbockers and red fezzes, and next in rank behind them over two hundred porters from several tribes whose job was to skin and bone the animals shot by the expedition and pack them for shipment back to the United States.

During its year in Africa, the Roosevelt safari leisurely circled the

Kapiti Plains, going from there to Nairobi, then to Lake Victoria, then down the White Nile to the Congo, and from there to Khartoum. As the trip fell into its own distinctive rhythm, TR not only enjoyed getting to be a boy again himself but also watching the effect of the trip on his own boy Kermit. He had taken his second son because he seemed stuck in mid-passage, obviously talented but floundering academically and to some degree personally, and showing no evidence of Ted's resilience, Archie's flinty resolve, or Quentin's ironic independence. TR made it clear, however, that while the trip was for himself a payment for years of effort in public service, Kermit would have to work doubly hard when he returned to Harvard because he was getting his reward in advance of the work that would justify it.

TR's intuition about Kermit proved right. Not long after arriving in Africa, he wrote home about him, "The rather timid boy of four years ago has turned out a perfectly cool and daring fellow." Kermit volunteered to be the official photographer in charge of "Kodaking" the expedition. In this capacity he captured a bizarre moment that occurred when a hyena came into camp one night, gnawed his way into the stomach cavity of an elephant they had shot that afternoon, and got stuck there when the dead animal's intestines dried and shrank. The hyena was trapped inside the elephant's ribs the next morning, snarling from behind the vitreous membranes, when TR discovered it and, after Kermit had shot a picture, dispatched the animal with a bullet to the head.

Kermit became a dashing character in TR's letters home, taking spills from his horse and recklessly mounting up again, racing through the veldt shooting game buffalo-hunter style from the saddle. The porters were closer to him than to TR, partly because of the rewards he gave in the form of tea and sugar and money, but also because he took the time to learn Swahili. Like his father, Kermit gloried in the dangers of the trip, gloating in one note to his sister Ethel that he and their father were now hunting a man-eating lion with twenty-five natives to its credit. As his self-confidence grew, Kermit decided at one point in the expedition to go off by himself for a month, and spent his twentieth birthday in isolation in the bush with one porter as his only companion. His romantic daring deepened the bond with his father, who proudly wrote home to Bamie about his son: "Two days ago he killed a leopard which charged him twice but he stopped it each time. It got up and mauled one of our bearers."

Africa appealed to the Colonel's taste for the exotic. He breakfasted on crocodile eggs and celebrated the kill of his first lion by doing a savage moonlight dance. But the trip had also engaged his naturalist's mind as was shown by the precise inventory he made of the contents of the stomach of a crocodile Kermit shot: "sticks, stones, the claws of a cheetah, the hooves of an impala, the big bones of an eland, together with the shell plates of one of the large river tortoises. . . ."

The Dark Continent called forth some of TR's most evocative prose when he came to write *African Game Trails.* ("In these greatest of the world's hunting grounds there are mountain peaks whose snows are dazzling under the equatorial sun; swamps where the slime oozes and bubbles and festers in the steaming heat; lakes like seas; skies that burn above deserts where the iron desolation is shrouded from view by the wavering mockery of the mirage. . . .") For years afterward, when he went out onto the patio at Sagamore to drink his coffee and watch the twinkling lights on Long Island Sound, he would inevitably reminisce about Africa, theoretically directing his comments to Kermit but actually speaking to anyone within earshot. "Do you remember that night in Sotick when the gunbearers were skinning the big lion?" he would begin, in an opening line that showed how attentive he had been to the story-telling art of the Victorians. Or: "What a lovely time that was in Lado when we were hunting the Great Eland. . . ."

In theory he had gone to Africa to cleanse his palate of the taste for power and thus be able to return home with a diminished appetite for elective office. Yet even in the Dark Continent he had been regarded—and to some extent regarded himself—as a once and future President not so much out of office as on a leave of absence. His tent was like a traveling White House. Every morning, the stars and stripes was run up a flagpole planted outside the entry. Foreign dignitaries always seemed to be visiting, and African children arrived to serenade him with "The Star Spangled Banner" in phonetic English ("O se ka nyu se bai di do nesli laiti . . .").

He kept in touch with developments at home well enough to know that there was a battle brewing inside the Republican Party between the progressive-minded Insurgents and the Old Guard. He had been able to create a balance of power between them by the force of his personality. But Taft, despite good political instincts, was a lazy man who had capitulated to the special interests in such matters as the tariff and conservation. (He had fired Chief Forester Gifford Pinchot, architect of

TR's conservation revolution.) For the time being, TR did nothing, knowing that the lackluster Taft administration made his own shine by comparison. Aware that he continued to hang like a charge of static electricity over American politics, TR artfully crafted his absence. He employed an aide in Nairobi who dispatched almost daily reports back home about the number and kinds of animals he and Kermit had killed (by the end of the safari their joint tally was 512) along with other news from the safari. If it was true, as he claimed, that he was using these releases to take incentive away from the newspapermen who had tried to shadow him to Africa, it was also the case that his public relations campaign kept him squarely in the public eye back home.

When TR and Kermit came out of the bush at the end of a year, Edith and Ethel were waiting for them in Khartoum. They all went to Cairo to prepare for a Grand Tour of Europe that would allow him to meet the crowned and uncrowned heads of the Continent and give a delayed Nobel Prize acceptance speech in Oslo. It was a trip that went well everywhere except for an at times strained meeting with the Kaiser, after which TR wrote, "Germans did not like me, and did not like my country."

If the tour of Europe was supposed to be a delayed victory lap for his presidency, it also became a warm-up for the trip home. TR claimed that his interest in political developments that had occurred during his absence was merely abstract. In fact, however, visits from Gifford Pinchot and other of his loyalists who had been purged from the Taft administration convinced him that he alone could close the fault line opening up in American politics between conservatives and progressives. Yet he acknowledged that even thinking in these terms was a kind of betrayal of the man he had chosen as his successor. One of the reasons he had gone abroad for a year, after all, was to give his old friend and colleague a chance to establish himself in the White House. Roosevelt wanted to remain loyal to Taft, but he was vulnerable to those who said that Taft's failure merely demonstrated his own indispensability.

The dozens of people—family and friends—who claimed a special relationship with Theodore Roosevelt were allowed to crowd onto the cutter that he transferred to from the German liner that had taken him across the Atlantic. As the vessel steamed into the Battery, lost in the crowd were Eleanor and Franklin. Insouciant in a white boater, FDR was anxious to let his idol know that he had tired of the desultory law practice he had entered after graduating from Harvard and had decided to follow him into politics by running for the New York State Senate.

Franklin's decision had a certain psychological urgency, as he had become squeezed by the conflict between the two women in his life. He saw that his mother ruthlessly dominated Eleanor, but he himself was barely able to challenge Sara directly where his own autonomy was concerned, let alone protect his wife. Sara still held the financial reins in the family. She had bought two interlocking brownstones on 65th Street where they all lived, a situation that allowed her to intrude into Eleanor's privacy at all hours through entryways linking the houses at both the second and third floors. She lectured her daughter-in-law on how to serve tea, how to furnish her bedroom, how to dress, and how to raise her children.

While Eleanor was secretly resentful, she was abjectly dependent on her mother-in-law to run her house because she felt helpless in her domestic life. She was unable to cook and uneasy directing servants. By her own admission, she had no idea how to raise children. ("I never had any interest in dolls or in little children," she said later on, "and I knew absolutely nothing about handling or feeding a baby.") Indeed, because of her own grim upbringing she seemed at times like one of those lab animals of a later age that has had love and caring withdrawn during infancy and as a consequence grows up deprived of parental instincts.

When her first child, Anna, born in 1906, was an infant, Eleanor hung her out the window in a box made of wire mesh each day because she had been told that babies required plenty of fresh air, a practice she stopped only after a neighbor, seeing the screaming child turn blue, threatened to call the Society for the Prevention of Cruelty to Children. In another well-remembered incident, Eleanor had scheduled a dinner party on the same night that the nurse was off and had to take care of the baby by herself. When little Anna began to cry, Eleanor panicked and called the doctor, who asked if she had burped her. Eleanor had not, but the lesson she carried away from the experience was not the obvious one about becoming more adept with her child's needs. "Never again," she vowed, "would I have a dinner on the nurse's day out."

Later on, when Anna was three, in a traumatic circumstance she would remember the rest of her life, Eleanor began tying her hands to the bedposts at night to keep her from masturbating.

After Anna came Jimmy. Then, in 1909, Eleanor's third child, Franklin Jr. She called him "the biggest and most beautiful of all my babies," but he failed to thrive, dying at the age of seven months of heart failure. This sent her into a tailspin of guilt and she allowed Sara to take even more control over the child-rearing duties. Later on she would say,

"Franklin's children were more my mother in law's children than mine."
It was a sentiment in which Sara concurred, sometimes telling her grandchildren during explanations how much she loved them, "Your mother
only bore you."

Franklin was caught in the emotional crossfire between the two
women, but he loved the children, especially Anna, whom he played
with on the floor and packed around Hyde Park. (Eleanor wrote her
mother-in-law, "F. carries her up the hill on his back with two short
legs sticking out on either side of his head.") But he had seen from
growing up with his mother that his only freedom lay in removing
himself from conflict and so he did not try to break the oppressive
triangle linking his wife, his children, and his mother. He tried to carve
a life for himself out of the world of affairs where he could be free.

He knew that his mother had hoped he would pick up his father's
identity as Squire of Springwood and live in Hyde Park. But he wanted
to escape her authority. Politics, which TR had not only made a legitimate profession, but an honorable one, was a way out. One day Franklin was talking to some of the Democratic Party operatives in
Poughkeepsie about a vacant seat in the New York State Senate. When
they offered it to him in behalf of the power brokers of Dutchess
County, he said that he would have to ask his mother. One of the men
responded by pointing at a bank across the street from where they were
conferring: "Frank, the men who are looking out that window are
waiting for your answer. They won't like to hear that you had to ask
your mother."

FDR replied, "I'll take it."

The *New York Times* referred to the Colonel's arrival back in America
as a "return from Elba." And there was something in it of the exile's
homecoming. The minute he landed, Roosevelt was once again the
center of attention and political speculation, with newsmen rushing up
breathlessly and delivering such statements as, "All Jersey's for you!"
There were thousands of people waiting on Fifth Avenue for the parade
of welcome, and the Roosevelt family was not able to be alone until a
special train had deposited them back at Oyster Bay.

In his first days home, TR was struck by how much they had all
changed during his absence. He noted glumly that Alice still gave no
indication of wanting to have children, although she appeared happily
married. (She had, in fact, commemorated their fourth anniversary with

Nick by writing, "A rather vivid four years—may the next four be forty times more so!") She chafed at the traditional role of the good wife, and when Longworth referred to her as "a nice young girl," she bristled, noting in her diary, "My instincts and desires were at least half in the other direction. Always wanted to know about everything personally—from my own experience. . . . I don't imagine I could ever be absolutely contented, no never contented but sometimes gloriously happy."

Having established herself in her father's absence as one of the arbiters of Washington's political society, Alice continued to measure everything by the prelapsarian standards of her family's days in the White House. This included the President. "Rather pale and fat," she wrote after an evening of bridge with the man who had nervously chaperoned her to the Far East five years earlier, "so discouraging." She was amused to hear how the three-hundred-pound Taft padded around the White House late at night in his size fifty-four underwear worrying if Roosevelt's return posed a challenge to him. While she had missed her father during his African sojourn, she did not spare TR the sharp cutting edges of her ambivalence. "No one can ever know how I long to see him, or how much I care for him," she confided in her diary upon his return, then adding the characteristic thrust, "when I care for him at all."

Ethel was the exact opposite of her sister—emotionally steady and reliable, the one child whose unconditional love TR could always rely on. A young woman who had unfortunately inherited TR's stocky build but had a pleasant face and was admired by everyone for the sweetness of her temperament, Ethel was anxious to try her wings just as her brothers were doing. She told TR upon his return home that she wanted to go to work with Jane Addams in Hull House. But he worried that she was too young and Chicago was too far away, and while he was an ardent supporter of suffrage for women in other contexts, he managed to convince Ethel to stay closer to home.

It was Archie who had changed the most in the year of TR's absence. During the Africa trip he had written enviously to Kermit, whose cast-off clothing he wore at Groton, "My, but you are a lucky dog," and pathetically asked him to bring back as a remembrance of Africa "any queer stones you find." Admittedly beset by "dullness and lethargy," Archie had sunk into despondency at Groton, a thin-faced little boy with skin so pale that it made his lips look rouged by comparison. Worried about reports he had gotten about his third son, TR had finally made the long-distance prescription of some Western therapy, and

Archie had transferred to the Evans School in Arizona in the shadow of the Superstition Mountains. There he had managed to reorient himself, and was soon writing Ethel, "The desert is perfectly wonderful. Sometimes you will go for miles and never see a soul. . . ."

His ties with Groton were cut when a letter to a friend containing the sentence "How's the old Christ factory" was discovered by Headmaster Peabody, who expelled him. Returning home for a fresh start after several months away, Archie enrolled at Andover, winning his father's respect by his tenacious independence there. "He is sometimes a little short on pure intellect," TR wrote Ted, "[but] he is long on character, which is a mighty sight more important."

There was never any doubt that Quentin would succeed at Groton or wherever else he went. (When TR said as his son was leaving for prep school that he wouldn't bother to tell him to be good, Quentin replied urbanely, "No, that would be a bromide.") He had none of Archie's difficultly adjusting, and quickly gathered a close circle of friends. One family friend was amazed at the eclectic way Quentin spent his spare moments—rebuilding old motorcycles and reading Turgenev and Racine—and said, "There is something very *Theodore* about all this."

As he had promised his father, Kermit began immediately to concentrate on his studies after returning from Africa. (He would repay TR's confidence in him by completing the four-year curriculum at Harvard in a little over half that time.) But in addition to toughening him, his experience in the Dark Continent had deepened his literary sensibility, and addicted him to a wanderlust he would never be able to shake.

In his spring recess in 1911, Kermit went on a moose-hunting expedition in New Brunswick that he eventually wrote up in a entertaining article for *Collier's* magazine. His next adventure was to go off to do some sheep hunting in Mexico by himself, writing in *Scribner's* about the dangerous trek across the Sonoran desert (the way was marked by nearly a hundred graves of others who had died from thirst or from attacks by the bandits who controlled the area) to the mountains whose deep craters, filled with rainwater, attracted bighorn sheep. The adventure impressed his father, who wrote an envious letter to Kermit in Mexico: "The papers have continually had stories that you were in danger of being captured by insurrectos and that American relief parties were being ordered to your rescue. . . ."

It was Ted of all the boys who understood his role most clearly: to help his father in politics. After graduating from Harvard in 1908, he had left his checkered academic career behind him and gone directly to work at the Hartford Carpet Company in Connecticut at seven dollars a week, five dollars of which went for room and board. Proud to have gotten the job on his own, he did everything from clerical work to hand-washing the newly woven carpets. He enjoyed the anonymity of the job, but he could not escape the heavy responsibilities that came with the dynastic name. Newspapermen hung around the carpet company and hounded him for stories. When a photographer snapped a photo of him lighting a cigarette on the way to work, the picture appeared in papers all over the country as a testament to tobacco's ability to corrupt even the children of the upright.

Somewhat suspicious about girls who showed interest in him, Ted had nonetheless become intrigued by a cool and collected young woman named Eleanor Alexander. Raised by her mother (who had divorced Eleanor's father, remarried him, and then gotten divorced again), she was independent and intelligent. Ted first met her at a social weekend at the home of Mrs. Alfred Dodge when he gallantly came to her rescue one morning on the bridlepath after a small catastrophe in which she had lost control of her horse and was unable to keep her hat from flying away in the wind, after which her hair had tumbled down and her riding habit had come unbuttoned.

The experience made an impression on Ted, and when he saw Eleanor Alexander again a few weeks later at his sister Ethel's coming-out party, they began a courtship in which he had to overcome the doubts of some of Eleanor's relatives, Wall Streeters who considered TR a class traitor, and of the spirited Eleanor herself, who rebelled when he addressed her in one letter as "Dear Goldilocks" instead of "Dear Miss Alexander," and reacted by tearing up the note and accepting no others until he apologized for being "fresh."

Writing in her diary, Alice said that Eleanor Alexander was "the type of mother and Ethel rather than the ecstatic and brilliant me." Indeed, this young woman did have a strong-mindedness that resembled Edith's and a comparable ability to devote herself totally to her husband and his career. And in time, she would fall almost as much in love with the rest of the Roosevelt clan as with Ted himself, but she still felt very much *sui generis* when she arrived for her first afternoon at Oyster Bay. Edith took one look at her formal attire and sighed, "White kid gloves in the country? Dear me." After this oblique notification that nobody put on airs at Sagamore, Eleanor (to avoid confusion, Oyster Bay clan would henceforward refer to FDR's wife as "Eleanor Franklin") was swept up into the nonstop activity. She wrote later on of the chaos she experienced during her first stay: "Every night they stayed downstairs until nearly midnight, then, talking at the top of their voices, they trooped . . . upstairs. For a brief moment all was still, but just as I was dozing off to sleep . . . they remembered something they had forgotten to tell one another and ran shouting through the halls." She put cotton in her ears and tried to sleep until the next morning when everyone got up at dawn for a picnic involving a two-hour row to a sandbar, a lunch of rubbery clams, and then a four-hour row home against the wind. After her first extended stay of better than three weeks at Sagamore, the already slim Eleanor discovered that she had lost twenty-six pounds.

She and Ted were married shortly after TR's return from Africa. He put out the call to his Rough Riders, five hundred of whom struggled into uniforms that had fit well ten years earlier and came as an honor guard for the bride and groom at the Fifth Avenue Presbyterian Church, staying on to eat most of the hors d'oeuvres and wedding cake. On the honeymoon trip out to the West Coast, the newlyweds were dogged by reporters. They got off the train and registered at a hotel under the assumed name of Mr. and Mrs. Winthrop Rogers, but the journalists tracked them down. After they had banged on the door of their hotel room for half an hour Ted finally answered with a "prodigious grin" and said, "I can't talk with you now, I'm busy." That next spring Eleanor gave birth to a daughter, Grace, TR's first grandchild.

The family had hungered for TR's return to the public arena almost as much as he himself did. In his first months back in the United States, Alice functioned virtually as his agent in Washington, gathering intelligence at the bridge parties and dinners and sending it home to Sagamore, all the time pushing hard for the Restoration. This made for divided loyalties in her own married life. Nick, a fellow Ohioan and Republican leader in the House, was a Taft loyalist, but the only party of which Alice was a member was the Roosevelt Party.

On the opposite coast, Ted and Eleanor had finished their honeymoon in Santa Barbara and then moved to San Francisco. Their home, rented from the Spreckels family, overlooked the Golden Gate and they had a Chinese houseboy for a few weeks until Eleanor found him in the kitchen biting apart with his front teeth pieces of parsley she had asked him to chop for a dinner dish. Ted wrote his father about his ambitions for a family of his own and got this letter in return: "Tell [Eleanor] that as regards the size of the family we rather agree with you. Four—five at the outside limit! And four is a *very* good number. . . . Home, wife, children—they are what really count in life. I have heartily enjoyed many things; the Presidency, my success as a soldier, a writer, a big game hunter and explorer; but all of them put together are not for one moment to be weighed in the balance when compared with the joy I have known with your mother and all of you. . . ."

Ted took a job in a San Francisco stock brokerage and acted as an informal advance man for his father's reentry into politics by making a contact with California's progressive Republican Governor Hiram Johnson and arranging for TR to give an important address at the University of California at Berkeley. Seeing that Ted wanted to become a political apprentice, TR wrote him a series of Lord Chesterfield–like letters combining advice with commentary about the contemporary political scene. In one of them, he called Taft "a flubdub with a streak of the second rate and the common in him . . . [who] has not the slightest idea of what is necessary if this country is to make social and individual progress." In another he gave his son an idea of the political razor's edge he himself was trying to walk: "I note what you say about your thinking of supporting Wilson if he runs next year. Don't make up your mind yet and remember that to say anything in public or to take any stand against Taft, especially by supporting his Democratic opponent, would cause me very great embarrassment. . . ."

In the months after his return from Africa, TR found himself becoming the equal and opposite reaction to his old friend. As Taft drifted rightward, TR veered to the left. By the end of August, while stumping for hand-picked candidates in the 1910 off-year elections, he delivered a speech at the John Brown battlefield at Osawatomie, Kansas, that would later be called the most radical ever given by an ex-President. Calling for a "New Nationalism," he outlined the stakes in America's increasingly intense social struggle as a "conflict between the men who possess more than they have earned and the men who have earned more than they possess." In what had the feel more of a platform than a pronouncement, he called for a graduated income tax and for inheritance taxes (to prevent "swollen fortunes"); for new conservation laws, restraint of corporate political power, and the creation of presidential primaries.

Over the next few weeks TR campaigned hard for candidates like Henry Stimson, running for governor of New York, who agreed with these ideas. He was so active, in fact, that he worried his young cousin Franklin, who had launched his own campaign, as a Democrat, for the State Senate throughout Dutchess County and was barnstorming his district in a red Maxwell bought for the occasion. He was concerned enough that TR might campaign against him that he got Bamie to write her brother and ask him about his intentions. Calling Franklin a "fine fellow," TR said that he "ought to go into politics without the least regard as to where I speak or don't speak." It was tantamount to a safe conduct pass and Franklin waged a spirited battle in which he constantly played on his relationship to his cousin and attacked his opponent for aligning himself with the Republican Old Guard instead of upholding the principles of TR.

Eleanor later recalled FDR as being "tall, thin, high strung, and at times nervous" during his campaign. But he also had a spark of that divine fire which had been attracting voters for years and managed to win a narrow victory. Afterward, one old pol in Albany, remembering TR's appearance there thirty years earlier, quipped, "You know these Roosevelts. This fellow is still young. Wouldn't it be safer to drown him before he grows up?"

Most of the candidates TR backed in 1910 were roundly defeated, leading him to comment, "I think that the American people are a little bit tired of me, a feeling with which I cordially sympathize." But private life was no longer an alternative. The forces propelling him back into the arena, internal forces working in synchronicity with the external ones, were irresistible. By mid-1911, he had already made up his mind to try to wrest the nomination away from Taft in 1912. He knew that he would be attacked as an egotist. (His response to the criticism about reneging on his promise about a third term was legalistic: he had meant three *consecutive* terms.) He knew too that he was jeopardizing the place in history he had so artfully crafted for himself, and that he would be opposed by his oldest friends, people like Elihu Root and Henry Cabot Lodge who had stood beside him since the beginning of his political career and who must now stand with Republican Party regulars. Nonetheless, he took the plunge with a phrase that would become famous: "My hat is in the ring."

Since Taft men controlled the official party machinery, he would have to travel the untried route of the state primaries, many of them being held for the first time, to establish a rival base of support. And so he stormed through the country, winning one primary after another. By the time the last state voted, he had amassed over one million more votes than Taft and fatally wounded the candidacy of Robert La Follette, his competitor for the support of progressives, although la Follette would stay in the race until the bitter end.

In August 1912 he came to Chicago for the Republican convention with 278 delegates and in fighting form, framing the nature of his crusade in the starkest of terms: "We fight in honorable fashion for the good of mankind; fearless of the future; unheeding of our individual fates; with unflinching hearts and undimmed eyes, we stand at Armageddon and we battle for the Lord!"

Making their case, his supporters pointed out that if Roosevelt was nominated and merely held on to the states whose primaries he had already won, the Republicans could beat the Democrats in a national election. But his nomination was never really a possibility. The outcome was settled before the balloting, in a struggle over seating of a handful of disputed delegates who could tip the balance between Roosevelt and Taft. When the Roosevelt forces lost out, they claimed that their candidate had been railroaded. Alice and her friends were in the gallery rubbing pieces of sandpaper together to simulate the sound of a locomotive. When Warren Harding, a Taft lieutenant, offered Nick Longworth the Ohio nomination for governor as a peace offering, Alice quickly interjected that her husband "didn't accept favors from crooks" and refused to apologize as Nick ordered.

As the Republicans were taking their final ballot, TR was in another place in Chicago overseeing the birth of an insurgent movement filled with revival tent fervor. It was the Progressive Party, and when it convened a few weeks later, it nominated him as its presidential candidate and California Governor Hiram Johnson as his running mate. That the new movement would be engaged in a fratricidal struggle could be seen by a development in TR's own family. Nick Longworth, congressional leader of the Republicans, had to remain loyal to Taft, while Alice, of course, wanted to be her father's lieutenant. TR was sensitive to his son-in-law's dilemma. He and Nick held "a court of justice" on Alice and prohibited her even from attending the Progressive convention. But it was clear to everyone that politics was affecting the marriage, and Alice admitted later on that she had gone so far as to mention divorce in 1912, and that her family had told her that it was not a possibility.

When the Democrats passed over conservative Champ Clark in favor of Woodrow Wilson as their candidate, TR realized that he probably could not win. Yet he took a grim satisfaction in holding his own in what soon became an ugly contest. He wrote Kermit, who had gone to Brazil to take a job superintending a railroad construction gang, "Taft and his managers are as shameless as so many baboons, and Wilson has headed the campaign of lying by indirection and innuendo. I fight back and hit them always fairly but always much harder than they hit me."

The Roosevelt family all worked for the holy cause—all except Franklin, who was finishing his first term in the New York State Senate with enough success in baiting Tammany that he received a congratulatory note from TR ("We are very proud of the way you have handled yourself."). He had gotten to know Wilson and discovered that the Democratic candidate was intrigued at the idea of having a Roosevelt in his corner. FDR campaigned for Wilson until he fell ill from typhoid, which jeopardized his own reelection campaign for State Senate. Eleanor had to appear as a stand-in. She was coached by Louis Howe, a gnomish, leathery-faced newspaperman who had been attracted to Franklin as a result of his battle against the bosses. Able to turn out a poem and a press release with equal ease, Howe was a misanthrope who admitted with no apparent concern, "I am hated by everybody, I have always been hated by everybody, and I want to be hated by everybody." Brusque and rude, he was nonetheless a keen observer of human nature and had seen something beneath that charm everyone else remarked on as Franklin's leading quality—a steely determination to get his own way—that could lead to power. He and Eleanor collaborated in the campaign that got Franklin reelected.

It did not go unnoticed that while others of the family were spending themselves for TR (Conie's son Teddy Robinson and her son-in-law Joseph Alsop, who had both embarked in politics at the same time as Franklin, had hurt their own promising careers by supporting TR in the Progressive cause), FDR was looking after himself. Yet what some members of the family were calling Franklin's "betrayal" in not supporting TR—even Sara had urged her son at least to seek the Progressive Party endorsement—did not hurt Franklin in the larger political world where he was seen as his cousin's heir. Newspapers from out of state had picked him out as someone special. ("May it not be possible that this rising star may continue the Roosevelt dynasty?" the Cleveland *Plain Dealer* asked.) And in a slightly smutty yet accurate Oedipal quip, a friend wrote a letter of congratulation for his reelection to the state legislature: "We hope your Big Stick grows to be as mighty as that other Big Stick we hear so much about."

TR had the power to inspire an almost religious commitment. But like other "hot" political personalities, he also inspired irrational hatred as well. At a campaign stop in Milwaukee on the evening of October 14, 1912, a deranged former bartender named John F. Schrank, who later claimed that he'd been having dreams in which President McKinley appeared to demand revenge against Roosevelt for assassinating *him,* emerged from a crowd and shot TR point-blank in the chest. Buckling from the impact, TR righted himself and calmly put his hand inside his coat to verify that he was bleeding. "They have pinked me," he said, and then put his hand to his mouth and coughed. Seeing no arterial blood, he calculated that he was not hit in the lungs and the wound was probably therefore not fatal. He called out to the men beating his would-be assassin, "Don't hurt him; bring him to me." After giving Schrank a dismissive stare of contempt, he told aides who were clamoring for him to go to a hospital, "You get me to that speech. It may be the last one I shall deliver and I am going to deliver this one myself."

Bleeding heavily, he began his appearance by gesturing at the crowd: "Friends, I should ask you to be as quiet as possible. I don't know if you fully understand that I have just been shot, but it takes more than that to kill a Bull Moose." He lost color during the speech and twice had to keep aides from stopping him.

Edith, in New York at a theater performance when she heard the news, rushed to TR's side. Ethel was also in New York, staying at a friend's house. She was just getting ready for bed, in fact, when she heard a newsboy outside the window yelling about a newspaper extra. She said to the friend, "Extras frighten me so—but I will not be foolish this time but go to bed." The next morning she saw the banner headline she had missed the previous night: "Roosevelt Shot!"

Recuperating in his hospital room, TR was in high spirits, exulting again in that sense of invulnerability that had been with him since San Juan Hill. ("Well, the campaign proved as exciting and as dangerous as any of our African hunts!" he wrote his old "side companion" in adventure Kermit.) Three weeks later, back home at Sagamore, he reenacted the shooting in a tableau staged for the benefit of the family. After watching his father describe with gestures and comments what had happened, Archie took his cousin Nicholas up to TR's dressing room, rummaged in the bureau for a moment, and then said, "Oh, there's the speech," dragging out the folded manuscript and spectacles case, both with a dime-sized hole through them, which had slowed the bullet and saved his father's life.

TR was able to resume campaigning at the end of the month, and although certain now of defeat, he pushed himself to the limit in a way that made the Bull Moose campaign one of the greatest of lost political causes and bound people to him as a prophet as well as a politician. As journalist William Allen White, one of the converted, wrote years later: "I doubt if anyone today can realize [the emotion] that came from direct contact with TR or can appreciate the fervor that [entered] those of us who shared the early Progressive Party years."

Wilson won in November, although TR beat Taft, and, if the Republican total was added to his own Progressive count, he would have been elected. He wrote to Kermit, "Well, we have gone down to a smashing defeat; whether it is a Waterloo or Bull Run, time only can tell. . . . In one sense, of course, this is bad for my reputation, for it rather diminishes the sum of my achievement, which is the only heritage I leave you children. After one has been a conqueror it is never pleasing to have a second installment of one's career as a leader of lost causes. On the other hand I do not sincerely feel that there was ever a cause so well worth fighting for as the cause of ours this year."

Immediate implications of the battle were seen in Alice's domestic life. Nick Longworth was bitter about the Progressive Party; it had not only taken his friend Taft out of the White House but cost him his congressional seat. Now he and Alice went into exile in Cincinnati, where her mother- and sister-in-law made clear their dislike for her. As Edith wrote Bamie, "I am afraid Alice is having a hard time with Nick's family and we can't help her in any way, I fear."

TR was publicly upbeat, but privately unsettled. As much as he had relished the idea of fighting the good fight, and as much as he had told himself that he was prepared to lose everything on this single roll of the dice, he was dismayed to lose political allies of a lifetime and to be regarded as a pariah. When one old friend visited him at Sagamore after the defeat TR told him, "You cannot imagine how glad I am to see you. You don't know how lonely it is for a man to be rejected by his own kind. I have just come from Boston where I attended a meeting of the Harvard Overseers. They all bunched up at one end of the room away from me. . . ."

He said that he intended to hold the Progressives together, but he knew it would not be possible. Within weeks after the election, radical elements in the party were already alienating the moderates Roosevelt had brought to the coalition. With the passage of time, rather than seeing himself as the magus who had created it all, TR would start to think of himself as a victim of circumstance. "When I got back from Africa," he wrote Kermit in a summary of what he came to believe had happened, "I found that everything had slipt. Taft had thrown in his lot with the sordid machine crowd, as had most of my former efficient political supporters. On the other hand, the reformers of the type of good Gifford Pinchot had begun to run wild and associate with a set . . . who came dangerously close to lunacy. I spent eighteen months in the vain effort to get them together on some kind of basis that would permit of efficient joint action. It proved impossible; and when the break had to come, I had to stand by the reformers against the sordid apostles of self interest. . . ."

A rite of passage within the family offered a respite from defeat. Ethel was getting married. Her fiancé, a physician named Richard Derby, had first become acquainted with the Roosevelts years earlier when he was one of the hand-picked Harvard students who had been invited to Sagamore for a seminar on government TR decided to give when he was vice president. During one of those sessions, Derby, already a tall and lanky young man, had come around a corner of the house when Ethel, a sturdy nine-year-old, barreled into him from the other way. He saw her again when he visited the White House later on, a tomboy racing with her brothers on stilts.

After going to medical school, Derby became reacquainted with Ethel when he met her in Berlin during TR's Grand Tour. When Derby began to court his daughter, TR enthusiastically backed him. Ethel was initially somewhat standoffish, but as she got to know Dick Derby she saw the qualities that made her father admire him—a steadiness and dependability. Best of all, he would be willing to relinquish some of his own family claims and fit right in with the Roosevelts. In the first days of her honeymoon, Ethel wrote her father reassuringly that they would still be one big happy family: "Dick feels just the way we all do about you and mother. It is just the same thing with him."

Almost unnoticed in the excitement about Ethel was news that the new President Wilson had plucked Franklin out of the New York legislature and appointed him assistant secretary of the navy. TR must have been amused by the statement FDR made upon sitting down at the same desk he himself had used some fifteen years earlier: "There's a Roosevelt on the job today. . . . You remember what happened the last time a Roosevelt occupied a similar position." He dropped Franklin a line to say that he was "pleased" by the appointment: "It is interesting to see that you are in another place which I myself once held. . . ." FDR's mother, Sara, took it to be a much more momentous development and wrote her son admonishing him to "try not to write your signature too small. . . . So many public men have such awful signatures and so unreadable."

When TR and Edith sailed for Brazil aboard the *Vandyck* on October 3, 1913, their departure was far from the national event that the send-off for his Africa trip had been four years earlier. The precipitousness of his fall as a national hero was suggested by the going-away party the night before, a function confined to members of the Progressive Party, a few hundred of whose diehards had appeared at the pier when the ship set sail. None of them admitted it, but TR was not only leaving America but leaving them and their cause as well. Edith wrote Bamie from shipboard that TR was "like Christian in *Pilgrim's Progress* when bundles drop from his back, [except that] in this case it was not made of sins but of the Progressive Party."

TR's stated purpose in making the trip was to speak to the legislatures of the major countries of South America. But the real purpose was to explore a continent only somewhat less dark than Africa. His initial idea was to travel up to one of the sources of the Amazon and then go down that great river in canoes. He did not want a "game butchering" trip and had arranged with the American Museum of Natural History to collect plant and animal specimens in return for partial sponsorship. He was pleased that Kermit would once again be his partner.

The second Roosevelt son had been in Brazil since graduating from Harvard in 1912. His plan, as he expressed it to his sister Ethel, was to stay in Brazil for ten years or even more. He knew that his absence perturbed Edith. ("I'm afraid Mother thinks I'm hopeless," he admitted to Ethel, "what they call down here a vagabond, which means a peculiarly useless sort of tramp.") Moreover, it represented a break in family solidarity: he was the only Roosevelt child who had not participated in the 1912 campaign, the only one who had not been able to rush to TR's bedside when he had been shot. Yet some spirit of adventure in Kermit had been touched by the Africa experience and he now saw himself not just a member of the small and exclusive Roosevelt clan, but also a citizen of the world.

He could not help but compare himself to Ted, who had recently moved back to New York from San Francisco to work for the brokerage house of Berton Griscom. His elder brother sent letters to Buenos Aires telling Kermit how he had doubled his salary in 1913 and gotten a 100 percent bonus and urging him to consider some lucrative venture they could do together. But Kermit wasn't really interested. In another letter to Ethel, he said, "[It] would seem as inapt as anything to fit me for Ted's plan for my life which is to return to New York in ten years to spend the rest of my life commuting. I'm afraid that no matter what I did, I wouldn't be able to fit into that."

He had been fascinated by the saga of the Panama Canal when he was young, associating TR with the actual physical construction of it, and in Brazil he became involved in his own version of that epic enterprise. He had started working as a supervisor of a railroad gang for the Brazilian Railroad Company cutting a track deep through the jungle. Tropical fever and snakebite were only a small part of the danger he faced. (Once he wrote home casually that he hadn't been able to go hunting lately "because the Indians are up and have killed several engineers with their long arrows.") Another time he narrowly escaped death when he was knocked off a derrick that was setting a timber in place on a bridge, miraculously suffering nothing more serious than cracked ribs after falling to rocks forty feet below. Upon recovering from the fall, he had gotten a new job with Vaughan Brothers, an English construction firm that was working in less remote sites. This pleased Edith, who wrote Bamie, "I am thankful he is off that feverish river."

Kermit knew that while his mother might worry, his father would be pleased. Indeed, Ted had written him that TR was taking a "grim pride" in the way he was putting himself "in harm's way." In fact, Kermit's only moment of pause in Brazil had come when he finally got word of the attempt on his father's life: "A big, up-from-the-soil sort of foreman . . . looked rather embarrassed and then said to me, 'Well, I guess they've shot Roosevelt all right!' " But like his brothers and sisters, he felt that TR led a charmed life.

All his adventurousness notwithstanding, Kermit had been ambivalent about accompanying his father on the new trek through South America. It was not because of his work but because he was in love. Shortly before leaving the States he had met Belle Willard, a stunning blonde debutante whose family owned the historic Willard Hotel in Washington (the first Theodore Roosevelt had stayed there when he went to work for Lincoln) and whose father, Joseph Willard, former lieutenant governor of Virginia, would soon be appointed U.S. ambassador to Spain in return for his early support of Woodrow Wilson.

Belle was different from Ted's wife, Eleanor—flirtatious and somewhat distracted, yet calculating enough to know that one way to win Kermit was by writing regular reports charting her increasing proficiency as a hunter *and* her progress in reading Ronsard and Racine in the original French.

Before he left for South America, Kermit had been alone with Belle during a long ride and hunt at her family's estate and had experienced a "summary moment" often alluded to in their correspondence. But for the most part it had been an epistolary romance, both writers breathlessly in love with being in love. Belle told Kermit that her days were long and dull, coming alive only when the mail arrived bearing word from him. In return, he confided in her that she'd had a talismanic effect on him when, after his fall off the derrick, he first went back to work and had to ride the same span that had previously taken him down: "I was afraid I had lost my nerve so I determined to walk across it . . . where it had fallen with me before. If it hadn't been that I had your picture in my pocket and kept thinking hard of you, and how I must try to live up to you if I was ever to hope for your love, I think I should have fallen."

After a year of increasingly intimate correspondence, Kermit had finally worked himself up to ask Belle to marry him. She quickly responded, "I do love you and *will* marry you. I don't know how or why you should love me [but] . . . my heart is very full. What have I done that God should choose me out of all this world for you to love?"

By the time TR told him of his plans for South America, Kermit was making secret plans with Belle for their wedding. But because of the bond of Africa (they sometimes addressed letters to each other by the titles the natives had given them on that trip—*Bwana Makuba,* the Great Master, and *Bwana Merodadi,* the Dandy Master), Kermit felt he had no choice but to accompany his father. Reluctantly, he wrote Belle that their marriage would have to be postponed.

He was there to meet his parents when they landed. Edith immediately began trying to commit him to TR's expedition. As he wrote Belle, "[She] took me aside and told me that I must go to manage the trip and take care of father. . . ." His next letter pursued the same subject: "Yesterday morning, Mother gave me another long talk about Father, and about some other ways I must look after him. She's dreadfully worried about him and there's nothing for me to do but go; I couldn't do anything else and really I ought to be very glad for any chance to help him."

Edith's sense of foreboding about the enterprise gradually spread to Kermit himself. In planning the trip, TR had been meticulous as always about some things—he did pack his usual eight spare pairs of glasses in

various parts of his traveling kit, for instance. But otherwise there was
an extemporized quality about the adventure, almost as if the purpose
was escape rather than discovery. Indeed, after arriving in Brazil, TR
had changed the trip from a relatively simple transcontinental trek to
something far more dangerous. During a diplomatic meeting, Lauro
Miller, the Brazilian minister of foreign affairs, happened to describe the
previous explorations of Colonel Enrique da Silva Rondon to the headwaters of the unexplored Rio da Divuda. TR listened intently and when
Miller was finished he said impulsively, "We will go down that unknown river!"

TR spent six weeks fulfilling his speaking engagements. He appreciated the countries he visited, particularly Brazil, whose frontier spirit—
produced in part by American cowboys who had gone south to work on
Brazilian ranches after the closing of the West—reminded him of his
days in Dakota Territory. Early in December, after Edith returned to
the United States, Kermit and naturalist George Cherrie, working with
Rondon, finished gathering supplies. Kermit's concern about what was
to come broke through the usual debonair tone of his letters to Belle:
"The trip has not been well planned and I have been a good deal worried
about father." He didn't specify what these worries were, but like Edith,
he sensed that TR, just turned fifty-four, was not physically up to a trip
such as this one might be, and that he was looking to the unknown for
a meaning it might not be able to give him.

But all this worry was in the background on February 27, 1913,
when, shortly after noon, the Roosevelt party finally nosed its dugouts
into the murky current of the River of Doubt and began to paddle
downstream. TR felt confident in the composition of his expedition,
particularly the native boatmen who were "lithe as panthers and brawny
as bears and swam like water dogs." Birdsong rained down from the
trees along the riverbank; gnarled vines hung like ropes along the water's edge. Roosevelt saw that they had entered a completely aqueous
environment with water from heavy rainfall rising up into marshy areas
that backed up from the river for hundreds of feet on both sides. He was
entranced, as he later wrote, "to drift or paddle slowly down this beautiful tropical river," which was so placid and becalmed in its early stages
that it gave no hint whatever that the party had embarked on what
naturalist George Cherrie would later call "a journey of peril and adventure such as none of us had ever contemplated."

What they all presumed would be the routine of the journey was established that first day. Kermit went ahead in his own dugout, planting sighting rods at regular spots in the river's course that Rondon and his men, in the canoes behind him, used for their surveying calculations. TR followed in a canoe with Cherrie and when the party landed for the night helped make camp.

The third day out, Cherrie shot a monkey and made a stew that everyone in the party ate with gusto. The only problem so far was the constant rain, which forced them to work in wet clothes and the mosquitoes and other insects which congregated so thickly that it was necessary for TR to wear a veil over his pith helmet and heavy gloves when sitting at his portable table writing his daily account of the trip.

The first sign that things might not go smoothly came on the fourth day out when the river's course began to twist and turn, doubling back upon itself, as the current gained momentum. They heard a distant roar. It became louder and as they rounded a sharp bend, they saw it was the sound of rapids and quickly paddled to shore. Upon reconnoitering, the party found that the stretch of white water ahead was about one mile long and went through a series of falls and rapids, pouring its fury into a gorge so narrow that at one point Cherrie was able to kneel and touch the rocks on the other with the end of his rifle. TR was taken aback. It seemed almost impossible, he thought, that "so broad a river could in so short a space of time contract its dimensions to the width of the strangled channel through which it now poured its entire volume."

It took a portage of three days to get around this part of the Divuda, a difficult process at one point requiring that numerous small trees be cut down to make a rolling skidway for the dugouts. The members of the expedition all felt relief when they got back on the water, but then, after a day and a half, they had to make another portage. This one took four days. It was clear that they had suddenly entered, as TR later wrote, "a land of unknown possibilities."

A new routine was established in which the party would paddle for a couple of hours, portage for a day or so, and then enter the water again, proceeding only a few kilometers before they were forced to pull out once more. At times they had to lower the canoes into the water by ropes from falls above. On March 11, two of the canoes carrying supplies were swamped and lost in a rainstorm. Stopping to make new dugouts, all the members of the expedition were aware of the situation: they had begun with short rations for fifty days and now part of these had been lost while more were being eaten up by delay.

On March 14, they started again, but the following day tragedy struck anew when Kermit, scouting the river ahead, was suddenly caught in a violent whirlpool that flung his canoe over a low falls and dashed it against a rock in a pool below. His boatman, a native named Simplicio, disappeared under the water and never came up. Kermit was almost lost too. "The water beat his helmet down over his face and drove him below the surface," TR later described his son's struggle. "When he rose at last he was almost drowned, his breath and strength almost spent. . . . His jacket hindered him but he knew he was too nearly gone to be able to get it off. With that curious calm one feels when death is but a moment away, he realized that the utmost his failing strength could do was reach the branch [above him]. He reached and clutched it and almost lacked the strength to drag himself to land."

Kermit got to shore, but all the equipment and supplies in his boat were lost, including the prized Winchester rifle he had carried all through Africa. TR was distraught, saying later on that if Kermit had died he did not know how he would ever have faced the guilt of having to tell his son's fiancée as well as his mother what had happened.

The next day, after another exhausting portage, there was yet another portent. Colonel Rondon was walking downstream with his dog looking for their next possible put-in point on the river. Suddenly, he heard the animal yelp. He ran ahead and found the dog dead, pierced by a pair of Indian arrows. Fearing that he himself or the others might be the next target, Rondon sprayed the air with rifle fire and ran back to the camp.

From this time on, the Roosevelt party was acutely aware that they were in hostile territory. They never caught sight of the natives, but they saw footprints and abandoned camps and sometimes heard voices just behind the green curtain of the jungle. They always posted an armed guard and slept with a sense of invisible menace all around them.

On March 19 they discovered a major tributary flowing into the Divuda, and as the ranking representative of the Brazilian government, Rondon christened it the Rio Kermit. On the same day he insisted on renaming the Divuda itself Rio Roosevelt in a sparse ceremony followed by three cheers for all involved. These gestures of bravado were intended to mute the note of desperation that had entered the expedition. The party had been out for eighteen days. It had already used one third of its food although it had covered only one fifth of the distance it had to go. Rondon now told the others about a sinister precedent for their trip. In 1899, a Brazilian party exploring another wild and uncharted river lost its canoes and supplies in the rapids and only three men out of an expedition of some two dozen survived.

They had four remaining canoes, which they lashed together into a pair of *balsas* carrying the men who were too feverish or whose feet were too swollen from cuts and bites for them to walk. Several hours of smooth water raised their hopes, but then the river fell into more white water. TR worked hard to keep everyone's spirits up, but he too had become solemn. It was about this time that he stopped reading the only two books he had brought—works by Epictetus and Marcus Aurelius— because the trip had grown depressing enough without the company of these two gloomy philosophers.

On March 26 they spent the entire day dragging their boats and supplies around a series of rapids. The next day, when they got into the water again, TR, seeing that one of the boats was about to capsize, rushed into the river to help stabilize it and gashed his leg against a sharp rock. In a matter of hours the wound had begun to fester, and proud flesh was ringing its edges.

During the next few days, they were on land more than in the water. To make the portage easier, they jettisoned more equipment, then began hacking their way through heavy undergrowth to circumvent the rapids. Although he would scarcely mention it in the account of the trip he wrote later on, the cut on TR's leg became a suppurating wound that the Brazilian doctor repeatedly lanced and tried to drain by inserting a tube.

Supplies were now so limited that they dined each night on one soda cracker, a few bites of monkey stew, and a cup of coffee. They all fantasized constantly about food. Kermit said that if he could have anything it would be strawberries and cream, while his father said that for him it would be a lamb chop. They were brought back to reality when one of the boatmen picked up a rifle during a petty dispute and shot one of his comrades. The murderer vanished into the jungle and there was no time to hunt him down and bring him to justice.

His leg wound badly swollen, TR became feverish and began to slip in and out of delirium. (Doggedly continuing to write the account of his trip commissioned by *Scribner's*, he penciled in an apology in the margin of his manuscript to the copy editor for his straggling handwriting, explaining that he was working with a temperature of 104.) On March 31, Kermit found his father sitting against a tree during a driving rainstorm deliriously reciting Coleridge: "In Xanadu did Kubla Khan a stately pleasure dome decree. . . ." Intermittently lucid, TR insisted that since he couldn't work he would take no food. George Cherrie wrote in his diary that he didn't believe Roosevelt could last through the night, and he and Kermit sat up in what both feared might become a death watch.

The next morning, having rallied somewhat, TR called his son and the naturalist to him: "Boys, I realize that some of us are not going to finish this journey. I know that I am a burᴅ ...ɪ to the rest of you." Then he took Cherrie aside away from Kermit's hearing and made his choice of suicide more explicit: "I will stop here." He asked the naturalist to take his son and go on without him. Kermit refused to listen to such talk. With grim humor he told his father that he would have to keep going, for while TR might have lost weight on the trip he was still too heavy for him to pack out of the jungle on his back.

Now in full beard, thin and intense, struggling through his own intermittent fevers and bouts of dysentery, Kermit fought to keep his promise to his mother to bring his father back alive. At the darkest moment, when the river seemed one long stretch of unnavigable white water and the jungle too thick to hack through, Rondon argued that they should abandon the canoes altogether, split up the food, and fight their way individually through the forest, every man for himself. Calling this a death sentence, Kermit refused to allow it. The other men rallied around him. Although he still deferred to his father, it was clear that he had become the leader of the expedition.

The next few days passed in an exhausting monotony of brief stretches on the river and long portages to bypass white water. TR was conscious but so weak he could hardly move. On April 9, it was Kermit who was down with a raging fever. Then, suddenly, the party noticed a subtle change. The roaring sound that had been with them almost since the beginning was subsiding somewhat. The river was growing quieter.

On April 12, Easter Sunday, they were in the water for a total of ten minutes, spending the rest of the day in portage as TR fantasized about how he would conquer the river if he only had a good Maine birch canoe. ("It would have slipped down these rapids as a girl trips through a country dance.") But the next day, almost magically, the river began to lengthen and slow. There was, for the first time in weeks, no white water. Fish and birds, rare in the deᴀᴛhscape they had just passed through, began to reappear. The boatmen fcᴜnd a grove of nut trees on shore and gorged themselves, later becoming sick.

April 15 was a "red letter day" because they saw a stake into which initials had been cut by some rubber gatherer defining his territory.

They were reentering the inhabited world. Shortly afterward they discovered a primitive dwelling, which buoyed their spirits higher, although the occupants had apparently fled at their approach. Only TR was unable to participate fully in the enthusiasm that now swept over the expedition because he was in the middle of another bout of fever, stretched out in the bottom of one of the boats daydreaming of a "wonderful northern spring of long glorious days, of brooding twilights, of cool delightful nights."

They drifted easily down the river during the next two weeks. Portages were still necessary, but they were short in duration and took place over blazed trails. The Divuda was no longer a river of doubt for them. They understood now that it was a branch of the Aripunta that flowed into the Madeira, which eventually fed into the Amazon itself.

By the time they reached civilization, they were all sick and exhausted. TR had lost thirty-five pounds; lines were deeply etched into his face. He carried away no luggage on the return trip to America; just a parcel comprising the manuscript of what became *Through the Brazilian Wilderness*. It was hard for him to leave Kermit, who was staying behind to sort out his affairs so he could finally get married. He knew his son had saved his life.

It *had* been a great adventure. TR had cheated death once again. His expedition had put a river the size of the Rhine on the map. Yet the trip had not led him out of the complexities that would continue to besiege him. What he had once called the romance of his life had become a modernist work whose narrative was now filled with strange twists and ominous subplots.

*H*is sister Corinne later said that when Theodore came back from Brazil he was "a man in whom a secret poison still lurked." She was referring to the tropical fever whose recurrences would indeed afflict him episodically for the rest of his life. However, he carried toxins of another, more metaphorical kind—a new sense of limits, and a growing awareness of the difficulty of impressing himself upon the world, something that had always come so easily to him earlier in his life. The *New York Times* reporter who met TR when his boat landed inadvertently put his finger on the change. The weight loss sustained in the tropics was perhaps to be expected, he noted, but what surprised him about the ex-President was that there was now "something lacking in the power of his voice."

Roosevelt counted on his loved ones and the familiar surroundings of Sagamore to bring him back to himself. And when he arrived at Oyster Bay, he was pleased that Ethel came running down to the dock to meet him, anxious to show off her first child, a boy named Richard who had been born during his absence. Soon he and Edith and Alice were packing for the trip to Spain, where Kermit was to marry Belle Willard in June. The wedding was taking place abroad because Belle's father was the

U.S. ambassador in Madrid. He had convinced King Alfonso to issue a decree allowing for a non-Catholic civil ceremony, which made everyone happy except for Queen Maria Christiana, who could not bear to be in the same country with the Rough Rider who had once savaged her nation's soldiers, and so arranged to be vacationing in Vienna when he arrived.

When he returned from Madrid, TR spent the fall doggedly stumping for Progressive candidates in the 1914 off-year elections, although he understood that the third party cause was now lost. Feeling that he had probably burned all the bridges that led back to political power, he began to talk about his long-range plan—to work for the next few years as an editor at *The Outlook* until he was sixty. Then all the children would be grown and on their own and he could finally consider retirement. But for now he was still the paterfamilias, as was clear in the description of Christmas 1914 he wrote to Kermit, who had somewhat reluctantly taken a managerial job in the First City Bank's Buenos Aires branch and was unable to come home for the holidays because Belle was still recuperating from a miscarriage she had just suffered. With the exception of his absence, TR noted, things were the same as always. Ted and Eleanor had come to Sagamore for the celebration, along with their new son, Theodore III; Alice and Nick were there too, as were Archie and Quentin: "We did the thing in regular fashion. They all hung up their stockings the night before and in the morning, everybody except little Ted, who was sleeping the sleep of the just, gathered in Mother's and my room and sat on the bed."

To the degree that this holiday season was different from others, it was because of international events that seemed to have pushed the world into a new frame of reference. At first TR, like most, had missed the significance of the assassination of Archduke Franz Ferdinand at Sarajevo. But when the inexorable consequences of this apparently random act led to a German invasion of Belgium, he moved, slowly at first, to back the English and French. The Kaiser probably accelerated his commitment by sending a representative to TR to say pointedly that he still treasured memories of their 1910 meeting and hoped he could count on Roosevelt's "sympathetic understanding." TR looked his visitor squarely in the eye and gave a brilliantly ironic response: "Pray thank his Imperial Majesty from me for his very courteous message; and inform him that I . . . shall never forget the way his Majesty the Emperor received me in Berlin, *nor the way in which his Majesty King Albert of Belgium received me in Brussels.*"

TR would have liked to support the U.S. government's position. But Woodrow Wilson's policy of obdurate neutrality, reiterated with great fanfare from the onset of the crisis, was calculated to rub him the wrong way. Quiescence was not in his nature, and it was not in the nature of his family either. Within months of the outbreak of hostilities, Ethel and Dick Derby rushed off to France to help set up a mobile surgical unit. Once there, Ethel bought supplies ranging from pillow cases to surgical instruments with her own money, backing up the strong statements her father had begun to issue and making it amply clear where the Roosevelts' sympathies were.

At first TR tried to moderate his public comments, although he excoriated William Jennings Bryan, Wilson's inept and unqualified secretary of state, as "a professional yodeler [and] human trombone" and Wilson himself "almost as much of a prize jackass." But soon he was in the trenches of opinion about the war with his columns in *The Outlook,* vigorously attacking the administration. U.S. neutrality, he said, was "unworthy of an honorable and powerful people." He sneered at Wilson's "loquacious impotence" and said that in the administration's response to events he heard "the shrill clamor of eunuchs." He was not advocating a hard line simply out of truculence. He believed that an early U.S. commitment would blunt the Germans' appetite for aggression.

Yet it was also true that his words grew sharper in direct proportion to his inability to affect events. Dismayed to see exactly how out of power he was, TR wrote Kermit early in 1915, "My bolt is shot! I wish it were not, for I abhor the way in which Wilson and Bryan drag our honor in the dust; but I am out of touch with the popular sentiment and can no longer influence it." That he felt even more out of touch with the elite than the popular culture was shown by his comments about two brothers who helped arrange a bird-watching trip he took to the Gulf of Mexico that summer and who were ready to volunteer in the Allies' cause: "At a time when so large a section of our people, including especially those who claim in a special sense to be the guardians of cultivation, philanthropy, and religion, deliberately make a cult of pacifism, poltroonery, sentimentality, and neurotic emotionalism, it was refreshing to see the fine, healthy, manly young fellows who were emphatically neither 'too proud to fight' nor too proud to work. . . ."

He kept hoping that unfolding events would collaborate with him in prodding the administration into a response. When the *Lusitania* was torpedoed, for instance, TR said, "It seems inconceivable that we can refrain from taking action in this matter, for we owe it not only to humanity but to our own national self respect." But always the President temporized in words that TR, as a connoisseur of the power of language, came to loathe. Alice, who sometimes sneaked along Pennsylvania Avenue late at night to throw pin-spiked voodoo dolls bearing Wilson's likeness onto the White House lawn, was at Sagamore with her father on a day when the papers reported that the administration had delivered yet another note of protest over some German atrocity. She read the account of the note to her father, who replied bitterly without looking up from what he was doing, "Did you notice what the serial number was? I fear I have lost track myself, but I am inclined to think it is No. 11,765 Series B."

Contemplating a time when the United States would be drawn into the European conflict despite the tactics of the Wilson administration, TR wrote Rudyard Kipling that he had always hoped that if there was a war in their generation his boys would be able to explain why they had gone, not why they hadn't. He had no reason to worry on this account. His sons were all ready to follow his lead.

Ted was beginning to assert himself as a leader of his generation of Roosevelts, as TR recognized when he wrote Kermit, "Not only do I feel that you can count on him, but, thank Heaven, I feel he will be a competent advisor for Archie and Quentin when they are launched into the world." In 1912, he and his wife, Eleanor, had moved from San Francisco to New York where he took another job in the bond business. It was not particularly good timing, since TR was just then flailing Wall Street as the candidate of the Progressive Party, and often Ted would enter some executive's office only to have the man snap, "I never expected to see the son of your father here. Kindly make your call brief." But he had persevered, having committed himself to making enough money during his twenties to carry on his father's work in politics later on as an independently wealthy man. By 1914 he had moved into a partnership in the Philadelphia brokerage house of Montgomery, Clothier, and Tyler and was plowing his salary back into the business while borrowing enough for the family to scrape by on. As his wife Eleanor later noted, in 1915 they had lived like paupers even though Ted made over $150,000.

He had parlayed his new financial connections into relationships with those TR lightheartedly called "the plutocrats." It was no joking matter

for Edith, however. When Ted's third child, Cornelius, was christened
with Grace Vanderbilt as godmother and a roomful of Fifth Avenue
financiers in attendance, she and Ethel "sat ceremoniously apart on a
sofa" in mute condemnation of such wealth (as TR wrote in his amused
account of the event) and "pointedly refused to go upstairs to see the
presents."

Ted and Eleanor had booked passage for a future trip on the *Lusitania*
and after it was torpedoed he wrote Kermit in Argentina that the incident, "combined with the other attacks, have caused a serious crisis
here. I believe war is thoroughly possible. . . . Should war be declared
of course we all will go."

By early summer 1915, Ted had joined others in forming a committee
of young businessmen and executives to attend a military training camp
in Plattsburg, New York. The idea, as he wrote Kermit, was to provide
instruction to "a lot of us who will of necessity serve as officers, but
who have no technical knowledge." The head of the Plattsburg camp
was General Leonard Wood, TR's commanding officer in Cuba, who
was still on active duty. Wood expected a hundred or so young men to
show up, but there were over a thousand, each of them paying his own
way to attend an event that became a rebuke and embarrassment to the
Wilson administration.

The equipment at the training camp was primitive, but the Regular
Army officers brought in to instruct the volunteers had all seen some
kind of action—skirmishing on the Mexico border, fighting in the Philippines insurrections, even involvement in the Boxer rebellion. TR was
invited to speak and out of respect for the delicate position General
Wood was in, tried to be politic in his remarks, although he could not
help interrupting his speech when he spied a dog lolling on its back near
the speakers' platform with all four feet up in the air in a gesture of
supplication. "That's a very nice dog," TR pointed at the animal, "and
. . . his present attitude is strictly one of *neutrality*."

After the camp was over, he wrote that it had been a good experience,
but was no substitute for what the country really needed: universal
military training. When administration officials blustered that ten million men would spring to arms at the call of the President, the Colonel
replied with disgust that some "might spring to squirrel pieces and fairly
good shotguns . . . [but the rest] would spring to axes, scythes and
hand saws."

Archie shared Ted's enthusiasm about a U.S. entry into the war. By
his own estimation, he had been ineffectual in his first years at Harvard,

having no athletic ability (he confessed to being a "dismal failure" even at managing the crew team) and not even making the editorial staff of the *Crimson*. He had a streak of moral severity in his character that alienated classmates, and it hadn't helped his reputation when it was discovered that he had informed on a pair of students who had brought "a loose woman" to their campus lodgings, instituting proceedings that ultimately got them expelled. His unyielding qualities had led him to be rejected by all the final clubs at Harvard, including the exclusive Porcellian, although TR had leaned on his brother alumni in his son's behalf, and Ted, who had also been a member, took a train to Cambridge to lobby for him. But Archie, who told his father that he "didn't give a continental whoop" about the rejection, refused to try to help himself. As TR noted afterward, "Archie's virtues and to a small extent his excess of virtue, tend to keep him out. He won't yield in the smallest degree to anyone from any feeling for his own interests. . . . He is hardly politic enough, but it is a fault on the right side, and I am very proud of him."

Archie shared his father's opinion about the pusillanimous spirit reigning in Washington. ("For a short time up here things looked like war," he wrote Kermit late in the spring of 1915, "but as usual the dear old administration has managed to back out of it and fool everyone into the fact that we have acted in a magnificent manner.") He jumped at the opportunity to attend the student training camp that preceded the businessmen's camp at Plattsburg. He was galvanized by the experience. He performed so well that he was invited to stay on when the businessmen began training and amused TR by earning a rank at the camp that was higher than Ted's.

Given a new sense of direction by this summer soldiering, Archie redoubled his efforts at Harvard so that he could graduate ahead of schedule and be ready to volunteer if war was declared. He got General Wood to help him get together some surplus rifles and uniforms and set up an army training program at the university. Harvard President A. L. Lowell didn't like it and threatened to suspend him but Archie persisted. By the spring of 1916, the Harvard Regiment he had helped start staged a grand review at the school stadium and thousands of people attended. As a student officer, Archie was mounted in front of the ranks. At one point during the ceremonies, a paper blew into the path of the drill. He gained applause by nonchalantly leaning down from the saddle in a fluid movement to pick it up. But then a little later on he tried the maneuver again and slipped off his horse.

After graduating in June 1916, Archie followed Ted's path by going to work for the Bigelow Carpet Company in Thompsonville, Connect-icut. He lived at the YMCA in Springfield and hitched a ride to work every morning on a bread truck, spending his evenings writing letters to his new girlfriend, Grace Lockwood, whom he addressed as "most Felicitous Madam."

By mid-summer 1916 he was back at the second Plattsburg training camp. Quentin, who was there serving under his brother, wrote a friend: "The only drawback to my being under Arch is that I always have to work about twice as hard as I would ordinarily, thanks to Arch's horror of being accused of favoritism."

Famed journalist Richard Harding Davis had criticized the first Platts-burg camp as a haunt of fox-hunting squires and Ivy League dilettantes. (Ted had unintentionally confirmed such a view by writing Kermit in 1915, "I am delighted to say that Yale is justifying the low opinion I have always had of her. I believe that the numbers of people coming from that glorious institution are given less than from Princeton.") The second camp was more serious. By 1916 the Wilson administration had recognized the likelihood of U.S. involvement in Europe and was be-ginning to institute measures TR scornfully described as "half prepared-ness." News about the kind of war being fought in Europe had made its way home, and the campers spent their summer learning how to dig trenches and go over the top.

TR was in an increasingly bellicose mood himself. He could see that his nonstop agitation was beginning to bear fruit. The Preparedness Parade staged in the fall of 1916 was one of the largest demonstrations in the history of New York City, beginning at Fifth Avenue at 9 A.M. and still going late at night, when the Women's Battalion organized by Ted's wife, Eleanor, appeared in white dresses carrying lanterns.

But if he was hitting a nerve among the people with his denunciations of "broomstick preparedness," Roosevelt was unable to translate it into a political comeback. With the Progressive Party in ruins, he attempted to insinuate himself back into the good graces of the Republican Party for 1916, which seemed likely to choose Supreme Court Justice Charles Evans Hughes as its candidate. Ted worked as his right-hand man, trying to organize members of the financial community to support his father. In one memo to Frank Vanderlip, head of the First City Bank, Ted described what he called the "four classes of opinion" in the Re-publican Party: those who wanted to beat Wilson by whatever candidate was strongest; those who were for Hughes; those who didn't like his father or Hughes; and "people who feel that in this crisis of international affairs there is one man and one man only who can handle the situation and that man is Roosevelt."

But the Old Guard could not forgive TR for 1912 and pretended not to see the hat he tried to throw into the ring. When Hughes was chosen, TR (who referred to him as "the bearded lady" because of his facial hair and elegant good looks) fumed that America was "passing through a thick streak of yellow in our national life." But he was enraged by the Wilson reelection slogan—"He kept us out of war"—and resolved to campaign against the President, if not for Hughes.

He was asked to appear at Cooper Union by Henry Stimson and other young men who would be influential in government for the next thirty years. At the end of his speech, he put away the text and began to speak extemporaneously. Alluding to the President's summer home at Shadow Lawn, New Jersey, he said: "There should be shadows enough at Shadow Lawn—the shadows of men, women and children who have risen from the ooze of the ocean bottom and from graves in foreign lands; the shadow of the helpless whom Mr. Wilson did not dare protect lest he might have to face danger; the shadows of babies gasping pitifully as they sank under the waves. . . . Those are the shadows proper for Shadow Lawn; the shadows of deeds that were never done; the shadows of lofty words that were followed by no action; the shadows of the tortured dead. . . ."

When Wilson was narrowly elected, TR steeled himself for another four years of bitter opposition. He wrote a supporter: "I very gravely question whether I can be of any assistance in shaping, or appealing to, or representing public sentiment for some time to come—that is, until after my death."

Always before he had expressed the temper of the time. Now time seemed to have bypassed him. He might have been the first President to go up in an airplane and down in a submarine, but this keen appetite for new experience was that of an Edwardian man who was nonetheless philosophically out of step and out of sympathy with the modern world. Exactly how out of step he was sometimes surprised even those closest to him. After leaving the White House, for instance, he allowed Edith to remove the telephone, which he believed to be a barbarous invention, from Sagamore, replacing it only when his children rebelled. And on his visit to Ted and Eleanor in San Francisco in 1911, he was called to the phone to speak to University of California President Benjamin Ide Wheeler. Fifteen minutes later, his daughter-in-law passed through the hall and saw the receiver still dangling from its cord. She found TR sitting up in a bedroom reading and when she asked why he hadn't taken the call he said apologetically: "Darling, I like President Wheeler, but I dislike telephoning. I thought if I went quietly away, he would get tired of waiting and perhaps come to see me."

A recurring metaphor in Roosevelt's speeches and letters throughout the difficult years of 1915–17 was that of a kaleidoscope that had suddenly been shaken, reconfiguring orderly and familiar patterns into a jagged asymmetry. History as he had previously understood it—as a participant and as a scholar—had been jarred cataclysmically with the advent of War War I. There was now "new combinations" someone like himself could not expect fully to understand. He could only fear future developments, which was one reason he wanted to get the United States involved in the European conflict. "If we don't get into the war now," he said to one acquaintance in 1916, "Russia is going to blow up and you'll have Bolshevism, communism, spreading all over the world." (The threat of communism was a theme he returned to in his wartime writing: "The followers of Trotsky and Lenine, just like the followers of Robespierre and Marat, have just one lesson to teach the American people: what to avoid.")

Fearing that he would be paralyzed by the ambiguity that enfolded him, TR reacted as he always had before—by trying to impress his will on the situation. His sons' involvement at the Plattsburg military training camps, in fact, had blended with an idea that had been forming in his mind since the beginning of the war: to lead a volunteer regiment to Europe. It would be a way of asserting that old self that had served him so well. It would also be a way of showing England and France that the American people cared about what was happening to them, even if their leaders did not.

As early as the fall of 1915, TR had decided on the exact composition of the outfit—a cavalry division (although he knew his men would probably have to fight mostly in the trenches) with support troops, and a command structure including military men he knew, some old Rough Riders, longtime friends, and of course his own sons. As Wilson continued to temporize, the Colonel gave some thought to offering this unit to the Canadian Army, even going so far as to design a flag with a bison on it. (Cruel Alice, unable to keep from trying to puncture her father's posturing, said that he would have done better to select the dodo as his symbol.) But he soon realized that it was impractical not to wait for U.S. involvement, and he began to raise money to train the regiment while Washington dithered.

Someone said that TR seemed almost "Shakespearean" during this time. If so, the tragic figure he most resembled was Othello, trying to rehabilitate an epic persona from the past and constantly reminding himself and others that he had "done the state some service and they know it." TR soberly told his friend, the French ambassador Jules Jusserand, "If I were allowed to go I could not last; I am too old to last under such circumstances. I should *crack,* but I could arouse the belief that America was coming. . . . That is what I am good for now, and what difference would it make if I cracked or not?" But while he was contemplating an apotheosis of romantic self-sacrifice, Roosevelt had also made a hardheaded calculation about international politics. He now believed that even a tardy U.S. intervention would alter the Germans' war aims just as an earlier show of strength might have altered German adventurism. If he went abroad as a hostage to his country's honor, he would show the enemy that the hard-pressed Allies intended to fight on until fully mobilized American troops finally arrived.

What might otherwise have seemed romantic quixotry suddenly became real early in 1917 when Wilson finally broke relations with Germany. Shortly afterward German submarines sank three American merchant vessels, and by early April, the pressure for intervention was finally too much for the administration to resist and Wilson went to Congress and asked for a declaration of war "to make the world safe for democracy."

By this time, TR had already been badgering Secretary of War Newton Baker for months about his volunteer brigade, receiving polite but firm rebuffs in the form of notes that said his offer was unnecessary, although his patriotism "was much appreciated." Now Roosevelt moved decisively, praising Wilson's declaration as "a great state paper," and, when that did not win him his regiment, traveling to Washington for a last desperate effort to get the command that would allow him, like Tennyson's Ulysses, in a poem he loved, to set sail on a final quest "to strive, to seek, to find and not to yield."

The evening of April 6, 1917, was chilly and damp in the nation's capital, but TR exuded a warmth of purpose as he banged on the door of his sister Bamie's stately four-story house on N Street. The place was connected with his myth: he had lived there briefly after McKinley's death before taking up residence in the White House a few blocks away and had returned periodically during his presidency for intimate moments with friends. Now another Roosevelt, his cousin Franklin, was living in what his wife, Eleanor, called the "dear, bright home."

It appeared to be a happy household. Every morning Franklin came down after shaving to find the family already at the table, usually eating some of the dairy goods and produce his mother shipped down almost daily from the bounty of Hyde Park. Kissing Eleanor on the forehead he would say, "Good morning, Babs." And then he would look at his children and say, "Good morning, chicks, how are we today?"

Her mother-in-law had said to Eleanor after her marriage in what passed for a discussion of sex that it was "an ordeal to be borne." She had done it well. There were now five children in Franklin's family. In addition to the daughter Anna, there were four sons—James, Elliott, Franklin Jr. (the dead child's name had been used again), and John. Too embarrassed to talk about birth control with her husband, Eleanor had simply broken off conjugal relations after John's birth in 1916. However upset this might have made Franklin, he had at least equalled TR by siring six children.

In the family portraits around the house there were all the outward appearances of normality, yet deepening tension had developed during the family's three years in Washington. There was still the problem between Eleanor and Sara. (At breakfast, for instance, Eleanor sat at the chair across from FDR only when her mother-in-law was not visiting.) Even when she was temporarily away from Sara's domineering hand, Eleanor still could not feel that the house was hers. Sara had come to visit the N Street house shortly after Franklin got the job as assistant secretary of the navy and the diary entry she made showed the power she had in the family: "moved chairs & tables & began to feel at home." Eleanor dared not rearrange the furniture to her own liking.

In addition to being dominated by her mother-in-law, Eleanor was so ill at ease socially that she was forced to use a formula for initiating conversation given to her by one of her aunts that was based on the alphabet: "A-apple: Do you like apples, Mr Smith? B-bears: Are you afraid of bears, Mr. Jones?" She followed the empty Washington social convention of filling up her days by going around town to leave calling cards at the homes of acquaintances. (She was envious of her cousin Alice, the one woman in Washington who refused to engage in this charade but nonetheless the one woman to whom everyone arriving in the city most coveted an introduction.) Eleanor's parochial narrowness, an outgrowth of her sense of inadequacy, could be seen in her anti-Semitism. After going to a gathering organized by her husband's new friend Bernard Baruch in 1915, she wrote, "The Jew party was appalling. . . . I never wish to hear money, jewels, and . . . sables mentioned again."

Eleanor also felt powerless when it came to the children. She had largely left the upbringing of the children to the succession of governesses that Sara had helped her select. Some of them had been vicious and sadistic. One in particular, called "Old Battleax" by the children, had instituted a reign of terror. For some small offense, she had once thrown Anna to the floor, sat on her chest, and pummeled her face. When Jimmy happened to stare at the way she slathered hot mustard on her sandwich, Old Battleax had forced him to eat the entire jar, causing the beginning of stomach problems that would torment him the rest of his life. She locked Elliott in a closet for three hours and ignored his terrified screams until Franklin came home and let the traumatized boy out. On another occasion, when Jimmy fibbed about brushing his teeth, the nurse forced him to stand outside the house in a girl's dress wearing a sign around his neck reading "I Am a Liar." When Eleanor finally fired the woman it was not for any of these acts but because she found a bottle of whiskey in the drawer of her dresser.

Conie's daughter, Corinne Alsop, later said, "She did her duty. Nobody in the world did her duty more than Eleanor Roosevelt. But with the children, I don't think you can have an understanding of them unless you enjoy them. . . ." Eleanor's children were confused primarily by her lack of warmth. Anna never forgot how her mother once came into the bedroom where her brother Jimmy was suffering horribly from a rash of poison ivy and instead of comforting him said dimissively, "You silly boy, whatever did you do that for?" They learned to be wary of interrupting her when she was engrossed at her desk because her "What do you want, dear?" had a special coldness. The only one of them she indulged was Elliott and that was because she had been carrying him when the first Franklin Jr. died and she worried that she had communicated her misery to him in the womb. Her guilty attention merely made Elliott into the most difficult of the children, giving him (as Eleanor admitted) "a rather unhappy disposition" that expressed itself in furious temper tantrums, wantonly hurting the others, and defying her attempts to control him.

Although Eleanor and Franklin were the subject of gossip by members of his own family, TR probably did not know about the peculiarities of their domestic life, and if he had known about them probably would not have said anything, especially on this particular evening. When Eleanor came to the door to greet him, he insisted that she take him up to the fourth-floor nursery where Bamie's son, Sheffield Cowles, Jr., had been born. Now it was the room of Eleanor's two youngest children, Franklin Jr., almost three, and John, not quite a year old. They were just dozing off when their Uncle Theodore threw open the nursery door and stood there for a moment, the backlight making his bulky, silhouetted figure seem even more formidable than usual. Then he advanced on the boys' beds, his teeth bared in a ferocious grin.

"Oh, ho, ho," he roared, "these two little piggies are going downstairs." Then he tucked one child under each arm and, with Eleanor looking on in dismay, charged down three flights of stairs in a terrifying ride that the boys remembered the rest of their lives.

Coffee was served in the drawing room. But soon TR was on his feet, pacing in front of Franklin and making short pistonlike gestures with his arms to emphasize his points. The subject was war.

Franklin might be a Wilson man, but he was also a Roosevelt, and TR believed that the blood they shared was thicker than the watery substance of politics. There had been a momentary contretemps between them during the campaign of 1916 when FDR, defending the Wilson administration against Republican charges of lack of naval preparedness, had charged that when TR sent the Great White Fleet on its around-the-world voyage in 1907, its sixteen battleships were fitted out with officers and matériel scavenged from other vessels. Taking the charge personally, TR had cuffed his young cousin gently: "My memory was not in accord with the statement as you made it." Flustered by the reproach, Franklin had apologized and said that he would "take the first opportunity to say something about the correct figures."

TR was understanding because he knew that Franklin had been walking a thin line: working for preparedness within the administration without alienating Wilson. It had involved what others felt was treachery toward his good-natured and indulgent boss, Secretary of the Navy Josephus Daniels, who was a determined opponent of U.S. involvement. While blandishing the older man to his face and playing the role of slightly mischievous son, FDR had undercut Daniels when his back was turned, doing "killing" imitations of him before members of the Metropolitan Club and writing Eleanor on one occasion that his chief "had about as much conception of what a General European War means as Elliott has of higher mathematics."

Following TR's lead, Franklin had tested his limits within the administration in pushing for a navy buildup. He had created a naval rescue squadron of private boats and had them train like the Plattsburg soldiers. In fact, not long before TR's visit, he had gotten an appointment with the President and requested permission to bring the fleet north from Guantánamo Bay so it could be fitted out in case of an outbreak of hostilities with the Germans, only to have the President solemnly rebuff him and say that whatever happened in the future he himself intended "to come into the court of history with clean hands."

Both Roosevelts knew that Franklin had taken risks in the assistant secretary's office to stay as close as possible to TR's view of the war. Even when his own hands were tied as far as changing policy was concerned, FDR had sometimes passed secret information to his cousin and functioned as something like his "mole" within the administration, flirting with insubordination but always managing to save himself from a confrontation with Daniels or Wilson by a sudden burst of charm. Just recently, in mid-March, with events moving the reluctant Wilson inexorably toward war, Franklin had secretly attended a meeting of interventionists at New York's Metropolitan Club. Republican Party figures like Elihu Root were there, along with General Leonard Wood, George von Lenzerke Meyer (Taft's onetime secretary of the navy), and TR himself. After the meeting, FDR had jotted an entry in his diary: "Root inclined to praise administration's present course—TR wanted more vigorous demand about future course—less endorsement of past. I backed TR's theory."

Part of TR's message the evening of April 6 was that Franklin, like his own sons, ought to prepare to get into the conflict. "You must resign!" he told Franklin. "You must get into uniform at once!" It was an admonition that annoyed the pacifistic Eleanor (she kept a tiny plowshare pounded out of an old gun that William Jennings Bryan had given her), although her husband shook his head in agreement when TR smacked a fist into his palm and told him again, "You must get in!" But he had not come on a recruitment drive. TR needed Franklin's help in another matter: gaining a hearing with the administration he had been savaging for the past four years so that he could raise a regiment of volunteers.

At the end of their conversation, Franklin agreed to help and the next day he talked with Secretary of War Newton Baker, who agreed to give

TR an audience. After this meeting, Baker set up an appointment for TR
to see Wilson the following afternoon. It was a measure of his desire to
fight abroad that he was willing to humble himself before the President.
Roosevelt tried to resolve his long-standing differences with the President through a gracious sentiment: "Mr. President, what I have said and
thought and what others have said and thought is all dust in a windy
street." He went on to say that once it was implemented, he believed
Wilson's war message would rank with the great state papers of Washington and Lincoln. All he himself asked was "to help to get the nation
to act, so as to justify and live up to [your] speech. . . ."

Wilson heard him out and then curtly reminded him that this war was
not going to be like Tennyson's "Charge of the Light Brigade." He
noted that his own developing plans centered on a draft army, not a
band of amateurs. Roosevelt emphasized that he understood volunteers
could not replace the regulars but insisted that they could become sym-
bols of American commitment. Wilson said that he would consider the
matter.

TR did not feel optimistic. Walking out of the White House with
presidential advisor Colonel E. M. House, he said plaintively, "I don't
believe he will let me go to France. I don't understand. After all, I'm
only asking to be allowed to die." (According to Winston Churchill,
who had the story from House and later passed it on to Kermit's wife,
Belle, at this point House had paused for a beat before replying to
Roosevelt, "Oh? Did you make that point quite clear to the President?")
TR returned to the Longworths', where he was staying, "in a very
unhappy mood," Eleanor later said, knowing that his request would
probably be rejected.

Over the next few weeks, TR worked tirelessly to force Wilson's
hand. He was behind the amendment calling for four volunteer regi-
ments that Ohio Senator Warren Harding attached to the draft bill that
was sure to pass the Congress. When his plan to raise a regiment became
public, he was deluged by applications from men who wanted to join
him. Soon, he was getting two thousand letters a day, including offers
to serve from descendants of Civil War generals Philip Sheridan, Stone-
wall Jackson, and Nathan Bedford Forrest. The response was so overwhelming that he finally had to open an office on Fifth Avenue and hire
a secretary to process the correspondence. TR himself continued to send
almost daily petitions to Secretary Baker at the War Department, pointing out repeatedly that if preparedness had begun two years earlier there
would be a reservoir of trained men and no reason for a volunteer force,

but now, even though there were no trained troops, there must be something.

Then on May 18, Wilson dashed TR's remaining hopes in a telegram that had a cutting edge: "It would be very agreeable to me to pay Mr. Roosevelt this compliment, and the Allies the compliment, of sending an ex-President, but this is not the time for compliments or for any action not calculated to contribute to the immediate success of the war. The business now at hand is undramatic, practical and of scientific definiteness and precision."

Roosevelt struggled to overcome the decision, but it was clear that he could not outmaneuver the President. His vision of heroic self-sacrifice in a Roosevelt battalion with his sons serving under him was dashed. Now they would have to go into war alone, prosthetic devices for him and proxies for his desire to serve his country and perhaps have one final apocalyptic moment of glory.

On April 14, 1917, the war was momentarily forgotten as Archie married Grace Lockwood, a good-humored and unaffected young woman (some of the Roosevelts would eventually compare her to comic strip character Blondie) who came from a solid Boston family and had been "finished" in European schools. As always, Edith's reaction to a newcomer knocking at the family door was a subject for trepidation. ("We are going to spring it on her quietly. . . ." Archie had told Ethel about his engagement. "It will be a touchy business with her.") Equally predictable was the fact that TR would be "dee-lighted" that another of his children would have a chance to be fruitful and multiply.

The clan gathered at Sagamore for the celebration. Kermit and Belle had arrived from Buenos Aires with their new baby, Kermit Jr., known as "Kim" in part because of their love for the Kipling stories. Because of Kermit's long sojourn in South America, it was the first time they had been with the rest of the family. It was also the first time Belle had spent time with her in-laws and her aristocratic airs did not go over well with Edith. (Years later, when Belle was having difficulties with one of her own daughters-in-law she wrote about this time: "My mother in law made whatever criticisms she had of me to Kermit, except in the misbehavior of the children when we were at Sagamore, or in lapse of anything with respect. . . . Ethel repeated to me with considerable acidity and pleasure that [Edith] was exasperated beyond words that I was always all which seemed inexcusable. . . .")

While the two women sorted out their problems, Ted worked with Kermit as representative of his investment banking house to negotiate a $15 million loan from the First City Bank for the Argentine government. He told Kermit that he had become close to his boss, Frank Vanderlip, head of the National City Bank, and knew that the higher-ups there were grooming him to play a bigger role. ("Mr. Vanderlip told me the other day that at any time when I wished you to have some particular position to come to him right away.") But Kermit was still lackadaisical about his career and uncertain of the future.

Quentin, now midway through Harvard, was Archie's best man. Alice came down from Washington with Nick, who had been elected to Congress again in 1914 after serving his two-year exile in Cincinnati and who was now trying to patch things up with his in-laws after not showing up for Ethel's wedding. Alice thought that Archie was grown into quite a handsome man, although his high brow and hawk nose gave his thin face a decidedly "Semitic cast" that made her wonder about Edith's forebears.

They were all pleased to be together again, but as Alice said later on, "There was little of the gaiety of other family weddings." With American involvement in the war now certain, this remarkable family, which had known so much happiness and so little tragedy, felt a shadow pass overhead.

Now that it was clear that he would be unable to go to war himself, TR moved to get the boys into the center of the struggle. As Archie noted later on, they were all ready, perhaps too ready, for military action: "to see what it was like, I suppose, and also to see if we had the courage to stand it." They wanted to serve for their own reasons, but they also wanted to serve for TR, who "never wanted to be put in a position of looking like he was refusing a war because of his father." Thus the weight of an imagined sin stretching back to the Civil War weighed heavily upon their shoulders as they prepared to enter the conflict that would so much resemble it in terms of the suffering and carnage it caused.

Although he was thirty years old and had three children, Ted was the most anxious to go. He had saved over $500,000 to use to enter politics and was anxious to get the war over with. In June, he and Archie were given orders to report as reserve officers because of their training at the Plattsburg camps. Ted feared that they would spend the war at home training conscripts. So did Archie. And if this happened, they would miss an opportunity to measure themselves against their father. In an unpublished memoir he wrote later on, Archie said: "Since our earliest days it had been the ambition of my brother [Ted] and I to 'beat out father,' as we called it. I remember one moose hunt where we let several moose escape just because they were not quite as big as the moose my father had killed. We could not bear the thought of going home with a smaller specimen than his. . . . And now again it looked as if father would 'beat us out.' In the Spanish American war he had been among the first to land in Cuba. It seemed that we were doomed to remain home training while other American soldiers were fighting in Europe."

Knowing how his sons felt, TR wrote General John J. Pershing, commander of the American Expeditionary Force, to ask that Ted and Archie be allowed to enlist in the regular army as privates and thus go to France with the first contingent of American troops instead of remaining behind. Pershing, whose early career TR had advanced during his presidency, agreed that this would be a waste and brought the matter up with Secretary of War Newton Baker, who ruled that the Roosevelt boys should be allowed to enter regular army combat units as officers.

News that he had gotten his sons put in harm's way where he could not join them was bittersweet for TR. "The big bear was not, down at the bottom of his heart, any too happy at striving to get the two little bears where the danger is," he wrote Ted. "Elderly bears whose teeth and claws are blunted by age can far better be spared. . . ."

Ted and Archie left for Europe in late June 1917, after a somber family lunch. During the Atlantic crossing, they studied French. When they arrived in France and marched down through Paris, the streets were thronged by bystanders who knew of their father's efforts to come to their rescue. They shouted at all the American troops, *"Vive les Teddies!"*

By this time, Ted's wife, Eleanor, was sailing for Europe to work for the YMCA there. At first, TR had been against her decision to go abroad. But he understood that Eleanor, of all his sons' wives, was the one who had a partnership with her husband most resembling his own with Edith. He could see that she was determined to be near Ted, even though it meant leaving their three children with her mother, and he supported her when she departed hurriedly to avoid a new regulation about to go into effect forbidding army wives from going to Europe. He was pleased to hear that in Paris she often found herself embraced by strangers once they found out who she was because they had heard that

Ted, offered a staff job, had insisted instead on being sent to the front. When it was announced with considerable fanfare that President Wilson's son was going abroad to work for the YMCA, TR commented acidly to journalists, "How very nice. We are sending our *daughter in law* to France in the YMCA!"

Kermit, meanwhile, was still odd man out. Alone of TR's boys he had not gotten caught up in the push for preparedness or gone to the Plattsburg camps, preferring to stay with Belle in Buenos Aires. This made him a subject of speculation among the Roosevelts when he returned to America, especially with Quentin, who was coming of age and trying to unravel for himself the opposing claims of self and family. "He is far less ambitious than the rest of the family," Quentin wrote a friend about his older brother. "I really think that work, so far, hasn't meant anything to him and that what he has been doing has been merely because he felt he had to. . . . That's the trouble with . . . Kermit—his life's aim was accomplished when he married—but it is no incentive in his work and Belle doesn't supply it!"

In early June, with Ted and Archie only a few days away from leaving for France, Kermit wrote his father a letter that hinted at his ambivalence about the looming struggle and also indicated the bond their adventures had created between them: "I shan't feel happy seeing [Ted and Archie] go over with me left behind; but now that I have Belle, the only way I would have been really enthusiastic about going would have been with you. After Africa and South America, it makes me feel unhappy and small to be going off without you. . . . I wish you were in this war so that I could go off with you again and try for the malevolent hyenas with the courage of simba. . . ."

Kermit considered enrolling in the third Plattsburg camp scheduled for the summer of 1917, but now that the country was officially at war he was afraid that it would be too slow a route into the service. He may have been more ambivalent about this great adventure than Ted and Archie, but he was not anxious to take a back seat to them. "I've never been behind before and don't like to begin," he wrote his father. "I don't like the war at all because of Belle and Kim, but as long as it's going on I want to be the first in it."

A few days later, Kermit had lighted on an alternative that would get him into the action quickly—going to serve with the British in Mesopotamia. His imagination was fired by the romance of it, and he wrote his father with excitement, "Wouldn't it be wonderful to be at the fall of Constantinople? . . . The whole thing appeals to me much more than trench warfare." TR immediately began working to get Kermit into the British Army. He got the influential publisher Lord Nothcliffe, who had dined at Sagamore the night after Ted and Archie left for Europe, to promise to recommend Kermit to Lord Derby, British secretary of state for war. Not taking any chances, TR also wrote directly to Prime Minister David Lloyd George: "He was my companion through Africa and South America. He is very hardy and cool and resourceful and exceptionally fit by aptitude to handle Arab auxiliaries or native troops. . . . I pledge my honor that he will serve you honorably and efficiently. . . ."

Early in July, TR told Kermit the good news: "Well, you are not to be left behind!" A commission in the British Army had been arranged. When Kermit left for England to arrange his service in Mesopotamia, he was accompanied by Belle and Kim, who were going to spend the war in Madrid with Ambassador and Mrs. Willard. Alice saw them all off at the port and carried away an image of her brother's family jammed into a taxi headed to the ship with Kim's toilet training seat dropping out of the door as the vehicle pulled away from the curb.

Soon Ethel's husband, Dick Derby, who had done two summers with his brothers-in-law at the Plattsburg camps, went to Fort Oglethorpe, Georgia, and after a few weeks' training as a combat surgeon, left to serve with the American Expeditionary Force in France. Now only Quentin was left.

As the youngest of the children, he had a somewhat different perspective on his role in the family from his brothers'. He admired his father, but questioned the obligation to act out TR's commitments in a way that the others didn't. During much of the spring of 1917 he had sat in his room at Harvard trying to sort out the correct path to take. Even though he liked to "analyze" Kermit's flaws, he was far more like him than he was like Ted and Archie, with their iron sense of duty and discipline. Quentin was far less ready than any of his brothers to march to the family drummer, far more introspective, and in touch with the ironies that informed the sensibility of his sister Alice.

He had grown into a stocky young man with a face capable of suddenly coming alive like his father's, although the two of them did not really look alike. His cousin Nick called him "the most whimsical and the most promising" of all the boys. Quentin had a mechanical bent, but he was also the son who had most inherited TR's literary abilities, although his short fiction and essays published in Groton's literary magazine had a dreamy quality that distinguished them from his father's brainy and spirited prose.

If he was not particularly enthusiastic about the army, Quentin had subtly broken ranks in another area as well—the girl he had fallen in love with. She was Flora Payne Whitney, an elegant young woman who was not just a member of a wealthy family like Kermit's wife, Belle, but part of the ruling class, eldest child of Gertrude Vanderbilt, whose great-grandfather, Commodore Vanderbilt, was the original robber baron, and Henry Payne Whitney, whose father, William Whitney, was a wealthy lawyer and businessman who had served as secretary of the navy in the Cleveland administration.

While Quentin was growing up in the rough-and-tumble atmosphere of Sagamore Hill, Flora Whitney had been a lonely child living a wholly different kind of life with her brother Cornelius ("Sonny") either in the family mansion on Fifth Avenue, at the seven-hundred-acre estate on Long Island, or at the immense vacation home on the gold coast of Newport called "The Cliffs," or at one of the several other residences her parents owned.

As a girl Flora was silent and withdrawn, spending most of her time with governesses while her parents traveled or tended to their complicated social life. Once when Gertrude Whitney became seriously ill and thought she was dying, she wrote what was supposed to be a last letter to her husband about their daughter: "She has the possibilities of lots of unhappiness in her. She will be moody and fearful and inclined to think too much about things which will only make her unhappy." But Flora defied the prediction and grew up to be lively and imaginative, her dark hair framing a frank, inquisitive face. Making her way through school, first at Brearley and then at Foxcroft Academy, where she was part of the first graduating class, she developed a humorously self-deprecating manner to offset her wealth.

Flora's parents might be plutocrats, in TR's lexicon, but they were not without accomplishment. Gertrude was a talented sculptor as well as a leading patron of the arts. (Her collection would become the nucleus of the museum bearing her name.) Harry Whitney was a polo enthusiast who had committed himself to bringing home the American Challenge Cup, which had been in England for almost twenty years, and succeeded in recapturing it in 1910 after painstakingly assembling a string of ponies and legendary team of riders known as the Big Four. Yet in contrast to the Roosevelts, the Whitneys had lived in a world that revolved around society instead of family and rigorously excluded their children. Even more than the other women who became involved with TR's sons, Flora was attracted to the intense relationships and sense of camaraderie that characterized life at Sagamore.

When he met her, Quentin was in his second year at Harvard taking courses that would allow him to be a mechanical engineer. He had actually been romancing another girl named Leslie Murray and at first maintained only a friendly bantering relationship with Flora, to whom he sent a Valentine's Day card "from a platonic heart" on Valentine's Day 1916. But he was attracted to what Flora's classmates at Foxcroft had called "her soulful beauty and playful personality." And while she was attracted to the eccentric sense of humor that had characterized Quentin since he was a little boy playing pranks in the White House, she also drew out his more serious side. In fact, her ability to penetrate the protective cuticle of his ironic detachment alarmed Quentin. In one of his early letters to her, he wrote: "I don't feel particularly like being funny tonight, and then, anyhow, I am trying to make my mind up about you. I don't exactly know how much to say to you, for the same reason that I'm not yet quite decided how 'safe' you are. . . ."

By the time of Flora's coming-out party at Newport in the summer of 1916, Quentin was a frequent escort. It was a memorable occasion dominated by the intentional magnificence of the Whitney estate, the smell of the ocean, and of the sea of flowers imported for the occasion. Flora was striking in a dress of white and silver trim and before the midnight supper served to hundreds of guests in the tents scattered around the property, she danced repeatedly with Quentin, called "a Teddy Bear of a young man" by some of those his father had attacked as malefactors of great wealth. After the party was over, Quentin wrote Flora to say that while his family might feel that he had "committed the individual sin of staying at Newport for more than three days," his memories of the event would always center on a memorable image of her "in the Scripps [automobile] and the ocean drive [the two of them took]—all accomplished by a pleasant, subdued tinkle, as of ice against the side of a cocktail shaker."

The romance became increasingly serious during the fall of 1916 when Flora finally screwed up the courage to tell her mother how she felt about Quentin. That the Whitneys were even more disturbed than the Roosevelts by the possibility of such a match was indicated by the sparse entry Flora jotted down in her line-a-day diary: "Took Mama out in motor and told her: *oh!—ooh!—oooh!*"

When he was with his family, Quentin might make fun of "the Newport horrors" and of the Whitneys' "excesses of wine and morals." But his increasingly divided loyalties were seen in the outsider's description he wrote to Flora of Christmas 1916 at Sagamore, an experience dominated by the competition being fomented among the five Roosevelt grandchildren: "The women were all feeling certain that her infant had a little edge on the other two tribes and was keeping a sharp watch." He felt that the only kindred spirit at the celebration was Alice, who liked starting "various degrees of trouble and then getting out and watching the fun. She makes a very valuable ally on such occasions."

A few months later on Valentine's Day 1917 Quentin was still writing tongue-in-cheek "To Flora Payne Whitney from her eldest son Window Pane. Alas the poor thing is cracked tho' it has a glassy stare." But they were growing closer, close enough that she was now (and always would be) "Foufie." One night at a dinner party he looked at her and realized, as he put it later on, that his feelings were not "at all Platonic." In a note to his mother, Quentin described what he was feeling. Edith advised him to tell Flora. Quentin agreed that this was the reasonable thing to do, but admitted that he feared exposing himself to possible rejection. Finally Flora took the initiative in a letter whose beginning words he never forgot: "And what if we both should fall in love with each other?" He replied immediately, glad that things were finally in the open: "Ah Fouf, I don't yet see how you can love me—still I feel as tho' it were all a dream from which I shall wake to things as before." He was particularly jocular when he wrote Kermit and Belle a "Dearly Beloved" letter: "The scripture moveth us . . . to confess our manifold sins and wickedness, and, that being the case, we—Flora and Quentin—do regretfully announce that we have decided for our sins to become engaged. . . ."

Quentin watched developments in Europe and Washington without Archie's sense of duty, Ted's enthusiasm, or even Kermit's anxiety about being left behind. Yet he agreed with his father's view of the Wilson administration ("We *are* a pretty sordid lot, aren't we?" he wrote to Flora after reading one of TR's jeremiads) and wanted to do his part. Always inseparable from Archie, at first he tried to get into his brothers' infantry unit but was unable to pass the eye test. Because he had loved airplanes since first seeing one in 1909 in Paris, he decided to become an aviator.

He considered going into the Canadian Air Force to speed his entry into the war. But then his father, worried that he would have to accept

Canadian citizenship, helped him get into the U.S. Signal Corps (which oversaw the fledgling air corps). Quentin memorized the eye chart and lied about his bad back and was accepted. He was stationed at Mineola, Long Island, for training at a time when his brothers were about to head for Europe. One day after Ted and Archie had shipped out for France, TR was holding a patriotic rally for several hundred visitors at Sagamore. The crowd watched enthralled as an army airplane appeared overhead and began doing a series of looping stunts over Oyster Bay. TR found out later that it was Quentin.

Because of their youth and the war, the relationship between Quentin and Flora came to involve both of their families in a way that threatened to make the two of them into a Roosevelt-Whitney version of Romeo and Juliet. The families were far apart in background and philosophy, and divided by a mutual suspicion. Additionally, TR was particularly scornful of Harry Whitney's frantic attempts to keep his son Cornelius out of the service. Nonetheless, the Colonel decided to make peace with the Whitneys. After visiting Gertrude in her studio in Greenwich Village, he came away more impressed than he thought he would be with her sculpture and with the fact that unlike most people with inherited wealth, she was at least trying to do something of consequence with her life. For their part, the Whitneys did not try to keep Flora away from Sagamore, where she became something of a fixture in the summer of 1917.

It was a bittersweet time for Edith particularly. She was watching her last born fall in love. The Mineola air base where he was training was near enough for Quentin to come home frequently. She would listen for his late arrival and sometimes actually get up and go to his room to tuck him in. Later on, when he was at the battlefront, she wrote him, "The months you were in Mineola . . . were very happy. The evenings when Father and I sitting alone in the North room we would hear your footsteps on the piazza and when I laid my head on the pillow I knew you were safe in the next room."

By mid-summer, it was time for Quentin to ship out. He and Flora bought a gold piece and had it split in two, and then each wore half of the coin on a chain, pledging to weld it back together when Quentin came home. On the day he was to ship out, he handled himself well at Sagamore until Ethel's three-year-old son, Richard, his favorite among his nieces and nephews, hugged him tightly and Quentin had to turn quickly and leave before he began to cry. Flora had her chauffeur take the two of them to the pier where the troop transports were docked.

They sat on a large smelly wooden case holding hands and watching other servicemen leaving their loved ones. After Quentin left, she immediately wrote him, "All I do from now on will be for you and I'm going to—I *will* do something—wait and see so that when you do come back I will be more what you want—more of a real person and a better companion and you will care for me as much as I care for you."

Flora wrote to Edith to let her know that she had been emotional at Quentin's departure, although she had forced herself not to cry. "It has gone deeper than I imagined anything ever could," she wrote of their love, "entirely new lands inside of me have been discovered by it." Edith replied with a letter of appreciation: "His love for you has made a man of Quentin. Before it came to him he was just a dear boy, and now you two children have found the greatest thing in the world." On the same day, TR sent Flora a note that was also meant to lift her spirits, although it had a strangely fatalistic undertone: "You and [Quentin] have had some golden moments, whatever comes hereafter; and many people never know anything except years that are all gray or tawdry." But Flora was unable to hold off thoughts that she might lose Quentin. "Can it be for any ultimate good that all the best people in the world have to be killed," she wrote him. "It isn't possible that you will be— no, I don't honestly believe for a minute that you will be, but there is bound, at times, to come the frightful supposition."

Now that all his sons were hostages to the fortunes of war, TR put a flag bearing five gold stars into the bay window at Sagamore. Then he sat back and waited. "All I can do is wade into the pacifists," he wrote Archie in France, "the pro Germans and rioters here—which is a pretty poor substitute for work at the front." The combative brio of his correspondence hid his feelings of lonely impotence. One night during a patriotic rally at Madison Square Garden he had just begun to speak when a heckler shouted, "What have *you* done for the war effort?" Taken aback for a moment, TR paused, blinking nearsightedly out into the darkness before replying in a voice breaking with emotion: "What am I doing for my country in this war? I have sent my four boys, for each of whose lives I care a thousand times more than I care for my own, if you can understand that. . . ."

$\mathcal{U}$nable to fight against the Germans, TR continued to wage his own private war against the Wilson administration at home. He was so perturbed at being out of formal power and, as he saw it, out of luck, that he didn't realize how much influence he actually had. He didn't see that despite all the defeats he had suffered since returning from Africa in 1910, he had nonetheless set the national agenda all those years and, more than any other figure, had awakened the country to the fact that it could not remain aloof from events in Europe.

He had functioned for years, in his own mind, as "an elderly male Cassandra." Now that his prophecies about American slackness and lack of preparation were coming true, he saw his role as more that of a Jeremiah, and although he sometimes felt that his jeremiads were regarded by those in power merely as an "awful nuisance," he was aware that he was in greater demand than he had been in years—"driven to death by speaking invitations," as he told one supporter. Wilson himself tried to dismiss TR's unrelenting attacks: "I really think the best way to treat Mr. Roosevelt is to take no notice of him. That breaks his heart and is the best punishment that can be administered."

Being behind the lines was an uncomfortable position for him. In the first months after America's entry into the Great War, TR struggled to cope with his role of noncombatant. He constantly referred to himself in melodramatic terms as a cornered bear or an old lion at bay. Guilty at being out of uniform while his boys were in danger, he obsessed over his impotence to affect events in letters to them filled with passages that had the sound of libretti from tragic opera. He wrote Kermit, for instance, that what bothered him, was "the horror of having you four, at the onset of your lives, exposed to death, while I, whose life is behind him, live softly at home."

Having rushed to get his sons into the front lines, he now had doubts. The *experience* of war was good—proving oneself equal to a task that others shirked. Yet as the boys got closer to the fearful slaughter whose statistics now glutted the newspapers of America, TR found himself trying to limit their jeopardy. Thus he wrote Archie to remind him that showing courage was good but being foolhardy was not: "Of course we wish you to get into the fighting in the line. That is the first thing to be done; you would never be happy if you hadn't done it, and neither would I in your place. If *after* you have been in the fighting line—whether for a long or short time matters not—you are offered a staff place *where you can be useful,* it would be foolish to refuse it merely because it was 'less dangerous.' "

He kept thinking of what might have been: "I wish I were over myself, not that I could do very much . . . but I would have had at least a hundred thousand volunteers, of just the type of those in my regiment. . . ." Often his mind drifted back to his own military exploits. Shortly after Archie arrived in France, for instance, TR wrote him a letter that gradually swerved into an account of the charge up San Juan Hill, which became so detailed that he finally became embarrassed and stopped himself: "Well, *that* skirmish seems about as far off as Bunker Hill."

He was right. A new kind of war had been born in the trenches of France. If he hadn't known this before, TR must have realized it when he received a letter from Kermit, who was training in England before shipping out to the Mideast. The second Roosevelt son wrote that he and other officer candidates had been required to put on masks and submit to simulated attacks in which real poison gas was used, first in a small room and then in a sample trench. After this, they had to endure being "bombed" by artillery, an experience realistic enough that two of the men training with him died of heart attacks during the shelling.

The boys were very much aware that they represented him and were, in effect, his stand-ins. Writing to Ethel, Archie said, "I am certainly proud of the way our family all stepped up to the fore. . . . We have been able to show people [Father] meant what he said." In cinemas in the working-class sections of Paris, audiences applauded enthusiastically at newsreels showing the four young Roosevelts in uniform and hissed as the image of Woodrow Wilson flashed onto the screen.

But while they knew they were regarded as "The Fighting Roosevelts," in the phrase of one French magazine, symbolically settling TR's scores and vindicating his views, the boys also sensed that the war was an opportunity for them to come of age apart from his titanic presence and sort out the order of precedence among themselves for the next generation. And while they may have entered the service fired by his vision of glory and heroism, they soon understood that this was *their* conflict with its own distinctive character. Their first few weeks in Europe showed them that this was a war of alienation, a war of attrition against that sense of gallantry and romantic sacrifice their father embodied. Not long after being put in the trenches, Archie, whose wife, Grace, was expecting their first child, wrote home forlornly about how the children born while he and his brothers were away would seem like "outsiders" to them and that these children would look at their fathers as "odd birds picked up out of the military scrap heap" if they managed to get back home at all.

While Archie and Ted were working their way into infantry units outside of Paris—Ted as commander of the 1st Battalion of the 26th Infantry and Archie as a captain serving underneath him—Quentin was trying to cope with the aviation bureaucracy that was keeping American airmen from the front. Kermit, on the other hand, was indulging his appetite for romance. Always something of an Anglophile, he had now adopted a military mustache to go along with the hint of a British accent. Stopping in London after completing his initial training, he had a pair of dress uniforms tailored and negotiated with Secretary of War Lord Derby about what rank to accept in Mesopotamia. He chose captain rather than major, a decision he forwarded to his father for approval, noting that he thought TR would agree that it was a bad idea to jump in rank over men who had fought since the beginning of the war.

On his way to the Mideast, he stopped in Paris, rendezvousing at the Ritz with Belle, who had come up from Spain with their son, Kim, for a last visit. Theatrical and demanding in her love, Belle sometimes brought out an uxorious streak in Kermit his brothers felt trivialized him. She was pregnant again, and as Kermit tried to get ready to leave for the front, he worried constantly about her having the baby on the Continent where chloroform was not typically used during childbirth. He insisted on telling her doctor that if it was a choice between her life and the infant's, the latter must be sacrificed.

One afternoon shortly before he left Paris, Kermit went out to see Ted and Archie at their battalion headquarters. While he was there, Quentin turned up too. It was a sentimental moment of reunion; the brothers didn't know it was the last time they would all be together.

After this meeting, Kermit wrote home exultantly to his father: "It seems that I shall after all be the first of the boys in action." And soon he was on his way to the Mideast, catching a train out of Paris in the middle of the night. Belle wrote him the next day that the last moments in each other's arms had made the darkened hotel room seem "golden [and] filled with brilliant radiance" after he left, although this reverie was broken not long afterward by a cacophony of sirens, whistles, and clanging bells signaling an attack on Paris by a German zeppelin that sent her scrambling with Kim and the nurse down to the wine cellar in the basement of the hotel.

Kermit's wartime experiences, which TR later described as the most distinctive of any of his sons', began when he boarded a converted ocean liner in the Italian seaport of Taranto that left for the Mideast escorted by a pair of Japanese destroyers. They convoyed at night to avoid German submarines. At one point in the voyage, there was a loud noise and everyone was ordered to lifeboats only to discover that the liner had not been hit by a torpedo, but rammed above the waterline by one of the escorts. A crisis occurred at Port Said, when some of the stokers deserted. Kermit volunteered to go below and take their place even though the ship was entering the Red Sea in the middle of a sweltering August. Joining him was a new friend, Denys Finch-Hatton, who shared Kermit's fascination with Africa and, after the war, would have his own adventure there as a big-game hunter and lover of Isak Dinesen and Beryl Markham.

After the undermanned ship finally docked at Basra, Kermit and Finch-Hatton traveled to Baghdad and then on to Samarra aboard a train with anti-aircraft guns on flatcars protecting against attack by Turkish planes.

Alive to the strangeness of his new surroundings, Kermit also quickly accommodated to British military fashion by getting a pair of horses to ride when he was off duty and also acquiring a Sikh groom to look after them. ("A wild unkempt figure with a long black beard," was how he described the man, "a dervish by profession.") Soon he was spending his days chasing after "Abdul," as the British called the Turks, and trying to lure the dispersed and cautious enemy into a massed battle. At night he sat in front of his tent drinking toddies and playing piquet with Finch-Hatton, whom he described in a letter to Belle: "He has read and can talk and we have a lot of friends in common. . . . He is very anxious to take up flying and expects to leave for Egypt soon to go to the aviation school there."

He worked to add Arabic to the Romany he and Alice had learned from Gypsies when he was a boy in Washington and the Swahili he had picked up when in Africa with his father. To keep up his Greek he had a friend in Cairo give a copy of the *Anabasis* to a British pilot, who dropped the book in front of his tent when he passed overhead. The British contingent of which Kermit was now part was soon joined by some Cossacks who had left Russia after the takeover of the Bolsheviks—stolid horsemen on squat ponies who inspired Kermit to study Russian too.

He was entranced by the exotic atmosphere in which he found himself and wrote home that he had learned to fear the Turks less than the Arabs, who sneaked through British lines after dark, crawled into the medical tents, and slit the throats of the wounded.

Beginning as an infantry officer, Kermit was soon drawn to a new weapon that had made an appearance in the British arsenal. It was the Light Armoured Motorized Car, a Rolls-Royce with heavy plate armor and machine guns. Seeing the LAM cars as a new kind of cavalry, he went out for a test drive and was so taken by the experience that he asked for a transfer. He was put into a motorized unit commanded by the grandson of Lord Raglan, the man who'd been in charge of the Light Brigade that had plunged into the Valley of Death during the Crimean War. In his LAM car, Kermit spent his first months of war looking for a similar defining moment. When nothing offered, he contented himself, as he wrote Belle, with cruising through the timeless desert with its exotic biblical place names and "noting what is happening."

As Kermit disappeared into a romantic haze, his brothers agreed that they would not change places with him—the Mesopotamia campaign was, after all, only a sideshow to the central event taking place in Europe—but they did regard him as fortunate to be fighting in warmth while they were shivering in the rain and mud of their first French winter. ("You are lucky in one respect," Archie wrote Kermit. "You do not have a cold rain every day while you live in muddy trenches. I hope the next war that the U.S. goes into will be somewhere in the tropics. No more cold weather for your 'uncle Dudley. . . .' ")

Like other American soldiers, Ted, Archie, and Quentin lived for the times they could get to Paris. The city was the center of the wartime universe. In the first days of the war, it had been deserted—the theaters and cinemas closed, the cafés shuttered, the streets empty. Searchlight beams probed the darkened sky for zeppelins, and the best officials could do to stop the expected arrival of German cavalry was cut a few big trees and place them across the Avenue de Neuilly.

By the late fall of 1917, Paris no longer feared being overrun and had come to life again, although it was encased in a grim ambiance Quentin captured in a letter written during his first visit: "There are no young men in the crowds unless it is in uniform. Everywhere you go you see women in black and there is no more cheerful shouting and laughing. Many of the women have a haunted look in their eyes as if they have seen something too awful for forgetfulness."

Ted's wife Eleanor had taken over a house on the edge of the Bois de Boulogne owned by her aunt, which became the Roosevelts' home away from home. Eleanor had quickly become a leading figure in the YMCA, helping establish canteens in Paris and planning to set up others in the French provinces as well. But while she had her father-in-law's strong patriotic commitment, she made no secret of the real reason she had gone abroad: to be near Ted and to be of help to him. He was only two hours away from Paris at Demange-aux-Eaux, and although it was forbidden for her to go there, she efficiently supplied him with whatever he requisitioned for his men, using her own money to buy barrelfuls of soft drinks, tobacco by the pound, baseball equipment, and boxing gloves.

It wasn't until late September, after they had all been in Europe for three months, that she finally saw Archie, who arrived at her house on leave to take his first hot bath since landing in France. He was already disillusioned, having experienced firsthand the lack of military prepared-ness TR had been warning about for so long. When he led his men in a raid against the Germans, they had been outfitted in French helmets and English gas masks and worst of all American boots that didn't fit. (He was a 9E and had been forced to cram his feet into size 6½C with the result that his toes and heels had gotten festering sores.)

A few days after Archie left, Ted turned up. Eleanor found him looking "very, very brown and . . . like he was made of steel." Cocky as a bantamweight fighter, Ted sported his father's clenched grin as they took a promenade on the Champs-Elysées. Since there were so few American wives abroad, the soldiers who passed them eyed her carefully, not knowing, as Eleanor wrote her mother, "whether I was respectable or not. They usually decided I was not. . . ."

After their brief interlude Ted went back to his battalion. He faced the same problem in the military that he had always faced as his father's namesake: proving himself without being high-handed about it. His immediate task was to disarm resentment coming from members of the regular army who grumbled that TR had gotten him his command. Because he was so closely watched, Ted knew he could not go by the same book as other officers. So he devised unusual forms of discipline to avoid having to initiate the court-martial proceedings his colleagues routinely used to combat insubordination. Finding that some of his men had stuffed their knapsacks with hay on a conditioning march, for instance, he ordered them to fill the packs with rocks far heavier than the infantryman's normal load and do the drill again. When he discovered that the regimental band was using time allotted for practice to sneak inside out of the cold weather and sit by a fire, Ted made them climb trees with their instruments and practice there in the chill where the other soldiers could see them.

He was not above making fun of himself. He liked to tell how he had been riding the full-blooded mare Tamara Eleanor had bought for him during a military parade for French Marshal Joseph Joffre. A sudden flourish of trumpets sounded just as he came even with the reviewing stand, spooking Tamara and causing her to bolt. The next thing he knew he was leading a one-man cavalry charge up the backs of the unit marching in front of his own.

On his second leave in Paris shortly before Thanksgiving, he and Eleanor had dinner with General John Pershing, who, midway through the meal, looked over imperiously at Ted. What he said sounded like a pronouncement from the God of War himself: "You have had a chance and so far you have made good. I am pleased."

*   *   *

Like other soldiers, the Roosevelt boys felt lonely and out of touch their first winter abroad. It took weeks for word from home to find them; much of their correspondence had to do with missing or out-of-order letters that produced a feeling of isolation Archie compared to being buried alive.

Quentin was one of the major subjects in the family's correspondence. Those at home were concerned because he was the youngest and wholly on his own. Quentin's brothers were interested in how he was faring because he had always been so precocious and independent. Writing to Kermit early in the fall, Archie said with a touch of condescension that he had just heard from their younger brother, who was frustrated to be stuck in a job behind the lines: "The poor lad is both homesick and I think a little discouraged."

Indeed, from the time he first left America in his troop ship to find the loaf of bread and bar of chocolate Edith had placed on his bunk as going-away presents, Quentin had been tortured by thoughts of home. The voyage to England had been a nightmare of seasickness and ominous knocking sounds against the ship's hull that called up the specter of U-boat torpedoes. He clung to Flora Whitney as a symbol of what he had left behind and what he was fighting for. "Sometimes I wonder whether I shall ever see you again," he wrote her soon after debarking, "or feel your lips on mine. . . ." He kept mulling the correctness of their decision not to get married, as TR had urged them to, before he shipped out. He thought they had made the right choice ("Suppose we were married and I came back here in a month to be killed"), yet the fact that their relationship was not consummated gave it a feeling he compared to Poe's "nevermore."

Eventually Quentin began to enjoy the camaraderie of the other men, who began by calling him "Baby" and then, when they saw that he could take their ribbing, changed his nickname to "The Babe" or "The Kid." He cultivated a mustache for a few weeks and then shaved it off when he decided that instead of making him look older, it only made him look like a debauched youngster.

After landing in England his group was shipped across the Channel to France where one of Quentin's first acts was to borrow a motorcycle and drive to the Seine so he could bathe. It was not yet clear what use would be made of aviators, for whom Pershing had an infantryman's disdain. Because he was one of the few Americans who could speak French, Quentin was appointed supply officer for the Issoudun aerodrome, which was a few hours from Paris. Charged with scrounging

spare parts that would keep the planes running, he made wild motorcycle trips through the French countryside, walking away from two
separate crashes that could have been fatal.

He wrote Flora that at times he wished he had let his bad back keep
him out of the service, but acknowledged that this was not possible
because of what he called "noblesse oblige." His brothers often cited
TR's physical courage in their letters; for Quentin his father was a *beau
ideal* more because of his moral comportment. He admitted to Flora that
some of the other men considered him priggish because he refused to
accompany them to the brothels of Paris. (He had been fooled the first
time when some English officers said that they were taking him to a
"hotel," but when scantily clad women appeared to serve champagne he
quickly made a getaway.) He told her that his notion of "what constitutes a gentleman does not allow of treating women as animals. . . ."
He added, "I've always felt Father was the truest gentleman I knew and
all he ever said to me was—be true to your sister and mother so that
when the time comes and you know what love is, you can come to the
one you love with a heart as clean and pure as the one she brings you."

Quentin had not been as vocal about the war as the rest of the family,
and had in fact used Harvard as a refuge from his father's passionate
commitments. But now he concluded that everything TR had been
saying was right. The aviators being sent over from the States were not
well trained. Even worse, the planes they had been promised did not
arrive. He cherished the moments when he was able to get some flying
time in the French Nieuports his pursuit squadron was using.

He was often out of touch with his brothers. Letters from home were
his lifeline. When Edith sent him a note into which she had pressed some
marsh rosemary picked on the shore of Oyster Bay, he was overjoyed.
Through his mother he heard that Ted and Archie were seeing action.
Galled by the succession of desk jobs he had been given, he begged his
commanding officers to get him to the front too. But the more he
struggled to be sent into combat, the farther away he seemed to get.
Shortly before Thanksgiving he was transferred to a job in the Signal
Corps purchasing department, which involved commanding fifty men
in a mechanical supply operation requiring constant travel between England and France. One of his jobs was to travel to Marseilles to assemble
some Hudson touring cars that had been shipped over for the high
command and then convoy them to Paris. He wrote Flora: "It's a beastly
job, far afield from the flying for which I came and it makes me feel
more and more that I am an *embusqué*."

This French word for "slacker" had become a sinister one for Quentin, who was as fearful that he would never get a chance to test himself as he was that if tested he might fail. More than his brothers, he was able to admit and articulate the fears he felt, although sometimes this resulted in a deep pessimism. ("Sometimes I catch myself wondering whether the happiest ones now are not those who are dead," he wrote Flora. "They have at least finished with all the ceaseless war and all the rest. . . .")

The word "death" appeared frequently in his letters. He began to have a "horrid recurrent dream" that he finally described in detail to Flora: "It's always the same now. I arrive back in the States, wounded, and with a bad leg. For some reason the ship docks at Hoboken and there is no one to meet me. I hunt and hunt and yet can find no sort of auto to take me to New York. Then, as I am still trying hopelessly, a huge military policeman . . . comes up and asks what I am doing. I tell him, tho' I know it is of no use, and finally, with that awful helpless defeat you feel in dreams, I am put on board a transport outward bound and just as I began to realize I shall never come back home, I wake up."

Quentin made enough noise about being stuck in supply that his superiors revised his orders and sent him back to Issoudun in charge of a detachment of cadets. Grousing that it was "no job for a flying lieutenant," he was thankful at least to be airborne every day in work that he was at pains to convince his family was more difficult than it might look. ("When you get up in the air trying to keep a hundred twenty horsepower kite in its position in a v-formation with planes on either side of you, you begin to hold different ideas as to its easiness.") It was so cold at ten thousand feet that he felt frozen by the time he landed, even though he had been bundled up in his "Teddy Bear," as the insulated flying suits were called. (He told Ethel that the experience had challenged his belief in angels, which he doubted could survive such temperatures.) He had an accident during a landing when he hit a patch of mud, causing his plane to nose down and break off the propeller, a fragment of which hit the fuel tank and started a fire he barely managed to escape.

In one of his letters, Quentin admitted that before coming to Europe he had not been particularly close to Ted's wife, Eleanor, feeling that she was somewhat remote and condescending. But in the fall of 1917 he began visiting her regularly at her Paris house, which served as family headquarters in France, and soon struck up an intense relationship. She became a surrogate mother and sister, escorting him around the city when he got a weekend pass, filling him in on family gossip, and listening to him pour out his hopes and fears about Flora. Most of all, he was surprised to discover, she was fun to be with.

Just before Christmas, not having heard from Quentin in a while, Eleanor went up to Issoudun to find out what the trouble was and found him shivering in bed with "a touch of pneumonia" in a long narrow barracks with a stove at one end that did not begin to cut the cold. She convinced the air corps doctors to give him three weeks' leave and took him back to Paris.

That winter was unusually cold and grim. Eleanor had difficulty getting coal for her furnace; she occasionally found a few sticks of wood to burn and often slept in hooded woolen pajamas with mittens on her hands. But Quentin said her house felt like the Ritz. After his fever abated, the two of them bundled up and walked all over Paris, stopping at La Belle Jardinière to buy Christmas presents for Ted and Archie. Then Quentin discovered the Grand Guignol. Seeing in this theater of sadism and extravagant violence an exaggerated echo of the war, he insisted on going to it over and over and surprised Eleanor by saying that it was his favorite Paris attraction.

Feeling better, Quentin took a train down to the Riviera for a few days of sunshine. By the time he returned to duty at Issoudun, he felt that he was getting a new perspective on his situation. He wrote Flora about the necessity of resigning himself to leading a double life: "On the one hand there is the life that war forces on one—drills, flying, and the reports. On the other hand there is the life I have inside myself and that is you."

If Quentin was depressed at spending his first holiday away from home, the family at Sagamore also experienced a "stingy little Christmas," as Edith wrote to Archie. Alice was there with Nick, and with Ethel and her children. But still this amounted to "only two daughters to enjoy the pig and not a single son to ply a valiant knife and fork."

Nonetheless, the home front was getting interesting. Now that American forces were engaged there was finally a debate about the war and war aims. In addition to flaying Wilson, TR turned his fire on every evidence he saw of defeatism or divided loyalty. One phrase that began to appear in his speeches was a demand for "One Hundred Percent Americanism" and he strongly challenged any group (such as the German-Americans) who wanted to maintain a "hyphenated identity" when the country was at war. Some criticized him for jingoism and questioned the authenticity of his patriotism. Yet TR's love of country was as constant and sincere a theme of his letters as was his alarm over the actions of those he saw trying to sabotage the war effort. "These last five years have made me bitterly conscious of the shortcomings of our national character," he wrote Ted, "but we Roosevelts are Americans and can never think of being anything else and wouldn't be for any consideration on the face of the earth. A man with our way of looking at things can no more change his country than change his mother. . . ."

TR followed his sons' every move, often going to the map to pinpoint exactly where they were at a given moment and what enemy forces they were facing. When Archie was denied the captaincy for which he had been recommended TR became enraged, certain that his son was being punished by the administration to get at him. But then he was "electrified" when word came through that Pershing had personally okayed the promotion. He was determined that Archie should prove himself as an officer who cared for his men and reminded him, "Remember, if you want shoes for the men, get them in Paris and I'll pay for them."

Archie's curmudgeonly streak made him a perfect sounding board for TR's complaints about the pace of things at home: "Our national army, the draft army, has only begun to learn its rudiments. The spirit of the men is simply fine; but the shortage in even the most necessary arms and equipment is appalling. Lockwood's artillery regiment still has only wooden guns *and wooden horses!* Imagine trying to train for modern warfare with such equipment!"

His only function, as he now saw it, was the limited one of acting as a prod to the national conscience and thus making the government "do one fifth of what it ought to do instead of one twentieth." Sometimes he felt that he had achieved results. ("They are afraid of me," he wrote Archie about the Wilson administration, "and they do endeavor to hurry up the troops, to hurry the building of ships, guns and airplanes, and to make for a reasonably serious effort just in order to neutralize what I say. . . .") Yet for the most part he felt that his chief role would be to bear witness in the future to what he regarded as the past and present crimes of the President: "It is a very unjust world in which my sons and their wives and their mother and I have to pay for the slothful and utterly selfish ambitions of a cold blooded and unprincipled demagogue. History *may* never discover it; but when the war is over I shall write a full and truthful record of why we went in so late and so unprepared, and of the incredible baseness which lay behind."

But despite his grim and unrelenting pursuit of the men in charge of U.S. policy and the radicals in the street who tried to sap morale, TR was actually in better spirits than he had been in years. He had begun to sense a change in the national attitude toward him. His reputation, which had fallen to its nadir after the Progressive Party defeat and his rejection by the Old Guard Republicans in 1916, seemed to be enjoying a rehabilitation. In the first stages of the war he might have been regarded as an irritating national nag talking too loudly about things the public didn't want to hear, but by early 1918, as much of what he had been saying proved to be right, he found himself coming back into fashion. He was mobbed by newspapermen wherever he went. There was already so much talk about Roosevelt in 1920 that he had begun to seem the Republicans' only possible candidate.

Only his physical condition was a question mark. Since the summer of 1915, when he made a trip with the Audubon Society to bird nesting grounds in the Gulf of Mexico and, a few months later, went on a moose hunting expedition near Quebec (in which a rogue moose actually "hunted" him by repeatedly threatening to attack his canoe and keeping it from landing on the shore of the lake), he had decreased his outdoors activities. Someone reading between the lines of some of his magazine articles about the outdoors might see a sad admission that he had now reached a point in his life where he could no longer engage in the Strenuous Life. ("Older men can find joy in such a life," he wrote, "although in their case it must be led only on the outskirts of adventure, and although the part they play therein must be that of the onlooker rather than the doer. . . .")

In the fall of 1917, feeling out of shape and lethargic, he had checked into a health farm run by Jack Cooper, a "retired middleweight skin glove fighter," and spent his time there grousing about the "irksome monotony of exercises" he was forced to undergo, although the regimen did take off a few pounds.

Then, in February 1918, TR was forced into the hospital with a recurrence of the fevers he had acquired on the River of Doubt. He underplayed the seriousness of this episode in his letters to the boys, some of which actually had to be written by Ethel because he was too weak to lift a pen. In fact the illness was so bad—both ears were deeply infected and the abscesses that had tormented him periodically since the Brazil trip had reappeared—that at one point he believed he was dying and roused himself from a deep fever to whisper what he thought might be his last words to his sister Corinne: "I am so glad that it is not one of my boys who is dying here, for *they* can die for their country."

Eventually he rallied, although by the time he left the hospital two weeks after entering he had complete deafness in one ear to go along with the blindness in one eye he had acquired while boxing in the White House. He couldn't get rid of a nagging anxiety and sometimes woke in the middle of the night, as he wrote Bamie, "wondering if the boys are all right, and thinking how I could tell their mother if anything happened." Nonetheless, he was surprised and perversely gratified by the outpouring of concern on the part of the American people over his illness. "It suddenly came over them," he wrote Archie, "that if I died there might not be anyone who would tell the truth. . . ."

Back home at Sagamore, he recuperated and often managed to annoy the nurses hired by Ethel and his daughters-in-law by making unscheduled trips to the nursery where he waited until no one was looking and then woke up his infant grandchildren so he could hold them. One of his letters to Archie, who had just recently become the father of a little boy, broke off abruptly. "Here I had to stop," TR noted upon resuming, "for Gracie appeared with wee Archie and I was allowed to take him in my arms and cuddle him and play with him."

The various women in his life superintended him back to health. Bamie was too crippled by her various disorders to leave her Connecticut farm and be with him. But the faithful Corinne was there, along with Edith, Ethel, and, periodically, the ever ambivalent Alice.

Alice had actually been enjoying herself in wartime Washington where she could engage in a distant collaboration with her father in blackguarding Wilson's reputation. She got together with like-minded female friends and spent evenings skewering the President's pietisms, joking about how he sanctimoniously charmed women "and said his prayers before leaping into bed with them." Unlike Franklin's Eleanor, for instance, who had earnestly volunteered for Red Cross relief work soon after the United States declared war, Alice refused to commit herself to wartime charity. She said she had tried it a time or two but had then been forced to back out because of "canteen elbow," which she said made it impossible to ladle coffee and soup. As usual, Eleanor was scandalized by Alice and charged that she "hadn't a conception of any depths in any feeling. . . ."

Eleanor was perhaps striking preemptively because she knew how critical Alice was of her. (Indeed, Alice had constantly mocked Eleanor's idea of Washington social life—going out every day on meaningless missions to leave calling cards at the homes of acquaintances, and staging "solemn little Sunday evenings with warm roast, indifferent wine, and a good deal of knitting.") Eleanor was also jealous because her acerbic cousin and Franklin were collaborating in a project of wartim ' counterespionage. Alice had been enlisted to help place a bug in the home of a social acquaintance named May Ladenberg, a wealthy and sexually voracious German-American socialite who was suspected of spying. FDR agreed to supply some phony but authentic-looking "sensitive" documents from the Navy Department that could be left "accidentally" by someone visiting the house. One afternoon when Alice and FDR listened in on the hidden microphone, Ladenberg became engaged in an amour with financier Bernard Baruch. In between sounds of kissing she asked about troop movements in Romania. Franklin and Alice both hooted when they heard Ladenberg chide Baruch, while *in flagrante,* "You are a coward, you don't dare look!"

Later on, Eleanor reproached them: "You know, Alice, I have always disapproved of what you and Franklin were doing." The way Alice defended herself was calculated to annoy her cousin all the more: "All I was being asked to do was to look over transoms and peep through keyholes. Could anything be more delightful than that?"

As it worked out, Alice was also acting the part of spy in her cousins' private lives. It was no secret in the Roosevelt family that there had been problems between Franklin and Eleanor. But now something more substantial was happening, as Alice had discovered: Franklin was having an affair with a dark-haired beauty named Lucy Mercer.

The two of them were as well suited for each other as Franklin and Eleanor were mismatched. On the eve of the affair, Franklin was, as biographer Kenneth Davis later pointed out, almost a model of the Gibson Man with his chiseled looks and aristocratic bearing. A sympathetic newspaperman created a word picture of FDR standing dramatically in the light streaming in from a window. "The face was particularly interesting. Breeding showed there, cleanly cut features, a small, sensitive mouth, tiny lines running from nostrils to the outlines of his lips, broad forehead, close cropped brown hair, frank blue eyes, but above all the straight, upstanding set of the head placed the man."

With her tall, lithe figure and eyes sometimes described as "sapphire-like," Lucy Mercer had a beauty that complemented his. It was a beauty that seemed remote, but she was a sympathetic and clever listener who had the ability, as one friend said, "to mesmerize men."

Her once prominent Catholic family having fallen on bad times, Mercer had taken a job as governess for the children of Franklin and Eleanor in 1914, staying on for two years and eventually becoming part of the family's social life, sometimes serving as an "extra girl" when a single male guest came for dinner. Alarmed by Franklin's growing interest in her, Eleanor had finally dismissed Lucy. But she kept turning up in their social circle. After Wilson's declaration of war, Mercer enlisted in the navy and Franklin managed to get her assigned to his office. From there they had embarked on a clandestine romance that, in the summer of 1917, became recklessly public.

Once after Alice saw the couple together in a car out in Virginia, she called Franklin. "I saw you twenty miles out in the country," she said. "You didn't see me. Your hands were on the wheel but your eyes were on that perfectly lovely lady."

"*Isn't* she lovely?" Franklin responded, not bothering to deny what he was being accused of.

Using the polio epidemic that was sweeping Washington as an excuse, Franklin convinced Eleanor to spend the summer at Campobello Island where their children would be safe from possible contagion. After she was gone, he got Lucy Mercer invited to official Navy Department cruises, often enlisting a "beard" to serve as her escort. Distant echoes of his activities must have reached Eleanor. His absence became so lengthy that in mid-August she wrote a letter demanding his presence at Campobello: "Remember, I *count* on seeing you on the 26th. My threat was no idle one."

Franklin went up to the island and placated her and then returned to Washington. His love affair increased his desire for heroism and he began to talk again about volunteering for active duty. (FDR's superior in the Navy Department, Josephus Daniels, felt that FDR wanted to see action primarily because it was what TR had done: "Inasmuch as his cousin Theodore left the position of Assistant Secretary to become a Rough Rider . . . Franklin actually thought fighting in the war was a necessary step toward reaching the White House.") But Wilson would not hear of it: "Tell the young man . . . to stay where he is." The enjoyment of Lucy Mercer's charms the summer of 1917—a time when the other Roosevelt boys were all shipping out for Europe—was a compensation for remaining at home.

Alice went so far as to invite Franklin and Lucy to have dinner with her and Nick. Criticized later on for becoming complicit in the love affair, Alice defended herself in the usual irreverent terms: "Franklin *deserved* a good time. He was married to Eleanor." In fact, however, she was not the only one in the Roosevelt family who felt that the romance was good for FDR. Conie's daughter, Corinne Alsop, also saw a change in the young man the Oyster Bay clan had always ridiculed, saying of the affair: "It seemed to release something in him." He gained a new power and sense of himself.

Anxious to provoke a reaction, Alice hinted broadly to Eleanor about what was happening. Eleanor wrote Franklin about this conversation: "She inquired if you had told me and I said no and I didn't believe in knowing things which your husband did not wish you to know. . . ." Franklin did not accept the invitation to confess and Eleanor's powers of denial were such that she let the matter ride.

Rumors of Franklin's parlor games made their way to Europe where they were regarded with scorn by the Roosevelts involved in the war their cousin had not yet joined. The brutal realities of that war were every day becoming clearer to all of them. Ted's Eleanor had gone down to Aix-les-Bains to help set up a YMCA canteen there. One of the things that struck her was that the American soldiers, about to be sent back to the front after rest and rehabilitation, were almost pathetically grateful for the attention they had received. "The YMCA women see every trainload off," she wrote her mother. "We stand and wave as long as the train is in sight and we can see the figures in khaki hanging out of the windows. I think the men like it as much as anything else we do, and of course we all realize that we may be the last American women who will wave goodbye to these boys."

Like Quentin, Eleanor too was having a recurring dream now. It was not about death, however, but about dislocation. It involved being back in the little house in San Francisco she and Ted had rented when they were first married. In the dream, she found herself walking through the rooms feeling "only bewilderment" at the idea that she ever "lived at a time when there was no war." Disturbed, she wrote her mother, who was taking care of her children, about the dilemma she felt was causing her distressed sleep: "I could not possibly bear not seeing [the children] for a year, and at the same time I can't imagine leaving here and going home with Ted in the trenches."

In the first months of 1918, the war had come to saturate completely Eleanor's life and the lives of Ted and his brothers. Death, an odd and exotic concept when they had first arrived in France, had become domesticated. Ethel's husband, Dick Derby, had finished his "triage training" with French doctors, becoming a specialist in matters ranging from trench foot to gunshot wounds in the chest. Shortly after he was appointed assistant surgeon to the American 2nd Division, he was standing beside a mule talking to a pair of men when an enemy artillery shell hit. The men were killed by shrapnel, and so was the mule, although its body shielded Derby from injury.

About this time, Ted closed a fatalistic letter to Kermit about the "dull and unromantic" work of the trenches by saying that he was prepared for the worst: "There is one consolation we will have. We have left sons behind."

All they could do was seize life where they found it. Archie, for instance, was in charge of finding billets for U.S. officers in between engagements with the enemy. He found one for himself in the small town of Re with a miller and his three grown daughters. There, he tried to make the war go away by occasionally pooling his rations with some of the French family's supplies and having a good meal and then spending the evening singing songs in French and English as the miller played a foot organ. When one of the daughters had a baby, Archie became its godfather.

But death was a casual occurrence even behind Allied lines. Early in the spring of 1918, Quentin wrote Flora that he had just been watching his cadets doing close formation flying when the wings of one man's plane suddenly "folded like a fan and came down and [he] was killed instantly." A few weeks later, he described a particularly hectic day in which he had pulled three dead American aviators out of their planes during separate accidents in training exercises.

Quentin's sensibility had made him especially vulnerable to the disillusionment of war. Lighthearted in his surface personality—he had found it necessary to assure Flora early in their relationship that it *was* a surface and that he just "played the fool" to keep people at arm's length—he was also by nature the most philosophical of TR's sons, a trait that deepened as a result of his experience away from home. Before he had never had to challenge his defined position in the family as the little brother—impishly precocious, always able to generate a laugh, taking for granted the freedoms his brothers had won with some effort. Now he was wondering where he really fit in.

During one of his visits to Paris to see Eleanor, for instance, he discovered that she and Archie had been "holding court" on his character. Archie's verdict, transmitted by Eleanor, was that he had more brains than anyone else in the family but less drive. Writing Flora what had been said about him, Quentin admitted that there was something to the charge, although he resented being labeled as "the family ne'er-do-well." After engaging in a lengthy self-inventory, he said that he knew this much about himself: he wouldn't be as unmotivated as Kermit "when I've been on my own as long as he has," and he was capable of wanting something as deeply as Ted and Archie, although "I don't grit my teeth like they do."

He was attempting to get distance from the family, to find room to maneuver within the strong ties that bound them all so closely together. But while he sometimes sought a subversive self, he could not help caring about what the others thought. He continued to be depressed by the fact that his brothers were already in the thick of the fight, while he was still stuck in the "mudhole" of Issoudun. He had tried every avenue to get into a combat situation, but he kept running up against a wall of bureaucracy.

In February he heard that the first American air squadron was going to the front and demanded to be put in it. But his commanding officer denied the request and told him why: "That squadron is going out merely as a political move—sent so we can say we have a squadron at the front. They haven't even got [airplanes] for them yet, or any sort of organization to allow for spare parts."

Soon afterward, Quentin was offered a good job as a plane tester in Paris, but he turned it down because while it would have been fine for someone "back from the front for a rest or one who's had a bad crash and lost his nerve," for him it would be just another detour.

Quentin tried to explain his desperation to see action to Flora, who was happy to have him on the sidelines: "I feel that I owe it to the family—to father, and especially to Arch and Ted who are out there already and facing the dangers of it. . . ." What he didn't tell her or anyone else was that he'd learned that Archie, the brother to whom he had always been closest, had been suggesting to Eleanor and others that he was avoiding combat. The accusation, combined with the bleakness of his prospects for getting to the front, finally brought Quentin low. He didn't write home for weeks, and the family back home became so alarmed that they sent out inquires to Eleanor in Paris to find out what was wrong.

Quentin finally brought the problem up in a letter to Ethel—telling her how Archie looked on him as the "slacker member of the family for not being at the front," and how he kept hearing from everyone "how interesting Arch and Ted's letters were and by contrast what I was doing seemed trivial and uninteresting." Against his wishes, Ethel showed the letter to her parents. TR immediately cabled Quentin from Sagamore Hill: "Am shocked by attitude of Ted and Archie. If you have erred at all it is in trying too hard to get to the front. You must take care of your health. Of course we are exceedingly proud of you."

TR's annoyance with Archie was dispelled a few days later by news that he had been severely wounded when a German shell exploded in his trench. He was hit by shrapnel in four places in his left knee and two places in his left arm, shattering the bone and severing the nerve. By the time he got to the operating tent fourteen hours later, surgeons had to work frantically to save the arm. Looming up above him as he was coming out of the ether, a French general standing next to the battlefield operating table placed the Croix de Guerre on Archie's chest while reading a citation calling him an *"officier de grande sang froid."*

The Roosevelts were at lunch when news about Archie arrived. Edith immediately stood up and drank the last of her Madeira and then dashed the wine glass on the floor with shining eyes: "This glass shall never be drunk out of again." Everyone else quickly followed suit. Not long after, a family friend who was in France censoring U.S. Army mail increased the Roosevelts' pride when he wrote to say that he had been noting that the men in Archie's unit were writing admiring letters home about him filled with phrases such as, "He is a gritty devil."

Archie soon became something of a celebrity as the first of the Colonel's sons to be blooded. But while someone else might have gotten pleasure out of the notoriety, he was all business. When Secretary of War Newton Baker was touring the front and stopped by to see Archie in the Paris hospital where he had been transferred, he asked what he could do for him. Rather than giving some personal request, Archie took the occasion to hit on TR's preparedness theme: "We need more machine guns and more automatics!"

Archie wrote home from the hospital to say that whatever else his wounds had accomplished, at least he felt that he had vindicated his father. Touched by the sentiment, TR replied, "It's rather rough on *you* to have vindicated *me* in such a fashion." Proud as he was of his son, however, he still could not suppress a smile at the notion of "this iron natured young Puritan's aspect when the French General kissed him on both cheeks" upon delivering him the Croix de Guerre.

While Archie was recuperating, the third and most nearly successful German offensive of the war began in early May 1918. The flashes of the big guns looked like distant lightning on the Paris skyline at night.

1

*The two tiny faces looking down at the Lincoln funeral
procession from the second-floor window of the brownstone are
believed to be Theodore Roosevelt and his brother, Elliott.*

The first Theodore Roosevelt.

2

Martha Bulloch Roosevelt.

The first
Theodore and his
beloved daughter
Bamie.

4

Teenaged Teedie, strengthened by exercise, with his brother, Elliott, his sister Corinne, and his friend and neighbor Edith Carow.

TR's first wife, Alice Lee.

Skinny and Swelly: Theodore and Elliott pose before leaving on a hunting trip.

TR's second wife, Edith Carow.

*The romance of his life:
TR poses in his Western
getup before leaving for
the Badlands.*

TR re-creates the capture of Redhead Finnegan.

Elliott Roosevelt home from India.

Elliott's wife, Anna Hall, "so beautiful that the poet Browning asked merely to be allowed to gaze at her."

Eleanor as a baby. Her mother called her "Granny."

Elliott as the reckless fox hunter.

*Sara Delano Roosevelt and
Franklin, "a very nice little boy."*

Franklin, in skirts, with his
father, James.

TR dressed for his "crowded hour."

TR's daughter Alice. "Sister" to
baby Ted Jr. (shown here) and all of
her father's other children by
stepmother Edith.

19

TR in Cuba surrounded by his Rough Riders.

20

Archie and Quentin (right) at attention with the White House guard.

21

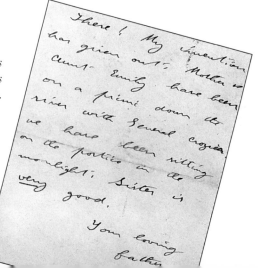

One of TR's "picture letters" to his
children, this one to Ethel about various
events at the White House.

22

Alice marries Congressman Nicholas Longworth in a White House ceremony.

FDR tends to Eleanor's knitting in a tranquil moment after their marriage.

23

2

TR reviews the Great White Fleet at the end of his second term.

Eleanor with "the first three," as James (left), baby Elliott, and Anna later called themselves.

26

25

Franklin Jr. and John, "the other two."

Kermit and TR in Africa, 1909.

27

TR in mosquito net along the River of Doubt, writing an account of the disastrous 1913 trip as it unfolded.

Quentin and Flora Whitney in a playful mood at Sagamore Hill.

Quentin as a cadet in the Air Corps.

31

Ethel pins a decoration on her husband, Dr. Richard Derby, as he leaves for the war.

32

Kermit's wife, Belle Willard, an artist's rendition.

Ted's wife, Eleanor Alexander, dressed in her YMCA uniform in France during World War I.

33

Kermit with his comrades during a quiet moment in the Mesopotamian campaign.

Archie on a street corner in Paris after being wounded in 1918.

An American doughboy marks Quentin's grave in liberated France.

FDR (third from right) on his inspection tour of 1918.

TR with Archie's wife, Grace, and baby grandson Archie Jr.

TR in 1918. One of the last photos.

Rumors of a possible German advance into the suburban *banlieues* spread through the city. Eleanor was working in her YMCA office when Ted suddenly burst in looking ghastly. His face was scorched, the skin peeling from his cheeks, and the whites of his eyes were bloody. He was covered with dust and racked by a deep rusty cough caused by the gassing he'd gotten a few days earlier.

"Are you safe?" he rasped. "What plans have you made in case anything happens? Oughtn't you to leave here at once? Who's looking after you?"

When she got him calmed down, she discovered that a few hours earlier he had been in hand-to-hand combat with the Germans at Cantigny, and after his unit had beaten them back he had heard that Paris was about to fall. Worried about Eleanor, he had begged a twenty-four-hour pass to see her from his commanding general, Francis C. Marshall.

Eleanor helped him bathe and dress in a clean uniform. She put on her prettiest dress and they ate dinner in the garden. Then they went to see Archie. She sat with the two men as Ted told his brother which members of their battalion had been killed at Cantigny. The litany of names of friends and comrades who were gone made all three of them fall silent. When Ted got up to leave she could tell by the film that came over Archie's eyes that he did not expect to see his brother again.

That night Ted had to sleep sitting up in order to breathe. Trying to get him in touch with life outside the war zone, Eleanor showed him recent photographs of their three children that she had just received from her mother. Ted studied the faces, so dramatically changed in the nine months he and Eleanor had been gone, and then handed back the pictures and shook his head sadly: "They are nice but they are not my children."

The next morning Ted went back to the front and the following day he led a dangerous raid into enemy territory that won him the Silver Star.

While his brothers were in close combat, Kermit was cruising over the vast and picturesque lands of the Tigris and Euphrates in his LAM car as part of the British offensive against the Turks. The armored Rolls-Royce was too light to function as a tank, but it was good for swift pursuit and surprise attack, moving in formation somewhat like the mounted cavalry charge this new kind of war had finally made obsolete. The crew rode on the running boards on both sides of the vehicle until engaged by the enemy, whereupon they slid inside and pulled the steel doors shut around them. A machine gunner looked through a slit in the armor to fire the LAM car's guns. Splinters of enemy lead sometimes got through the slits and during one engagement one of Kermit's men was hit in the face and killed.

He had gotten into his first significant battle in January in Tikrit. As news of the operation reached home, TR wrote: "Three cheers! You have proved yourself. You have made good. . . . It *is* better than drilling drafted men with wooden cannon here at home, isn't it?" Not long after, in three days of fighting with massed Turkish forces outside Baghdad, a battle Kermit always remembered as being marked by the stench of camels that had been killed in the fighting and gone bad in the heat, he came upon the remnants of a Turkish platoon holed up in a building. He jumped out of his car and kicked open the door. Forgetting to draw his holstered revolver, he pointed his swagger stick menacingly at a man he picked out as a possible officer and demanded that the group surrender. The Turks complied. As a result of this action, Kermit was awarded the British Military Cross.

As the Turkish forces in Mesopotamia began a swift collapse, Kermit started thinking about transferring to the European theater. He asked his father for help. By return mail TR wrote to say he had contacted General Leonard Wood and told him "of your eagerness to do some fighting under our flag . . . and your desire to be where the heaviest fighting was. . . ." Soon it was set: Kermit would travel to France and join the American Expeditionary Force there.

He went to Alexandria to try to get passage on a troop ship to Europe. But no convoys were ready, so he went up to Cairo to find a passenger liner. As gregarious as always, he struck up acquaintances with other soldiers. One of them was Major A. B. Paterson of the Australian Army, author of *The Man from Snowy River,* a Roosevelt family favorite. Another was into Colonel T. E. Lawrence, already almost as much of a mythic figure as TR himself and far more exotic. ("He dressed in Arab costume," Kermit later wrote, "but as a whole made no effort to conceal his nationality.") As they discussed the war, Lawrence told Kermit about the raids he had led against Turkish railroads and supply units. With a strange look in his eyes, Lawrence confided that what he had found hardest was killing his own wounded, but the fear of falling into the hands of the Turks was so great on the part of his Bedouins that this had been an absolute necessity. As he bid Kermit goodbye, Law-

rence of Arabia said in a resigned voice that "things had broken altogether too well [for him] and would not continue to do so."

On his way to France, Kermit stopped off in Madrid to see Belle and
Kim and to be introduced to his new son, Willard. There seemed to be
no reason to hurry. Early in 1918, it felt as though the war would last
forever. For Quentin especially, the concept of no-man's-land, describing the area between the trenches where nothing could survive, had
taken on an ominous personal meaning. As he told Flora, he felt that he
lived in a no-man's-land where he was in the war but not fighting, in a
kind of suspended animation. When TR wrote him what he thought
was reassuring news that spring had returned to Oyster Bay ("The
woods are showing a green foam; the gay yellow of the forsythia has
appeared"), it must have seemed like a description of a different planet.

Quentin could not conceive of a world other than the one that imprisoned him. With more time on his hands than he wanted, he had
begun to write short stories when he was off duty. Some of them were
in the naturalistic vein of Jack London. One called "The Service Revolver" described a young officer serving in a German U-boat who sees
a photo in a newspaper of a young woman killed in a passenger liner his
submarine had torpedoed. The picture obsesses him to such a degree
that he finally picks up his service revolver and shoots himself in the
head.

Some of the other short stories he wrote were allegorical. In one
haunting piece, the narrator is traveling through "life's bazaar" when he
walks into a surreal room filled with a strange pulsating light. He sees
a hideous crone with a crystal ball that is filled with images of people
living ordinary lives and lives of quiet desperation. After seeing the
possibly trivializing fate awaiting him, the narrator flees the room feeling that Death is not necessarily an enemy.

Caught up in that mood of nihilism that shaped the literary response
to the war, an emotion seen in the poetry of Wilfred Owen and the prose
of Robert Graves, Quentin was still enough his father's son to be stirred
by the pageantry and romance of battle and particularly of the air war
being waged by men he regarded as knights of the sky. In May, he
wrote home about the funeral of a French flyer who had been brought
down: "A Boche flew over his squadron's airdrome and dropped a letter
saying that his funeral would be on a certain date and that four French-

men would be given safe conduct to land on the German field and attend it. They accepted and the four flew over, landed and were received by the Germans. [They] attended the funeral and went home."

This chivalry was reciprocated by the Allied side. Not long before the event he described, Quentin pointed out, the German ace Baron von Richthofen was buried with full military honors by the English after they finally managed to bring him down.

His own experiences were more prosaic. The most excitement he'd had recently came when he was forced by a low ceiling to make an emergency landing in a muddy field. He slammed into a tree and when he came to after being unconscious for a few moments, he heard two French peasant women chattering over him. *"Il est mort!"* one kept saying. *"Mais, non!"* the other replied, pointing at him. *"Il vit encore!"*

Quentin continued to be bothered by the gap between himself and Archie. Never before had there been such an emotional distance between them. With time on his hands, he thought constantly about the experiences they'd had when Ted and Kermit were already off on their own and the two of them were left at home. He said to Flora that he felt that he and Archie "could settle up our row in an afternoon" if only he could see him in Paris where he was recuperating from his wounds.

Quentin finally did get a leave and found Archie wandering around the city killing time—"heartbroken," in Eleanor's estimation, because his arm would not heal and he could not get back to the front. Still resolved not to return home unless "forced to," he often went into restaurants to eat alone, and sometimes Frenchmen came up to him and insisted on paying his check because they had seen the Croix de Guerre on his chest.

Possibly because of TR's rebuke for his accusations regarding Quentin's courage, Archie was on his best behavior. He amused Quentin particularly by his dyspeptic reaction upon hearing that his wife, Grace, wanted to come to France. ("He was going to telegraph her that we were already encumbered with too many useless civilians," Quentin wrote home, "but the censor, not knowing him, deleted it.") It was ironic because at that particular moment getting Flora to Europe, almost as much as getting himself to the front, had become the focus of Quentin's life. He had become especially desperate in the past few weeks because, as he told Flora early in May, he was having difficulty in holding on to memories of her, and he feared that if he lost these memories of the past, he would lose his hold on the present.

TR sensed what his son was feeling. He said in a letter to Quentin,

"Why don't you write to Flora, and to her father and mother, asking if she won't come abroad and marry you. . . . As for your getting killed or crippled, why she would a hundred times have rather married you under these circumstances. . . . And anyway we have to take certain chances in life. . . ."

The Whitneys proved to be an obstacle. "Hon Ma and Hon Pa," as Quentin called Flora's parents, felt she was too young to be on her own. They feared that her brother, Sonny, training as a pilot in Texas, might be also sent abroad and then both children would be in the war zone. For a while Flora was afraid even to ask their permission. But Quentin kept pressuring her. ("They ought at least to give us a chance to state our case," he wrote to help her screw up her courage to make the request.)

Finally, TR weighed in on the side of the lovers. Although still scornful of Henry Whitney's desire to keep his son out of active duty, he used the fact that they both had sons who were aviators as a common ground from which he began to plead the case of Flora and Quentin. He helped bring Whitney around, and soon both men had joined in pressing the military bureaucracy in Washington to relax the rules that prohibited civilians from going to France. Flora applied for a passport and so did TR and Edith, who proposed to accompany her abroad as chaperons.

During the latter part of May it seemed that she and Quentin might actually be reunited after nearly a year apart. Quentin began to make plans for what they would do when she arrived. But then came Flora's grim telegram informing him that the State Department had finally turned down the passport request. Quentin was downcast: "It seems torment when it was almost in our grasp to have it taken from us." Back home, TR said of the ruling, "It is wicked; she should have been allowed to go and then marry Quentin. Then even if he were killed she would have known their white hour."

A few days later, though, there was consolation for Quentin when he received word that he was finally being sent to the front as part of a French *avion de chasse*. Galvanized by the news that he would finally be seeing action in a pursuit squadron, he made the rounds saying goodbye to fellow officers. In his last day at Issoudun there was an unexpected tribute from the men he had commanded for nearly six months when the truck driver taking him to his new post began by driving slowly in front of the hangars where all the aircraft mechanics had lined up to cheer: "Hip, hip, hooray for Teddy's boy!" Quentin's last sight of Issoudun was of a gruff American sergeant yelling, "Let us know if you're captured and we'll come after you!"

There was time for a last visit to Paris to see Eleanor, who had mothered and sistered him since he had been abroad. The two of them made the rounds, as they had for the past year, with Quentin insisting, as always, that they go to Montmartre to see the Grand Guignol. He also visited with Archie, who was about ready to undergo another operation to repair the two-inch gap between the atrophied ends of the severed nerve in his arm. Quentin was surprised at his stolid brother's gloominess. Archie admitted that he sometimes felt "that none of us are going to get back and that our one interest should be how soon we are going to die." But as Quentin was about to leave, Archie suddenly became uncharacteristically emotional and hugged him. "He evidently felt that he was saying a last fond farewell to me," Quentin wrote Flora.

Luck now seemed finally to be with him. Instead of being placed in a French unit, as he thought he would be, his orders were changed and he was put in the U.S. 1st Air Pursuit Group. He was assigned to the famous "Kicking Mule" Squadron headed by a morose officer Quentin quickly decided was "over here to get killed because he doesn't get on with his wife."

Now that he was finally engaged, the pessimism of the previous months lifted and Quentin felt at peace for the first time since leaving home. His first patrol was on July 1. He saw no German planes, but came back to base to find that holes from the fire of anti-aircraft guns (called "archies" by the pilots) had hemstitched his wing.

He fell into a new rhythm: flying missions and waiting to fly them. His plane had Doc Yak, a character from a Rube Goldberg cartoon, painted on one side and a figure in a racing car on the other. His squadron mates quickly christened Quentin "The Go and Get 'Em Man" because of his eagerness to engage the enemy.

When he was not in his plane Quentin tramped through the French countryside, seeing in the depths of summer "signs of renewal." Many of the men in his squadron were going down and he contemplated his own death with equanimity. "In case I do get it," he wrote Flora, "Ham [Hamilton Coolidge, his friend and fellow avaitor] is going to look after my things and send them home to the family—I'm leaving a letter in my trunk that he'll find when he goes through it."

On July 6, Quentin and his mates engaged the remnants of Richt-hofen's Circus Squadron in their red planes. "We circled and came back between them and the sun and then dove on them. They never saw us until we started shooting, so we had them cold. . . . I had my man right where I wanted him. . . . I set my sights on him and pulled the trigger.

My gun shot twice and then jammed." It was a disappointment to have missed a chance at one of the enemy, but at least he had proved to himself that he was not going to get "cold feet."

Five days later he wrote Flora in high excitement. He had just returned from patrol in which he had been separated from the rest of the flight by a billowing wind. He had decided to look around before heading back to base. As he circled around up near the cloud ceiling, he saw three planes below him, just north of Château-Thierry. Thinking they were part of his scattered squadron, he began to follow them. But then, as he drew close, he saw the black crosses on the planes' fuselages: "I was scared perfectly green, but then I thought to myself that I was so near I might as well take a crack at one of them, so I pulled up a little nearer, got a line on the end man, and pulled the trigger. . . . My tracers were shooting all around him but I guess he was so surprised that for a bit he couldn't think what to do. Then his tail shot up and he went down. . . ."

Back home, TR was excited when the telegram arrived announcing that Quentin had made his first kill. "The last of the lion's brood has been blooded!" he exulted in a letter to Ted. But a note to Ethel written at the same time had an oddly fatalistic undertone: "Whatever now befalls Quentin he has now had his crowded hour, and his day of honor and triumph."

Five days later, on July 16, another telegram arrived at Sagamore. This one had bad news: Quentin had been shot down behind enemy lines. From various accounts that began to arrive, the Roosevelts pieced together what had happened. Quentin had been on a patrol when his squadron was surprised by a superior force of German planes. ("Christ, there were Fokkers everywhere!" one of the other pilots later said.) Quentin immediately rose to engage two of the enemy. He held them at bay for a moment, but then they closed in. His plane was hit and began to cartwheel downward. American pilots who had seen it smash into the field below took heart only because there had been no fire or explosion.

Hoping against hope that he might have survived the crash and been captured, the family, with Eleanor working from Paris and TR and Alice using Washington diplomatic contacts, tried desperately to get reliable word about what had happened. In England, Rudyard Kipling wrote a letter to Kermit urging him to take heart because if Quentin had been taken alive the Germans, knowing the tide of war had turned against them, would treat him better than they might have earlier in the conflict.

TR had agreed to see a delegation of Japanese YMCA volunteers at Sagamore on the morning of July 22. He greeted them, took them through the bottom floor of his home, and then made a graceful little speech. As the Japanese were leaving, Trubee Davison, host of the delegation and an acquaintance of Quentin's, asked TR what news he had of his son. A look of pain suddenly crossing his face, TR handed Davison a telegram he had received just minutes before his guests arrived. It was confirmation from Washington that Quentin was dead. Davison said later on that TR's behavior that day was an example of self-control he never saw equaled in his life.

Quentin had been struck squarely in the forehead by a machine gun shell, the family learned later on, and had been dead before his plane hit the ground. He had been buried with full military honors by the Germans, although the code of chivalry was not so strong that it prevented an amateur photographer from snapping a close-up of the mutilated face. A German entrepreneur made it into a postcard which began to circulate in Europe. General John Pershing gave orders for the photos to be confiscated whenever the Allied soldiers encountered them. Nonetheless, some of the postcards ultimately found their way back to Sagamore Hill.

TR gave out a simple statement to the press: "Quentin's mother and I are very glad that he got to the front and had a chance to render some service to his country and show the stuff that was in him before his fate befell him." Before this he had taken Flora Whitney aside to tell her what had happened. She reacted with a Roosevelt's stoicism. (In fact, she would live with the Roosevelts as something like an in-law for the next year and a half, first moving in with Ethel for several months and then going to Washington to live with Alice.) In time Flora allowed her mother to sculpt her face—the sunken eyes and bowed head of the figure establishing it as a metaphor for undying grief.

TR and Edith rowed out on Oyster Bay the afternoon that the tragic news arrived and talked about their son. Later, Edith wrote Ethel that the two of them were like a house of cards, barely managing to hold each other up. They went to visit Ethel in her rented home at Dark Harbor, Maine. Edith had difficulty sleeping, wandering from room to room at night until she finally came to the bedroom of Ethel's four-year-old son, Richard. She lay down on his bed for a moment, and, as she told her daughter the next morning, the little boy, Quentin's favorite nephew, finally patted her to sleep.

* * *

The sadness over Quentin was so deep that the Roosevelts were almost anesthetized against the sequel. Five days after his death, however, Eleanor happened to pass by the window of her Paris house where she was in deep mourning for the brother-in-law who had been like a brother. Her eye was caught by a commotion outside. Looking closer, she saw it was Ted being lifted out of an automobile. She ran downstairs and flew out the front door. As she bent over to embrace her husband, she read the tag on his shirt: "gunshot wound severe." Through his jagged conversation she made out that he had been hit in the leg by machine gun fire during a raid, and, because of a scarcity of field ambulances, had made his way from Soissons to Paris by hitching a ride first in a motorcycle sidecar and then in a private auto.

Ted kept downplaying the significance of the field-dressed wound, but soon after she had gotten him comfortable, Eleanor summoned Dick Derby, who happened to be on leave in Paris. Derby's examination showed two bullet holes above and behind the knee. He said that Ted could possibly lose the leg if it wasn't treated immediately and made him go directly to the hospital. Eleanor sat outside the operating room where she was joined by Archie, who was himself recovering from another round of surgery on his shattered arm. After two hours, Derby, who had been inside assisting, came out to tell them that the procedure had been a success.

During the next few weeks, after Ted had left the hospital, he and Eleanor and Archie walked around Paris, Ted on crutches and Archie's arm akimbo in a huge cast. Living in the frozen shadow of Quentin's death, the threesome sometimes acted crazily. On the Metro, the brothers made a scene by pretending to be boorish Americans trying to pick up Eleanor. One afternoon on the Champs-Elysées, they suddenly started to pretend they were mental patients. Ted picked at imaginary butterflies in the air and Archie cried and howled at the top of his lungs.

They met up with Belle and Kermit, who had been appointed a captain of artillery in the American army and was on his way to gunnery school in Saumur. One afternoon after they had all eaten lunch, Ted started singing a marching song as he left the restaurant. He kept moving smartly on his crutches up a narrow street and some French *poilus* fell in behind him. Soon there was a parade of people stretching for over a block. One of the French soldiers yelled, *"Vive L'Amérique!"* Kermit vaulted into a cart and began to wave his cap and shout, *"Vive La France!"*

They all had a sense that they might soon die just like Quentin. Yet in some sense they were addicted to the war. Archie tried desperately to get reassigned to his battalion, but he was so thoroughly incapacitated that he was finally ordered home for further treatment. He tried to keep from going, not wanting to leave Ted in the trenches without him, but finally he could not put it off any longer. After his boat sailed, Kermit wrote TR to alert him to be wary of Archie's "nerves."

After Kermit had headed off for his unit, Ted was left alone. When Eleanor was at work at the YMCA, he wandered incognito through Paris. One day he ran into Georges Clemenceau, his father's old friend, who looked at his military decorations and then said, "But you have not the French War Cross! No one deserved the French War Cross more than you, Major!" Clemenceau then sent for another French general, who pinned the Croix de Guerre on Ted's chest on the spot.

Although still unable to walk without crutches, Ted got himself assigned as an instructor in an infantry school. He was bored by the duty and after a short time he disappeared. There was talk about him having deserted and his superiors were about to report him AWOL when they discovered that he had defied medical orders and gone back to the front to resume command of his old unit.

When Archie arrived home early in September, TR wrote Kermit: "Of our four hawks the hero has come home, broken winged, but his soul as high as ever." Yet after watching his son, TR noted apprehensively that Archie took only a "tepid interest" in his baby son, Archie Jr., who had been born while he was away. Indeed, there were invisible wounds that seemed as serious as the ones that had crippled him. Archie kept insisting that he was merely back for a visit and that he would soon return to the front. Unable to admit that the war was over for him, he began to resemble one of the dislocated veterans Ernest Hemingway would soon be writing about in his short fiction—subject to moments of emotional bleakness and filled with guilty longing for the relative clarity of battle. He wandered around Sagamore like a ghost. "Poor mother will never recover about Quentin," he wrote Kermit. "Indeed, none of us will, for I find that on going around, I keep remembering the time we were last together."

*   *   *

At this time of tragedy for the Oyster Bay family, their Hyde Park cousins were moving toward the denoument of their own closet drama.

After the fall of 1917 Franklin had no longer been able to carry on with Lucy Mercer in the Navy Department because she had been relieved of her duties, possibly because his chief, Navy Secretary Josephus Daniels, had gotten wind of the affair. But they still saw each other and, as Franklin would soon regret, still corresponded. Lucy continued to be a part of FDR's imagination as part of a possible alternative to the life he was leading.

Among the issues that agitated him in the spring of 1918 was the fact that he had still not seen the face of war. TR's sons were constantly in the news. TR himself had once again urged Franklin to get into active duty. But it was difficult for him to defy his President and resign from a position of power and influence. Then, in the early summer, Congress announced that it planned to investigate naval installations in Europe and Navy Secretary Daniels okayed Franklin's request to go there first to make sure that the Navy Department would not be embarrassed. Dramatizing the trip as a top secret mission, Franklin informed Eleanor that he would be sailing into danger in a note that ended, "Don't tell a soul—not even mama."

He was in a state of high excitement when he sailed aboard the USS *Dyer* on July 9. He had designed what he called his "destroyer costume," a uniform comprised of riding trousers, golfing stockings, flannel shirt, and leather jacket. Every time there was a submarine alert, he rushed up to the bridge to prepare for action and if he did not have time to put on his uniform he came in nightshirt and bare feet.

He landed in England the day that Quentin's death was confirmed. When he visited Buckingham Palace, King George V offered condolences about his cousin. Franklin talked to a variety of English politicians as part of his fact finding. One of them was Winston Churchill, who didn't make a good impression. "One of the few men in public life who was rude to me," Franklin described him.

A few days later he was on his way to Dunkirk. When his ship docked, a pair of limousines met his party and took them to Paris. He paid a visit to Eleanor and Ted, whose wounded leg was stretched out over a chair, and saw Archie, who, FDR wrote, was "looking horribly badly." Then, after experiencing the night life of Paris, he set out on a tour of the battlefields.

On August 4 his party approached Château-Thierry, which had just been regained from the Germans ten days earlier. Passing some captured

German soldiers being marched along the road, Franklin noted in the journal he was keeping of the trip that there was "an awful contrast between the amount of intelligence in their faces compared with the French Poilus." After a lunch with French officers, his American military escort tried to show him some of the villages around Château-Thierry, but Franklin became annoyed because he felt that he was being kept too far behind the lines. The French officers saw his irritation, as he noted with satisfaction in a letter home, and took him "as close to the actual fighting as seemed prudent."

He went on to Belleau Wood, where the U.S. Marines—FDR had taken to referring to them as "my Marines" on this trip—had recently fought with such heroism. Signs of the desperate struggle that had been waged there littered the ground. He made a catalogue: "In order to enter the wood itself we had to thread our way past water-filled shell holes . . . hastily improvised shelter pits, rusty bayonets, broken guns, emergency ration tins, hand grenades, discarded overcoats, rain-stained love letters. . . ." He could hear the distant thunder of the field guns. If this was not actually warfare it was the next best thing.

His automobile carried him farther west. On August 6, wearing a French helmet and carrying a gas mask, he crossed the Meuse. He was outraged to see the wanton destruction the Germans had inflicted on the small French towns. His party stopped in the village of Mareuil to look around. Suddenly there was a huge explosion. After diving for cover, he realized that it was not German artillery, but an American gun emplacement firing an outgoing round. Chagrined, he walked over and visited the battery of 155s and was invited to fire one of them, which was pointed in the general direction of the German lines. It would become the high point of his trip. He wrote portentously of the experience, "I will never know how many, if any, Huns I killed."

His party went on to Italy for consultations with the government, and then returned to Paris, had a press conference, and left for Bordeaux and Brest to complete his tour of Allied installations. Being close to battle and sensing the heroic dimensions of this war had made up his mind about one part of his future at least. He wrote Eleanor on August 20, "Somehow I don't believe I shall long be in Washington. The more I think of it, the more I feel that being only 36 my place is not at a Washington desk, even a Navy desk. I know you will understand. . . ."

The next week, Franklin and his party took a little side trip to Scotland where they fished for salmon and drank single malt Scotch whiskey. After more socializing in London, he began the trip home on

September 12, telegraphing Eleanor from the USS *Leviathan* to register him for the draft in Hyde Park. But on the trip home he became ill, sinking into a fever that quickly led to double pneumonia. He was not the only man on the ship to become ill. Several others had contracted the influenza that was sweeping through Europe. Some of them died on the passage home and were buried at sea.

When the *Leviathan* docked in New York, Franklin was still seriously ill. He was taken off on a stretcher and driven to his 65th Street brownstone in an ambulance. It was at this moment that the secret life he had been leading for more than a year finally came to light. In unpacking his suitcase, Eleanor came across some love letters from Lucy Mercer. The physical evidence of Franklin's affair finally broke down the denial by which she had kept herself from knowing what was going on all these months.

There was a series of emotional scenes, exactly the kind of conflict from which there was no exit that Franklin had always dreaded. Although devastated by her discovery, Eleanor did not demand that he choose between her and Lucy. She simply offered to step out of his life. She knew she had allies in Louis Howe, who pointed out the damage a divorce would do to Franklin's long range political hopes, and, more significantly, in Sara. Although normally chafing at her mother-in-law's dominance, Eleanor now saw her as her best hope. In one of the few times she ever denied him anything, Sara made it clear to Franklin that if he did not give up his lover and work to repair his marriage she would disinherit him. Chastened, he agreed not to see Lucy and to try to work things out.

One afternoon early in November a few weeks after his cousin's closet drama had ended, Kermit was standing in the desolate, shell-pocked town of Sandres St. George watching some doughboys coming up the road. At the head of the column, in a battered Dodge car, he recognized Ted. Still limping, his brother got out and came to greet him. While the two were talking, another car stopped and Dick Derby jumped out. There was a brief family reunion and then all three men were subsumed by the vast army chasing a retreating enemy toward the Rhine.

As he trudged toward Germany, Kermit recorded the pitiful sight of Frenchmen walking back to their recently liberated villages with wheelbarrows and baby carriages filled with possessions. But he also saw a determination in the scene. The image that summarized for him the resilience of the French in the midst of devastation was that of an elegant woman walking carefully through the mud in a moth-eaten fur coat and rickety high heels with a fox terrier on a leash.

Then, on November 11, with an eerie and disquieting suddenness, it was over. "What everyone was listening to was the guns," Kermit wrote Belle. "At almost eleven they began to stop and we went on, wondering whether they would open up again. Finally the news came through in a fairly definite shape. . . . I can't at all realize that the war is really over."

With the stilling of the guns came a momentary loss in the élan that had held the Roosevelts together during their time abroad. Annoyed that Belle and her sister, both of whom had sat out the war in the comfort of Madrid, were now hitching rides to Strasbourg, where Kermit and Ted were stationed, Eleanor wrote her husband: "I am willing to bet that they end by flagging a car that happens to be General Pershing's and . . . sleep in the Commanding General's tent. Also that they have grandstand seats for whatever show is going on."

Ignoring the cat fight that had broken out between his wife and sister-in-law, Kermit rounded up a Thanksgiving pig for his men and then ate a second dinner with Ted's officers' mess. On December 1, he wrote home about "marching beside the Moselle for some time before crossing over into Hunland. . . . We soon began meeting German soldiers on the road, on their way home, and still in uniform. They smiled and seemed most friendly, but of course my men did not respond. . . ."

If it was a victory for the U.S. Army, it was a victory for TR as well. He had fought as doggedly at home as his sons had in the trenches and suffered even more serious wounds.

The one that wouldn't heal, of course, was Quentin. TR referred to his fallen son as an eagle who'd had his moment in the sun and compared him to Robert Gould Shaw, commander of the Massachusetts 42nd Regiment of black soldiers in the Civil War, and other patriots who had also died young. He was pleased to hear that before the Armistice, when Allied soldiers were retaking territory once occupied by the Germans, Quentin's grave—marked only by a sign with his name and a piece of the propeller from his plane—had become a sort of shrine and that American infantrymen had beaten a path there through the grass and were leaving messages pinned to nearby shrubs. He wrote Ted and Eleanor when he heard the French might posthumously award a medal to "poor dead Quentin" and closed the letter by asking, "Perhaps if Cornelius or Willard or little Archie ever had a small brother, he might be named Quentin?"

But it was difficult to find an affirmation in this death that had struck down the one person who most embodied the Roosevelts' undiscovered promise. There were long periods of silence, and TR admitted that something in him had "shut down" after the boy's death. "There is no use of my writing about Quentin," he responded to condolences from his friend Edith Wharton, "for I should break down if I tried." He tried to keep up his public obligations, but in that fall of 1918, one acquaintance saw him on a train, staring out into space with an unopened book on his lap. "Poor Quenty-Quee," he was murmuring. As one acquaintance noted later on, with Quentin's death "the boy in Theodore had died too."

For the most part, however, TR soldiered on so well that few except for Edith saw the extent of his grief. He closely followed the endgame being played out in Europe and followed the progress of his two sons who remained in the war zone. He was gratified when Kermit got into the action as a commander of a field artillery battery in the battle of the Argonne. He was annoyed when Ted was held back from promotion to lieutenant colonel, and wrote him a letter of apology to say that while his influence had helped get him into the fighting it had probably held him back in terms of getting the rewards and recognition he had earned. But TR was no longer really interested in glory; he just wanted Ted and Kermit home. Initially anxious to have his sons discover themselves in battle, he was now pessimistic and told one visitor at Sagamore, "If this war continues, none of the boys will come home."

Nevertheless, he continued to strike out at Wilson. He tore into the President's plans for peace, especially the Fourteen Points, which he scornfully referred to as "fourteen scraps of paper." By October he was campaigning hard for Republican candidates in the 1918 off-year election. When the voters repudiated the administration, most political observers agreed that it was to some degree a Roosevelt victory and that TR, the only candidate for the Republicans in 1920, was likely to be President again. History, in one of its odd pirouettes, was facing his way once again, but TR wasn't in the mood for politics as usual and had a standard response for those who now offered to climb onto his bandwagon: "I am not in the least concerned with your supporting me either now or at any future time; all I am concerned with is that you should act so that I can support you."

In the middle of his political rebirth, there were other losses besides Quentin's. The most serious came in September, when his sister Corinne's husband died. "Good Douglas Robinson," as TR called him, had been the first outsider to enter the family; he had been the kindly loyalist who generously helped TR's brother, Elliott, in his declining days. His passing caused a metaphysical lurch. TR wrote Dick Derby in Europe: "It is in the nature of things we must soon die anyhow—and we have warmed both hands before the fire of life."

On October 27, he turned sixty. It was a symbolic moment for him, somewhat in the nature of a grand climacteric. He recalled to Corinne that as a young man just setting out, he had pledged to himself to work *up to the hilt*—he smacked a fist on his palms for emphasis when he used this phrase—until he was sixty. Now he had done it. He wrote a joint letter to Ted and Eleanor in France: "I hope that when you two come to this age, you will have had as happy a life as I have had, and above all I hope that your children will have given you the cause for pride that you, Ted, have given me."

Roosevelt was suddenly hospitalized the day that the Armistice was declared. The diagnosis was an especially serious case of rheumatism. But his condition was worse than these words indicated. His energy was gone; he was in constant pain. The timing of his collapse seemed to suggest that he had waited until the enemy was defeated to call an end to his own private war and give in to his failing body.

He was a bluff patient, never admitting how sick he was, holding court in the hospital for friends of a lifetime like Henry Cabot Lodge as well as for those like newspaperman William Allen White whom he had acquired more recently. He wrote Bamie that he was embarrassed to be getting any sympathy at all because she had smiled through pain all her life. ("My troubles are not to be mentioned in the same breath with all that you have gone through. . . .") But in a conversation with Corinne, he inadvertently indicated his fatalistic state of mind when, after again reminding her of his vow about turning sixty, he said: "I have kept my promise and now, even if I should . . . be an invalid or die, what difference would it make?"

He expected to be hospitalized only for a few days, but he was unable to rally and his stay stretched into weeks. Still he continued to make political plans. Some of them involved Ted, whom he urged to return and "come forward in public life." Some involved himself. When *Amer-*

ican magazine ran an article claiming that he had been infected with an illness during his South American adventure that was so serious that he would never be the same physically or mentally, he considered a suit, lest such gossip hurt his chances in 1920. He went so far as to jot down preliminary ideas for a platform while lying in his hospital bed—eight-hour workday, social security insurance, old age pensions—many of which would be noted with keen interest by his young cousin Franklin, who was already considering *his* next step. TR assured concerned friends that the need to settle a personal score gave him a good reason to get well: "I seem pretty low now, but I shall get better. I cannot go without having done something to that old grey skunk in the White House."

With the war over and her husband a survivor, Ted's Eleanor finally returned home from France early in December. She immediately went to her mother's house and reintroduced herself to the children she had not seen for a year and a half. Grace, at eight the oldest, remembered her, and Teddy, five, pretended to, although when she came into the house he gave her a peculiar look and asked why she was taking off her hat and coat. Three-year-old Sonny, as Cornelius was called, did not remember her or Ted. (In saying his nightly prayers, he had addressed him as "Our Father Who Art in France.") When Eleanor told the little boy that she was his mother and said that his father would be returning from the war soon, the little boy solemnly asked if Ted would be bringing home a stuffed German to add to the collection of heads on the wall.

Next Eleanor went immediately to the hospital to see TR. It was a touching moment for them both. Although initially opposed to her going, TR was immensely proud of his daughter-in-law, regarding her as much a veteran of foreign service as his sons. He was appreciative of what she had accomplished and for the love she had shown Quentin as well as Ted.

In their conversation, she told him something no one else ever had: that Ted worried constantly that he was not worthy of him.

"Worthy of me?" TR smiled. "Darling, I'm so very proud of him. He has won high honor not only for the children but, like the Chinese, he has ennobled his ancestors. I walk with my head higher because of him."

Eleanor immediately wrote Ted with news of her talk with his father, saying, "He is proudest of you than of everybody, and with reason." By this time, TR had added his own words of praise, writing Ted that being on the victorious march through the Rhineland was an "unbelievable historic experience" comparable to being at Waterloo.

One indication of how ill TR actually was came when he asked Archie to substitute for him in the annual Christmas celebration at Cove Neck School, for decades a high point of his holiday season. He sent both of the boys still in Europe one thousand francs apiece to buy Christmas food for their men.

On Christmas Eve, Kermit wrote home to Belle, "I'm afraid it won't be a very merry Christmas at Sagamore; there will be too many ghosts around." And indeed, TR himself seemed like one of them. It was not until Christmas Day that he was allowed to leave the hospital. He was glad to come home, but he saw a resonance with what he was feeling within in "the sad, frozen landscape" of Oyster Bay. For the next few days, he shuffled around the property on short walks. Not wanting to disturb Edith because of his broken sleep, he took the bed in Ethel's old room just off the main bedroom, and spent much of his time there. In a letter to Kermit just after New Year's Day, Edith said that he was "having a horrid painful time."

On Saturday, January 4, his valet James Amos washed TR and dressed him in clean pajamas and sat him next to the bay window downstairs where he could look out at the woods, which were petrified with snow. The next day he stayed in bed. He and Edith spent hours reading aloud to each other from favorite books. When she got up to leave for a moment late in the afternoon he gave her an odd look and said, "I wonder if you'll ever know how much I love Sagamore Hill." Edith later wrote to Ted about these special hours together: "He was very sweet all day. Since Quentin's death he has been very sad."

That night TR called to Edith in the next room at about ten o'clock and asked her to help him sit up, saying without any particular fear that he felt oddly as if his heart was about to stop. She gave him some sal volatile and he was peaceful until around midnight when she came in to check on him and asked the nurse she had hired to give him a shot of morphine. Shortly afterward, he began to drift off and said to his valet, who was sitting nearby, "James, will you please switch out the light?"

Around two in the morning Edith checked in on him and found him sleeping comfortably on his side. Two hours later she was awakened by Amos, who said that TR's respiration had suddenly become labored and spasmodic. By the time she got to his side, he was not breathing at all.

"Dear Kermit, I felt he was just asleep only he could not hear me," Edith concluded the letter she wrote her son describing the death of his father. By this time, of course, Kermit and Ted had already received Archie's one-sentence telegram: "The old lion is dead." They sat up all night on the German frontier after it had come, just the two of them, talking about the remarkable life he had led and the remarkable life he had given them. "The bottom has dropped out for me," Kermit later wrote to his mother, but added that he wasn't worried because he was sure that it wouldn't be long before "we are all joined together on the other side of the great adventure, and Quentin will be waiting over there with his usual smile."

Corinne came out to be with Edith the morning after Theodore's death. The two women, whose friendship went back half a century to a time when they were both under the spell of the charismatic little boy Teedie with his complicated games and fervid dreams, walked the frozen grounds of Sagamore in silence. They went down to the shore of Oyster Bay, then returned through the little forest, passing by the pet cemetery where all the family animals including Little Texas, the horse that TR rode to glory at San Juan Hill, were buried. At sunset they heard the sounds of airplanes and went out on the piazza to look up at the sky. Circling up above was a squadron of planes that passed overhead and began to drop laurel wreaths. Looking up, Edith said, "They must be planes from the camp where Quentin trained. They have been sent as an honor guard for his father."

People like William Allen White reported simply being stunned by news of Theodore Roosevelt's passing, feeling as if one of the forces of the universe had suddenly stopped operating. Vice President Thomas Marshall, perhaps trying to make amends for the parsimony of Woodrow Wilson's response, had this comment for the newspapers: "Death had to take him sleeping, for if Roosevelt had been awake there would have been a fight."

But of all the hundreds of thousands of words of praise and tribute heaped upon his memory, the ones TR probably would have liked best were in the announcement of his death sent out by Harvard's Class of 1880. They were the words spoken by Valiant-for-Truth in *Pilgrim's Progress:* "I am going to my Father's and though with great difficulty I have got hither, yet now I do not regret me of all the trouble I have been at to arrive where I am. My sword I give to him that shall succeed me in my pilgrimages and my courage and skill to him that can get it. My marks and scars I carry with me, to be a witness that I have fought His battles who will now be my rewarder."

PART FOUR

Nemesis

"There we were—*the* Roosevelts—hubris up to the eyebrows, *beyond* the eyebrows, and who should show up but *Nemesis* in the person of Franklin."

—ALICE ROOSEVELT LONGWORTH

$\mathcal{I}$t was August 10, 1921, and Franklin D. Roosevelt was doing one of the things that he loved best—sailing in the waters off Campobello Island. With the exception perhaps of Hyde Park, this rugged island across from Eastport, Maine, was his favorite spot. He had been coming to the area since 1883 when he was three years old and his father bought a place here. In 1910 his mother had helped him buy his own elaborate "cottage" for his growing family.

Franklin had sent his family here each summer from Washington for the last several years, a safari-like journey that involved a six-hour train trip to Boston and a continuation to Maine on a commuter line on which local Indians would pass through the passenger compartments selling their handicrafts. Arriving in Eastport, Eleanor, the children, and their governesses and nurses took a launch across the bay to the island, preceded by their baggage, forty or fifty trunks that would have been taken from the dock to the house in horse-drawn carts and finally, the last several hundred feet, in wheelbarrows manned by local residents hired to help.

Franklin usually stayed behind until the move was made, working by himself at the assistant secretary of the navy's desk in Washington and then showing up, usually after Eleanor's commands became too importunate to ignore any longer, to become master of revels on the island for a few days before going back to his other life.

But this summer, he was not reluctant to join the family. He genuinely needed the recreation and had been looking forward to the trip. He had been involved in nonstop activity since joining the Wilson administration eight years earlier. His talent for infighting and intrigue had made him enemies. The tensions of the war had taken a personal toll because of his inability to get into uniform at a time when others in the extended Roosevelt family were serving with such distinction. Deep and possibly permanent fault lines had opened up in his marriage. And then there had been the disappointment of an unsuccessful run in 1920 for the vice presidency.

The hectic pace hadn't stopped when FDR reentered private life six months earlier. He had spent the last two weeks in the malarial heat of Washington testifying about a scandal involving an alleged "ring" of homosexuals in the Newport Navy prison that had been simmering since his years as assistant secretary. He had been driven to exhaustion by the effort to combat what he regarded as a smear: that he knew about this immorality and had not only sent tender youths into the prison to entrap the deviants but then covered up the problem by putting the offending seamen on active duty.

But all these cares were left behind once he smelled the mentholated sea breeze of Campobello. His arrival at the island two days earlier, was, as always, an event for the children. They had crowded around him competing for his attention as if he was a god fallen from the sky. And in truth this is what he seemed. Tall and lean, with a springy step, he had retained his youth, although he was almost forty years old, and still had the looks that led one society matron to call him, on the occasion of his wedding, "one of the beautiful young men of his time."

After getting to Campobello, Franklin spent some time talking business with his gnarled political strategist Louis Howe, who, much to the family's dismay, had been there waiting for the man he called, with heavy irony, "master." But now, having gotten that out of the way, FDR was on the *Vireo,* slicing through Cobscook Bay. He liked to say that sailing was in his blood, and he would tell the children tales of how the Delanos, corsairs of the China trade, had survived hazardous journeys in their clipper ships. (In the time of the Civil War, his grandfather Warren Delano had once outraced a Confederate man o'war that shadowed him out of port in hopes of boarding and plundering his ship.)

And he tried to teach them all to sail, the one athletic endeavor at which he excelled. On this day he had the two oldest boys, James and Elliott, with him. Windswept and tow-headed, they were part of his brood—"the chicks," as he and Eleanor referred to them in their letters—that clustered around him in the family portraits.

Franklin had a model for his family—the Roosevelts of Sagamore Hill. Just recently TR's *Letters to His Children* had been published by Scribner's. It gave a different view of the man America had known as a soldier, statesman, and writer, by showing him also to have been intensely interested in the minutiae of his children's lives, guiding and advising them and writing them affectionate letters filled with amusing drawings and interesting glimpses of his life. (TR had gone over an early draft of the book shortly before his death and told the editor, "I would rather have this book published than anything that has ever been written about me.") Published as a sort of throwaway, *Letters to His Children* had become a best-seller, causing a new wave of nostalgia for TR as, above all, a family man.

In this, as in other things, Franklin liked to think of himself as being in his illustrious cousin's mold. He sent his own children witty letters and when he was with them he tried to be a palpable presence in their lives. The only problem was that because of his lifelong effort to gain independence first from a domineering mother and then from a wife whose needs were, if anything, even more consuming than his own, he was not there often enough.

He had mistakenly assumed, because he himself was supremely capable of suppressing the subject, that his children would not feel entangled in the dark undergrowth of emotion that characterized his relationship to Eleanor. But it was, of course, the dominating fact of their lives. It was the atmospherics of this perversity, more than their father's accomplishments, that defined them. It was what made the family, in Tolstoy's formulation, unhappy in its own distinctive way.

Fifteen-year-old Anna was a blooming teenager with hair so blonde that she looked Scandinavian and a forehead perpetually creased in a look of incomprehension. She smoldered with resentment and waged a guerrilla struggle with her mother, whose causes were obscure but whose skirmishes involved bitter combat.

James, thirteen, was a thin, nervous, nearsighted child also unstrung by the family situation. His constant childhood illnesses had included a heart murmur that made it necessary for his father and mother to carry him up and down stairs for a year. He had just finished a miserable first term at Groton after arriving at the school so shy and unhappy that he was unable even to ask where the bathrooms were, and, as a consequence, had relieved himself for weeks either in the bushes or in underwear that he quickly buried, finally making himself ill from what school authorities discreetly referred to as a "digestive complaint."

Nine-year-old Elliott was the only one of the children able to manipulate his mother, perhaps because he was in the womb when the first Franklin Jr. died and therefore the recipient of what she feared was bad energy from her own prenatal depression. Like the others, Elliott too had suffered from her neglect. (In one well-remembered incident, she had allowed him to fall into a campfire on the beach at Campobello and hot coals had gotten between his skin and the orthopedic braces she forced him to wear for his "bad bones.") But she seemed to feel a guilt with him that she didn't with the others. His sister and brothers resented Elliott's ability to get attention from Eleanor and also feared his explosive temper. In one of Eleanor's letters to FDR she described how the boy "went for me with both fists" when she tried to discipline his dog and later on she was astonished when he threw a hunting knife at a tutor who had pressed him too hard academically.

There were strong individual differences between the three older children, but they all remembered a distant time, before Lucy Mercer, when the family was still able to pretend that it was normal. The two younger boys had escaped the vicious governesses who had tormented the first three, but they had also missed the good times that preceded the fall. Exposed only to the denial and the long silences, they were growing up virtually without control. Franklin Jr., seven, was the madcap of the family, creating chaos wherever he went, usually with the Swiss governess in his wake shouting "Fraunklaine! Fraunklaine!" Five-year-old Johnny was given to bad language and tantrums and fought constantly with the others.

The children did not yet think of themselves as abnormal. A half century later, however, at the end of a long life marked by retroactive coping, James would say that they were all "accidents waiting to happen."

After the death of her Grandmother Hall, who had devoted her life to Eleanor as well as her own grown children, Eleanor made a point of saying that she would never "allow all [my] interests to center on [my] children." While they were young they sometimes felt that she did not love them. But as they grew older they realized that the problem was more subtle and intractable. Actually, she did love them but was unable to accept emotion in return because she felt so unworthy. As Jimmy said later on, "Mother did not know how to let her children love her."

They listened to her high-pitched voice for meanings in the tremulous rhythms that were not conveyed by the words themselves. Their father was more responsive. (Anna said later on that while Eleanor was unpredictable—sweet one moment and coldly withdrawn the next—FDR at least allowed them to count on "a consistency of affection.") They looked forward to little things like his good nights when he asked them if they were "snug as a bug in a rug." But they knew he was too committed to smooth sailing, at home in domestic affairs as much as on the bay.

He was Pa-*pa,* accent on the second syllable, not much help in adversity but the best companion in good times. A little like an indulgent uncle, he allowed his "chicks" to troop into his bedroom, play with the knickknacks on his dresser, and get under the covers with him. (None of the children recalled ever having been asked into their mother's bedroom.) Yet he was someone whose deepest wish was to avoid conflict—not only with their mother and his own, but with them too. Called upon by Eleanor once to punish Elliott, for example, FDR took him in his study, talked to him for a few minutes, and said, "Well, now I think it's time for you to let out a yell, and then she'll think I've hit you." When told to spank James, who had stolen ten dollars from his wallet, he instead took the boy aside and said that if such a thing ever happened again, "I shall have no choice and I shall not hesitate, though I would regret it, but to call the police. . . ."

He was a blithe spirit and a figure of tremendous power, yet paradoxically unable to protect them—not from the tyrannical nannies, not from their mother's painful deficits, and not from his own relentless desire to pretend everything was fine, his way of conserving the core of privacy he had won with such difficulty. As in so many other things, he had ceded control of his family to Sara, who was quite willing to treat her grandchildren as her own. She too was eccentric, demanding for instance that the boys all sleep in oversize beds (not because they were tall for their age, which they all were, but because she believed that normal beds stunted their growth) and insisting that they master Victorian etiquette. The children knew that Sara made their mother miserable. ("We recognized the hostilities existing among the grown ups," Elliott later said, "and exploited the Cold War to the hilt.") Yet in the maelstrom of family life, "Granny," who smothered them in her capacious bosom and spoiled them with her handouts, was, for all her flaws, the one predictable person in their lives. Her grandson Jimmy had no hesitancy about drawing the bottom line: "We were fortunate to have a grandmother who would do for us when we had a mother who could not and a father who would not."

All these ambiguities would surface later on in an interminable ongoing public recrimination that frayed beyond repair the already unraveling family ties of the Hyde Park Roosevelts. But on this splendid August morning in 1921, they were having one of those privileged moments of togetherness the children regarded as precious, "a gift of the gods" that pushed the demoralizing aspects of their lives aside for a time. As the *Vireo* darted lightly through the rocky islands surrounding Campobello, the boys, novice sailors themselves, marveled at their father's sailing skill, so effortless that it was easy to miss how capable he was.

At one point early in the afternoon, they saw smoke rising off one of the tiny islands dotting the bay and he brought the boat in close so that they could all get out and beat the fire out with pine boughs. Then they splashed back into the *Vireo* and headed for home.

The previous day FDR, intent on cramming as much activity as possible into the vacation, had accidentally slipped overboard while on a fishing trip with the new business associates of his post-Washington life and come up spluttering about how the freezing water had "paralyzed" him. He still felt an ache in his muscles and joints all morning. Yet when he docked the sailboat back at Campobello he insisted on going another round in the strenuous life his famous cousin made into a Roosevelt ritual and asked all the children if they wanted to swim in the warm freshwater pond on the other side of the island. When they said they did, he led them on a two-mile run there and back.

By the time they all returned to the cottage he was so tired he could only sit listlessly in his wet bathing suit shuffling papers. Feeling himself sinking into a fever, he dragged himself up to bed just before dinner and lay shivering under heavy covers.

The next morning, waking with an ache running the length of his spinal column, Franklin got out of bed and headed to the bathroom. His left leg crumpled. He got himself back into bed and Eleanor came in to find that his temperature was spiked at 103. After a while he tried to get up again. But now his legs wouldn't work at all. The old country doctor from the mainland Louis Howe summoned conducted a quick examination and said that it was only a bad cold.

By the next morning Franklin couldn't sit up. "I don't know what's the matter with me, Louis," he kept saying to Howe. "I just don't know." It took two days for the doctor Howe found at Bar Harbor to make his way to Campobello. When he arrived, Franklin was unable to move below the waist and unable to empty his bowels and bladder. Instructing Eleanor in the use of catheter and the administration of enemas, this new doctor said the problem was a spinal lesion whose effects would gradually diminish. But the fever continued to rage, at times driving him into delirium, and his body ached so painfully that he cried out when Howe and Eleanor took turns administering the deep massage that had been prescribed for him.

As the days passed, a hush settled down over the house that the children associated with death. Their father's health was not improving. Finally, two weeks after the initial symptoms, Dr. Robert Lovett, chief surgeon at Harvard, arrived for a consultation. After a brief examination that showed weakness of many muscle groups including the patient's arms and even his face, not to speak of the nearly destroyed muscles of the immobile legs, Lovett finally made the firm diagnosis everyone was dreading. Franklin Roosevelt had polio. As he was told what he faced, Eleanor saw a look cross her husband's face that she had never seen before and would not see again for another twenty years, when news arrived one Sunday morning that Pearl Harbor had been bombed.

The illness came at a moment when FDR was facing a transition he was not sure he could accomplish. His mother had been the great problem of the first part of his life. His wife had been the problem of his recent years. He and Eleanor strained against each other, opposites struggling against the magnetic force that locked them together. The lack of resolution in their situation, close friends believed, contributed to the impression FDR sometimes gave of being superficial and unfinished; a tentative man, for all his accomplishments and personal growth, a man unlikely to reach his high goals.

In the aftermath of the Lucy Mercer affair, Eleanor had become possessive, calling him at all hours and dropping in on him unannounced at his office in the Navy Department. But the breach of faith was too deep to be healed by the reassurance he tried to offer. In the months after she learned of the affair, her face had taken on a ravaged gray look and her weight had dropped so rapidly that she seemed suddenly spectral. She looked like a woman in mourning. Yet even in her pain she knew how to make a point, often going to sit at the quiet spot in Rock Creek Park where Henry Adams had placed a Saint-Gaudens statue of a female figure popularly thought to be modeled on his wife, Clover, after she committed suicide, possibly a result of *his* extramarital affair.

The betrayal was something she had so often imagined in the early years of their marriage that when it finally happened it had the force of a prophecy fulfilled. Eleanor might say that she could forgive if not forget the transgression. But in fact she was able to do neither. As one close friend later said, FDR "had taken from her an ideal and a concept of life together that could never be restored." He had committed a treachery against her and against his godfather, Elliott, that vision of perfection whose reincarnation he was supposed to be.

She had tried to be gay and accompany him on his social rounds in the winter of 1919, but her suffering and the restrained fury she could not acknowledge were too powerful for her to withstand. The result had been a descent into self-pity and alienation. In one famous incident gleefully recounted by Alice Longworth, Eleanor accompanied Franklin to a party at the Chevy Chase Club but when the women began to swarm around him as always, she left early, saying that she didn't want to diminish his social pleasure. Arriving home and finding that she had forgotten the house key, she lay down on the doormat. When Franklin arrived hours later, he found her there shivering melodramatically. He asked why she hadn't rung the bell or gone to one of their neighbors' homes, she shot him an accusatory reply, "I've been taught never to bother people if you can possibly avoid it."

Her two aunts, Bamie and Conie, were exemplars of graceful suffering, and Eleanor picked up her correspondence with both of them in the middle of her agony. Bamie's suffering was physical. Conie's was not only physical (her childhood asthma still afflicted her) but emotional as well, since she had lost one son, Stewart, in a freak accident at college, and seen another, Monroe, become an alcoholic. Eleanor wrote her: "I can never tell you what admiration I have for you and all you have been through and are bearing every day with such wonderful courage and forgetfulness of self." That was what she wanted to do: forget the gluttonous demands of self. But it was impossible. The image of Franklin's sin was too vivid. Sex was animality that entered the spiritual realm and trampled true love.

Eleanor agreed to accompany him when he returned to Europe early in 1919 to help prepare for the peace conference. She was appalled at the license she saw in the war-torn countries of France and Germany and wrote home to Sara, "Just wait till I get home and tell you what these respectable people . . . let their daughters do. Your hair will curl as mine did!" Depravity had been loosed on the world.

Over the next few months she and Franklin gradually arrived at what one son later called their "armed truce." The terms were never announced but both parties knew their roles: she to suffer in silence and he to pretend that everything was all right. The surreal quality this compromise injected into their lives found an objective correlative in an event in June 1919. James, then eleven, was with them in Washington studying for an exam, while the other children were with Sara in Hyde Park. A bomb exploded at the home of Attorney General A. Mitchell Palmer across the street. Franklin and Eleanor, returning from a social engagement a few minutes afterward, saw the blown-out windows in their own house. Franklin rushed upstairs to find the boy standing stunned in his bedroom but otherwise all right and gave him a "rib-crushing" hug. Eleanor walked in a few moments later and casually asked, as if nothing exceptional had happened, "Whatever are you doing out of bed at this hour, James?"

The next morning, the boy, rummaging in the debris outside the house, found an unusual object and brought it in for his father to see. Eating breakfast, Franklin paled when he saw what James had put on the tablecloth. It was a piece of the collarbone of the anarchist who had set the bomb and was blown up in the explosion.

They no longer had a common language of the heart. (Their son Elliott said later on that his father "very much needed the husband-wife relationship to exist again, but my mother could never bring herself.") It was politics, not love and forgiveness, that helped them learn to speak to each other again.

Franklin had gone to the 1920 Democratic convention as part of the New York delegation pledged to favorite son Al Smith. After the delegates deadlocked between McAdoo and Attorney General Mitchell Palmer, Ohio Governor James Cox was chosen as a compromise. Anxious to retain Wilson loyalists and also to lure progressive Republicans attracted by the Roosevelt name, Cox selected FDR as his running mate. This delighted Franklin, who pointed out that he was only thirty-eight and that TR had been forty-one when he was nominated as vice president.

At first Eleanor was filled with dread. As the Democrats began their national publicity, Howe wired for a photo and she wired back, "Are no pictures of me." She agreed to present a united front by accompanying Franklin on the campaign train, but she was miserable there too, powerless to keep herself from censuring her husband's behavior or from nagging him. (When he retired to a club car to have a drink and play poker with the campaign workers after a day's campaigning, she criticized him, but then said unconvincingly that she was concerned only for the black porters inconvenienced by the lateness of the card game.)

As Franklin's gray eminence, Louis Howe saw that Eleanor was a time bomb ticking inside his patron's career and would detonate sooner or later if something was not done. She had always disliked the misshapen little man who hung around her husband like his trained monkey, and agreed with her mother-in-law that he was "repulsive." But Howe, whose loyalty to FDR was such that he had forsaken his own career in journalism and neglected his family to be with him, now began to court her, spending time with her on the train, showing her drafts of speeches and asking her advice.

What began as an effort to neutralize her and keep her out of Franklin's hair soon became something else. Howe was one of the first political strategists to see the potential in the women's vote. (TR's sister Corinne had already become the first woman to appear at a Republican convention when she seconded the nomination of General Leonard Wood for President during the Republicans' 1920 meeting.) Quite sincerely, he praised Eleanor's political intuitions and noted how much those "clever grey eyes" remarked on by newspaper heiress Cissy Patterson and others managed to pick up. He saw that she had a deep desire—almost as deep as the need to be loved—to be taken seriously. He began to give her an ongoing seminar on politics as the Democrats' 1920 campaign train ran through the heartland of America. As Eleanor later said of Howe's attention: "I was flattered and before long found myself discussing a wide range of subjects."

Soon there were the beginnings of a conspiracy between this odd couple. Howe knew about the emotional bruises the Lucy Mercer affair had inflicted on her and used his rough newsman's humor to help Eleanor become amused rather than threatened by the women that now thronged around her husband. Each saw in the other a fellow outsider. The two of them made light of their physical limitations, engaging in a contest to see who looked uglier in the pictures that appeared in newspapers.

If one of the shadows that hung over FDR in the 1920 campaign was that of Eleanor, the other was Theodore Roosevelt's. In death TR had acquired a cult following. On the anniversary of his death, for instance, there was a pilgrimage to his grave site by friends and admirers who came to Oyster Bay from all over the country by train, the beginning of an annual event whose conclusion would always be marked by a return to Sagamore Hill, where Edith would serve refreshments and lead the talk about her husband's thoughts and deeds.

In his own way Franklin too was a member of the TR club, having joined as a boy and never let his membership lapse. As he entered the national limelight after the vice presidential nomination, the press noted the similarities with his hero that he had cultivated. ("Peculiar coincidences," in the words of the influential *Literary Digest,* which noted that both men had gone to Harvard, started politics in the New York state legislature, and been assistant secretary of the navy when their country was at war.) The similarity in résumés seemed like a prophecy of even greater things to come for Franklin. One newsman wrote him, "You are the political and spiritual heir of Theodore Roosevelt. . . . [TR] was an essential and fundamental democrat, exponent of liberalism and progressivism, and the Democratic Party inspired by Wilson now stands for everything the great Roosevelt represented."

Franklin moved to seize the TR heritage during the campaign, calling himself a "a progressive Democrat" (with the accent on *progressive*) as he whistle-stopped through the Western states, proven Roosevelt country, and hit the Republican nominee by saying that he couldn't help believing that TR, who had "invented the word pussy-footer would not have resisted the temptation to apply it to Mr. Harding."

It worked. Soon people at his stops were shouting out at him, "You're just like the old man!" and "I voted for your father!"

The Oyster Bay clan, seeing this as imposture rather than homage, rushed into the fray. TR had held the tensions between the two branches of the family in check during the war, although his sons had scorned FDR first for slacking and then for playacting at war when he did come to Europe on his inspection tour. But now TR was gone and the decorous solicitude he insisted on in interfamily matters was breaking down. Buried grievances were dug up again. The family had not forgotten, for instance, that in 1912, when Corinne Robinson's son Theodore and her son-in-law, Joseph Alsop, elected to the state legislature at the same time as Franklin, had thrown away equally promising careers to stand with TR at Armageddon, FDR had stayed safely in the Democratic Party and been reelected in a race where his Progressive and Republican opponents together got more votes than he did.

Until now, the Oyster Bay Roosevelts had taken out their irredentist fury on Woodrow Wilson. Alice Longworth had led this charge. After the President returned from Versailles, she drove by the White House intoning a curse ("a murrain on him, a murrain on him, a murrain on him . . ."). She had been with TR before his death when he denounced the proposed League of Nations because he didn't want the United States to have to depend on the trustworthiness of countries like Germany and the Soviet Union. (League opponent Henry Cabot Lodge got her to write an affidavit stating that this was the case.)

In the summer of 1919 she had made defeat of the League a holy cause. Sitting in the Senate gallery every day during the debate on the League, she was nicknamed "the Colonel" and her followers "the Battalion of Death." She celebrated each parliamentary victory over Wilson's proposals by having scrambled eggs with "irreconcilable" Senators Lodge, Harding, and William Borah. When the Senate Foreign Relations Committee issued a report on the League containing its reservations and amendments, she made it a point to be in New York watching members of the 1st Division—including all three of her brothers—march up Fifth Avenue behind General Pershing.

It was not just meanness. Alice believed that Woodrow Wilson's snubs had hastened her father's death. When Wilson had suffered his stroke in 1919, she exulted in a letter to Bamie, "Think of this week— the Peace Treaty debate, the illness of that sissie in the White House . . . yet Father in everyone's mind, his name on their lips, his memory in their hearts."

The Roosevelt legacy: that was uppermost in the minds of her brothers as well as Alice herself. And it was clear to them who should lead the family and come forth as the next Roosevelt. It was not Franklin, an outsider and a Wilson man. It was Ted. Archie had made that clear scarcely a week after TR's death when his brothers were still in Europe waiting to be mustered out of the army. "I am very anxious that Ted get started soon," he wrote Kermit, "and that he get the current that will allow him to catch father's thought. Neither you nor I possess his ability or his means to forge ahead in [this] time. . . ."

Ted returned to the United States later in the spring of 1919, after staying for several weeks in Paris where he, Colonel Bill Donovan, and twenty other officers had held a series of discussions regarding demobilization and the role of servicemen at home that led to the founding of the American Legion. Back home, Ted made his own political ambitions clear by staging his first public appearance before the Republican committee of his home district. Standing in front of a large crowd with hands on hips, pelvis thrust forward, and teeth bared in a reminiscence of the familiar grin, he announced, "It's bully to be home again!"

For TR loyalists Ted was not just a simulacrum like FDR, but the real article. There was immediately talk among party pros of running him for governor of New York. But Ted realized that he should start at a lower level and announced for the State Assembly from Nassau County. His right to the privileges of primogeniture within the Oyster Bay clan was reinforced by something that happened on the day of his election. His own wife, Eleanor, Archie's Grace, and Kermit's Belle had all been pregnant as the war ended and although never mentioned, it was understood that they were in competition to have the next male child in the family and thus the right to use the name of the fallen Quentin. When Grace had a girl early in July, this took her out of the running. Belle was due in November and Eleanor several weeks later, but by what Ted called "an act of will" his wife went into labor and had a boy on November 9, the same day he was elected to the New York State Assembly by the largest majority in the history of the district. It seemed like an omen. Edith gave the new baby Quentin the christening clothes TR had worn over sixty years earlier.

Just after FDR won the Democrats' vice presidential nomination, Ted came to the Republican convention a major figure. Although he only had a year's experience in the state legislature, his name gave him tremendous weight in the party. Along with the rest of his family he was behind the presidential candidacy of General Leonard Wood, TR's old friend and commanding officer in the Spanish American war. But Alice, best politician among them, did a nose count of delegates and decided Wood probably could not win. When Ohio Senator Warren Harding was finally chosen as a compromise candidate, the party bosses called her and asked how the Roosevelts had taken it. Alice's own opinion of Harding was unequivocal: "To call him second rate would be to pay him a compliment." But she made her peace and offered him the support of the "Roosevelt party" on the condition that he support Ted for the governorship of New York in 1924.

Alice and Ted agreed that their chief objective in 1920 was not only getting a Republican elected, but also defeating Franklin, who seemed to be purposefully creating confusion about who was the real Roosevelt heir in his vice presidential run. (Eleanor was aware enough of their feelings to write a letter to her Aunt Corinne: "I do see how annoying it must be to have people saying and thinking Franklin is a near relation of Uncle Ted's and I do hope they realize we personally never sail under false colors.") As Harding began his campaign, Ted volunteered to shadow Franklin for the Republicans and counter the growing impression, in the words of the *New York Times*, that "the Democratic Roosevelt is really the son of the late Col. Roosevelt."

Things immediately got rough on the campaign trail. Ted obviously had his cousin in mind when he said at one stop, "There was not a male representative of the national Democratic administration . . . during the war [who was] within range of a gun fired by the enemy." A few days later he struck out at Wilson and FDR together when he compared them sarcastically to his father. A woman in the audience yelled, "Hit them again, Teddy." Ted smiled at her from the rostrum and yelled back, "I like to hit them when they deserve it!"

Surviving a series of near accidents in the airplanes ferrying him to his campaign stops seemed to be proof of Ted's Rooseveltian manliness. In Joplin, Missouri, the pilot left the plane while it was warming up and it suddenly began to taxi by itself, forcing Ted to jump off a wing just before it struck a tree. In Tulsa a sudden lightning storm made the engine go dead twice before the pilot managed a precarious landing. Arriving in Wyoming Ted finally addressed the issue of his cousin's imposture head-on in a speech to a troop of Rough Riders in Sheridan. "He is a maverick," Ted said of FDR. "He does not have the brand of our family." Soon the *Chicago Tribune* was echoing Ted's charge by calling FDR "the one half of one percent Roosevelt."

Franklin tried to fight back. He pointed out that in 1912 the Republican nominee, Harding, one of the leaders of the Republican Old Guard, had compared TR to Benedict Arnold and then to Aaron Burr. "At least some members of the Roosevelt family will not forget," he said pointedly. But his counterpunching was inept and as Ted's attacks on the Democratic ticket began to have an impact, presidential candidate James Cox was forced to jump in: "It is a pitiable spectacle to see this son of a great sire shamelessly paraded before the public. Out of respect for the memory of his illustrious father someone ought to take this juvenile spokesman aside and in primer fashion make plain what really ought to be obvious."

A subtext in the developing competition between the cousins was the question of which had the virility expected of a Roosevelt. At the Republicans' New York State convention, a pair of Brooklyn delegates struggling for a standard accidentally fell against a woman from Nassau County and Ted immediately knocked both men down, saying later that he was protecting the honor of the woman as well as that of his home district. In reporting the event, journalists also noted that FDR had figured in a similar fracas at the Democrats' national convention in San Francisco, where Tammany bitter-enders had tried to keep the New York standard from joining Woodrow Wilson's victory demonstration, and FDR had made a foray into their midst and grabbed it for his party's nominee.

As the campaign got dirty during its last days, the Republicans, looking to counter Democratic-inspired rumors that the dark-complected Harding was a mulatto, revived the story that while he was assistant secretary of the navy, FDR had returned a navy man sentenced to ten years for committing sodomy in the navy's Newport prison to active duty. The account was now expanded to allege that Franklin had sent undercover "fairy chasers" into the prison to identify suspected homosexuals and these agents had themselves turned to vice.

To the degree that these innuendoes about FDR worked, it was because he was so attractive. (Traveling on the Democratic candidates' train, Eleanor watched from the shadows and criticized the "lovely ladies who served luncheon for my husband and worshipped at his shrine.") The vanity that gave him energy and charm also retarded the development of a countervailing sense of gravity, and as the campaign ground to an end, TR's old friend Henry Cabot Lodge pronounced what he obviously believed was a postmortem on FDR: "He is a well meaning, nice young fellow but light. . . . His head is obviously turned and the effect upon a not very strong man is obvious."

The result of the 1920 election was never really in doubt. The Republicans swamped the Democrats, and in the emerging contest between the Roosevelt cousins to see which of them could bottle the lightning in the name, Ted had clearly won round one.

As always when he suffered rejection, Franklin hid his hurt. He pretended to have been "delighted" by the campaign and said that it was a good thing Harding had won by a huge margin because now the Republicans would be solely responsible for what came next. He left Washington and returned to his old law firm in New York, and also agreed to work as vice president in charge of the New York office of Fidelity and Deposit, a large bonding company whose executives felt that his contacts in the world of politics and government would be useful. He was making $25,000 a year and thus financially self-sufficient for the first time in his life. His refusal to knuckle under to the Oyster Bay clan was shown in the spring of 1921 when he attended the wedding of

Bamie's son, Sheffield Cowles, Jr. Rather than deferring to Ted and his other cousins by staying in the background, as he had previously done in these large family affairs, FDR was in "uproarious" high spirits, making himself the center of attention and drinking enough to cause the women in the family to talk about his behavior in the flurry of letters that followed such events.

While the competition with Ted to see who would inherit the Roosevelt mantle might have been a burning issue for Franklin before August 10, 1921, it became irrelevant as he lay in bed at Campobello, his body wracked by pain and paralysis. Dr. Lovett held out just enough hope of recovery to keep him going in the first weeks of the illness.

Eleanor, for whom intimate touch with Franklin was only a memory, ministered to his most intimate needs. Howe was at her side. Because of Franklin's return to private life after the 1920 campaign, apparently for an indefinite period of time, Howe had been about to take a job with an oil company when the polio struck. But when Eleanor asked him about it now, he replied, "This is my job—helping Franklin." He was tough in speech and demeanor—still calling Franklin "you dumb Dutchman!" in moments of frustration—but sympathetic to suffering, having lost his own first child to meningitis and having once been told by doctors that because of his multiple disabilities he had only months to live.

In the first days of his illness FDR went along with all the false optimism and encouragement, but as he later told his future Secretary of Labor, Frances Perkins, in one of his rare discussions of the illness, he had spent his time staring at the flowered wallpaper, trying to lose himself in the leaves and petals. He worried that God had abandoned him, but then, as he worked through the first, worst hours of his dark night of the soul, he began to feel that this was perhaps God's way of chastening him and preparing him for some great task that had not yet come into view.

This was before the firm diagnosis of polio had been made. Now the hardest job Eleanor and Howe had was reassuring Franklin about the future and convincing him that he could be useful and not simply warehoused in one of the shadowy back bedrooms where most polio victims of the day lived the remnants of their lives as freaks and dependents.

He kept waiting for his condition to stabilize, but instead it continued to degenerate. Within two weeks his muscles had begun to atrophy; not only were his legs dead, but there was no movement below his waist. Once or twice he almost abandoned himself to despair, but each time he seemed to catch himself, saved by that determination not to let others see his true feelings that had always been the hallmark of his personality. (Yet his children certainly saw his state. "I'll never forget the terror I felt," Elliott later said. "I fully expected Father to die at any moment. He was so still—so very still—and it seemed that my world was coming to an end.")

By the time his mother returned from her summer holiday in France two weeks after his illness had been diagnosed, Franklin had mobilized his resistance well enough to put on the same debonair facade that he had used in letters sent to her all during his growing up when he was suffering rejection by the top social clubs and failing in sports and friendship. The decision not to wire Sara in advance about the illness had been made in concert with his half brother, Rosy, who agreed that she would "have forty thousand fits" on the return passage home from her trip. But now, as Sara hurried to Campobello she found him sitting up in bed "brave, smiling and beautiful." Before she could break down, he said brightly, "Well, I'm glad you are back, Mummy . . ." and made her tell him about her tour of the Loire Valley.

Sara was pained when she saw that her boy's legs, one of his features in which she had always taken particular pride, now had to be moved by others periodically because they ached if left too long in one position. But she too became caught up in the élan spreading outward from the sickbed and she wrote to an acquaintance after her first day home, "The atmosphere of the house is all happiness."

Trying to find some compensation in the disaster that had befallen Franklin, Sara fantasized about how her son would now have no choice but to come home and pick up his father's role as Squire of Hyde Park, the role she had always wanted him to play. Knowing what she was thinking made Franklin all the more desperate to get back to New York and to the promise of an independent life. Louis Howe arranged for him to enter the Presbyterian Hospital there, and on September 13, a month after he felt the first premonitions of sickness, FDR allowed himself to be strapped into a stretcher that six local man maneuvered down the Campobello cottage's narrow stairways at a precarious tilt.

With his hat balanced on the left hand that he still could not move, he was carried past his children, who had been kept at a distance from him for the last few weeks because of fear of infection. The sight of him would stay with them forever: the little Scottie dog riding on his chest; his jaws clamping at a jaunty angle the cigarette holder Howe had given him; a clenched smile on his face that could just as easily have been a grimace of pain. And then he gasped a cheery farewell—"I'll be seeing you chicks soon!"

Over the next months, Franklin's condition fluctuated. Sometimes the high fever would inexplicably return. The weakness in his arms and hands and upper body came and went, and his facial muscles would sometimes inexplicably go slack. His legs seemed to be wasting before his eyes, becoming ridges of bone with flesh hanging from them. Occasionally observers would catch him concentrating on his legs so hard that he broke into a sweat as he tried by sheer will power to make them move. His daughter, Anna, happened to be in his room on one occasion when she heard him squeal with delight after managing to elicit a muscle twitch.

Gradually he recovered some sense of control and after he had been released from the hospital to his mother's 65th Street house, took heart in little things—his developing ability to sit up, the fact that his feet felt warmer. He believed that he had entered that second stage of the disease when doctors told him there might be some improvement before his condition was deemed stationary.

Franklin was convinced that the disability that was afflicting his body was not *him*. It was something external, to be struggled against. He regarded the polio with that patrician hauteur some of his schoolmates had seen in his days at Groton, when he sometimes threw back his head and stared down his nose at them. He now said over and over again that he refused to be felled by "a *childish* disease." He had a trapeze installed above his bed. After several days of trying he managed finally to grasp it with one hand. Then he began to work almost demonically on the apparatus. Someone intimate with the saga of the Roosevelt family might have compared this activity with TR as a teenager when he worked at the home gymnasium to *make* a body to replace the one that had betrayed him.

The stakes could not have been higher. He knew that it was not just his public life that was in the balance, but his inner life as well. The polio threatened to bring back the dependency he had fought against all his life—on the wife who was compassionate out of duty; and on the mother who was a tyrant of love. He knew that even as he was trying to recover, Sara was having wheelchair ramps installed throughout Springwood.

As he fought against the diminished future that seemed to stretch out before him, he began to show a resilience and determination others hadn't even suspected he possessed. Early in his treatment an admiring doctor said something that must have heartened him: even if he had been the *son* of Theodore Roosevelt, Franklin could not have been more like him in the courageous way he had fought the disease.

His efforts to recover made him more selfish, but paradoxically also more aware of the needs of others. This was especially clear where the children were involved. Anna said later on that she was initially uncomfortable around him, "but gradually his gaiety and his ability to poke fun at himself" broke down the barriers. He brought the youngest boys, Elliott, Franklin Jr., and John, into bed with him to demystify his dead legs. When his troubled son James came home from Groton for Christmas and saw his father for the first time in over four months, FDR watched him for a moment standing at the doorway to the bedroom with a quivering lower lip and then said, "Come here, old man!" After tousling the boy's hair roughly, he engaged him in an eager conversation about the doings of Endicott Peabody, his own old headmaster, and other prep school matters. As if to indicate that whatever else might happen, there was still a continuity in the family, he gave his eldest son the tailored tweed suit his father had bought in Scotland in 1878 that he himself had worn since inheriting it.

In the days ahead, FDR would reassure James and the other boys about his physical durability by getting down on the floor and Indian wrestling with them so that they could feel the growing strength of his upper body. Yet what had happened to him was a blow that they too never got over. Many years later, when James was watching his father help decorate the lower branches of the Christmas tree from his wheelchair, he suddenly remembered an earlier time when FDR had been the life of the party, hopping around Christmas trees past and putting ornaments on the top branches. The physical sensation that came over him as a result of this memory was like "a blow in the stomach."

As much as FDR tried to convince them that everything was the same as it had always been, there was no denying that there had been a fundamental change. As James later said, "This was the time of the second father, the father with the dead legs." As if to mark the appearance of a new persona, there was also a subtle name change. No longer was he Pa-*pa*. Now he was plain Pa, the name, like the body, cut in half.

Before he was an Olympian figure whose lean physique the famous football coach Walter Camp had once praised; now he was humbled in a wheelchair.

His early efforts at rehabilitation were part of a primal drama at which the children were spectators, filled with pity and fear. Fire was one of FDR's phobias, perhaps because of the story he remembered from his boyhood about one of his mother's sisters, who had caught fire when alcohol had spilled on an iron she was holding and had run through Algonac, the Delano estate, in flames before collapsing charred and dying on the front yard. As FDR got down on his hands and knees and practiced the slither in which his increasingly powerful arms and shoulders pulled his dead nether parts along, he told his children, "If I ever get caught in a fire, I might be able to save myself by crawling."

In one sense, the illness was a godsend for the children, providing an explanation for what before had been inexplicable—the lack of intimacy between their parents, the fact that outsiders like Louis Howe were part of the daily life of the family. But it also increased tensions. Not only did Eleanor get ready to pack sixteen-year-old Anna off to Miss Chapin's School against her wishes, for instance, but added to the feeling of displacement by installing Howe in the girl's room. Already deeply ambivalent toward her mother, Anna went to her grandmother for comfort and of course Sara was only too pleased to egg her on. This led to shouting matches that ended with Anna slamming out of the room and maintaining a sullen silence toward her mother for months.

The children all resented the intrusive Howe. He was both the court dwarf and a Luciferian presence in the household—sitting at the breakfast table drinking black coffee and wreathed in the smoke from chain-smoked cigarettes whose ashes spilled down onto his vest and pants legs. There was always a look of sharp preoccupation on his pitted face as he scanned the daily newspapers for tidbits to feed FDR and keep him interested in politics. The boys played rough practical jokes on him that were meant to remind him he was an interloper. Others in the family were perplexed by his growing indispensability as well. Conie's daughter, Corinne Alsop, came away from a visit to the 65th Street house asking her mother, "Who is this little man who controls the whole of the Roosevelt family?"

Having changed over the years from a journalist to a personal assistant, Howe had come to believe that his own future was dependent on FDR's. Yet apart from self-interest, he was also a believer in Thomas Carlyle's theories about Great Men in History and felt that he had seen latent greatness in FDR, particularly in his theatricality and his ability to dramatize himself before an audience. Before the polio, perhaps, he had seen Franklin as a figure he intended to manipulate. But now, if he was a Rasputin, he was moved by pity rather than power. Visiting his own family only on weekends, Howe kept things going for Franklin, working as physical therapist, letter writer, and jester; trying to make FDR believe that he had something to live for, urging him forward and acting as his prosthetic device in New York politics. The harder he worked, the more he believed in what he was doing. Early in Franklin's convalescence, when the exhausted Eleanor asked Howe incredulously if he really believed that her husband had a political future, he fixed her with his glittering eyes and said, "I believe that some day Franklin will be President."

Eleanor had no choice but to believe him. Almost as much as Franklin, she needed a hope to cling to. In the crowded house that now combined the features both of a rehabilitation ward and political headquarters, she, like her daughter, Anna, was a displaced person, sleeping on a spare bed in the room Franklin Jr. and John shared. Initially galvanized by the prospect of self-sacrifice, she was eventually worn down by endless days spent exercising her husband's withering lower body. The tantalizing prospect of selfhood she'd seen during the vice presidential campaign, when she was out in the world doing something, now seemed like an illusion.

One afternoon in the spring of 1922, she was sitting on the floor with the two little boys, reading them a story, when she suddenly began to sob uncontrollably. The spectacle startled Franklin Jr. and John. At about the time they were creeping off to their room, Elliott came home from school, stumbled into his mother's pain, and made a quick exit, not realizing until later in life that he had seen her "at the nadir of her existence."

Unable to stop crying on this afternoon, Eleanor went to Sara's adjoining house to cry in privacy. The tears had to do with her past as well as her future, the years of being Elliott's tragic daughter and Franklin's betrayed wife. Finally she stopped crying, put a cold cloth on her face and looked at herself in the mirror with a sense of wonder. She had just experienced something unique: loss of control.

Once again Louis Howe came to her rescue. A kindred spirit, he seemed to understand that Eleanor, like Franklin, stood between two selves, the old one dead and the new one struggling to be born. At a more pragmatic level, he realized too that now, more than ever, she was pivotal to her husband's destiny. During the vice presidential run he had begun by trying to keep her from damaging Franklin's prospects. But he had seen that she could be an asset and had encouraged her to stay active in organizations like the League of Women Voters. Now he began to try to convince her to overcome her remaining reticence and get involved as a political operative in the women's organizations springing up around the Democratic Party. In them, as Howe made her understand, she could make a serious bid for power on her own at the same time that she was serving as a stand-in for her husband.

Over the next year, Howe became a Pygmalion sculpting Eleanor's public image. He tutored her in public speaking, bringing her high-pitched voice down a notch and forcing her to control the giggle of anxiety that appeared without warning. ("Nothing to laugh at!" he would admonish her. "Stop that!") He showed her how to keep an audience from knowing how nervous she was by gripping the rostrum with her shaking hands rather than the pages of her speech. Accompanying her to public appearances, he sometimes sat in the back of the hall coaching her with hand signals. He was a demanding mentor, but there was a tenderness in the relationship too. Once Anna walked unexpectedly into the parlor and saw her mother curled up at Howe's feet, in a languid trance as the gnomish figure sensuously brushed her hair. Eleanor later said, "He probably cared for me as a person as much as he ever cared for anyone & more than anyone else has!"

When once enumerating the unexpected good things about her husband's illness, Eleanor said, "It made me stand on my own two feet." The figure of speech may have been somewhat odd, but there was truth in the sentiment. What was a setback for him had allowed her to step forward.

There were new signs of competence throughout her life. Although she rammed into the brownstone pillars at the entry to Hyde Park and once ran into the back of the house itself, she finally learned how to drive. Because of Franklin's disability someone had to be able to get into the water in case the children got in trouble in the pool and so she made up her mind finally to conquer the fear of water that stretched back to the ocean liner accident of her childhood. She had her mother-in-law's butler suspend her by a rope from a long pole in the pond at Hyde Park and stand there watching her thrash in the water and jerking her up when she went under. The experience offered itself as a metaphor for her new life: at first it was a struggle to keep afloat, but soon she was moving through a foreign element on her own.

One sign of Eleanor's emancipation was her willingness to seize control of her life from her mother-in-law, whose domination she had not only tolerated but invited for so many years. The armistice the two women had declared when they joined forces against Lucy Mercer had long since been called off as Eleanor struggled for greater independence, going so far as to block off the entryway between her place and her mother-in-law's at the 65th Street house with a bulky sofa, thus ending Sara's unwanted intrusions into her privacy.

Another sign of the changes within was her new willingness to forge relationships outside the home. She made friends with women like political activists Esther Lape and Elizabeth Read, whom she met in the League of Women Voters. At first tentative in her overtures, she became emboldened as she struck up successful relationships with women her own age, acknowledging the deep hunger for friendship she had previously suppressed. She spent time with Lape and Read in their Greenwich Village apartment, not only talking politics but reading poetry and talking intimately about her life.

Lape and Read and some of the other women Eleanor met were lesbians for whom politics was both an expression of and an antidote for their status as outsiders. Although repelled by homosexuality (she expressed an almost phobic reaction to the subject when Lape gave her a copy of André Gide's "sensitive" treatment of the subject, *Les Faux-Monnayeurs*), Eleanor was strongly attracted to their strivings for independent lives.*

In 1923, Eleanor's *tour d'horizon* through the women's organizations within and around the Democratic Party brought her in contact with Nancy Cook and Marion Dickerman, a couple who would have a profound impact on her life. Dickerman was a tall woman with an equine

---

* The issue of Eleanor Roosevelt and lesbianism is a vexed one. In the first volume of *Eleanor Roosevelt,* Blanche Wiesen Cook tries to make the case that Eleanor was not only attracted to but sexually involved with lesbian friends. In light of what others close to Eleanor said about the matter, the case Cook makes seems at times overdetermined, filled with special pleading and a kind of genital reductionism. Interviewed for *Eleanor and Franklin,* Esther Lape told Joseph Lash, "She couldn't even bring herself to consider homosexuality. Generally her reaction [to controversial issues] was not so final, but in this case it was." All of her children not only denied that Eleanor had been sexually involved with her female friends but considered the suggestion more laughable than threatening. Elliott, who, along with Jimmy, was certainly not averse to writing something sensational about his mother if he thought it would sell books, said, "Her sensibilities were not tuned to sexual attraction of any kind, whether it existed between a man and a woman or between members of the same sex." Yet who can say for sure?

face whose melancholy features belied her high spirits. She had been getting a degree from Syracuse University when she met fellow suffragette Cook, her opposite in looks—"a short and somewhat toughish bobbed hair person," in the words of one Roosevelt in-law—but otherwise her soul mate for life. Dickerman was voluble and literary; Cook was more pugnacious about politics, but worked with her hands and often was content to let her craftsmanship do her talking for her.

Having met just before World War I, the women were self-defined "idealists" who committed themselves to teaching and women's suffrage and to a life together that they envisioned as a research and demonstration project in women's liberation. Because many of the young men they had taught in public school went into the army, they felt they had to support them and traveled to England to do hospital work and anything else that would advance the war effort. Dickerman offered her ability as an administrator; Cook's woodworking talents got her a job carving artificial limbs.

When the war was over they came home and were about to resume their teaching careers when they became outraged at the decision of Thaddeus Sweet, speaker of the New York State legislature, to kill a minimum wage bill. With Cook serving as her campaign manager, Dickerman decided to run against Sweet, who was then considered a possible future candidate for governor. Picking up endorsements from the Socialist and Prohibition parties, she gave him enough of a scare before finally losing to put an end to his aspirations for higher office.

After this Dickerman took a job in Trenton as assistant dean at the state college there, and Cook went to New York City to organize for the new Women's Division of the Democratic Party, although they still lived together on weekends in Greenwich Village, where they socialized with other lesbian couples like Lape and Read. On a whim, Nancy Cook, who had followed Eleanor's first halting advances into politics in the League of Women Voters, looked up her name in the phone book one day and called to ask if she would like to appear at a fund-raiser. Eleanor said she would. The luncheon was successful, and afterward Eleanor suddenly asked Cook what she did on weekends. Cook told her about her friend Dickerman and said they did "various things" together. Eleanor asked them to visit her at Hyde Park.

They showed up the following weekend and met the family. Sara instinctively liked Dickerman but did not hide the fact that she considered Cook mannish and unpleasant. FDR was also there. Dickerman, who later did an extensive oral history of reminiscences about the

Roosevelts, was surprised by two things when she first met him. First, that while she had been led by press accounts of his illness (for the most part written under the canny influence of Howe) to believe that he was only moderately disabled, she now found that he was almost totally crippled. Secondly, that although his body was profoundly affected by the illness, he had none of the psychology of the sick—no self-pity, no gamesmanship to elicit sympathy—and he made her forget almost immediately that there was anything wrong with him at all.

Dickerman and Cook provided a lifeline for Eleanor. For the first time since she was a teenager in boarding school with Madame Souvestre, she began to feel that she had friends and was part of a community. In the first days of this new relationship, in fact, there was something almost schoolgirlish in her behavior. Bamie, Corinne, and others in the Roosevelt clan were scandalized when Eleanor and Nan Cook showed up together at Oldgate dressed exactly alike in matching tweed knickerbocker outfits including vests and jackets. At one family get-together, Conie's daughter-in-law, Helen Robinson, happened to be staying in a room next to one occupied by Eleanor, Nan, and Marion, and was awakened in the middle of the night by the shrieking laughter of the three women, who were having a wild pillow fight. When Alice Longworth caught wind of Eleanor's new friends she immediately began caustically referring to them as her cousin's "female impersonators."

These relationships Eleanor forged were given intensity by a shared commitment to the new liberalism that was remaking New York's Democratic Party. Dickerman and Cook got Eleanor into the Women's Trade Union League and behind an agenda that included abolishing child labor, establishing a minimum wage, and a forty-eight-hour work week. There were still blind spots in her philosophy resulting from her class background (such as a lingering anti-Semitism and an even more stubborn anti-Catholicism), but the activism of Dickerman and Cook offered her a perspective she had never dreamed she would have. When younger she had opposed the women's movement Alice Longworth had supported. Now she saw that for a woman as well as a man, politics could be a life's work, conveying exactly that sense of relevance and personal authenticity that had always eluded her.

Her new friends completed the process of personal transformation begun by Howe. Soon Eleanor was holding classes for working women in the basement of the 65th Street house. Because of her name, the newspapers quoted her frequently on women's issues. She and Dickerman and Cook began calling themselves the "Three Musketeers" as they toured the state in a green Buick on speaking tours meant to bring the women's vote into the Democratic column. When the New York Democrats started the *Women's Democratic News,* Eleanor was named editor.

Before this, Eleanor had hoped merely for an absence of pain. ("Behind tranquility," went a quote she particularly liked, "lies conquered unhappiness.") Now the possibility of a different kind of life had been revealed to her—one of engagement and achievement. There was an uplifting zeal in what people like Dickerman and Cook did. Their work—unlike that of her husband and other male politicians—was defined by a disinterestedness; it was for a cause, not merely to advance a career, although Eleanor was aware that what she was doing would have a payoff for Franklin if he were ever able to pick up the pieces of his political life.

Speaking with a forceful new voice, in August 1922 she attacked New York Republicans, saying women should "go forward with the Democrats to better things rather than remain with the Republicans, futilely digging among war-destroyed ruins of ancient standards of civilization for some charred bits of salvage with which to create a pitiful imitation of our old industrial structures. . . ." Not long after this, she was appointed chairman of the Women's Platform Committee for the national Democratic Party.

With Howe and others, FDR joked about his wife's new "she-male" friends, yet he too became close to Cook and particularly to Dickerman. It was in his nature to build bridges and make people into resources he could use. He not only craved the approval of Eleanor's new friends but also recognized that they might have his future in common. He was, moreover, glad to have Eleanor find a life of her own because he knew he had to do the same. Neither of them fully appreciated the nature of the synchronicity that linked them, but it was there. Just as she was rebuilding a world destroyed by Lucy Mercer, so he was rebuilding a world destroyed by polio.

The regimen Franklin followed for the first two years of his recuperation was painful and demanding. He celebrated his fortieth birthday on January 30, 1922, in a painful hip cast that had been applied to keep his atrophied legs from curling up. Once the cast was removed, he was fitted with heavy braces stretching from his buttocks to his feet where they clamped onto his shoes. Wearing them, he began to learn a new kind of locomotion—thrusting his head forward, planting the crutches, and swinging his body forward and then repeat.

He practiced diligently, but he hated the stiff-legged, mechanical look the appliance gave him, the teetering sense of precarious balance, and above all the discomfort. He could not abandon the hope of recovering enough normal function that he would be able to dispense with all the hardware. Instead of practicing with the braces—which he felt symbolized acceptance of his state—he preferred to swim in the indoor heated swimming pool at the nearby estate of his friend and semi-relative Vincent Astor. (Astor's Aunt Helen had been the first wife of FDR's half-brother, Rosy.) He conceived an almost mystical belief in the healing powers of water. After one of his first swims in the pool, he said to Sara's chauffeur, who was taking him back home, "The water put me where I am and the water has to bring me back!"

Franklin tried to return to work in the fall of 1922 at the Fidelity and Deposit office in New York. Writer Turnley Walker later reconstructed his first day, beginning with the appearance of Sara's limousine at the curb in front of 120 Broadway. The chauffeur got out and came around to help FDR out of the back seat. Together they straightened his legs out and clicked the braces into the locked position. As they were swinging his legs out, one foot caught on the jump seat of the limousine. As both men worked to disentangle it, the drivers behind them began to honk their horns, causing a crowd to gather on the sidewalk.

As the chauffeur finally got FDR to a standing position, a gust of wind swept his hat off his head. A bystander returned the hat and because FDR's hands were full with his crutches, crammed it on his head askew. Looking down, eyes on the sidewalk, Franklin began laboriously making for the door of the building, the crowd parting to let him through. Once in the lobby he pointed himself toward the elevator. But then one of the crutches slipped on the polished marble and he began to teeter, slowly falling down despite the chauffeur's efforts to keep him upright. Hoisted to a sitting position after going down in a jumble of crutches and braced legs, FDR spoke to the crowd that had followed him inside with forced nonchalance, "There's nothing to worry about. We'll get out of this all right. Give me a hand there. . . ." Raised up to his feet again and sweating heavily, he resumed his struggle toward the elevator.

Experiences such as this one convinced him that he could not expect to have anything approaching a normal business career. During the next year, he severed connections with Fidelity and Deposit and also with his old law firm, where going to the office was even more out of the question because of a formidable set of stairs. With his friend Basil O'Connor, he formed a new law firm, Roosevelt and O'Connor. But he had never been much more than a dabbler at the law and over the next few months spent much less time building a practice than straining the family finances by taking unsuccessful plunges in the stock market and making a series of investments in unorthodox enterprises. (One manufactured a coffee substitute; another sought to create a fleet of dirigibles for passenger and mail traffic.)

Friends believed he was adjusting to his condition, but he was quick to drape a newspaper over his atrophied legs when a stranger came into his presence. As if to compensate for his disability, he began to acquire new capabilities. He used witty banter and conversation filled with puns and patter to mesmerize the people who came close to him, creating a heightened social atmosphere that made them forget he was in a wheelchair. He talked endlessly and found subjects that made others talk back. It was almost an exercise in the magician's art of misdirection—creating an illusion of competence and happiness that altered perceptions and affected his social reality itself.

People saw a new sensibility in Franklin. Bamie's son, Sheffield Cowles, Jr., watched when FDR came to visit his mother at Oldgate, her Connecticut estate. The Admiral, as everyone called Bamie's husband, Sheffield Sr., was there, a relic of a bygone era and now so old and infirm that he had become almost a humour character. (Once, upon leaving for a naval reserve meeting he'd allowed the butler to put on his hat and coat and gone out the door only to return a few moments later with a bewildered look saying, "Nobody put my scarf on me.") Bamie was bent almost in half now, immobilized by her arthritis, and so deaf that people had to shout into the boxlike hearing device called an accousticon she kept beside her chair. Franklin maneuvered his wheelchair next to hers, and shouted jokes into her primitive listening device to make her and the Admiral laugh. Sheffield Jr. was struck by the quiet courage with which these afflicted Roosevelts went about dealing with their ailments.

Eleanor was loyal, but no comfort to him emotionally. He had two people he depended on. One was Howe, his political eyes and ears, constantly giving him hope that he would return to the political arena. The other was his loyal secretary, Marguerite "Missy" LeHand. Just twenty-one when she had begun to work for him after the vice presidential run of 1920, Missy was a pleasant-looking but by no means beautiful young woman, who would become crucial to him in the years of his illness. She was his secretary and strong right hand, but she was also a devoted feminine presence. She had a room at Hyde Park and at the 65th Street house. She accompanied him everywhere. A shrewd politician in personal relations, Missy was at pains to maintain a good relationship with Eleanor, who was relieved from feelings of jealousy by Franklin's disability and in any case was now happy to have someone fill in for her so she could pursue her newfound freedom.

Missy encouraged FDR in his fantasies of recovery in a way that Eleanor, with her crueler sense of reality, could not or would not. She was with him in 1923 when he decided to rent a sixty-foot houseboat called the *Weona II* for a couple of weeks and meander along the Florida Keys. This was an important experience—not only the farthest he had ventured from home since his illness, but also the first real relief he had gotten from the pressures he faced. Being waterborne left FDR suntanned and hearty with the inkling of a new identity: the captain of the boat.

In the coming months, he continued to toy with the quack cures and novel appliances he hoped would make him whole again. (They ranged from bizarre exercise machines and locomotion aides, to supporting the Kansas City doctor who used oxygen in Aerotherapy, and interest in the theory of Emile Coué, French advocate of autosuggestion and author of the phrase "Day by day in every way, I am getting better and better.") But the sea continued to beckon. Finally, late in 1923, Franklin and a friend named John Lawrence bought a second-hand houseboat and named her the *Larooco* (for Lawrence, Roosevelt and Company). It looked like a "floating tenement," with peeling paint and a shredded canvas canopy and two ancient engines that coughed ominously, but FDR planned an extensive trip. The crew would include himself and Missy and his loyal valet, Roy, as well as an elderly couple serving as boatmaster and cook.

The first voyage of the *Larooco* began on February 2, 1924. Doctors had recently given him the gloomy news that they believed his condition was stationary, but Franklin didn't believe them. He had been at sea when the illness hit. He went to sea again to overcome its consequences.

$\mathcal{J}$f Ted and the other Oyster Bay Roosevelts did not vaunt when they learned of Franklin's illness it was only because they were concentrating on what they hoped would be their own destiny—to recapture the glory days of the past. They all tried to follow TR's injunction "to enjoy and make the most of life." Yet they would always have a parallax view of things, looking backward at the same time that they tried to look ahead. And at the center of the family's inner life was a shrine to the dead whose significance would always weigh heavily against the claims of the present.

In 1922, when Ethel's little boy, Richard, a favorite of the fallen hero Quentin, became ill and died, she wrote to her brother's former fiancée, Flora Whitney: "As I held [Richard's] hand I seemed to be with him as he crossed the border and had such a sense of father and Quentin being with him. . . ." Similar sentiments occurred to Ted when he wrote to console his sister for her loss: "For so many years we have been all together. Then, with the war, we began to lose those nearest to us. Now three of the most beloved are together and have left us."

Yet although the past continued to tug insistently at them, the Oyster Bay clan tried to move into the postwar world. While still in the army, for instance, Kermit had decided finally to get serious about a business career. The business he chose—travel—fit the wanderlust that had always dominated his personality. By the time he mustered out of the service, he had joined a friend named Alfred Clegg, who ran the Kerr Steamship Lines. Traveling with Clegg to South America to check prospective routes not long after returning home, he wrote to his wife, Belle, "I will be learning a lot about the shipping game and identifying myself with him in it in a way that I should not miss if I am to keep in the game as I want to." Shortly after this exploratory trip, he started his own firm, the Roosevelt Steamship Company.

In the midst of these moves, however, Kermit also kept one eye on the past. He put together a little book on Quentin comprised of family memories and fragments of his letters. And in his 1919 trip to South America, he took with him all the letters his father had written him over the years and tried to write about TR. "Try to think of a title for the Father article," he wrote Belle. "I can't seem to make any headway with it. If we collect the other articles on hunting in book form, I should like to use [the] Father article as the title of the book." When he finished the collection—a sentimental look back at the outdoor experiences he'd had with his father—Kermit called it *The Happy Hunting Grounds*.

Archie too launched himself into a business career as soon as war wounds allowed. Largely because of Ted's friendship with oilman Harry Sinclair, he got a good position with the Sinclair Oil Company. Yet he kept thinking about his father and took time to defend TR's views on the war in a series of biting articles in *Everybody's Magazine* about the consequences of America's lack of preparedness. He made it clear why he was taking the trouble: "I want the events on record for the pacifists of a later date, who will of course refuse, precisely as the pacifists of the war refused, to keep our nation in such a state that she can defy threats of armed force."

Ever the family loyalist, Archie was outraged when a biography of Woodrow Wilson appeared in which the author claimed that, during the 1912 campaign, then President Taft had compared himself to a tenderfoot in a poker game and someone had responded that if this was so, it was only because Roosevelt was dealing from the bottom of the deck. Taft was quoted in the biography as saying, "Well, that's all right, it's his deal." Archie was furious that his father had been compared to a card cheat and told his brother Ted that he was going to write Taft, now Chief Justice, a stiff letter of protest.

But it was on Ted that the burden of the legacy fell most heavily.

Even more than his brothers he was the keeper of the past—enough so that there was a momentary chill between him and his Aunt Corinne when she published her memoir about TR in 1921, which he felt was indecorous. But he was also the bearer of the flame into the future.

All those years of having been referred to as the Crown Prince had created a public persona—hearty but guarded, aggressive but secretly uncertain that he was equal to the huge task ahead. Some who were close to the family felt that Ted was better equipped for a career in the military than in politics. Like his father, his views were strongly held, but while TR's views were backed by impressive intellectual force, Ted often appeared simply opinionated when he tried to argue his case. One of his nieces put her finger on a deficit in him others also sensed when she said he was "lacking in subtlety."

Elected to the New York State Assembly in 1919, he arrived at Albany amidst speculation, repeated in the *New York Times,* that the Republican regulars were going to "take him into camp" and keep him from proposing "radical" social programs. But Ted was determined to emulate the independent stands his father had taken when he was first in politics. In his maiden speech, Ted came to the defense of five Socialist legislators the rest of the Assembly was trying to expel. This caused parliamentary chaos reminiscent of the days when TR, then a young man of twenty-three, would jump out of his seat periodically in the same chambers to yell, "Mis-tah Spee-kar!" Republican colleagues quoted his father to Ted on the need for "One Hundred Percent Americanism," but Ted demanded that the Socialists get "a square deal, a fair trial, and absolute justice." When the Assembly voted to expel the five men a few weeks later, Ted voted with the small minority opposing this move. For a time it appeared that his principled stand might be expensive. The mail he got was so abusive that he thought that his political career was over before it had begun.

He had other accomplishments in his brief time in Albany. He defended the cause of labor against the corporations. He introduced a bill to increase the exemptions per child on state income tax from two hundred to five hundred dollars, arguing, in sentiments straight from his father, that children are an asset to the state and parenthood ought to be rewarded. But he didn't have a chance to define himself as a legislator before he was called on to shadow Franklin in the presidential election of 1920. The *Manchester Union and Leader* gave the most balanced review of his bravura performance in that effort: "When some leaders found they could not use him for their own purposes they seemed to lose interest in him. Yet all over the country Col. Roosevelt was reported to have made a decided impression upon his audiences in the national campaign and some party leaders said they thought he had done more good for the ticket than any other orator who appeared."

After the election, Ted looked toward Washington for his reward. He and his family were not overly fond of Harding, but Alice particularly lobbied the new administration hard for a post for him. Ted was also the darling of the veterans' organizations. During the transition after Harding's election, John Mahrer, co-founder with Ted and other veterans of the American Legion, conferred with the President-elect and made it clear that appointing this Roosevelt to a significant position would be a sign that the Legion was being taken seriously in the new administration.

The announcement was made early in 1921 that Ted would be appointed to what had become virtually a Roosevelt family sinecure—assistant secretary of the navy. He would be backing up Edwin Denby, former head of the Huppmobile Automotive Company, who'd enlisted in the marines at the onset of the war and risen into the officer corps. After word came that he had been chosen for the position, Ted, exhibiting a rhetoric that would have pleased his father, gave the *New York Times* a summary of his thinking on one of the great issues: "We must not fatuously disarm ourselves and then blandly wait for the deliberations of the other armed nations."

He arrived in Washington amidst the speculation that had accompanied him since he was a boy. (One Washington paper referred to him as "a young man in a hurry.") Like his own father at a comparable time in his life, he brought a brood of children—Grace, ten; Teddy, seven; Cornelius, six; and two-year-old Quentin, namesake of his martyred brother.

Taking the assistant secretary's job was like participating in the saga of the eternal return. Ted may not have been pleased by the fact that Franklin had been there before him, but he was quite aware that this had been TR's springboard to national fame. So was everyone else. Shortly after taking office, when Ted sat in for the absent Secretary Denby at a cabinet meeting, the papers reported that it was a case of "history repeating itself," for it was thirty-three years ago to the month that his father had appeared before McKinley's cabinet with a message that a fleet of Spanish destroyers was heading toward Puerto Rico and then surprised all the senior men present by blurting out his opinion that this hostile act must be met by "armed intervention."

When he heard that Franklin had polio, Ted sent a brief note of sympathy—brief enough that in the middle of their troubles the cousins at Hyde Park put it into their store of grievances. But with his rival now apparently out of the political picture, Ted plotted his next moves, relieved that there was not now someone else with the same name creating confusion about the dynasty. He began a daily diary modeled on that of Samuel Pepys, another naval personality and man-about-town. If the pages were like the "posterity letters" his father had sometimes written—intended for future public consumption—there were also candid glimpses of the private person enjoying being at the center of things in the nation's capital.

Even if his name hadn't gained Ted automatic entry into the inner circle, the fact that he was related to Alice Longworth would have. With the Republicans back in office, she and Nick were now the most powerful of Washington's "cave dwellers." Nick was even more intimately connected to his fellow Ohioan in the White House than he had been to Taft. The President frequently showed up at the floating poker game that alternated between the Longworths' house and Ted's. The First Lady would show up too—the "Duchess," as Harding called her, who didn't play herself and had the job of tending bar during the game. When one of the players wanted another drink he would call out, "Duchess, you're lying down on your job!"

Multimillionaire Secretary of the Treasury Andrew Mellon once left one of these poker games with forty cents in his pocket. Senator Charles Curtis once cheated and Alice went to his office and braved the glint of his "Indian eyes" to ask him not to come again. She dominated these evenings so thoroughly with her wit and sarcasm that sometimes she forgot herself. Once a friend asked her the morning after one of the poker games if she realized that when she had spoken to the President the previous night her manner "was condescending if not downright contemptuous."

Ted was adept at the social whirl, but somewhat ambivalent toward what he regarded as effete entertainments. After his wife, Eleanor, had coerced him into going to see *Pirates of Penzance,* for instance, he wrote acidly of his dislike of musical theater: "I can generally bear up pretty well through the first part of the first act by looking at the audience and wondering what they are thinking and counting the number of Nordics and the number of Mediterraneans, reading the advertisements in the program, and other intellectual occupations. By the time the second act is on its way, however, I don't know whether to scream and kill someone or break down and be led from the theatre in tears. . . . All the chorus men looked like, and probably were, moral degenerates."

In his first months as assistant secretary, he concentrated on the Conference for the Limitation of Armament and played a pivotal role in working out the formula of tonnage for the fleets of the United States, Britain, Italy, France, and Japan. But in 1922 a wave of postwar pacificism was sweeping the country and some members of Congress were trying to cut U.S. navel personnel from the 87,000 allowed under provision of the conference to 67,000. Ted waded into the fray, giving speeches in which he contrasted the "soft headed pacifists" with "hard headed peace lovers" like himself.

Like his cousin Eleanor he was touched with the anti-Semitism of his class. (At one point in his diary he wrote nonchalantly about being on a train in a compartment containing "kikes.") Yet he scrupulously separated private prejudice from public policy. When a young man named J. L. Olmsted, editor of the yearbook at the Naval Academy, published a picture of the one Jewish cadet in the graduating class with perforations around it to suggest that it could be ripped out of the publication, for instance, Ted issued a strong rebuke and made it clear that such behavior was un-American and would not be tolerated.

Such outspoken positions did not make him popular in naval circles. But he had already decided that his time in Washington would be brief. He was looking to the next political goal, which for him, as for his father before him, would be the governorship of New York. His allies all over the country, remnants of the TR coalition, were solidly behind him. In far-off Wyoming, the *Casper Daily Tribune* predicted a Republican disaster in New York unless "Young Teddy" was chosen to head the state ticket. The *Manchester Union and Leader* was more pointed: "Twenty five years ago the Republican organization faced defeat [in New York]. At that time [the party's] astute leaders . . . tendered the nomination to Theodore Roosevelt. The maneuver proved successful, and the state, which under the normal conditions would have gone Democratic, was saved for the Republican Party."

There was pressure on him to declare for governor in 1922, but Ted felt that he needed to be "seasoned" awhile longer. The main difference between him and his father, he pointed out, was that he was serving as assistant secretary in a time when there was no war to help him distinguish himself.

*   *   *

The more Ted pursued a political future, the more he depended on Alice. There had been a strong bond between them since the days when he was a cross-eyed little boy she bullied into playing her tomboy games. Now she envisioned playing a role with him like the one Bamie had played with their father in his youth—special advisor, friend, and voyeur in his rise to power.

She spent almost as much time at Ted's house in Washington as at her own. For Ted's children she was "Auntie Sister," a droll and somewhat unpredictable addition to the family's games. When Ted's wife, Eleanor, decided to dress as an Italian peasant in a costume party she was having for the kids, for instance, she asked Alice to go as her dancing bear. Alice agreed on the condition that Eleanor make a little skirt for the bear costume that she felt would make its midsection appear more decorous.

Ted regarded her as his mentor and only dependable friend. Once when she was returning from a long trip to Europe, he wrote in his diary with anticipation, "I have missed her more than I can say. It will be like rain on parched ground to have her back here again with me."

A fanatical Roosevelt loyalist who protected herself by creating a facade of cynicism about the family, Alice believed in Ted, but even more in the destiny of her father's line. She had once thought of being a kingmaker for her husband but gave up on Nick as a "lost cause" after the initial excitement of being married to this roguish man wore off. Now she found him a bore. When he declared his desire to return home to Ohio to run for governor, she threatened to stand on the streets of Cincinnati smoking cigarettes to create a scandal.

Cosseted by his mother and sister, both of whom loathed Alice almost as much as she loathed them, Longworth had become flamboyantly unfaithful to Alice after TR's death removed the one restraining presence from his life. Despite his bald head and somewhat squat body, he was catnip for women, as Alice discovered on one occasion when she discovered Nick and her old friend Cissy Patterson in the bathroom, drunk and *in flagrante* on the bathroom floor.

Flailed by his wife's sharp wit, Longworth, a very clubbable man despite his other defects, had retreated into a persona, as one observer put it, that was comprised of equal parts liquor, violin, and fornication. He had become a legend of debauchery in Congress. In one famous moment, a fellow member of the House thought to twit Longworth by saying in front of a large assembly that he'd always wanted to tell him something but had never before had an occasion.

What was it? Longworth asked.

"That your bald head reminds me of my wife's behind," said the congressman.

Knowing that everyone was waiting for his reaction, Nick paused for a moment, then ran his hand over his bald head and said, "Yes, I'll be damned if it doesn't feel like your wife's behind."

Always a suffragette of the spirit, Alice was actually further liberated by her husband's philandering, and she took pride in the fact that she didn't crumble as Eleanor had when finding out about Franklin. She became somewhat notorious among the Oyster Bay clan for her own advanced opinions on sex. Archie's wife, Grace, was unpacking Alice's bag for her at the beginning of a visit, for instance, and was scandalized to find a diaphragm. Knowledge of the use to which the device was being put would have been far more shocking. For Alice had begun an affair of her own with one of the most powerful figures in Washington, Senator William Borah.

The Lion of Idaho, as Borah was known, was a square and burly man whose heavy face looked like a parody of TR's. He too was a powerful orator and had in fact been one of Roosevelt's supporters during the 1912 insurgency, although he hadn't followed him into the Progressive Party. This had caused a certain friction between the two men that became visible when TR made a campaign swing as a Progressive through Idaho, and Borah, in introducing him in Boise, happened to say that if Roosevelt had only been nominated on the Republican ticket he certainly would have swept the country. In his speech, TR said he would explain why he was not nominated and ask Borah to confirm it. Then he launched into a litany of specifics about the "stolen" convention of 1912, concluding each charge with a polite bow in Borah's direction and the rhetorical question, "Isn't that so, Senator Borah?" then waiting for Borah's uncomfortable assent before continuing.

If not the most popular man in the Senate, Borah was probably the most admired for his personal powers. Alice had gotten to know him well during the League of Nations debate. (As she wrote discreetly later on, "Occasionally I did not entirely agree with what Borah said . . . but he had a quality of earnest eloquence combined with a sort of smoldering benevolence, and knew so exactly how to manage his voice, that before he finished speaking I was always enthusiastic.") As she pursued their liaison, she found that she was not the only one infatuated with the senator. Once again her competition was her old rival Cissy Patterson, who once innocently asked if she could meet him in Alice's house. Alice agreed, but when she returned she found some of Patterson's hairpins in her bed and sent them back with a snide note saying only, "I believe these are yours," to which her friend replied immediately that indeed they were: "And if you look up in the chandelier you may find my panties."

Alice never really admitted the nature of her relationship with Borah. (Late in life she did say, when asked indirectly about it, "I suppose you could say I was adept at skating on thin ice and playing with fire.") Their assignations re-created some of the excitement she had experienced in the first days of her courtship with Nick Longworth. She was careless enough that the press printed blind items about the couple in the gossip columns and gave her a new nickname: Aurora Borah Alice.

Even Ted was privy to his sister's doings. As his diary reveals, he usually invited Alice and Nick to his poker parties, but sometimes it was Alice and Borah. At one point, when she had been forced to accompany Nick to Cincinnati ("Cincin-nasty," as she called it), Alice wrote Ted a note to say that she would not be back in Washington as planned because of what she called "affairs of Egypt." As Ted commented in his diary: "I spoke to Sister on the telephone. I found her 'affairs of Egypt' consisted of going to St. Louis to hear Bill Borah speak."

Early in 1923 Ted met with the other bright young star of the Republican Party, Herbert Hoover, who'd made a name for himself in war relief work in Europe and then as secretary of commerce. Like Ted, Hoover was bothered by the ineffectuality and moral laxity of the Harding administration. Both men were concerned about the Republican reverses in the off-year elections of 1922 and agreed that the party needed a "constructive program" that looked to the future. "He suggested that perhaps he and I and a couple of others might get together and work up such a program," Ted wrote of Hoover, "submit it to the President and urge it on him for adoption."

After working with Hoover on the memo, Ted showed it to Harding a couple of weeks later, but was rebuffed. Annoyed, he noted in his diary, "The President is fooling himself. He thinks that the last autumnal elections were not a repudiation of the national administration. . . . He plans to make about fifteen speeches this summer and expects that to arouse interest and support for the party. He can't possibly do this unless he can change his entire method of expression, for no one knows when he is through with a speech what he means."

Ted acknowledged that he was probably too impatient to be a successful politician. There were times he wanted simply to get away from everything, even his family. (In the summer of 1923 he confided to his diary that he was not sorry the press of events had forced him to cancel a family vacation in Nova Scotia: "It isn't my idea of a holiday to go to a semi camp with a lot of women and children. When I go into the woods I want to go, go hard, and go alone.") But he kept plugging in Washington, focusing on issues such as the intramural struggle in the navy over whether or not air power should supersede battleships in the national defense strategy, an innovation Ted believed would be a "national disaster."

But by 1923 he had made up his mind to go for the governorship of New York. He spent the spring making exploratory appearances in the state. After a forum in Albany with other possible candidates, he wrote in his diary, "There was a tendency to hit at me but I think I succeeded in turning most of the shafts reasonably well." In a speech in Manhattan a month later he got a sense of the chief problem his well-known independent streak would cause him: "Organization does not want me as governor of New York state unless they have to have me. If they think they can win with anyone else, they will try."

Ted felt he had other options. The *New York Times* ran an item saying that "progressive Western politicians" were pressing Harding to put him on the ticket in place of incumbent vice president Calvin Coolidge in 1924, an idea supported by New York Republicans who didn't want to have to deal with him as governor.

All this speculation became moot, however, in August when Harding died and Coolidge moved into the White House. Alice was convinced that this was a change for the better. (In an early conversation with the new President she twitted him about his celebrated taciturnity by saying that she had bet her friends that she can get him to say more than three words, only to have Coolidge go her one better by replying, "You lose.") Ted was not so sure. He had regarded Harding as an indifferent leader but at least he knew what to expect from him. He came away from his first interview with the Sphinx-like Coolidge not knowing what to think: "In so far as I am concerned, he is a sealed book. I know nothing of him. I have no personal relationship with him at all. I don't believe he has a personal relationship with anyone in the cabinet." He was hopeful, however, that with Harding gone, the party would now take on a "more liberal complexion."

All summer he shuttled back and forth between Washington and New York pressing his reform agenda as a prospective gubernatorial candidate. His appeal to the working man was based on "keeping out peon labor" and on support for the tariff. He was also developing a moderately "dry" position on Prohibition. (His mother was not supportive, having reacted to passage of the Volstead Act by beginning to serve cocktails for the first time at Sagamore Hill, fiery concoctions Alice compared to gasoline, although she acknowledged that the point was defiance of what Edith saw as a silly law, not pleasure.) On the issue of equal rights, Ted's position was simple: "The only way to treat the colored people is on the basis of merit, giving the good colored person a position regardless of his race and [letting] it stand there. . . ."

When the increasingly powerful New York branch of the Ku Klux Klan made tentative overtures offering to support him, Ted was enraged and issued a press release to all the newspapers in the state: "Americanism never goes masked and he who tells you it does lies."

By September 1923, Ted's plans were fairly well advanced. He was convinced that 1924 would be his year. Late in the month, he traveled once more to Albany for a conference with the man he regarded as his chief rival for the Republican nomination, New York Assembly Speaker Eddie Machold. He returned to Washington satisfied with the meeting, confiding to his diary that Machold had said that he would probably not be a candidate: "I was surprised to find that he had figured things out in terms of the future, namely if he and I were able to reorganize and get control of New York State, and if I was elected governor in 1924 and again in 1926, we might, according to his plan, make a bid for control of the national organization and the Presidency in Twenty Eight."

The grand plan had finally come into focus.

It was at this high point of his political expectation—the moment at which his success was beginning to seem inevitable—that Ted was caught in the oil slick of Teapot Dome.

The slow-motion scandal had begun in the fall of 1921 when the Harding administration decided to transfer the massive Wyoming oil reserves at Elk Hills and Teapot Dome from control of the navy to the Interior Department. In the behind-the-scenes maneuvering, Ted had actually opposed the decision because he believed it to be against national security interests. But once Harding acted he lost interest in the matter until one afternoon late in 1922, when he was coming back from one of his political excursions to New York and heard that Interior Secretary Albert Fall had just leased the Teapot Dome fields to oilman Harry Sinclair. Ted arrived home more upset, his wife, Eleanor, later said, than she had ever previously seen him. When she asked him what was wrong, he replied, "My career is over and done with. . . . The Sinclair Oil Company stock has jumped ten points on the strength of the lease, and we own a thousand shares. I can never explain it. People will think my price is ten thousand dollars and will never believe the truth."

"For heaven's sake, wait," Eleanor finally interrupted the gloomy monologue. "It's all right!" She reminded him that when he went into politics he'd given her power of attorney to control the family finances. Then she told him that she had sold their Sinclair stock, at a slight loss, a few months earlier to help cover their income taxes. Ted jumped up and hugged her.

He thought he was in the clear. But what began as a controversy over the Teapot Dome lease slowly developed into a national scandal during the next year. While he had been worried about owning Sinclair stock, Ted was not concerned about further possibilities of conflict of interest. He had been scrupulous in avoiding them. As part of his own work for Sinclair, for instance, Archie had once asked him to award the company a contract, but while Ted actually thought the proposal would be a good deal for the navy, he had rejected it because of appearances. In 1923, Harry Sinclair himself had asked for the use of a destroyer to ferry him to the U.S.S.R. so he could negotiate oil leases with the Soviets, but Ted had rejected the oilman's request, writing in his diary, "I don't believe this can be done. . . . I feel that the use of a destroyer for these particular civilians . . . would involve all kinds of difficulties."

The rumors of payoffs and fraud involving Teapot Dome continued to spread. Then, in October 1923, Ted was asked to testify at a Senate investigation into the scandal. He was not particularly forthcoming in his appearance before the committee, as he wrote in his diary, because he felt that his chief, Navy Secretary Denby, might have played a suspicious role in the affair and he did not want to appear to be "running out" on him. But the next morning, as the press began to dissect what he had said the previous day, Ted held a news conference and made a more detailed statement. Afterward he wrote, "I think this should finish it."

And in fact, the investigation did appear to bog down at the beginning of 1924. Ted continued to organize for his governor's race, scoring a coup when he got the New York branch of the Traveling Salesmen's organization to agree to back his candidacy and have their seventeen thousand members carry his literature. But then early on the morning of January 17, he got a call from Archie in New York that plunged him into panic.

Having served an apprenticeship in sales for Sinclair in Costa Rica and then going to Europe for a year to work in the export division, Archie was now a vice president of the company. A few months earlier Ted had written in his diary about how well his younger brother was doing, and how "he has got plans made to leave Sinclair unless he gives him a larger salary, after he has put through a couple of deals he is on." In fact, however, Archie had recently become disillusioned because he felt he was being used by Sinclair executives. ("I thought that the Sinclair Company wanted me because I was such a brilliant young man," he later wrote. "I didn't know that they had hired me because my father's name was Theodore Roosevelt and they believed they could use that name. . . .") Now he had discovered something that deeply alarmed him. "I'm afraid there's been dirty work at the crossroads in this oil business," he said cryptically to Ted when he called. "I don't want to talk about it on the telephone."

Ted immediately caught a train for New York. When he got there Archie said that "through a chain of accident" he had suddenly found out that the Sinclair company was "extremely questionable." He told Ted that he had been informed by Harry Sinclair's own private secretary, G. D. Wahlberg, that at the time of the signing of the Teapot Dome lease Sinclair had secretly sent Interior Secretary Albert Fall a check for $68,000.

Ted knew that this bribe was the missing piece of information needed to blow the investigation wide open. He knew too that he would be dragged back into it. But he asked Archie to come to Washington to testify about what he had learned. Archie, just thirty years old and still a partial invalid from his war wounds, knew his business reputation would suffer for informing on his employer, but he immediately agreed to reveal what he had learned.

Sinclair's secretary, Wahlberg, also agreed to testify and corroborate what he had told Archie. Knowing that Sinclair would try to get to Wahlberg, Ted hired a private investigator to shadow Wahlberg on the way from New York to Washington. But the detective never made contact and the minute Ted walked into the Senate hearing room, the

FDR with his "enormous Jewfish"
caught aboard the Larooco.

FDR afloat:
"The water
made me sick
and the water
will get me well
again."

Theodore Roosevelt Jr. on the campaign trail.

42

43

Eleanor, Belle, Ted, and Kermit riding an elephant on their 1925 expedition to India.

Eleanor (left) with the friends of her personal liberation, Marion Dickerman and Nancy Cook.

Archie and Kermit as successful young businessmen in the 1920s.

FDR and Elliott sail for France in 1931.

46

47

Presidential aspirant FDR celebrates his fiftieth birthday in 1932 with (standing left to right) Elliott and his wife Betty Donner, Jimmy and his wife Betsey Cushing, Anna and husband Curtis Dall, and Eleanor. Matriarch Sara Delano Roosevelt sits in the privileged spot beside her son.

48

49

Elliott and his second wife, Ruth Googins.

Anna and her second husband, John Boettiger.

Ted and his son Quentin training for the European campaign early in 1942.

General Theodore Roosevelt Jr. in 1944, riding in the jeep that served as an homage to his father. (Note the bullet hole in the windshield.)

Colonel Elliott Roosevelt (center) looking over a flight plan with crew members during the North African campaign.

53

*FDR and
daughter, Anna,
head for Yalta
early in 1945.*

54

*Eleanor with Elliott and his third
wife, Faye Emerson, 1946.*

*Elliott and fourth wife
Minnewa Bell, 1951.*

55

Young intelligence officers Kermit Roosevelt Jr. ("Kim") and Archie Jr. (in uniform) with an unidentified Egyptian contact just after the war. Both men were present at the creation of the CIA.

Eleanor in one of the last photographs taken with her four sons, John, Jimmy, Elliott, and FDR Jr.

Elliott and fifth wife, Patricia Peabody.

Alice Roosevelt Longworth: "the other Washington monument."

terrified look on Wahlberg's face told him that Sinclair had managed to "put the fear of God into him."

Archie took the stand and told what he'd heard about the bribe, adding a new tidbit of information that Harry Sinclair had hurriedly left for Europe without notifying anyone in the company a few days earlier. He was followed to the stand by Wahlberg, a round-faced and clerkish man, who, when asked by Senator Thomas Walsh if he had knowledge of the $68,000 check, turned gray and said in a barely audible voice, "Mr. Roosevelt is mistaken. I never mentioned a check for sixty eight thousand dollars. What I said was that Mr. Sinclair had sent Secretary Fall a present of six or eight cows and bulls." After the furor had died down in the hearing room, Archie was recalled. Asked if he was sure he had heard Wahlberg correctly, he replied, "Dead sure."

In the chaos of the following weeks, Interior Secretary Fall quit in disgrace. Navy Secretary Edwin Denby also resigned under pressure. Eventually attention shifted to Ted. Congressman William Stevenson of South Carolina said he should be forced out of government because his wife owned Sinclair stock. Alice got both her husband, Nick, and her lover, Bill Borah, to state publicly that Eleanor had long ago sold the Sinclair stock she and Ted owned, but Stevenson kept up the attack. Returning from a campaign trip to New York, Ted, hearing how his wife had been dragged into the Teapot Dome mess, lost his temper and said that he was going to beat up Congressman Stevenson. Eleanor tried to laugh it off, but Ted was ready to leave the house on his mission of vengeance. Unable to dissuade him, Eleanor quickly telephoned Alice.

"Sister?" she shouted into the receiver. "Ted is back. He's leaving to beat up Stevenson." Then, after listening for a moment, she handed the phone to Ted.

"I hear you're going to beat up Stevenson," Alice said. "Yes, of course he deserves it. . . . I know he's a rat. . . ." Then she paused for a moment before continuing. "By the way, he's a little elderly man and wears glasses. Remember to have him take them off before you hit him."

"Are you sure of that?" asked Ted, who'd never met the congressman.

"Positive."

"Oh, damn," he said with resignation. "Now I suppose I can't do it."

*   *   *

Ted's entanglement in Teapot Dome was the play within the play watched with careful attention by New York politicians of both parties. But Louis Howe was far more interested than most. "Louis the Giant Collar," as FDR sometimes called him because his skinny neck always made his shirt collars look too large, had realized that there was only room for one Roosevelt at a time in the country. He feared Ted as he feared no other potential competitor for Franklin. Now he was overjoyed as his man's rival for the Roosevelt political inheritance became tarred by the scandal. As Teapot Dome threatened to engulf Ted, Howe cut out newspaper articles and sent them to FDR. "I'm sending you clippings from which you will see that little Ted appears to be down and out as a candidate for governor," he wrote in a triumphant note sent shortly after the first of the year. A week or so later, after canvassing his contacts in the world of journalism, Howe added a jaunty postscript to his previous obituary: "The general position of the newspaper boys is [that] politically he is dead as King Tut, for the moment at least."

FDR found all gossip irresistible and was interested in Howe's news. But during the spring of 1924, his mind had drifted far from politics. He had allowed himself to become lost at sea aboard the *Larooco*, aimlessly cruising the Florida coast in and around Palm Beach in the rehabilitated houseboat, getting waylaid in mangrove swamps and running aground on sandbars and sometimes stopping to take aboard old friends who were willing to subscribe to the one basic rule of the voyage, which was that there was no destination.

Hyde Park and his mother's New York townhouse remained his home bases, but over the next two years he would take three lengthy trips on the *Larooco*. Aboard ship he didn't have to pay any attention to the doctors' gloomy predictions about his flaccid legs. He didn't have to use the crutches or braces his mother and wife had hectored him to wear. He was "the Admiral" on his flagship. People who were piped aboard saw a master of verbal sleight of hand who used brilliant conversation to create an illusion of normality. They didn't see the often disconsolate man who was so depressed that Missy sometimes couldn't drag him out of bed until noon.

He was quarrying out new places in the self to deal with his disability, yet he was also still trying to beat it. Convinced more than ever that water and tropical warmth would be his salvation, he anchored the *Larooco* outside deserted beaches and spent whole days slithering through the surf and crawling in the sand. He swam constantly, uplifted by the saline buoyancy. As he wrote his mother one afternoon, "I took the motor boat to an inlet, fished, got out on the sandy beach, picknicked and swam and lay in the sun for hours. I know it is doing the legs good. . . . I know the muscles are better than before."

Missy LeHand was his first mate. She was the perfect companion, as optimistic and convinced that he would walk again as Franklin himself was. Her heavy-jawed face was always composed in a smile. Her blue eyes were alight when she was with "Effdee," as she called him, and people were struck by the way her "trilling" laugh lit up the *Larooco*. In addition to accompanying him on his self-prescribed therapy sessions in the water, she was his companion in birdwatching for odd species that nested in the maze of inlets and islands, and fished with him for barracuda and mackerel.

She had learned to speak his lingo—a combination of Runyonesque patter and college puns in which Washington's Birthday would inevitably be transformed into "Birthington's Washday" and the famous parlor game was always called "Ma and Pa Cheesey." When someone sent a questionnaire about FDR's polio that was both intrusive and illiterate, the two of them collaborated on an irreverent reply. *Can you walk without a cain or some assistants?* "I can't walk without a CAIN because I am not ABEL. *Have pain below the hips? If so tell me where.* "My principal pain is in the neck when I get letters like this."

Informality ruled the boat—seminaked sunbathing and swimming—but the hedonism had a sort of innocence, even when Missy sat chattering on FDR's lap wearing only a nightgown. The question about whether or not there was physical intimacy between them (or whether Franklin was even capable of it) divided Roosevelt's friends. (Later on, when FDR, then President, suggested to Joseph Kennedy, about to be appointed ambassador to England, that he give up his affair with Gloria Swanson, the brash Irishman retorted that Roosevelt should set an example by giving up Missy.) Among his own children, James and Anna always denied that it was a sexual relationship, but Elliott, who spent more time aboard the *Larooco* than either of them, insisted that it was.

The question was not only moot; it was irrelevant. Even if Missy was not FDR's mistress, she was clearly his surrogate wife. She was his accomplice in his existential maneuvers; she gave him the intimacy and witty banter that Eleanor could not summon. Her love was unconditional, so unconditional, in fact, that Eleanor sometimes ridiculed Missy's selflessness in letters to her friends Dickerman and Cook on the rare occasions when she could be persuaded to join Franklin on the *Larooco*. Accustomed to odd domestic arrangements, the Roosevelt children accepted Missy and knew their father needed her. When ten-year-old Franklin Jr. wrote to his father he referred to her as a fact of FDR's domestic life: "I hope you are well and Misi is not home-sick. I hope you have fine swimming and Misi is not scared of the sharck. I gues your home-boat is comfy."

FDR himself was a distant figure writing letters filled with humor, gaiety, and solicitude. The children wanted more, and sometimes regarded what he offered them as a sham; but they seemed to understand that it was all that he was capable of giving at this time in his life. They were learning, as Elliott said later on, to be satisfied with the emotional crumbs that fell from their father's table.

He seemed to be on a perpetual vacation. They didn't feel the personal drama of his inner voyage or sense the purpose of the outer one. Neither, for all of the personal growth in her own life, did Eleanor. FDR constantly badgered her to visit him aboard the *Larooco*. When she could no longer decently refuse, she came for as brief a visit as possible, and while aboard wrote back snide letters to her friends about the mosquitoes, bad weather, and triviality, and how her life was "quite empty" without them.

When they were apart, her letters to Franklin typically began with the salutation "Dearest Honey," but they were primarily businesslike and the sentiment was perfunctory. She expressed her affection through politics, believing that what she was doing was helping him. "You need not be proud of me, dear," she wrote in response to his encouragement. "I'm only being active till you can be again. It isn't such a great desire on my part to serve the world and I'll fall back into habits of sloth quite easily."

Here she was being somewhat disingenuous. Far from simply keeping a seat warm for FDR, she was deepening her involvement in what she referred to as public service (and what her son Elliott called "the obtaining and exercise of power"). If deep and trusting love had left their marriage, the recognition was growing in Eleanor that she and Franklin had an identity of interests and her own success would always in some sense be dependent on his. As their daughter, Anna, later said, "The more she got involved in helping father, the more she gained her self confidence." The marriage had been replaced by a joint venture.

With her friends Dickerman and Cook, Eleanor had become an outrider for social causes, traveling all over the state calling on women to become politically involved and make their recently won right to vote count. They also had a legislative wish list that included the construction of more nursing facilities and parks and public playgrounds, as well as the demand for health and safety legislation and laws protecting children and female workers. Because their agenda intersected with that of Governor Al Smith they became a vanguard supporting his 1924 run for the presidency.

Smith was the most colorful politician New York had seen since Eleanor's Uncle Theodore conquered the state upon his return from San Juan Hill. Smith had been a youth when TR was making headlines prowling the streets of New York as police commissioner. He was in the Democratic Party machine as a leader when TR was fighting Tammany as governor. He was the accidental beneficiary of TR's decision to run as an insurgent presidential candidate in 1912 because Roosevelt's Progressives diminished the Republican vote in New York and allowed the Democrats to sweep state offices, thus putting Smith into a position he never expected to hold as speaker of the State Assembly. This was the platform from which he had run successfully for governor in 1918, unsuccessfully in 1920, and then successfully again in 1922.

Sara was appalled when Eleanor began inviting the governor to Hyde Park. He was boorish and uncouth. Yet like her son she always labored to find a silver lining when clouds gathered over her life, and so, when a social friend asked if it was true that Smith actually had spittoons in the Executive Mansion, Sara said it was, but then quickly added, "But I am reliably informed that when he uses them he never misses."

The relationship with Smith gave Eleanor and her friends a quick course in political pragmatism. They, in turn, provided a whiff of idealism for the Democratic machine. Eleanor began to work closely with the governor as he prepared for his 1924 presidential run. She scored a major victory when she faced down party boss Charles Murphy and won the right for women to pick their own contingent on the New York delegation rather than having men make the pick for them. Called "a prominent woman" by the *New York Times,* she said in an interview about Smith, "You may differ from his beliefs but you are never at a loss to know them if you take the trouble to ask and certainly their quality of honesty is vital in our next President."

As head of the Women's Platform Committee at the 1924 convention, Eleanor tried to press an ambitious social welfare agenda on the Resolutions Committee and was rebuffed because some of her ideas were seen as too great a burden for the party to carry in the general election. At the same time that Eleanor was suffering this setback, however, Franklin was on the way to a triumph. The Machiavellian Howe had convinced Al Smith that having FDR nominate him for President would be a dramatic event that would capture the attention of the country as well as the delegates. Smith agreed, having no idea that it was not at all certain that Franklin would make it to the podium.

Publicly displaying his disability created the possibility for disaster for FDR. But an appearance at the convention, now that his cousin Ted's career had hit a snag because of Teapot Dome, offered Franklin a chance to reestablish himself in the Roosevelt family sweepstakes. (Frances Perkins, then serving with Smith and later to be FDR's Secretary of Labor, said that one of his leading characteristics at this time was the desire "to outshine his cousin Ted," a quality that made Franklin very "active where there was a great deal of indolence in his nature.")

He was ambivalent about Smith, feeling the same desire to be the good son with him that he had with Josephus Daniels and other older men, and the same desire to be a rebellious son as well. But with Ted as his target, he began to choreograph his convention appearance as a campaign appearance for himself, not the governor. Not wanting to show up in a wheelchair, he conscripted his eldest son, James, now a strong sixteen-year-old, to help him. They marked out a fifteen-foot path in the 65th Street house, the same distance he would have to travel to the rostrum, and then, gripping James on his left and using a cane on his stronger right side, FDR worked at making the trip without appearing to struggle. To keep people from focusing on his halting progress, FDR instructed his son to make it seem that they were moving slowly on purpose and to engage him in laughing banter so that delegates would focus on their faces.

His appearance was as dramatic as Howe had predicted. Franklin got to the podium without mishap, although he was drenched in sweat by the time he arrived. As he began to speak the sun suddenly broke through the melancholy afternoon and sent a shaft of light down through the skylight of Madison Square Garden that drenched his imposing head. And when he urged a vote for "the Happy Warrior," the crowd erupted, in part because these words seemed to fit him far better than Al Smith. Marion Dickerman went to visit him back at the 65th Street house that evening and found FDR beaming with pleasure. "He was sitting in bed," she told an interviewer later on. "I remember him so vividly. He held out his arms and said, 'Marion, I did it!' "

The convention was deadlocked after 102 ballots, with Smith battling Woodrow Wilson's son-in-law William McAdoo. When neither of them could assemble a majority, the colorless Wall Street attorney John Davis was chosen as a compromise candidate. But if it was a loss for Eleanor's candidate (humorist Will Rogers, finding her in the gallery knitting furiously with a grim look on her face, asked if she were doing names for the guillotine), the convention was a tremendous victory for FDR. As the *New York Herald Tribune* editorialized, "From the time Roosevelt made his speech . . . he has easily been the foremost figure on the floor or platform. That is not because of his name." He had proved himself as a hope and a promise.

Franklin's triumph made the rough political weather Ted was facing all the more difficult. His prospects, which had seemed so bright a few months earlier, were dimmed early in 1924. In the spring, the *New York Times* wrote that the "boom" for his candidacy, which had been almost feverish before Teapot Dome, had died down almost to nothing. He got a boost early in the summer when the Senate committee investigating the scandal issued a report that completely exonerated him. But while friends in New York like old wartime comrade Bill Donovan were trying to keep his name alive in party circles, he now seemed at best a long shot.

At the Republican presidential convention in June, Ted watched the renomination of Silent Cal Coolidge, thinking back to two years earlier, just before Harding's death, when he himself had been mentioned as a replacement candidate for vice president. The delegates "accepted him as logical, inevitable," Ted wrote about Coolidge in his diary, "a good man but one they did not particularly warm to."

After the Republicans finished, Ted watched the Democrats. His dismay at Franklin's bravura performance was compounded by Al Smith's failure to get the nomination, which meant that Smith would now run for reelection as governor of New York as a strong incumbent. Ted's sense of urgency about his future was behind the request for a private audience with Coolidge. "I was absolutely frank," Ted wrote of the meeting. "I said both administratively and politically I felt I ranked a cabinet position, if I was not going back to run for Governor of New York. He nodded his head and said he agreed with me." But the President did not offer to make him secretary of war or even to keep him on in the Navy Department. And so, nervous and edgy, Ted decided to stake everything on one roll of the dice in New York.

As he began to move toward an official announcement of his candidacy, the family got a shock when forty-year-old Alice informed them that she was pregnant. Knowing of the growing estrangement between Nick and Alice, and having heard rumors of the Borah affair, the Roosevelt women were scandalized. Edith reacted by saying she was glad she happened to have scheduled a trip to Cuba at this time.

Alice did her best to help Ted from Washington, contacting an old ally in New York politics, Senator James Wadsworth, to drum up support for her brother. Some Republican strategists were looking for a candidate who could compete with Smith by trying to cut into the mammoth vote of New York City, but Ted concentrated his efforts elsewhere in the state. The *New York Times,* which since the first of the year had been doubting his viability, wrote in late July that his candidacy "appears to have been revived during the last two weeks" because of his appeal to upstate voters and "his winning ways with political audiences."

When the state convention met in September, the favorites in the race for the governor's nomination were Assembly Speaker Eddie Machold and U.S. District Attorney William Haywood, who had been boosted by an endorsement by kingmaker William Randolph Hearst. But then, after ferocious back-room bargaining, Ted called upon Machold to honor the deal they made a year earlier and the speaker withdrew with "dramatic suddenness," as the *Times* said the next morning in an article that went on to note that "equally startling was the 'come back' of Colonel Roosevelt, whom the party leaders had virtually left out of the reckoning altogether."

Ted was chosen the Republican candidate for governor on the first ballot. He resigned his post as assistant secretary of the navy and was replaced by his Aunt Corinne's son Teddy Robinson, thus keeping the position in the Roosevelt family. The telegram of congratulation from Alice suggested the hard road ahead: "They have certainly handed you a fight!"

Transfigured by his illness, Franklin had finally shaken the ghost of TR and found a political persona of his own. But Ted was stuck with being TR's son. Those who felt that he was trying to capitalize on his father's image did not realize that what might seem an imitation was actually an act of homage. The morning after his nomination, the *Times* editorialized that he must "leave off special efforts to look like his father and sound like him. The truth cannot too soon be impressed upon him . . . that no mere simulacrum, no echo of a dead voice can defeat Governor Smith." This view was reinforced by a cruel cartoon in the *New York World* prefiguring others to come that showed Ted as a tiny figure looking ridiculous with his father's Rough Rider uniform draped over him.

On the day after the state Republican convention adjourned, the Democrats nominated Al Smith for another term in office. The national Democratic party, having assumed that Speaker Machold would be the nominee and state issues would dominate the contest, had planned to stay out of New York. But now that Ted was the man, the national party entered the fray using the Harding administration's corruption against Ted. He hit back hard, attacking Smith's boss-ridden administration and claiming that the governor had placed political hacks in every appointive office, even in the public schools. "I cannot eliminate Tammany Hall on 14th Street," he said in laying out the dominant theme of his campaign, "but by George I will eliminate the branch office of Tammany in Albany."

The stakes of the election transcended control of the governor's mansion in Albany. In the words of the influential *Literary Digest,* what was at issue in New York was "the making or breaking of the political career" of Theodore Roosevelt, Jr.

Smith was wary about personally using Teapot Dome against Ted lest this inadvertently create sympathy for him. But there were others to make sure the relationship with Harry Sinclair remained in the public eye, as Ted discovered on one of his first campaign swings through the state when an elderly heckler planted in the audience yelled up at him from the rear of the hall, "How's the oil, Teddy?"

Taken aback for a moment, Ted recovered himself and yelled back, "Clean as a whistle! The Democrats . . . brought out [in] the only report any honest man could bring out on it that I was clean as a whistle! I am honest, and if you, older timer there in the back, had bothered to read the report, you would not have asked the question."

But Louis Howe saw Teapot Dome as the defining issue of the campaign and made sure that it would not die. He did not particularly care whether or not Al Smith won, but he wanted Ted to be defeated. Franklin was back at sea with Missy LeHand, unable and unwilling to enter the fray. And so Howe enlisted Eleanor to smear her cousin.

At first she expressed halfhearted qualms. But it didn't take much for Howe to convince her. If Ted was elected it would mean the end to Franklin's hopes and thus the end also of her own newfound power in politics. Howe knew there was antagonism between the branches of the family. He had probably heard of how Conie's son Teddy Robinson had put a disc on the Victrola at a recent family gathering and asked Eleanor to dance. The record was not music, but rather his mother's voice giving her speech at the 1920 Republican convention and he whirled his irritated cousin to the opening words, "I am one who believes there is a difference between the Republican Party and the Democrat Party. . . ."

In choosing Eleanor as his instrument, Howe may also have seen the quality in her that Marion Dickerman had glimpsed when she said that her friend may have seemed "kind and compassionate but when certain matters touched her personally she could be very hard and sometimes cruel."

It was not hard for him to convince Eleanor to try to bring Ted down. Her attack began at the state Democratic convention when she seconded Smith's nomination for governor and caustically observed that he had already been assured of victory by his opponents, who, in nominating Ted, "had done everything they could to help him." As the campaign began in earnest, she took to the road. With Howe's help, she fitted out her car with a papier-mâché "bonnet" in the shape of a teapot whose spout emitted steam. Denouncing Ted as "a personally nice young man," but a political weakling "whose public service record shows him willing to do the bidding of his friends," she began to tour the state in her odd vehicle with her friends Dickerman and Cook, shadowing Ted and parking the teapot car at several different stops each day at places where it would draw a crowd and allow her to launch into a bitter attack on her cousin that focused on the Teapot Dome scandal.

People close to the Roosevelt family were shocked. It seemed so out of character for the long-suffering Eleanor to do such a thing. They rationalized the behavior as vengeance for the attacks on FDR by the Oyster Bay branch when he was running for vice president and for Nick Longworth's recent slur that Franklin was no more than a "denatured" Roosevelt, a nasty if oblique reference to his paralysis.

But if Eleanor was looking for revenge, it was perhaps for an offense more profound than political attacks against her husband. Wounding the hopes of TR's heir was a way of equaling the score with TR for triumphing so flamboyantly over her father. It was vengeance, even if pursued unconsciously, for what she could not help but regard as the brutal treatment of Elliott during his last years, and also a chance to pay back the Oyster Bay clan for half a lifetime of slights, real and imagined, that went back to the days when Edith forbade Alice to play with her and she was passed around from aunt to aunt like a bad penny and allowed to come within the golden circle of her Uncle Theodore's family only on their sufferance.

One of the stops made by the teapot car during the campaign was at Oldgate, Bamie's Revolutionary War era retreat in Connecticut. Bamie was alone now, Admiral Cowles having died of a stroke the previous year. She was so crippled that her butler often had to carry her from room to room. Eleanor and her lady friends surprised the gnarled old lady by their getups—tweed suits and plus fours. Too genteel to say so, Bamie was even more deeply upset at their mission—opening a jagged breach in the laws of clan solidarity and shared experience that had been the foundation of the Roosevelt family since even before her father's time. After the anti-Ted caravan moved on, she wrote a letter redolent with the dismay of the *ancien régime* to her niece Corinne Alsop: "I just hate to see Eleanor let herself look as she does. Though never handsome, she always had to me a charming effect, but alas and lackaday! since politics have become her choicest interest, all her charm has disappeared, and the fact is emphasized by the companions she chooses to bring with her."

Later on, Eleanor would say she was "ashamed" of what she had done to Ted, although she had carried out her campaign with gusto. Ted did not publicly respond to her, although his wife, doubly angry because of her misfortune to have the same name as their antagonist and thus constantly be mistaken for her, hoarded such bitterness as a result of the 1924 campaign that she would refuse to be introduced at a public function in Texas over twenty years later by FDR's son Elliott.

Ted reacted to Eleanor's attack by campaigning harder, setting himself a killing schedule that involved as many as twenty speeches a day. Most of them were given from the back of a train on a whistle stop tour pausing at every small town in the upstate area. To be sure of making his next appearance, Ted arranged with the conductor to have the train pull out prematurely from each stop. As he began to disappear down the track he would placate the crowd by turning around and yelling in the direction of the locomotive, "Wait! Wait! I haven't finished! Stop the train!"

The people liked him. But he was outgunned by Smith's far bigger organization and superior political savvy. In one meeting in a small town, for instance, Ted complimented the townsfolk about a victory of their high school football team. When told that the team had in fact recently lost, he turned to an aide and said about his misstatement of fact, "I wonder who told me that?" Smith heard about the remark and in a later speech "correcting" Ted for all the errors he had made on the campaign trail, said after each one, *"And* who told him that?" The audience soon made this refrain into a derisive chant.

Ted won fifty-six out of New York's sixty-two counties. But he lost in the county of Albany and in the five counties of New York City and lost the 1924 governor's race by one hundred thousand votes out of the three million cast. Because he was a winner in the middle of a Republican landslide, Smith immediately became a powerful national figure and an almost certain nominee for President in 1928. But his biggest accomplishment was one he didn't see at the time. He had recalled FDR to politics and allowed Eleanor a taste of blood. He had smashed Theodore Roosevelt, Jr.'s, dream of picking up the fallen standard of his father and someday restoring the Oyster Bay branch of the family to the White House.

$\mathscr{A}$ few weeks after the 1924 election Alice reserved a room at the Chicago Lying-In Hospital to await the birth of her child. Those who had been cut by her sharp tongue over the years gossiped vengefully about how Nick Longworth, now a habitual drunk, probably could not have fathered the child even if he and Alice had been sharing a bed, which they hadn't for several years. (In fact, while Nick's drinking had become more extreme, his amours had continued unabated.) Some insisted that Alice had had herself artificially inseminated. Most said that the father had to be her lover, Senator William Borah.

The baby, a girl, was born on February 14, 1925, which Alice took to be a portent, for it was on Valentine's Day that her mother had gotten engaged to TR and on Valentine's Day that Alice Lee had died. A few of those who saw the infant talked about its "round, Borah-like face," but Nick immediately claimed the role of father. He vetoed Alice's malicious suggestion that they name the baby Deborah, instead compromising on Paulina, after St. Paul, who was Alice's favorite figure in the New Testament and Borah's too.

Edith and Kermit had been at Alice's bedside when the baby arrived. Ted had not. The special relationship he and his sister had shared over the years had been strained by his loss to Smith; Alice had pinned her hopes for a restoration on him and saw, even more clearly than he did, that his defeat had killed this hope. But Ted was not with her in Chicago primarily because he was busy planning an adventure designed as a reprise of his father's hunting trip to Africa in 1909.

With financial backing from the Field Museum of Natural History in Chicago, he had decided to stalk the *Ovis poli,* the fabled wild sheep of Central Asia first described by Marco Polo and scarcely seen since then. The trip he designed was to last for almost a year and take his party over the Himalayas into a terra incognita within Chinese and Russian Turkestan, which Ted called somewhat grandiosely "the Mecca of my desires."

In toying with the odd name of Ted's quarry, humorist Will Rogers wrote, "What is an ovis poli? It is a political sheep. You hunt it between elections." With Ted, however, it was not clear that there would ever be another election. So the trip was a time to take stock about his future and also to give himself a reward for years of hard work in trying to shoulder his father's bulky legacy.

He had decided to make the expedition with Kermit. Archie was not a candidate. Forced to quit his job at Sinclair Oil following his testimony about the bribe to Interior Secretary Fall, he was having a hard time supporting his family, having lived for several months off savings until his cousin Emlen gave him a job in the family investment firm of Roosevelt and Son whose existence went back to the days of C.V.S. Roosevelt. He felt that he had been shunted into the family backwaters. But he accepted the fact that it was his lot to be the "stay at home Roosevelt brother," helping Ethel take care of Edith.

Kermit, on the other hand, was the perfect companion. His résumé of adventure included risky trips with TR to Africa and Brazil, and many on his own since then. He was gregarious and debonair, a great talker who had maintained the family friendships with Kipling* and Edwin Arlington Robinson, and established himself as a minor literary figure in his own right. Since returning from the war, Kermit had written numerous articles and three books—*War in the Garden of Eden,* an account

---

* Kermit corresponded regularly with Kipling about a variety of matters. One of their subjects was the geography of "The Road to Mandalay." Kermit questioned Kipling about the accuracy of some of the directional references and the poet admitted that he had gotten many critical letters on the subject, such as the one from a colonial captain in Rangoon complaining of the dreadful situation *he* was in because of travelers who had taken Kipling's directions and gotten lost.

of his involvement in the Mesopotamian Campaign; *Quentin Roosevelt: A Sketch with Letters,* a tribute to his younger brother; and *The Happy Hunting Grounds,* a collection of pieces about his hunting trips, especially ones with his father.

In addition to their sons Kim and Willard, he and Belle now had a daughter, Clochette, and a new baby named Dirck. The chaos of the household was something of a family legend. Kermit was often gone for long stretches of time, and Archie and others in the family felt that Belle was so preoccupied with an ambitious social life that she didn't make sure that the children were properly cared for. Archie conspired with Edith to get Kermit's children to Sagamore periodically where they would be sure at least to get a regular bath.

In choosing to travel with Kermit, Ted had picked someone, as he wrote, "whose campfires have been seen on every continent." The steampship business had taken Kermit all over the world in the years since the war. In 1922 he went to the Orient to set up business relationships with the Japanese and managed to schedule a winter hunting trip in the snows of Korea. In 1923, he took Belle on a tiger shooting expedition in India. This trip particularly had been a homage to TR. In an article about the trip Kermit wrote, "I had read a great deal about hunting in India, chiefly books from father's library filled with delightful colored illustrations of wounded tigers attacking elephants. The first hunting book I ever remember reading was the classic of Samuelson's *Thirteen Years among the Wild Beasts of India.* Father had given me his copy not long after I learned to read."

Archie might be the one who took most seriously the workaday responsibilities as son, but Kermit knew he was his mother's favorite and took steps to include her in the romance of his life. In 1924, while Ted was getting ready to run for governor, Kermit, who had just been in the Far East for ten months, had to go back to Japan again on business. This time he took Edith with him for company. They went from Japan to the Soviet Union, taking a ride on the Trans-Siberian Railroad. Plowing through snow drifts in the dead of winter, the train went through crystal forests of icicles hanging from beech trees. Amazed at the beauty outside, Kermit and Edith were forced to hold their breath when they walked through third class on the way to the dining car because of the stench of unwashed bodies. One man on the train died of smallpox during their trip.

In Moscow, as in the frozen countryside, there were signs all around of the civil war that had followed the Bolshevik revolution. In Moscow

Kermit and Edith were housed in a home formerly belonging to an aristocrat. Everything was there—knickknacks and photos with personal inscriptions from famous opera and ballet stars of the Romanov era—but the owners of the house had vanished. They saw a number of arrests by the secret police, and after returning home Kermit wrote of the postrevolutionary terror with alarm: "No one can be certain of his immunity, neither prominence nor obscurity can guarantee it."

It was the sort of exciting life—"a work in progress," as one friend called it—that he had crafted for himself since he was a teenager. Yet those familiar with the patterns in the Roosevelt family noted a disturbing parallel with something that had happened a generation earlier, when TR was becoming a national figure and his brother, Elliott, rather than supporting him in his rise or even competing with him for achievement, had begun to travel compulsively. Archie might have been glad to have his older brother seize the reins of the dynasty, but Kermit was not ready to subordinate everything to Ted's quest for office. To him, the Roosevelts were a network of personal loyalties that took precedence over politics, and it seemed natural to him to try to use family connections in his business.

In 1922, for instance, Kermit had written Archie, then stationed in Paris working for Sinclair, to thank him for using Roosevelt ships to move the company's oil: "That was grand of you. . . . It is all loaded and I hope it gets up to Rouen without any trouble. We have had a hard time for this steamer, but both coal and railroad strikes have combined against us." A few weeks later, Kermit was prodding Nick Longworth to give him inside information about what items would be classified as duty-free in the bill about to be voted on by the House. In return, Kermit, who was close to Tex Rickard, heavyweight champion Jack Dempsey's manager, provided Nick with ringside seats for the Dempsey-Carpentier title fight.

It did not occur to Kermit to exempt Ted from his maneuvering, despite his brother's sensitive political position. While he was on his first trip to the Far East signing a contract with representatives of the Japanese Steamship Company, he got Archie to write their brother, who had just been installed as assistant secretary of the navy, about an executive in the Japanese firm, a man named Komatsu, who "like all Japanese, is very proud of his acquaintance with our family." The Japanese planned to send Komatsu as a part of a trade delegation to Washington and Kermit said that it would help his business if Ted wrote a letter asking Komatsu to call on him in Washington and saying he was pleased about the contract.

This was innocuous enough, but Kermit kept upping the ante. Just as Ted's campaign for governor was beginning, Kermit asked him to intervene with a member of the New York Shipping Board with whom he was trying to cut a deal. Ted said he couldn't because of possible conflicts of interest, which led to an angry exchange. "He feels that I have insulted him by doubting the propriety of the proposition he is making and refusing to back him," Ted wrote in his diary. "He is absolutely unable to catch what is on my mind. . . ."

When he heard that Kermit had gotten on a train for Cincinnati to try to get Nick Longworth to help him, Ted wrote Alice to try to end the misunderstanding: "When you see him, will you be kind but firm. . . . And will you try to make him understand the difference between politics and business. . . . [And] will you also explain to him that among the other things he has in his keeping is the good name of father and that at all times he must guard that good name."

Alice mediated between her brothers and a few days later, after things seemed to have been patched up, Ted was relieved: "Last evening Kermit and I went out and played tennis first, then we had dinner at the house together. . . . His was a perfectly legitimate request, but my original stand is no less legitimate. The real problem, I think, with Kermit was that he felt I was not interested in his work." With things back to normal, Kermit visited Washington and Ted found him "as delightful and inconsequential as ever."

Now that his political career was on hold, Ted could afford to improve his relationship with his brother. In fact, it was almost as if, in planning this trip with him, Ted was trying in a different way to assume the role of their father, who had previously been Kermit's companion in adventure. He seemed to understand how different he and Kermit were—he a man of action who had tried to cultivate a contemplative side, and Kermit basically a bookish man who'd put himself in challenging situations because he felt they would develop his character. The trip to hunt *Ovis poli* would not only cement their bonds, but also become something they would be able to talk about when they had "qualified for the grandfather class."

That this was a reprise on one of their father's trips became clear when the brothers enlisted George Cherrie, the venerable naturalist who had accompanied TR down the River of Doubt, to go with them. After months spent assembling gear and getting travel permits from India, China, Kashmir, and the other countries they would pass through, they set off in April 1925. The first stop was Europe. After landing in France, Ted got up before dawn one morning and took a train to the small town of Chambrey where he visited Quentin's grave, writing in his diary about the beauty of the early spring countryside. At the well-kept grave site, "three partridges flushed and rumbled into the woods" almost as if Quentin's slumbering spirit itself had been aroused.

They went to Italy and set sail from there, passing Stromboli at night and watching the volcano throw red flames up into the night. When they reached Port Said, some "shady characters" tried to sell Ted "French photographs." After he said no, a man offered to sell Ted his "little sister," and, as he wrote in his diary, "as a last resort, 'my little brother' was suggested."

They landed in Bombay on May 11 and two days later were in Rawalpindi, traveling from there to Srinagar. As their party reached Kashmir, Ted, under Kermit's influence, had "gone native," growing a beard and wrapping his head with a turban. They hired local guides, purchased pack ponies, and uncaged the four cougar hounds they had brought from Montana.

Ted felt he was getting to know Kermit all over again. More than just a sophisticated traveler, his brother was an adventurer in the class of Richard Halliburton. Ted was amazed at his facility with languages ("Hindustani comes so much slower to me than to Kermit") and by the amount of ethnographic lore he picked up as they went along.

In early June they went through the Khardung Pass, climbing to nearly eighteen thousand feet. At night they shivered in their eiderdown sleeping bags and tried to cook in the pressure cookers they had brought for high altitudes. Nearing the top, they saw the bones of pack animals from other expeditions picked clean by wolves and snow leopards. At the summit, the pack ponies bled from the nose and Ted collapsed into the snow while Kermit supported himself on walking sticks, both men suffering splitting headaches as a result of the altitude.

By August, they had descended through the Himalayas into the desert plain of Turkestan. Exchanging their pack ponies for yaks, they began to seek their elusive quarry, the great horned sheep. In the end they bagged eight *Ovis poli,* along with some two thousand specimens of small mammals, birds, and reptiles, all of which were sent back to the

Field Museum. They celebrated their success by giving their native
bearers the evening clothes they had brought with them in case they had
meetings with local dignitaries.

Back home the trip was an event. Each week the Associated Press
carried a report of the progress of "the Roosevelt boys" that readers
followed as if it were a serialized fiction. Calling it an adventure in "the
Roosevelt tradition for 'mighty hunting,' " *The Literary Digest* detailed
the incredible hardships of the expedition and then said, "Just why
meeting such conditions is docketted under the head of sport and stirs a
ripple of [sympathy] is not clear. But it does."

Ted and Kermit had arranged before they left for Eleanor and Belle to
come to meet them after they had bagged their *Ovis poli*. The wives
sailed from the United States in October. They had spent a good deal of
time together over the years, but they were not really compatible. The
blonde, eye-catching Belle was scattered and aristocratic, having depended on servants to organize her life since she was a little girl. Eleanor,
on the other hand, while somewhat plainer, was competent and self-
sufficient and had developed into a cunning political wife who had
helped plot her husband's career. Having caught the Roosevelts' competitive spirit in her fifteen years of marriage to Ted, Eleanor worried
that Belle would outdo her in the hunting the foursome planned, and
had hired a marksman to help her practice with a rifle for weeks before
their departure.

Retracing their husbands' steps, the women arrived in Bombay by
ship in early November, then took a train to Rawalpindi, and, after
staying there overnight, left at dawn the next morning to drive by car
to Srinagar. It took a whole day to come down through the steep
mountain pass on a road that hung out over a precipice much of the
time. At sunset, the glare of the headlights caught a pair of figures in
sheepskin coats, boots, and heavy woolen caps, with great bushy beards.
Eleanor asked the driver to stop. He protested that the ragged men were
Pathan tribesmen and possibly dangerous. Eleanor and Belle got out of
the car and ran to embrace Ted and Kermit.

The two couples spent a month hunting in Kashmir. The competition
Eleanor had foreseen did develop with her sister-in-law. Belle got the
first barasang, a native deer, but when Eleanor got hers she wrote home
to her mother that it had "ten points, one less than Belle's, but the
antlers are longer and wider than hers."

The competition involved more than shooting. In Delhi, Ted decided
to buy Eleanor an emerald necklace with stones the size of pigeon eggs,

rationalizing that he could use the fee *Cosmopolitan* had promised him for an article about the trip to pay for it. Kermit wanted to buy Belle the companion necklace, but she wasn't interested. As Eleanor wrote home, "The necklace we got is a little the prettier of the two. . . . [Instead, Belle] says she will wait until she gets to England and get a Joshua Reynolds. Kermit is hoping she won't do this. . . ."

After the Roosevelts went through the Khyber Pass and through the Allapilli Forest in central India, they went to Nepal for a tiger shoot, hunting from howdahs on the backs of elephants. Each of the four made a kill and described their success over dinner with the Viceroy of India before returning to America.

Arriving back home after almost a year abroad, Ted was anxious to revive his political career, but unsure quite where to start. Others in the family saw possible pitfalls. The prospect that he would become merely a name and a face used by other men, for instance, bothered his mother enough that she sent a note of caution: "All that I wish you to guard against is being on call, so to speak, so that they feel at [Republican] headquarters that they can send you around to all the doubtful districts and county fairs to speak for the other men."

Ted thought about running for governor again in 1926 and had a conference with President Coolidge, but received no encouragement. He decided to wait. Later on he remarked to one of his children that at this point he still felt that there was hope for him. As long as Franklin was still mired in his disability he didn't have to worry about his own diminished prospects. What he didn't know, however, was that his cousin was indeed progressing—not in politics, perhaps, but in the larger project of the self.

With the possible exception of his son, James, who had helped him to the podium, no one but Franklin himself knew how hard it had been to create the illusion of physical competence at the 1924 convention. He wanted a career in politics, but he also wanted to walk again. He felt that if there was conflict between these two goals, then at this point in his life he would have to choose the latter.

The search for health had shifted from sea to land, although it still focused on water. In the fall of 1924, he had heard about the Warm Springs Resort, not far from Bullochville, Georgia. When he was told that other polio victims had experienced a dramatic improvement in

their condition after swimming in the hot springs of the spa, he asked to
go there immediately.

Warm Springs was set in a thick pine forest. The waters were heated
by a subterranean passage and gushed out of a rock at the foot of a
mountain range that had been visited for hundreds of years by Creek
Indians seeking cures for a variety of ailments. In 1889, after the old
hotel that had stood near the hot springs for years burned down, a new
three-story Victorian, surrounded by a colony of cottages and complete
with an outdoor therapeutic swimming pool, was put up in its place. It
had been a fashionable resort until the coming of the automobile made
other destinations on the coast equally accessible. By 1924 Warm Springs
had taken on an aura of shabby gentility.

The resort was run by an old newspaperman named Tom Loyless
who had heard of FDR's struggle to overcome polio. Looking for a
famous customer who would boost business at the resort but also truly
believing that the waters were curative, he wrote Roosevelt about the
benefits some patients had experienced there and got him to agree to
visit in October 1924.

Arriving with Missy and Eleanor, Franklin rhapsodized about the
setting on the drive in to the hotel: "That air! Makes a man feel ten years
younger." He got into his swimsuit almost immediately upon arriving
and was sitting on the edge of the pool with his shrunken legs dangling
in the water when one of the polio victims Loyless had described as
having experienced such a remarkable recovery, a man named Louis
Joseph, came walking up on canes, his upper body swaying with the
effort, but his footsteps firm.

As writer and fellow polio sufferer Turnley Walker later reconstructed
this meeting, FDR looked Joseph up and down and asked, "No braces
at all?"

"Not any more," Joseph replied.

"Won't you need help?" FDR asked as the young man began to climb
a course of stairs leading to a terrace.

"Watch me," Joseph replied, negotiating the steps slowly but with
authority.

"How did you get to be able to do that?" Roosevelt asked.

Joseph described what he'd done to improve his condition: three years
of constant swimming and water exercises at Warm Springs. FDR asked
to go into the pool right away so that he could get started on the task
ahead. He found that the warm, slightly sulfurous water had a feeling of

buoyancy. In up to his neck, he flailed his arms with his useless legs dangling below, the toes dragging on the floor of the pool, and was able to move forward. It was almost like walking with the water serving as a medium of locomotion.

Eleanor left for New York the next day to pick up her role as hatchet woman in the gubernatorial campaign against Ted. Staying on with Missy, FDR wrote her, "The legs are really improving a great deal. The walking and general exercising in the water is fine and I have worked out some special exercises too. This is really a discovery of a place." Soon he was writing his mother: "I feel that a great 'cure' for infantile paralysis and kindred diseases could well be established here."

Over the next three years, FDR fell into a ritual of health: a brief time during the winter months in New York; a spring cruise on the *Larooco;* and then summer and fall at Warm Springs. During this time, he would spend more than half his time—116 out of 208 weeks—away from his family, by the later reckoning of biographer Geoffery Ward. Eleanor would be with him for only two weeks; Missy would be away only for a total of six.

FDR tried to keep in touch with his brood of "chicks" by mail. He used his witty letters to amuse the children, to show his continuing love, and also to keep tabs on them. In a "Dear Bunny" letter to Elliott, the problem child who was now deep in conflict with his older brother, Jimmy, at Groton, he said: "Jimmy says you are in the squad of which he is corporal. Don't try to beat him up while you are a mere private in the ranks. You might get court martialled and shot!" It was a typical communication in that he acknowledged that there was a problem but also made it clear that he could not help solve it.

The three older children were more closely bonded to Franklin than his two younger sons, who lacked what Elliott later defined as a "communion of the spirit" with him. John, his youngest, sometimes sent FDR pictures he had drawn. One showed his view of his father—a pumpkinlike figure with a gigantic body and sharp-toothed grin and shrunken limbs like stunted tentacles.

There were, however, some situations FDR was capable of finessing for his children. Understanding the bitter estrangement between Eleanor and Anna, who was resentfully finishing up at Miss Chapin's, he worked to get his daughter into a short course in agriculture at Cornell so that if nothing else she could retreat to Hyde Park and take care of the animals there. When Elliott, the former runt of the family who was now over six feet, got in trouble at Groton, FDR reassured Headmaster

Peabody: "Perhaps his great physical growth has slowed up his mind, but he has stopped growing and will, I think, speed up mentally from now on. . . ."

But it was not in his nature to confront problems directly and so his children were never quite sure where he—and they—stood. When James had a conference with him in which he gave a prepared speech on how he wanted to break with family tradition and not go to Harvard, for instance, FDR heard him out patiently and even agreed that somewhere like Williams College or the University of Wisconsin might be better. Then he began "hypnotically" to talk about his own days in Cambridge—about experiences on the *Crimson*, in the Fly Club and Hasty Pudding, etc., and before James knew it he had changed his mind and decided to go to Harvard after all. Afterward he wondered how this had happened.

Almost everything between FDR and his children was done by long-distance now, and without personal connection. Often the children felt *managed*. Anna, who would grow up to be a heartbreakingly articulate critic of her parents, later described her growing feeling that FDR, like Eleanor, had "the ability to 'relate' to either groups of people or individuals who had problems . . . [but] the apparent lack of ability to 'relate' with the same consistent warmth and interest to an individual who was their child."

Warm Springs played into two strains of FDR's character. On the one hand it was what Uncle Remus might have called his laughing place. He *believed in* the resort the way he believed in his luck in draw poker and believed in private lucky numbers, lucky days, and lucky clothing like the shoes he had bought on his honeymoon in London in 1905. (Conversely, he would not travel on Friday the 13th and never lit three cigarettes on a match and became upset when someone else did in his presence.) Warm Springs also appealed to the fondness for get-rich-quick schemes. Between 1925 and 1928 he would take loans from his mother in making a significant financial investment in the resort.

But while he never lost the belief that it would be a tremendous money-maker, Warm Springs stood for something larger than that—a cause and a calling. A newspaperman happened to be present when FDR first tested its waters, and the article he wrote ("Swimming Back to Health") caused several other polio victims to make a pilgrimage to Warm Springs. They arrived helpless and without support. Because there was no one else to take responsibility for them, FDR stepped forward. Thus something that had begun as being about him and his problems took on larger implications that drew out his compassion for others. Without realizing it he began to turn Warm Springs into one of those spas he had visited as a child when his father was seeking health in Europe and began to think of creating something like a utopia for "cripples."

Writer Turnley Walker, himself a polio victim, later described how Franklin began to adopt the persona of "Doctor Roosevelt," caretaker of the patients of Warm Springs. One of his first was a man named Fred Botts who had lived with his disability in the back room of a relative's house for nine years before coming to the resort. FDR got Botts into the pool, along with a pair of giggling and overweight women who were also trying to cope with the effects of polio.

"I think you'd better be ready with a pitch fork to remove drowning people from the pool," Roosevelt called out to a bystander as he got the ladies to hold on to the side of the pool and thrashed his way through the water to reach the apprehensive Botts.

"Do you trust me?" he asked.

"Absolutely," Botts replied.

"All right. You'll be my first patient."

He maneuvered so that he was sitting on the bottom of the shallow part of the pool and got Botts to lie out on his back, with his arms over his head and his hands holding on to the coping. Then FDR began to manipulate Botts's legs, pumping them up and down in the water.

"How does it feel?" he asked.

"Wonderful," Botts replied, sensing, or at least thinking he did, a new tingling feeling in his feet.

With Missy at his side, Franklin threw himself into this paramedical practice. He tried to get Eleanor to come down to Warm Springs to help, but her experiences with Sara had made her conscious of the relationship between geography and power, and she felt she would be under FDR's thumb at the resort.

Franklin hired a doctor and nurse and devised a chart for each patient showing the muscle groups in the body color-coded to indicate the level of strength in each ranging from none to normal. Then he helped the patients through a series of water exercises, often working with them in the pool himself, and, after a few weeks, measured the muscle strength again. When an aide noticed that FDR was grading the tests leniently and asked if this was right, Roosevelt shrugged and replied, "We've got to keep them *believing* that they'll improve!"

He grew tan in the sun and worked hard in the pool, further developing the bulging shoulders and arms he had acquired from his exercises. Seeing how much time he devoted to the others, a nurse asked him, "What about your own legs, Mr. Roosevelt?"

She saw his face, always so genial, harden into a look of determination: "I'll walk into a room without scaring everybody half to death. I'll stand easily enough in front of people that they'll forget I'm a cripple!"

When Tom Loyless died after FDR's first year at Warm Springs he decided to buy the resort outright. ("It looks as if I have bought Warm Springs . . ." he wrote his mother. "I feel you can help me with many suggestions and the place, properly run, will not only do a great deal of good, but will prove financially successful.") He showed a determination and entrepreneurial skill that suprised those close to him. When the American Orthopedic Association met in Atlanta, for instance, he asked to be allowed to appear to describe the successes of Warm Springs. When word came back that the doctors were not interested in having a paraplegic address the convention, FDR had his chauffeur drive him to Atlanta. Crashing the meeting, he buttonholed doctors and showed them his tests and gave anecdotes about how the condition of his "patients" had improved. Finally, the directors of the Orthopedic Association approved Warm Springs as a treatment center.

He looked forward to returning to Warm Springs after political missions to New York and always greeted his fellow polio victims, "Have you been good boys and girls when Papa was away?" As a result of his enthusiasm, the resort became a sort of Lourdes, drawing polio sufferers from as far away as Europe. "Push boys" were hired to help the wheelchair patients get around. Egged on by Franklin, some of these young men adopted an irreverent swagger. A couple of them took it too far when they were sitting at the fountain near the entrance of the resort watching some pilgrims who came to examine the treatment. One of the push boys began talking loudly about how he was "a cured polio." The other one, saying he was desperate for treatment, pretended to fall into the fountain and rose spluttering, "I'm cured! I'm cured!" and began leaping all over the lawn to the astonishment of the onlookers.

For reasons of cash flow, FDR had to keep his clientele of "normal" customers and worked hard to lessen their fears of being infected by the polio victims. Keeping the two groups separate, he ordered a new treatment pool to be built in the basement and enlarged the living space allotted to the disabled. But when there was a conflict between the well customers and the polio victims, he resolved it in favor of the latter. In addition to being "Doctor Roosevelt," he was also "Vice President in charge of Picnics," and began to arrange recreational outings for them in the woods around the resort.

Warm Springs became his equivalent of TR's Badlands experience—a place where he found that he had something in common with common men and women and where he toughened his soul as well as his body. No one would again charge him with being effeminate after his days at the resort. The "streak of vanity and insincerity" that Frances Perkins saw as his chief quality was still there, but it had been subordinated and controlled. He learned lessons of sensibility as well as survival as a result of his involvement with others.

"It was as if he was looking for the first time into the recesses of the human heart," said one paraplegic who came to Warm Springs because of Roosevelt. There were flashes of anger, as when he was told by one of his patients how doctors had urged him to have his useless legs amputated. There was compassion too. Amused by the romantic intrigues that sprung up among the residents of the resort, Roosevelt once told the nurse who worked there that it was inevitable that love would bloom—young crippled men loving their female therapists and young crippled women loving the push boys he had hired to help them get around in their wheelchairs.

"Not if I can help it," the nurse joked, thinking that FDR was trying to set her up for some witty rejoinder. But then she realized that he was serious. She saw him looking across the valley of pine trees, his face touched by that sadness it always acquired in repose.

"Love is a good thing," he said, "a healthy thing, and thank God, something that's practically inevitable."

The love between him and Eleanor had been blocked and rechanneled so often that it now no longer resembled love. Although he was now confined to a wheelchair, the distance between them was as much symbolized by their physical dissimilarities as it had been when they were married. When British politician Oswald Mosley and his wife, Cynthia, traveled to America in the mid-1920s, they spent time with the Roosevelts and Cynthia later recalled their lasting impression of this odd couple: "What a contrast between this magnificent man with his fine head and massive torso, handsome as a classic Greek and radiating charm though completely immobile, and the exceptionally ugly woman, all movement and vivacity within an aura of gentle kindness but without even a reflection of his attraction."

Yet if there was not love—at least not love as commonly defined— between them, there was a deep chemistry that went past their shared history or even their pragmatic need for each other. They had both embarked on parallel journeys to rebuild selves damaged by cataclysms of illness and emotion. Each had even created an ideal community and alternative family. FDR built his at Warm Springs. Eleanor built hers at Val-Kill, an idyllic area a mile or so behind the big house at Hyde Park where she had decided to have not only a room but a house of her own she could share with her friends Dickerman and Cook.

The origins of Val-Kill were in the antagonism between Eleanor and Sara. Eleanor felt that whenever she had her friends at the Big House at Hyde Park, her mother-in-law always treated them like interlopers. In addition, Sara controlled such basic decisions as when Springwood would be closed for the winter. Once Eleanor said sadly to Franklin that she and her friends had just had the last picnic of the season. Ever on the lookout for ways to keep her happy, he suggested that she build a place of her own and offered to give her the land.

There was a perfect site about two miles from the Big House. A frustrated architect, Franklin himself designed a "cottage" to be built from fieldstone, a plentiful native material. Construction began in the summer of 1925 while Eleanor and her two friends, along with Franklin Jr. and John, were vacationing at Campobello. The housewarming took place on New Year's Day 1926.

Built within the shelter of a stand of trees, Val-Kill had vistas of the rolling hills of Hyde Park. There was a large pond and water was channeled into a rock pool designed to look like a swimming hole. Eleanor would stay at Val-Kill episodically; Cook was more a full-time resident, and Dickerman joined her when her work permitted.

Eleanor's son Elliott later compared Val-Kill to a kids' clubhouse, and it did have something of the same sense of exclusivity and make-believe self-sufficiency. His mother crocheted doilies bearing the interlocked first initials of the threesome's names—EMN. The monogram was also engraved on the silverware. Nancy Cook built furniture by hand for the cottage in imitation of the work of local craftsmen. Her design was so pleasing that the three women decided to build a workshop and began Val-Kill Industries to sell Early American furniture.

Eleanor's lifelong sense of displacement would never completely leave her. (When Franklin was governor, Frances Perkins complimented her on her willingness to give up her own room at the Executive Mansion in Albany to visitors. "As a matter of fact, you know, this isn't my home," Eleanor replied. "That isn't my room that I sleep in down there. . . . I've never had a home of my own. . . .") But Val-Kill was the first place where she felt she belonged. It was here that also deep confessions were exchanged between the three friends, including Eleanor's story of the Lucy Mercer affair.

In the same way that Eleanor was faintly ironic about Missy but at the same time recognized her value, so FDR conditionally embraced the community of women at Val-Kill. He wanted Eleanor to be happy not only because of his generalized commitment to equanimity, but also because he cared about her. Gaily condescending to "the girls" in his chosen role as "Father Roosevelt," he involved himself in the details of their life together. He made suggestions to improve their sense of well-being and occasionally had to smooth out misunderstandings.

A dispute arose, for instance, over who would pay for the upkeep on the pool, for example, and Dickerman wrote an angry letter saying that perhaps she and Cook should simply leave Val-Kill. FDR wrote back to say that there was no real problem and that he would pay for the cleaning of the pool: "Why the injured tone . . . O, ye of little faith! Don't you poor idiots realize how much I care for you both and love having you at Val-Kill! . . . If I had you here I would spank you both and then kiss you!"

As much as Franklin, Eleanor had undergone a remarkable personal transformation. If his involved the emergence of a charismatic gallantry, hers involved the acquisition of an iron resolve. Most people didn't see it because of that facade of gentleness that captivated people like Cynthia Mosley. But the perceptive Marion Dickerman saw it: the ability to bear a grudge; the unrelenting will that took over once she had made up her mind about something.

The Roosevelt children, however, could not appreciate the limited partnership that had evolved between their parents. Not perceiving the subtle network of intersecting agendas, they experienced only the long separations and the inability of their parents even to have intimate moments like Christmas without a gang of nonfamily members present as insulation between them. They felt the hypocrisy in their mother being lionized as a spokesman for family values, as when she responded to an interviewer from *Good Housekeeping* who had asked her for a definition

of "the ideal modern wife" that while once she would have said mother
was the most important role, she had come to understand that "everything else depends upon the success of the wife and husband in their
personal relationship."

Anna still went through long periods where she barely spoke to her
mother. Instead of encouraging her in the courses she had taken at
Cornell, Eleanor, who elsewhere was pushing for women to have
greater access to higher education, wrote FDR of their daughter that she
hoped college would at least "get some of the foolishness out of her." A
patient listener for her friends, Eleanor did not listen to her daughter.
Once, after she had eavesdropped on Anna and Al Smith's daughter
complaining about the way politicians' families were deformed by outside pressures, Eleanor told the *New York Times* that it was a shame that
these young women were not more like the daughters of British families
who "not only take a keen interest in their fathers' careers but go out and
help in the political battle."

Desperate to get out of the family, Anna began looking for a husband.
She met Curtis Dall, an investment banker at Lehman Brothers who
was ten years her senior, at a deb dance late in 1925. When he asked who
this striking blonde with a look of habitual concentration on her face
was, a classmate said, "Anna Banana, that's what we call her at school."
Anna invited him to spend New Year's at Hyde Park. Dall was struck
by the chaos created by Franklin Jr. and Johnny, both home from Buck-
ley School. He was staring at a formal portrait of Franklin's formidable
great grandfather Isaac, called "Isaac the Patriot" because of his involvement in the American Revolution, when FDR wheeled up beside him
and said, "Curt, I think we should button up our coats very tight before
talking with him, don't you?"

Jimmy and Elliott showed their hostility to the outsider by purposely
tripping Dall in a pickup game of hockey, opening a deep gash on his
chin, but four months later Dall asked FDR for Anna's hand. The night
before the wedding, Eleanor had a talk with her daughter in which she
wondered if there was anything she'd like to know about "the intimacies
of marriage." Considering the source, Anna said no. The next day
Jimmy walked her down the aisle, a stand-in for their father. It was
portrayed as a joyous occasion by New York newspapers, but for those
close to the family there was a somber undertone to the event. Anna had
married, as she said later, "to get out of the life I was leading."

Eleanor was outraged when Sara secretly gave the newlyweds a co-op
apartment in New York as their wedding present without telling her.

No longer willing to suffer her mother-in-law in silence, she wrote
FDR, "I've reached a state of such constant self control [with her] that
sometimes I'm afraid of what might happen if it ever breaks." Alienated
particularly from her two older children, whose upbringing she felt had
been taken out of her hands, she sometimes seemed to be looking for
flaws in both of them. When Jimmy, who was trying to find a niche at
Harvard, wrote her a chatty letter about how he had just gotten over the
bacchanalia that functioned as an initiation for Hasty Pudding and added
the customary college student's postscript about needing money,
Eleanor forwarded the request to Warm Springs with a cold note to
Franklin: "Too bad James needs the money. You can never get away
from your many gold diggers, can you? I can't say that three nights
drunk fills me with anything but disgust!"

Eleanor was determined to have greater influence over the last two
boys than she'd had on her first three children. She made them go to
dance class wearing periwigs so they could learn the minuet. Along with
Dickerman and Cook, she took Franklin Jr. and John on tours of the
Statue of Liberty and other sights. In the summer of 1925 the five of
them went on a camping trip through Canada. Despite the fact that the
boys squabbled constantly and Franklin Jr. cut his foot with a hatchet,
Eleanor regarded the outing as a success. However, the boys told their
sister, Anna, that they believed that she planned the trip out of duty, not
love, and Marion Dickerman later said that even on this holiday she had
seen the wall of resentment growing between mother and sons.

This wall thickened when Eleanor took a part-time job teaching at
Todhunter, a fashionable girls' school where Dickerman was assistant
principal. She was there three days a week, shepherding wealthy girls on
field trips to slums and settlement houses and giving them more attention than she gave her own children.

By the time news of his family reached him at Warm Springs FDR
could not hear the resentment and rancor in the distant voices. The
atmosphere he tried to maintain there was that of a sort of Shangri-la,
the name he would later give to his presidential retreat. Anxious to share
the resort's curative powers with others, he wrote his crippled cousin
Bamie, "Oh, I do wish that you could be wafted from there and placed
gently in a chair and slid gracefully into the water."

He oversaw every detail at Warm Springs, spending long hours planning a preserve for the quail shooting, a man-made lake, and two eighteen-hole golf courses—all of which he planned to make available to the disabled as well as the regular clientele. He had a Model T outfitted with hand controls that allowed him to drive and he went around the area to design these improvements, most of which would never be finished. He was master of ceremonies for the musical nights staged by the polio victims, which centered on jokes about the "ABs" (able bodied persons) and skits such as the one where a group of paraplegic ladies were rolled onto the stage in wheelbarrows and holding up signs reading, "I Won't Dance, Don't Ask Me."

He involved himself in the lives of all his patients. Yet he was still intensely committed to his own case and to walking again. In the privacy of his own cottage, he practiced standing with his back to the wall, stiff in his braces. Upon achieving precarious balance, he would throw away the crutches and usually teeter there for a moment, sweating with apprehension, until he toppled over and came crashing down. His neighbor at the resort, Leighton MacPherson, once came onto the porch and was about to knock when he heard FDR call out urgently from within: "In here, Leighton, in here!" MacPherson went in and saw Roosevelt against the wall, his arms held out: "Look at me, Leighton, I'm standing alone!"

Behind the dream of standing was the contingent dream of politics. Louis Howe kept the political pot boiling with communiqués and visits. As a result of Howe's efforts, the uneasy coalition with Al Smith continued. Although FDR knew the Irishman considered him a lightweight who could be easily used, Eleanor was strongly behind Smith's decision to try for the Democrats' nomination for President again in 1928, and FDR agreed to go to the national convention in Houston and nominate him once again.

For a time he considered trying to get to the podium by himself, with a cane in his right hand and a crutch under his left arm, but it was too risky and this time he decided to use Elliott, now a strapping young man of eighteen, as his escort. They practiced for days at Warm Springs, the boy flinching as his father's powerful fingers dug into his left arm for support as they coordinated their shuffle. "Don't look at me, son," FDR kept telling him. "Keep your head up, smiling, watching the eyes of the people. Keep them from noticing what we're doing."

Once again he was a tremendous success, stealing the show from Smith, who was chosen this time as the party's nominee. As one delegate said, "Roosevelt was a heroic figure. His whole appeal was of overcoming adversity, telling people by example that they could do the same thing."

Starting as an underdog to the Republican nominee Herbert Hoover, the desperate Smith, in an acknowledgement of FDR's growing status, begged him to run for governor of New York and help him to carry the state. But Howe firmly believed that there would be a Republican landslide in 1928 and didn't want Franklin's future jeopardized. And for his own part, FDR didn't want to leave the healing powers of Warm Springs. He believed that it was not merely wishful thinking when he said he knew his condition was improving. The day he returned from the Houston convention, the resident nurse at the resort did an exhaustive test of his lower body and claimed that every muscle had picked up strength since the last measurement.

The hope of recovery had come a step closer to reality because Henry Ford's son Edsel had donated $25,000 so that a glass enclosure could be built around the hydrotherapy pool. Now, instead of having to shut down in October, the resort could remain open for polio victims all year long. FDR claimed that the doctor at Warm Springs told him that he would perhaps be able to discard his right-hand cane if he worked in the pool through the winter. When Smith asked him again about running for governor, FDR dictated a letter saying that he hoped to be able to get rid of his braces if he worked year-round at Warm Springs for the next two years.*

Eleanor was strongly behind Smith, her women's committee having been given significant power by his campaign brain trust. Yet although she knew it would help Smith's cause, she was ambivalent about her husband's possible candidacy for governor because she feared that if he were elected, her maneuverability would diminish as she was shoehorned into the symbolic role of governor's wife. But Missy had no doubts; she was flatly opposed to FDR's running. If he won the governorship, their idyllic days in searching for a cure would be over.

As the New York Democrats began their convention, FDR's coy refusals to accept the nomination made him all the more attractive. Desperate to get ahold of him for one last talk, Al Smith called Warm Springs and got no answer. Fearing that FDR was ducking him, he got

---

* In *A First Class Temperament,* Geoffery Ward, after doing considerable research about whether or not FDR's condition was permanent and stationary, argues convincingly that he would have experienced no marked improvement from further treatment at Warm Springs.

Eleanor to call for him. She reached her husband at a public telephone outside a drugstore near a hall where he'd been giving a talk. FDR got on the line and began to explain cheerfully how tough he'd been making it on Smith. Annoyed at having had to wait so long for him to get to the phone, Eleanor curtly said she had to leave and handed the phone to Smith. Smith shouted over the poor connection that he had to be the candidate, and FDR shouted back that he couldn't.

In another long conversation after FDR returned to the resort, Smith begged him to reconsider and also made a subtle threat—if FDR didn't cooperate now it could affect his future. Smith insisted that FDR would still be able to spend most of the year at Warm Springs once he was elected. The only thing necessary would be to appear in Albany and sign some bills and then let his lieutenant governor (presumably to be hand-picked by and loyal to Smith) take care of the details. Finally, incapable of saying no any longer, Franklin agreed not to turn the nomination down if it was handed to him.

Now that the decision had been made, a pall descended over the evening as Missy realized that their long holiday together was over. The chauffeur took her and FDR back to their cottage. Oppressed by the downcast atmosphere, FDR remarked cheerily, "Well, if I've got to run for Governor there's no use in all of us getting sick about it!"

Once nominated, he threw himself into the fray with enthusiasm. Standing in the rear of a convertible supported by a specially made bar running along the back of the front seat, he campaigned vigorously throughout the state. Rather than ignoring his disability, he made it part of his pitch. "Well, here he is, the helpless cripple my opponent is speaking about," FDR would sometimes tell a crowd. "This is my sixteenth speech today!"

As the early returns came in on election night several weeks later, it was clear that Smith had been swamped by Hoover and it seemed that FDR would lose too. When Eleanor and Anna wheeled him off to bed at around midnight, he had the cigarette holder clamped in his jaw at a defiant angle but he was prepared for defeat. But his vote count began to rise after he went to bed, and just before daybreak it was certain that he would win the election by a narrow margin.

Sara had stayed up alone until the victory was certain, then went to bed happy. Eleanor woke up the next morning and was irritable in an appearance before the press. "No, I am not excited about my husband's election," she snapped at a reporter. "I don't care. What difference can it make to me?"

Both of them were aware that a process had gotten ahold of them now, something that was beyond their conscious control. It was history, and they could feel themselves being integrated into its flow. The days of the Oyster Bay clan's ascendancy began to seem like a prologue to their drama.

During Franklin's first year in office at Albany, Jimmy became engaged to Betsey Cushing, daughter of famous surgeon Harvey Cushing. (The irrepressible Sara, introduced to her grandson's fiancée, said, "Surgeons always remind me of my butcher.") After the marriage, there was a reception at the Executive Mansion and FDR stole the show. Later on, Jimmy reproached him playfully and his father laughed, "Oh, that was nothing. When your mother and I were married, her uncle, President Theodore Roosevelt, gave the bride away. After the ceremony, when TR moved into the library for a sip of punch, the crowd followed him as if he were the Pied Piper, leaving your mother and me standing all alone and forlorn."

Ted watched the emergence of Franklin and Eleanor with a silent dismay. His own political attractiveness had always depended on two factors that were beyond his control. One was his name and the other was his ability to keep the power inherent in that name in the Republican column. FDR's election compromised this second element.

Ted's wife, Eleanor, would later call the years 1927–29 one of the most difficult periods in his life. He was a politician without a clear political future. The warning his mother issued after he lost the 1924 governor's race—that he must not allow himself to become just a famous name wheeled out periodically by the party to support others—now seemed like a prophecy.

He wrote a couple of books that drew on the two aspects of his life in which he could take unalloyed pride—his family and his service in the Great War. *All in the Family* was a sentimental chronicle of life at Sagamore, and *Rank and File* was a series of vignettes about episodes of bravery in the war, including the story of Sergeant Alvin York.

He did not buy a house at Oyster Bay because he assumed that someday he would inherit Sagamore. But he spent time with all the others of his generation who had made Long Island the family seat. (Ethel's husband, Dick, had taken a position on the staff of Long Island Insane Asylum; Archie had a house in Cold Spring Harbor; and Kermit had one in Oyster Bay called Mohannes, the second part of the name of the

Indian Chief Sagamore Mohannes.) Ted tried to fulfill the expectations his name carried with it. Every Christmas Eve he went to the Episcopal Church his father had attended, arriving in a car instead of a sleigh, and gave a short address just as TR always had.

Ted continued to spend time with Kermit, whose business took him in and out of New York. "Both of them were drinking more than was good for them," as one family member put it later on, "although Ted didn't hold it as well as Kermit and was intelligent enough to know this and so drank less." To have a place to drink conveniently in the middle of Prohibition, the brothers joined with Vincent Astor, Nelson Doubleday, Marshall Field, and several other prominent figures whose commond bond was membership in the Knickerbocker Club, and rented a floor in a brownstone on 62nd Street. "The Room," as their private club became known, had an antique mahogany bar and was soon filled with stuffed animal heads and other trophies and memorabilia donated by the twenty members. (The Roosevelt brothers gave a Remington bronze that had once belonged to TR, along with captured enemy flags they had brought back from Europe.) Each member had his own key and a mug embossed with the club logo, a bear and deer holding a cocktail glass. Chief among the rules of The Room, as Vincent Astor reminded Kermit in a letter, was the fact that "ladies, or at least society ladies, should not be brought in as guests."

Ted had been the Republican hatchet man against Smith in 1928, beginning to attack him as soon as it seemed likely he would be the Democrats' nominee. "For the first time in the history of the nation," he had begun his address at the 1927 state Republican convention, "the shadow of Tammany lies athwart the White House." The speech was so hardhitting, the *New York Times* reported the next day, "that it made some of those who listened gasp in amazement."

Still nursing his own furtive ambitions, Ted went on a cross-country speaking tour after the first of the year to repeat the anti-Tammany speech. He secretly hoped for another call to run for governor but told political allies that he was willing "to skip over that link in the chain" if Hoover selected him to be his vice presidential running mate. But while the party valued him as a speaker it was not interested in him as a candidate and the call he was hoping for did not come.

Before the 1928 election was over, Ted and Kermit had started planning another trip. Again it would be a trip reminiscent of TR's, but again it would be to a part of the world he had not visited, allowing them to extend his tradition. They began by simply unrolling a large

map and examining the uncharted spaces on it. First they thought of
Borneo, but other explorers had just made the trip. They discussed
Angola. They finally settled on an area northwest of Indochina where
the Himalayas descended into the tropical plains.

Supported once again by the Field Museum, they would go into this
area by the trail that later became known as the Burma Road. They
planned to do some rough mapping and shoot rare animals for the
museum's collection. Their primary quarry was something more mysterious than the *Ovis poli* of the last expedition: a giant panda. No
specimen had been taken by a sportsman in over fifty years. A few
panda skins had made their way to the West, but there had been no
skeletons. The aim of their expedition was to settle the zoological debate
over what exactly the animal was, a bear, a giant raccoon, or some
hybrid species.

Eleanor and Belle were to accompany Ted and Kermit to Paris, return
home, and then journey to Saigon several months later to meet them
again when they emerged from the jungle. Somewhat jealous at his
brothers' freedom, Archie saw the party off at the dock in early December and then wrote Ethel, the other stay-behind, a letter filled with
ironic observations: "To the vast disgust of Kermit and Belle, Ted
appeared flanked with two reporters demanding interviews and pictures . . . and was 'airing off' to them."

When the party docked in London, Ted went to the British Museum
to interview the director about pandas. He jotted down an entry in his
diary: "Got some information from him by promising him the penis and
testicles of a male Panda if we got it. They apparently will [use these
body parts] to determine whether it is a panda or a bear. Such a science!"

After the wives went back to America, Ted and Kermit pushed on to
Indochina. They arrived in March and spent weeks trekking through the
high jungles, taking specimens along the way. But the world had become somewhat smaller since TR's trip to Africa twenty years earlier.
Moving pictures now allowed people to see exotic animals without
visiting museum dioramas, and it was more difficult for them to believe
that "collecting" was an important public service. Instead of what TR
had once called "game butchering," the trip came to center on the search
for the giant panda.

Exploring the mountainous area on the Chinese border, the brothers
went native, both brothers wearing Robinson Crusoe beards and following guides carrying antique matchlock rifles and smelling of opium.
Ted promised to give whichever guide flushed a panda for them a

pearl-handled .38 revolver that had belonged to TR. But the creatures were elusive and they had almost given up finding one of them until one morning in mid-April when they decided to separate and hunt up parallel gorges in the mountains.

Late in the morning, Kermit suddenly spotted a panda foraging in a bamboo thicket—"very large and like the animal of a dream." He sighted the animal with his rifle; he was in range and considered taking a shot, particularly when it seemed that the panda would "vanish like smoke into the jungle." But since this was a joint venture, he decided to send a runner for Ted. Ted came up about half an hour later, just as the animal was starting to move on. The brothers fired at exactly the same instant at the end of a countdown and killed the panda together.

They had planned to hunt their way to the Cochin area and then meet their wives in June. But word arrived that Kermit's shipping business had fallen into deep trouble and so he left early to return to the United States. Ted's wife, Eleanor, decided to make the trip alone.

While Ted was on his adventure, she and Alice had been lobbying hard to get him a position in the Hoover administration. Their sights had been set on the high-profile job of governor-general of the Philippines. But this proved to be out of reach and in May Eleanor cabled Ted that the best they had been able to do was governor-general of Puerto Rico. His first response, brought out of the jungle by a runner, said that he believed the office was beneath him and felt he should turn it down. Alice supported this decision, but Eleanor urged him to take the job because it was the only hope he had.

"You are absolutely right," Ted wrote back contritely after considering her advice. "I have got to get into the line of officeholders again or I am going to be forgotten. . . . It may be that Porto Rico will lead to nothing, but it may lead [somewhere] else. I need a longer record of positions held."

As soon as the issue was resolved, Eleanor boarded a steamer and headed for Shanghai. The ship cut its way through a typhoon and landed on time. A telegram was waiting for her from Ted saying that he was having problems hacking his way through the jungle and would be late for their rendezvous in Saigon. She went along at a leisurely pace, stopping for a few days in Hanoi. Arriving in Saigon, she stayed with the U.S. consul there. There was no word from Ted and she began to worry. She did not know that his expedition had been stopped by sickness, and that two of the men he and Kermit had taken with them had died while several others had become gravely ill.

Finally one night during dinner at the consulate, everyone was disturbed by strange howling noises outside. Eleanor went to the window with the other diners and saw an emaciated figure in torn clothing hanging from the grillwork of the iron gates and yelling at the top of his lungs. The U.S. consul thought it was just another crazy beggar, but Eleanor recognized her husband. Ted had just emerged from the jungle. He was wasted from fever and, she decided after examining him, looked worse than any time she could remember, including when he was gassed in the trenches of France in 1918. His temperature was 105. He had lost forty-two pounds and was suffering from malaria and dysentery. One of the scientists he had carried out with him had been hospitalized in Hanoi with a jungle fever which so deranged him that he jumped out of a hospital window and killed himself.

After several days of bed rest, Ted was strong enough to accompany Eleanor on a tour of Saigon, a city of whitewashed buildings with yellow trim where rickshaws thronged the streets and coolies carried bales of produce on either ends of poles balanced on their shoulders. Then they boarded a ship for home. Ted weighed only 102 pounds, and was still so weak that members of the crew, Eleanor learned later on, had established a betting pool so that they could wager on whether or not he would die before they docked back home in America.

After building up his strength, Ted went to San Juan to take up his new job. Strangely garbled information about his appointment was circulating in the island. A reporter for the *New York Times* jotted down the following conversation he heard between two Puerto Ricans:

"Roosevelt is coming to be governor."

"What Roosevelt?"

"The son of the President."

"The son of the President is the Governor of New York."

"That's one son, the other's coming here, the younger one."

"I thought he was commissioner of the War or the Navy."

"That's another son, still younger."

Ted was sworn in as governor-general of Puerto Rico wearing the cutaway in which he'd been married and the top hat he'd bought for Harding's funeral. He told newspapers that he intended to be a "people's Governor General," and gave his inaugural address in hastily learned Spanish, the first American administrator to do this on the island. The speech caused such a stir of approval that Ted decided to go all over Puerto Rico with his military attaché giving extemporaneous speeches in Spanish to the villagers. After his tour was over, Eleanor sent her mother a progress report: "[He] was getting along well until in one place full of children he told them that he had four children of his own, but phrased it in such a way that what he actually said was that he had given birth to four. . . . Waving to the audience, he introduced General Parker, intending to say he was a bachelor. By mistake he used the wrong word and introduced him as a tapeworm!"

In a letter written to a friend during the first year of his governorship, Franklin wrote about how the family had come through a series of near disasters: "Jimmy is getting over pneumonia; Elliott is about to have an operation; Franklin Jr. has a doubly broken nose; and John has just had cartilage taken out of his knee . . . and I am in one continuous glorious fight with the Republican legislative leaders."

Eleanor was a little harder to categorize. Still teaching at Todhunter School three days a week, she was unreconciled to her new role and to the increased domesticity it demanded. (She was also unreconciled to herself. During a family dinner the first year they were at Albany, James and Anna unveiled a portrait they had commissioned of her. Eleanor took one look at the oil painting, said, "It's hateful!" and ran crying from the room. This event was considered noteworthy because family activities were generally so highly planned that there were no such spontaneous episodes that might cause such an explosion.)

Yet there were compensations. FDR had assigned Eleanor a body-guard from the State Police named Earl Miller. A boxer and judo expert who was vain about his good physique, Miller, twelve years younger, became a close companion for Eleanor. She basked in his rough-hewn gallantry. The two of them traveled together, Miller becoming an escort more than a bodyguard. He taught her to shoot and rode with her and flattered her with the first male attention she had gotten since Franklin courted her. She mothered him and integrated him into her family of nonfamily members. Irritated that Miller had risen to a position of such first-name intimacy in the Governor's Mansion, taking meals and so-cializing there, Sara delivered a huffy pun, "He used to be Sergeant and now he's Earl."

FDR had said in his inaugural in Albany that he wanted to unite the factions of New York in an "era of good feeling." Observers of the Executive Mansion felt that he had demonstrated a knack for gover-nance in his first two years in office, but it was hard for him to define himself politically because Al Smith had held the office for eight years and had such a significant legislative accomplishment. Yet he instituted fireside chats on the radio in an attempt to circumvent a largely Republican press. And as the country stumbled into hard times, he exhibited a stirring optimism.

Raymond Moley, Rexford Tugwell, and the other brain-trusters who had joined Louis Howe on FDR's staff agreed that the Depression could be interpreted as the birth pains for a new order that would require new leaders. But the Oyster Bay Roosevelts looked at the same social and economic conditions and saw only the death of their world. Part of their alarm came from the diminution of the prerogatives they had enjoyed. Kermit's lighthearted comment to his mother—"Old Brother Economy makes it preferable to entertain now at lunch rather than at dinner"—hid the fact that his shipping business, which he had come home early from Indochina to rescue, was seriously affected by the economy and he found himself eating into his wife, Belle's, family money to keep the ships afloat.

Archie too had been hit hard. He had managed to right himself from the aftereffects of the Teapot Dome scandal and his dismissal by the Sinclair Oil Company in his work for the stock brokerage house of Roosevelt and Son when the Depression hit. Now, to make ends meet, he was operating a school out of the garage of his home in Cold Spring Harbor and inveighing against national fiscal irresponsibility as a member of an organization called the National Economy League, which Ted believed was valuable primarily in "keeping Archie's mind from dashing itself to pieces against an impossible set of business problems."

But over and above the personal setbacks they all suffered was the disturbing sense they shared of a world reconfiguring itself into new and ominous shapes. It was a moment for them like the beginning of the First World War had been for TR when he had compared history to a kaleidoscope whose glass had suddenly been shaken and rearranged into unfamiliar patterns.

One casualty of the times was that perception of shared history and uniqueness that had always contained the disagreements of all branches of the Roosevelt family. The remarkable group whose spiritual center TR had been, a family that had always made a point of embracing not only lineal relationships but lateral ones as well, had now divided into two bitter warring camps—the one side simmering with resentment over stolen birthrights, and the other taking pleasure in vengeance for past slights. Like Old World clans struggling for territory, they were known by their locale—the Oyster Bay Roosevelts versus the Hyde

Park Roosevelts. The geographic emphasis was appropriate, for it was no exaggeration to say that the ground they fought over was America itself.

In this fierce contest, the generous gesture—always before a Roosevelt hallmark—was now such a rarity that it required comment when it occurred. After the elections of 1928, for instance, Eleanor wrote Corinne Robinson, "You have always been wonderful to Franklin and *about* Franklin. I think it was wonderful, your voting for him. I never expected it, dear." Yet Corinne was one of the only Roosevelts for whom family still took precedence over party. One of Ethel's daughters recalled later on the time when the FDR family had stopped to visit the Derbys during the gubernatorial campaign: "We were *awful* to those Franklin children. And after the family left, we took all the Franklin Delano Roosevelt buttons they left with us and stamped on them with glee!"

The sense of transition inside the family was dramatized by losses along the way. First came Nick Longworth, who died unexpectedly of pneumonia in early April 1931. In his last years he had reached the apex of his power as speaker of the House. And in a curious reversal of roles, he had become somewhat domesticated, not only accepting paternity for the baby, Paulina, but becoming a doting father. Longworth had frequently taken the child with him to the speaker's office, happily indulging her whims (Paulina molded cookies on his bald head) and getting her to perform for his colleagues.

Alice had remained aloof from both of them. Her daughter seemed to bring out the long-buried conflicts of her own motherless childhood and the two of them were not close. With Longworth, the passionate love from her days as Princess Alice, the relationship had degenerated into one of cordial hatred. When Alice went to Cincinnati for the funeral, one of Nick's mistresses showed up at the Longworth estate and assumed the wife's role of taking the last grieving look at the casket. One gossip claimed that Alice had burned her husband's beloved violin after returning home.

At the time of Nick's death, a far more monumental figure was ready to topple. It was Bamie, who lay dying at her Connecticut estate. She had been sinking for some time, almost totally deaf, and so deformed by arthritis that she appeared petrified. But she had faced her disabilities with courage and humor. "She was like a ship," said one female friend, "a battleship that might be going down, but every flag was flying and the band was playing." Virtually paralyzed by pain, she still insisted on putting on her entertainments, although she had to be moved by her butler after guests were ushered out and sometimes she could be heard gasping to him as he carried her from the sofa to her wheelchair, "Oh Hopkinson! Oh Hopkinson!"

As she sank toward a coma, her son, Sheffield Jr., and his wife were at her bedside. After several days, they sought a brief respite from the death watch and went out to play golf. At the second hole someone drove up and told them that they must return because Bamie had decided that she would rise from her deathbed. As they came running into the house, she was out of bed and ready to preside one final time over tea. "You thought I'd die and I fooled you," she smiled at them.

The next morning she told them that she would probably die that day and she did. Her niece Corinne Alsop, who was also present at the end, said that her aunt's exit was the most dramatic thing she'd ever experienced.

A year later it was Conie. She had become a little scattered in her old age, writing notes to herself. ("Remember to see Mary," went one entry, and then, right under it, came the next, "Who's Mary?") A poet with a minor reputation, she had become a literary lioness after the publication of *My Brother Theodore Roosevelt* in 1921. She had terrible asthma attacks, but carried on just as Bamie had. To the end, she continued to hold dinner parties. Her illness forced her to stay in an adjacent room, gasping for air as she breathed noxious powders, but she sent in poems by runners written for the occasion for each of her guests—"wheezy and breathless," but still the life of the party.

With her passing, the last remnant of the remarkable family of the first Theodore Roosevelt was now gone.

The economic chaos now gripping the country, background for the passing of these figures who were so deeply implicated in family history, further contracted the world of the Oyster Bay Roosevelts and made them feel even more alienated. From his isolation in Puerto Rico, Ted watched bitterly as the processes that were hurting his own family buoyed the fortunes of his rival, Franklin. On the day after the 1930 midterm elections, when the Republicans were buried by a landslide and FDR was reelected governor by a huge margin, making him almost the inevitable nominee for the Democrats in 1932, Ted wrote his mother sarcastically, "Well, as far as I can see, the ship went down with all on board. Your cousin Franklin now, I suppose, will run for the Presidency, and I am already beginning to think of nasty things to say concerning him."

He was popular in Puerto Rico. His stumbling but always enthusiastic Spanish was appreciated. He was a passionate advocate for the people. When he wrote a much noticed article in the *New York Herald Sunday Magazine* about the children of the island going hungry and suffering from disease, there was a storm of protest in Washington from those who denied that such things were possible under the American flag. But Ted continued in his role as advocate for the residents of the island. In an effort to increase tourism, he personally went to the docks to welcome the boats. Meanwhile, his wife, Eleanor, tried to create a market for Puerto Rican crafts by getting the chic stores in Manhattan to carry them. When there was a run on the banks in 1931, he got the U.S. Treasury to put $100,000 of government money into the Puerto Rican central bank and backed it with his own note.

The *Baltimore Sun* called him "one of the finest, and perhaps the finest colonial governor in our history." He thought his performance might help him claw his way back to political prominence. But two years after arriving in Puerto Rico he had not been offered another post by the Hoover administration. As anything other than a temporary position, the job seemed a humiliation, and late in 1931, Alice began to insist that he resign. (His sister's advice was so apocalyptic, in fact, that he thought it might be evidence of menopause: "She has evidently gone completely wild. . . . Is it her physical condition? She must now be forty eight. . . .")

Ted considered his options and wrote his wife, Eleanor, who was back on the mainland for a visit, "I believe that what I should do is come north for Christmas as you suggest. . . . I do not believe, however, that I should ever go back to Porto Rico again. . . . I think there is a limit beyond which I should not be kicked around, and I think that limit has been reached." The strategy paid off. Just after the New Year's holiday the beleaguered Hoover administration, increasingly worried about defections, told Ted that he would be appointed governor-general of the Philippines.

It was a position that resonated with family history. It was his father, after all, who had helped secure the islands for the United States. As a homage to TR, Ted detoured to Japan on his way to Manila and visited Admiral Takishta, who had come to Sagamore a quarter century earlier as part of the delegation settling the Russo-Japanese War. "He had pictures of Father given him in Washington," Ted wrote his mother, "and the photographs taken at Oyster Bay when the mission called. The old boy . . . came down to the train with me with a large bamboo walking cane [that he called] 'The big stick of old memories.' "

Arriving in Manila, Ted made plans to visit all the major islands of the Philippines. He went into the back country provinces to speak, talking to townspeople from early morning until midnight about their grievances. Everywhere he stopped he went on hunts, no longer particularly enthusiastic about killing animals but conscious, as he told Eleanor, that the reputation he had acquired as a result of his trips with Kermit made it neccessary to demonstrate his skills.

The *Philippines Herald* called him "a Governor General who does not mind being bitten by jungle mosquitos, who can fall into wild carabao wallows and like it, who can drink Igorot wine and lick his chops, who can be really human without losing his grin. . . ." One gesture that particularly impressed the people came when Ted went to the leper colony on the island of Culion and reviewed a troop of leper Boy Scouts, shaking the hand of every one of them.

He tried to defuse the pressures for independence by designing a Reorganization Act. The idea was to aid the small farmer and thus both improve public education and also make it available to every primary student. Everywhere Ted went in the islands, he tried to sell the plan. In his appearances he was always conscious that he was a representative of TR. "I have been smart as a monkey at times, father's own son," he wrote his mother. "Yesterday they read a quotation from a speech Father made in North Dakota wherein after paying a tribute to Jose Rizal, the national Filipino hero, he said the United States would always live up to her obligations to the people of the Islands. When I came to speak, I quoted to them in Spanish a sentence from Jose Rizal's famous novel in which he said, ". . . I believe that realizing the ideals of your father is far more valuable than mourning him.' "

This job thrust Ted into the periphery of the nation's vision once again. He began to grasp at straws, thinking almost irrationally that the high political office on which he had set his heart was still a possibility. When he heard rumors that aged Vice President Charles Curtis was undecided about seeking another term, he wrote Eleanor, "To nominate him would be a crime. He is such an old man now that should Hoover die it might be a national calamity to have him as President. Furthermore, it seems to me that what the Republican ticket will need next autumn is not an old gentleman, dry, from Kansas, but an active, younger man, preferably an ex-service man with wet leanings, possibly from the Northeast. . . ." He assured his wife, not very convincingly, that he wasn't thinking of himself.

He was making a mark, as the *New York Times* indicated in an editorial: "Men who have had many years in the islands say no other governor has achieved such quick popularity." But time was running out. The American economy was sinking deeper into chaos, and the Democrats were sensing an opportunity for victory in 1932.

Ted followed from afar the drama of the Democrats' convention. He had come to believe almost as much in his cousin's inevitability as did people like Senator Henry Ashurst, who surprised his colleagues in Washington by saying that FDR was the man who could lead the United States out of the Depression because "Providence does not drag a man back from the grave unless it has a special purpose to be served."

Franklin arrived in Chicago with more delegates pledged to him than any other candidate. But Al Smith was there working against him, joining forces with crafty Texan John Nance Garner, speaker of the House. After several ballots, with FDR apparently stalled, Howe was desperate. Working around the clock, he was even more ashen-looking than usual, panting as he lay on the floor of his hotel room and let a fan blast air into his asthmatic lungs and at one point climbing up on top of the chest of drawers to lie there with the ventilation beating on him. Finally, as Franklin went over the top in the delegate count, there was one last crisis as Eleanor, panicked once again at the thought of losing her freedom, wrote a letter saying she "couldn't live in the White House." Howe ripped it up and tossed it in the wastebasket, saying harshly to a bystander, "You are not to breathe a word of this to anyone, understand? Not to *anyone*."

Hoover wanted to recall Ted from Manila to campaign against FDR. Always before Ted had welcomed such opportunities. But now he resisted the call, feeling that partisan politicking would compromise the dignity of the office he held and make the people of the Philippines, who had come to regard him as "the poor man's Governor," think he had deserted them in their time of need. But Republican campaign officials insisted in an angry conversation over an unsecured telephone line that soon leaked to the press. Placed in an impossible position, Ted wrote his mother, who had replaced Alice as his confidante: "I resisted to the point where I would either in my opinion have had to resign or go to campaign. . . . What idiots they are! They have been trying in the most insincere manner possible to make it look to the public as if I . . . intended to come home and campaign for personal reasons. I don't think anyone is fooled."

The *New York Times* supported him in an editorial arguing against using in this way "a man who has shown his administrative talent and who holds one of the greatest administrative offices in the world. . . ." Finally, in an uncomfortable compromise Ted agreed to make a campaign broadcast for Hoover from Manila, the first such message beamed across the Pacific.

Edith acted as his proxy. At seventy-one, still deep in mourning for TR, she was a symbol of widowhood itself. (She wore a long black veil to church in the winter and a white one in summer, garb her grandchildren referred to as her "widow's weeds.") Over the years, prospective biographers had often asked for her help in writing books about TR, but as she had written Corinne about one writer, "I helped him as much as I could, but I just cannot read the book. It is terribly painful to me to read about Theodore."

She had stayed out of the public eye for over a decade. But after the nomination of FDR, when she received several hundred letters and telegrams congratulating her as the mother of the next President, she had gone public with her support of Hoover. In addition to sending all her correspondence in envelopes bearing his picture, she boarded a plane at Roosevelt Field on Long Island (renamed for Quentin, who had learned to fly there) and traveled to Washington for a publicized visit with the President, and later caused a stir by appearing to speak for Hoover at a huge rally in Madison Square Garden.

Yet TR was increasingly a memory, which made Edith a memory of a memory. Her political appearance was little more than a curiosity. She was unable to do much more than write melancholy letters to her eldest son about the increasing likelihood of their relative's election.

Ted was whistling in the dark when he wrote his mother from Manila, "I have a distinctly hopeful feeling about November. Franklin is such poor stuff it seems improbable that he should be elected President." In a less self-delusive moment, though, he realized that the seesaw he had shared with his cousin had now risen for good on Franklin's end, sending him down: "I believe that the Governor Generalship of the Philippine Islands may well mark the end of my active career as a public servant. Should it do so . . . I would like to feel that I had done the best that lay in me. I do not feel now that I have anything to be ashamed [for] having gone into public life or that Father would feel other than that I have done well."

A couple of weeks later, Ted wrote his mother with a postscript for his political obituary: "These last few years in Porto Rico and the P[hilippine] I[slands] have given me enough in the way of accomplishments to make me feel I have left sufficient to the children in that way. That chapter of our lives is definitely closed. I believe the chances of me 'coming back' politically are almost nonexistent."

Shortly after Franklin was elected, Edith journeyed to the Philippines to be with Ted. In joining him at this critical juncture in the family's history, she was validating the effort he had made to seize his father's standard. She wanted to stand together with him against the dark future that stretched out ahead, a future in which the prerogatives and expectations they had enjoyed would be eroded and power would pass to the hands of the groups that had buoyed Franklin's candidacy.

But Edith and Ted were also standing together against what both regarded as treason from within their family. It involved Kermit, who had opened secret lines of communication with the enemy. They expected Belle's family, old-line Democrats, to support FDR. They did not imagine that Kermit too would break ranks, although it was true that as a boy he had been closest in age and temperament of all the Oyster Bay boys to Franklin, and closest in terms of friendship.

Edith and Ted did not know about the unctuous letter of congratulation he had written to FDR after the election. ("I can say with absolute truth that, although I have been a Republican all my life, I am tremendously relieved and pleased that you were elected.") Or that in this letter he had also offered ideas on how to revive the economy that seemed to suggest he would be willing to become a consultant. But what they did know was bad enough. Shortly after the first of the year, Kermit had written Ted to say that he had accepted an invitation from Vincent Astor to go on a two-week cruise to the Caribbean aboard the *Nourmahal*, Astor's extraordinary, German-made yacht, which the *New York Times* had described as "the biggest and fastest ocean going motor yacht ever built." It was only after he'd agreed to go, Kermit insisted, that he found out that FDR had also been invited. "Personally I would rather the situation hadn't come up," his letter said, "but there was nothing to do but to make a quick decision and I am convinced it would have been stupid to have decided any other way. . . ."

The truth was that FDR had not only been involved in the cruise from the beginning, but Astor had set it up to give the President-elect a good rest before his inauguration, and Kermit had obviously known this. Going through her husband's papers later on, Ted's wife, Eleanor, found Kermit's letter informing him of the trip and typed in the margin: "I do not remember anything that hurt T as much as this particularly when we heard that the trip had been planned for FDR. . . . It was known at this time that T was to be recalled from his position in the Philippines by the new President."

Kermit's presence on board the *Nourmahal* led to a front-page story in the *New York Times* headlined, "Rift between Roosevelt Families Bridged." This was salt in Ted's wounds. The disloyalty destroyed the strong connections built by the brothers' treks into foreign countries on hunting trips. Not understanding that Kermit needed to feel part of an inner circle, Ted saw only an unprincipled attempt on his brother's part to blandish his rival, the man who had displaced his own family. Going on the cruise, moreover, was a gesture that compromised him personally by making it appear that he was using his brother to try to save his job. Edith agreed with her eldest son, sternly telling newsmen who inquired about why Kermit had gone, "Because his mother was not there." The meaning was clear: if she had been able to talk to Kermit she would have put her foot down and kept this faux pas from happening.

It didn't save the situation that Kermit became a witness to history. At the end of the pleasure part of the cruise, the *Nourmahal* stopped in Miami so that FDR could make a brief speech on the evening of February 13, 1933, to a crowd of twenty thousand American Legionnaires. Kermit was in the limousine right behind FDR's open car watching Chicago Mayor Anton "Tony" Cermak come up to the President-elect just as an Italian bricklayer named Joseph Zangara rushed out of the crowd with a .32 pistol and began firing. Cermak took the bullet intended for Roosevelt. FDR cradled the wounded man in his arms as his car screeched toward the hospital. "Tony, keep quiet," he said softly to the dying Cermak. "It won't hurt if you keep quiet." (Afterward, brain-truster Raymond Moley asked the President how he had managed to remain so calm and FDR replied that he had lived with such an event in his mind because TR once told him it might happen and he should prepare for it.)

Ted wrote Edith, who by this time had returned home from the Philippines: "I was shocked at the attempted assassination of Franklin Roosevelt. After deep thought I gave out a short statement for the press here. It seemed to me that I could not let the matter go for fear of being called surly but at the same time I must not slop over and give anyone the chance to say that I was endeavoring to curry favor."

The contretemps cast a shadow over the brothers that would lengthen in the years to come as the Oyster Bay clan became divided over how to deal with Franklin. For weeks it was the primary topic of discussion in the family, causing irritation and disagreement. Back home at Sagamore, Edith wrote Ted about the latest chapter: "Sister was here yesterday and could not understand why Kermit's fishing cruise with FDR should have hurt us. I mentioned there were others I had met coming across the country who felt that way and those she dismissed as low, vile trash with whom only I would consort. I think however she saw a dim light at the end for 'tho quiet I was firm and gave her no chance of one of her bitter temper fits."

Ted was listening on the radio as FDR took the oath of office on the old Dutch Bible that had been in the family since the time of Issac the Patriot. Radio commentators said that tears were pouring down the faces of some of the thousands who had gathered in Washington to hear him. Some compared it to a revival meeting atmosphere. Eleanor stood beside him, looking out at the solemn, hopeful faces and wondering, she later said, how these poor people would ever pay for their hotel bills.

Interviewed about his new home, Franklin said of the White House, "You know how it was when Uncle Ted was there—how gay and livable. Well, that's how we mean to have it." That night Alice was invited to dinner as a peace gesture. She flounced in, looked around haughtily and said, "Well, Eleanor, I wonder how you're going to be able to handle this?" Other ironic comments followed, and by the end of the evening she had her cousin on the verge of tears.

The following day, Ted cabled from Manila asking that the Philippines be exempted from the bank holiday that the new administration had announced as its first order of business. His request was granted, and the resignation he submitted was also immediately accepted. As he began to settle his public and personal affairs, walking through the capital city in a white summer suit, one hand in the side pocket and the other holding a cigarette, Ted was asked by newsmen to specify once again exactly what his relationship was to the new President. "Fifth cousin about to be removed," he answered wryly.

He had come back from the war ready to defeat the usurper. But like the rest of his family, he had always underestimated Franklin. In the resilient and courageous way he had handled personal tragedy and in the way he had allowed it to temper his spirit, Franklin had actually become more like TR than any of them could have imagined. Like his cousin, FDR had a feel for history. While TR had been the last man of the old age, he had positioned himself to become the first man of the new one.

He could not have done it without Eleanor. She had brought him close to the TR family and this experience had lit a slow fuse in him. She had entered public life in a way that brought luster to the name. Unlike Franklin, Eleanor had motives for success that transcended simple ambition, motives that involved revision of the family history. Her daughter's husband, Curtis Dall, only heard her mention her father once in all the time he knew her, but then it was to say that Elliott had been charming and popular, a "more attractive social personality" than TR.

When it seemed certain that FDR would be elected, Eleanor conspired with Charles Scribner about printing a collection of her father's letters, which would help restore his reputation. Publisher to the Oyster Bay Roosevelts for years, Scribner hesitated for fear of offending his other clients, but then, after the election, said that he would do the book, and *Hunting Big Game in the 'Eighties,* a chronicle of Elliott's travels as seen through his letters, appeared shortly after the inauguration.

In the space of little more than a decade, the tables had been turned in the Roosevelt family. Now the Oyster Bay clan had become the *other* Roosevelts. It was evident everywhere, but perhaps no place more than in one newspaper's reference to Kermit as being a representative of "the steamship company branch of the family."

There was no public acknowledgment of the transition but an incident that summarized what had happened occurred one afternoon in September 1933 when the liner *Manhattan* docked in New York harbor. Nineteen-year-old Franklin Jr. was one of the passengers, returning home after a summer's trip to Europe. Ironically, Ted and Eleanor were on board too, having booked passage home after spending six months touring Europe following Ted's resignation as governor-general of the Philippines.

Edith was there to meet her eldest son, along with his children Theodore III and Quentin, and his sister Alice. As they were all getting ready to debark, Eleanor showed up with her son James and daughter, Anna, to meet Franklin Jr. She walked over to where Edith was standing and kissed her on the cheek and then collected Franklin Jr. As she left, the newsmen who had been talking to Ted about his views on world affairs before she arrived scurried after the First Lady and her children. Although none of them reported the event as such, what they had just seen, as one of them said later on, were two families within one dynasty passing in the dark.

PART FIVE

The Children of
Presidents

"One of the worst things in the world is being the
child of a President. It's a terrible life they lead."

—FRANKLIN D. ROOSEVELT

*E*arly in 1939, while he was juggling so many other problems, Franklin Roosevelt had another troublesome request from his most troublesome son, Elliott. Living in Texas apart from the rest of the family, Elliott was also apart from his father politically, having fallen in with conservative oilmen and power brokers who had made him their mouthpiece in attacks on the New Deal and in opposition to the third term he knew his father wanted.

His son's political disloyalty did not particularly bother FDR. He was nothing if not a pragmatist, and he knew that his children might have to disagree with him to make their way in the world. His dynastic impulses were surprisingly weak; his notion of the family was of a collection of individuals happily pursuing separate lives rather than a group with its own internal order. He was sometimes disturbed by Elliott's lack of discipline, but unlike Eleanor, who disapproved of their son but felt a guilt about his growing up that he was able to manipulate with an adroitness sometimes bordering on cruelty, FDR was actually fascinated by Elliott and drawn to the whiff of amorality in his character.

At six three and two hundred pounds, Elliott was the best-looking and most athletic of Franklin's boys, with hooded eyes and a wolfish grin that gave his face a sensual animation. FDR appreciated Elliott's easy camaraderie with men and effortless success with women, and he was aware of the fact that although he had been through more scrapes at the age of twenty-eight than all his brothers combined, Elliott retained an element of innocence that they didn't possess. FDR admitted that he forgave his second son things he shouldn't have—not only to maintain the surface equanimity that was so important to him in all his close relationships, but also because he suspected that the emotional disorganization in his family, a disorganization largely created by his own unusual relationship with Eleanor, had somehow affected Elliott more than the others.

The other children had also had a hard time of their own growing up. Confused by the inexplicable silences and vast emotional distances dividing the adults in the family and invited to choose sides between them without having a clear understanding of what was at stake, Elliott's brothers and sister had all grown up uncertain about their place in the world and about whether those outsiders who now competed for their favor did so out of genuine affection or from more cynical motives. They had all been conned during their coming of age; but they had also all taken whatever advantage they could of their name and position. The result was personal and married lives of such chaos that one writer had used the famous passage from *The Great Gatsby* to describe them: "They were careless people. . . . They smashed up things and creatures and then retreated back into their vast carelessness, or whatever it was that kept them together, and let other people clean up the mess they had made."

But while the others had paid some deference to propriety, Elliott seemed at times to place himself beyond good and evil. For the past few years, he had milked his position as the President's son with gusto, trading shamelessly on the family name and not hesitating trying to make his father complicit in his schemes. All during the first term he had badgered FDR to receive his wealthy Texas friends in the White House. But at least these oilmen, once the President sat down with them, had served FDR's interests too, raising millions for his 1936 reelection campaign in return for access to the presidency and solidifying the power of the Democratic Party in the Southwest.

This current request was different. In making it, Elliott had explained to his father that he felt that he was on the edge of attaining real wealth and power. Having assembled a chain of radio stations, he now wanted to form what he called the Texas State Network, but he needed a large loan to put him over the top. He had found a potential lender in John Hartford, head of the Great Atlantic & Pacific Tea Company, who was considering putting up $200,000—not necessarily because he believed in Elliott but because he felt that if he backed a Roosevelt family member there might be relief from a proposed chain store tax that would cost A&P over $6 million in the coming year.

Now Elliott was sitting in Hartford's office ready to clinch the deal. By prearrangement, he called the White House and got his father on the line and then handed the phone to Hartford. The gay and comforting voice, familiar to the nation because of the fireside chats, came on the line. After an exchange of pleasantries, FDR told the A&P president that he knew about the loan and approved of it because the Texas State Network looked like such a sound business proposition. He said that he would appreciate whatever Hartford could do for his son.

"After the President was so enthusiastic about it," Hartford said later on, when this deal, like others FDR's children made, had erupted into unpleasant headlines, "I felt that I was on the spot and I had to make a decision right then and there, and I did not want to do anything to incur the enmity of the President."

Being asked to cooperate with questionable schemes like this one was just part of the ambiguity Franklin faced in 1939. Although the country was far healthier than it had been when he had taken office six years earlier, the dark days of the Depression sometimes seemed almost preferable to the present. Back then things had at least been black and white instead of a muddy monochrome of gray.

The national economic disaster had prepared the stage for him to enter office with unparalleled drama. The situation was so stark and the need so great that some, like his cousin Ted, had actually worried that FDR would take advantage of the chaos and desperation to become a strongman on the European model. Franklin himself had wryly addressed and dismissed the possibility: "I have none of the requirements which would make me a successful dictator."

His other critical cousin Alice Longworth thought she was insulting him when she quipped that he "had polio and had to wear a brace; [and] now he wants to put the nation in a brace." In fact, the role of good Doctor of the New Deal, trying to nurse the nation back to health just as he had nursed his patients a few years earlier at Warm Springs was just the one he wanted to play—always encouraging his countrymen and spreading hope and optimism, and never telling them exactly how serious their condition was. Looking back, he could feel that he had perhaps succeeded too well. One of the sentences in the first draft of his second inaugural speech of 1937 had compared the Washington of four years earlier to an emergency hospital whose patients were now "doing very well, some of them even well enough to throw their crutches at the doctor."

By 1939, the First Hundred Days was a period already suffused with nostalgia. FDR could look back sentimentally at the excited improvisation that had led to an alphabet soup of emergency agencies like the AAA, CCC, TVA, and RFC that led to an economic resurgence, and at the existential brio of young aides whose outlook was summarized by brain-truster Rexford Tugwell's brash notion that the venture they had undertaken amounted to nothing less than "doing America over." (If they were doing it over, some observers pointed out, they were using a model TR had provided them, for much of the New Deal's program was a delayed implementation of the 1912 platform of the Progressive Party.)

History usually took its time in reaching a verdict, but by 1939 Franklin could see that the achievements of his first few years in office were already settled. The New Deal had accomplished a basic alteration in the terms of the social compact in the United States, creating a new set of relationships between workers and employers, rich and poor, small businessmen and bankers, the government and those it governed. The break with the past was seismic. America would never be the same.

And he himself had been at the center of it all—mercurial, devious, reassuring, and agreeably overbearing—exemplifying the temper of the time as much as his cousin Theodore had during that equally crucial American moment at the turn of the century. After visiting him in the White House, Bamie's son, Sheffield Cowles, Jr., observed of FDR, "Power released something essential in him." It was a confidence and joy, a reminiscence of that tireless ardor that had characterized TR in his day.

The two Roosevelt Presidents had taken different paths—the path of cunning for Franklin rather than of confrontation, the path of ethical sinuousness rather than what TR would have called moral righteousness. But no less than the cousin he had always admired, Franklin had made himself into the right man at the right time, a man thoroughly in control of his persona. He felt that he had finally stepped out of TR's giant shadow.[*]

When his 1932 opponent, Herbert Hoover, had called FDR "a chameleon on plaid," this was a negative interpretation of a quality others saw as a virtue—the protean ability to be all things to all people. He had used the political stage like a superb actor. (He was "all the Barrymores rolled into one," one admiring newspaperman said of him.) He did not always follow the script, perhaps, but he always managed to *be* the leading character. Tossing his head, allowing an incandescent smile to light his face, wagging the cigarette holder like a semaphore in his clenched jaw—he had created a larger-than-life figure. When he went on radio for his fireside chats, his hands moved to help him make his point and he smiled and gestured at the microphone as he spoke as if it were a live audience capable of being *persuaded*.

From the day he took office he seemed made for the presidency— splashing happily in the White House pool, dictating witty and compelling notes, riding the updrafts of intrigue within his administration, and relishing the gossip that he demanded be brought him from all corners of his Washington kingdom. He seemed simple and sincere in his ineffable good humor, although his complexities were actually quite Byzantine. Those close to him soon learned the truth of newspaperman William Allen White's comment: "His smile is from the teeth out."

Franklin's chief trait was the one Homer had attributed to Odysseus: he was, above all, a "deep devising" man. For him, the presidency was not a bully pulpit from which he could beat people into acquiescence by the strength of his character, as it had been for TR, but rather a court where he got his way by charm and conspiracy. People who came away from discussions convinced that they had persuaded Franklin to support their cause would later find that he had only been, in the phrase of an aide, "pleasantly present" during the conversation and had in fact already decided on a course of action far different from the one they had assumed he would take as a result of their meeting.

During those first years of his presidency he had won the adulation of

---

[*] The time seemed to be right finally to make such a move. In 1931, author Henry Pringle had published a revisionist biography, *Theodore Roosevelt,* which portrayed TR as egotistical and capricious. It had won a Pulitzer Prize, an indication that TR's stock was falling. FDR felt that he had an opportunity to be judged on his own, not as a successor. In fact, during the early days in the White House, he frequently became impatient with Eleanor when she sang the praises of her uncle too loudly.

millions of Americans who would always think of him as the father of the new country they inhabited after the Depression. There were also those who despised him. He was amused by some of the hate mail that cascaded into Washington and he kept the most imaginative of the letters (ones addressed to "Dishonorable Franklin Deficit Roosevelt," for instance, and to "F.D. Russianvelt, President of the USA/CIO"). He relished the acquisition of enemies like Huey Long, who ridiculed him as "Prince Franklin of the Nourmahal" and said that the initials of his NRA did not stand for National Recovery Act but for Nuts Running America. The Kingfish was dead now, but Father Coughlin, Gerald L. K. Smith, and others were still snapping at Franklin's heels, along with Al Smith, the Du Ponts, and even John Davis, the Democrats' candidate in 1924 whose view of FDR was that someone ought to "teach him respect for the rights of person and property."

It was not his enemies who bothered FDR now, however, but rather the sense of inertia slowing his administration and the accumulation of petty obstacles that continued to get in his way. He had overreached in trying to pack the Supreme Court to keep it from invalidating his emergency measures, and had also overshot the mark when he went on a crusade to purge the Democratic Party of the conservative congressmen who obstructed him. But more damaging than these political reverses was the sense that the magic show over which he had presided was running out of tricks. He might have appeared to his opponents to have a plan (some of them went so far as to call it a plot), but, ever the sailor, he had actually only been tacking from one crisis to another. In the beginning this technique had worked, but by 1939 the economy was not only stagnating but beginning to dip downward again and people were doubting that happy days were here again and whispering about a Roosevelt recession.

And there was also the vexing question of a third term, which at times it seemed that he alone supported, and the deteriorating international situation with which his reelection was intimately involved. By 1939, as one biographer later observed, he "seemed to float almost helplessly on the flood tide of isolationism." He had made a mistake in thinking he could win over international political figures as easily as he had some of his domestic opponents. (Despite letters to "My Dear Duce," for instance, Mussolini had engaged in one aggression after another and made common cause with Hitler.) FDR thought he could use his wiles to maneuver the United States into a greater engagement with the fate of Europe, but the country did not seem to be interested.

When Franklin now grumbled, as he frequently did, that the presidency was no longer "fun," however, he was not only referring to politics. During the first term, life at the White House had frequently resembled one of those zany screwball comedies everyone was talking about, a scenario snapping with brittle dialogue and interesting characters making unpredictable entrances and exits.

There was Louis Howe rising like a corpse out of the Lincoln bed, which he had commandeered as his own, issuing orders and, when he encountered resistance, bellowing, in words no one else would have dared to use, "You can tell the President to go to hell!" Or his daughter, Anna's, kids Sistie and Buzzie, the White house mascots, getting into bed with FDR every morning when he was attended by government officials (in sessions Dean Acheson later compared to seventeenth-century levees at Versailles), and making a game of clapping their hands over the presidential mouth when he was in the middle of some important policy statement. Or Missy wandering the halls in nightgown and peignoir. Or Lorena Hickok, Eleanor's friend, a big heavy woman one writer pictured as following the First Lady around "like a St. Bernard" and hiding in her room whenever the President was near. Or the colorful aides, all with Runyonesque nicknames. And above it all had been FDR himself, orchestrating events like Prospero on his enchanted island.

This atmosphere had now vanished. Louis Howe was dead. Anna had divorced and remarried and taken FDR's grandchildren to live with her on the West Coast. Missy was less available than in the old days, having acquired friends of her own and embarked, with FDR's approval, on flirtations with Eleanor's courtier Earl Miller, diplomat William Bullitt, and others. (The loss of her constant closeness, in speechwriter Sam Rosenman's opinion, deprived FDR of the one figure who was not a "yes-man," in that Missy could always be depended on to tell him her true opinion, rather than saying what she thought he wanted to hear.) Even some of the brain-trusters had moved on.

Feeling lonely and needing someone close to him he could trust, FDR had turned to the family. He tried periodically to close the gap with Eleanor. But this was no longer possible. (She had written a friend at the end of the first term, "I realize more and more that FDR is a great man & he is nice to me but as a person I'm a stranger & I don't want to be anything else.") So FDR had begun to groom his eldest son, Jimmy, as an aide after Howe's death, beginning by getting him commissioned as a lieutenant colonel in the marines so that he could accompany him on his goodwill tour of South America and then offering him the job of presidential assistant in 1937. This had been a controversial move—not only in the press, which criticized the nepotism and inquired somewhat too closely into Jimmy's finances, but also in the family itself. Jimmy's brothers had feared he would steal a march on them. And Eleanor, worried that their son would use his office to engage in the same sort of shady dealings that had characterized his business career up to that time, had argued against the appointment, putting such pressure on FDR that he finally exploded, "What good is the Presidency if I can't even have my son near me?"

FDR had used Jimmy during the time he was an assistant. Indeed, he had almost used him up, for his eldest son had become afflicted with such painful ulcers that it took him two hours to get going every morning and he needed to gulp down three quarts of milk during the day. Ultimately, FDR had come to rely as much on Jimmy's wife, Betsey, as on Jimmy himself. One of the three remarkable Cushing sisters who would ultimately count among their husbands (in addition to the son of the President), an Astor, a Whitney, and a William Paley, Betsey was exactly the kind of woman FDR adored—blonde and emerald-eyed, flirtatious and witty. He looked forward to her visits at the White House late every afternoon when she would arrive to preside over cocktail hour and make his cares disappear.

But even though Betsey was taking on duties she herself disdained, Eleanor deeply resented the access her daughter-in-law enjoyed, once blurting out with unusual asperity, "Betsey just thinks she *owns* him, you know!" And his father's dependence on his wife caused problems for Jimmy too. Coming from a Republican family, Betsey had begun by being somewhat aloof from the New Deal. But once she achieved the status of an intimate of the President, she had become as mesmerized by politics as any of his blood kin. Coming home after his own long day at the White House, Jimmy often found a note from her saying that she was presiding over some function for her father-in-law and would not be there until later.

He began to feel that she was not involved with him, but with the life of power emanating from his father, which had such a powerful hold on them all. He began to bicker with her and his stomach problems worsened. Fearing that he had cancer, he had checked into the Mayo Clinic in July 1938 and underwent an operation that resulted in two thirds of his stomach being removed. While recuperating, Jimmy fell in love with his nurse and decided to divorce Betsey. FDR was so alarmed by the prospect of yet another emotional subtraction from his life that he sent chief aide Harry Hopkins on a diplomatic mission to try to convince Jimmy to change his mind. When Jimmy refused to give in, the President was annoyed enough that he hired his old friend and law partner Basil O'Connor to represent Betsey in her divorce proceedings against his son.

If it was true, as Missy LeHand once said, that FDR never really allowed anyone to get close to him, that he had no intimate friends and treated everyone, even those closest to him, with the same surface gaiety and good humor that he used on potential voters, then by the end of his second term, as the contretemps with Jimmy showed, his family had become his most difficult constituency.

The presidency had finally insulated him from his mother. Having disdained politics as a gaucherie when Franklin first chose it as his life, Sara had long since accommodated to dealing with the lower classes. (Once at a Hyde Park get together, Eleanor's friend Marion Dickerman watched as one of the union men invited for dinner scooped ice cream into his finger bowl and Sara, sitting next to him, immediately followed suit without missing a beat.) She was now her son's most dedicated fan. She listened to every one of his radio speeches with rapt attention, commenting every once in a while as if speaking to him personally, "Good!" or "How true that is!" or "I know some people won't like that!"

The imperiousness that had intimidated him when he was young was now the subject of amusement. When she traveled abroad she sent detailed messages to the White House in which she told her son that Mussolini engendered "devotion in all classes," and said that a Franco victory was "the only hope for poor Spain. . . ." Franklin read these "Assistant Secretary of State letters," as he called them, aloud to Jimmy and other family members amidst gales of laughter.

But while his charm worked better on his mother than it ever had before, it continued to fail utterly on his wife. White House routines rationalized the frozen spaces between them, yet there were constant reminders of those icebergs of feeling whose tips alone were visible. Unbeknownst to Eleanor, for instance, FDR had provided limousines so that Lucy Mercer (who had since married and was now Lucy Rutherfurd) could be present at his first two inaugurals. For her part, Eleanor let him know in subtle ways that she too had not forgotten the traumatic denouement of their life together. In the first draft of her autobiography *This Is My Story,* she wrote, in a discussion of her brother, Hall's, marital problems, "Infidelity, under certain circumstances, need not ruin a relationship." Given the manuscript for review, FDR crossed the sentence out with a blue pencil.

Eleanor was unwilling and unable to give FDR the lighthearted enjoyment he required. Making one of her rare visits to his winter White House at Warm Springs during the first term, she confessed in a letter to her daughter, Anna, that she was functioning during the brief vacation as "a spoil sport and policeman." She admitted that she had lost her temper the previous evening with FDR: "He's been giving Nan [Cook] a cocktail every night & for two nights it went only a little to her head but it was so strong last night that she not only talked incessantly much to their amusement but couldn't talk straight & I feel he did it on purpose. . . . I feel revolt physically from anyone in that condition."

Eleanor had initially hoped that Franklin would take her on as his official secretary in the White House, but when she asked him about this job shortly after the 1933 inauguration, he shot her one of his quizzical, arched-eyebrow looks and said that such an arrangement would not do because it might upset Missy. So she had been forced once again to make a place for herself.

At first she concentrated on the political clubs and other aspects of the women's movement that had been her chief focus since getting involved in politics. But gradually she expanded her interests to include a variety of social welfare issues with national implications.

One project that particularly helped Eleanor define her role developed out of a visit she and Dickerman and Cook made to some unemployed miners in Morgantown, West Virginia, in the heart of Appalachia. Many of the workers had been blacklisted by mine owners because of union activities. They all lived in filthy hovels with no sanitation or running water. After seeing their plight firsthand, Eleanor and her friends returned to Washington determined to do something. Seeing a chance to create a model for the large-scale homesteading program Louis Howe was just then trying to design, Eleanor got the government to purchase a nearby estate owned by a family named Arthur that was on the market, and set out to make a new community called Arthurdale where the miners' families would live in fifty prefab homes ordered at a cost of two thousand dollars each.

Guided by her teaching experience at Todhunter School, Eleanor helped set up a school for the miners' children based on John Dewey's principles of progressive education. She spent time getting to know the people there, encouraging a renaissance of spirit and culture and urging them to develop folk arts and preserve their folkways as they became integrated into the modern world. She worked with government officials to provide employment by setting up a factory in Arthurdale that would produce furniture for post offices across the country. She poured thousands of dollars of her own from speaking engagements and magazine articles into the community.

Despite several years and huge expenditures of government money as well as intense effort on Eleanor's part, Arthurdale never quite became the laboratory for social uplift she had envisioned. The prefab homes didn't fit the climate (or, for that matter, the foundations that had been poured for them) and wound up costing sixteen thousand dollars apiece instead of the budgeted two thousand. (Hearing of the cost overrun, FDR commented to Interior Secretary Harold Ickes, "My missus, unlike most women, doesn't know anything about money at all.") While appreciative of Eleanor's effort, the miners and their wives were suspicious of the program of progressive education she tried to implement in their schools, demanding instead the 3 Rs for their children. And Congress killed the subsidy for the furniture factory. But if there was a daunting disparity between the dream and the reality at Arthurdale, the experiment helped establish Eleanor's identity. If Franklin was Doctor of the New Deal, she would become the Head Nurse.

She traveled nearly fifty thousand miles during the first term alone, becoming an outrider for the administration, extending its reach and presence, demonstrating sympathy for the suffering and support for those trying to get back on their feet after the worst days of the Depression. She journeyed to rural black communities, Indian reservations, poor white areas. Franklin encouraged her, recognizing that having someone close to him function as "the conscience of the New Deal" was a significant asset and also appreciative of the fact, as his son Jimmy later said, that these long trips got his wife out of his hair.

The creation of a public persona for Eleanor was one of the unheralded triumphs of the New Deal. By the end of the second term, she had found her voice. It was as familiar as the one her husband presented in his fireside chats, a voice often heard on radio, but speaking primarily through print. The publishers of Ladies' Home Journal paid $75,000, at the time an enormous sum, for serialization rights to Eleanor's autobiography, This Is My Story. And by 1936, her influential syndicated column, "My Day," was appearing in over sixty newspapers.

"My Day" became the cornerstone of Eleanor's influence, and when it was time to file she would drop whatever she was doing and disappear with her secretary Malvina "Tommy" Thompson to write it. The column was read for her comments on books, films, and other cultural and social phenomena to which she applied her liberal views. But administration-watchers learned to read it for clues about what was happening inside the White House. Eleanor often quoted her husband or other administration figures in her pieces, as in 1938, when FDR was trying to build up Harry Hopkins as his possible successor: "It was good to see Mr. Hopkins yesterday and to have him spend the night with us. . . . He seems to work because he has an inner conviction that much needs to be done. I think he would be that way about any job he undertook."

An added dividend came from the fact that "My Day" allowed Eleanor to score a triumph over her cousin Alice, who happened to have been given her own syndicated column at about the same time. (In some cases, the columns ran side by side on the same editorial pages.) It was assumed that Alice's deft wit would allow her easily to outshine Eleanor once again, but it turned out to be a wit that could not express itself on paper.

In an effort to capture the quality of Alice's distinctive verbal style, editors tried having Alice dictate the column to a stenographer. When the prose still sounded stilted and unnatural, they moved the stenographer behind a curtain so that Alice would not be distracted by her presence. But nothing worked and her column was soon canceled. Trapped now in a game of tortoise and hare, Alice was forced to watch as the more prosaic Eleanor outdistanced her again.

With Eleanor's success came drastic changes in her personal life. Her friend Earl Miller had been left behind in New York with the job of personnel director for the State Department of Corrections. Marion Dickerman came back from a fact-finding trip to England (where FDR had asked her to study industrial policy) and found that her partner Nan Cook had quarreled with Eleanor. Money was the presenting cause—Cook apparently felt that she and Dickerman were being forced to bear too large a part of Val-Kill expenses—but the fact was that Eleanor had outgrown her old friends. Dickerman had seen the warmth in Eleanor suddenly freeze in her relations with others she had cut out of her life. Now she experienced the same thing herself. She tried to patch things up, but Eleanor rebuffed her.

Part of the reason that Eleanor felt she could afford to sever the most meaningful ties of her recent life was that she had embarked on an even more intense friendship. This time it was with an Associated Press reporter named Lorena Hickok. Novelist and foreign correspondent Martha Gellhorn, who worked briefly at the White House, found Hickok to be "ugly and boring," a squat woman who resembled a "walking tank." But Eleanor had become intensely attached to her almost overnight, finding in her someone who had her own hunger for friendship and ability to return it.

Hickok had been born and raised in South Dakota, part of a poor and abusive family. She had grown up worshipping Theodore Roosevelt, an independent young woman with an ambition to be a writer. Becoming a newspaperwoman, she had taken on the persona of a character out of *The Front Page*—smoking immense cigars in the newsroom and allowing tears of sadness to run down her face when she was typing out a tragic human interest story and jiggling with laughter when the piece she was writing was humorous. She was also a lesbian who conceived of possessive crushes on a number of women during her life.

Hickok was covering the 1932 campaign for the AP when she first saw Eleanor. It was the day after FDR was nominated in Chicago and after watching Eleanor in her first appearance before the press, she said to a colleague, "That woman is unhappy about something." This *aperçu* would initiate the bond between them. Hickok made a point of meeting Tommy Thompson, Eleanor's private secretary, on the campaign train. She told her the story of how she herself had been sexually molested as a girl. Tommy passed some of what Hickok had said to Eleanor and the stage was set for their first interview, which involved an exchange of confidences about past disappointments and future hopes and ended with Eleanor coyly inviting further contact.

Hickok was one of the most intelligent and the most intense woman to come into Eleanor's life. ("I adore your ability to feel deeply," she told the journalist soon after their first meeting.) She came along at a time when Eleanor was feeling particularly vulnerable—not only because she feared the loss of her hard-won independence in the new role she was assuming of President's wife, but also because three of her children were already talking about divorce, a development that made her feel "soiled," as she told her new friend.

Over the next two years, a deep bond was forged between the women. Because she felt her objectivity as a journalist was compromised by her feelings for Eleanor, "Hick" (as she would soon become) quit her job. For long periods of time she had her own room in the

White House. She was loud and tactless and extremely possessive of Eleanor, jealous of Dickerman and Cook, whom she referred to snidely as "the Val-Kill ladies," and jealous even of Eleanor's own children when they took the precious time she had planned to spend with her friend in travels or private moments.

The correspondence between them was passionate. ("I couldn't say je t'aime and je t'adore as I longed to do," Eleanor wrote hurriedly from the White House in a typical passage, "but do always remember I am saying it & that I go to sleep thinking of you & repeating our little saying.") On Hick's part it was filled with physical longing for kisses and hugs.

Generalizing from the letters (which were not opened to public view until sixteen years after Eleanor's death), a later age would rush to judgment about the lesbian nature of the relationship. (When the same suggestions were made at the time, Martha Gellhorn and others dismissed them as "contemptible stuff.") That it should become one was certainly Hickok's intention. But, while filled with a variety of suggestiveness, the correspondence also shows Eleanor pulling back after two years of intense companionship following a summary moment, possibly a request for consummation. "It won't help you," Eleanor wrote her friend in 1934, "but I'd never do to anyone else what I did to you. . . . Why I didn't know I couldn't give you (or anyone else who wanted and needed what you did) any real food I don't now understand."

As time went on, while Eleanor continued to relish the companionship, what can only be called a heterosexual condescension entered some of her correspondence with the hapless Hick. On one occasion she wrote: "I think you will remember that once I told you I wished you had been happy with a man. . . . I rather think the lack of that relationship does create emotional *in*stability. . . ." And later she returned to the same theme: "Of course you should have had a husband & children & it would have made you happy if you loved him & in any case it would have satisfied certain cravings. . . ."

Yet whether or not Lorena Hickok was Eleanor's lover, she was a mentor and then her colleague in her new identity as journalist. She led her toward greater sophistication in her social views and toward an expansion of her inner circle of friends and confidants, as well as toward an independence in her interpretation of what it meant to be the President's wife.

*   *   *

By the end of the second term, Eleanor had become something more than a particularly active First Lady. She was a countervailing center of power in the White House, appealing to the "idealists," while the far more numerous "realists" gathered around FDR.[*] (One reason that Jimmy's first wife, Betsey, irritated Eleanor was that she was seen as being "pro-FDR" in the unspoken choosing of sides.) Eleanor knew that there were certain people in the administration like the curmudgeonly Secretary of the Interior Harold Ickes who did not take her seriously. She fought with him over projects like Arthurdale, holding her own well enough that at one point Ickes feared he would be removed from the cabinet. Those like Agriculture Secretary Henry Wallace who blandished her about their shared liberal agenda found her effective in promoting their careers in the administration's power struggles.

Eleanor willingly served as an agent for her husband—his "eyes and ears," it was frequently said—but was often frustrated by the fact that her power ultimately flowed from him and she had no right to what she had to convince him to give her. On one occasion she entered the White House living quarters when FDR was talking to some publishers. Seeing that he had a drink in his hand she asked, "Are my friends included in this?" FDR said no and Eleanor, annoyed that her entourage was excluded from this social moment, immediately left the room. On another occasion, a man who was close to the family later reported being told by Eleanor's secretary, Tommy Thompson, that she had once come upon Eleanor looking blankly at a wall. Asked what was wrong, Eleanor replied: "I've just lost a friend." It turned out that she was referring to Harry Hopkins. Eleanor had cultivated Hopkins and thought that he was someone she could rely on, but it turned out that he had "betrayed" her in favor of her husband.

An episode in 1939 showed that the policy and ideological differences between FDR and Eleanor could cut as deeply as the emotional ones. Members of the left-wing American Youth Congress, one of the "idealistic" groups in which Eleanor was involved, had been called before the House committee chaired by Representative Martin Dies that was investigating fascist and communist subversives. On the first day of the hearings, Eleanor appeared in the gallery with her knitting to lend moral support to Joseph Lash, her future biographer, then one of the most influential of the young activists in the group. At the noon recess, she

[*] Louis Howe was apparently somewhere in the middle. Eleanor claimed in one of her letters to Lorena Hickok that Howe once indicated to her that he was interested in making her President after FDR left office "and insisted he could do it."

invited some of them to the White House for a well-publicized lunch that amounted to a vote of confidence.

FDR regarded the Youth Congress as malicious for the way it had changed overnight from a popular front organization opposed to Hitler to an isolationist group after the signing of the Hitler-Stalin pact. But to appease Eleanor, he agreed to speak to the young people three months after their appearance before the Dies Committee when they staged a rally in Washington in an attempt to head off any U.S. support for Finland, which had just been invaded by the Soviets.

The night before his speech, there was a meeting of the Youth Congress at which the feud between the branches of the Roosevelt family surfaced indirectly as Archie Roosevelt's son, Archie Jr., rose to denounce Eleanor's naïveté about communism and tried to introduce a resolution condemning Soviet aggression in Finland but was first shouted down and then wrestled to the floor and thrown out of the room. (Later on, Archie Jr. ran into Franklin Jr., who was about the same age, and said he was surprised by the way Eleanor apologized for the communists. "I'm not too happy with Mother either," said his cousin.)

When nearly five thousand Youth Congress members showed up on the White House lawn the next day, Franklin appeared at a balcony and in effect repeated what Archie Jr. had already said. He called the Youth Congress charge that a proposed U.S. loan to Finland was an act of war "unadulterated twaddle." He said that he too had been sympathetic to Russia twenty years earlier but because of intervening events had acquired a different view: "I disliked the regimentation under communism. I abhorred the indiscriminate killing of thousands of innocent victims. I heartily deprecated the banishing of religion. . . . The Soviet Union, as anybody who has the courage to face the facts knows, is run by a dictatorship as absolute as any dictatorship in the world."

He was booed and hissed by his guests. Eleanor later tried to explain her friends' behavior: "Some members of the American Youth Congress view the Soviet experiment in communism as having made headway in solving problems of Russia's millions of underprivileged." She invited a delegation of the young people to come to the White House for tea. When FDR made an appearance, members of the group again harangued and insulted him. With Eleanor beside her, her secretary "Tommy" Thompson stormed at them, "How *dare* you be so rude to the President of the United States!" But while she defended her husband publicly, privately she still had her doubts. Soon after the incident, she

wrote Anna, "Many of them are youngsters who are inclined to believe
well of Russia but that is because they are so afraid of all propaganda and
feel Russia in Finland may be a victim of that. . . . Pa lost their support
and will have to win it back."

And so the differences in politics in the White House functioned as a
continuation by other means of the old emotional war between Franklin
and Eleanor. The terms were the same as always: FDR giving no more
than he had to; Eleanor wanting far more than he could give.

Bamie's son, Sheffield Cowles, Jr., and his wife came to Washington
in 1935 for a visit and witnessed a closet drama countless others would
also see in the future. The Cowleses were in the private quarters listening raptly to FDR as he gave a sophisticated *tour d'horizon* of world
events while Eleanor, obsessively busy as always, kept coming in and
out of the room and the conversation.

"Can't this bill go through?" she finally interrupted, referring to a
matter she and Franklin had apparently been discussing before the
Cowleses' visit.

"No, it is *not* going through," FDR answered resentfully.

A few minutes later, Eleanor entered the room again, ascertained that
her husband was now speaking about Japanese ambitions in the Pacific,
and said, "Oh, you should not talk about this, Franklin."

FDR replied firmly, "It's on my mind and I'm going to talk about it."

She was persistent and he was stubborn. She sent memo after memo
on issues in which she had a stake. He often ignored them. Then she
would phone and he would arrange not to take the call. Finally she
would drop a note onto his nightstand and he would dictate a response
for Missy to send her.

She thought his friends frivolous and he thought hers tedious. He
sometimes began work in the morning commenting sourly to Missy or
his secretary Grace Tully, "Well, Eleanor had a group of her do-gooders
in for dinner last night." He craved a lighthearted social atmosphere in
the White House, but, as brain-truster Rexford Tugwell later said,
"Eleanor, so humorless and weighed down with responsibility, made
this difficult."

While Franklin defended his wife and appreciated her loyalty and the
real political benefits her activism for liberal causes provided for him, he
was not altogether unhappy when someone else ridiculed her. (Presidential aide Marvin McIntyre had an imitation of her FDR found particularly funny in which he would trill, "Franklin! Something *has* to be
done! The Negroes are *not* getting a square deal!") A piece of doggerel

parodying Poe's "The Raven" that someone sent Franklin must have struck a responsive chord, for he slipped it into a top drawer of his desk and kept it there:

> And despite her global milling
> Of the voice there is no stilling
> With its platitudes galore.
> As it rushes on advising,
> Criticizing and chastising,
> Moralizing, patronizing,
> Paralyzing—ever more
> Advertising Eleanor.

Eleanor climbed onto the list of the Most Admired Women during the White House years and did not relinquish this position during the rest of her life. Yet like her husband, she acquired passionate enemies along the way. Some, like her cousin Alice, derided her as the "Great White Mother" and asked, "Who elected her?" Others, more virulent in their hatred, composed savage lampoons like the notorious rhyme directed at Eleanor and Franklin jointly:

> You kiss the niggers
> And I'll hug the Jews
> And we'll stay in the White House
> As long as we choose.

Ironically, however, Eleanor's severest critics, if not always her most vocal ones, were her own children. When they read her "My Day" column, as Elliott said later on, they "marvelled how she created the image of a total stranger, not the detached, hurried, fault-finding wife and parent we knew." Her sons made jokes about Joseph Lash and the other bright young men of the American Youth Committee, seeing Eleanor's search for protégés as an attempt on her part to make up for the botched motherhood that had had such disastrous consequences for them. They were equally cynical when she would insist on dropping whatever else she was doing during the White House years to try ineffectually to help them through the crises that chronically afflicted their lives. It was a surprise, as Elliott noted laconically, that she did not see that "the damage had been done."

The FDR children were different from that other Roosevelt family that had lived in the White House with whom they were always compared. It was true that America had been a simpler and more innocent place at the turn of the century, and the TR children had been younger and more endearing when they were in the public eye. Yet it was also true that those other Roosevelts, whatever their individual differences, had all been obsessed with living up to their heritage. The FDR children had no such tradition to follow in making their way to self-definition. Their parents' example suggested that life was a matter of every man and woman for him- and herself—a scramble to satisfy personal needs and appetites. From their earliest memories, the children had always been left to flounder in the wake behind FDR and Eleanor. It was no surprise, therefore, that during the presidency, the "chicks" started coming home to roost.

The two younger boys had not fully experienced the family trauma begun by FDR's affair with Lucy Mercer and completed by his polio, and thus had little of the wounded nostalgia that Anna, James, and even Elliott felt for the ideal family that never was.

At six five, John had grown up to be the largest of the boys, with toothy features somewhat resembling Eleanor's. His hair-trigger temper was legendary in the family and soon became legendary outside it. At Harvard, John saw a photographer covertly snap a forbidden picture of Franklin Jr. as he was being initiated into Hasty Pudding wearing a sign reading, "I'm the nation's leading capitalist's boy"; he savagely attacked the man and smashed the camera. Yet, as a counterpoint to his outbreaks of temper, John also had a dreamy, solitary quality that went along with his desire to escape the pressures of the family name. All through college, he could be seen at deb parties on weekends slow-dancing with his eyes closed and his feet shuffling in a state approaching self-hypnosis.

The others had been granted at least a small piece of their father when they were young, but the polio had taken him completely away from John at a critical moment in his childhood. As a result, John had grown up with less emotional connection with his parents than any of the others. When he was a junior at Harvard, FDR got him a summer job working in the forests of Tennessee for the Tennessee Valley Authority. At the end of the experience, his supervisor felt compelled to write Eleanor to say that her youngest son seemed to believe in "the psychology of making one's way by influence and association rather than by hard work and personal achievement." In fact, however, John was the most autonomous of all the boys and least inclined to trade on his name.

Knowing that politics was the lifeblood of the family, he framed his rebellion by antagonism to the aims of the New Deal. When Eleanor confided to the antiwar leftists and young communists of the American Youth Committee that one of her own sons had isolationist tendencies, she was referring to John.

In 1938, when he married a North Shore socialite named Anne Sturgis Clark whose father, a financier, was bitterly opposed to administration economic policies, John, then twenty-two, became a secret Republican, although he resolved not to make his affiliation public during his father's lifetime. Seeing how hard it had been for his sister and two older brothers to leave their orbit around FDR and find lives of their own, he also took a job as far from the administration as possible—selling lingerie in Filene's department store in Boston.

John later said that the only person in the family to whom he really felt close was Franklin Jr. Deemed the most like his father in looks and temperament, with a voice that sounded almost like an imitation, "Brud," as FDR called Franklin Jr., also had the same quick charm and easy assurance. He was the favorite of Nancy Cook and Marion Dickerman, the lesbian couple having functioned somewhat as surrogate mothers for him and John during the mid-1920s.

A close observer of Eleanor's children, Dickerman later described Franklin Jr. as "happy, delightful, thoroughly lovable." Yet she also recognized the danger signs in his personality: a narcissism and almost pathological carelessness. While at Groton he had tried to seduce a girl at a debutante party, getting her so drunk that she vomited in the back seat of the car when Franklin and Eleanor had to drive her home.

He had continued this wild behavior at Harvard, where he smashed cars and staged loud parties. By his senior year, he was dating Ethel Du Pont and once got her to leave school early, claiming a dentist's appointment, so that they could go to a boxing match. The inevitable photographer was present, and, in behavior that would be repeated, Franklin Jr. punched him and smashed his camera. Afterward, he went to Marion Dickerman to ask if he had done the right thing. When he admitted under her questioning that he had gone into the event on free tickets, she pointed out that since he was using his prerogatives as the President's son to get into the boxing match, he had entered the public domain when he went into the building and should not have acted as he did.

When he married Ethel Du Pont in 1937, her father, Eugene, a bitter opponent of the New Deal and member of the Liberty League along with his cousin Pierre, said of young Franklin, "He's a good egg, but it would be better if he had a different last name." FDR went to Wilmington for the wedding, portrayed by newspapers around the country as a Capulet and Montague union, and enjoyed his day in the lion's den, charming his Du Pont enemies by inviting them to come down and see him in Washington and discuss their grievances now that they were all "family."

Like John, Franklin Jr. also saw the rootlessness and confusion of his older brothers and made an effort not to fall into the same pattern. Enrolling at the University of Virginia law school, he joked cuttingly that he, at least, wouldn't "have to rely on Pa for business opportunities." Yet he couldn't break the mold in other respects and a few years after their marriage, when he brought Ethel to live for a time at the White House, staff members were soon gossiping about how another of the female houseguests staying with the Roosevelts had ordered a maid to tell Franklin Jr. that she was waiting for him in her room. After this, Ethel could be seen wandering through the third-floor residence area twisting her hair in distraction, even pulling out hanks of it, and talking aloud to herself. Concerned about her but not knowing what to do, FDR began referring to his unhappy daughter-in-law as "our hothouse flower."

If John and FDR Jr. were closest to being Eleanor's children, the three older children were closer to FDR. The pressures of office made it impossible for him to focus on any one of them for long periods of time, but he did try to attend to each of them when they sank into emotional or financial trouble. Elliott later compared this effort to the performer who gets three plates spinning on sticks: "As soon as one of us started to tilt Pa got him going again, and then had to go to work on one of the others."

Anna was his favorite, "tall, blonde, and graceful," in the words of her brother Elliott, "much prettier than mother and not cursed with her high, irritating voice." FDR had never been particularly fond of her dour husband, Curtis Dall. (And neither were Dall's own children: Eleanor Anna Dall, known as "Sistie," later said they had "*no* affinity for him at all.") Even Eleanor was unable to be kind to her son-in-law. In June of 1929, Jimmy insisted that Dall invest the $1,000 college graduation present he had gotten from his grandmother in the stock market. Dall bought him Du Pont, which, along with all other stocks, was swamped a few months later in the crash. After the money was lost, Eleanor came to Dall and said, "You certainly know Jimmy planned to go abroad next January, so I think *you ought* to return his money to him!"

Knowing that his daughter had married largely to get out of the emotional maelstrom of his own marriage, FDR did not encourage Anna to remain in what had obviously become a loveless relationship by 1930. In fact, he and others in the family participated with vicarious enthusiasm in the romance she struck up with a *Chicago Tribune* reporter named John Boettiger during the 1932 presidential campaign. It was like falling in love for the first time for her; the experience was so exciting that the whole family was swept up in the romance of the secret assignations and hurried meetings. FDR himself finally took Curtis Dall aside and told him that Anna wanted a separation.

The dashing Boettiger was on the rebound from his own unhappy first marriage when he met Anna. He had been a successful reporter, but once he became close to the Roosevelt clan he could no longer stay with the *Tribune,* whose publisher, Colonel Robert McCormick, was a rabid opponent of the New Deal. Also, Boettiger was a little like Anna's own brothers in that he wanted to parlay his connections with presidential power into something big. He allowed Joseph Kennedy, one of the opportunists nibbling at the edges of the Roosevelt family, to use his Hollywood connections to help him get a job with Will Hays, the film industry's czar and censor. But Boettiger was a newspaperman at heart. Soon he quit Hays's operation and he and Anna worked out a deal with FDR's arch-enemy William Randolph Hearst to take over the *Seattle Post-Intelligencer.*

Anna was always her father's partisan and co-conspirator. When he was lonely at Warm Springs, she acted as a go-between trying to convince Eleanor to spend time with him there ("Pa seems to want you [there] so badly . . ."). She had mastered the anger toward her mother that had characterized her teen years, and now strove for civility in letters that often began with the salutation "Darling." And while she often talked to Boettiger about what she had suffered as a girl and vowed that things would be different, especially after the birth of their child John Jr., she found herself powerless to keep from reproducing some of the traumatic circumstances of her own upbringing.

One of the things that shocked family friends was the discovery that Anna had tied her infant son, Buzzie's, hands to keep her from masturbating just as Eleanor had tied her hands when she was a baby. And after she and Boettiger had moved to Seattle to go to work for Hearst, Sistie, now twelve years old, reported to her that her stepfather was coming into her room at night to molest her. Insecure and groping in the second marriage, Anna practiced a denial worthy of

Eleanor herself by raising the issue timidly with Boettiger and then doing nothing when he dismissed the issue, "It's time Sis learned a little about sex."

Jimmy was like his sister—anxious to please and easily upset by emotional conflict. Peering uncertainly out of thick glasses and running his fingers nervously through his thinning hair, he did not handle the role of "Crown Prince" very well. People close to the family believed that he had been weakened by his precocious ability to play his parents off against each other and his grandmother off against them both. Sara's favorite among all her grandchildren, he had taken whatever she gave him—a new car when he left the top down on his own roadster and snow destroyed its interior; an apartment and a monthly allowance when he was in his mid-twenties and married to Betsey Cushing. Yet still he complained about how she squeezed him in "a golden loop of money."

After graduating from Harvard, Jimmy attended a year of law school at Boston University. He left to go to work for an insurance company because he thought that being in business would teach him how to be more comfortable with people and thus better able to pursue the political career that had been his ultimate ambition since he was a boy. But Marion Dickerman was right when she said, "A great number of people inveigled [Jimmy] into enterprises that were uncomfortable."

He proved to have little instinct for the political game his father played so masterfully and was an easy mark for pros like Boston Mayor James Curley, who used him to try to get leverage on his father, and for a political predator like Joe Kennedy, who used him financially as well as politically. In 1933, Kennedy paid for Jimmy and Betsey to accompany him to London when it seemed certain that Prohibition would soon be repealed and then paraded them before Haig & Haig and other distillers in a way that suggested a presidential endorsement to his efforts to get a monopoly on liquor distributorships in the United States. After getting the contracts, Kennedy did not even give Jimmy's company the insurance on his new business.

Jimmy used his position as first son to score lucrative commissions off a $2.5 million life insurance policy for George Hill of the American Tobacco Company and over $2 million for blanket coverage for CBS. He was perpetually ensnarled in conflicts of interest, and by the time FDR asked him to come to work in the White House in 1937, Jimmy, although barely thirty, had already acquired such a legend of shady doings that he had to reveal his tax returns to a reporter for *Collier's* to dispel rumors that he had illicitly made millions of dollars during his father's first term in office.

He sincerely wanted to help his father and wrote him not long after going to work at the White House, "Just to be able to be near you and hope to make you feel how fully you can depend on us who love you is what we want so much. I often fear so greatly of doing something big or small which will bring some hurt to you, and I pray so hard that somehow it may never happen." Yet he understood that psychological dilemma in which he was trapped: he "had the yen to look at anything anyone came up with, an idea or a project," and although he worried about "getting into a situation that would embarrass [FDR]," he found it hard to resist easy money. While working as a White House aide to his father, he once went to William O. Douglas, then head of the Securities and Exchange Commision, and asked him to help Charles Schwartz, a businessman who was trying to arrange with various companies to become their "fixer" in cases that came before the SEC. When Douglas refused, Jimmy told him that now that the Democrats were in office after a long Republican dominance, it was *their* turn to make money. Douglas was so disturbed by the conversation that he made an appointment with FDR to tell him about it. FDR listened, Douglas later wrote, and then put his head down on the desk and cried.

It was a pattern that continued after Jimmy recovered from his stomach operation in 1938, divorced Betsey and married Romelle Schneider, one of the nurses who had taken care of him at the Mayo Clinic. Moving to California, he used the good offices of the ever willing Joseph Kennedy to meet Samuel Goldwyn and take a job with him as a producer at $40,000 a year. But it was not long until Jimmy was in contact with his father again, pleading the case of movie mogul Joe Schenck, who was facing prosecution for income tax evasion.

For the most part, Anna and Jimmy were willing to pretend they were part of one big happy—if somewhat eccentric—family. Perhaps because he had been separated from the others by temperament and ill health while growing up, Elliott alone seemed willing to perceive the realities of the Hyde Park Roosevelts without flinching. He was the id of the family—the one who understood most clearly the nature of the "deal" Franklin and Eleanor had made. What he had seen exonerated him in advance, he seemed to believe, for whatever he did or said later on.

He watched as his older brother and sister were forced into situations

they disliked. Anna had not wanted to go to Miss Chapin's School or
have a coming out, for instance, and Jimmy had initially not wanted to
go to Harvard and never wanted to go to law school. Finally they had
both capitulated to please their parents. Elliott was unwilling to do this.
As a friend related, "He said early on that the name of the game was
taking care of number one." He decided that he would be his own man,
playing a role he defined as "the maverick" and others saw as the spoiler.

When Elliott looked back on his life later on, he decided that the
crucial moment had come in 1924 when he was fourteen and his father,
following the family tradition of giving Roosevelt sons an early dose of
"Western therapy," sent him and Jimmy for the summer to Charlie
Moore's Ranch for Boys near Du Bois, Wyoming. They were picked up
at the railroad station along with some other campers in a rickety bus.
Midway to the ranch, there was a stop so that the passengers could all
relieve themselves. Not realizing he was squatting in a cactus field, Elliott got his backside stuck with dozens of needles. When he tried to
brush them off he only forced them deeper into his flesh. Fearful that
his bullying brother would call him a sissy, he buttoned his jeans and
got back on the bus, although in agony. By bedtime that night he was
feverish and nauseated and woke up shortly after midnight vomiting
uncontrollably. When he asked his brother for help, Jimmy only
forced him out of the tent where they were sleeping and made him
stay outside.

The next morning the camp doctor was summoned, removed the
cactus spines, and forbade Elliott from riding for several days. When the
others went on a trail ride, he hung around the corral. He met a wran-
gler named Hank who took pity on him and spent the next few days
teaching him to rope and, when he could sit on a saddle, to ride. As the
friendship deepened, the cowboy took Elliott into town with him on
weekends so that he would have someone to guide him home from the
saloons when he got drunk.

The West offered a vision of independence and anonymity that galvanized Elliott just as it had his grandfather and namesake some fifty
years earlier. Every summer from this point on, when Sara took his
brothers and sister to Europe, Elliott insisted on going back to Wyoming or Colorado. He became a good enough cowboy that he was on
the rodeo circuit by the time he was sixteen, traveling from California
to Canada. Completing his escape from the family, he competed under
the name of Robinson, bringing home a wad of prize money at the end
of each summer. The year FDR won the governorship, he and Eleanor

went to the annual rodeo at Madison Square Garden and watched from the Governor's Box when a young man who looked familiar but was called "Robinson" by the announcer was gored in the side by a bull and rushed to the hospital.

After his second summer in the West, Elliott wrote his father in Warm Springs, "I have never enjoyed myself so much in my life. I do feel though that I've enjoyed myself so long now that I'd like to see what real work was like. Could I leave school for the next year and have some sort of job? Of course I know what you'll say. Impossible. I must finish out Groton etc. etc., but really pa I don't think it will do me any good and I would like to show you I can work at something I like. . . ."

He was right: FDR did say that it would be impossible for him to leave Groton. By this time, Elliott, the runt of the family as a child, had grown into his size—not the biggest of the Roosevelt boys but the roughest. Jimmy had stopped bullying him after Elliott had bloodied his face in a fight over which of them was the better stroke on the Groton crew. His classmates learned that they could no longer tease Elliott with impunity as they had when he arrived at school as a scrawny twelve-year-old.

By 1927 his size and aggressiveness had made him a star on the school football team. In the game against Milton, he fell with both knees on the back of an opposing player who was already down, putting the boy in the hospital with a kidney injury. Headmaster Endicott Peabody wrote FDR an alarmed letter about the incident and got a reply from Warm Springs suggesting the the proper response to Elliott was "patting him on the back occasionally and if anything goes badly . . . [giving] him a chance to explain instead of assuming he is an 'angry spirit.' " Peabody remained concerned about Elliott, calling him "a fierce player who does not care particularly whether he hurts people or not."

Among his other ambitions was the desire to be a pilot, and while at Groton he hung around Long Island's Roosevelt Field, named for his cousin Quentin. He met Lindbergh when he was preparing for his flight across the Atlantic, and cadged flying lessons from World War I veterans now barnstorming around the country. His father encouraged him in his desire to fly but refused another request to leave school. The summer of 1928, when FDR was scheduled to nominate Al Smith for President, Elliott and some Groton friends decided to ship out from Boston on a freighter bound for the West Coast via the Panama Canal. The night before departing they all got drunk on rum and Coke and wound up in a Chinese tattoo parlor. One of the boys betrayed his class origins by getting a fox hunt tattooed on his chest. Elliott settled for a screaming blue eagle on his forearm.

Unable to stand working in the boiler room of the freighter, he jumped ship in the Gulf and went to Houston to support his father as he struggled to the speaker's podium to nominate Al Smith at the Democratic convention. But politics didn't interest Elliott as it did Jimmy, and he wrote home that the whole affair had been boring except for when they arrived at the convention site with a police motorcycle escort and blaring sirens.

After the convention, he continued west. He did not write or notify his parents of his whereabouts. After three months, Eleanor finally grew worried enough to ask the New York State Police to launch inquiries. About this time Elliott sent a breezy letter summarizing the adventures that had begun after the convention, when FDR put him on a train for Phoenix and gave him seventy-five dollars to fly from the Grand Canyon to Salt Lake City. He found that the flight cost more than he had been given and so he used the money getting to Colorado and found a job at a working ranch where he had spent the summer.

"Do you think I could have a little money to come home on," he concluded his letter. "I'm afraid I haven't a cent. I've managed to last out by selling one by one my articles of clothing so I'd have some money on hand. . . . I hope you really will forgive me for no[t] writing before. Of course I suppose you told everybody how terrible I was and that I hadn't written so I suppose there is no use in asking you to keep my defects and faults quiet but I do hate to have that sort of thing told to people it doesn't concern."

The end of the letter was typical of Elliott—apologetic and defiant at the same time.

Picking his next fight in advance, Elliott informed his parents before graduation from Groton that they should not expect him to go on to college. FDR remonstrated with him in a way that might have convinced his elder brother, James, but only made Elliott more rebellious. "I hope in the future you won't bother 'to lean over backwards to please' me," he wrote FDR after one such attempt at persuasion had resulted in an exasperated standoff. "I'll do my best not to give you any chance to do that. . . . Maybe I have been 'selfish' in my decisions but I must say that I am not intentionally so as seems to be your opinion."

Ultimately Elliott tried to make the question of higher education moot by simply turning in a blank college exam book at the end of his senior year. But Eleanor put her foot down and forced him to spend a year raising his grades at a Philadelphia preparatory school. He finally agreed to try college only because he wanted to play football. He spent a semester raising his grades and then went West for a vacation with a friend, which was highlighted by a night in a Juarez jail after a drunken brawl in a Mexican cantina.

Enrolling at Princeton, he spent his first month on campus playing weekends for a Brooklyn semi-pro football team at twenty-five dollars a game. When this was discovered, he was ruled ineligible to play for the university during the regular season. He left the school without completing a course.

He got a job for thirty dollars a week working for a New York ad agency. One of the customers he got to know was the famed car designer E. L. Cord, who allowed Elliott to chauffeur him on weekends in his Duesenberg. Elliott would always remember driving this car to the Army-Navy game of 1929. He got a speeding ticket on the way home but when the policeman saw that he was the son of the governor he gave him a motorcycle escort into the heart of Manhattan.

FDR had a way of allowing Elliott to get only so far away before reeling him back into the family through one of those offerings of intimacy all his children coveted. In 1931, for instance, when Sara fell ill during her annual summer trip to Europe, FDR decided to go to France to look after her and asked Elliott to go with him. They were like a pair of bachelors on the crossing. FDR was amazed at the way his son attracted women. He convinced Elliott to dance with a hefty opera diva they met and was delighted when the ship lurched and the woman pinned his son against the railing.

In Paris, the two of them shopped in the curio stores FDR loved. Elliott desperately wanted a bronze statuette of a horse he saw in one shop but didn't have enough money to buy it and put it out of his mind. Then, several months later, it arrived on his birthday with an affectionate note from his father.

That fall of 1931, Elliott started his own ad agency with two acquaintances, Jack Kelly and Jim Nason. Kelly brought the account of Grace Lines to the venture; Nason brought the New York Catholic Charities; and Elliott got Louis Howe to give him the account of the Democratic National Committee. He made one hundred dollars a week.

In his last year at Groton he had discovered girls when his Aunt Polly (Sara's sister, Laura Delano) introduced him to a young woman named Jane Wyatt and he took her to his prom. The two of them became inseparable for a time, but then Wyatt said that she wanted to be an actress and didn't have time for a serious romance.

On the rebound, Elliott started dating an ethereal brown-haired woman named Elizabeth Donner he had met at a coming-out party. She was a wealthy Philadelphia Mainliner whose family owned the Donner Steel Company, and when Elliott ran out of money on their nights out, she charged their evenings on her father's accounts around New York. Later on Elliott would say that he had doubts he could ever support her in the style to which she was accustomed the first time he visited the Donner house and saw over a hundred pair of shoes in her closet, but he asked her to marry him anyhow. They were wed in 1932.

Their honeymoon, an ocean cruise, was paid for by Betty's father. So was the apartment they moved into on Park Avenue. His new father-in-law also invited him into the family business as a vice president. As Elliott later said, "I saw my life laid out ahead of me." It was the same vision of responsibility and respectability that had driven him West when he was a boy. Six weeks after the marriage he was telling friends that he had made "a terrible mistake." (Belle Willard, Kermit's wife, heard that another reason he had second thoughts was that the honeymoon had been a sexual fiasco.)

By the time his son William was born ten months after the wedding, Elliott was already spending long periods of time away from his wife. Four days after FDR's inauguration, he decided to go West again, heading his yellow Plymouth coupé for California with the idea of taking a job there in a small airline company run by a friend of his mother's. In the words of one White House employee, he "dumped" Betty there and then took off. He told his wife he might send for her; she knew he probably wouldn't and in a painful scene returned some family pearls Eleanor had given her as a wedding present.

Elliott was short of cash by the time he hit Little Rock and placed a collect call to the White House.

"How are you, Bunny?" his father answered in his usual debonair manner.

Elliott told him his predicament.

"How much money do you have?" FDR asked.

"Thirty dollars," Elliott replied.

He heard the jingling sound of coins being counted. "I have only eight dollars myself," his father said, "and I've just shut down the banks. I suggest you stop at some prosperous farmer's house and perhaps earn enough money to continue your trip."

Elliott decided to keep going.

The Little Rock papers reported that he was heading west and as he approached the outskirts of Dallas a motorcycle policeman pulled him over, verified his identity, and then escorted him downtown to the Baker Hotel where a group of local businessmen including American Airlines vice president C. R. Smith were already waiting for him. They gave him a lunch and the next day took him to Fort Worth, where they presented him with a pearl-handled revolver, put him on a palomino horse, and gave him the title of Grand Marshal of the "Fat Stock Show" taking place there.

The next day C. R. Smith got an American Airlines pilot to fly Elliott across the border to Mexico, where a fiesta was staged in his honor followed by a visit to a huge distillery manufacturing bourbon by the barrel in anticipation of his father repealing Prohibition. Before letting him go on his way, Smith introduced Elliott to Sid Richardson, Clint Murchison, and other oilmen who would soon become legendary figures closely identified with the rise of Texas as a power center in the national Democratic Party.

"I was vaguely aware that I was being sized up," Elliott said later on about his experience in Texas. If so, women were watching him as steadily as the small group of power brokers. During the dance that took place on the night of the Fat Stock Show, Elliott found himself doing the Texas slide with a vivacious dark-haired woman named Ruth Googins whose father had come to Texas at the turn of the century to set up a meat packing operation for the Swift Company.

Ruth was unlike Betty Donner—down to earth and able to talk horses and ranching. She was certainly on his mind, although he didn't mention her by name when Elliott sent a note to Eleanor on the letterhead of the El Paso Club: "Gosh, but this is what I should have done three years ago! Nothing could pay me to go back east again. The people, the spirit of hospitality and friendliness are marvellous and so different from New York."

He kept moving west, feeling that he had embarked on his life's journey. Indeed, it was the beginning of an adventure some observers would later term "picaresque." By this they meant merely that it was episodic and involved constant movement from one place to another, but the term fit in another way as well. His odd upbringing had given Elliott some of the features of the picaro—an impatience with traditional morality and a willingness to get his way by hook or crook.

*   *   *

He arrived in California two days after leaving Fort Worth and went to work as manager of Gilpin Airlines, a failing operation owned by an old friend of Eleanor's. Headquartered in Burbank, Gilpin's small fleet of rickety planes made charter trips to Tijuana and elsewhere in the Southland. One advantage of the job was that every couple of weeks Elliott was able to hitch a ride to Texas to visit Ruth Googins.

Gilpin Airlines' business didn't pick up, and after he had worked there about three months, the company shut its doors. But by this time, Elliott had met a reporter for the *Los Angeles Examiner* who urged him to contact the paper's owner, William Randolph Hearst, for a job.

Elliott met Hearst in Marion Davies's elegant bungalow on the MGM lot. Apparently he was not aware of the ungainly *pas de deux* in which the newspaper tycoon had been engaged with FDR since 1914 when he had opposed him for the U.S. Senate nomination from New York. Hearst had been an enemy since then except for a brief honeymoon after the 1932 Democratic convention when he had accepted Roosevelt as the lesser of several evils. But soon after the inauguration, Hearst had gone on the attack again, sending a memo to all his papers saying that henceforward the New Deal would be referred to as the "Raw Deal."

A few months after meeting Elliott, Hearst would invite Anna and John Boettiger to take over his *Seattle Post-Intelligencer*, partly out of perversity, but also because the paper was beset by labor problems that were costing millions of dollars a year and he thought that hiring these "spotlight people" might help generate advertising and circulation as well as causing the unions to have second thoughts.

Hearst never made any bones about his attitude toward the President. "The real candidate, the unofficial candidate of the Comintern," he said in the mid-1930s, "is Franklin D. Roosevelt." When he offered Elliott fifty dollars a week to be the *Examiner*'s aviation editor (with a raise to one hundred dollars if his pieces were picked up by the other Hearst papers) it was because he saw him as a subtle instrument to use against the administration.

By the time he went on Hearst's payroll just after his father's inauguration in the spring of 1933, Elliott had decided that he must marry Ruth. He called his distraught wife, Betty, who had no idea what he was doing in California, and told her he was going to get a divorce in Reno. He also informed his parents. They told him that Anna was first in line, having postponed her divorce from Curtis Dall and marriage to John Boettiger for over a year out of deference to FDR.

Bothered as much by Elliott's plans for immediate remarriage as by the divorce itself (although he would be the first White House child to go through this procedure), FDR sent Anna to California to try to convince him to wait. Elliott refused, and FDR's irritation was compounded by the fact that there were reporters hiding on the fire escape outside the hotel room where he and his sister had their family discussion who immediately broke the story.

Anna was the only family member present when Elliott married Ruth Googins in Iowa five days after getting his Reno divorce in July 1933. FDR showed his displeasure in the same way he would later on when Jimmy disappointed him with Betsey Cushing—by not inviting the newlyweds to Christmas at the White House. But Elliott was not as easily cowed as his older brother. He struck back at his father by devoting one of his first columns for the Hearst papers to an attack on the administration for canceling air mail contracts with the commercial carriers and giving them to the military.

FDR was still annoyed at his second son early in 1934 when he was cruising in the Bahamas on Vincent Astor's *Nourmahal* and word came that Elliott had inveigled his way onto the seaplane bringing the diplomatic pouches. FDR told Astor not to let his son on board and then made a point of going fishing for the day in a smaller boat. Elliott added insult to injury by arriving monumentally hung-over. Astor disobeyed the President to the extent of letting him come aboard the *Nourmahal* and take a shower, but then put him back on the plane and sent him on his way.

By the mid-1930s newspaper reports on the details of Jimmy's insurance deals in Boston were causing him and his parents discomfort. But Elliott was at the same time engaging in financial maneuvers that were far bolder and more questionable than his brother's. In 1934, while still working for Hearst, he worked out a secret deal to sell fifty military planes designed by the famous Dutch aircraft designer Anthony Fokker to the Soviet Union. The plan had some of the features of a conspiracy. The planes were fighters but would be camouflaged as civilian aircraft. In the code used for communications between the principals, Moscow was "Mosley," FDR was "Rochelle," and Elliott was "New Rochelle."

In a deposition given later on, Fokker claimed that Elliott called FDR in his presence from California about the deal, which was to net him personally a $25,000 payoff. In this conversation, FDR forbade Elliott from going to the U.S.S.R. to tie up the details, according to Fokker, but did not oppose the arrangement itself. The deal ultimately fell through only because the Soviets decided that the $58,000 price tag per plane was too high.

In 1935, after Hearst put him in charge of his radio operations at $50,000 a year, Elliott decided to set up his headquarters in Texas, buying the Rolling R Ranch outside of the small town of Benbrook. He began to do commentaries with an anti–New Deal slant on a local station. He criticized the administration in terms that reflected the view of Hearst and the Texas oilmen whose "tool" he confessed to having become—that the crowd in Washington was too power-hungry, too bureaucratic, too radical.

At the same time that he was criticizing his father, however, Elliott also served his interests. He arranged for Clint Murchison, Sid Richardson, and Charlie Roesser, whom he called "my three oilmen," to meet with FDR. Roesser and Richardson spent two days at Warm Springs expressing their opposition to any changes in the oil depletion allowance and then, once they felt comfortable with the President, pledging to raise large sums for his 1936 reelection drive. They were present in 1937 when FDR made a tarpon fishing trip to the Gulf of Mexico and stopped for a barbecue at Elliott's ranch. They brought some of their friends from the cattle industry to try to convince the President to ban the import of Argentine beef.

Although Elliott was portrayed in the press as the "black sheep" of the family, he still considered himself an integral part of the Hyde Park clan. In 1937, he entertained his grandmother on her first trip to the American West. He was amused to see that Sara had packed as if going to Indian Territory, never counting on being invited to elegant garden parties in Fort Worth where her "farm clothes" would embarrass her. But as usual she left her mark on the situation. As news of her visit reached Washington, Eleanor wrote Anna, "Elliott says Granny has tried Ruth to the breaking point because she *always* talks about [his first wife] Betty."

By this time, FDR had long since relented and allowed Elliott to bring his new family (Ruth gave birth to a daughter, Chandler, in 1934 and a son, Elliott Jr., in 1936) to the White House. On one of those trips Eleanor arranged to have little William Donner Roosevelt, Elliott's son by his first marriage, there to meet his father. Although he had not seen the boy since he was an infant, Elliott took little notice of him, and after the social occasion was over and he and Ruth had returned to Texas, White House staff members heard Eleanor dictating a memo to her son reminding him to try to be at least a little affectionate to the child if he ever saw him again.

By 1937, Elliott had assembled four radio stations for Hearst in Texas and one in Oklahoma. When Hearst had to sell them to raise cash for his hard-pressed newspaper chain, Elliott decided to try to buy them himself and set up what he called the Texas State Network. He was already living as if he were as rich as the other Texas entrepreneurs in his circle and this was his chance to make it to their level. He even entertained the possibility of a political career, and had become head of the state's Junior Chamber of Commerce and gotten himself appointed a regent at Texas A&M. It was the moment when he stood on the edge of realizing the only ambition he would ever have—an ambition he defined later on when he said, "All I ever wanted out of life was to be a really big man."

He began impatiently bombarding the White House for help. Eleanor was as always on his side and wrote FDR to try to cut through the license-granting bureaucracy of the FCC: "Couldn't you or James [at this point still a presidential assistant] say a word which would hurry them? You know Elliott's disposition, he is beginning to think you are both against him." At one point there was a disturbing call from Texas that led Jimmy, at least, to think that Elliott might take his own life if help was not forthcoming. It was in this context that FDR got involved in the deal for the $200,000 loan with John Hartford of A&P.

At the same time that he demanded help from home, Elliott kept up the drumbeat of criticism. In one of his radio commentaries, he said of the Dies Committee, whose investigation of subversives was making life miserable for Eleanor's leftist friends in the American Youth Congress, "It has done more for the U.S. in the last two years than many able and sincere statesmen achieve in a lifetime."

He was also critical of the interventionist forces working with Franklin to push the United States toward involvement in Europe, and, as 1940 approached, opposed a third term for his father. As he and his Texas friends backed Vice President John Garner for President, FDR's supporters got nasty. Their attacks on Elliott became so intemperate that FDR finally had to authorize his press secretary to reply to one person who had complained about his son, "Mr. Elliott Roosevelt is an

American Citizen—free and of adult age. He therefore enjoys, among other things, the right of free speech and is entitled to the exercises of that right."

When his father was nominated in 1940, Elliott was at the convention as part of the Texas delegation. FDR wanted Henry Wallace as his vice presidential candidate, but Wallace was anathema to Texas conservatives. Elliott again lined up with his friends against his father, not only backing Texas financier and RFC chief Jesse Jones for the post of vice president (although FDR had said he would not run if not given Wallace as a running mate) but even agreeing to give a seconding speech for Jones. He was ready to mount the podium when Eleanor suddenly appeared and ordered him not to defy his father any further.

After the convention, Elliott was at the end of his string. The radio stations were still promising but not yet profitable. His marriage to Ruth was under pressure because he was so heavily in debt, never having paid back any of the money he had borrowed from John Hartford of A&P a year earlier. When he told his father about his problems, FDR called Jesse Jones: "Elliott has a serious financial problem that I wish you would help him straighten out." The financier convinced Hartford to retire his $200,000 debt for $4,000 and got another man who had lent Elliott an additional $10,000 to settle for a single payment of $500.

A dangling man caught between alternatives, Elliott looked to the military as a way out. As he said later on, "It was clear there was going to be a war, so I figured I might as well get a head start." He enlisted in the air force and managed to get himself appointed a captain. News that he had been appointed an officer caused such an outcry that he tried to resign. But the top brass decided to ride out the storm of protest.

At a party at Hyde Park in late September 1940 celebrating Elliott's thirtieth birthday, FDR raised a glass in a toast: "To Elliott. He's the first of the family to think seriously enough, and soberly enough, about the threat to America to join his country's Armed Services. We're all very proud of him, and I'm the proudest."

As Elliott Roosevelt prepared for war, young men all around the country began forming chapters of the "I Want to Be a Captain Too" Club.

$\mathcal{T}$he Oyster Bay Roosevelts watched the emotional chaos emanating from the First Family with a perverse sense of satisfaction. This was a confirmation of what they had been saying for almost twenty years: the Hyde Park branch was not just an inferior copy of the original, but a forgery. Elliott, who may have seemed at first glance to be the exception, was actually the rule, exemplifying the world Franklin and Eleanor had created. Thus, in 1940 Ted gleefully wrote his son Cornelius, "Your cousin Elliott has put his fat foot in it. What he did about being made a captain in the Air Corps has . . . hurt your other cousin, his father, more than any other single incident. When I go speaking, I am going to say his mother's favorite song is 'I Didn't Raise My Boy to Be a Private.' "

There was a strong sense among members of the Oyster Bay clan that the Roosevelt family name, whose conscientious custodians they felt they had been so long, was being degraded by the financial misdeeds and especially by the marital failures of these other Roosevelts. (As late as 1950, when Archie's son announced that he was getting a divorce, Archie responded bitterly, *"We* don't do that sort of thing. That is what *they* do.") But the heirs of TR could not afford to be too smug because they had disturbing problems of their own. One that they talked of in whispers was Alice's cruel treatment of her daughter, Paulina, a plain and unhappy girl with a debilitating stutter that rendered her virtually mute, especially in the presence of her mother, who had shocked family members by telling Paulina that she was illegitimate. But a far more daunting matter that implicated them all was Kermit's long night of the soul.

In a better time he had been the liveliest and most attractive of them all—so adventuresome and poetic, in the words of a friend, "that he seemed to dance on air." His nieces and nephews looked forward to Kermit's visits, for he always brought them some gift picked up on his exotic travels—a Sumatran knife for the boys, perhaps; an ivory chicken from China nesting in a handmade basket for the girls. He always arrived with new stories, and his relatives were not alone in being mesmerized by his narrative powers. It was said that the Knickerbocker Club fell into silent anticipation whenever Kermit walked in the door after a long absence, the members putting down their newspapers and waiting for the tales to begin. He was one of those personalities everyone wanted to know, a collector of literary friendships that now included modernists such as William Butler Yeats, whom he had to lunch during the poet's tour of America, and Gertrude Stein, whom he had looked up in Paris, as well as Kipling and Robinson.

But by the mid-1930s something was wrong and everyone in the family knew it. Once his eldest son, Kim, was driving down Park Avenue and the door accidentally opened and his mother, Belle, fell out, not injuring herself seriously but narrowly avoiding being hit by following cars. In writing one of his brothers about the incident, Ted's son Cornelius noted, "Things like that always happen to that family."

It was true. There was now a star-crossed quality in Kermit's life. He was not particularly well. He had never been able to shake the malaria he contracted on his voyage down the River of Doubt with his father, although this illness, because it was a reminder of that prestige moment in his life, had acquired the paradoxical feel of an old friend. During the 1920s he had developed warts on one of his hands, and a doctor, overly enthusiastic about the newly available radium treatment, had so overdosed him that he got cancer and had to have a thumb amputated.

It was also indisputable that his business was failing. In 1930, using his wife, Belle's, inheritance as collateral, Kermit and two partners had obtained the International Merchant Marine Company. He had folded his own Roosevelt Steamship Company into the larger venture and started the United States Lines, one of the biggest in the world.

But work had never meant much more than meeting people and letting them see the son of Teddy Roosevelt; taking exotic trips; and going with his children to spend the afternoons at the docks watching the ships come in. Success had seemed guaranteed. When the Depression changed all that, Kermit found it hard to cope. His alarm was clear in a letter he had written to Belle's sister Elizabeth Herbert in 1932: "As you probably know, both passenger and freight carryings have fallen off at a perfectly appalling extent. Trans-Atlantic travel is approximately 53% less than it was two years ago. As a consequence we are obliged to lay up ships and turn the crews loose and also to curtail our shore staff."

It was a condemnation as well as a nuisance not to have money. When his fourteen-year-old son, Willard, wrote from Groton asking for a loan, Kermit sent an embarrassed reply saying it was impossible: "Don't speak of this to Mother or anyone. I confide my troubles in you so that you may understand why I haven't done even the things I formerly did for you. . . ."

His income tax return from 1933 showed that he made $20,004 and was selling for $3 a share International Merchant Marine stock valued at $28 when issued. The following year he had to write a vice president of the Chase Bank who had asked for a "substantial reduction" in the principal of his outstanding $140,000 personal loan: "At the time when I saw you . . . you explained fully to me how greatly disturbed the Executive Committee is at the position of my loan. . . . Under the circumstances the best thing for me to do would be to appear before the Executive Committee and explain to them the situation." A measure of his distress could be seen in the fact that he had been forced to rent out Mohannes, his Oyster Bay estate, and Belle had to sell for $350 a diamond bracelet appraised for $4,000 at the time of their marriage.

Some close to the family felt that Kermit was very much the moth to his own flame—an Edwardian romantic who had grown up thinking he would plot an exciting existence for himself and then had suddenly awakened to find himself trapped in the same viscous expectations that constrained other men. He was guilty over losing Belle's money, but alienated by her persistent social climbing, a trait that became particularly marked after FDR was elected President and she began to bombard the White House with unctuous notes of congratulation and support.

Kermit was amused at being regarded as a society figure. (He served as master of ceremonies for socialite Elsa Maxwell's famous 1933 Halloween party and allowed her to make a hair from his mustache one of the items required to complete the scavenger hunt.) But he was well aware of the triviality of such affairs. People at parties would sometimes watch as he started off being the center of attention but then, by choice, ended the evening on the periphery of things, quietly watching everyone else. As one friend said of Kermit, "He didn't fit in. He seemed to float. He didn't like the type of life he was leading but didn't quite know how to get out of it."

He might have coped with his problems if he had not crossed the line that separated social drinking from alcoholism. Over the years, as he had gotten older and heavier, Kermit had come to resemble TR so much that his mother, once catching sight of him after a long absence, had gasped in surprise as if seeing a ghost. But by the mid-1930s he was pale and bloated, resembling a caricature of his father. As in the case of his work and his marriage, it was a surprise for him when this part of his life went out of control. "My father always thought he could handle liquor," his son Willard later said, "and when it dawned on him that he couldn't he reacted with bewilderment."

Much of the drinking was done at The Room, the brownstone Kermit and his friends had outfitted as a private club in the late 1920s to circumvent Prohibition. After a while, instead of merely drinking once he got there, Kermit began showing up drunk. On one notorious occasion, a party was staged for Admiral Richard Byrd at which Kermit got so drunk that he passed out in a corner of the room and was not discovered until late the following day.

In the beginning, his relationship with Belle had been a joint poem they had written together—a breathless courtship when Kermit was a young man in Brazil, wartime heroism and moonlit tiger shoots after that. But she had wanted him to be a Roosevelt just as he had been when they met—at the center of things, the focus of attention. As the changing times and his own problems made this impossible, he became acutely aware of how much he disappointed her. Gradually Kermit began to seek the company of women one friend called "ladies of the night"— women who allowed him to be anonymous and who had no expectations.

In 1936 he had entered a long-term relationship with a German masseuse named Carla Peters. Blonde and earthy, Peters once asked him what he saw in her and he laughed and said, "Relief." He took her to The Club occasionally. Sometimes the two of them disappeared for days, registering at hotels as "Mr. and Mrs. Hilton," the pseudonym coming from the name of James Hilton, author of *Lost Horizon* and one of Kermit's literary acquaintances. ("James would certainly be amused," Kermit once told Peters when he was signing the hotel register.)

At first Belle denied what was happening. Then she became obsessed with preserving appearances. Finding out who Peters was, Belle invited her to their apartment and introduced her as "a family friend." She insisted on meeting Peters in public places like the River Club and Rainbow Room where they could be seen together and introducing her to social acquaintances. She expected the mistress to cooperate in every detail of the charade. Once Peters balked at some request while they were sitting in the bar at the Waldorf-Astoria and Belle suddenly grabbed her arm and bit her, leaving deep teeth marks in the skin. She demanded that Peters accompany her to a psychiatrist so they could discuss their sex lives with Kermit, and afterward she sent him the bill. Sometimes Belle called Peters in the middle of the night, hissing into the phone, "If I can't sleep, I don't want you to sleep either."

Kermit accepted all this with his usual equanimity, never mentioning the schism in his emotional life. He could not break with Belle because she was his "soul mate" and because he too wanted to believe in her apologia for him as someone too poetic and easily bruised to tolerate the brutalities of modern life. In the spring of 1937, Kermit took her on what was supposed to be a trip of reconciliation to Europe, but midway through the holiday she had to enter a Swiss sanatorium for treatment for exhaustion and he came home without her.

That romanticism that was always the strongest part of their bond would not allow Belle to forget the dashing young man with whom she had shared adventures for half a lifetime. For her, the man who was now her husband was an imposter. But for Kermit it was the real self. Something had snapped—the assumption that the world would always be his oyster—when his father died. At that moment "the bottom dropped out," as he said at the time, and he had not been able to build a stable foundation under his life since. In the late 1930s he sometimes took Carla Peters to visit TR's grave in Oyster Bay where they would sit quietly picking at a few straggling weeds. (Thinking the site barren, Peters once suggested they put in some crocus bulbs and Kermit got a stricken look on his face, "Oh no, mother wouldn't like that!") Once they were on a picnic in the Delaware countryside when Kermit's car broke down and he asked a farmer to tow him to town. After looking at him for a long time, the farmer said, "I hope you won't mind if I say this, but darned if you don't look like Teddy Roosevelt." Kermit threw back his head in a laugh edged with pathos: "You know, people have been telling me that all my life."

His two older children, having come of age before his life began to disintegrate, did well. Kim was a brilliant student at Harvard and by the late 1930s was in California working at the Huntington Library on a thesis about war propaganda in seventeenth-century English politics. Willard was a promising music composer who went off to Paris to study under Nadia Boulanger.

But his younger two children exemplified that star-crossed quality that others in the Oyster Bay clan saw as having overtaken his family as a whole. His daughter, Clochette, who had suffered a brush with polio as a girl, had an accident in 1935 when she was bending over the upstairs banister of the family home, lost her balance and fell down to the marble floor below, suffering injuries that took years to heal. His last child, Dirck, born in 1925, was the one whose own experience mirrored with disturbing fidelity the disorganization that had entered Kermit's life.

A strange, gangly boy, oddly un-Roosevelt in appearance, Dirck defied every expectation. Sent away to school like his brothers and cousins, he began his first letter home, "Groton disappoints me greatly," and his second, "Groton disappoints me still more."

By his second term, Dirck had begun to act in a bizarre fashion, mordantly isolating himself from school activities and conceiving possessive crushes on his classmates. At one point in 1938, as Kermit's alcoholism was reaching a destructive crescendo, Dirck and one of his only school friends, a boy named Henry Distler, sneaked away from Groton. They registered as Dick and Harry Godenick in a Springfield hotel and slipped out when they saw that the management had become suspicious of them. By the time they were apprehended after showing up in Baltimore two days later, an eight-state alarm had been issued amidst fears of another Lindbergh case.

When the two boys were brought back to Pennsylvania Station, the episode reached a surreal conclusion. The Roosevelt chauffeur, trying to shield Dirck from the mob of photographers that had gathered, quickly grabbed him. The Distler chauffeur, thinking Dirck was being kidnapped, punched his opposite number and tried to disentangle Dirck from his grasp. As the New York Times reported the next day, the Roosevelt driver "Kehoe returned the blow and the chauffeurs exchanged punches while young Distler fainted and young Roosevelt became hysterical with excitement."

Thinking to toughen his son through the family tradition of Western adventure, Kermit sent Dirck to a ranch in British Columbia in the summer of 1938. The miserably lonely thirteen-year-old wrote pathetic letters asking to come home. Kermit answered by reminding him that the rest of the family was not having an easy time either; he had been forced to rent their home at Oyster Bay and had recently himself been hospitalized for a recurrence of malaria. But he was unable to offer solace to his son. ("Once I get out my plans are exceedingly vague and I don't at the moment see how you could fit in them.") And two weeks later he wrote again to say that Belle was off traveling and he had taken a room for one on East 83rd Street for nine dollars a week and thus literally had no room for Dirck.

Desperate, Dirck wrote to a former governess: "If I don't go home soon . . . I fear I may have to break my promise and go so far as to leave the world by violent methods such as 'falling' off a building." He was more explicit in a letter addressed to his parents: "If I am not away from here by June 20 at 8pm—11pm your time—I swear you will never see me alive again. . . . If you say no also say goodby. You will hear maybe that I was burned to death or got a cramp and drowned." The deadline came and went and the boy continued to write threatening notes.

One reason Kermit ignored his youngest son was that he was busy crossing his own personal Rubicon in the summer of 1938. Earlier that spring, Belle had tried to separate him from Carla Peters by getting Vincent Astor to invite him on an extended cruise. The *Nourmahal* sailed the South Pacific for three months. (The nature of the itinerary was such that some observers thought that FDR had asked Astor and Kermit to spy on Japanese war preparations.) But when he returned home, Kermit went back to his mistress as before.

Belle got FDR to have a conversation with him, which Kermit immediately related to Carla Peters, quoting the President as having said to him, "Why can't you just keep your women on the side like the rest of us?" Next Belle took her problems to John Franklin, president of the United States Lines, who gave Kermit an ultimatum to shape up or ship out. Indignant that his private life had been discussed with a business associate, Kermit resigned from the company he had helped found and left for California taking Peters with him.

It was a traumatic moment for the family. Edith particularly had come to love and dread the visits of her favorite son. After one of them, a granddaughter staying at Sagamore saw the iron-willed old lady break into tears: "Grandmother knew about Kermit's masseuse. She was too moralistic to let the woman come to the house. But she was also appreciative of her because she took care of Kermit."

Kermit rented a house in Palo Alto with Peters in the summer of 1938. He took a job working a few hours a day on the San Francisco wharf with his old friend Alfred Clegg of the Kerr Lines, the man who had originally brought him into the shipping business right after World War I. The salary was just enough to live on and Kermit wasn't under any illusions about the significance of the work, telling Peters, "Alfred is just making a gesture. It's good of him, but I have nothing to do, really. I just sit there and meet people." Sometimes he and Peters went to the zoo. Once they took a train to Los Angeles and toured the movie studios.

Trying to dry out, Kermit watched the gathering storm in Europe. He agreed with the elliptical maneuvers by which FDR was trying to bring the United States into the conflict. "Franklin is quite right," he said to Peters out of the blue one morning. "We'll have to go after Hitler some day, and you know, of course, that I'll have to be part of it."

Belle continued to stay in contact, pretending to others—and to him— that his absence was merely a temporary sojourn. She wrote chatty letters keeping him informed of family business matters, such as her decision to sell their 69th Street brownstone and auction the contents. The language of her correspondence contained the same romanticism as it had twenty years earlier when they were courting. Shielding him from matters she thought would upset him, she wrote her sister Elizabeth to say that Dirck had now been expelled from Groton for good and was under a psychiatrist's care: "The most difficult thing is to explain to Kermit so that he will not be worried or frightened."

If she was solicitous about Kermit, however, Belle had no compunctions about laying out the facts of their life for her in-laws. At this high point of her personal drama, she wrote an angry letter that was addressed to Ethel's husband, Dick Derby, but meant for all of the Oyster Bay clan. She said that she had tried to elicit concern for what was happening to Kermit, but that the family—particularly Ted and Archie —had ignored her:

> We who love Kermit hope and believe that he will get well. The family, however, have said to me as well as to others that they didn't believe, *even that they did not hope*. I can't explain to you what this attitude of the family has done to me and to Kermit's children. For

years he has been a very sick man. You only had to look at him to see
the agony of mind and body he was suffering. . . . It will serve no
purpose to enumerate the times when the family's attitude has caused
trouble and unnecessary pain. . . . Criticism by the family has come to
us very strongly through various sources. If the family will search their
mind and conscience they cannot deny that. . . . Neither my sons nor
I can . . . meet the family until we are convinced that such talk is at an
end.

The response from Ted was immediate: "I don't know to what you
refer when you say that the family has been speaking ill of Kermit. I
discuss him with no one and write him regularly once a week. Naturally
I will be sorry if Kim and Willard feel they do not want to see any of us.
I am very fond of them."

It was disingenuous of him not to acknowledge that there was a
problem. If Kermit's failure was primarily a moral one as far as the rest
of them were concerned, for Ted there was also a political dimension.
He was aware that Belle was constantly blandishing Franklin and
Eleanor and conniving to get invitations to the White House. He had
seen an example of what he regarded as Kermit's defective will when his
brother accompanied FDR in his 1933 cruise aboard the *Nourmahal* and
then went further by becoming part of what the press called "the *Nourmahal* gang." Ted also knew that his brother had asked FDR for financial
favors as the shipping industry fell on hard times, writing him in late
1933 to urge a "war" on British shippers cutting into the business of the
International Merchant Marine Company.

From Ted's perspective all this amounted to a treason of the heart. He
felt that FDR had manipulated the relationship with Kermit to make it
seem that there was no opposition to him from the Oyster Bay
Roosevelts. For his own part, however, opposition was implacable and
unyielding. Even before getting home from the six-month world tour
that followed his resignation from the governor-generalship of the Philippines in 1933, he was on the attack, writing his mother from Italy that
he had just had an audience with Mussolini "and he told me in almost
so many words he considered Franklin his pupil."

All through the first term, Ted had pressed the attack on his cousin.
"Our liberties are being violated," he warned a Republican youth group
in a speech at the beginning of the first term, "cast aside and disregarded." A progressive Republican who opposed the Old Guard in his
own party, he was nonetheless deepy disturbed by the "coercion" prac-

ticed by FDR's administration. Ted accused the New Deal of "making false promises to the needy," of administering relief in such a way as "to leave a stench in the nostrils of decent people," and of destroying the country "morally and spiritually and ruining it materially." Finally, he addressed Franklin himself in a Pennsylvania speech in 1935: "You have been faithless. You have usurped the functions of Congress, hampered the freedom of the press. . . . You have urged Congress to pass laws you knew were unconstitutional. . . . You have broken your sacred oath taken on the Bible."

Others saw a coherence between the first and second Roosevelt presidencies. In fact, several figures who had originally entered politics as a result of TR's Progressive crusade—Harold Ickes, Henry Wallace, and others—had also become stalwarts of the New Deal. But as Ted noted, there were far more who had not gone over to Franklin than who had. For most of the old Progressives, government now occupied the same menacing position that business had a quarter century earlier, and the New Deal emphasis on reform through materialism rather than through a structure of ideals was anathema to them. The social programs of the New Deal, they believed, amounted to "equality conquering liberty."

George Creel, a muckraking journalist and editor of the Progressive era who was now one of those criticizing the New Deal, expressed the common complaint of the old Progressives when he wrote, "Where once [liberalism] stood for the dignity of men—the rescue of the spirit from the debasements of materialism, it now stands for the obliteration of individualism at the hands of a ruthless, all powerful state."

Guarding the TR legacy as if it were a saint's relics, Ted called a meeting on the twenty-fifth anniversary of the Progressive Party on his father's birthday in 1937. At the end of his meeting, Ted issued a statement saying that while TR had fought for "reform under the Constitution," the New Dealers wanted to "destroy democracy." The idea that FDR resembled his father in any way was not just wrong, it was heresy.

Alice was also actively working against the New Deal, although in her case this involved constructing malicious bon mots about her cousins and passing them on to other conservative cave-dwellers in Washington. When she said that they ought to get the pants off Eleanor and onto Franklin, for instance, she managed to allude to his paralysis in the same sentence that she alluded to her association with lesbians. Soon after FDR took the country off the gold standard, Alice showed up at a White House party festooned in gold jewelry. She made a point of calling him "Franklin" in public, and she had perfected her cruel imitation of Eleanor that involved sucking in her lower lip and putting her front teeth over it to make them look like they protruded. At a White House luncheon one day Eleanor said to her, "Alice, why don't you give one of your impersonations of me now?" Alice did it immediately and Eleanor laughed along with everyone else but was clearly hurt.

Yet Ted was such a hardliner that the mere fact that his sister set foot in the White House, even if it was to make its occupants uncomfortable, was evidence that she was willing to "snuggle up" to FDR. "I could not help feeling it was like behaving in like fashion to an emeny during a war," he wrote his mother after one such visit. "More so, for enemies generally only fight for territory, trade or some material possessions. These are fighting us for our form of government, our liberties, the future of our children. I did not expect Kermit to see—for that's his blind side. But I did expect her to see this, for she's acute and her life has been politics."

His own family cooperated in his obsession. When his wife, Eleanor, made an appearance at a Fort Worth Town Hall meeting in 1936, Elliott was set to introduce her but she asked him not to, causing the other Eleanor, Elliott's mother, to write a letter of complaint to their mutual cousin Corinne Alsop: "It seems to me unfortunate to harbor that kind of a political feeling in personal relationships."

Because of the effectiveness of his concentrated attack on FDR during the first term, Ted was once again briefly mentioned as a possible candidate for New York governor in 1936. An even more elaborate scenario had him challenging FDR as vice president on a ticket headed by Senator William Borah. It was a crucial moment in the Republican Party's future—a choice between "modernizing" and taking on a progressive identity, or staying with the Old Guard. As the convention approached, Alice's former lover Borah launched a ferocious attack on corporations that irritated the party's Old Guard and effectively dashed his chances and Ted's as well.

Other old Progressives, his brother Archie among them, rushed toward the extreme right as a result of their fear of the New Deal. Ted tried to stay in the disappearing middle. He felt that he had not only lost in politics, but lost out. There were only two alternatives, neither of them palatable—the dangerously power-hungry New Deal and an increasingly predatory Wall Street.

Somewhere along the line, Ted seemed to have resigned himself to becoming a ceremonial figure, his father's heir rather than his political heir apparent. He encouraged people to call him "Colonel" Roosevelt, the same title TR had taken after leaving the White House. While he was still a committed opponent of FDR, Ted was otherwise an ecumenical figure—involved with the NAACP, national chairman of the Boy Scouts, and on the board of the National Council of Christians and Jews. (When songwriter Irving Berlin chose three trustees to administer the royalties from "God Bless America," Ted was one of them.) It was as much for social relationships as income that he accepted jobs first as chairman of the board of American Express and then as a vice president of Doubleday Books.

Ted was bothered by Kermit's decline, although he tended to see it as yet another symptom of a time that was out of joint. He was involved in other conflicts within the family, notably with his other brother, Archie, which also occupied his attention.

While Ted and Kermit had been off on their exotic adventures, it had fallen to Archie, along with the ever reliable Ethel, to keep the home fires burning and to look out for Edith. By the mid-1930s Archie had managed once again to dig himself out of the financial troubles that had plagued him for a decade. A ramrod-straight man of middle years, with a fierce raptor's nose defining a face that his teenaged nieces all felt was handsome, he had become the most conservative of the Oyster Bay Roosevelts. Yet it was a libertarian rather than authoritarian conservatism. He had created an ethic of independence in his own family that one of his children later said was symbolized by family sailing vacations where everyone was encouraged to swim and sun themselves naked.

His son, Archie Jr., who had eschewed the "manly" Roosevelt image and become a brilliant linguist at Harvard, was an anti-Stalinist when Stalinism was chic. One of Archie's daughers, Theodora, was a modern dancer who went to Rio de Janeiro in the late 1930s and raised such controversy with her provocative performances that Under Secretary of State Sumner Welles at one point wrote the White House to tell Eleanor that the U.S. ambassador to Argentina was worried that the performance might be "seized upon with alacrity by Nazi propagandists" to prove the decadence of America.*

---

* There was a limit to Archie's tolerance of iconoclasm within his family. When Archie Jr. married and had his first son in 1940, his mother, Grace, came to San Francisco where he was then living to see her grandchild, bringing with her family

Archie had always been the ultimate loyalist. (Never, while Edith was alive, did he ever fail to send her a telegram on the anniversary of Quentin's death.) He had always deferred to Ted as the leader of his generation. But now, as his elder brother settled into the role of Colonel Roosevelt, an unsolved matter of family business caused bitterness between them.

In response to a suggestion by Edith, Ted was ready to move into Sagamore Hill in the mid-1930s. The house was no bargain. When Kermit's son Kim first brought his fiancée, Polly, to stay there on Thanksgiving 1936 she was struck by how cold and drafty it was and how uncomfortable, with the mattresses feeling as though they had been stuffed with corncobs and the hot water gurgling slowly into the antique bathtub. Making small talk with Edith during the weekend, Polly remarked on the animal skins on the floor and was surprised by the response. "Do you think I like all these rugs around here with their awful open mouths and shining eyes?" asked Edith. "No, I don't like them at all!"

Yet if it was somewhat run-down, the family home was still a symbol of their joint past and their common heritage. Archie's son, Archie Jr., always remembered going there as a boy and feeling the presence of TR: "He was our hero and our playmate. All the activities of the house followed the patterns he had set during his lifetime there." It was like a museum. The taper Quentin had used because of his fear of the dark was still on an upstairs nightstand. The sword TR had worn on San Juan Hill hung in its rotting scabbard. His trophies of war, diplomacy, and the hunt were everywhere. It was as if time stood still: the clocks had not been wound since the day of TR's death. Archie Jr. felt that his grandfather was particularly present in the southwest bedroom where the bedcover was in the design of an American flag. And once he had what he later described as a near out-of-body experience in which he found himself in this room speaking aloud to TR and asking for his help to be worthy of him.

Given such strong associations as these, it was no surprise that Archie resisted Ted's move to take over Sagamore. Edith had originally offered to move out and deed the place to Ted. Archie's strong feelings made her equivocate. Then Ted became angry, causing Edith to write Kermit, "As far as he is concerned, it had been better if I were dead."

---

silver. When she was told that the baby had been named Tweed instead of Archibald Bulloch Roosevelt III, she turned around and took the silver back home.

For a brief time, the issue became almost as divisive for the Oyster Bay family as Kermit's tragic deterioration. Determined "to set the record straight," Ted drafted a letter to his brother in 1937 that revealed his own sense of hurt and, between the lines, his frustration at having spent his life chasing his father's ghost in his own way:

> I am the only one in the family who has no home of his own. All the rest of you have your houses. I have no home because it was understood that some day I was to move into Sagamore. It was not merely understood, it was told me that this course represented the wish of the family and especially mother.
>
> I am now in my fiftieth year. Eleanor [his wife] is approaching the same age. We have never known what it meant to do as all the rest of you have done, namely plan and work on improvements on your own home. As a matter of fact, we have received far less from the family than any of the other children, with the exception of Sister. [Crossed out at this point are the following sentences: "You yourself were given approximately $200,000. You and others have made it a practice to stay at Sagamore with your family for long periods of time. The produce of the place goes in part to you. It does not go to me."]
>
> . . . There is a consequence which of course you must have realized when you took your position with mother, and that is that Sagamore will now be sold on mother's death. . . . I am the only one in the family now who has the means to take it over. Naturally I know the financial affairs of my brothers and sisters. You for example could not take it over. . . . Kermit has two houses already and is not in a business where much money may be made. Both Ethel and Sister have homes of their own and fixed incomes which will not increase.

The struggle for Sagamore was a lacerating experience and it left scars. But by 1937 Ted solved his housing crisis by purchasing the old apple orchard adjacent to Sagamore. He had architect William Mc-Millan, husband of his daughter, Grace, design an immense Georgian house with high ceilings and a wide hallway running from the front of the house to the back. In it he put the portraits of four generations of Roosevelts and curios collected from his world travels. As one of his friends said, "It looked like a museum of past dreams."

Life at Old Orchard, as Ted named the new house, was good in the late 1930s. His work as vice president of Doubleday led him into literary associations. He staged softball games with teams led by Lowell

Thomas and Thornton Wilder. Literary wit Alexander Woollcott was a frequent houseguest and Ted and Eleanor returned his visits by journeying to the Woollcott estate in Vermont where on occasion Harpo Marx strummed his instrument while the guests played croquet on spacious lawns.

But Ted's vendetta against FDR took on a new life as another war began to loom on the horizon. He was enraged at his cousin's statement, "I have seen war in land and sea. I have seen blood running from the wounded. . . . I hate war." Not only did he know that FDR had avoided combat in World War I, but he also doubted the antiwar sentiments themselves.

It was he and his brothers who had seen war. And his own family had just seen a preview of what was to come. Eleanor and their youngest son, Quentin, were visiting Shanghai in August 1937 when they witnessed an attempt by Chinese airplanes to attack Japanese gunboats that ended in a tragic fiasco with the bombs landing on the city itself. Eleanor described the incident over NBC radio in a broadcast with antiwar overtones: "Bodies in the street were frightfully mangled, stray arms and legs, charred cars and the people in them disfigured beyond recognition. I was in Paris all through the bombardment of 1918 and though at that time I was looking at the face of war it was a tea party compared to what went on in Shanghai these three days."

Ted thought that entering a European war would backfire on the United States just as this attack in China had backfired on the Chinese. And so he took up the fight to keep the United States out of the looming international conflict.

Those close to the Roosevelt family were struck by the paradox: Franklin, who was a noncombatant in World War I (despite his relentless revisionism of his personal history since then) was pushing for U.S. involvement, and Ted, the highly decorated war hero and son of TR, was opposing it. Behind the contradiction was the issue that had divided the two men all along: which of them truly represented the Roosevelt tradition? Ted seized on small things such as TR's opposition in his last days to the League of Nations to justify his position and square it with what he claimed would have been his father's attitude toward the new conflict. But it was clear to Henry Stimson and others who had been close to his father that in this matter TR would have stood with Franklin and not with Ted.

As the European situation deteriorated, Ted plotted with Borah and the other leading isolationists in Congress. For him, no less than for his close friend Charles Lindbergh, keeping the United States out of war was a holy cause. "Our frontiers are not in France," he said in a 1939 address to the Irish Historical Society. "Our frontiers are on the shores of this hemisphere." He derided FDR's idea of collective security as a matter of the U.S. "furnishing the security while others do the collecting."

Not long after this he gave his ideas more scope in a speech to the University of Virginia in which he stated: "The only thing worth fighting for is our free institutions and our representative democracy, our own integrity and the Monroe Doctrine." He worried that FDR was conspiring to manipulate foreign affairs as he had the domestic scene: "I believe most emphatically that no further powers should be granted to the President. . . . No small group of men should have the right to decide for the American people questions of this sort in secret."

Ted was no reactionary. He had gone to England in 1937 to deliver a series of lectures at Cambridge about colonialism and had criticized the "empire complex" that had overtaken people like his father fifty years earlier. Published as *Colonial Policies of the United States,* his speeches brought praise from Walter Lippmann, who saw the book as an enlightened document—"the history of one family, of the father who was touched with the imperialist vision and of his son who has dealt with it as Governor General of our two greatest colonial possessions."

While his campaign against interventionism was in large part a campaign against Franklin and indeed against the very *idea* of Franklin, it also had a heartfelt component of fear. It was not fear of combat. Ted had maintained his position in the army reserves since coming home from World War I. It was fear that another global war would accelerate the social changes he had seen taking place during the last decade and wind up midwifing a brutal society like those already under arms on the Continent. In a letter to Alexander Woollcott, Ted wrote, "I can remember the last war. I remember that I felt when I came back that no matter what we might have failed in doing, at least we stamped out intolerance in the United States, for our common service, shoulder to shoulder for the common cause, could not help but accomplish this. The [actual result] was the Ku Klux Klan and bigotry, hooded and rampant."

At the same time he was crisscrossing the country issuing warnings about the war, Ted was rallying the Roosevelt family as well. To his son Cornelius, temporarily working as an engineer in Mexico, he wrote: "I am doing my level best to stiffen the country in a determination to stay out of war. I have made speeches and at the American Legion I succeeded in getting the stiffest kind of a resolution passed." He wrote to Alice as well: "Like you I am bitterly fearful of Franklin. I am confident he is itching to get in the situation, partly as a means of bolstering himself and partly merely because of megalomania. . . ."

His sister didn't require any pep talk. Asked for her views on the third term, Alice said, "I'd rather vote for Hitler." When this and other verbal assaults were reported to him, FDR finally decided he'd had enough, roaring, "I don't want to have anything to do with that damned woman again!" As the invitations to the White House finally dried up, Alice shrugged, "They might have said, 'Look here, you miserable woman, of course you feel upset because you hoped your brother Ted would finally achieve [the presidency] and now he hasn't. But after all, here we are. Come if it amuses you.' But they took it all seriously. They took the meanness in the spirit in which it was meant."

The night England declared war on Germany, Ted and Eleanor sat in their living room with their sons Theodore III and Quentin somberly leafing through scrapbooks they had kept during World War I. A few months later Ted formally joined America First. Alice was already a founding member of the organization, a name on its letterhead and a familiar figure on its speakers' platforms. But while for her it was mainly malicious ("Anything to annoy Franklin"), Ted saw the success of the organization as a matter of life and death for the country. "We are working like beavers to get America First going in this community," he said in a letter to Cornelius. America First was the only hope for stopping the juggernaut Franklin had set in motion.

As he took up the isolationist crusade, often portraying it to himself and others as one of those doomed good causes like TR's Progressive Party fight in 1912, Ted was also in contact with Kermit, who had returned home from California as war threatened. Their brother seemed "broken down in pieces," Archie sadly noted, but Ted's letters to Kermit warily skirted personal issues and Kermit reciprocated by pretending that the family was still intact. He wrote about how impressed he was with Ted's son Quentin, now a brilliant Harvard student who'd taken his junior year off in 1939 and traveled alone to the Tibet-China border to pursue his thesis about the spread of Buddhism from India to China. Kermit had heard how Quentin had eaten locusts and caterpillars and traded sunglasses and raincoats for ancient scrolls and prayer wheels and recognized a kindred spirit. "It's interesting that he, of all the boys," Kermit wrote in allusion to the epic trips he and Ted had made in the mid-1920s, "should be the one who on his own initiative goes after what you and I did."

But when Ted wrote of his alarm about war, Kermit answered him far differently than others in the family: "Looking at it offhand, I should believe that we were all slated to be over there before long. . . . I don't see how we can keep out of it without heaping up more and worse trouble for ourselves and our sons in the future."

This, of course, was FDR's line. But Kermit saw the international situation in personal as well as political terms. Torn between his wife and his mistress, watching his own deterioration and its effects on his children, he had come to see the war as a last desperate chance to reconstruct the heroic image he had so carefully constructed as a young man. Late in the fall of 1939, he enlisted in the British Army.

Belle supported him. She too believed that the war might allow him to reassemble those pieces of self his brother Archie had seen as being so tragically fragmented. At least it would get him away from his mistress. She accompanied Kermit when he sailed for England at the end of the year and was with him when he fell ill from the effects of his alcoholism early in 1940 and had to be hospitalized in London. He emerged suffering from a variety of complaints, not the least of which were badly abscessed teeth. Doctors counseled against having a dentist pull them for fear of loosing a generalized "septic poisoning" throughout his body; instead he had a large volume of pus drawn from his gums every day as he tried to regain his strength.

After weeks of negotiating over the terms of his service, it was finally settled that Kermit would lead an expeditionary force into Finland to try to repel the Soviet invasion. Winston Churchill was solidly behind him and on March 5, 1940, they lunched together at the Admiralty. Belle found the free-flowing conversation between the two men to be "reminiscent of [the] sparkling quality at Sagamore long years ago." One of the subjects broached was why TR had disliked Churchill. Kermit said he didn't know. Churchill claimed that Alice had once told him that it was because TR had heard that he had once disregarded the health of his native bearers during an African safari and knowingly exposed them to tsetse flies, a charge Churchill now vigorously denied.[*]

_____

[*] Apparently the distance between TR and Churchill had begun during a visit Churchill made to Albany when TR was governor. During lunch Churchill had

Before Kermit could ship out, however, the Finns were forced to sign an ignominious peace treaty. As he again waited for British authorities to find him a role, he and Belle were called to Buckingham Palace for an audience in which King George VI talked earnestly of the need for U.S. support. During the conversation the monarch kept coming very close to Kermit to emphasize his point while Kermit kept retreating to maintain a dignified space between the two of them, with the result that at the end of a half hour's conversation they had traversed the entire reception room and Kermit was backed against a wall with the King inches from his face.

Finally his posting was set. He would be part of a raid into Norway, taking in wireless equipment and operators and serving as liaison officer between the Norwegians and the British War Office as they tried to fight the Nazi invasion. Belle helped Kermit dress before he shipped out, straightening the Sam Browne belt and holstering his pistol, loading the old musette bag left over from World War I, and handing him his swagger stick. As he left, she gave him a St. Christopher's medal.

Kermit performed well in Norway, but the mission was doomed. The British expeditionary force was outnumbered and overmatched by German power. Kermit watched as wave after wave of Stukas dive-bombed his positions. (In one particular strike he described in affecting letters home, German planes methodically demolished a Norwegian hospital despite the large red cross painted on its roof.) Later on, Belle would describe his "amazing feats" during the evacuation from Norway: "He was fifty and had been an ill man for years, yet not only did his own job but labored unremittingly in aiding other men to get themselves and then their equipment out, in many cases carrying the wounded on his back."

Extracted from Norway with the rest of his outfit in the early fall, Kermit was next sent to North Africa to join British forces there. Trying to maintain relations with Ted, he wrote his brother, "I certainly never expected to be back here again. I expected this war to be fought in France, but here I am back in the desert. The final showdown may be anywhere, and I shall hope to be in on it."

---

talked about an incident in the Boer War that had taken place at the town of Bloemfontein. TR had interjected, "I beg your pardon, but that particular incident, if I am not mistaken, took place at Magersfontein." Flustered, Churchill at first insisted that he was right and then, after thinking about the matter during the rest of the lunch, blurted out, "You are right, Governor, it was Magersfontein and I am mistaken." But it was not the disagreement but rather the fact that Churchill did not stand when ladies entered the room that apparently made TR dislike him.

At the same time that he was sending chatty letters home, however, Kermit turned his back on everything Ted and other Republicans were trying to do. "Wish absolutely withdraw from Republican Party," he cabled FDR. "Can you effect this? Deeply grateful." Franklin was interested enough in the prospect of one engaged Roosevelt brother discrediting the isolationism of another that he had his press secretary, Steve Early, pursue Kermit's request.

In the previous war the desert had been an epic theater where Kermit had played a dashing role. But this workaday war offered none of the drama now necessary to sustain him. With time on his hands, he resumed his heavy drinking. By the end of 1940 he was sent back to England where doctors were alarmed at the enlargement of his liver. Despite personal pleas to Churchill for reinstatement, Kermit was released from the British Army early in 1941.

By the time he arrived at La Guardia Airport that June, his dreams of self-regeneration having crumbled, Kermit was so sick that Belle feared he might die in a matter of days. In addition to the effects of alcohol, he had suffered a recurrence of his malaria and was "shaking like a leaf [with] his teeth chattering around in his head."

After a few days in a hotel, he told Belle he was going to check into a hospital, but after she put him in a cab he disappeared without leaving a trace. She knew he had hooked up with Carla Peters again and was probably living in the demimonde he had inhabited before leaving for England. Alarmed, Belle called Eleanor at the White House and described what had happened. Eleanor wrote her a simple note of sympathy that obliquely alluded to her own past crisis: "I understand what you are going through." She then wrote her husband's aide Edwin "Pa" Watson: "Remind the President . . . that he must think of something which will take Kermit Roosevelt out of the country immediately." A week later, Watson contacted the president of the American Museum of Natural History to say that Kermit was about to leave the country for South Africa and FDR wanted him to have a letter "with a line of [scientific] investigation you would like him to cover."

But Kermit was still missing and had not been informed of the trip to Africa, let alone consenting to it. FDR turned the matter over to their joint friend Vincent Astor and asked him to get J. Edgar Hoover on the case. With several FBI agents looking for Kermit, Astor happened to see him and Peters sitting outside a sidewalk restaurant having a drink while he was out for a drive. He stopped and got the two of them to come up to his apartment. He pleaded with Kermit to enter the U.S. Army, claiming that American forces would inevitably be going into battle in North Africa and would need his experience.

"You go!" Carla Peters interrupted. "Can't you see that Kermit is sick?"

Astor told her to shut up and continued badgering Kermit, pointing out to him how he was embarrassing his family.

"You just sit here with the millions you inherited from your German ancestors," Peters interrupted him again, "and you try to tell other people what to do."

As they were walking out of the apartment, Kermit was delighted. "That was wonderful, darling," he said to his mistress. "I don't think anyone has ever talked to Vincent like that."

FBI agents continued to search for him. The accumulating paperwork on the case showed one agent asking another if Kermit's problem was his heart. "His liver," was the reply, "and he has got a dose too [of syphilis] so he is pretty well washed up."

On July 7, Kermit finally showed up at the hospital with cuts on his face from a fistfight with a cab driver whose taxi he had hit while driving Peters's car. An FBI man wrote a memo that his supervisor summarized for Hoover: "[The agent] stated that Roosevelt had such an odor about his person that he almost turned the stomach of the agents when they got in an elevator with him. The agents state that he is in terrible shape and can barely walk."

After checking into the hospital, Kermit was dozing in his bed when a party of men suddenly appeared in his room and began lifting him onto a stretcher. He yelled for help and they ignored him. Then, in a scene eerily reminiscent of TR's attempts to control his brother, Elliott's, self-destructiveness fifty years earlier, Archie stepped into the doorway and sternly directed the orderlies to tie Kermit down on the stretcher and take him out. Kermit asked what was happening; Archie looked away, refusing to answer him.

Yelling loudly that he was being kidnapped, Kermit was loaded into an ambulance and taken to Hartford, Connecticut, where he was placed in a sanatorium called the Hartford Retreat. He immediately sued for "unjust incarceration." Belle appeared to testify in the family's behalf in the hearing that ended with Kermit being put under a conservatorship and being committed indefinitely to the sanatorium.

In the days ahead, Carla Peters was allowed to visit Kermit only because she was the one person who could pacify him. Depressed, he told her that at least he had been vindicated in his decision to join the fight against Hitler. Indeed, several weeks earlier, in the spring of 1941, Ted too had seen that war was inevitable. He had taken steps to dissociate himself from America First after attending a meeting of the organization that unsettled him. "I found that three out of four with whom I was sitting at the table were all for everyone refusing to cooperate, enlist or fight in case we did get into war," he described the scene to his brother's son, Archie Jr. "That in no way represents my feeling. I have fought and will fight our entrance, but if and when we are committed, then I feel that every last one of us have got to do all he can to bring the war to a successful conclusion."

Not long after this letter, Ted, although he was fifty-four years old, asked Army Chief of Staff General George Marshall to take him out of the reserves and put him on active duty. In late April 1941 he was given command of his old unit, the 26th Infantry. Bitter over the fact that all those who had attacked him for cowardice were now scrambling for cushy jobs for themselves and their children, he nonetheless felt the ambiguity of the past few years begin to melt away. When the 26th was sent to North Carolina for training, his wife, Eleanor, wrote their friend Alex Woollcott, "Ted is very well and far happier than he has been for some years. He has got his teeth into something he knows he can do supremely well."

Family members who saw him were surprised by how cheerful he seemed. Archie Jr. realized why the change had come over his Uncle Ted. For years he had been in a situation where he couldn't feel like his father's son. Now he was ready to fight his country's enemies and this was a sort of "emotional homecoming."

*A*lice Longworth was hosting a brunch when the news came of the attack on Pearl Harbor. After listening to the radio bulletin, she paused for a moment and then said, "Well, friends, Franklin asked for it, now he's got it."

It was true that FDR had worked hard and resourcefully for U.S. involvement in the European situation. He had been forced to deal not only with outright opposition but also with the inertia of those who should have been sympathetic to his cause. His own family's reaction to events showed what he was up against. After England and France declared war on Germany Eleanor was still doubtful about the United States getting in. Her feelings were mirrored by at least two of her sons. As late as 1938, Jimmy, still in the marine corps reserve, asked her apprehensively if he should be prepared to go on active duty, and when Eleanor said yes he replied fatalistically that he didn't believe U.S. entry into the war could make a difference. And John had gone so far as to consider filing for status as a conscientious objector before she talked him out of it.

Yet Franklin had been steady of purpose, using the patience and guile he had learned as much from being a son and husband as from being in politics, and insisting, as he had since he was a boy, on getting his own way. He brought interventionist Republicans like TR's old friend Henry Stimson and former Rough Rider Frank Knox into the cabinet. With equal aplomb he got rid of people like Joseph P. Kennedy, his appeasement-minded ambassador to the Court of St. James, who had impeded his purpose. (When Kennedy tried to justify himself to John Boettiger in a carom shot letter aimed ultimately at the President, FDR told his son-in-law that Kennedy had "a positive horror of change in the present methods of life in America. To him, the future of a small capitalistic class is safer under a Hitler than a Churchill.")

After the Japanese attack, FDR continued to make astute moves. One of the most notable was raising Ted Roosevelt in rank to brigadier general four days after Pearl Harbor, a gesture his cousin understood perfectly for what it was: "It will do something to make people feel that in this war the hatchet has been buried." As far as the public knew, the Roosevelts were united for the struggle at hand—a symbol for the country to contemplate.

Franklin's resolve was all the more admirable for having been achieved against a backdrop of loss in his personal life. The first was Missy, who had suffered a stroke in the spring of 1941. He sent her to Warm Springs to recuperate and she came back to the White House for a brief time in braces and using a wheelchair, almost as if she was recapitulating his own ordeal. She assumed that they would function again as a team, as they had for nearly twenty years, but her condition continued to deteriorate, reaching a point where she was unable to carry out any duties at all and finally she had to be sent home to live with her family.

And that summer Sara died. As much as he had chafed against her, Franklin had always enjoyed the role of son. Sara's unconditional love not only comforted him but also gave him an opportunity for mischievous rebellion. (Almost sixty years old, he was still pleased to be able to scandalize his mother by serving the King and Queen of England cocktails and hot dogs when they visited Hyde Park in 1940.) Although she had sometimes tormented him with her domineering love, Sara was a breakwater against his own mortality, and when he heard that she had died he was unable to keep from weeping.

For Eleanor, however, this death produced a joyless relief. ("I couldn't feel any emotion or any real grief or sense of loss," she wrote Anna, "and that seemed terrible after 36 years of fairly close association.") It was a reaction family members could not help but contrast to FDR's gesture when the distraught Eleanor came into his office in tears a few weeks later and told him her beloved brother, Hall, had just died from the ravages of alcoholism. He struggled to her side in his wheel-chair, urged her to sit down beside him, and then cradled her head on his chest and comforted her.

As he led the country into war, Franklin was more alone than he had ever been during his presidency. Yet he was finally undertaking the heroic role he had fantasized about since threatening as a teenager to run away and join the Rough Riders. After Pearl Harbor his own family fell quickly into line. The idea of conflict was so painful for her that Eleanor occasionally had quixotic ideas about how to end the war quickly. (A few months after Pearl Harbor, she forwarded to FDR a suggestion she had received from one of her correspondents: "Suppose we collected as many hornets, bees and wasps as we could possibly get. Keep them in their hives and put them in a plane. Have the plane fly as low as possible and drop them over enemy lines. I think they will retreat in utter con-fusion.") But the boys were all in uniform—Elliott in the air force, Franklin Jr. and John in the navy, and Jimmy on active duty in the marines.

FDR urged them on just as TR had urged him on at the onset of World War I. When Anna's husband, John Boettiger, hinted that he would like to be present at some of his father-in-law's diplomatic sum-mits, FDR gave him one of his impenetrable looks and said that unfor-tunately this would not be possible. When Boettiger asked why, FDR shrugged, "Well, you're not in uniform." Boettiger got the hint and quickly enlisted.

Elliott was ahead of them all, of course. After the controversy over his captaincy had subsided, he was sent to Newfoundland in the spring of 1941 to help locate sites for fighter aircraft being shipped from the United States to England. As part of this mission, he had to go to London to negotiate with his opposite numbers in the British military. Arriving during the Blitz, he was invited for a weekend to Chequers, Churchill's country retreat. Having brought nothing more than a tooth-brush, Elliott was given a pair of the Prime Minister's expensive Chi-nese silk pajamas, and, almost immediately after putting them on, he split the seat.

Back in Newfoundland, Elliott was suddenly ordered to report to the USS *Augusta* in late summer. When he arrived he found his father on board. The press had been told that FDR was on a fishing trip in the Bay of Fundy, but he was actually preparing for his first official meeting with Churchill. He wanted Elliott to witness the making of history and to watch him performing his leading role. It turned out to be a strange moment for his son. Always before his father had dominated every gathering, but here Churchill was in command, a rhetorical one-man show, outclassing the Americans in discussions about the war and the shape of the postwar world. "A real old Tory of the old school," FDR described the Prime Minister to Elliott after the Atlantic Charter had been signed.

After this Elliott was ordered back to Texas for bombardier school at San Antonio's Kelly Field. He was there when the attack on Pearl Harbor occurred. After he heard about the bombing he put a call through to Washington. FDR asked him how the news was affecting people there. Elliott told him that there was a rumor that a Japanese landing force was in Mexico ready to invade Texas. FDR replied laconically that for all he knew this might be happening and asked his son to keep him posted.

Early in 1942, Elliott was ordered to Africa to fly photo reconnaissance. Before leaving he stopped in Washington and told his father that he was disappointed by what seemed like such an insignificant mission. FDR told him he was wrong and gave him a lecture about the war to come: "The Chinese are killing Japanese and the Russians are killing Germans. We've got to keep them doing just that, until *our* armies and navies are ready to help. So we've got to start sending them a hundred—a thousand times as much matériel as they've gotten from us so far. Africa is our insurance they'll get it."

One trait Elliott shared with his father was an inclination to fabulate his experiences. All through his postwar life he would embroider on his combat experiences, making them seem ever more dangerous and grandiose than they had actually been. One of the stories he told was of flying into China on board a B-17 outfitted for reconnaissance to do a photo survey of Chinese supply lines and then being ambushed by Messerschmitt fighters on the way back and being forced to crash-land in British West Africa. This experience was not officially confirmed, but it was true that Elliott flew hazardous missions and his unit suffered heavy losses. On one mission, one of his gunners was killed and he was the only member of the crew not to suffer a wound of some kind.

In July 1942 he was back in the United States hospitalized for amoebic dysentery. It was a time when the war was not going well, and while Elliott didn't spend much time alone with FDR he was the first to notice the gray pallor of his father's face and begin to guess at the toll the transition from "Doctor New Deal" to "Doctor Win-the-War" was taking on him.

After recovering, Elliott was sent to England and given command of the 3rd Photographic Reconnaissance Group. This unit was involved in the invasion of North Africa in November, and his planes began flying out of a captured, bomb-cratered airfield the day after the Allied landing.

In November he was invited to meet his father at the second of the great wartime conferences at Casablanca, a locale that delighted FDR because the name of the city meant White House. Franklin Jr. was there too, having been given leave from his post aboard the destroyer *Mayrant* to attend. During one dinner at which Eisenhower and George Marshall were present, Franklin Jr. described how his ship had performed under heavy enemy fire. FDR listened admiringly and then reminded everyone that he too had been at the front in the last war, adding, "And I'm going up front in this one too." At this point the generals glared at him and began explaining why getting him close to the front lines in North Africa would be far too dangerous even to contemplate.

At Casablanca, Elliott spent afternoons with General George Patton, who lectured informally on the Punic War and took him to see the site of the ancient city of Carthage. The tension that had arisen between FDR and Churchill in the Atlantic Charter meeting over the future of colonialism returned under a different guise in heated discussions over the question of who would be recognized as the leader of the Free French. Churchill was a partisan of Charles de Gaulle, while the American side, worried that de Gaulle wanted one-man rule in postwar France, favored General Henri Giraud. Amused by this competition between Frenchmen, FDR sent a letter to his son John that gave his distinctively jaundiced view of the contest: "General de Gaulle was a thoroughly bad boy. . . . The day he arrived, he thought he was Joan of Arc and the following day he insisted he was Georges Clemenceau. Winston and I decided to get him and Giraud to come to Casablanca to hold a shotgun wedding. I produced the bridegroom from Algiers but Winston had to make three tries before he could get the bride."

Although not present at any major diplomatic events, the Oyster Bay clan was as fully mobilized as Franklin's family. All three of TR's sons were in uniform, along with six of his grandsons. (Only Kermit's son Dirck, sixteen when the war began, had not joined up.)

It had taken time for them to get into action. In the spring of 1942, six months after Pearl Harbor, Ted was still at Camp Blanding. With him was his son Quentin, who had enlisted in the 1st Division so they could be together.

Hearing that Quentin was preparing to go overseas, the former Flora Whitney contacted him. Her life had been difficult since the death of the first Quentin in World War I. Her postwar marriage to Roderick Tower, a man who had been Quentin's friend and rival at Harvard and in the air corps, had collapsed. A few years later she married again, this time to an architect named G. Macullough Miller and together they had gotten involved in the administration of her mother's Whitney Museum. It was a good relationship, although Flora's own children felt she had never fully recovered from the events of 1918.

With another war beginning, her old connections with the Roosevelts, kept alive all these years by cards and letters, became important again. Flora sent Ted's son—Quentin II, she called him—a copy of a prayer that she had given his uncle and namesake when he too went off to war and told him that she wanted him to come back safely.

With Quentin in his unit and his oldest son, Theodore III, who had just recently married, stationed near him in a Florida navy installation, Ted got his wife Eleanor to rent a cottage on the beach at Ponte Vedra so they could all be together. She bought ironing boards at the local dime store for the young people to surf on when they got weekend leaves.

The war seemed far off during this brief moment of family reunion. Then one night after dinner they all went outside to watch the distant flames coming off the ocean and learned the next day that an American oil tanker had been torpedoed and the whole crew lost. Not long afterward, a German submarine landed a contingent of saboteurs who passed right by the Roosevelt's cottage before being apprehended.

As Ted went off to England with a small advance guard of the 1st Division, Eleanor searched for a way to be with him just as she had in the prior war. She joined the Red Cross and got herself posted to England in the summer of 1942. Although they were in the same country, however, they saw each other only rarely. Finally Ted got leave in the early fall and they went on a brief holiday to Scotland. They would always remember how bizarre these hours together were—the filthy railroad station in Glasgow; the garish rain-slicked streets teeming with servicemen looking for prostitutes. Ted told Eleanor later on that this was the moment that he realized they had gotten themselves involved in another generation's war.

A few weeks later he was on board a ship being convoyed to North

Africa. During the brief voyage, he and Quentin drew close to each other. With all the panache and quick intelligence of his namesake, the twenty-two-year-old delighted Ted. He was already something of a public figure in his own right, having been profiled by *Life* magazine in 1940 after returning from his expedition to China with a priceless collection of antique manuscripts. As they talked, Ted was drawn back to the last war, when his brother Quentin was going abroad filled with the same fears and excitement as his son.

One of the subjects they talked about was picking up in public life after the war. As Ted wrote Eleanor, "Q. thinks we go back into politics. Poor lamb! He does not realize that we are done. This war effort will finish us. When it's through, if we survive, we'll be considered too old. All we'll want to do is get a chance to be a little quiet and sit in the sun."

Three days later, his regiment landed off the coast of Tunisia amidst heavy resistance. Wading ashore with the first wave as fellow officers fell from enemy fire, Ted hit the beach. A German soldier loomed up in front of him and he killed the man with the first shot from his carbine.

After U.S. forces had captured the heights above the city of Oran, Ted drove a jeep down into the city flying a dirty undershirt as a flag of truce and convinced the defenders to surrender rather than risk annihilation. Once victory was assured he unburdened himself to a young officer who was so struck by Ted's words that he wrote them down: "War is an abomination. Everybody loses in a war. I was an American Firster and against going to war. I received a lot of flak for it. But when the balloon went up, my friends and I rallied to the colors and joined up. Where, where were those noisy interventionists? I suspect you'd find a lot of them still fighting their war back in New York in the Stork Club bar."

As his unit moved through North Africa, Ted took a grim satisfaction in the dirty daily work of war, but he also relished moments of tranquillity as when he was sitting outside his tent one morning having coffee and a tiny finch flew up and perched on his table, ruffling his feathers and bursting into song in a way that immediately transported him back to Oyster Bay.

Near the end of the North Africa campaign, at a place called El Guettar, he was awakened one night by machine gun fire and rolled out of bed to find a German counterattack on the verge of overrunning his position. His command post was destroyed, and he climbed to the top of a ridge to direct Allied counterfire. When an enemy Panzer unit seemed about to break through his line, Ted stood up and yelled at his men, "I'm staying in this position! You leave it and you leave me behind!" The Americans held fast and repulsed the German attack.

Late in February 1943 he learned that Quentin, who had just made captain in an infantry unit, had been hit by a German plane strafing his position and had shell fragments in his lungs and liver and might be dying. Unable to reach his son for twenty-four hours because of the heavy fighting, Ted finally drove his jeep to the field hospital and found Quentin just out of surgery with a fever of over 104. Doctors told Ted that his son, now asleep, had been calling for him deliriously. Ted stood over the hospital cot, afraid to wake him; but then Quentin suddenly opened his eyes and Ted bent over to kiss him "as if he were a little boy again." When he wrote Edith about the incident he said, "Father would be very proud of him. . . . As Father wrote in the last war, 'Only those deserve undying glory and fame who stand where the danger is sorest.' "

As Quentin rallied and began to gain strength, Ted and Eleanor decided that she should resign from the Red Cross and return home so she could help him through his convalescence. Almost losing his son made Ted realize the peculiarity of the situation he was in. "Do you realize it's 26 years ago this month that I went abroad with the 26th Division," he wrote Eleanor, "and 26 years ago next month that you arrived? Couple of old idiots, that's what we are."

Archie had hoped to be fighting shoulder to shoulder with his brother as they had in the previous war. But it hadn't worked out. Unlike Ted, he had not maintained his military status in the reserves and thus was not associated with any unit. He had trouble getting into the army because of his age. When he had still not managed to get into uniform two months after Pearl Harbor, some people assumed that he was malingering because of his well-known opposition to the New Deal. But of all the innuendoes directed at him, nothing hurt as much as an envelope he received that contained only a single white feather. There was no doubt that it was from Kermit and that it was a allusion to the symbol of cowardice in the novel *The Four Feathers*.

In fact Archie had already gotten his own son Archie Jr. into military intelligence by pulling strings with General Truman Smith. He wanted to get in himself badly enough to swallow his pride and write FDR for help, the beginning of a distant collaboration between the two men that would grow into a wary friendship as the war progressed.

Archie began a letter to the President with a reference to their common interest in Kermit, whom he said had improved physically at the sanatorium but not "mentally and morally." Then he went on to his own problem. At forty-six, he was too old to be an enlisted man but probably not qualified for anything else. He didn't want to ask favors, but after giving the matter long thought he had figured out a rationale for an appointment as an officer: "There may come many places and many times in the war where you would like to have the son of the former President and someone with your name to share the dangers of soldiers or sailors or marines in some tough spot. . . . I would be perfect for such a job. . . . You would not be throwing away [someone] who was useful elsewhere."

FDR passed the letter on to his aide Pa Watson for an opinion. Watson told him that because of Archie's age and the ongoing effects of the wounds he had suffered in the last war it would be better for him to stay home and do civilian defense work. But Archie persisted. Having served under General George Marshall, now Army Chief of Staff, twenty-five years earlier, he applied to him for help in getting active duty. Marshall finessed Archie into the army and he was sent to the Pacific.

One of his stops on the way to duty was at Christmas Island. His feeling of unreality at being there was accentuated when his plane was about to land and he looked out the window and watched a shark take a lazy bite out of a sailor swimming in the surf. As he explored the ring-shaped atoll during his few hours there he found that it looked exactly like the illustrations in the geography book he had used at Cove Neck School forty years earlier and this made him feel like he was back in Oyster Bay.

Archie reported personally to General Douglas MacArthur in Australia. MacArthur had once served as a military aide to TR and wanted to be helpful. Assuming Archie wanted a staff position, he made arrangements to get him a job behind the lines, but Archie insisted on being sent to the infantry. MacArthur assigned him to the 41st Division and then to a combat unit in New Guinea.

At first he was given the job of a supply officer and spent his spare moments writing dyspeptic letters to Ted about how they were not fighting for democracy at all but for the "orgy of socialism" that would characterize the postwar world. He kept pressing to be sent to the front lines. In the meantime he proved himself to be his father's son in the way he spent his spare time inspecting the flora and fauna of the jungle. "I have been trying to collect some of the insects to send back to the Museum," he wrote Edith. "Entomologically speaking, this country is a paradise. The trouble is, of course, most of them bite and sting."

Ever the dogged loyalist, he kept in close contact with his aging mother, who, as his sister Ethel wrote, had her "ups and downs," sometimes thinking clearly and sometimes drifting. Finally about to go into combat, Archie wrote Edith a note apologizing for not sending a telegram on the anniversary of his brother Quentin's death, the first time he had ever missed this remembrance. And a few months later, on TR's birthday, he wrote to reassure her he had arranged for the chaplain to give a special sermon of commemoration.

Not wanting to worry his mother, Archie didn't mention his experiences in the field. But by this time his regiment was in heavy fighting and had pushed the Japanese out of Nassau Bay and then Salamauna, where Archie's heroism in the battle was such that Australian soldiers fighting alongside him named one peak "Roosevelt Ridge" in his honor. At one point he was in combat continuously for seventy-six days.

He volunteered for exotic jobs. Made into a one-man surveying team, he explored the jungle looking for areas to put troops in forward positions. Carrying only his rifle and a small pack, he found himself in places that no white man had ever seen before and was met by natives who fed him melons and huge red bananas.

Because of his sailing experience in Oyster Bay, Archie was also asked to do reconnaissance along the island's coastline and up into the mouths of its rivers. He wrote home about how he had run into swarms of huge bats during night voyages in which the moonlight created such a bright phosphorence in the wake of his boat that it seemed possible almost to read by it.

At times he was low, writing his wife, Grace, in July 1943 that he was "exhausted by problems beyond my ability to handle." The same note of despondency entered a letter he wrote Ted: "All of us look twenty years older and I doubt if I can stand more than one more campaign like the last one." Yet he closed on a plucky note: "I am sending this in an envelope picked off a dead Jap."

He was proud of his ability to bear up and soldier on and shared Ted's bitterness at how many of those who had criticized the two of them were now enjoying the good life at home: "I can't help thinking of all our friends who kept saying you & I were quislings when we said it was folly to become involved in Europe. They are all of them in nice bullet proof places telling us how to do the job."

After a stint as executive officer Archie was given another of the missions he loved—going out on the water again, this time during the day, to pinpoint Japanese gun placements. His technique was primitive: standing up in the boat with a map and field glasses and marking down the flashpoints of the guns as they fired at him. One of the enlisted men who accompanied him on one of these missions later told an AP reporter: "While Colonel Roosevelt was standing there deliberately encouraging them to fire at us, I was crouching on the bottom of the boat praying for all I was worth. He looked down and said, 'You're safe with me. I was wounded three times in the last war and that's a lucky charm.' "

One of the continuing motifs in Archie's letters home was guilty anxiety over Kermit. Where was his brother? What was he doing?

Kermit had been released from the Hartford Retreat in the fall of 1941 and disappeared again. Belle asked for FDR's help once more in locating him and FDR got Pa Watson to get Hoover on the case again. ("I know he's worthless, this fellow, and it makes me sick to my stomach," Watson wrote the FBI chief.) Two days later, Hoover's agents found Kermit in his old haunts with Carla Peters and noted in their report that he was also being shadowed by two private detectives, apparently hired by Belle.

Early in 1942, Kermit went to California with Peters again but he was drinking so heavily now that even she left him and returned to the East Coast alone. It was hard for the family to trace him.

One of the reasons he had been so upset when Archie had him committed was that he thought people would assume he was malingering. His two oldest sons had enlisted. Willard was in the navy. Kim had come to the attention of Bill Donovan before Pearl Harbor because of an article he had written after finishing his Ph.D. thesis on war propaganda in the English Civil War. This article was a blueprint for building a secret intelligence service. Donovan, about to become head of the OSS, asked Kim not to publish the piece but instead to consider coming to work for his agency. (Donovan was renting space for his fledgling espionage organization from the Willards, Belle's family, in Fairfax, Virginia.) Kim enlisted and Donovan sent him to Cairo. When Kim telegraphed a cryptic message, "Send trunk of civilian clothing," his wife, Polly, understood that it meant he had joined up with the OSS as a spy.

Even Dirck was in uniform by 1942, Belle having marched him down to the recruitment center, although the boy had become physically ill at the prospect of fighting and was sent to one military hospital after another for treatment for emotional difficulties during the next year.

Left behind, Kermit became demoralized, talking of the hopelessness of his life and sometimes reciting "Richard Cory," his old friend Edwin Arlington Robinson's poem about the man who "one calm summer night/went home and put a bullet through his head." Stumbling through deep depression and alcoholism, he was recommitted to the Hartford Retreat.

Worried about her husband, Belle now asked FDR to help Kermit get into the military. Ever loyal to TR's boys, General George Marshall offered him a job as information officer in Washington, but Kermit insisted on being put in a situation where there was at least the possibility of combat. Finally, it was arranged for him to go to Alaska.

He was sworn into the army on July 15, 1942, after a physical examination marked by dozens of X-rays and radiocardiograms, all of which had to be repeated when the shutter on the camera malfunctioned. He had no khaki shirt or tie, so Belle had to go shopping for him. She recorded in her diary how well he looked in his uniform. When he boarded a train to leave her, he was "excited and delighted—but very emotional when saying goodbye—which undid me completely. . . ."

The alleged reason for sending him to Alaska was that it would keep his tropical disorders from flaring up. The real reason was to put him in the deep freeze for the duration in a place where he could not harm himself. Once he had been an asset to FDR—the only member of the Oyster Bay clan who supported him—but now he was a liability whose flamboyant self-destructiveness might become public at any time. Yet while he wanted him out of sight, FDR was still loyal to Kermit and after he was on duty in Alaska agreed to attend the wedding of his daughter, Clochette. (As Belle noted proudly, "Because of her infantile [a light case of polio] and her accident FDR had always felt especially drawn" to their daughter.)

Kermit tried to get into action in Alaska. He convinced U.S. pilots to take him along as an observer during bombing runs of Japanese positions in the Aleutians. Then he got himself appointed to help the legendary "Muktuk" Marston establish a Territorial Guard comprised of Eskimo and Aleut soldiers who would become guerrilla fighters in the event of a major Japanese invasion. It was exactly the sort of duty his travel and adventure experiences equipped him to carry out. But his physical condition was so poor that he was now unable to handle anything this demanding and he had to drop out.

Early in 1943, nine months after arriving in Alaska, he was flown down to Vancouver on a stretcher to be treated for internal bleeding at Burney General Hospital. Further complicating his life, both Belle and Carla Peters immediately rushed to his side. Because Belle reminded him of a past he now realized he could never live up to, he chose to be with Peters. The two of them began taking day trips around the Northwest, which caused a new round of concern in the family. When Archie heard of this new development, he wrote his wife, Grace, from New Guinea, "I heard about Kermit's sickness. I have not yet written him as I am afraid the poor boy would not like to hear from me. I do hope they can send him back to Alaska. I am afraid he will get into trouble back in the states."

This was what happened. As his condition improved somewhat, he and Peters began taking longer trips. Since he was on extended leave, they decided to go cross-country, taking a train from Portland to Los Angeles and on to El Paso and finally winding up on the East Coast. Kermit told friends that he was finally ready to get a divorce. Belle, who wanted him away from Peters and charged that the decision of a medical board to approve Kermit for duty only in the continental United States was "heartbreaking for every reason," tried to get different orders.

She succeeded in getting the War Department to send him back to Alaska. As he left, Edith had a premonition about her favorite son. "I seem to feel anxious about you," she wrote, and, as if to draw him close to her one last time, told him that spring was unfolding at Oyster Bay—forsythia fading and dogwood beginning to bloom—as it had when he was a little boy away at school and homesick for the beauty of Sagamore.

Back in Alaska and stationed at Fort Richardson, Kermit spent the lengthening spring nights playing chess and poker. A shambling figure with a distended stomach and sticklike arms and legs, he haunted Anchorage. His favorite place was Nellie's Diner, and he went there two or three times a week to drink wine, the only liquor his body could now take, and chat with Nellie Brown, the proprietor.

He and Muktuk Marston made the rounds of the blacked-out city on the night of June 3, 1943. When it was time to return to the post, Kermit asked his friend what he was going to do.

"Go to sleep," replied Marston.

"I wish I could sleep," Kermit said wistfully as the two men parted.

He went back to his quarters that night and got out the service revolver he had kept from his days in the British Army. Perhaps remembering the time nearly thirty-five years earlier on the River of Doubt when he and his father had reached what seemed to be an impasse and TR had contemplated suicide as the honorable way out when one had become a burden, Kermit shot himself in the head. The telegram sent to FBI headquarters in Washington said that the suicide had been "due to despondence resulting from exclusion from combat duties."

The next day an inventory of Kermit's personal effects yielded a briar and corncob pipe, two pinochle decks, a backgammon set, and an engraved silver napkin holder once given to him by Belle. Kermit was buried at Fort Richardson in Grave 72, Plot A, with a simple marble headstone no different from those marking the other soldiers at rest there.

As his affairs were unscrambled, it was discovered that he had made Carla Peters the beneficiary of the $10,000 life insurance policy that was virtually his only asset, and left her the two rifles he had used when he and his father went to Africa. "If feelings are permitted in the hereafter," read the handwritten note he had appended to his will, "you will honor my wishes regarding Miss Peters."

Archie's wife, Grace, geographically closest of the dispersed family to Edith, was appointed to tell her that Kermit had died, but not how it happened. After finally getting the news, Archie wrote home to Sagamore: "I know it is the best thing that could have happened, but could not help feeling sad. All the good times we used to have together. The family parties. The clamming and joking. Those weird automobiles crammed full of children that he used to drive around at breakneck speed. After all, it was only a few years out of a long and useful and attractive period that he had trouble and that we had trouble with him. Everything we get in this world we have to pay for, and we paid very little compared to what we got from Kermit."

The tragedy of Kermit was the conclusion of a decline and fall that had largely taken place out of public view. Those who knew about his failings tended to make allowances: he was a son of Theodore Roosevelt, after all. But the children of Eleanor and Franklin had no such safe conduct pass. The scrutiny and criticism that had dogged their steps before the war continued after Pearl Harbor. When Jimmy, on leave from his marine unit, was traveling from Washington to California and asked that a train be held for a few minutes in Chicago so that he could make his connection, the other passengers booed as he was escorted to the platform. When Franklin Jr. had appendicitis early in the war and had to be given a few weeks' leave, the newspapers pummeled him mercilessly for slacking. He came to tea at the White House after the appearance of a particularly brutal article and was so dispirited after he left that Eleanor, tears welling up in her eyes, said to her secretary, "They won't let up on my boys until they are all killed."

Elliott said during a get-together with his brothers that perhaps it would be better for FDR if one of them *was* killed in battle.

All the boys had close calls. Franklin Jr. saw heavy action in late July 1943, when the *Mayrant* was partly disabled by a German attack and towed to Palermo for repairs to its hull. While it was docked there, the Germans staged an air raid. An ammunition train near the docks was hit by dive-bombers, sending shrapnel flying in all directions. Franklin Jr. was on the bridge of the ship trying to direct anti-aircraft fire when he looked over at the seaman next to him and saw that the man's leg had been taken off just below the knee. He went for help but the doctors were all busy. He brought back morphine, gave the sailor a shot, and then hoisted him over his shoulder and carried him across the deck to the sick bay, shells bursting all around him.

By this time, Jimmy had also seen heavy combat as a member of Carlson's Raiders, the famous commando unit whose raid on Makin Island was the subject of the wartime film *Gung Ho!* John had received the Bronze Star for bravery aboard his aircraft carrier. And Elliott was piling up missions. After the invasion of North Africa, his unit was losing planes at the rate of twenty a week and only 10 percent of the pilots who entered that campaign at its inception were able to answer the roll three months later.

Yet Elliott had a life apart from his service life that continued to fuel the criticism of his family. In North Africa, for instance, he had gone weeks without writing his wife, Ruth, while engaging in a prolonged and public affair with a WAC that made the gossip columns back home. Ruth, who had given birth to their third child, David, not long after Pearl Harbor, had become so distraught over the rumors that she went to her father-in-law. FDR counseled her, "Don't worry about this. Things happen in war and this is nothing to worry about."

But he had no ability to control his son, and Elliott's extramarital behavior became more egregious. With reports filtering home to Ruth about his doings, he asked a fellow pilot named Harry Eidson who was going home on leave to look in on her and try to mitigate her anger. Eidson was involved in a minor crash on landing in San Antonio and hospitalized there. Ruth visited him. They began to talk about Elliott, and Eidson, who had begun as his friend's ambassador, wound up falling in love with Ruth himself. Claiming that when he next saw two-year-old David, the boy called him "Harry," Elliott postured as the wronged party in the disintegrating marriage and made it seem that Ruth was responsible for their troubles.

In the summer of 1943 he came home on assignment to the War Department to help select the air force's next generation of reconnaissance aircraft. Dropping in on his parents, Elliott talked flippantly about the end of his marriage. FDR argued against another divorce because of adverse publicity and Elliott put off a decision for the time being. Eleanor was shocked by Elliott's attitude, writing to Anna: "Fundamentally we think so little alike on many things that tho' I love him, I have to be careful when with him & that means that short visits are better than long ones!"

The War Department sent Elliott to Southern California to look at the D-2, a prototype of a new plane designed by Howard Hughes's company. Knowing of Elliott's appetite for a good time, Hughes had him met on his arrival by an employee named John Meyer. Meyer, whom some called Hughes's "official pimp," took him to the Hughes home in the Hollywood Hills, where a bevy of starlets were tanning themselves around the pool. Hughes introduced Elliott around. When he came to Jane Russell he spent several minutes describing the special bra he had designed for her. Finally he gestured for her to pull off her blouse. "Jane, show Elliott those amazing breasts of yours."

One of the women at Hughes's house was Faye Emerson, a $500 a week starlet appearing in B movies at Warner Brothers. Coolly intelligent, with style and ambition, she allowed Hughes to put her together with Elliott. John Meyer paid their hotel bills over the next few days and financed a holiday to Catalina Island. On August 1, Hughes himself took Elliott to his aircraft plant and testing grounds. He showed off a prototype of the D-2. A few days later, when Elliott left for the East Coast accompanied by Emerson, he was singing the praises of the plane. John Meyer followed the couple and paid for their nightlife at the Copacabana, Stork Club, and other New York nightspots before Elliott flew to Washington and recommended to the brass that they purchase Hughes's plane. After directing Hughes to make a few design revisions, Air Force Chief "Hap" Arnold ordered one hundred of the planes for $43 million.

Elliott returned to duty in the Mediterranean where his unit was doing aerial mapping of Italy. He wrote passionate letters to Faye Emerson, which were infrequently answered. He also lobbied with his mother regarding his military career, ending one letter by saying, "Somebody told me I had been recommended for a decoration at the close of the Tunisia campaign, which has to go back to Washington for approval by the President. I hope he approves. I think it is the Legion of Merit."

One day he got word to fly to Eisenhower's headquarters in Tunisia. There he met his father, who was on his way to Cairo for a meeting with Chinese leader Chiang Kai-shek. After sitting in on these meetings, Elliott accompanied his father to Teheran, where FDR and Churchill were having their first meeting with Stalin.

Having become a sort of Kilroy figure at these conferences, Elliott took everything in at Teheran, getting his father's reactions to the diplomatic minuet whenever there was a recess. The large subject of this conference was the long-delayed opening of the second front. Churchill floated his plan to invade through the "underbelly" of the Balkans as well as through France. Without acknowledging that he knew it was a ploy to cut off the western advance of Soviet troops, Stalin parried the thrust. He and Churchill carried on an oblique debate with FDR on the sidelines enjoying their single combat.

In the one moment at Teheran where the latent tensions between the leaders almost overflowed, Stalin offered a toast to swift justice for Nazi war criminals with the hope that fifty thousand of them would be put in front of firing squads. Churchill was immediately on his feet protesting: "Any such attitude is wholly contrary to our British sense of justice. The British people will not stand for mass murder!"

Stalin asked FDR what he thought. Amused by Churchill's discomfort, Roosevelt said that his role was obviously to compromise between the Prime Minister and the Soviet Premier. So instead of fifty thousand to be executed, he said, "Shall we say forty-nine thousand five hundred?" Relishing the moment, Stalin went around the table asking everyone present how many Nazis should be killed. He came to Elliott, who replied: "Russian, American and British soldiers will settle the issue for most of those fifty thousand in battle and I hope that not only those fifty thousand criminals will be taken care of but many hundreds of thousands more Nazis as well."

Delighted by the bloodthirsty response from the President's son, Stalin proposed a toast to him while Churchill shouted: "Do you know what you are saying? How can you even say such a thing?" Although he was posted to England shortly after this meeting, Elliott was never again invited to the Prime Minister's residence and had no further contact with him.

FDR went back home from Teheran thinking things had gone well, although some observers would later make the case that his flippancy at this meeting would lead to disaster in the sequel at Yalta. On the way back home, he became sick and arrived in Washington suffering from the flu and from exhaustion. He didn't pay much attention when Elliott casually informed the family of his irrevocable decision to divorce Ruth, but Eleanor was aghast. "It takes my breath away," she wrote Anna, "for one would think divorces & one's 3 children are a mere incident not to be mentioned. . . . I've an idea Elliott may cut loose & live in China or Russia [after the war]. I'll be sorry, but I guess there is a streak of unruliness in some of us."

One of the few people in whom Eleanor confided her fears about her children was Kermit's widow, Belle, with whom she shared a bond of marital betrayal. Yet Belle, a frequent overnight guest at the White House, preferred being with FDR. She was one of those attractive, garrulous women he found diverting. She gave him cocktail shakers and other little presents, gushed over his accomplishments, and drew him out when he wanted to talk and then recorded his conversation in her diary when she returned home.

One night soon after the Teheran conference, for instance, the after-dinner conversation at the White House involved a lengthy discussion about who was shorter, Churchill or Stalin. Other candidates for shortness were mentioned. Belle jumped in and delighted the President by saying that she had always felt that her brother-in-law Ted, barely five seven, suffered particularly from being "a little man."

Since their confrontation five years earlier over the family's attitude toward Kermit, the chill between Ted and Belle had intensified. In fact, in writing home to register his sadness at Kermit's passing, one of the things Ted had said to his mother was that he supposed Belle and her children would now "drift away" from the family.

Ted had no choice but to regard the relationship with his sister-in-law as yet another casualty of war. But as one of the few "fighting" generals in the army, he was in the thick of things and not able to devote much attention to repairing damaged emotions on the home front. While nostalgic for the world he was helping destroy, he was nonetheless fully engaged and intensely present in the conflict.

He had been overshadowed by his father in the first half of his life and by his cousin in the second half, but now he was in his element, racing to the front of every battle in a jeep with the words "Rough Rider" painted on the side and a starburst from an enemy shell in the middle of the windshield. His battered face, wide-mouthed grin, and gamecock manner had made him a folk figure with his men. They were amused by the way that all poetry learned at the childhood dinner table rolled out of him during heavy fighting, as the New Yorker's A.J. Liebling said, "with the large facility of a jukebox full of quarters."

After fighting his way through North Africa he had hit the beach with the 1st Division at Sicily, having to use a cane as he waded ashore because of crippling arthritis in his hip. (Pinned down behind a crumbled stone wall at one point during the Sicily invasion with bullets zinging all around him and everyone else flat on their stomachs, Ted had begun telling stories in a booming voice: "On the boat from Kolee to Singapore in 1926. . . .") He had repeatedly drawn reprimands from superior officers for recklessly exposing himself to enemy fire, but he joked that he was invulnerable, an assertion that seemed confirmed during the Sicilian campaign when he was hit in the face by a spent fragment from a German mortar shell and suffered only two cracked teeth.

His bristling pride made him annoyed by news that his name never appeared in battlefront dispatches printed in the papers back home, although what were only vague suspicions about FDR enforcing a news blackout on him would have gained weight had he known of the mysterious directive issued by the British, apparently in response to requests from U.S. intelligence, that his name and that of his son Quentin were to be censored out of all press reports.

But a far more serious problem had occurred after Sicily was secured, when he was removed from the line of command and made liaison officer between the U.S. 5th Army and French forces under General Alphonse Juin.

Ted was told that the move was part of a "normal rotation," but as he probed deeper he discovered that it had been instigated by his superior, General George Patton, who claimed that Ted was not "technically qualified" for command because he had been out of the army between the wars. Ted believed the real reason for the demotion had to do with a moment in North Africa that Patton would have preferred to forget: as German fighter planes had launched a strafing attack Ted had offered Patton his place in a small foxhole and Patton had surprisingly (and ignominiously from Ted's point of view) taken it.

"I don't think that F. [Franklin] had anything to do with it," Ted wrote his wife about being removed from command, "except by [listening to] people thinking they could make a hit with him by slapping me down." He confessed that he was "heartbroken" by this turn of events and told Eleanor of a plan he was hatching: to get himself and Quentin, who had returned to the front after a too brief convalescence in the United States from his wounds, transferred to China where they could serve there with the legendary General Joseph Stilwell.

As 1943 ended, Ted was still working with the French. Although not in command, he was still at the center of the fighting in Italy:

I'm just back from the front . . . [he wrote Eleanor]. It has been bitter, with every foot of ground paid for in blood. Attack and counter attack have succeeded one another in unending sequence. Day has merged into night and night into day until time seemed to have no periods. I've been at the front every day, usually with Juin—he's a front-fighting general—often alone. . . . This country we're fighting through has to be seen to be believed. It is a jumble of sheer rocky hills and mountains so steep that they seem about to tumble down on you when you get among them. The soldiers assault them in the face of hostile fire, often climbing hand over hand in rain or snow. . . . And always after days of battle the weariness—the desperate weariness. Sometimes you'd rather take a chance of being hit than throw yourself down and have to get up again.

He felt that the Germans were "in a bad way" because they were leaving their dead behind for the first time in the war and also because duds were becoming a larger proportion of their artillery. He knew this from personal experience: he had been standing on a ridge helping direct a French offensive when twelve German shells fell nearby; of the two that didn't explode, one of them landed only thirty yards away from him.

As Christmas came, Ted allowed a touch of pathos to enter in his letter home to Eleanor: "I know one old bald headed General who keeps thinking of Christmases at Oyster Bay, the carols, the stockings, the wind sighing around [the] eaves—and the family. But let's forget about him. He's old anyhow and has always liked to pretend he's tough."

At the beginning of the new year, Ted's anxiety about being side-tracked with the French was compounded by rumors he was hearing that the Allied invasion of Europe was finally going to happen. Desperate to be part of it, he wrote his friends and fellow generals Omar Bradley and Matthew Ridgway (once his attaché in the Philippines but now in command of the 82nd Airborne) to enlist their help. He also got his wife working on the problem in Washington, and as before in his career, Eleanor proved an effective diplomat, contacting George Marshall and others in the War Department in Ted's behalf. Finally, in February 1944, he got the good news: he had been ordered to England to help prepare for D-day under the command of General Raymond "Tubby" Barton.

Quentin was already there when Ted arrived, having been transferred to England several weeks earlier. His son also had news: he had fallen in love with a Red Cross nurse from Kansas City named Frances Webb. After meeting her, Ted wrote Eleanor about this turn of events: "She is 26, 5'7" tall, and a fine looking, healthy girl, well formed with good legs and a deep chest. Her hair is dark brown, her eyes hazel." He added gruffly that while he personally felt incompetent in these matters of the heart and wished that she was present to handle things, he had talked to Quentin to make sure that he felt he had found a partner for life and to Frances to make sure that she understood what an extraordinary person she was marrying.

Unable to get to England for the wedding, Eleanor called the Webbs, who had not yet heard the news about their daughter's engagement, and told them how pleased she was about the match. She detected a peculiar coldness on the other end of the line, as she wrote Ted, which she did not understand until a few days later when Mrs. Webb wrote to say that she and her husband had been confused at first and thought they were being told that Frances was marrying *Elliott* Roosevelt. The ceremony took place at a small church in the English countryside with Ted as best man and a makeshift reception afterward at Quentin's officer's mess.

As the preparations for the Normandy invasion went forward, Ted learned that Archie, who had been seriously wounded in the Pacific by shrapnel from a grenade, was now agitating to get back to the front lines although he was far from recovered. Given a desk job, Archie wrote irritably: "I feel like the nurse of a lot of very small children. Inspection for hair cuts, clean socks, fingernails and all sorts of similar silly things. I suppose in the Brave New World, with its paternalistic government, such will be the usual course of things." He also wrote Ted about politics, saying he was glad Wendell Willkie, too much of a "one worlder," was out of the running as FDR's opponent in 1944: "I don't know enough about [Thomas] Dewey to be any judge but my guess is that if the people want a change at all, they want the direct opposite of Franklin."

Although his brother never mentioned his physical problems, Ted had learned that in addition to his wounds, Archie had dropped forty-one pounds by the end of the Solomon campaign. He wrote Edith, "I wish Archie would call it a day and not go on in the battle over there. . . . He's done more than any other man of his age." He also worried about his son Cornelius, who was using his engineering degree from MIT to work on top secret weapons research for the navy. Cornelius was now the only one of his children not yet married and Ted urged him to find a wife and start a family—the only things, he said, that would not fail him in life.

When Eleanor sent him photographs of the apple trees in full bloom at Old Orchard, the home he had lived in only for three years, Ted wrote back, "Let's hope God will let us enjoy them together some time in the future. . . ."

He didn't tell her about the sense of forboding that had come over him. But Kenneth Davis, an OSS man who had gotten to know Ted in North Africa, saw the change when he ran into him again in London. The bulldog face and booming voice were the same, but Davis found Ted much frailer than before, emotionally as well as physically. Summoned to his quarters for what turned out to be an unexpected conversation, Davis found him propped up in bed recovering from a bout of pneumonia. "I asked you over today to ask a favor," Ted said, hacking on a forbidden cigarette. "The coming operation will be my last one. I won't come back from this one. No, no don't interrupt, please listen to me. When I am dead, I want you to get Quentin transferred to OSS. . . . He was pretty badly hit in Tunisia and is not strong enough to serve in an infantry division."

Davis was aware that there were many melodramatic conversations taking place on the eve of the Normandy invasion. But he was struck by the matter-of-factness and complete lack of self-pity in Ted's voice. It was as if he were describing something that had already occurred rather than a premonitory fear. Davis said he would do what he could.

Ted was well enough recovered from his illness by May to participate in the final stages of preparation for the invasion. He had asked General Barton to allow him to go ashore with the first wave. When the request was turned down, he put it in writing and sent it through channels. He didn't know when it was finally okayed that the request had gone all the way to Eisenhower himself. At fifty-seven, Ted would be the oldest man in the invasion. He and Quentin were, he believed, the only father and son who would land together at Normandy.

The night before the cross-Channel sailing, he wrote home to Eleanor: "We are starting the great venture of the war, and by the time you get this, for better or worse, it will be history. . . . I go in with the assault wave and hit the beach at H-Hour. I'm doing it because it's the way I can contribute most. It steadies the young men to know that I am with them, to see me plodding along on my cane. We've got to break the crust with the first wave or we're sunk, for the following groups won't get in."

Then he added something personal to the woman who had been his "old girl" for so long, a partner as well as a wife: "We've had a grand life and I hope there'll be more. Should it chance that there's not, at least we can say in our years together we've packed enough for ten ordinary lives. We've known joy and sorrow, triumph as well as disaster, all that goes to fit the pattern of human existence. Our children are grown and our grandchildren are here. We have been very happy. I pray that we are together again."

As Ted went ashore with the first wave on Utah Beach, he saw immediately that a mistake had been made. His men had been landed almost a mile south of their targeted position and were badly exposed to enemy fire. Immediately organizing a counterattack on German machine gun positions raking the beach from less than a hundred yards away, he began personally shuttling groups of soldiers to the protection of a sea wall, returning for more as he got the previous ones safely settled. He was under constant enemy fire for several hours, propping himself up on his cane as the bullets whined around him, showing the soldiers the son of Theodore Roosevelt and gesturing at them to follow him. Years later, at the end of a long and distinguished military career, General Omar Bradley was asked about the bravest thing he had ever seen in wartime and replied without hesitation that it was Theodore Roosevelt, Jr., on Normandy Beach. For his actions that day, Ted would ultimately be given the Congressional Medal of Honor, the great award his father had coveted but been denied for political reasons.

After the beachhead was secured, Ted was relieved to find that Quentin, who had landed on Omaha Beach, had also come through unscathed. But there was only a short time for them to be together. Ted was already beginning to press his forces inland. He stormed a little town whose name he didn't mention in the letter he wrote to Eleanor, but he told about seeing American soldiers dead in the streets after their siege of the place, and how, before his men could move them, French women had come out of their homes to stand above them crying as they scattered rose petals and flowers over their bodies.

Rooting out pockets of resistance in another town, Ted's forces got about one hundred Germans to surrender, but fifteen more refused to be taken alive. After praising the resisters for their bravery, Ted sent in his men to kill them.

He was appointed temporary military governor of Cherbourg. A captured German truck outfitted with a desk and bed and electric lights served as his headquarters. After fighting constantly for over a month, he was exhausted. After a particularly bad day, he wrote Eleanor on July 11: "I was a pretty sick rabbit and it had been raining for God knows how long. . . . After I got in and was dry I summoned up energy to take off my drenched clothes. The doc came in and said with little embarrassment that my troubles were primarily from having put an inhuman strain on a machine that was not exactly new."

He was still concerned about Quentin's future, and when he ran into OSS man Kenneth Davis again after the invasion, he reminded him of the promise he had made in England. Davis was accompanied by David Bruce, theater commander of the OSS, and Bruce personally pledged that he would get Quentin into the OSS and then send him to China.

On the evening of July 14, Quentin left his unit to visit his father. He and Ted spent three hours in the captured truck talking about family and home, speculating on the way things would look at Oyster Bay at the height of the summer growing season. Neither of them was aware that Eisenhower had that morning signed the papers promoting Ted to major general and putting him in charge of a division. Ted admitted to his son something he had told no one else: that he had been suffering a series of mild heart attacks. Not wanting to dwell on the subject, he went on to say that he felt "whole." He said that one of the most gratifying things that had happened to him in this war was that everywhere he went soldiers told him how much they had loved his father. He told Quentin how proud he was that he and Archie and Kermit had all stepped forth to serve their country in the two wars fought by their generation.

Back with his own men that night, Quentin was awakened from a deep sleep at three o'clock and told that his father had died of a heart attack. The letter he wrote to his mother began with exactly the same words that Archie had used when he informed Ted and Kermit of TR's death nearly twenty-five years earlier: "The old lion is dead. . . ."

Ted was buried in the town of Sainte-Mère-Église with a dozen ranking generals as his pallbearers. As his casket was lowered into the ground, sounds of battle rumbled in the distance and the military band played "The Son of God Goes Forth to War."

He was the most decorated soldier to serve in the war, having won every combat medal awarded by U.S. ground forces. Journalist A. J. Liebling saw at least one of the conclusions that could be drawn from Ted's lifelong dialogue with his heritage when he wrote that while TR had been "a dilettante soldier and a first class politician; his son was a dilettante politician and a first class soldier."

It was left to Archie, now the sole surviving son, to try to comfort his mother: "We have all the memories of a large, quarrelsome, fun-loving and united family, and Ted died spending himself to the limit. These are the things we must always remember."

When Quentin got leave, he came home to see Edith and tell her about his last visit with his father. His grandmother was eighty-two. She listened to Quentin while looking at him through clouded eyes. Then, suddenly enveloped in confusion, she said to him, "You were the first of my babies to die."

The efforts of his sons in battle suggested that this was Theodore Roosevelt's war as well as Franklin's. Indeed, this seemed to be the point Secretary of War Henry Stimson was making early in 1945 when he called Chief of Staff George Marshall and Air Force General Hap Arnold to his office, along with John J. McCloy, Robert Lovett, Henry Bundy, and other of the "bright young men" he had collected. When asked the purpose of the meeting, Stimson said that it was the twenty-fifth anniversary of the death of Theodore Roosevelt and that he felt it was appropriate, now that the U.S. appeared to be driving this war to a conclusion, to take a few minutes and commemorate this great American leader. Stimson reminisced at length about his own experiences as a disciple of TR and then read the eloquent address given by Elihu Root at the memorial service following Roosevelt's death in which Root said that his break with TR was one of the saddest experiences of his life and his reconciliation with him one of the happiest. The little ceremony finished, Stimson dismissed his colleagues and told them to get back to the business of victory.

A more subtle affirmation of the TR tradition had come from FDR himself. He had felt shame after the previous war in not heeding TR's call to action. But in this one he had made up for it, "spending himself and being spent," in the TR formula, as surely as his cousin and onetime rival Ted had done, and proving himself as much a soldier of freedom as TR himself.

By 1945, the toll the war had taken on Franklin was fearsome. He had changed significantly, becoming ashen-faced, his skin discolored by liver spots and purple smudges beneath his eyes. He was so gaunt that he seemed to have shrunk, and his clothes seemed sizes too big. People who saw him up close came away with the same thought: this man is dying.

The physical deterioration had begun the previous spring after he returned from Teheran. Unable to shake his flu, he had grown listless. Alarmed at his condition, his daughter, Anna, had come to the White House to brighten as well as organize his life. For others the gray pallor was the most worrisome change in FDR; for her it was her father's signature—once a bold flourish of assertion that now trailed off weakly into self-cancellation.

Desperate to get relief from the pressures he faced, FDR had arranged for Missy to come down for a visit in the spring of 1944, but Eleanor found out about the trip and delayed it, telling Missy that she too wanted to be present when she came and was too busy over the next few weeks. A few months later Missy was dead, never having seen FDR again and never knowing that he had made her the beneficiary of one half his estate in gratitude for the commitment she had made to him when polio had threatened his future.

The cocktail hour had become the most important moment of the day for FDR—a time when he could try to relax and lose himself in the frivolous conversation that had become his only recreation. He would sometimes hand out "Uncle Joe's Bounty," as he called the caviar sent by the Soviet leader, and occasionally Eleanor would cook her one dish—scrambled eggs, which he would eye distastefully as they lay "like lead" in their chafing dish.

Writing in her diary, Kermit's widow, Belle, captured the quality of the meandering talk—usually about himself and those close to him—

that FDR so enjoyed and required to keep him going. "She was right in a way," FDR laughed after Belle once started him off by mentioning a comment his mother had once made to her about the Roosevelt part of his character not having contributed much to his vitality. "What vitality I have is not inherited from Roosevelts—our branch of the Roosevelts haven't got vitality and mine, such as it is, comes from the Delanos and is a very convenient type because it can be turned on and off at will." He then digressed to talk about his grandfather Isaac, describing him as a man trained as a doctor who so abhorred suffering that he gave up his profession in favor of a life spent in philosophical speculations. "From here," Belle concluded her entry, "he went on to a lively discussion of concentration and memory."

Anna set up occasions such as these, which she believed helped her father cope with the burdens thrust upon him. With Missy gone, there weren't that many people who could provide the sprightly familiarity he craved. Anna went so far as to allow Lucy Mercer Rutherfurd, recently widowed, to come to the White House for discreet visits about which Eleanor was never informed. Lucy and FDR sat together with Anna as a distant chaperone chatting about old times and about the lives they had led since they had known each other.

But even diversions like this did little to rehabilitate FDR. When Elliott came home on temporary assignment to the War Department in November 1944, Anna warned him about the changes that had come over their father. Even so, Elliott's face betrayed such surprise when he came into the office that FDR looked up at him for a second and then shrugged and said, "Well, what did you expect?"

While he was home, Elliott asked for a forty-eight-hour leave and flew to California to see Faye Emerson again. He begged her to marry him and she finally agreed. Howard Hughes flew them to the Grand Canyon where they said their vows in an observation tower providing a breathtaking overlook.

Afterward, Elliott went back to his unit. As part of his divorce from Ruth, he had given her and the children all the assets remaining in his Texas State Network, saying that it did not matter because he did not expect to survive the war anyhow. Some of that fatalism was present in a letter he wrote his mother: "I have about 25 more combat hours to do to reach 400 and I will have flown about seventy-five missions in all. . . . I never used to be afraid in the pit of my stomach before taking off on a flight, but now I get that feeling and I guess I'm beginning to push my luck."

Soon after this two separate pieces of news broke about Elliott that came to seem related in the public mind. First he was named brigadier general, an elevation in rank that caused comment because nonpilots almost never made general in the air force. And then it was revealed that three servicemen, one of them on his way home to see his dying father, had been bumped from a flight on Elliott's authority so that Blaze, a bull mastiff he had bought Faye, could be flown to her in California.

The furor was immediate. Archie was expressing the general opinion when he wrote Edith, "What a shocking scandal of Eliot [sic] Roosevelt. That whole family were certainly most brazen in the way they exploited the office." There was little reaction from Franklin and Eleanor about Elliott's follies, however. They were resigned to the adverse publicity he produced. In addition, they had come to rely on him as a go-between in their own tangled relationship. Before he returned overseas after marrying Faye, FDR had said to Elliott, "You know, I think that your mother and I might be able to get together now and do things together and take some trips, maybe, learn to know each other again." Elliott immediately took this news to his mother, who said wistfully, "I hope this will come to pass."

But while there may have been a desire to close the gap, there was no ability to accomplish it. And family politics ultimately made the problem worse instead of better. Eleanor was now jealous of the access her daughter had to FDR. (Perhaps jealous himself, Elliott said, "Anna was pushing herself as power behind the throne and playing Eleanor.") But Eleanor failed to acknowledge that her daughter had power only because she herself refused to play the part of wife.

Anna had seen the potential for trouble with her mother, writing her husband, John Boettiger, after her father invited her to come to work in the White House, "I pray I don't get caught in the crossfire between these two!" But it was inevitable. Anna was presiding over the cocktail hour one afternoon when her mother showed up late, as usual with a sheaf of papers. She sat down across from FDR, who was chatting with various people, and began to badger him: "Now Franklin, I want to talk to you about this. . . ." Before she could finish, he exploded, throwing the papers Eleanor was pressing on him toward Anna: "Sis, you handle these tomorrow morning!" With her monumental self-control, Eleanor stood up, said, "I'm sorry," and walked away to begin talking to someone else.

It was as if the two of them were locked in a deathly embrace they could not break. One of the physicians brought in to examine the Pres-

ident felt that nothing could be done for him "unless he were rescued
from certain mental strains and emotional influences." Despite the eu-
phemistic language and despite the huge strain of directing the war, it
was clear that he meant Eleanor.

She had hoped to accompany FDR to Yalta. But he asked Anna to go
with him instead. What Eleanor didn't know was that Anna had actually
campaigned for the trip, knowing that only one of them could go and
pointing out to her father that Churchill and Averell Harriman, two
other leading players, were bringing their daughters and not their wives.
("I wanted desperately to go," Anna said later on. "But I also knew that
if I went, Mother couldn't go.")

As he set out on the voyage to the meeting that would determine the
shape of the postwar world, FDR sat bundled up on the deck of the
destroyer heading into the Atlantic and began to talk in his usual meandering way to Anna. Gesturing in the direction of the Virginia coastline, he spoke knowledgeably about the birds that nested there. As he
spoke he pointed at the foothills above the shoreline and interjected
casually, "Over there is where Lucy grew up," and then talked about
her for a moment before letting the conversation find another subject.

It was an oblique acknowledgment of what the love affair had meant
to him, one of a handful of relationships that had made him what he had
become, although it, like so much that was important to him, could
never be openly discussed. It was also an acknowledgment of the conspiracy into which he and his daughter had entered, which involved not
only secret visits by Lucy Rutherfurd to the White House but also a
meeting at Warm Springs the previous Thanksgiving. FDR had taken
his old lover for a drive up into the hills surrounding the resort, engaging in a rambling monologue about world affairs that he interrupted
occasionally to point out some landmark involved with his work with
other polio victims some fifteen years earlier.

The Yalta meeting was filled with ambiguities and unresolved questions. Franklin was as charming as ever, but Churchill remarked on the
"far away look" in his eyes and a strange thickness in his voice. FDR had
prided himself in these wartime meetings on his abilities to act as an
opportunist in behalf of democracy, but the British delegation and even
members of his own felt that this time he was consistently outmaneu-
vered by Stalin and had relied too heavily on being able to smooth out
the rough spots in the negotiations later on by exertions of personality
during the remainder of his fourth term.

Franklin returned from the meeting so pale that his skin appeared almost transparent. But he moved back into his White House duties. Most of his responsibilities he regarded as onerous. But he took great pleasure in acting the part of Father Roosevelt—not only for his own wayward brood with their multiple marital and public relations problems, but also for his Oyster Bay relatives when they would let him. He gave constant advice to Belle, who was trying to make a life for herself without Kermit. And he also tried to make sure that Archie got through the war in one piece.

After having been wounded and hospitalized, Archie was told that he would not be able to command a battalion again. Confined to a desk, he let off steam by writing mordant letters containing his views about issues that concerned him. ("Vice President Wallace has the simplest solution," he wrote one friend. "Turn over all the machinery, produce and work of the U.S. to Jo Stalin. . . . I wish we could export him to Russia under Lend Lease and leave him there. Something tells me that Brother Jo would know how to handle him.")

Without Archie's knowledge, his wife, Grace, had been writing FDR to tell him that Archie was hanging around division headquarters "desperately unhappy and very bored." His wounds had made him 100 percent disabled (he was the only U.S. soldier to have a complete disability in both world wars), but she knew that "unless ordered home, Archie will expend himself the way Ted did."

He came home on leave in the fall of 1944 to attend his daughter Nancy's wedding. Then, after his thirty days' leave was up, Archie prepared to return to the Pacific. But FDR was receptive to Grace's fears and concerned about the possibility that the last of TR's sons would die in battle.

"What do I do about Archie?" he wrote his aide Pa Watson. A few days later, Watson replied, "I have put the case of Archie Roosevelt in the hands of General Marshall." Marshall decided to buy time by sending Archie to the hospital for a lengthy exam. While he was there, he had a sudden recurrence of the malaria he had contracted while fighting in the jungle and this postponed a decision on how to handle the case.

After he had finally recuperated from the malaria, Archie went to the White House for a meeting about his military future. Afterward, FDR wrote Grace that the two of them had had a "nice chat." It marked a moment of partial closure in the long conflict between the Roosevelt branches. As he was about to leave the Oval Office, Archie, seeing a crumpled pack of cigarettes on FDR's desk, pulled out the battered metal cigarette package holder he had carried all through the Pacific campaign and gave it to his cousin. FDR was touched by the gesture, which he knew was meant as a homage from one old soldier to another. But he nonetheless sent the holder back to Grace a few days later: "I am quite sure that you have nothing which has been so intimately associated with his Second World War days and I want you and the children to have it. *But* do not, for heaven's sake, let him know that I have given it to you. I merely thought it would be a nice memento to have of his service in a war which he was much too old to undertake anyway."

Archie and FDR were still separated by political ideology and by a host of unresolved—and probably unresolvable—family issues that had festered over the last quarter century. But they were joined as comrades in arms, two of the last Roosevelt males of their generation left standing after two wars. For the next few months they engaged in a pleasurable and often humorous correspondence about Archie's desire to get back in the action.

"Since you have taken so much time 'brooding' over me," he wrote FDR shortly after his return from Yalta, "I'm going to ask you to 'brood' some more. . . . It seems to me that regardless of the bitterness that many people feel toward the 'Hyde Park' Roosevelts or the 'Oyster Bay' Roosevelts, they have to admit that the whole clan has turned out to a man. . . . It is [something] in which I think we can take a certain amount of pride, and I want to live up to it."

Once again the President turned to George Marshall, writing his leading general that while Archie was "an awfully nice fellow and an excellent soldier," he believed him to be too old and sick to go back into battle. On April 9, 1945, Marshall replied that they would have to discuss the matter further and figure out a way to overcome Archie's persistence.

His cousin's future was one of the things on FDR's mind when he went to Warm Springs three days after the note from Marshall. With Anna's secret cooperation, along with assists from Alice Longworth and Laura Delano ("Aunt Polly"), Lucy Rutherfurd was scheduled to spend a few days there. In fact, she had commissioned a friend of hers, Elizabeth Shoumatoff, to paint a portrait of Franklin she could hang in her home. He was sitting for the painter wearing his Harvard tie and old navy cape and talking to his old friend and lover on the morning of April 12 when he suddenly put a finger to his temple and said he had a terrible headache. Then he collapsed. Doctors were summoned and after working feverishly for an hour to revive him pronounced Franklin Roosevelt dead.

Eleanor was told about Lucy's presence at Warm Springs by Aunt Polly when she arrived there close to midnight after a journey of several hours. She went into the bedroom where his body lay and shut the door behind her, emerging five minutes later dry-eyed and stony-faced.

The anger she turned on her daughter was like cold fire, an intensity of emotion Anna had never experienced before. Anna had known she was betraying her mother by countenancing Lucy's presence, but she had been convinced that her father needed the life-giving companionship and warmth that Eleanor herself could not give. Distraught over FDR's death and guilty over what her mother claimed was treachery, Anna found no consolation until she received a letter from Lucy herself a few days later. It was the sort of letter, she thought later on, that a mother might write a daughter:

"He said you had been extraordinary," Lucy wrote of FDR's appreciation for what Anna had done for him in the last year and a half of his life, "and what a difference it made to have you. He told me of your charm & your tact & of how *everyone* loved you. . . . The world has lost one of the greatest men that ever lived—to me the greatest. . . . Now he is at peace—but he knew even before the end—that the task was well done."

*F*ranklin had left detailed instructions for his funeral in an envelope with Jimmy's name on it. Jimmy started home from the Philippines immediately upon hearing that his father had died, but because of weather delays his plane did not arrive until after the ceremonies were over. Even so, everything was almost exactly as FDR had wanted it. His body had lain in state in the Capitol (the casket closed because the stroke had caused the blood vessels in his head to burst, swelling his face and turning it purple) and then there was a somber death march to the railway station, with most of the thousands who lined the streets weeping but a few exulting over "that bastard Roosevelt" as the caisson passed by. And then the long trip to Hyde Park for a final interment.

Franklin Jr. and John also couldn't make it home because they were both involved in the Okinawa invasion. Elliott was the only son present. He and Anna accompanied Eleanor on the funeral train. She was silent and remote, the deep tension she felt apparent only in the constant movement of her fingers, which appeared to be tapping out an arcane rhythm of grief in her lap.

Her anger toward her daughter over the final betrayal with Lucy Rutherfurd had not thawed. ("Boy, am I in the doghouse!" Anna had blurted out to Elliott when he arrived home.) Their conversations since the death had been brisk and businesslike. But Eleanor's primary emotion was actually one of self-blame over what now seemed like a tragedy of lost opportunities. When she collected herself a few days after the funeral, she would have a talk with Elliott, go-between in the final attempt FDR had made shortly before his death to establish better relations with her.

"I should have tried much *harder* to help him through the awful war," she told him. "I was pigheaded! Unbending during all those years since the first war. Always so insistent on doing what *I* wanted to do. . . . If only I had found the *courage* to talk to Franklin as I wanted to do, I could have said, 'Let us bury this whole matter and begin over again.' I ought to have done that when I said I would. But I left it too late. . . ."

Once the funeral procession reached Hyde Park, there was a brief ceremony attended by the new President, Harry Truman, along with representatives of the international community and Roosevelt stalwarts from the past fifteen years. As the casket was lowered into the ground in the rose garden Franklin had loved, a squadron of cadets from West Point fired a salute into the air. Then came two minutes of silence as planes across the nation rested on their runways, trains paused on the tracks, and radios went silent. Afterward, Eleanor returned immediately to Washington to remove her belongings from the White House. On the way, she was badgered for an interview by a handful of reporters. When they asked what was next for her, she shook her head and said simply, "The story is over now."

She was not quite right. One final chapter remained to be written, and Eleanor would be the central character. The postwar years, in fact, would mark her apotheosis—as U.N. Human Rights Commission leader, partisan of Israel's nationhood, and ultimately, in Harry Truman's phrase, as First Lady to the World. Never pretending to be an original or even a particularly forceful thinker, she would nonetheless become a symbol of the FDR legacy, while also redefining and extending that legacy in her own image.

It was the final flowering of a process begun twenty-five years earlier when Louis Howe had decided to make her a public figure. And yet, in all those years, as much as she had come to depend on success in the political domain for her sense of self, there had always been a restless searching in the private realm—for friendship and love, and also with

less drama perhaps but greater emotional urgency, for family. If the
world was now to see her dramatic emergence as the figure called Mrs.
R., widow of the New Deal and the conscience of liberalism, Eleanor
herself put equal energy, albeit with less rewarding results, into the role
of Mother R., bewildered *materfamilias* trying to deal with the fractious
and unhappy children who floated unanchored through her life.

There was a huge backlog of unresolved family issues at the time of
FDR's death, issues that had been waiting for his intervention to get
solved. Now Eleanor was left to handle them. Her problem was that she
had never acquired Franklin's authority within the family because of her
emotional ineptitude and unpredictability, and also because at a certain
point in her life she had started to look outside the family for satisfying
relationships. Her children still resented the profligacy of Eleanor's affection for others. The generation of her mother's friends they had first
been jealous of in the past had moved to the corner of Eleanor's affections. She didn't speak much to Marion Dickerman and Nancy Cook;
Earl Miller and his third wife had moved to Florida, where Eleanor had
helped him buy a home; Hick was becoming infirm and had taken a
room near Val-Kill.

These relationships still sometimes resurfaced in a dramatic way. In
1948, for instance, Earl Miller's latest wife left him and began flourish-
ing affectionate letters from Eleanor and threatening to name her as
co-respondent in their divorce suit. When Franklin Jr., who was handling legal negotiations, asked if there was anything to the accusations,
Eleanor smiled and replied, "In the sense that you mean, there was
nothing." But it was such a devastating episode in her life that Elliott
believed his mother was at one point close to suicide, although she
steadfastly denied that there had been any impropriety between her and
the onetime state policeman, and did not rest until Franklin Jr. finally
worked out a solution by which "a sum of money" was passed to the
woman and the letters were returned.

But now, at the very time she wanted to close the gaps that divided
her from her children, Eleanor was also moving toward a new generation of intense friendships—younger people like Joe Lash and his wife,
Trude, whom some of her children regarded as parasites, and Dr. David
Gurewitsch, a man she met on a trip to Israel and became intensely
involved with, making him her personal physician and confidant.*

---

* The friendship with Joe Lash, begun in the prewar era, had grown during the war
after he was drafted—he suspected as a result of FDR's own request—and made into

These people and others were present during her workaday life and at every holiday—a layer of insulation between her and the family. Anna later called them "hangers on" and said that she felt her mother's attachment to them defined Eleanor's two principal problems: that she had to be "adored," and that she couldn't stand to be alone.

But while she was reluctant to give up these friends she trusted and depended on, Eleanor redoubled her efforts to bring the family back together in the years after FDR's death. Although tightly scheduled in her new role as U.N. diplomat and Democratic Party power broker, she allowed an element of sentimentality to enter her life. Pictures of the family when the children were young, before Lucy had cast a shadow on her life, appeared on her desk and on her walls. Not otherwise given to reminiscence, Eleanor occasionally talked about incidents from those times at family gatherings. She even took to FDR's dog, Fala, whom she'd previously regarded as a pampered nuisance. Now she adopted the animal as a sort of talisman, taking it with her on solitary walks through Val-Kill and letting it sit next to her in the evening. (When the irritable little Scottie died in 1951, Eleanor buried him at FDR's foot in the rose garden and finally gave in to the tears that hadn't come six years earlier.)

The attention Eleanor began to pay her children in the postwar years was sincere, but it would always have the feel of emotional reparations. She could not fill the void left by FDR. Jimmy best expressed their common disorientation without their father when he said later on, "As long as [he] was alive, I had a feeling of security. There would always be some way I could earn a living. If the chips were down I could ask him to introduce me to so and so to get a job and he would do it. . . . When he died I suddenly had a feeling I'm cast out into the cold. I'm on my own. What do I do? Where do I start?"

But if FDR's memory was a lost sense of security to be mourned, it was also an asset that could be sold. Jimmy and Franklin Jr., the most political of the brothers, made it clear upon mustering out of the service that they intended to run for office as inheritors of their father's legacy. And Jimmy and John, both of whom had settled in Southern California before the war, immediately opened negotiations after returning to civilian life with several Hollywood producers for rights to an unnamed

---

a weather forecaster. Lash had been under surveillance by army agents as a result of his left-wing political beliefs, and he was taped in hotels making love to his future wife, Trude (who was then married to someone else). In one instance, the surveillance accidentally caught Eleanor in Lash's room crooning maternally to him as he went to sleep.

project about FDR. There were interminable discussions within the family about how the royalties would be split and who would control the script. The discussion of bottom lines finally brought an anguished dissent from Anna: "I still feel as strongly as ever that the family should not receive remuneration for such a movie or from it. I recognize Jimmy's and Elliott's and Johnny's feelings . . . but do feel so darn strongly that we have no right to capitalize on father's accomplishments in life."

This was a minority opinion and as her own financial problems grew, Anna would abandon this principled stand and herself look for parts of the legacy that could be easily liquidated. The movie would continue to be discussed over the next few years. (By 1951 it had a name—"The Roosevelt Story"—and possible director in Stanley Kramer.) But despite often desperate maneuvering by Jimmy and John, and eventually Franklin Jr., it did not come to fruition until the play *Sunrise at Campobello* provided a vehicle that delivered handsome royalties to each of the children.

Despite her troubles with her Oyster Bay cousins over the years, Eleanor had always admired the way that they had protected the TR legacy from exploitation. Yet when her own children wanted to cash in on the FDR heritage—one writer compared it to insects who hatch inside the corpse of a parent and eat their way out—she was powerless to stop it. It was something her husband had tacitly encouraged during his life by participating in their shady deals. Moreover, she had gotten in a position, as she admitted to friends, where she could not deny her children anything.

She was particularly unable to say no to Elliott, the child who best understood her weaknesses and most adroitly played on her guilts and aspirations.

After his father's funeral he had asked to be reassigned to the Pacific so he could be part of the endgame of the war to be played out there after Germany's capitulation. But news of the loan his father had helped him get right before the war from A&P President John Hartford had just broken, and this, combined with the lingering after-effects of *l'affaire Blaze* (as Elliott blithely referred to the incident in which he had caused enlisted men to be bumped so that he could send the dog to Faye Emerson), kept him at a desk job at the War Department. Restless there, he had asked Henry Morgenthau if he would help get him a job training Jews in what was to become Israel so they could form an air force. This fantasy came to nothing and he stayed in Washington for the duration.

As his brothers came home and began talking about selling film rights and making other deals, Elliott already had his sights on the most significant asset the Roosevelts owned, the estate at Hyde Park.

He had first raised the subject of the disposition of the family home in the spring of 1945 when he was watching the war wind down and wondering how he would support himself in peacetime. Writing his mother, he asked her if she'd talked to FDR yet "about what we could do with the property" and if she'd circulated his "proposition" to his brothers. It was a touchy subject: Sara had been desperate to keep Springwood in the family and before her death had tried, unsuccessfully, to groom Jimmy to take it over. FDR had recognized that it would be impossible to keep the Big House itself, which he was deeding to the government for his presidential library, but he had hoped to keep the estate in the family's hands.

Once he was out of the air force, Elliott was ready to pursue the subject again. He had grown heftier during the war and wore his hair slicked back and nervously fingered a new mustache. He had alert eyes and a sullen mouth, a face that lit up when he was smiling but was grim in repose. He did not have Jimmy's charm, Franklin Jr.'s banter, nor John's mordant wit. Yet he was still the most appealing of them all—his hustler's aggressiveness somehow managing to coexist with a kind of naïveté. "Elliott had big appetites for everything," a wartime friend later said, "for women, liquor, and for work. He was an *enthusiast*. Everything he did, even the questionable things, he did wholeheartedly and without cynicism."

He had blown his inheritance from Sara on a prewar 1941 Cadillac and was penniless, living off Faye as she attempted to restart her movie career. He had reached something of an impasse with his mother during the war years as a result of his divorce from Ruth Googins, but in 1946 he began trying to ingratiate himself back into Eleanor's favor. He had also returned to his idea about capitalizing on Hyde Park, as Eleanor indicated in a letter she wrote Anna: "Elliott and Faye are in Los Angeles and she's doing a picture. . . . I'd like him to tell you about his troubles and I'd like your reaction about his state of mind and real desire to run the HP place."

Elliott alone of her children sensed Eleanor's new vulnerability and understood that FDR's death had liberated a sentimentality she could not afford to feel during his life. He understood too that Hyde Park presented his mother with a problem. While she was not at all unhappy to see the Big House go to the government, she loved Val-Kill and all the surrounding lands and pictured it as the center of a reunified family in the future.

Elliot began to court his mother after she mentioned coquettishly that she would need a "resident son" if she were to continue to live at Val-Kill. Soon he was swarming her with attention and enthusiasm. Eleanor was bowled over by him. In addition to being grateful for his sudden outpouring of emotion, she saw an opportunity in their renewed relationship to make amends for the past and make good on her vow to bring the family together again. Elliott's irrepressible faith in the future—a trait he had inherited from his father—was so persuasive that she implored him to help her before he had to ask her for the favor. "Would you consider coming back to Hyde Park and working with me?" she asked. "I don't think I could live there unless you do."

The terms of FDR's will said that the Hyde Park lands should be sold to the highest bidder. With Elliott as her silent partner, Eleanor decided to buy a large plot herself, paying $87,000 for 744 acres she immediately deeded to her son. (Another 258 acres would be purchased from his father's trustees in 1948.) She tried to calm the other children's suspicions about Val-Kill Farms, as Elliott called their new venture, by writing a letter reassuring them that they would all get their patrimony. And when others outside the family also questioned the wisdom of her decision, she made it clear that she was not interested in debating the matter. "If Elliott were not at Hyde Park I could not live there," she wrote to her old friend and colleague Henry Morgenthau, "in fact I would not want to."

Settling in with Faye at Top Cottage, the place on the estate about a mile from Val-Kill FDR had built as his own private retreat, Elliott plunged into the role of Squire of Hyde Park—a role Sara had always hoped FDR would play—with his usual gusto. (There was a contretemps when Blaze, Faye's notorious bull mastiff, tried to eat Fala and had to be destroyed.) Faye was an asset—an intelligent woman who courted Eleanor as assiduously as Elliott himself did. In previous years, when FDR had hosted Katharine Hepburn and other film personalities, Eleanor had been somewhat aloof. But as a family friend said, "She let Faye's glamor wash over her. She was so pleased that Elliott had married someone so beautiful."

Elliott's first task was to get rid of Marion Dickerman and Nancy Cook, who had continued to live at the Stone Cottage at Val-Kill despite several years of cooled relations with Eleanor. Unlike his younger brothers, Franklin Jr. and John, Elliott had never been particularly close to the two women. Sensing that they would be "hard to get out," he negotiated a buyout of their interest in Val-Kill for $30,000. They left the property where they had lived for two decades without even a final goodbye from Eleanor.

Elliott made Val-Kill Farms into a reprise on his ranching days in Fort Worth. And the enterprise he envisioned was Texan in scope. He started with forty dairy cows, one hundred beef cattle, twenty-five hundred laying hens, and forty pigs. (He planned to use the latter for Val-Kill hams, part of a sideline of products he planned to develop.) More ominously, as part of his wheeling and dealing, Elliott also began selling off large parcels of the Roosevelt land to a developer who put in a shopping center including a Howard Johnson's and a movie theater not far from the Big House.

"This was hard to take," his brother Jimmy later said, "but then of all of us Elliott seemed to have the least connection with Hyde Park. To the rest of us it was a place that had produced our father and our family. To him it was just land."

Elliott had assured Eleanor that Val-Kill Farms would pay for itself. But the only thing that made money were the Christmas trees that FDR had planted on the property years earlier. The first harvest was in 1947 and Faye, dressed in a fur coat and high boots, helped Elliott sell the trees to passing motorists on the road bordering Hyde Park. The following year the operation was more ambitious, as Elliott opened a series of twenty-four-hour-a-day lots in Manhattan that were supplied with freshly cut trees by trucks leaving Hyde Park every two hours. Elliott made a point of being there to talk to reporters, condemning the product of competitors as "needle droppers," and touting his Norway spruces as "the original Christmas trees in Germany, where Christmas trees originated. . . ."

Eleanor was charmed not only by her son's energy and drive but also by his flattery. (He did make something of a faux pas in 1946 after she was in a head-on auto crash that knocked out her front teeth when he said she was now "much better looking" because of her dentures.) She was also touched by his intellectual pretensions. It was a paradox: he was the least educated of all her children, but he was also the one who seemed most interested in ideas. His mind was littered with misinformation whose truth he asserted with dogmatic insistence, but he was as passionate about thought as he was about action. Consequently, when he asked to be allowed to take on the FDR literary legacy, Eleanor named him editor of Franklin's letters.

For the first volume Elliott received an advance of $10,000. Anna immediately wrote asking querulously how the money was to be spent. Elliott replied patiently that research expenses—much of it to their mother's friend Joseph Lash—would exceed the advance, and Eleanor jumped to his defense by censuring Anna for having written a "critical and almost hostile letter."

But Elliott was already involved in a far more audacious book. Because FDR had left no memoir, there was enormous interest in what he had thought about the great events of his presidency. So Elliott, working with several ghost writers, produced *As He Saw It,* purportedly an intimate look at FDR's attitude toward the secret diplomacy of the war years, some of which Elliott had witnessed firsthand when he accompanied his father to the wartime conferences at Cairo and Teheran.

Based on re-created scenes and reconstructed dialogue (Elliott claimed to have lost his diary documenting what he had seen and heard), the book caused a furor. It was not stylistic invention that led to the most serious criticism, however, but political views that were methodically anti-British and pro-Soviet. Elliott highlighted and celebrated FDR's differences with Churchill over the future of colonial nations and the second front. He portrayed the British Prime Minister as arrogant and pompous, a figure whose posturing had irritated his father and whose postwar plans FDR intended to block. He portrayed the Soviets as rational allies FDR had believed he could work with in winning the peace.

Appearing at the onset of Cold War tensions in 1946, the book became part of the emerging debate. "Progressives" around Henry Wallace (who had resigned from the Truman administration over policy toward the Soviets at about the time *As He Saw It* appeared) saw Elliott's work as a confirmation of their fears that the United States was provoking the Soviets into a crisis. Intellectuals like Arthur Schlesinger, Jr., on the other hand, criticized the book as clumsy propaganda supporting "the current communist line." Other commentators went even further, asserting that Elliott had been duped by his unidentified ghost writer, who had put a frosting of Soviet disinformation on the final draft of the work.

The strongest criticism came from two of Elliott's cousins on the

Oyster Bay side, political commentators Joseph and Stewart Alsop, grandsons of TR's sister Corinne. Using information about Elliott secretly supplied to them by Franklin Jr., they wrote, "Few people could admire Elliott Roosevelt's behavior while his father lived, but this business of turning a dubious penny by putting *Daily Worker* words into the mouth of the great and helpless dead is just too ghoulish to be borne in patience. . . ."

Eleanor, who had doggedly read and approved each draft of the book, immediately fired off an angry letter to Joseph Alsop defending her son and saying she was "quite horrified" by the review. She did not mention the fact that in the byzantine atmosphere of intrigue and competition that marked her own family, some of the damning material the Alsops had printed about Elliott had been given to them by Franklin Jr., who was annoyed by the adverse impact his brother's work might have on the political future he contemplated for himself.

Others in the family were more direct than Franklin Jr. Jimmy criticized Elliott for *As He Saw It* (although those close to the family felt that he was more annoyed at his brother for making money than for the actual content of the book). And Anna, asking in effect who would be allowed to sell future versions of FDR to the public, wrote Jimmy saying that as the two oldest they should call for a moratorium on all such exploitation, in books as well as movies. Jimmy replied that he agreed with her, but admitted sheepishly that if this principle were to be stringently applied, not only would Elliott have to stop selling *As He Saw It,* but he, Jimmy, would also have to give back an advance he had taken for his own FDR book and back out of contracts he had already signed for several articles on his father.

As a compromise he suggested that after all present contracts were fulfilled, everyone in the family should "agree to make no further commitments for a period of ten years" and then submit contested projects to the arbitration of neutral third parties.

For all the internal criticism it generated, Elliott's book was a best-seller as well as a cause célèbre. Because of its success, Gardner Cowles, publisher of *Look* magazine, asked him to go to the U.S.S.R. to interview Stalin. Elliott accepted the assignment and enrolled in a crash course in Russian at Columbia University. Then in the summer of 1946, he and Faye flew to Moscow aboard an Aeroflot jet outfitted for VIPs with a plush red interior that Elliott felt made it look like a turn-of-the-century Pullman car.

He'd had some contact with Soviet authorities since accompanying his father to the Teheran conference. Toward the end of his service in Europe, he had been sent to Russia to help design up-to-date landing fields for Soviet military planes, and, mired in his wartime marital woes, had briefly thought about going to live in the U.S.S.R. after peace broke out. And right after FDR's death, Stalin's representatives had made a secret contact with Elliott to demand that their doctors be allowed to examine his father's body. He had turned them down then and discovered now why Stalin had made the request. He had been convinced that "Churchill and his Gang" had poisoned FDR and would try to do the same thing to him in order to take over the postwar world.

While in Moscow, Elliott had an audience with the Soviet Premier. Midway through their conversation, he noticed that Stalin was preparing a response before the translator finished with the question. He asked him if he spoke English, and Stalin, who had previously denied it, admitted that he did. Then Elliott observed that this must have given him an advantage at Teheran and Yalta and Stalin replied that it did, adding emphatically, "and I needed every advantage I could get!"

As his trip was coming to an end, Elliott attended a cocktail party the Soviets gave in his honor. Somewhat in his cups and unaware that American reporters were present, he began to hold forth on international affairs and was overheard to say, as he became carried away by his own enthusiasm, that he believed there was as much freedom in the Soviet Union as in the United States; and that he felt the Soviets had never broken their word in postwar dealings, while the United States and Great Britain had been systematically violating pledges made at Yalta and Potsdam. After reporting this conversation, *Time* magazine observed tartly: "The Russians and their admirers in the United States were completely delighted."

Back home more contempt was heaped on Elliott, who was once again portrayed as the Roosevelts' black sheep. Yet in fact he was not the only one in the family to see the Truman administration as having strayed from the "liberal" FDR heritage. In Los Angeles, one of Jimmy's first postwar political efforts, as he gathered support to run for statewide office, was to head the Independent Citizens Committee of the Arts, Sciences and Professions, later revealed as a communist front organization. Even after leaving this group, Jimmy continued to attack the Truman administration's responses to the Soviets' hardening line and joined with Elliott and Franklin Jr. in an attempt to draft Eisenhower as the Democrats' presidential candidate in 1948, an effort that led Truman to corner him during a campaign swing to California and give him a dressing-down: "Here I am trying to do everything I can to carry out your father's policies. You've got no business trying to pull the rug out from under me!"

Eleanor too had qualms about the administration's foreign policy. In clashes with the Soviets at the organizing assembly of the United Nations in London in 1946 she strenuously defended the West but nonetheless admitted privately that she had trouble believing Stalin was as evil as some of her diplomatic colleagues claimed. After a debate on the fate of the one million postwar refugees in Europe in which the brutal Soviet position for forced repatriation to country of origin was argued by Andrei Vishinski, she commented about the man who had been Stalin's prosecutor at the Moscow Purge trials, "Mr. Vishinsky really isn't any different from any of the communists I used to meet in the American Youth Congress."

Eleanor believed, as she made clear to Elliott, that the Cold War might have been avoided if she had been allowed to sit down with Stalin right after FDR's death, and, as her husband's stand-in, make "the first moves toward mutual trust." She was so uncomfortable with anti-Soviet views that when Churchill came to Hyde Park in 1946 to lay a wreath on FDR's grave after giving his Iron Curtain speech at Fulton, Missouri, she began her welcoming speech to him by saying pointedly, "No matter how much any of us may differ at times with the ideas which Mr. Churchill may hold. . . ."

Yet, partly because of her prewar experiences with the American Youth Congress and other such groups, Eleanor was under no illusions about domestic communists. ("Because I have experienced the deception of the American communists," she said, "I will not trust them.") Along with Franklin Jr. she was at the founding conference of Americans for Democratic Action, a group formed to hammer out the principles for "an American non communist left." She was initially sympathetic to Henry Wallace's policy split with Truman, saying of her old friend when he left the cabinet in 1946 that he was "peculiarly fitted to carry on the ideals which were close to my husband's heart." But while she was scarcely more enthusiastic about the beginnings of the policy to contain the U.S.S.R. than Wallace himself, in the end she was unable to support him in 1948 because of the domination of his campaign by communists.

And in time, her experiences at the United Nations would make her realize that the U.S.S.R. was "nearly always obstructionist" and that it had "an expansionist program and somewhere it had to be stopped." By 1949 she stated sadly but emphatically, "The Cold War must be won." It was this sentiment that led Stalin's propagandists to denounce her as "a garrulous, feeble old woman consumed by anti-Soviet fever."

While Eleanor and her children were part of a drama of gossip and expectation that occasionally took on international overtones, their Oyster Bay cousins were fading from view, completing the long withdrawal from public life that had begun in the 1930s. It was a recessional symbolized by the passing of Edith in 1948.

In the years since TR's death in 1919 she had been a keeper of the flame and also a symbol of duty for her children as they pursued their father's ideals. She had emerged from the war frail and aged, having lost two more sons. Barely able to take care of herself, her memory failing, she had called members of the family together at Sagamore in 1946, showed them through the house, and encouraged them all to carry away some small memento. Depending on her daughter, Ethel, who had come to function even more than before as the family anchor, Edith had spent her last days burning a lifetime of letters from TR. At her death in 1948, however, there was still one packet on her nightstand, love letters so dear to her that she was unable to bring herself to destroy them.

The tragedies that now afflicted the Oyster Bay families were private ones with no implications for the state of the nation. An example was Kermit's troubled son Dirck who had never managed to escape the riptide of his father's decline. He went to Oxford after the war and studied there with Lord David Cecil, eventually graduating with high honors. Yet he was rootless and disturbed, never able to make good on his promise. He wandered around Europe, cultivating a brush mustache and wearing a waistcoat and pince-nez in imitation of TR. In 1951, he was arrested in Spain for making a homosexual advance to a young man in a hotel and expelled from the country. Eventually he returned to the United States and, in what was euphemistically termed "a household accident," committed suicide at the age of twenty-eight in 1953 at his mother, Belle's, house in an event that was largely ignored by the press.

Dirck's death came the same year that a restored Sagamore Hill was dedicated by the Theodore Roosevelt Association and opened to the public with President Eisenhower and other dignitaries in attendance. Belle complained bitterly to Ethel, who was in charge of the ceremonies, that Kermit's family had been slighted in terms of seating and tickets, and threatened to boycott the event before finally being mollified. For Alice, Archie, and Ethel, the surviving children of TR, it was a moment when the house of their youth was transformed from the seat of family life into a national monument commemorating a time that was now time past.

Rather than producing a sense of failure, this transition was accompanied by a sense of relief among family members. Politics had become an onerous responsibility. Ted's son Theodore III ("Teddy") came back from the war feeling that he should pick up the burden of the family's political destiny. After joining his father's brokerage house in Philadelphia and becoming active in Republican Party circles, he was appointed to a vacant seat as Pennsylvania State Secretary of Commerce. Because of the dynastic name, he was automatically regarded as a contender for higher office. But the prospect filled him with dread, and at one point he came to his mother and said, "You know, I literally get sick to my stomach when I have to get up and give a political speech." Understanding that this was a veiled request for permission to lead the family toward anonymity, Ted's widow, Eleanor, replied, "Well, for heaven's sake, don't do it any more." Teddy quit.

One of Ted's daughters-in-law was once denied permission to cash a check because a shopkeeper mistakenly thought she was Elliott's wife. But for the most part the two branches of the family were no longer in each other's way. With the Oyster Bay group's retreat from the limelight, the long competition seemed to be over. There was no great political division. In fact there were crossovers on both sides. John Roosevelt finally made public his membership in the Republican Party and Belle became an even more active Democrat.

Those who studied the Roosevelts closely, however, discerned one remaining area of conflict. It was an intellectual one and it centered on the Cold War.

While Eleanor and some of her family saw FDR's liberal legacy as having been sullied by an aggressive competition with the Soviets, the sons of Archie, Kermit, and Ted saw the Cold War as their generation's call to duty. As in the case of their fathers in two prior hot wars, they volunteered for service in the trenches, except that in this case the front line was the CIA and the shadowy world of espionage where the two antagonists did their fighting largely out of sight of the rest of the world.

Archie Jr.'s first steps toward intelligence work, although he hadn't known it at the time, had come in 1939 when he fought the attempts of the communist-dominated American Youth Congress to keep the Soviet Union from being censured for its brutal occupation of Finland. Small and unathletic yet tough-minded with strong convictions, he had been a distinguished linguist at Harvard whose selection as a Rhodes Scholar was postponed and then canceled by the war. He had served in the war in military intelligence and afterward was recruited by "Wild Bill" Donovan (who used his strong connections with the Oyster Bay Roosevelts to establish a sort of employment agency among them) for the OSS.

In Iran in 1947, Archie Jr. studied Middle Eastern languages and watched Soviet attempts to penetrate the infrastructure of the country. He grew a beard so that he would fit in better in Teheran, but found that when he returned home to Oyster Bay he was ridiculed for "trying to look mysterious." He also had to deal with his father. Archie had become increasingly anticommunist and pro-McCarthy after the war and irritated him by making comments such as, "Owen Lattimore is the number one Soviet agent in the U.S." As Archie Jr. said later on, "I knew that Lattimore was a sympathizer but not much more than that, certainly not the number one Soviet agent, but even if I had been able to explain the facts to my father they wouldn't have changed his mind."

His career in the CIA would take him to Beirut, Lebanon, where he was chief of station. Next he went to the Middle East section of the Voice of America because of his proficiency in languages. In the 1950s and 1960s he was a runner of agents in Turkey and Spain, engaging his Soviet opposite numbers directly.

Ultimately he wrote about his experiences in the game of cat-and-mouse that had him scrambling to alert at potential flashpoints such as the Berlin Blockade and the Cuban Missile Crisis in *A Lust for Knowing*. In this book he issued what amounted to a credo for all of his Roosevelt generation who served in the CIA: "[The intelligence officer] must believe in his society, his country and its form of government. . . . [He] must not only know whose side he is on but have a deep conviction that it is the right one."

Archie Jr. had hoped to be head of the Middle East Section. But in this region he always played second fiddle to his cousin Kim. The eldest child of Kermit and Belle, Kim had been present at the creation of the spy corps that would evolve into the CIA. One of Donovan's cloak-and-dagger men during the war, he had worked for the OSS in Italy after a transfer from his first assignment in Cairo and had been scheduled to parachute into Yugoslavia to help organize the resistance until Tito's partisans took control.

As the war was winding down, Kim had been involved in a serious jeep accident and suffered head injuries that would require a lengthy recuperation and leave him scarred for life. During his year-long convalescence, he thought about his time in Cairo and the importance of the Arabs in the postwar world and wrote a series of articles espousing the cause of Arab nationalism for *Collier's* and *Harper's,* which formed the nucleus of a later book, *Arabs, Oil and History*.

Although not the linguist that Kermit had been, Kim had some of his father's literary abilities and had inherited a full share of his appetite for the exotic. Stationed in the Middle East when he returned to the CIA during the postwar era, he "went native," smoking opium and disappearing for long periods into the folkways of the area. He used his famous name to hobnob with opinion-makers and formed some deep friendships with leaders in the region, particularly people around the young Shah of Iran, who was walking a political tightrope in an effort to establish his right to lead his country.

Rotated back to Washington in the early 1950s, Kim became an ally of the peculiar James Jesus Angleton, who had risen to the top of counterespionage in the Agency and whose conviction—some would call it an obsession—that the Agency had been penetrated by a high-level mole would eventually make him a legend and lead the CIA into a destructive identity crisis.

He and Angleton grew particularly suspicious about the behavior of another Kim, Kim Philby, who was stationed in Washington as liaison between British intelligence and the CIA. During Philby's stay in the United States, Roosevelt and Angleton noticed that Guy Burgess, another British intelligence officer in Washington, had begun staying at his house. And Burgess, as Roosevelt later said, had been distinguishing himself for several months by making careless remarks, after getting drunk at parties, about how he and his friend Donald McLean were secretly working for the Russians.

Kim Philby managed to get out of Washington before the suspicions of Roosevelt and Angleton became decisive. And he escaped from the clutches of British intelligence before it could be revealed that he was the highest ranking and most strategically placed Soviet double agent in the Cold War. But in their brief brush, Kim Philby had acquired a healthy respect for Kim Roosevelt, describing him later on from exile in Moscow as "a courteous, soft spoken Easterner with impeccable social connections. . . . In fact the last person you would expect to be up to his neck in dirty tricks."

Kim's dirtiest trick ranked close to Philby's own treason against the West as one of the great espionage coups of the Cold War. It came in Iran after Dr. Mohammed Mossadegh, masquerading as a nationalist when he came to power as the country's premier, began to make common cause with Iranian communists and a growing alliance with the Soviets. The British were alarmed at the prospect of Mossadegh's nationalization of the Anglo-Iranian Oil Company; Kim convinced CIA chief Allen Dulles and his brother John Foster Dulles, secretary of state, to be concerned by the prospect of eventual Soviet control of the Persian Gulf. After drafting a plan for the removal of Mossadegh, code-named Ajax, he presented it to the Dulles brothers and got a go-ahead.

Just as the effort to bring down Mossadegh was about to begin, Kim got a kidney stone and had to be operated on. (The Agency supplied a nurse with top secret clearance lest he mutter classified information while under anesthesia.) As soon as he recovered from the operation, he resumed preparations for what he would later call his "counter coup" in Iran.

Working under the code name Rainmaker and using a pseudonym on his passport, Kim crossed the Iranian border in July 1953 and began to put the pieces of the plot in place. He found a Teheran so full of U.S. and Soviet agents, each side working to get its own Iranians in control, that one foreign correspondent said that the Americans and Russians ought to share a large apartment and save time and money from keeping each other under surveillance.

After a final conference with Kim, the Shah flew out of the country in August so that he could deny complicity in what was to come. Two weeks later, amidst the sounds (as one observer quipped) of ignorant armies clashing by night, Mossadegh was in flight and the pro-Western forces were in control of the country. With the Shah returning to head the government, Kim sent a jaunty telegram to the Dulles brothers in Washington: "Love and kisses from the team."

On his way back to the United States after pulling off his counter-coup, Kim stopped off in England to see Winston Churchill, who was just then recovering from a minor stroke. The British leader, who warmly remembered the first Kermit Roosevelt's gesture of solidarity in joining the British Army at the beginning of World War II, insisted that Kim tell him the entire story of the action in Iran even though he occasionally drifted off to sleep during the conversation, forcing himself back awake intermittently to pick up the narrative. When Kim finished Churchill told him, "If I had been but a few years younger, I would have liked nothing better than to have served under you in this great venture."

If the Oyster Bay branch had successes in this invisible war waged by the CIA, however, they also suffered casualties. One of them was Ted's son Quentin.

Along with his brother Cornelius, who served in the technological branch of the CIA, Quentin had been involved in the Agency since the end of the war. In 1945, he was transferred from the European theater to China (just as Ted had been promised by the OSS after Normandy) and had worked as a liaison officer there between the U.S. army and high-echelon Chinese leaders.

When the war ended, Quentin came home and took a temporary job with Pan American Airways. Because of his wartime experiences and his reputation as a Sinologist, he returned to China in 1948 with his wife, Frances, and their three little girls to head China National Aviation, Pan Am's Chinese affiliate. Quentin was also working for the CIA.

Since it arranged all official passenger and freight flights in the country, the airline gave him an overview of the situation in China. His job was also the perfect cover, allowing him to help arrange airlifts of food to cities besieged by Mao's forces. In 1949, during the communists' final push against the disintegrating forces of Chiang Kai-shek, Quentin was on a routine commercial flight from Shanghai to Hong Kong. Part of the flight plan involved passing over communist territory and using communist air controllers. When his plane crashed into the mountains, killing all aboard, it was officially classed as an accident, although his wife, Frances, also working with the CIA, was convinced that the communists had deliberately given wrong flight information in order to kill her husband.

With Shanghai about to fall, Frances had no time to try to do anything about Quentin's death. Her brother-in-law Cornelius happened to be in China too and he helped her and her three little girls get back to America. Without a home of their own, they went to stay temporarily at Old Orchard with Quentin's mother and wound up remaining there for the next ten years, a small society of women practicing the arts of survival and self-sufficiency.

*   *   *

Unlike the Oyster Bay cousins, FDR's sons had no reticence about making a bid for political power. It was what their upbringing had taught them to do. And for a time it seemed that their ambition had a kind of inevitability about it. By 1948 news magazines were speculating about how Jimmy and Franklin Jr. had established themselves, respectively, in California and New York as potential candidates for governor and thus appeared to have the Democratic Party in a pincers movement. Outsiders assumed that there was a detailed blueprint for family power similar to the one that would later exist among the Kennedys, the dynasty that succeeded the Roosevelts. But in fact there was only the magic name and an ongoing and often bitter struggle in the family's smoke-filled rooms over who should have the right-of-way in using it.

Jimmy felt that he, as the oldest, should be allowed to go first. Politics was, as he said, in his blood. His earliest memories were of Albany, when his father was serving in the state legislature and he had toddled around the city watching dray horses pull their cargo. He also pointed out in family meetings that he was the one son to have served an apprenticeship to FDR in the White House, devoting himself to politics for two years before his divorce from Betsey Cushing precipitated his California exile.

Franklin Jr., on the other hand, said that the family should be "a democracy of talent," an allusion to his acknowledged superior personal skills as the Roosevelts' "sunshine boy."

The rest of them sniped from the sidelines at both brothers. Elliott wrote Anna about Jimmy's second wife, Romelle, who was against his running for office. "[She] is a very ambitious little biddy. Right now she doesn't think Jimmie can pull it off and seems scared that failure might hurt her security, but if he makes the grade watch her take the bow!" Meanwhile, John wrote Anna that watching the maneuvering of Franklin Jr., who had finally divorced the increasingly disturbed Ethel Du Pont and remarried, was similar to "watching Sammy run" in the Budd Schulberg novel. He went on to note with gleeful anticipation, "Brothers Jimmie and F Jr. are going to collide in their ambitions one of these days if they are both successful. . . ."

At one level the competition was amusing: at family get-togethers, all the boys would sit around doing imitations of FDR and arguing lightheartedly about whose voice was most like his. But at another level the quarrels were quite serious, causing a backbiting that frequently leaked into the public domain. Eleanor eventually tried to control the divisiveness by sending a directive to all her children: "I want you to agree that

you will never say anything about each other or make any kind of
remarks that can be so construed and you will never allow people in
your presence to say anything that will reflect on the integrity and
character of the family." But this admonition did little good.

Franklin Jr. was the first one to take office, winning a congressional
seat in New York in a special election in 1949 and putting himself on the
first rung of the Roosevelt ladder that had twice led to Albany and
ultimately to Washington. The following year, in an effort to jump over
his younger brother's achievement, Jimmy announced that he was challenging popular incumbent Earl Warren for governor of California.

Jimmy had worked hard—taking the job of state Democratic Party
chairman and solidifying the Hollywood connections he had made before the war. But he acknowledged that whatever appeal he had came
from his parents when he begged his mother to come to California to
appear at his fund-raising events. Eleanor also acted as an ambassador to
Truman, who was still miffed about Jimmy's attempt to draft Eisenhower in 1948. She even threatened to resign from her job at the United
Nations when the President endorsed Helen Gahagan Douglas, who
was running for the Senate against Richard Nixon, but ignored Jimmy.

Yet Eleanor was not particularly close to her eldest son and saw what
he could not see for himself: that he did not have it as a political figure.
The fact that he was running against her advice, his son, Jimmy Jr.,
believed, was responsible for the "cloud" that hung over his family's
annual summer visit to Hyde Park in 1950. Eleanor was right: Jimmy
was swamped by Earl Warren in the November election.

Jimmy went to the 1952 Democratic convention and after supporting
Tennessee Senator Estes Kefauver through the primaries, agreed to give
a seconding speech for his mother's candidate, Adlai Stevenson. Franklin Jr., meanwhile, had lined up behind the presidential bid of New
York's Averell Harriman. In giving his seconding speech for Harriman,
he pointed out in a sarcastic aside that his brother Jimmy, who had just
spoken, had never been elected to office while he, Franklin Jr., was in
the Congress.

The political squabbles gave the public a hint of a family that, far from
being an invincible juggernaut, was in serious disarray. Even Anna,
who, more than her brothers, wanted members of the family to love
each other and respect the memory of their father, was affected. She and
her husband, John Boettiger, had also allowed themselves to be caught
up in the notion of a generational seizure of power. At the war's end,
they left Hearst's *Seatttle Post-Intelligencer* and bought a small weekly

shopping paper in Phoenix with the idea of turning it into a major daily and creating a beachhead for liberal ideas in a conservative hinterland. But despite huge infusions of money from Bernard Baruch, Henry Morgenthau, and other family supporters, the *Arizona Times* proved to be a disaster. Anna and John were unable to generate ad revenues and didn't have enough capital to hire an adequate staff. A good reporter who had no talent for business and who had been disoriented by attempts to become an important figure in an important family, Boettiger was devastated by the costly failure. He began seeing other women and finally, as the paper ceased publication, he took off, leaving Anna holding the bag of debts accumulated over two erratic years.

It was a nightmare time for her. She told friends that everything had been going downhill since her days as her father's private secretary and chief aide. (Nonetheless, she blamed FDR in some degree for the failure of her marriage because of his insistence that Boettiger enlist in the army, the event, she believed, that had begun his personal disintegration.) Now, faced with abandonment and financial ruin, she became listless and ill, losing weight and becoming so weak she was barely able to get out of bed. At first it seemed an emotional breakdown. Then for several weeks during the spring of 1949, doctors tried without success to diagnose what was wrong. Finally specialists discovered that she had contracted coccidiomycosis, desert fever.

Nearly destitute, Anna teetered on the edge of personal and financial disaster. Eleanor rushed to her side and the illness became the occasion for a partial healing of the rift between them. Writing in his new capacity as interpreter of their mother's thoughts, Elliott assured Anna that she should not feel bad about accepting the help: "Mother would like to knit us all together as a family united, united in good times as in bad. If she helps you today, maybe you'll help her some other day." Then he added a typical afterthought that brought the generous sentiment down to a more prosaic level: "If Mother didn't do this for you, she'd probably do it for someone like a Lash or Gurevitch [sic]."

Actually, Elliott was in no position to offer anyone else in the family advice. His own personal life was becoming unraveled once again and he was headed for yet another marital breakup. Bright and exceedingly ambitious, Faye had wanted Elliott to outshine all of his brothers by being a true *Roosevelt*. (She even talked about him running for political office.) This was exactly the kind of summons he had always rejected in the past. This pressure came at a time when Elliott was feeling generally unanchored, having lost interest in Val-Kill Farms once he realized that it would not lead to the apocalyptic financial success he had always envisioned for himself.

He became by his own admission "a poor excuse for a husband." Seeking to get away from him, Faye began spending time with her acting friends in New York. Elliott followed her there, haunting the city's nightspots and taking up with chorines. He was drinking heavily and, by his own admission, ignoring Faye. Soon she turned her attention back to her career, and the private eye Elliott hired to follow her caught her in bed with another man.

In November 1948 Faye slashed her wrists during a family Thanksgiving celebration at Val-Kill and was rushed to a hospital. Nine months later she filed for divorce after telling reporters, "It's not easy voluntarily to give up being the daughter-in-law of Eleanor Roosevelt."

Eleanor was stricken by this development. Cornering Elliott, she apologized for having failed him.

"None of you children experienced security," she insisted when he tried to brush off her concern. "You couldn't ever count on a father and a mother. All you could possibly see in me was the disciplinarian and bad tempered too. Father was the one who could comfort all of you, and he fell ill before your eleventh birthday. . . ."

Elliott said that actually he'd had a rather good time during his youth, particularly the days he'd spent in the West. But Eleanor insisted on blaming herself for what had become of his life:

"Where was the *guidance* you should have had from father and equally from me? Anna and Jimmy suffered just as you did. *Nobody* was willing to devote the time to provide you with a proper upbringing. I did begin to realize my mistakes and made an effort with Franklin and Johnny. But it wasn't enough. . . ."

In the middle of her efforts to deal with the political bickering of Jimmy and Franklin Jr., Anna's health problems, and Elliott's marital woes, Eleanor was badly shaken by what seemed the final blow. It was the progressive deterioration of former son-in-law John Boettiger. He had stayed in touch with Eleanor after divorcing Anna and remarrying. She had watched from afar as he tried desperately to stabilize his life. But he could not take hold. ("I'm too big for the reporting jobs I started out with," he candidly explained his situation, "and not big enough for the jobs I had when I was part of the Roosevelts.") He had gone from job to job, dragged downward by the feeling that having once been a demi-Roosevelt, it was hard to settle for anonymity again.

In October 1950, Boettiger tried to commit suicide by overdosing on sleeping pills, leaving behind the message, "I have thought this all out. I have explored every detail and this is the thing to do." Revived and put under close observation by a male nurse, he vowed to try again. And two days later he managed to get to the window of his seventh-floor room in the Weylin Hotel and jump.

The police telephoned Elliott and asked him to go to the morgue and formally identify the smashed body. When he talked to Eleanor about the suicide, she was deeply depressed, flaying herself because of the desperate letters from her former son-in-law that she had brushed off in the past months.

After Boettiger's death (later on, Ethel Du Pont, Franklin Jr.'s ex-wife, would also commit suicide) and Elliott's divorce from Faye, Eleanor became obsessed with what she began referring to as "the problem." At a musicale staged by Belle Roosevelt, she met a psychiatrist named Dr. Lawrence Kubie. In the course of the evening, she questioned him closely and then asked if he would come to Val-Kill for a weekend so they could continue the conversation. At that meeting, she talked with him in greater depth about the family's past and how each of her children had been affected by their upbringing. Kubie later told Eleanor's biographer Joseph Lash that at times during that conversation, she had seemed on the verge of a breakthrough understanding the role of the dark forces of the unconscious in human behavior, but each time had pulled back. In the end, she could not agree that anything counted except for the individual will. She had quarried a life for herself out of the most difficult circumstances; others could do the same if they were determined enough.

In her discussions with the psychiatrist, Eleanor had said that she felt Elliott particularly had been "destroyed" by his upbringing, which was why she had continued to devote such attention to him. She was now at the high point of her public career, deeply involved in helping draft the United Nations' Declaration of Human Rights. But she was also focused on her relationship with Elliott and apparently convinced, according to a close family friend, that if she could just get him established it would release her once and for all from the guilt she felt about the family's early days.

Keeping a diminished version of their operations going at Val-Kill, Elliott began to spend more time in Manhattan. Eleanor gave up her apartment in Greenwich Village and rented a suite at the Park Sheraton.

She would take the one bedroom; Elliott could have a daybed in the living room. She agreed to let him represent her in her public life and they began an organization called Roosevelt Enterprises. The exact nature of the business was not specified, but those close to the family saw what was happening: having sold off Hyde Park, Elliott was now going to sell his mother.

It was not simply exploitation. Elliott demonstrated immediately that he could do some good for Eleanor's career. Although nearly seventy years old and beneficiary of trusts left by her father and her husband, she still had to make money, in large part because of the constant needs of her children. She had recently completed her second book of memoirs, *This I Remember,* but her editors were not particularly enthusiastic about it, feeling that in comparison to *This Is My Story* it was dry and uninteresting. But Elliott would not accept the verdict. Acting as his mother's agent, he convinced *McCall's* to pay $150,000 for serial rights to the book and additionally to run a regular column of advice from Eleanor for which they would pay another $3,000 a month. He got her better rates for the syndicated column "My Day."

Elliott understood far better than Eleanor herself did how marketable her growing reputation was. He got ABC to buy a weekly television show featuring her having Sunday afternoon chats sitting on a living room couch with the likes of J. Robert Oppenheimer and Albert Einstein and talking about world problems. Acting as her producer, he began sending out telegrams in his mother's name inviting top entertainers and political figures and even European royalty to come on the program. ("I was appalled to learn that a telegram using my name had been sent to Mrs. Truman," Eleanor had to reprimand him at one point. "I must know what messages are being sent in my name!")

Elliott also arranged to produce a daily radio show for her, forty-five minutes of talk and advice. Eleanor was glad to do it, not only because it gave her an opportunity to popularize ideas that were important to her, but also because she knew that it helped her son continue to live in the style to which he was accustomed. Explaining the new venture to Anna, she said, "Anything to help Elliott with his money problems!"

It was almost as if Elliott, single again, had decided to romance his mother. In addition to squiring her around New York and managing her career, he made her laugh and played possessive little jokes on her such as making one of his father's favorite drinks of brown sugar and orange juice, which disguised the two jiggers of rum, and then solemnly insisting that there was no liquor in it as she drank it down.

Eleanor was excited by this closeness with one of her children—the first time her maternal feelings had really been requited—and also proud of the success of Roosevelt Enterprises. Always happiest when her hours were overbooked, she wrote Anna in California that she was now working at the United Nations by day and recording her radio shows at night. "We have our 12 sponsors and . . . in about three weeks you should get the show on the [west] coast."

When listeners tuned in the radio show, they heard not only advice from Eleanor but also commercials delivered by Elliott himself. He told the audience that "Mother eats" a certain kind of soup (more information could be obtained by "dropping a card to the Roosevelts"); that "Mother uses" a certain kind of bobby pin; and that "Mother washes" with a certain brand of soap. In its review *Billboard* said that what the show proved above all else was that "a boy's best friend is his mother." There were even more negative reviews from within the Roosevelt family, as Franklin Jr. scornfully dismissed as disguised greed his brother's rationale that he was "bringing Mother's voice and educational ability to the American people."

Oblivious to how her special relationship with Elliott looked to the other children, Eleanor made him her ambassador to the rest of the family. He flew to California to see how Anna was doing and reported back that not only was she recovering from her illness, but she was in love again, this time with a Veterans Administration physician named James Halsted. While in the Los Angeles area he also saw Jimmy, who was making money in another insurance business, and John, who had graduated from working in a department store to running his own financial firm. But the youngest of the brothers was not doing particularly well.

After conferring with Eleanor, Elliott invited John to come to the East in 1952. He was made an equal partner in Roosevelt Enterprises and given half of the Val-Kill property that remained after Elliott's land sales, about three hundred acres.

Elliott began to date a woman named Minnewa Bell, whom he had met through John and John's wife, Anne, in Southern California. Tall and lithe, with austere features that justified her Indian name, Minnewa came from money, her father, Alphonso Bell, having developed Bel Air in Southern California. Elliott liked her plainspokenness, especially in comparison to what he was now calling Faye Emerson's "staginess." There was also an excitingly clandestine quality to the romance. Minnewa was in the process of divorcing her first husband and her son Rex always remembered crouching with her on the floorboard of a car driven by a chauffeur so that they would not be seen by detectives his father had hired to keep her away from Elliott. After a wild ride they stopped and Elliott loomed up in the night to open the car door for them and bring them into the light and warmth of his brother John's Pasadena home.

In a stunning feat of courtship, Elliott drove the power boat he had bought with his profits from Eleanor's radio and television programs all the way from New York to Florida, where Minnewa had a winter home. "This seemed to cinch the deal," as one observer said. They were married in the spring of 1951.

Elliott and Minnewa lived most of the time at Top Cottage, and John and his wife Anne moved into Stone Cottage. It was like a family compound. Eleanor had moved into the converted workshop and everyone used her place as the center of family life, the grandchildren padding over to use her swimming pool and her sons and their wives having dinner together with her in her dining room. For a brief moment it seemed that she had finally created the utopian family community she had always imagined residing at Val-Kill.

But there were warning signs about the impermanence of this arrangement. Much as she had suffered under Sara's strictures, for instance, Eleanor nonetheless sometimes badgered John's wife, Anne, on issues like whether or not the children should be required to attend church. And in the 1952 presidential contest, when John and Anne supported Eisenhower over Eleanor's protégé Adlai Stevenson, Eleanor humiliated the two of them when Stevenson came to Val-Kill for dinner by seating them at the children's table, well away from her friend. When the results of the election were in, John rubbed his mother's nose in her defeat: "You just don't know how to pick the right horse."

There was also building tension between the brothers primarily over what to do with Val-Kill. But there was also a personal dimension. John's wife, Anne, was still a friend of Faye Emerson's and frequently invited her to Stone Cottage, causing Minnewa to become jealous and setting the two couples at each other's throats.

All this time, Elliott, in an effort to impress his new wife, was "going through money like water," as his sister, Anna, said later on. When Eleanor gave him title to the family's Campobello vacation property, he sold it to oilman Armand Hammer for $12,000. Things that she or John loaned to him he disposed of. He began selling off Val-Kill furniture made during the days of Eleanor's partnership with Marion Dickerman and Nancy Cook, some of which was now considered collectible. Other items of value that had once been in the Big House at Hyde Park were sold to the curious as Rooseveltiana.

At first Eleanor defended him. In the words of one relative, "She did not think the Val-Kill or Roosevelt things were all that important, and she wanted the boys to make money." She felt herself to be on shaky grounds to reproach any of them, knowing that she and FDR had both set an example of self-gratification for the children. But then she was jolted into an appreciation of the magnitude of the problem when she discovered one day that Elliott had sold, without her knowledge, a tea set dating back to the time of the Revolutionary War that she had inherited from her Livingston forebears.

The arguments that now echoed at Val-Kill were nasty and loud, political arguments and personal ones. Eleanor and John squabbled over national politics; Minnewa and Anne squabbled over sexual politics; and Elliott and John over family politics concerning the division of the remaining Hyde Park property. (The two brothers once came near a physical confrontation and when Eleanor tried to separate them they both turned on her.) Anna, Jimmy, and Franklin Jr. were not present for many of the confrontations, but they worried from afar about whether or not their interests were being protected.

Holidays and family gatherings became difficult. One of Eleanor's grandchildren later recalled Thanksgivings and Christmases at Val-Kill with Eleanor's house "burstingly full" of large Roosevelt boys with booming voices and broods of children by various wives. The celebrations always began well. Eleanor had relaxed her attitude toward liquor enough to have a blonde Dubonnet during the cocktail hour. Then she would lead the way to the dinner table, standing to offer two toasts—one to the President of the United States and the other to family members who were not present. Yet there was also a "shadow side" to these gatherings. The children would be bundled off to bed soon after dinner. And as they lay there trying to sleep, the would hear the clashing sounds of "conflict and competition" as family elders turned on each other.

One day Eleanor read in the papers that Elliott had sold Top Cottage. It was the final betrayal: getting rid of the place that FDR had designed as a retreat for himself when his days in the White House were over. "She was terribly disappointed in him," said Maureen Corr, Eleanor's new secretary. "She felt that he had deceived her." She terminated Roosevelt Enterprises. She decided to phase out the television and radio programs.

Elliott accused his mother of being "disturbed, angry and disappointed" in him. She wearily replied that she was not: "You have weaknesses and I know them, but I never loved you less because I know them." She even tried to find some way to restore the relationship. But it was too late: a moment in their lives had passed.

Tony (Elliott Jr.) and Ruth Chandler, Elliott's children by Ruth Googins, had been visiting him during what turned out to be his last summer at Val-Kill and always remembered Elliott driving them back home to Fort Worth without stopping and once falling asleep at the wheel and almost rolling the car in the soft shoulder. Preparing to resume the picaresque life that had been interrupted by six fairly stable years with his mother, Elliott made plans to leave for Florida with Minnewa. Soon Eleanor named Franklin Jr. and John as executors of her will, telling Jimmy that she had excluded Elliott because she no longer trusted him. As Elliott himself said later on, from this point onward, he and his mother were never really close again.

This emotional transition in Eleanor's family was paralleled by a sea change in the outer world. A reaction against the FDR era could be seen in the resurgent conservatism of the 1950s and in the emergence of Senator Joseph McCarthy. It could be seen, for that matter, in the Roosevelt's own extended family. Following other onetime Progressives who were traumatized by what they regarded as the New Deal's assault on individualism, Archie was now a hardened right-winger, writing broadsides about socialism and eventually joining the John Birch Society, and even holding a testimonial for Roy Cohn. Alice too was at times an ultraconservative, although when she met Joseph McCarthy at a social function and he greeted her by her first name, she quickly put him in his place: "The trash man may call me Alice and so can the clerk in the store and the policeman on the beat. But *you* may not call me Alice."

Eleanor too was caught in this political undertow. After Eisenhower's election, she was not asked to stay on at the United Nations, less for political disagreements than because the new President was annoyed at an unflattering comment he heard that she'd made about his wife's drinking. Eleanor would continue to be an unofficial ambassador for the United States in her travels abroad, but hold no more high government positions.

If the dream of a reunified family centered around Val-Kill was now gone, the hope of a Roosevelt renaissance in politics was also evaporating. By 1954, Franklin Jr., who had served three terms in the House, was ready to make his move for higher office. And in California, Jimmy was also going to run again—this time for Congress. The problem was that his second marriage had failed and as part of divorce proceedings, his second wife, Romelle, had made public a letter Jimmy had written her in 1945 in which he admitted having had adulterous affairs with nine women during the first years of their marriage. (Eleanor had known about the couple's problems then: the same year as Jimmy's letters were written, 1945, she had gotten in touch with Anna and asked her to find out if Jimmy was beating Romelle.)

Jimmy replied weakly to his wife's revelations by saying that Romelle had been "insecure" in the mid-1940s and he had signed the confession of infidelity only to reassure her and keep her from embarrassing his father at a crucial moment in the war effort. Eleanor had loaned him $100,000 against his inheritance with the proviso that he not run for office until the debt was paid. Jimmy gave Romelle a settlement of $75,000 to buy her silence and then announced his candidacy.

Anna's new husband, Dr. James Halsted, although still something of an outsider in the family, was expressing the sentiments of others when he begged Jimmy to drop out of the congressional race and get his house in order: "Your obsession to be elected to Congress . . . will aid the forces of McCarthy because you [open] your father's name and his administration . . . to nefarious attacks resulting from your personal difficulties. . . . You may subconsciously believe that your rehabilitation is only through the ballot and public appeal, but don't forget . . . that people will give their approval . . . only because you are your father's son."

Jimmy replied by return mail that he was running because he had to. Politics, he said, was "the only thing for which I have any fundamental training."

Still scarred by memories of John Boettiger's quiet desperation, Eleanor relaxed her displeasure with Elliott enough to ask him to go to California to make sure that Jimmy was not suicidal. Elliott flew to Los Angeles and wrote her his evaluation of his older brother: "He has embedded in his soul the desire to compete with Father and now with Franklin. . . ." At about the same time, Franklin Jr. was writing Anna to say that their only alternative with Jimmy was to remain silent: "To oppose him would be disloyal. To support him would be hypocritical."

Franklin told his sister that he didn't feel that the bad publicity surrounding Jimmy would hurt his own bid for governor of New York.

This was not an accurate analysis: the prewar perception of the Roosevelt boys as pampered and irresponsible remained in the public consciousness during the postwar era and each one of them was burdened with the others' failings. But a more serious difficulty for Franklin Jr. than the spillover from Jimmy's misdeed was his own character flaws.

He had established a poor record in the House because, as Jimmy later said, he considered the job "beneath him." In his three terms, Franklin Jr. had been one of the least effective members, earning the contempt of colleagues and of many constituents alike for his laziness and absenteeism. Equally damaging, he had not played ball with party bosses—partly out of principle but also because of his assumption that his name put him beyond their reach. As he made his move for higher office in 1954, Tammany chief Carmine DeSapio got even by steering the governor's nomination away from him to Averell Harriman. Bitterly disappointed, Franklin Jr. allowed himself to be convinced to run for attorney general in the general election. Then the bosses got their ultimate revenge by putting out the word that he should be ignored, and he lost badly to Republican Jacob Javits, running far behind Harriman and other victorious Democrats on the ticket.

Eleanor had virtually ignored Jimmy in his 1954 congressional bid, but had campaigned strongly for her younger son. Disappointed over his loss, she couldn't keep a trace of the old anti-Semitism from creeping into her evaluation of events: "F Jr. was defeated because they put a *very good Jew* against him."

Franklin Jr. would run for office again and again in the future, each time finishing further away from the victory that had once seemed assured. Ironically, however, Jimmy won his congressional seat in California. When he arrived in Washington House Speaker Sam Rayburn told him, "Don't make a fool of yourself the way your brother Franklin did. . . . Franklin wasted his time and our time and I don't want you to make the same mistake." Jimmy didn't make the same mistake, but his effectiveness was limited by revelations about his private life. He would always be a follower in Congress, considering himself lucky to keep his seat, let alone think of higher office.

Living in Miami now in Minnewa's house there, Elliott had not been much concerned with his brothers' political fortunes. He was pouring all his energy into a new scheme—organizing a chain of radio stations in Cuba for an American investment group with an eye to eventually

introducing television to the island. In 1953, he and Minnewa moved to
Havana where he worked on the plan for several months. As front man
for his investors, he finally had a summary conference with Cuban
dictator Fulgencio Batista—"short, swarthy and looking like a thug," in
Elliott's later description—who spent one part of their meeting talking
of his admiration for FDR and the other part demanding to be bought
off with a half interest in the network. Elliott refused to grant him such
a big cut and left Cuba immediately.

After this, he and Minnewa were nomadic, living their lives in year-
long segments. They built another house in Florida but never occupied
it, having decided to move to Los Angeles by the time it was completed.
They lived for a time in one of the Bell family homes in Bel Air. While
there, as Minnewa's son Rex said later on, "They did heavy partying. A
lot of times they would have games at the parties and the games would
go on and on until it was like watching *Who's Afraid of Virginia Woolf?*"

Elliott entertained his friends with knowledgeable political mono-
logues. Occasionally after a few drinks, he would climb up onto the
coffee table and deliver a riotous parody of a stump speech. In the
marathon, all-night sessions, Elliott was indefatigable, always the last
person standing.

In addition to drinking he began to chase women. ("He was just a lost
child," Minnewa said later on after they had parted, "who turned from
woman to woman for love.") To keep him away from this temptation
and to keep herself from "becoming as sunk as he was," Minnewa got
him to agree to move to a ranch she owned near Meeker, Colorado, in
1954. It was called the Bar Bell, but Elliott changed it to the Rolling R,
the name of his old ranch in Fort Worth.

He took up ranch life with the enthusiasm he displayed in all of his
new beginnings. "Elliott is in wonderful shape now and really does love
his ranch work so much," Minnewa wrote Eleanor. "Being 'just ranch-
ers' is a happy life for both of us, although it took a long time to see
that." For a while they were a happy family. Minnewa's son Rex admired Elliott because he was "a straight ahead guy" who was always
candid and also because "he seemed to know everything."

But soon he was seized again by the desire that had dogged him all his
life—to be a "big man." The West still seemed like a land of opportunity, just as it had when he was a teenager thirty years earlier fleeing his
parents' expectations. But now it was the financial opportunity rather
than the psychological one that appealed to him. He began to invest in

uranium and oil leases, putting up $200,000 to go into partnership with local entrepreneurs. Adding to Minnewa's land holdings, he conceived a grandiose plan of building a four-seasons resort—skiing in the winter and hiking in the summer and hunting and fishing in between. He bought a twin-engine Bonanza airplane so he could keep track of all the property he intended to own.

After using up all his own resources, Elliott began to run through Minnewa's money with alarming speed. Looking back on their years together later on, she remembered once sitting in the middle of the living room floor in the Colorado ranch house with what seemed to be a thousand bills all around her and not only not knowing how to pay them but not even having enough money to buy clothes, although Elliott always seemed to be standing over her saying cheerfully, "Oh, we're doing awfully well. It's just a matter of time." Unable to reconcile his optimism with her sense of their reality, Minnewa began to drink heavily.

As things got tight, Elliott hocked his plane and the Thunderbird Minnewa had bought him. When he couldn't pay an interior decorator, he settled the debt by giving the woman a "Roosevelt piano" he said had been in his family. He used his inheritance as collateral for loans and quickly spent his one fifth of the stage and screen rights for *Sunrise at Campobello*. He continued to ask Eleanor for money, causing her at one point to say in anguish, "It seems the best thing I could do for my children would be to die so they could have their inheritance from me."

Elliott later claimed that in 1958 he was so needy that he swallowed his pride and asked his estranged brother John for a $20,000 bridge loan to pay off losses he'd suffered speculating in uranium and oil. The youngest Roosevelt brother was now making good money on the East Coast, having first acquired the rights to sell confiscated German stocks of cologne and perfume and then going on to brokering the sale of Toni hair products to Revlon. Eventually he had become a vice president to Bache and Company where he had brought the pension funds account of the Teamsters. (This was a payoff from Jimmy Hoffa, Elliott later insisted, in return for John's appearances for Republican presidential candidates Eisenhower and Nixon.)

John gave Elliott the loan, but demanded that he pledge his remaining interest in the Hyde Park property as collateral. When the loan came due, Elliott, who did not have enough cash to pay his brother, assumed that John would carry the relatively trivial debt. Instead, John immediately foreclosed and then, in a moment of jubilation, exulted over his brother in front of Jimmy: "I've finally done it to Elliott! I've gotten all the Hyde Park property."

Desperate now, Elliott went to the trust department at the Bank of Colorado without Minnewa's knowledge and convinced bank officers to allow him to invade her trust funds. She was disturbed when she discovered what he had done. Yet Minnewa was like Eleanor: appalled by Elliott, yet believing that he couldn't help what he was doing. "[He and his brothers] wanted to be *somebody*," Minnewa stated later on. "Everybody *expected* them to be outstanding in every way and then to have no money. . . . Perhaps this is why Elliott didn't mind using my money. . . . He felt that he had to. He didn't expect to lose it."

Her drinking became worse, beginning early in the morning rather than at the cocktail hour. Elliott could function while drinking; she couldn't. She switched to wine, but drank two quarts a day. The ranching experiment in Colorado having failed, they bought a place in Phoenix. Minnewa was in and out of the hospital. Finally Elliott put her in a sanatorium and authorized doctors to give her electroshock therapy. While she was undergoing this treatment, he tried to get a conservatorship that would have allowed him to control all her assets. When she discovered what he was doing, it ended their relationship. As Rex Ross, Minnewa's son by her first marriage, later said, "My mother spent a lot of time after that digging through old pictures of Elliott and cutting them to pieces with scissors."

When Eleanor saw Elliott in Los Angeles at the 1960 Democratic convention where he was a delegate from Colorado pledged to John Kennedy, she was once again pushing Stevenson and was deeply suspicious of JFK because of his Catholicism and what she had regarded as his weakness in dealing with McCarthy. ("All profile and no courage," had been her bon mot about the Massachusetts senator.)

She had been disturbed at the way Franklin Jr. had allowed himself to be used by the Kennedys during the primary in West Virginia, where he had attacked Hubert Humphrey's "draft dodger" war record in letters that were sent out over his signature from Hyde Park as if posted by the dead President himself. And she was seething over what John was saying in *his* campaign appearances: "If my father were alive today he would vote for Nixon." But she was worried most of all by her middle son's new failure in matrimony. She took Elliott aside in the middle of the presidential drama and begged him to try to make another go of it with Minnewa: "All of us have feelings, you know, but in time a husband and wife get to make *allowances* for the other's faults as long as they refuse to be *selfish*."

But Elliott already had a replacement wife in the wings. It was Patricia Peabody, a thirty-eight-year-old divorcee with four children. They had met the previous winter when Patricia was chosen as the estate agent to list his Phoenix house. The first meeting was inauspicious; Patty was doing a room-by-room evaluation of the house and happened to step into the bathroom at the moment Elliott was emerging naked and dripping from the shower. "Get the hell out of here!" he growled, terrifying her. But then, after getting dressed, he came to the living room and talked with her for a long time and so flustered her by his charm that she kept calling him "Mr. Rockefeller."

The acquaintance grew as she sold the house and helped him and Minnewa buy a new one near Camelback Mountain, following Elliott's directive to find a place that would allow him to "spit down on Barry Goldwater" so literally that the Arizona senator became a close neighbor.

In response to Eleanor's efforts to bring order to his marital life, Elliott wrote her, "There is nothing you can do to alleviate my situation. Don't feel sorry for me because this is the great challenge. . . ."

Invited to JFK's inauguration, Elliott decided to make a stop first in New York so that he could introduce Patty to the family. Filled with enthusiasm about being part of the Roosevelt clan, Patty had a momentary setback when she and Elliott happened to run into Alice Longworth, whose only comment, after looking her up and down, was to shake her head and say, "I can see why Eleanor is so disappointed in you."

This dinner at Eleanor's Manhattan apartment turned out to be an even ruder introduction to the Roosevelts. Eleanor was distantly friendly, but Elliott's brothers and sister did not make an effort. Jimmy and John did not even bother to come. When Patty tried to make conversation with Anna by saying that she thought they might have met briefly when they both lived in Seattle, Anna said dismissively, "I don't remember seeing you." Approaching Franklin Jr., who had recently become the Fiat distributor for the East Coast, Patty said that one of her children was a car enthusiast. "Bring him around sometime," her new brother-in-law said without much interest, "and I'll have one of the men give him a ride."

Later on, after everyone had had a few cocktails, Franklin Jr.'s mood changed. When Elliott was occupied elsewhere, he took Patty aside and said warmly, "We'll have to get together sometime." Not getting his drift, she asked him why. "Because you're the only sister-in-law I haven't had," he replied.

Eleanor was dismayed when Elliott adopted his fifth wife's four children. Not particularly fond of Patty, she nonetheless made an effort and agreed to fly to Miami Beach to visit them in their new home there. But when Patty's children ran out onto the tarmac to meet her plane yelling, "Grand-mère!" she was horrified that they used the familiar term of her natural grandchildren. Recently Eleanor had become so hard of hearing that she'd gotten thick glasses with hearing aids embedded in them. Observers noted that whenever her new daughter-in-law came into the room and began to chatter, Eleanor would take off her glasses and sit there smiling blankly at her.

History seemed to have whiplashed the Roosevelts. The son of FDR's onetime friend and opponent was in the White House now, and FDR's son and namesake was rewarded for his service to the Kennedy campaign with the disappointing job of under secretary of commerce.* The sensation was not only of time passing, but of time doubling back upon itself.

A bit old-fashioned in the world of the 1960s, Eleanor still secured her hair into a braid every night at bedtime, got into a long gown (wool for winter and cotton for summer), and knelt beside the bed for her prayers. She reeked of garlic from the pills her young friend and physician David Gurewitsch had prescribed as an aid to memory. She had learned to enjoy food in her old age, and would eat enthusiastically enough to gain weight and then, through an exercise of that iron will, make herself lose it by going on a virtual fast. Her longtime secretary Tommy Thompson was dead now and she no longer saw that much of Lorena Hickok. She spent more time by herself, sitting in her room late at night taking care of her correspondence while records of Gregorian chants played in the background.

---

* FDR Jr. actually hoped to be secretary of the navy. According to Justin Feldman, JFK had sent Secretary of Defense–designate Robert McNamara to check him out. Going to the office Franklin Jr. maintained in his Fiat distributorship, McNamara asked to speak to him but didn't identify himself by his position in the new administration. So when Roosevelt's secretary buzzed him that "Mr. McNamara of the Ford Motor Company [where he was still technically employed] was calling, Franklin Jr. let him cool his heels in a waiting room for nearly an hour, thus killing his chances at a higher position.

The children of John, who was now the "resident son" at Hyde Park, saw Eleanor at her most informal. When she was staying at Val-Kill, they would get up and run over from Stone Cottage to have breakfast with her. They went out in the car with her, regarding this as an exciting and somewhat dangerous adventure. (In one typical maneuver, she would come to a stop at an intersection, carefully look both ways as she had been taught, stall the car, restart it, and then shoot forward without remembering to look both ways again.) On sunny days, they watched her get into her baggy black swimsuit and bathing cap, come to the edge of the pool, point toward the water with her bowed head and clasped hands, do a painful belly flop, and then swim laps in the deliberate crawl of one who had never overcome her adversary relationship with water.

For all her grandchildren (except the ones Elliott had adopted) she was "Grand-mère," a formidable, iconic figure who tried to be unassuming but couldn't help carrying a sense of history with her. Jimmy's son, James Jr., always remembered that on her annual visit to California she would start the day with hot water and lemon juice and spend a long time sitting alone and knitting in silent self-absorption except when she was reading to him and his sisters, an activity into which she poured energy and enthusiasm.

A few of the grandchildren she hardly knew. Others she took with her on the unstinting world travels that consumed her later years. For a few like Tony and Chandler, Elliott's children by Ruth Googins, she seemed to have a special affection. When Tony was going off to Andover, she took pleasure in outfitting him with proper Ivy League clothing on a shopping expedition he never forgot. And while Chandler was a teenager, Eleanor, surprisingly old-fashioned about a girl's coming of age, took pleasure in buying flatware and other items for her trousseau and in counseling her about being a debutante.

Eleanor understood that some of the chaos in her children's lives had been transmitted to their families. Not knowing how exactly to counter it, she talked constantly to her grandchildren about *un droit*—a term that meant to her something different from the French translation of "a right." It was the conscience, involvement, and, above all, the duty that goes with privilege.

The younger Roosevelt generation learned that the best avenue to Grand-mère's attention was through political and social concerns. When John's son, Haven, became involved in a Harvard project for African relief in the late 1950s, for instance, Eleanor put together a dinner of influential people for him and made a fund-raising pitch for his organization. When Franklin III came back from South Africa in 1960 galvanized by the horrors of apartheid, she spent hours with him discussing strategies for change.

For a few of them relating through politics left a bad taste. For instance, Anna's daughter Sistie never forgot being dragged off by her grandmother to a Christmas party in New York for underprivileged children at which she got the worst cold of her life and became too sick to enjoy her own holiday. But most of the grandchildren believed that such activity connected them with a Roosevelt tradition their own parents had ignored.

Eleanor did not encourage them to offer confidences to her. But she was a patient listener and occasionally capable of an emotional breakthrough. Anna's son John Boettiger, Jr., never forgot one particular visit. Describing the work he was doing in college in an organization that supported the activities of the United Nations, he showed his grandmother a draft of a letter he was going to send to campus groups across the country. Eleanor took a long time reading it and then praised it generously, telling him that the style reminded her a good deal of the writing of his dead father. She then went on to talk of the respect she'd had for John Boettiger as a journalist and of her affection for him as a man. It was a "magical moment" for John Jr.—the first time he had really been able to talk about his stigmatized father and the first time he'd gotten a sense of him as a real person.

Her grandchildren watched Eleanor deal with adversity the only way she knew how: by marching straight ahead. Nina, one of John's two daughters, caught a glimpse of the ferocity of her will one day when she saw her grandmother inadvertently sit on a radiator after getting out of the bathtub, burning her backside badly. The girl saw how painful it was; she was amazed when Eleanor kept going as if nothing had happened.

When John's other daughter, Sally, was killed in a horseback riding accident, Eleanor told Nina that now she must be especially brave. In the ensuing conversation about what bravery was, Nina got a sense that she was faced with *un droit*—not only to face her grief with courage, but also to be sensitive to the pain of others, particularly her parents, who were devastated by this death.

As she got older all those who had always thought of her as part of the FDR side of the family realized how profoundly Eleanor was associated with the psychology of the Oyster Bay Roosevelts. Her celebrated social conscience resembled that of her grandfather, the first Theodore

Roosevelt; her inclination to confront her demons without flinching was akin to a similar quality that characterized her Uncle TR. And in some sense, despite all her achievements, she was still Little Nell, orphan of her father's stormy passage. When she was seventy-seven years old she took a battered Bible that had belonged to her father and showed it to an Episcopal priest near Val Kill to ask about getting the cover repaired. This led to a lengthy conversation in which Eleanor described her father's failings and asked if they were such as to bar him from heaven. When the clergyman said he thought not, Eleanor was visibly pleased at the thought that she would see her father again someday.

When Eleanor got sick early in 1962, it first seemed simply like old age. She was nearly eighty years old, after all. But the fatigue and lethargy was so deep she would sometimes nod off during a lull in a conversation. After lengthy testing, the malady was finally diagnosed as a tuberculosis that was destroying her bone marrow—a disease, ironically, that physicians theorized might have lain dormant in her body since the summer of the FDR-Lucy affair, when Eleanor had been afflicted by what she dismissed at the time as a particularly bad flu.

Having initially misdiagnosed the illness, her friend Dr. David Gurewitsch still believed he could save Eleanor with extreme remedies after she entered the hospital for the last time. But her secretary Maureen Corr heard her say repeatedly, "No, David, I want to die," the intonation making it clear that it was not a matter of simply not wanting to go on living but rather of actually wanting to die.

Hospitalized at the time that the Cuban Missile Crisis was unfolding, Eleanor clenched her teeth when pills were offered and removed the IV tubes inserted into her arms. In her surreal hospital dreams, her son Elliott and her tragic brother, Hall, who had wasted his life so profligately, were conflated into a single oppressive figure. In and out of coma, she had everyone waiting for some last pearl of wisdom to fall from her lips. When Joe Lash was doing a turn at her bedside she suddenly began to gasp, "All I want . . ." As her future biographer immediately bent over her expectantly, anxious to catch the pearl, Eleanor finished the sentence: ". . . is to be turned over."

As the end approached, she made it clear that there were two family members who were not welcome in her room: "I do not want to see Elliott and I will not see Patty." When Anna passed her mother's wishes on to her brother, Elliott reacted by saying he would never speak to her again.

When Eleanor died on November 7, 1962, there was a sense of something ending, a process that had framed and organized her life and the lives of other Roosevelts with whom her destiny had been entwined. That divine fire that had ignited by spontaneous combustion in the family of the first Theodore Roosevelt nearly one hundred years earlier had finally burned itself out. The long journey of two young boys who called themselves Skinny and Swelly—a journey that had led to power and glory for two families that could never shake off their intimate ties with each other—had finally come to an end.

$\mathcal{W}$hat was left was an enterprise in aftermath, something like the ending of a Victorian novel after the main action has concluded—individual lives tying up the loose ends of a larger story.

Kermit's son Willard spent his life composing music that was performed to small and select audiences. Kermit Jr. (Kim) retired from the CIA before the Bay of Pigs invasion because he believed that the Agency, as a result of his own success in Iran, was about to catch overthrow fever despite his own strenuous attempts to caution his superiors in the Agency against taking such actions without the certainty of success that had surrounded his countercoup.

Belle died in 1968. She was survived by Kermit's mistress, Carla Peters, who lived on into the 1990s. (She had seen to it that the two hunting rifles Kermit left her in his will were given to Kim and Willard.) Peters told people who discovered that she'd once had a connection to the Roosevelts that Kermit had been the love of her life and that knowing him had been like knowing history.

Ted's widow, Eleanor, lived on at Old Orchard with her son Quentin's widow, Frances, and her three daughters until her death in

1960 at the age of seventy-five. Frances then moved to her own home in Oyster Bay where she worked as an artist. When her daughters married they were given away by her dead husband Quentin's brother Cornelius—"Unk," as he was known in her family. Cornelius had made a large sum of money after retiring from the CIA and he willed it to his nieces. One of them, Dr. Anna Roosevelt, became an anthropologist who ultimately won a MacArthur "genius" award. Another, Susan, was a scholar in Chinese who married Massachusetts Governor William Weld and gave campaign speeches for him in Mandarin in Boston's Chinatown.

Ethel Derby's husband, Dick, died in 1973 after a long and productive career as a physician on Long Island. Ethel herself became unofficial curator of the museum of family memories. She was the driving force behind the donation of the Theodore Roosevelt Birthplace in Manhattan and Sagamore Hill, along with Old Orchard, to the National Park Service, and lobbied for their designation as National Historical Sites, a status finally granted in 1963. When there was talk that the Theodore Roosevelt Association, founded shortly after her father's death, had outlived its function, Ethel insisted that it stay in business to continue its educational and historical function (and its enthusiastic spreading of the word about TR), and she was its mainstay until she died in 1977 at the age of eighty-six.

During her lifetime, Ethel had willingly allowed herself to be over-shadowed by her brothers. Many of those close to the Roosevelts, however, felt that she should have been counted a significant public figure. Edith Wharton, for instance, often said that Ethel was one of the leading Americans of her age. It was perhaps fitting, therefore, that the actors in the film version of *Age of Innocence* were given a recording of Ethel's voice to study as an example of how a well-bred, intelligent New Yorker sounded in the early part of this century, when Theodore Roosevelt was the dominating figure in American national life.

Archie rehabilitated his finances once again after he came home from World War II by forming Roosevelt and Cross, a brokerage house specializing in municipal bonds. With his narrow-faced, ascetic hand-someness, he seemed to have an unapproachable hauteur. And he was a man of ramrod integrity, always paying the debts he felt as well as those he actually owed. (Perhaps because of Kermit's tragic end, for instance, and his own unwilling role in institutionalizing him, for instance, Archie became involved in Alcoholics Anonymous and was one of the non-alcoholics invited to sit on the board of directors.) But those who got to know him appreciated his wicked sense of humor and his ability to quote poetry learned at the dinner table of his youth.

The postwar years were difficult for him. He was the only surviving son of a great man, and everyone had expectations for him. Everywhere Archie looked he saw the wreckage of a past that made the present seem tawdry by comparison. Beached on the shoals of the TR legacy, he tried to affect his world, speaking out on the issues of urbanization and over-population and especially communist subversion.

During the 1950s he volunteered to appear before the House Un-American Activities Committee to testify as an "Episcopal layman" about communist attempts to undermine religion. ("There is only one way we can stop and reverse the trend in our churches," he testified, "and that is complete exposure and pitiless publicity.") In the 1960s he became an early supporter of the John Birch Society and wrote friends letters filled with gloomy warnings about the beachheads that communists had established in democratic institutions.

In 1971 Archie was driving with his wife, Grace, near their home in Cold Spring Harbor when he accidentally veered into a bus. Grace was thrown from the car and killed. After this, Archie retreated from his business and social world and went into exile at his winter home in Hobe Sound, Florida. As one business associate said, "For years, nobody could approach him. Nobody could make a dent in that terrible depression."

The wounds he had suffered in two wars prevented him from going bird hunting and engaging in the other outdoor pursuits he liked. He began a memoir in the late 1960s and sometimes tried to work on it. It never quite came together as a statement about his unique life, but it did convey the melancholy and displacement of one who had been born at the center of things and, as a result of a process he didn't quite under-stand, been shunted to the periphery after being whirled in the centri-fuge of history. "I realize how little, when we were younger," he wrote in a hard-won perception about himself and his brothers, "we realized that nothing is permanent and that there is constant change." Archie died of a stroke at Hobe Sound late in 1979 at the age of eighty-five.

One of the sadnesses of his life was that he was temperamentally incapable of making the kind of connection with his own children that his father had made with him. This was particularly true in his relation-ship with his son, Archie Jr., whom he continued to regard as "soft on communism" even though Archie Jr. was in the front line of the Cold War in covert actions with the CIA.

By the time his father died, Archie Jr. had resigned from the Agency to work in the foreign division of the Chase Manhattan Bank. Having inherited the family appetite for irony, he took it as an indication of the fading importance of the Roosevelts that the barber who had a shop in the bank's headquarters called him "Mr. Rockefeller" and that his wife, Selwa, also called "Lucky," was sometimes introduced as "Happy," the name of Nelson Rockefeller's wife.

When Lucky was named chief of protocol by Ronald Reagan, Archie Jr. was sometimes invited to the White House for dinner. On more than one of these occasions, he found himself looking up at one of the portraits of TR and imagining, during a lull in the conversation, what his grandfather might say to him if the painting could speak: "I worked hard to get here and what have you done with the talents you were born with? You're here all right, but only as a guest."

Alice Longworth outlived all of her half-siblings. Her own family life was chaotic. She was unable to draw close to her daughter, Paulina, a tragic young woman, silent and self-effacing, who never identified as a Roosevelt and never took hold in Alice's social world. At the age of nineteen Paulina married a former CIA employee named Alexander Sturm, an eccentric and recluse who drank himself to death a few years after Paulina gave birth to a daughter, Joanna. In 1957, Paulina died as the result of an overdose of alcohol and barbiturates, although the coroner did not call it suicide.

Speaking of Joanna as her "second chance" to be a successful mother, Alice focused an iconoclastic love on the girl—half playmate and half grandparent—and formed a strong and lasting bond.

Washington society knew little about Alice's domestic drama, which was odd given the fact that she was the ultimate insider—someone who had been an insider for longer than anyone in the history of the city. She became a fragile heirloom whose daily activities yielded epiphanies that were passed around by word of mouth. One of the small events that became part of Alice's legend occurred in the late 1950s when her Negro chauffeur was taking her someplace and accidentally cut off another motorist who yelled, "Where do you think you're going, you black bastard?" Whereupon Alice rolled down the window in the back seat of the car, where she was sitting in the lotus position, and shouted back, "He's taking me to my destination, you white son of a bitch."

Like Archie, she was at times a supporter of extreme right-wing causes, although she decided she didn't like Barry Goldwater and voted for LBJ in 1964. Unlike her brother, however, the opinions she acquired seemed to flow less from a coherent worldview than from a reflexive hatred of anything historically connected to the New Deal. Nor did her unpopular opinions ever make her unpopular. She was courted by Presidents from Kennedy to Carter, an ornament at social functions of the White House.

Alice's home on Massachusetts Avenue, friends said, had the dual nature of a junk store and museum. There were few reminders of Nick Longworth. But oddments of the Roosevelts were everywhere, artifacts like Proust's madeleine that had the ability to call forth another era: Sargent watercolors once owned by her father, historic old photos of her 1905 trip to the Orient, knickknacks that had once sat on TR's desk.

She specialized in Dorothy Parkeresque quips. When she was forced to have a mastectomy in the late 1960s, she called herself "the only topless octogenarian in Washington." The message needlepointed on her pillow was famous: "If you don't have anything nice to say about anybody, come and sit by me." She liked bizarre events. A friend once made Alice's day by bringing over a severed toe she'd somehow gotten from the morgue.

In her late eighties, Alice still did yoga and could touch her toe to her nose without bending forward. She was still strikingly beautiful, with clear agate eyes and facial bones that made younger women stare enviously at her. (Yet when she caught sight of a photograph of herself, she grimaced: "I look like an aging Eurasian concubine!")

Alice took pleasure in having outlived her old rivals. When author Michael Teague was interviewing her for the book *Mrs. L* and mentioned that he was also doing research on the China clippers operated by Warren Delano, Alice immediately replied, "Do let me know if you discover whether they had any dealings with the opium trade because, you see, that would make Franklin a *criminal*."

The subject of Eleanor brought out a particular meanness, particularly as her cousin became a model of the *femme engagée* for a new generation of feminists. Alice was quite pleased to oblige when people asked her to do her notorious imitation of her cousin, deforming her face into a buck-toothed, recessive-chinned look. Yet as senility overtook her and she became "crazy," as she called it, Alice would sometimes look around the room in confused alarm and ask whoever was with her if Eleanor was still alive.

The day before she died in 1981 at the age of ninety-six, Alice was visited a last time by her granddaughter, Joanna's, fiancé. As he was leaving he turned for a last look and saw her stick out her tongue—not at him, he knew, but at life itself.

For the TR family, it was always a matter of living with the memory of a man who seemed to ask them, as he seemed to do to Archie Jr. at the White House dinner, what they had done with their lives and why they hadn't managed to be as happy and productive as he had been.

For the children of Franklin and Eleanor the task was even more daunting. They felt they had no tradition, nothing to guide them, nothing to measure themselves against. There was such a difference between their view of their parents and how the world regarded them that they lived in a perpetual state of cognitive dissonance.

They fought over their monetary inheritance because it appeared to them to be the only inheritance there was. On the day of Eleanor's funeral, there was a terrible quarrel between Anna and Jimmy. Jimmy had borrowed money from Eleanor before her death, and Anna had been made her beneficiary. Now she demanded the money from him—immediately.

This process would continue during the twilight years ahead—fighting over the scraps Franklin and Eleanor had left behind. In an attempt to deal with the rancor, Franklin Jr. sent a memo to his sister and brothers in 1964 before a family meeting. He laid out an agenda that touched on joint investments and other matters, but then quickly came to the main issues: "Methods of achieving close connection between members of the family in order to avoid actions which appear at cross purposes." And also: "The immediate airing of and a possible resolution of any differences or of specific actions which caused irritation between members of the family."

But the animosities between them—resulting from too long a competition for scarce emotional resources—could not be healed by a memo. Franklin Jr. received only criticism for his attempt to bring them all into harmony. As Elliott said of his brother: "[He] appointed himself head of the family after Mother died and tried to boss the rest of us around. We had shouting matches over the attitude of his and our relationship was quite cool after that." The last time they all got together was in 1972, ten years after their mother's death, when the Eleanor Roosevelt wing of the FDR Library was dedicated. But as Elliott said later on, at this point "there was no trace of kinship. We had broken with each other as we had with her. . . ." Family, the power and glory of the Roosevelts since the arrival of Claes Martenszen van Rosenvelt at New Amsterdam in the seventeenth century, had become the viper at the heart of their enterprise.

They all kept an eye on what would sometimes be referred to as "the body count" of their generation: nineteen marriages for the five of them, two suicides among the people they had married. Puncturing the myths that others created about their parents became for them an obscure way of asserting a principle of justice. As Anna said, "We all turned out to have long memories. It was impossible to discount the coldness with which Mother treated us when we were young or to be immune to the animosity we observed between the adults in our family."

Those memories were put into the public domain during their lifetimes as a way of making profit and cutting their parents down to the size in which they saw them. After Joseph Lash published his *Eleanor and Franklin*, for instance, Elliott, annoyed that an outsider was profiting on the family and also feeling that his father had been slighted in the book "because he disliked [Lash] thoroughly," wrote his own memoir, *An Untold Story: The Roosevelts of Hyde Park*, which also became a bestseller. In it he portrayed his mother as cold and ineffectual and his father as vivacious and attractive, and, most controversially for the rest of the family, as capable of having had a physical relationship with Missy after his polio. Anna and his brothers issued a press release: "We four of the five children of Franklin and Eleanor Roosevelt . . . are deeply troubled by reports of sensationalism and misrepresentation in the book by Elliott Roosevelt. We therefore dissociate ourselves from the book."

Franklin Jr. lobbied the rest of the family to denounce Elliott, going so far as to try to enlist Elliott's children Tony and Ruth Chandler against him. Jimmy waded into the fray with *My Parents: A Differing View*, a book that basically recycled his earlier *Affectionately FDR*, except that it added a denunciation of Elliott for the inference about Missy, while trying to trump his brother by suggesting that Eleanor had an affair with state trooper Earl Miller.

Anna tried to live around the posthumous dissection of her parents' marriage. She managed to achieve an angle of repose in her life with her third husband, Dr. James Halsted, after they moved from California to upstate New York. They lived in a remodeled farmhouse in Syracuse. Anna had a public relations job and did her own gardening and housekeeping and was "almost happy," in the words of a relative. She died in 1976 of throat cancer.

John had prided himself on being the only Roosevelt son to achieve financial stability and the only one not to be divorced. Yet after Eleanor's death, his marriage (which his own children believed had been empty for some time) ended and his estranged wife, Anne, went to Majorca to live with Faye Emerson. John remarried and finally sold the remaining family holdings at Val-Kill. He was the first of the boys to die in 1981.

Franklin Jr. had not been given the post he felt he deserved in the Kennedy administration, but he was a member of the in crowd at the White House and had a sense of reflected glory there. He hitched his star to JFK's (just as Joseph Kennedy had once hitched his to FDR's) and hoped ultimately to get a more visible appointive post that would jumpstart his political career. When Kennedy was assassinated, Franklin Jr. was left out in the cold.

He ran for office again—for mayor of New York and then governor on the Liberal ticket in 1966, but with ever decreasing vote totals until he was in danger of becoming, in the words of one commentator, "the Harold Stassen of New York." He had five marriages, tying Elliott for family honors in that category. He died in 1988 on the day he turned seventy-four.

Jimmy served six terms in Congress. But he fell under the influence of powerful Democrats like Adam Clayton Powell, who used him in their schemes. He left Congress to run for mayor of Los Angeles in 1964 and lost. He then took a job with Investors Overseas Services, a shady business venture of renegade financiers Bernie Cornfeld and Robert Vesco, which was ultimately the subject of a government investigation. While in Switzerland working for Cornfeld, Jimmy informed his third wife, Irene, without warning that he was seeking a divorce and she stabbed him eight times in the back, miraculously managing not to hit a vital organ.

Of all the children he seemed to have experienced the most and learned the least. "People ask me why didn't you become President," he observed near the end of his life, "and I always say I didn't push the right button." It was a comment that showed how distant the sons of Franklin D. Roosevelt were from him and the reality of his life.

Jimmy ended his shady business career as a spokesman for an organization called the National Committee to Preserve Social Security and Medicare. He made public appearances and signed the fund-raising appeals. There was a congressional seal on the letterhead of these letters, and Jimmy's words began, "My father started Social Security. Now we must act to save Social Security and Medicare!"

After serving as front man for this series of old-age scare messages that netted millions for the entrepreneurs who paid handsomely for the use of his name, Jimmy was called before a congressional committee at the age of seventy-nine and asked to testify about what some would refer to as a "scam." When one questioner accused him of committing "geriatric terrorism," Jimmy tilted up his chin and gave the radiant smile that made him look exactly like his father.

Elliott continued to think of himself as the "maverick" of his Roosevelt generation. After Eleanor's death, he continued on his picaresque way, always searching for new beginnings. Chronically out of money but without his mother to borrow from any longer (she had kept him on a $150 a month allowance until the day of her death), he undertook a series of jobs in which he tried to sell his name.

First he was a consultant for a fertilizer company in Shelton, Iowa, that was marketing a secret enzyme product for improving the egg production of cattle breed stock. But within months of his arrival, the company had gone bankrupt as a result of an embezzlement scandal. Then he took a job in Minneapolis at $12,000 a year doing public relations work for the state police. By 1964 Elliott was in Miami Beach working as a greeter for the convention center there.

He decided to run for mayor of Miami Beach in 1965 and was elected. Momentarily he contemplated a political career, but then he was defeated in his reelection bid because his wife, Patty, had been overheard making remarks some interpreted as anti-Semitic, a charge Patty denies. There were rumors during his Miami days that Elliott had become close to gangster Meyer Lansky. (In 1976 he was questioned and ultimately given a clean bill of health by a Senate subcommittee investigating the charge that he had been involved in a plot to assassinate Lydon Pindling, President of the Bahamas.)

In the late 1960s, he set up a consulting firm to take advantage of money being poured into the Alliance for Progress. He wanted to move to Costa Rica, but Patty refused, saying that she would move only to Europe. They bought a copy of *Fodor's* and decided that Portugal sounded like a promising country.

Elliott scratched together enough money to buy a ranch outside of Lisbon, which he named Quinta Las Cadras. He added to his land holdings until he had 171 hectares. He and Patty began to breed Arabian horses. Elliott made friends in the government of dictator Antonio Salazar and began to work as a lobbyist for Portugal, traveling back and forth between Washington and Lisbon. As Patty said later on, "He finally made it. He was a big man, just as he always wanted to be. He had a ton of money."

He was beginning to feel that he had left all the ambiguities of his past behind him and achieved something on his own. But always there was a Roosevelt gravity that pulled him backward. One day he caught an elderly American woman staring at him in a Lisbon bookstore. "Don't you recognize me?" she finally asked. He looked at her closely and said, "You look familiar. Who are you?" The woman smiled, "I'm your first wife."

After the Salazar government fell, Elliott decided to leave Portugal. He sold his ranch at a loss and flew to England after a humiliating episode in the airport in which he and Patty were strip-searched for contraband by the members of the new socialist militia.

Looking for a way to make a living in England, he began writing books about his mother. After *An Untold Story: The Roosevelts of Hyde Park* came *A Rendezvous with Destiny: The Roosevelts of the White House* and *Mother R: Eleanor Roosevelt's Untold Story*. Elliott called this his Eleanor Trilogy. "See, she's still supporting me after all these years," he would sometimes joke.

He had a heart condition that required two dangerous operations, the first of which nearly killed him. And in the early 1980s, he was diagnosed as having colon cancer and needing a colostomy. He told Patty, "I want to go home to die." She responded, "Where's home?" It was a legitimate question: in the years of their marriage they had lived in thirty-five separate residences.

They finally returned to America, living first in Seattle and then settling once again in Phoenix. Elliott continued to live with the enthusiasm he had never lost, not even in the darkest days. He continued to try to strike it rich, becoming involved in a venture seeking to build a world-class race track in Palm Springs. He became a Roman Catholic and befriended Barry Goldwater, claiming that he had become a Reagan Republican. He joined the local Rotary Club and said that the people he met there were the best friends he had made in his whole life. He had no contact with his brothers, saying, "I'll never forgive what they did to me until my dying day," although what exactly their offense was he had trouble explaining.

Elliott continued to sell his mother. After talking to Margaret Truman, who had written best-selling mystery novels about Washington, he embarked on a series of ghost-written mystery novels of his own whose central character was Eleanor, now a sleuth solving crimes while maintaining her role as First Lady. ("She was a detective of sorts in real life," he said. "She had a great sensitivity for things felt and unsaid.") Periodically, in exchange for free passage to Europe, Elliott would lecture about Franklin and Eleanor aboard cruise ships, with Patty acting as his shill asking questions from the audience.

As he turned eighty, Elliott said that his one remaining ambition was to outlive Jimmy, the only other member of his family still standing. But he died in 1990 and Jimmy lasted until the following year.

All these Roosevelts, who had been touched by the divine fire of their predecessors, lived out their lives feeling the burdens of history and inheritance and engaged in a dialogue with parents who were long gone. Pursuing their individual causes and trying to achieve something significant within the context of their legacy, they seemed largely unaware that what they were actually doing was negotiating a withdrawal for the family from its passionate encounter with American history, which it had dominated for half a century. A measure of how well they had succeeded could be seen in the way that the TR heirs now responded to invitations to appear at public events or ceremonies. They would talk among themselves about who should go and typically, one would say to the other, "Do you want to be a Roosevelt today or shall I?"

Something else had happened too—a gradual conclusion to the bitterness that had driven the two branches of the Roosevelt family apart and created a state of civil war between them.

For those who had witnessed this conflict, the event that took place at Hyde Park in the summer of 1989 was extraordinary. It was a peace meeting between the descendants of Theodore and those of Franklin and Eleanor. It had been developing for several years, at least since 1976 when the Hyde Park and Oyster Bay clans decided they had a mutual interest in cooperating in the hiring of a pair of researchers to produce a comprehensive and accurate genealogy of the family.

The spirit of cooperation established in this project (which would eventually be published by the Theodore Roosevelt Association) had deepened when both branches were convinced to work together to establish the Roosevelt Study Center in the Netherlands, a place where Europeans could study the neglected subject of American history.

Franklin Jr. had represented the Hyde Park branch at the opening of the Study Center in Middleberg in 1986, and P. James, grandson of TR's closest cousin Emlen and a near-son to Ethel and Archie in their last years, had represented Oyster Bay. The rapprochement the two men presided over was referred to, only half humorously, as "the Peace of Utrecht." After ceremonies attended by Princess Margiet and other dignitaries, Franklin Jr. told P. James that it was time the Roosevelts became one family again.

And so it was that on a weekend late in June 1989, approximately forty members of each side of the family journeyed to Hyde Park for a two-day reunion. There was an organized schedule: dinner on the lawn at Springwood, lunch at Val-Kill, Sunday service at St. James Episcopal Church. In a solemn moment that symbolized the end to the hostilities that had caused such pain to so many over the years, there were formal speeches.

On Friday night, Elliott, representing the Hyde Park branch (Franklin Jr. had died the previous year), rose to speak of what a great man Theodore Roosevelt had been. He told about his own memories of his great-uncle and emphasized that his mother and father had revered him. The following night, P. James, representing the Oyster Bay branch, delivered a moving speech about the contribution to American history of Franklin and Eleanor and underlining the courage they had each shown in overcoming the obstacles life had placed in their paths.

At the conclusion of this speech there was a torchlit meeting on the lawn of Springwood. It was supposed to be a social occasion, but it began somewhat stiffly, with people mingling and chatting but not knowing quite what was expected of them. Then, quite spontaneously, the older men on both sides of the family—individuals who had actually experienced the rivalry that split the Roosevelts and destroyed a unique family feeling—began to come together in a knot. Suddenly they were not only shaking hands but clapping each other on the back and giving hugs and laughing in delight. All the younger members of the family then moved forward and joined them.

As one of the few non-Roosevelts present at the event said, "It was remarkable. The Roosevelts together again and everyone so happy. Just like it must have been at get-togethers a hundred years ago before all the trouble. And smiling! You wouldn't believe it. All those Roosevelt teeth!"

The story of the Roosevelts has been marked at almost every step of the way by excellent literature, beginning, of course, with TR's own early works about his personal Wild West show in the Badlands.

The good books have continued into the present. Edmund Morris and David McCullough, whose major works on TR appeared almost at the same time, rescued him from feckless revisionism and placed him once again in the epic tradition of self-madeness and rugged individualism where he had in fact placed himself and where he belongs.

The Rise of Theodore Roosevelt and *Mornings on Horseback* did more than this, of course. Each in its own way also documents the emergence of a subtle and powerful personality and of the vanished world that produced him. Alongside them must be placed *Edith Kermit Roosevelt,* Sylvia Morris's biography of the woman who complemented and in some sense completed TR—a book that sees a life clearly and sees it whole, and also portrays the development of the family that TR believed was his most enduring creation.

In *Before the Trumpet* and *A First Class Temperament,* Geoffrey Ward chronicles the rise of FDR. This two-volume biography is a brilliant cumulative portrait of the amusing, selfish, attractive, and devious young man who fooled most of his contemporaries with his personal legerdemain and with his impressive stock-pile of hidden resources. Ward's volumes join Joseph Lash's works on Eleanor in providing the most subtle illumination of the inner life of the Hyde Park Roosevelts.

I am indebted to all these books and thank the the authors. There are other works worth noting. The best full life biography of TR, until Edmund Morris completes his projected three-volume work, remains William Harbaugh's *Power and Responsibility: The Life of Theodore Roosevelt* (New York, 1961). The most recent is Nathan Miller's *Theodore Roosevelt* (New York, 1992). Two good one-volume works on FDR are Frank Freidel's *Franklin D. Roosevelt: A Rendezvous with Destiny* and Ted Morgan's *FDR: A Biography.* Also see multi-volume works by Freidel, James MacGregor Burns, Kenneth Davis, and Arthur Schlesinger.

My own effort has been to try to treat the story of the Oyster Bay and Hyde Park branches, usually seen as two casually related stories, as one complex dynastic drama. It is a saga filled with character and event, hoarded grievances and petty vengeance, magnanimity and self-sacrifice. There is a familial civil war at the heart of the story; there is an enduring engagement with the American enterprise at its outer edges. There is nothing else like it in American history.

The rise and fall of the Roosevelts poses the issues surrounding the question of generational inheritance with a special clarity. Members of powerful public families usually have no choice when it comes to whether or not they want to be dragged into "history." Ambitious and charismatic figures like TR and FDR (and ER too) make that decision for them. Those who come after are left to cope as well as they can with the burdens they receive. In that coping hangs a tale. In the case of the Roosevelts, the saga is particularly interesting for the way the children dealt with the fathers and mothers, and for the way the family as a whole negotiated its exit from the spotlight. I have written about other great families over the years—families like the Rockefellers and the Kennedys—but the Roosevelts were the first ones for whom the term *dynasty* was a completed act rather than a concept in transition.

TR's letters, along with those of Edith, Bamie, Corinne, Ethel, and other family members, are part of the Theodore Roosevelt Collection at Harvard's Houghton Library. Some of Archibald Roosevelt's papers are also at Harvard. I was able to see something of the inner lives of TR's sons TR Jr. and Kermit (and their wives Eleanor and Belle) through their papers at the Library of Congress. FDR's and Eleanor's letters, along with those of the first Elliott, Sara Delano, and other Hyde Park Roosevelts, are at the Franklin Roosevelt Library. I learned about the relationship of Quentin Roosevelt and Flora Whitney through Flora's papers, which her daughter Flora Biddle graciously allowed me to see. I got an additional insight into the life of FDR's son Elliott (and the lives of his brothers and sister) through the unpublished biography on which he collaborated with Dean Smith, which Mr. Smith kindly allowed us to examine.

I am grateful to my good old friend David Horowitz for his help in rounding up some of the material in the first stages of this book. It would have joined our other coauthored family biographies if events had not intervened. But we are always collaborators—on those projects we do separately as well as those we do together.

Wallace F. Dailey, curator of the Theodore Roosevelt Collection at Harvard, was generous in his efforts to make the subtleties of that extraordinary resource available to me. I also want to acknowledge the significant contribution of Jim Silberman, formerly at Summit Books, who first saw the merit in this project, and the efforts of Dominick Anfuso finally to bring it forth. Cassie Jones got it into production despite the obstacles I put in her way. The process of writing this book was made easier by the fact that I have Georges Borchardt as an agent and a friend. He and Anne Borchardt and Denise Shannon are part of my creative process, such as it is.

Jim Denton, Scott Kellermann, John and Laverne Vaughan, Richard and Julie Cobden, Keith Andre, Barry Miller, and Bill Cerveny are among those who stood behind me and my family (probably without knowing it) in troublous times. So did Pamela Collier and Clarissa Cooper, and Louis and Frances Giachino. Debbie and Jim Luckinbill gave me some interesting Rooseveltiana. Bill Schambra shared his work on early twentieth century Republican Party politics. My children, Andrew, Caitlin, and Nicholas, and my wife, Mary Jo, are the lights of my life.

—February 1994, Nevada City, California

SOURCE NOTES

Abbreviations

TR[1]—The first Theodore Roosevelt
MBR—Martha Bullock Roosevelt
TR—Theodore Roosevelt
E—Elliot Roosevelt
ARC—Anna Roosevelt Cowles (Barnie)
CRR—Corinne Roosevelt Robinson (Conie)
ALR—Alice Lee Roosevelt
EKR—Edith Kermit Roosevelt
ER—Eleanor Roosevelt
ARL—Alice Roosevelt Longworth
TR Jr.—Theodore Roosevelt Jr.
KR—Kermit Roosevelt
ERD—Ethel Roosevelt Derby
EAR—Eleanor Alexander Roosevelt
BWR—Belle Willard Roosevelt
ABR—Archibald Bullock Roosevelt
QR—Quentin Roosevelt
FW—Flora Whitney
SDR—Sara Delano Roosevelt

St. Patrick's Day, 1905

16 "whenever two Roosevelts met": Nathan Miller, *The Roosevelt Chronicles* (Garden City, N.Y., 1979), p. 108.

16 "our *very* common ancestor": Theodore Roosevelt, *Autobiography* (New York, 1913), p. 1.

16 The first Roosevelt to be removed: *The Roosevelt Family in America: A Genealogy,* edited by John Gable and published in the *Theodore Roosevelt Association Journal,* volume 16 (1990), no. 1, p. 8.

16 Roosevelt ancestors: See *Genealogy,* nos. 1, 2, and 3 of the *Theodore Roosevelt Association Journal.*

19 "His polished, pointless": Cited in Nathan Miller, *Theodore Roosevelt* (New York, 1992), p. 222.

19 Delano family: For backgrounds, see Geoffrey Ward, *Before the Trumpet* (New York, 1986, paper), p. 61ff.

20 "Poor little soul": EKR to ARC, 5/18/1894.

20 "I shall never": Michael Teague, *Mrs. L: Conversations with Alice Roosevelt Longwood* (New York, 1981), p. 158.

21 "He is a Delano": Joseph Lash, *Eleanor and Franklin* (New York, 1971, paper), p. 205.
23 "So uniquely gifted": Fanny Smith Parsons, *Perchance Some Day* (privately printed, 1951), p. 18. Cited in David McCullough, *Mornings on Horseback* (New York, 1981, paper), p. 143.
23 "Well, Franklin": Lash, p. 205.
23 their gift: "A Dutch genre painter called Blommer sent Theodore a sketch for which we had to pay $20 duty. . . . I am having Blommer's sketch . . . framed for Eleanor R's wedding present. It is really good of its kind, but a kind I don't happen to care for!" (EKR to her sister Emily Carow, 2/7/05.)

Chapter 1

28 "a Hindoo idol": Allen Churchill, *The Roosevelts—American Aristocrats* (New York, 1965), p. 104.
28 "Economy is my doctrine": Cited in McCullough, p. 24.
29 "that lovely Mrs. Roosevelt": Corinne Roosevelt Robinson, *My Brother Theodore Roosevelt* (New York, 1921), p. 3.
30 "My boys at the Lodging Home": See *Hunting Big Game in the Eighties: The Letters of Elliott Roosevelt, Sportsman* (New York, 1933), ed. Eleanor Roosevelt, p. 13.
30 "maniacal benevolence"; McCullough, p. 28. The friend was John Hay, private secretary to Abraham Lincoln and eventually TR's own Secretary of State.
30 Joseph Brady: TR mentions Brady in his *Autobiography,* p. 13.
31 "Poor Topsy": Details about Robert Barnwell and "Aunt Lizzy" are in Anna Roosevelt Cowles ("Bamie") memoir, TRC.
31 "Sweet little Dresden": Edmund Morris, *The Rise of Theodore Roosevelt* (New York, 1980, paper), p. 49.
31 Archibald Stobo: For Bulloch family backgrounds, see McCullough, p. 39ff.
32 "I shudder to think" Lawrence Abbott, ed., *The Letters of Archie Butt* (New York, 1924), p. 278.
33 "He always afterward felt": Bamie memoir.
33 "I know you will not regret": TR [1] to MBR 1/1/62, cited in E. Morris, p. 59. (The letters of the first Theodore and of Mittie are part of the TRC.)
33 "Are me a soldier laddie": Cited in E. Morris, p. 40.
34 Mittie's odd behavior: See McCullough, p. 67.
35 "caustic disapproval": Nicholas Roosevelt, *Theodore Roosevelt: The Man as I Knew Him* (New York, 1967), p. 30.
36 "What was it, ma'am?": The story is told by Alice in *Mrs. L,* p. 26.
36 One of the stories about Ellie: The story of his giving the coat to the urchin is in *Hunting Big Game,* p. viii.
37 Teedie's asthma: For the best insights into the nature of his disease and attitudes and treatment in nineteenth-century medicine, see McCullough, p. 90ff.
37 "defeating the ends of science": Theodore Roosevelt, Jr., *All in the Family* (New York, 1929), p. 59.

37 their neighbor Edith Carow: For Carow backgrounds, see Sylvia Morris, *Edith Kermit Roosevelt* (New York, 1980, paper), p. 9ff.
38 "Conie and I want you": TR to EKR, 5/29/1869.
38 "Ellie was on me": 1/15/1870 diary entry from TR's Grand Tour, cited in McCullough, p. 87.
39 "fed them like chickens": Ibid.
39 "Theodore, you have the mind": Robinson, p. 50.
40 "Boxing is one": Robert J. Moore Jr., *Chronology 1858–1919*. TRC. (A chronology of TR's life using letters and diary entries; hereafter referred to as Moore *Chronology*.)
41 "My father—he got me breath": Cited by Lincoln Steffens, *Autobiography* (New York, 1936), p. 349.
41 "I had to train myself": TR, *Autobiography* p. 50. His sister Corinne records Teedie's unhesitating response to his father's injunction: *"I'll make my body!"* (See Robinson, p. 50.)
41 "At present I am writing": TR to ARC, 6/20/1875. In *The Letters of Theodore Roosevelt*, ed. Elting Morison (Cambridge, Massachusetts, 1951), vol. 1, p. 13.
41 "There was an old fellow": E to Archibald Gracie, 9/5/1873.
42 "My body is getting so thin": E to TR, 11/22/1874.
42 "Lately I have been feeling": E to MBR, 3/6/1875.
42 "Oh father": E to TR[1], 3/6/1875.
43 "I can't remember": E to TR[1], 10/1/1875.
43 "Oh dear splendid old pater": E to TR[1], 2/20/1876.
43 "I have gone through": E to TR[1], 1/12/1876.
43 "partly for warmth": ibid.
43 "I feel well enough": E to TR[1], 1/14/1876.
44 "I believe you could live": Hermann Hagedorn, *The Roosevelt Family of Sagamore Hill* (New York, 1954), p. 10.
44 "As I saw the last": TR[1] to TR, 9/28/1876.
44 "I do not think": TR[1] to TR, 10/22/1876. *Letters of TR*, vol. 1, p. 18.
45 "looked quite like Edith": TR to CRR 1/14/1877, cited in S. Morris, p. 53.
45 "If I were writing": Robinson, p. 96.
45 "Thank God I am pure!": Cited in E. Morris, p. 88.
46 1876 Republican presidential convention: For background on the efforts of TR1 to fight the Conkling machine, see McCullough, p. 169ff.
46 "The machine politicians": TR[1] to TR, 12/16/1877.
46 "I am very uneasy about Father": TR to ARC, 12/16/1877. *Letters of TR*, vol. 1, p. 31.
46 "his young strength": Robinson, p. 104.
46 "He never said anything": Elliott's account of the first Theodore's passing, written the day after he died, is quoted almost in its entirety in McCullough, p. 183.
47 "if merely as talismans": Robinson, p. 106.
47 "He was the best man": TR, *Autobiography*, p. 8.

Chapter 2

48 "After his death": Bamie memoir.
48 "How doth the busy bee": Corinne Alsop Oral History, TRC.

48 "How I wish": Moore *Chronology*, 1/8/1878.
48 James Roosevelt: For James Roosevelt's background, see Ward, p. 21ff.
49 "a corrupted Dandy": Ibid., p. 26.
51 "Tell her that I hope": TR to CRR, 5/20/1879. Various explanations have been advanced to explain the contretemps between TR and Edith, in addition to his possible overimpetuousness, ranging from her father's feeling she was too young for a commitment to his father's displeasure with Charles Carow's excessive drinking. See S. Morris, pp. 58–59.
52 "See that girl?": McCullough, p. 222.
52 duck hunting trip: TR's account of his perilous sail with Elliott was recently rediscovered and published as "Sou Sou Southerly" in *Grey's Sporting Journal*, Fall 1988.
52 "As athletes": TR Diary, 7/30/1879, cited in E. Morris, p. 116.
53 "Attractive without great depth": E. Morris, p. 244.
53 "He made us understand": TR, *Autobiography*, p. 7.
53 "I am all the time thinking": TR to ALR, 6/8/1880. The correspondence between TR and Alice Lee (Roosevelt) is a relatively recent addition to the TRC. For a summary of its contents see Michael Teague's "Theodore Roosevelt and Alice Hathaway Lee: A Perspective," *Harvard Library Bulletin,* vol. 32, no. 3, Summer 1985.
53 "My own sunny faced queen": Ibid.
54 "Despite what you have said": James Roosevelt with Bill Libby, *My Parents: A Differing View* (New York, 1976), p. 9.
54 "He is the first person": Lash, p. 172.
54 "old Miss Delano": Kenneth Davis, *FDR: The Beckoning of Destiny* (New York, 1971), p. 35.
54 "It is great fun": Moore *Chronology*, 8/17/1880.
54 "I try to keep him": E to ARC, 8/29/1880.
54 "Get plenty of sleep": TR to ALR, 8/15/1880.
55 "Don't you think": ALR to TR, 8/30/1880.
55 "How I wish": ALR to TR, 10/6/1880.
55 "I am just longing": ALR to TR, 10/17/1880.
55 "I worship you": TR to ALR, 10/17/1880.
55 Teddy's way of paying homage: Nicholas Roosevelt, p. 21.
55 "the soles off": S. Morris, p. 64.
56 "maddened him": Corinne Alsop Oral History, TRC.
57 "glorious freedom": E to TR, 8/24/1881. Cited in McCullough, p. 240.
57 "I would not trust myself": E to MBR, 1/31/1881. See also *Hunting Big Game*, p. 64.
57 he became so ill: E to MBR 8/1/1881. See also *Hunting Big Game*, p. 89.
57 "I have good broad shoulders": E to MBR 2/22/1881. See also *Hunting Big Game*, p. 64.
57 "I shall need you": E to TR, 8/24/1881. Cited in McCullough, p. 242.
57 "I am going to bed": TR to ALR, 3/28/1889.
57 "I don't think I ever saw": TR to CRR, 8/23/1881.
58 "a chubby Minerva": TR to CRR, 8/24/1881. *Letters of TR*, vol. 1, p. 82.
58 TR used a "jimmy": TR, *Autobiography*, p. 63.
58 "saloon keepers, horse-car conductors": Ibid., p. 63.
59 "totally unable to speak": E. Morris, p. 162.
59 "By God, if you try": E. Morris, p. 166.
59 "His plans for occupying": Lash, p. 7.

59 "he would wish to surpass": Anna Bulloch to E, 1/8/1882. See also *Hunting Big Game*, p. 141.
59 "All the small curs": TR to ALR, 3/6/1883.
60 TR and cigar workers: See TR, *Autobiography*, p. 88.
60 "I then made up my mind": Ibid., p. 95.
61 "If I were to do something": CRR to Douglas Robinson, 3/19/1881. Cited in McCullough, p. 274.
62 Hall family backgrounds: See Lash, p. 40ff.
62 "I hated so to leave you": ALR to TR, 2/11/1884.
63 "I *love* a little *girl*": Anna Bulloch Reminiscences, TRC.
63 "There is a curse": Corinne recalled Elliott's words for TR's biographer Henry Pringle in a letter of September 1930. Cited in McCullough, p. 283.
63 "She was beautiful": TR's literary epitaph for Alice Lee is in the TRC. Moving as it is, this threnody is one of his last written references to his dead wife. Alice Lee is not mentioned at all in his *Autobiography*, a document, some scholars have pointed out, that is almost as interesting for what TR excludes as for what is included.
64 "He feels the awful loneliness": Conie to E 3/4/1884. See also *Hunting Big Game*, p. 156.
64 "The romance of my life": Hermann Hagedorn, *Roosevelt in the Badlands* (Boston, 1930), p. 466.
64 "That's it exactly": Ibid., Preface, p. x.
65 "as grim and desolate": Cited in McCullough, p. 330.
66 "I have just come in": TR to ARC, 6/17/1884. Cited in Hagedorn, *Bad Lands*, p. 104.
66 "It would electrify": Cited in E. Morris, p. 281.
67 "Four Eyes": TR, *Autobiography*, p. 136.
67 "I wear a sombrero": TR to ARC, 8/17/1884.
68 "The bullet hole in his skull": TR to ARC, 9/20/1884.
68 "I understand you have threatened": Hagedorn, *Bad Lands*, p. 208. (In this work, Hagedorn changed some of the names of the principal figures.)
69 "I do care about being pretty": EKR to TR, 6/8/1886.
70 Redhead Finnegan: For the story of TR's pursuit of the outlaw, see Hagedorn, *Bad Lands*, p. 372ff. See also TR's own *Ranch Life and The Hunting Trail*.
70 TR "reenacts" the capture: Author's interview with Wallace F. Dailey. (Dailey, curator of the TR Collection at Harvard University, discovered that the photo was posed when the descendant of one of TR's employees wrote to say that the figure identified in a book as one of the renegades TR hunted down was actually that of her father.)
71 "I do not undervalue": Cited in Hagedorn, *Bad Lands*, p. 407.
71 "You will be President": Hagedorn, *Bad Lands*, p. 411.

Chapter 3

72 "I always knew": Author's interview with Nancy Roosevelt Jackson.
72 "You could not reproach": TR to ARC, 9/20/1886. Cited S. Morris, p. 90.
73 "had a gift for making her own people uncomfortable": Teague, *Mrs. L*, p. 37.
73 "a girl whose main characteristic": Nicholas Roosevelt, p. 23.
73 "She was the only person": Cited S. Morris, p. 195.

73 "She would have bored him": Teague quotes Alice about Edith: "I think she always resented being the second choice and she never really forgave him for his first marriage." *Mrs. L,* p. 37.

73 "live to oneself": Hagedorn, *Roosevelt Family,* p. 18.

73 "Had she not done this": Ibid.

74 "If you are unhappy": Teague, p. 12.

76 "Every time he opens his mouth": E. Morris, p. 414.

76 "that quality that medieval": Henry Adams, *The Education of Henry Adams* (New York, 1974), p. 417.

76 "little brother in a blanket": TR to ARC, 10/13/1889.

77 "When I think": S. Morris, p. 133.

77 "It was just heart breaking": TR to ARC, 10/23/1890, cited in Hagedorn, *Roosevelt Family,* p. 21.

77 "Your father thinks of you": TR to TR Jr., 8/8/1892.

77 Kermit and Mame: See Kermit Roosevelt, "Down to the Sea," *Scientific American,* February 1937.

77 "Ted got no mufstache": Hagedorn, *Roosevelt Family,* p. 21.

78 "Sissy had a sweat nurse!": From Alice's point of view, this was something more than an amusing malapropism on Ted's part. In this comment, her half brother was actually emphasizing that she had lost her mother at birth and that she had been nurtured by a stranger, which distinguished her from him and from the rest of TR's children.

78 "sickness present": *All in the Family,* p. 45.

78 the spelling of "chaps": *All in the Family,* p. 170.

78 When Rudyard Kipling came to visit: Teague, p. 46.

79 "A cow, a calf, a pony": TR to TR Jr., 7/11/1890.

79 "A beaver had built": TR to TR Jr., 7/23/1891.

79 "I loved the picture letter": KR to TR, 4/29/03.

80 "Baby does not want": Lash, p. 59.

80 "There was a thump": CRR to ARC, 8/1/1888, cited in Blanche Wiesen Cook, *Eleanor Roosevelt* (New York, 1992), p. 51.

80 "very unhealthy": Lash, p. 60.

81 "Eleanor, I hardly know": Joseph Alsop, *FDR: A Centenary Remembrance* (New York, 1982), P. 39.

81 "sink through the floor": Eleanor Roosevelt, *This Is My Story* (New York, 1937), p. 18.

81 "always disgracing my mother": Ibid., p. 17.

81 "Feeling that I was useful": Ibid., p. 13.

82 "But I am not going to speak": E to ARC, 5/2/1890.

82 "Ask Theodore": Anna Hall to ARC, 7/21/1890.

82 Eleanor and the coin: *This Is My Story,* p. 11.

82 "Anna must be made": Cited in E. Morris, p. 438.

83 "I wish emphatically": Elliott's letter was published in the *New York Herald* on 8/21/1891. It is printed in its entirety in Cook, p. 68.

83 "not as she last saw me": Lash, p. 71.

83 "Did she say": E to Mrs. Hall, 11/26/1892.

84 "It is most horrible": E to Mrs. Hall, 12/7/1892.

84 "She always had a string": Hagedorn, *Roosevelt Family,* p. 50.

85 "Shake *me,* father!": Ibid., p. 24.

85 Milton readings: Archibald Roosevelt, unpublished autobiography (hereafter referred to as ABR Ms).

85 "Father! Don't talk": *All in the Family*, p. 27.

85 Cove Neck public school: ABR Ms.

86 Eleanor and the "begats": Teague, *Mrs. L,* p. 57. At the end of her own long life, Alice said of Eleanor, "I had a lot of admiration for her. But I did—still do—get bored with her type. . . . I can still see those large blue eyes fixed on one, worrying about one, and wanting you to know that in her you had a friend." (Ibid., p. 155.)

86 "Dive, Alicy": Teague, *Mrs. L,* p. 42.

86 "While I always admired": Lash, p. 61.

86 "Maybe soon I'll come back": E to ER, 10/9/92. See also *Hunting Big Game*, p. 168.

86 Her mother's death meant nothing: *This Is My Story*, p. 19.

87 "Somehow it was always": Ibid., p. 20.

87 "feeling the awful night": TR to ARC, 8/18/1894. This letter to Bamie on the death of Elliott, both affecting and ambivalent, is printed in its entirety in S. Morris, pp. 143–44.

87 Elliott became gripped by delusions: CRR to ARC, 8/15/94.

87 "he cried like a child": S. Morris, p. 143. There was an element of relief within TR's grief. After Elliott's death, he wrote Conie, "There is one great comfort I already feel; I only need to have pleasant thoughts of Elliott now. He is just the gallant, generous, manly boy and young man whom everyone loved." *Letters of TR,* vol. 1, p. 397.

Chapter 4

92 relationship between the Rough Riders and Cody: Author's Interview with Paul Fees, curator of the Buffalo Bill Museum.

92 "Nine tenths": TR to TR Jr., 10/4/03.

92 "Nobody can tell": TR to CRR, 6/7/98. *Letters of TR,* vol. 2, p. 836

93 "The enemy were hidden": Richard Harding Davis, *The Cuban and Porto Rican Campaigns* (New York, 1898), p. 291.

93 "Colonel, isn't it Whitman": Theodore Roosevelt, *The Rough Riders* (New York, 1923), p. 105.

94 "They put their heads in my lap": EKR to TR, 6/18/98.

94 "I shall speedily assail": Cited in E. Morris, p. 491.

95 "Never, never": Steffens, *Autobiography,* p. 258.

95 "If it wasn't wrong": TR to ARC, 1/19/98.

96 "When war comes": E. Morris, p. 595.

96 "For two weeks": TR to CRR, 3/16/98.

97 "no more backbone": E. Morris, p. 610.

97 Kermit knocked down a classmate: EKR to TR, 5/20/98.

97 "You know what my wife": Archibald Butt, *Letters* (New York, 1924), p. 146.

98 "Captain, a bullet": *The Rough Riders,* p. 124.

98 "Are you afraid": Ibid., p. 127.

98 "I am the ranking officer": Ibid., p. 129. See also *Autobiography*, p. 264.

99 "No one who saw Roosevelt": *New York Herald,* 7/14/98.

99 "Look at all these": TR made the comment to his friend Robert Ferguson, who repeated it to Edith in a letter of 7/5/1898. Cited in E. Morris, p. 656.

100 "rather have led the charge": TR to Douglas Robinson, 7/27/1898.

101 "My little man": Cited in Ward, p. 124.

101 "Poor little boy.": Ibid., p. 116.
102 "Consider yourself spanked": James Roosevelt and Sidney Shalett, *Affectionately, FDR* (New York, 1959), p. 20.
102 "What's the matter, Mummy?": Davis, *Beckoning*, p. 69.
102 "Mama has left": FDR to JR, 6/7/1890. *FDR: His Personal Letters,* ed. Elliott Roosevelt (New York, 1947), vol. 1, p. 16.
103 "a small boy [who] took special delight": *Affectionately*, p. 45.
104 "not a ball of fire": Helen Robinson Oral History, TRC.
104 Cowles saw the *real* Bamie: Mrs. Richard Aldrich Oral History, TRC.
105 "It makes me miserable": Ward, p. 198.
105 "I have been playing baseball": FDR to SDR and JR, 5/7/1897. *FDR Letters,* vol. 1, p. 92.
105 "The only ball I received": FDR to SDR and JR, 5/14/1897, *FDR Letters,* vol. 1, p. 96
106 "Please don't make any arrangements": Cited in Ward, p. 194.
106 visited Franklin from a rickety ladder: Ward, p. 201.
107 Franklin and the Italian boy: Earl Looker, *This Man Roosevelt* (New York, 1936), p. 35.
107 "A cyclone from the West": TR to TR Jr., 2/19/04. See *Theodore Roosevelt: Letters to Children,* ed. John Bucklin Bishop (New York, 1919), p. 91.
108 "He has had this time": SDR to FDR, 11/21/1900.
108 "not a race to do good": SDR to FDR, 1/9/1900.
108 "be a good man": SDR to FDR, 11/30/04, cited in Ward, p. 231.
110 "You see, it represents": TR to Elihu Root, 12/5/1900. *Letters of TR,* vol. 2, p. 1450.
110 "A great work lies ready": S. Morris, p. 298.
111 "Do you realize": Robinson, pp. 206–7.
111 "I think there is": Ibid.

Chapter 5

112 "had now acquired": *New York Times,* 9/26/01.
112 "He laughed": Steffens, *Autobiography,* p. 503.
113 "Of all forms": Cited in Miller, *Theodore Roosevelt,* p. 365.
113 "controlling the big companies": TR to Trevelyan, 3/9/05, *Letters of TR,* vol. 4, p. 1133.
114 "If we have done anything": See John Bucklin Bishop, *Theodore Roosevelt and His Times* (New York, 1930), vol. 1, p. 184.
114 "by the seat of the breeches": See Henry Pringle, *Theodore Roosevelt: A Biography* (New York, 1956, paper), p. 190.
115 "His tendency": FDR to SDR, 10/26/02, *FDR Letters,* vol. 1, p. 481.
115 "A revolution?": David McCullough, *The Path Between the Seas* (New York, 1977), p. 351.
116 "If I had followed": Joseph Gardner, *Departing Glory: Theodore Roosevelt as Ex-President* (New York, 1973), p. 53.
116 "the most perfectly equipped": E. Morris, p. 17.
116 "You can't believe": EKR to TR, 9/21/01. Cited in S. Morris, p. 221.
117 "Alice is exceedingly pretty": EKR to Cecil Spring-Rice, 1/27/01, cited in S. Morris, p. 233.

117 "If you send me": Hagedorn, *Roosevelt Family*, p. 69. See also Alice Roosevelt Longworth, *Crowded Hours* (New York, 1933), p. 26.
117 Alice and Ted do a jig: Teague, p. 62.
118 "I can do one": Owen Wister, *Roosevelt: The Story of a Friendship* (New York, 1930), p. 87.
119 "What effect would it have": Teague, p. 73.
119 "well after noon": TR to TR Jr, 1/8/03, *Letters of TR*, vol. 3, p. 402.
119 "The wife of the President": Hagedorn, *Roosevelt Family*, p. 189.
119 Bamie and Harriman: From Sheffield Cowles, Jr., Oral History, TRC.
119 "Alice has been at home": TR to CRR, 9/23/03, cited in S. Morris, p. 271.
120 One journalist kept track": Hagedorn, *Roosevelt Family*, p. 186.
120 "As you truly say": EKR to ARL, 8/2/03.
120 "to try not to buy": EKR to ARL, n.d.
120 "Father doesn't care": ARL Diary, 1/27/03, Alice Roosevelt Longworth Papers, Library of Congress.
121 "the second period of my life": *This Is My Story*, p. 52.
121 "Cousin Eleanor": Lash, p. 150.
121 "grandmotherly concern": Ibid., p. 155.
122 "I am as fond": cited in Ward, p. 337.
122 "startling announcement": Lash, p. 159.
122 "I know just how": ER to SDR, 12/2/03, cited in Lash, p. 161.
122 "Alice is looking well": Lash, p. 178.
123 "No one would know": Teague, p. 157.
123 "I am sending": ERD to KR, 9/18/02.
123 "It was a friendly": TR to ERD, 6/20/06. See also *Letters to His Children*, p. 167.
124 Hunting with Seth Bullock: Kermit Roosevelt, *Happy Hunting Grounds* (New York, 1920), p. 7.
124 Kermit skins a jungle mouse: *All in the Family*, p. 61.
125 "Hereafter I shall never": TR to ARC, 2/19/1898, cited in Hagedorn, *Roosevelt Family*, p. 50.
125 "He bit or clawed": TR to TR Jr., 1/14/01, *Letters to His Children*, p. 20.
125 "fighting proclivities": Hagedorn, *Roosevelt Family*, p. 103.
125 "In boxing": TR Jr. to TR, n.d.
125 "disinherit" any son: E. Morris, p. 477.
126 "Athletic proficiency": TR to TR Jr., 10/4/03, *Letters to His Children*, p. 63.
126 "My darling": TR to EKR, 2/16/02.
126 The Norman Baron's Prayer: Theodore Roosevelt, Jr. Papers.
126 "I believe you have": TR to TR Jr., 1/11/04.
127 "I have had": TR to TR Jr., 11/1/03.
127 "Very few outsiders": S. Morris, p. 298.
127 "I got the water pistol": KR to EKR, 4/26/03.
128 "I am not the age": TR to KR, 3/5/05.
128 "The last two or three": TR to KR, 2/1/03. See also, *Letters to Kermit from Theodore Roosevelt*, ed. Will Irwin (New York, 1946), p. 27.
128 "The more I read": KR to TR, n.d.
129 "I do not like": EA Robinson to KR, 2/23/13. KR Papers.
129 "The packers have been": TR to KR, 6/3/06.
129 "If things go wrong": TR to KR, 10/26/04. See also *Letters to Kermit*, p. 81.

130 "There was a young lady of Clare": Earle Looker, *The White House Gang* (New York, 1929), p. 165.
130 "posterity letters": The children sometimes joked about these posterity letters. They recognized that the picture letters would be particularly valuable and as Alice later noted, sometimes jokingly said to TR as they got older, "Do us one of those so we can cash them in later on." Teague, p. 44.

Chapter 6

131 "sex was an ordeal": Lash, p. 211.
131 FDR night terrors: See Cook, p. 170; also Davis, *Beckoning,* p. 195.
132 "clairvoyant lady": FDR to SDR, 8/14/05, *FDR: His Personal Letters,* ed. Elliott Roosevelt (New York, 1948), vol. 2, p. 66.
132 "Everyone is talking": FDR to SDR, 9/7/05, Ibid., p. 84.
132 "The more I see": TR to Henry Cabot Lodge, 6/16/05, *Letters of TR,* vol. 4, p. 1230.
133 "It's a mighty good thing": Cited Hagedorn, *Roosevelt Family,* p. 230.
134 It was Teddy doing "Teddy": O.K. Davis, *Released for Publication* (Boston, 1925).
135 Vitagraph motion pictures: E. Morris, p. 629.
135 TR and the press: Author's interview with John Gable, Executive Director, Theodore Roosevelt Association.
136 "a less *jeune fille* version": *Crowded Hours,* p. 77.
136 Alice in China: Ibid., p. 93ff. For insights into TR's use of Alice in matters of State, see Stacey Rozek Cordery, "Theodore Roosevelt's Private Diplomat—Alice Roosevelt and the 1905 Far East Junket," in *Theodore Roosevelt—Many-Sided American* (Interlaken, NY, 1992), ed. Natalie A. Naylor, Douglas Brinkley, and John Gable.
137 "to show us": *Crowded Hours,* p. 100.
137 "You know, your friend": Cited in Carol Felsenthal, *Princess Alice* (New York, 1988, paper), p. 85.
137 "Oh, why am I": ARL Diary, 5/3/04, ARL Papers.
137 "——— has told me": ARL to NL, n.d., ARL Papers.
138 "in conversation on subjects": Cited in William Manners, *TR and Will* (New York, 1969), p. 11.
138 "I think I ought to know": *Crowded Hours,* p. 88.
138 Longworth background: See *Crowded Hours,* p. 130ff; also Felsenthal, p. 87ff.
139 "Isn't it extraordinary": Teague, p. 139.
139 "Though I have not": *Crowded Hours,* p. 116.
140 "Let me congratulate you": Cited in Felsenthal, p. 115.
140 "The thing to do": TR to TR Jr., 10/2/05, *Letters to His Children,* p. 137.
140 Ted and fracas at Cambridge: *New York Times,* 10/4/06.
141 "We are often defeated": TR to KR, 3/5/08, *Letters to Kermit,* p. 236.
141 Ted writes in blank verse: Eleanor Alexander Roosevelt, *Day Before Yesterday* (New York, 1959), p. 42.
141 "He bids fair": *New York Times,* 10/10/07.
141 "the young man's face": *New York Times,* 8/28/08.
142 "a beautiful idiot": Author's interview with Nancy Roosevelt Jackson, Archie's daughter.

142 "Kermit the Hermit": *White House Gang,* p. 118.
143 "a *fine* bad little boy": S. Morris, p. 316.
143 Quentin at Force School: See ABR Ms.
143 "Stop that!": *White House Gang,* p. 65.
143 TR apologizes for Quentin: Ibid., p. 44.
144 "Guy Fawkes?": Ibid., p. 197.
145 "See, the moth balls": Ibid., 80.
145 "I love all these children": TR to Emily Carow, 8/6/03.
145 "That bell's tolling": Ibid., p. 33.
145 "They played hard": TR to ABR, 1/2/08. *Letters to His Children,* p. 217.
146 TR carries pistol: Miller, *Theodore Roosevelt,* p. 70.
146 "felt like a bull dog": Cited in Pringle, p. 346.
146 "I have had": TR to KR, 1/14/09, *Letters of TR,* vol. 6, p. 1476.
146 "There is a little hole": Hagedorn, p. 278.
147 "No one will ever know": *Crowded Hours,* p. 148.
147 "This, my darlings": Ibid., p. 158.
147 "I could not ask": S. Morris, p. 339.

Chapter 7

151 Rio da Duvida: For details about the Brazil trip, see especially Theodore Roosevelt, *Through the Brazilian Wilderness* (New York, 1919), and George Cherrie, *Dark Trails* (New York, 1930).
153 "Kermit shows": *New York Times,* 8/2/08.
155 Kermit would have to work doubly hard: *Happy Hunting Grounds,* p. 15.
155 "The rather timid boy": TR to TR Jr., 5/9/09, LC.
155 Kermit's photograph: See Theodore Roosevelt, *African Game Trails* (New York, 1919), p. 403.
155 lion with twenty-five natives to its credit: KR to ERD, 8/13/09.
155 "Two days ago": TR to ARC, 8/17/09.
155 "sticks, stones, the claws": *African Game Trails,* p. 341. For a contemporary Roosevelt's perspective on the Africa trip, see Tweed Roosevelt, "Theodore Roosevelt's African Safari," in *Theodore Roosevelt—Many-Sided American,* op cit.
156 "In these greatest": Ibid., Introduction, p. ix.
156 "Do you remember": *Happy Hunting Grounds,* p. 22.
157 "Germans did not like me": Gardner, p. 159.
158 "I never had any interest": Elliott Roosevelt, *An Untold Story: The Roosevelts of Hyde Park* (New York, 1973), p. 32.
158 Eleanor and baby Anna: Geoffrey Ward, *A First Class Temperament* (New York, paper, 1990), p. 52
158 "Never again": Elliott Roosevelt, *Untold Story,* p. 33.
158 Eleanor ties Anna's hands: John Boettiger Jr., *A Love in Shadow* (New York, 1978), p. 53.
159 "Franklin's children": Lash, p. 274.
159 "F. carries her": ER to SDR, 7/14/07, *FDR Letters,* vol. 2, p. 91.
159 "Frank, the men": Ted Morgan, *FDR: A Biography* (New York, 1986, paper), p. 112.
160 "A rather vivid four years": Alice Diary, 2/17/10, ARL Papers.
160 "No one can ever know": Alice Diary 1/23/10.

160 "My, but you": ABR to KR, 9/26/09.
161 "The desert is perfectly": ABR to ERD 12/28/10.
161 "He is sometimes": TR to TR Jr., 9/22/11, *Letters of TR,* vol. 7, p. 344.
161 Kermit moose hunting: See *Collier's,* 4/16/12.
161 Kermit sheep hunting: See *Scribner's,* 6/12.
161 "The papers have continually": TR to KR, 8/22/11.
162 "the type of mother and Ethel": Alice Diary 2/9/10.
163 "Every night they stayed": *Day Before Yesterday,* p. 160.
163 "as regards the size of the family": TR to TR Jr., 1/14/11.
164 "a flubdub": TR to TR Jr., 8/22/11, *Letters of TR,* vol. 7, p. 336.
164 "I note what you say": TR to TR Jr., 9/22/11, *Letters of TR,* vol. 7, p. 344.
165 "ought to go into politics": Ward, *First Class,* p. 119.
165 "You know these Roosevelts": Miller, *The Roosevelt Chronicles,* p. 275.
165 "I think that": Cited in Miller, *Theodore Roosevelt,* p. 517.
165 TR and Progressives: For the best treatment of this subject see John Gable,
     The Bull Moose Years (New York: Kennikat Press, 1978).
166 "didn't accept favors from crooks": *Crowded Hours,* p. 203.
166 "court of justice": Ibid., p. 211.
166 Alice mentioned divorce: Teague, p. 158.
166 "Taft and his managers": TR to KR, 10/11/12.
167 "We are very proud": TR to FDR, 1/29/11, *Letters of TR,* vol. 7, p. 215.
167 "May it not be possible": Ward, *First Class,* p. 152.
167 "We hope your Big Stick"; Ibid., p. 153n.
168 "They have pinked me": Eyewitness account of assassination attempt in
     memo by journalist O. K. Davis, TRC.
168 "Well, the campaign": TR to KR, 10/19/12.
168 "there's the speech": Nicholas Roosevelt, p. 69.
169 "Well, we have gone down": TR to KR, 11/5/12.
169 "I am afraid Alice": EKR to ARC, 11/23/12.
169 "You cannot imagine": Hagedorn, *Roosevelt Family,* p. 328.
169 "When I got back": TR to KR, 1/27/15.
170 "Dick feels": ERD to TR, 3/14/13.
170 "There's a Roosevelt": Ward, *First Class,* p. 202.
170 "It is interesting": TR to FDR, 3/18/13, *Letters of TR,* vol. 7, p. 714.
170 "try not to write": SDR to FDR, 3/17/13.
171 "like Christian": EKR to ARC, 10/15/13, cited in S. Morris, p. 398.
171 "I'm afraid Mother": KR to ERD, 5/12/13.
172 "[It] would seem as inapt": KR to ERD, 9/9/13.
172 "because the Indians": KR to BWR, 10/10/12.
172 "I am thankful": EKR to ARC, 5/29/13.
172 "grim pride": TR Jr. to KR, 9/9/13.
172 "A big, up-from-the-soil": KR to BWR, 11/26/12.
173 "I was afraid": KR to BWR, 12/4/13.
173 "I do love you": BWR to KR, 8/22/13.
173 "[She] took me aside": KR to BWR, 11/15/13.
173 "Yesterday morning": KR to BWR, 11/22/13.
174 "The trip has not been": KR to BWR, 11/15/13.
174 "lithe as panthers": *Brazilian Wilderness,* p. 250.
174 "a journey of peril": *Dark Trails,* p. 250.
175 "so broad a river": *Brazilian Wilderness,* p. 258.
176 "The water beat his helmet": *Brazilian Wilderness,* p. 276.

177 he threw away the only two books: *Happy Hunting Grounds,* p. 30.
177 TR gashed his leg: *Dark Trails,* p. 251.
177 fantasized constantly about food: Ibid., p. 306.
178 Cherrie didn't believe Roosevelt could last: Ibid., p. 253.
178 "Boys, I realize": Ibid., p. 309.
178 "It would have slipped": *Brazilian Wilderness,* p. 322.
179 "wonderful northern spring": *Brazilian Wilderness,* p. 324

Chapter 8

180 "a man in whom": Robinson, p. 278.
181 "We did the thing": TR to KR, 12/28/14.
181 "Pray thank": *Day Before Yesterday,* p. 68.
182 "a professional yodeler": Gardner, p. 323.
182 "My bolt is shot!": TR to KR, 2/22/15.
182 "At a time": Theodore Roosevelt, *A Book Lover's Holiday in the Open* (New York, 1916), p. 293.
183 "Did you notice": Pringle, p. 409.
183 "Not only do I": TR to KR, 10/15/15.
183 "I never expected": *Day Before Yesterday,* p. 57.
184 "sat ceremoniously apart": TR to KR, 11/10/16.
184 "combined with the other attacks": TR Jr. to KR, 5/29/15.
184 "a lot of us who will": TR Jr. to KR, 5/22/15.
184 "That's a very nice dog": Gardner, p. 339.
184 "might spring to squirrel": Ibid., p. 326.
185 Archie a "dismal failure": ABR Ms.
185 Archie and "a loose woman": TR to KR, 3/15/15.
185 "Archie's virtues": TR to KR, 2/22/15.
185 "For a short time": ABR to KR, 5/19/15.
185 Archie slipped off his horse: ABR Ms.
186 "most Felicitous Madam": ABR Ms.
186 "The only drawback": QR to Flora Whitney, n.d., Biddle Papers. (The correspondence between Quentin and Flora has recently become part of the TRC.)
186 "I am delighted": TR Jr. to KR, 7/21/15.
186 "four classes of opinion": TR Jr. to Frank Vanderlip, 3/14/16, Vanderlip Papers, Columbia University.
187 "passing through a thick": TR to ARC, 6/16/16, *Letters of TR,* vol. 8, p. 1063.
187 "There should be shadows": Cited in Gardner, p. 357.
187 "I very gravely question": TR to Frank Vanderlip, 1/16/17, Vanderlip Papers.
188 "Darling, I like": *Day Before Yesterday,* p. 57. Sometimes TR was curt in his dismissal of the modern world. After seeing the revolutionary painting "Nude Descending a Staircase" at the famous Armory Show of 1913, he said of it, "Obviously mammalian, but not necessarily human." (Teague, p. 112.)
188 "If we don't get into": Cited in William Savacool Oral History, Columbia University Oral History Project.
189 "If I were allowed": Robinson, p. 330.

190 "You must do your duty": Bernard Asbell, ed., *Mother and Daughter: The Letters of Eleanor and Anna Roosevelt* (New York, 1982), p. 20.
190 FDR and ER break off conjugal relations: Elliott Roosevelt, *Untold Story*, p. 77.
190 "A-apple": *This Is My Story*, p. 138.
191 "The Jew party": Ward, *First Class*, p. 252.
191 "Old Battleax": James Roosevelt tells the story of his abusive governess in *Affectionately*, p. 39ff.
191 "You silly boy": Asbell, p. 14.
192 TR visits FDR: See Ward, *First Class*, p. 344; also Davis, *Beckoning*, p. 458.
192 "My memory was not": TR to FDR, 5/26/16, *Letters of TR*, vol. 8, p. 1046.
193 "to come into the court of history": Ibid., 338.
193 FDR as TR "mole": Author's interview with John Gable, who had this information from FDR Jr.
193 "Root inclined": Ward, *First Class*, p. 340.
193 "You must resign!": Ibid., p. 346.
193 "Mr. President": Ibid.
194 Churchill comment: Belle Willard Roosevelt, London Diary, 3/5/40, BWR Papers.
195 "We are going to spring": ABR to ERD, 2/17/17.
195 "My mother in law": BWR to Nancy Thayer Roosevelt, n.d.
196 "Mr. Vanderlip told me": TR Jr. to KR, n.d. [October 1915].
196 "There was little of the gaiety": *Crowded Hours*, p. 254.
196 "to see what it was like": ABR Ms.
197 "Since our earliest days": Ibid.
197 "The big bear": Hagedorn, *Roosevelt Family*, p. 367.
198 "How very nice": Gardner, p. 376.
198 "He is far less ambitious": QR to FW, 8/8/17.
198 "I shan't feel happy": KR to TR, 6/4/17.
198 "I've never been behind": KR to TR, 6/19/17.
199 "Well, you are not": TR to KR, 7/3/17.
200 Flora Payne Whitney: For Whitney backgrounds, see B. H. Friedman, *Gertrude Vanderbilt Whitney* (New York, 1978). Also, author's interview with Flora Biddle.
200 "She has the possibilities": Friedman, p. 205.
201 "from a platonic heart": QR to FW, 2/13/16.
201 "I don't feel": QR to FW, n.d.
201 "committed the individual sin": Friedman, p. 381.
201 "Took Mama out": Flora Whitney Diary, 10/29/16, Biddle Papers.
202 "the Newport horrors": BWR to KR, n.d.
202 "The women were all feeling": QR to FW, 1/17/17.
202 "To Flora Payne Whitney": QR to FW, n.d.
202 "And what if": QR to FW, 5/2/18 (recalling the event while stationed in wartime France).
202 "Ah Fouf": QR to FW, n.d.
202 "The scripture moveth us": QR to KR and BWR, n.d. [June 1917].
202 "We *are* a pretty sordid lot": QR to FW, n.d.
203 Quentin flies over Sagamore: "Personal Glimpses," *Literary Digest*, 8/3/18.
203 "The months you were": QR to FW, 5/18/18 (quoting Edith's letter from memory).
203 Flora takes Quentin to pier: FW to EKR, n.d.

204 "All I do": FW to QR, 7/19/17.
204 "It has gone deeper": FW to EKR, n.d.
204 "His love for you": EKR to FW, 7/28/17.
204 "You and [Quentin]": TR to FW, 7/28/17.
204 "Can it be": FW to QR, 7/31/17.
204 "All I can do": TR to ABR, 7/8/17.
204 "What am I doing": Hagedorn, *Roosevelt Family*, p. 376.

Chapter 9

205 "driven to death": TR to Frank Vanderlip, 6/19/17. Vanderlip Papers.
206 "the horror of having you four": TR to KR, 9/1/17.
206 "Of course we wish": TR to ABR, 10/7/17.
206 "I wish I were over": TR to ABR, 8/8/17.
206 "Well, *that* skirmish": TR to ABR, 8/2/17.
206 Kermit's training experiences: KR to TR, 8/2/17.
207 "I am certainly proud": ABR to ERD, 8/11/17.
207 "odd birds picked up": ABR to ERD, 10/11/17.
208 "It seems that I": KR to TR, 8/12/17.
208 "golden [and] filled with": BWR to KR, 8/18/17.
208 Kermit's wartime experiences: See Kermit Roosevelt, *War in the Garden of Eden* (New York, 1922), p. 6ff.
209 "He has read": KR to BWR, 11/14/17.
209 "noting what is happening": KR to BWR, 11/15/17.
210 "You are lucky": ABR to KR, 11/17/17.
210 "There are no young men": QR to FW, 8/18/17.
210 Eleanor in Paris: See *Day Before Yesterday*, p. 76ff.
211 "whether I was respectable": EAR to Mother, 9/22/17.
211 "You have had a chance": EAR to Mother, 11/26/17.
212 "The poor lad": ABR to KR, 11/7/17.
212 "Sometimes I wonder": QR to FW, 7/29/17.
212 "Suppose we were married": QR to FW, 9/9/17.
213 "what constitutes a gentleman": QR to FW, 10/6/17.
213 "It's a beastly job": QR to FW, 10/31/17.
214 "Sometimes I catch myself": Ibid.
214 "It's always the same": QR to FW, 10/18/17.
214 "no job": QR to FW, 12/18/17.
214 "When you get up": *Quentin Roosevelt: A Sketch with Letters,* ed. Kermit Roosevelt (New York, 1921), p. 89.
215 Eleanor and Quentin in Paris: See *Day Before Yesterday,* p. 80ff.
215 "On the one hand": QR to FW, 12/22/17.
215 "only two daughters": EKR to ABR, 12/30/17.
216 "These last five years": Cited in *Day Before Yesterday,* p. 100.
216 "Remember, if you want": TR to ABR, 12/31/17, *Letters of TR,* vol. 8, p. 1280.
216 "Our national army": TR to ABR, 12/20/17.
216 "They are afraid of me": TR to ABR, 5/23/18.
216 "It is a very unjust world": Hagedorn, *Roosevelt Family,* p. 392.
217 "I am so glad": Robinson, p. 338.
218 "It suddenly came over them": TR to ABR, 2/15/18.
218 "Here I had to stop": TR to ABR, 5/23/18.

218 "and said his prayers": Teague, p. 169.
218 "hadn't a conception": Ward, *First Class,* p. 372.
219 "solemn little Sunday": Felsenthal, p. 137.
219 "You know, Alice": Teague, p. 163.
219 "All I was being asked": Ibid., 162.
219 "The face was particularly": Davis, *Beckoning,* p. 482.
220 "I saw you": Morgan, p. 205.
220 "Remember, I *count*": Cited in Ward, *First Class,* p. 369.
220 "Inasmuch as his cousin": Ibid., p. 346.
220 "Tell the young man": Davis, *Beckoning,* p. 460.
220 "Franklin *deserved*": Lash, p. 309.
221 "It seemed to release": Ward, *First Class,* p. 414.
221 "She inquired if you": Lash, p. 309.
221 "The YMCA women": EAR to Mother, 3/2/18.
221 "only bewilderment": Ibid.
221 "I could not possibly bear": EAR to Mother, 1/5/18.
222 Derby almost killed: For Richard Derby's wartime experiences, see *Wade in Sanitary* (New York, 1923).
222 "There is one consolation": TR Jr. to KR, n.d. [3/18].
222 Archie and the miller's family: ABR Ms.
222 "folded like a fan": QR to FW, 3/2/18.
222 Quentin pulls out three bodies: QR to FW, 5/18/18.
223 "when I've been on my own": QR to FW, n.d. [5/18].
223 "That squadron": QR to FW, 2/11/18.
223 "back from the front": *Quentin Roosevelt,* p. 118.
223 "I feel that I owe": QR to FW, 3/5/17.
223 "slacker member": QR to ERD, 2/1/18.
224 Archie's Croix de Guerre: *New York Times,* 3/12/18.
224 "This glass": TR and ABR, 3/13/18, *Letters of TR,* vol. 8, p. 1301.
224 "He is a gritty devil": Sherrard Billings to TR, 3/21/18.
224 "We need more": Archie's response is reported by Eleanor in a letter to her mother, 3/13/18.
224 "It's rather rough": TR to ABR, 4/28/18.
224 "this iron natured": TR to TR Jr., 3/17/18.
225 "Are you safe?": The anecdote is described in a letter by Eleanor to her mother, 6/4/18.
225 Kermit in battle: For details, see *War in the Garden of Eden.*
226 "Three cheers!": TR to KR, 2/2/18.
226 Kermit demands Turks surrender: *War in the Garden,* p. 122.
226 "of your eagerness": TR to KR, 4/4/18.
226 "He dressed": *War in the Garden,* p. 201.
227 "The woods are showing": Cited in Hagedorn, *Roosevelt Family,* p. 400.
227 Quentin's short stories: The stories are part of the Biddle Papers.
227 "A Boche flew": QR to FW, 5/15/18.
228 *"Il est mort!"*: Quentin's accident is described in a letter by Eleanor to her mother, 4/21/18.
228 "could settle up our row": QR to FW, 5/17/18.
228 Archie "heartbroken": EAR to her mother, 5/2/18.
228 "He was going to telegraph": QR to FW, 5/27/18.
229 "They ought at least": QR to FW, n.d.
229 TR and Henry Whitney: Interview with Flora Biddle.

229 "It seems torment": QR to FW, 6/2/18.
229 "It is wicked": TR to ARC, 7/6/18, *Letters of TR,* vol. 8, p. 1347.
229 last day at Issoudun: QR to FW, 6/18/18. See also S. Morris, p. 420.
230 "that none of us": Ibid.
230 "over here to get killed": QR to FW, 6/23/18.
230 "signs of renewal": QR to FW, 7/1/18.
230 "In case I do": QR to FW, 7/3/18.
230 "We circled": QR to FW, 7/6/18.
231 "I was scared": QR to FW, 7/11/18.
231 "The last of the lion's brood": TR to KR, 7/13/18.
231 "Whatever now befalls": Cited in Gardner, p. 390.
231 Rudyard Kipling wrote: Kipling to KR, n.d. [7/18].
232 German postcard: Interview with John Gable. Along with the postcards, pieces of Quentin's downed plane, taken by soldiers as battlefield souvenirs, also made their way back to Sagamore over the years, and Edith had parts of the fuselage framed and placed in the North Room of Sagamore Hill along with the plane's axle.
232 "Quentin's mother": This statement, which TR composed for the press on the day Quentin's death was made public, can be found in Hagedorn, *Roosevelt Family,* p. 412.
233 Ted wounded: EAR to Mother, 7/18/18.
233 Ted, Eleanor, Archie in Paris: EAR to Mother, 8/13/18.
233 Ted and Kermit march: *Day Before Yesterday,* p. 100ff.
234 Ted and Clemenceau: EAR to Mother, 8/17/18.
234 "Of our four hawks": TR to KR, 9/8/18.
234 "Poor mother": ABR to KR, 10/23/18.
235 "Don't tell a *soul*": Ward, *First Class,* p. 384.
235 FDR's "destroyer costume": *Affectionately,* p. 74.
235 "One of the few men": FDR made the comment to Joseph P. Kennedy. See Michael Bechloss, *Kennedy and Roosevelt* (New York, 1980), p. 230.
235 "looking horribly badly": FDR tells of meeting Archie and Ted and Eleanor at Eleanor's house in Paris in the diary he kept during his inspection trip to Europe. See entry for 8/3/18. The diary is reprinted in *FDR: His Personal Letters,* vol. 2, p. 412.
236 "an awful contrast": Ibid., p. 417.
236 "as close to": Ibid., p. 416.
236 "In order to enter": Ibid., p. 417.
236 "I will never know": Ward, *First Class,* p. 401.
236 "Somehow I don't believe": FDR to ER, 8/20/18, *FDR Letters,* vol. 2, p. 420.
237 the pitiful sight of Frenchmen: KR to BWR, 11/8/18.
238 "What everyone": KR to BWR, 11/11/18.
238 "I am willing to bet": EAR to TR Jr., 11/23/18.
238 "marching beside the Moselle": KR to TR, 1/2/18.
239 "Perhaps if Cornelius": TR to TR Jr. and EAR, 8/29/18.
239 "There is no use": S. Morris, p. 426.
239 annoyed when Ted was held back for promotion: TR to TR Jr., 9/9/18.
239 "I am not in the least": *Crowded Hours,* p. 270.
240 "It is in the nature": Cited in Gardner, p. 402.
240 "My troubles are not": Cited in Gardner, p. 397.
240 "I have kept my promise": Robinson, p. 362. Corinne asked TR if he felt

the same as he had the previous spring when he thought he was dying and said he was glad that it was he and not one of his boys. TR replied, "Yes, just the same way. I wish that I might, like Quentin, have died for my country." Ibid., p. 363.

240 "come forward in public life": TR to TR Jr., 10/27/18.
241 he considered a suit: ABR to TR Jr., n.d. [12/18].
241 "I seem pretty low": See Margaret Chanler, *Roman Spring* (Boston, 1934), p. 202.
241 "Worthy of me?": *Day Before Yesterday*, p. 118.
241 "He is proudest": EAR to TR Jr., n.d. [12/18].
241 "unbelievable historic": TR to TR Jr., 12/7/18.
242 "I'm afraid": KR to BWR, 12/24/18.
242 "the sad, frozen landscape": TR to KR, 12/29/18.
242 "I wonder if": EKR to TR Jr., 1/12/19.
242 "He was very sweet": Ibid.
242 "Dear Kermit": EKR to KR, 1/12/19.
243 "The bottom has dropped": KR to EKR, n.d. [1/19].
243 "I am going": Cited in Gardner, p. 401.

Chapter 10

247 August 10, 1921: The most thorough account of FDR's bout with polio is found in Ward, *First Class*, p. 576ff.
249 "I would rather have": *Letters to His Children*, p. 10.
250 James at Groton: *My Parents*, pp. 60–61.
250 "went for me": Lash, p. 272.
250 "accidents waiting to happen": Interview with James Roosevelt.
250 "allow all [my] interests": *This Is My Story*, p. 300.
251 "Mother did not know": Asbell, p. 19.
251 "Well, now I think": Elliott Roosevelt Oral History, FDRL.
252 "We were fortunate": *My Parents*, p. 29.
252 "I don't know": Ward, *First Class*, p. 586.
253 Same look as Pearl Harbor: Robert D. Graff Papers, FDRL.
254 ER and Clover Adams: See Cook, *Eleanor Roosevelt*, p. 235ff.
254 "had taken from her": Marion Dickerman Oral History, Columbia University Oral History Project.
254 "I've been taught": Lash, p. 332.
254 "Just wait till I": Elliott Roosevelt, *Untold Story*, p. 106.
255 "Whatever are you doing": *My Parents*, p. 44. Coming home from a separate dinner party with her husband, Nick, at about the same time, Alice Longworth was told by police that one of the anarchist's legs had been found up the street and a fragment of his head on the roof of a nearby house (*Crowded Hours*, p. 283).
255 "very much needed": Elliott Roosevelt Oral History.
255 "Are no pictures": Ward, *First Class*, p. 516.
256 "I was flattered": *This Is My Story*, p. 316.
256 who looked uglier: James Roosevelt describes this odd competition in *My Parents*, p. 110.
257 "You are the political": See Morgan, p. 229.
257 "invented the word": Ward, *First Class*, p. 510.
257 "You're just like": Ibid., p. 531.

258 "a murrain": *Crowded Hours*, p. 285.
258 "Think of this week": Cited in Ward, *First Class*, p. 463.
258 "I am very anxious": ABR to KR, 1/14/19.
258 Ted and the American Legion: *Day Before Yesterday*, p. 119.
259 Edith gave christening clothes: *All in the Family*, p. 50.
259 Alice and General Wood: *Crowded Hours*, p. 306–7.
260 "the Democratic Roosevelt": *New York Times*, 8/14/20.
260 "There was not a male": *New York Times*, 8/31/20.
260 "Hit them again": *New York Times*, 9/6/20.
260 "He is a maverick": *New York Times*, 9/9/20.
260 "At least some members": Lash p. 345.
260 "It is a pitiable spectacle": *New York Times*, 10/10/20.
261 "fairy chasers": Elliott Roosevelt, *Untold Story*, p. 128ff.
261 "lovely ladies": *This Is My Story*, p. 319.
261 "He is a well meaning": Davis, *Beckoning*, p. 616.
262 "uproarious" high spirits: Lash, p. 359.
262 "This is my job": *Affectionately*, p. 144.
263 "The atmosphere of the house": Ward, *First Class*, p. 594.
263 The sight of him. Elliott made this comment in an unpublished biography by Dean Smith, hereinafter referred to as the Smith Ms.
265 "Come here, old man!": *Affectionately*, p. 146.
266 "If I ever get caught": *Affectionately*, p. 156.
266 "Who is this little man": Corinne Alsop Oral History, TRC.
267 "I believe that some day": Ward, *First Class*, p. 617.
267 "at the nadir of her existence": Elliott Roosevelt, *Untold Story*, p. 177.
268 Howe as Pygmalion: Howe's tutoring of ER has been commented on by all who have written books about her, including Eleanor herself in *This Is My Story*. For an interesting view of the relationship, see Marion Dickerman Oral History.
268 "He probably cared for me": ER to Lorena Hickok, 11/15/40. Cited by Doris Faber in *The Life of Lorena Hickok, E.R's Friend* (New York, 1980), p. 281.
268 "It made me stand": Lash p. 373.
269 Cook and Dickerman: For the couple's biography and life together, see Marion Dickerman Oral History. Her extensive reminiscences form the basis for Kenneth Davis's *Invincible Summer: An Intimate Portrait of the Roosevelts Based on the Recollections of Marion Dickerman* (New York, 1974).
270 "somewhat toughish": Curtis Dall, *FDR: My Exploited Father in Law* (Washington, D.C., 1970), p. 45.
271 Dickerman on FDR lack of self-pity: *Invincible Summer*, p. 16.
272 "go forward with the Democrats": *New York Times*, 8/7/22.
273 "The water put me": *Affectionately*, p. 162.
273 "There's nothing to worry about": Turnley Walker, *Roosevelt and the Warm Springs Story* (New York, 1953), p. 8.
274 "Nobody put my scarf": Mrs. Richard Bissell Oral History, TRC.

Chapter 11

276 "As I held": ERD to FW, 11/14/22, Biddle Papers.
276 "For so many years": TR Jr. to ERD, 11/15/22.
277 "I will be learning": KR to BWR, 1/5/20.

277 "Try to think": KR to BWR, 11/21/19.
277 "I want the events": See Archibald Roosevelt, "Lest We Forget," *Everybody's Magazine,* 5/19/19.
277 "Well, that's all right": ABR to TR Jr., 11/23/21.
278 Chill between Ted and Corinne: See letter from TR Jr. to EKR, 10/26/21.
278 "lacking in subtlety": Author's interview with Nancy Roosevelt Jackson.
278 "a square deal": *New York Times,* 1/24/20. For insights into Ted's career, see Charles W. Snyder, "An American Original—Theodore Roosevelt, Jr.," in *Theodore Roosevelt—Many-Sided American,* op cit.
278 "When some leaders": *New York Times,* 12/3/20.
279 Mahrer made it clear: *New York Times,* 12/29/20.
279 "We must not fatuously": *New York Times,* 2/28/21.
279 "history repeating itself": *New York Times,* 3/20/21.
280 "Duchess, you're lying down": *Crowded Hours,* p. 322.
280 "I can generally bear up": TR Jr. Diary, 7/23/24, TR Jr. Papers.
281 "soft headed pacifists": *New York Times,* 3/22/22.
281 Academy Yearbook: *New York Times,* 6/16/22.
281 "Twenty five years ago": *New York Times,* 12/31/21.
282 Alice as dancing bear: *Day Before Yesterday,* p. 140.
282 "I have missed her": TR Jr. Diary, 9/26/23.
282 Nick *in flagrante:* Ralph Martin, *Cissy* (New York, 1979), p. 190.
283 "That your bald head": William "Fishbait" Miller, *Fishbait: The Memoirs of a Congressional Doorkeeper* (Englewood Cliffs, N.J., 1977), p. 104.
283 Grace finds a diaphragm: Author's interview with Nancy Roosevelt Jackson.
283 "Occasionally I did not": *Crowded Hours,* p. 300.
284 "I believe these are yours": Martin, *Cissy,* p. 189.
284 "I spoke to Sister": TR Jr. Diary, 5/17/23.
284 "He suggested that": TR Jr. Diary, 1/22/23.
284 "The President is fooling himself" TR Jr. Diary, 2/9/23.
285 "It isn't my idea": TR Jr. Diary, 6/6/23.
285 "national disaster": *New York Times,* 5/27/23.
285 "There was a tendency": TR Jr. Diary, 4/13/23.
285 "progressive Western politicians": *New York Times,* 4/4/23.
285 "In so far": TR Jr. Diary, 8/3/23.
286 "The only way": TR Jr. Diary, 10/4/23.
286 "Americanism never goes": *New York Times,* 11/30/23.
286 "I was surprised": TR Jr. Diary, 9/23/23.
287 "My career is over": *Day Before Yesterday,* p. 148.
287 Ted rejects Archie's request: TR Jr. to ARL, 7/11/24.
287 "I think this": TR Jr. Diary, 10/26/23.
288 "he has got plans": TR Jr. Diary, 2/23/23.
288 "I thought that": ABR Ms.
288 Archie's appearance before Senate: *New York Times,* 1/22/24.
289 "He's leaving to beat up Stevenson": *Day Before Yesterday,* p. 157.
290 "I'm sending you clippings": Ward, *First Class,* p. 684.
290 "The general position": Ibid.
290 "I took the motor boat": FDR to SDR, 2/22/24, *FDR Letters,* vol. 2, p. 543.
291 Missy aboard the *Larooco:* See Ward, *First Class,* p. 711.

291 FDR and Joseph Kennedy: For an overview of relationship, see Peter Collier and David Horowitz, *The Kennedys* (New York, 1984), p. 72ff.
292 "I hope you are well": FDR Jr. to Missy LeHand, 4/23/24.
292 "You need not be proud": ER to FDR, 2/6/24.
293 "But I am reliably": *Affectionately*, p. 55.
293 "You may differ": *New York Times*, 6/8/24.
294 "to outshine his cousin": Frances Perkins Oral History.
294 "He was sitting": Dickerman Oral History.
295 "accepted him as logical": TR Jr. Diary, 6/10/24.
295 "I was absolutely frank": TR Jr. Diary, 7/16/24.
296 "appears to have been revived": *New York Times*, 7/25/24.
296 "equally startling": *New York Times*, 9/23/24.
296 "leave off special efforts": *New York Times*, 9/23/24.
297 "I cannot eliminate": *New York Times*, 10/10/24.
297 "How's the oil": *New York Times*, 10/18/24.
298 "I am one who believes": The anecdote is related in Corinne Alsop and Mr. and Mrs. Sheffield Cowles Oral History, TRC.
298 "kind and compassionate": Dickerman Oral History.
298 Howe enlists Eleanor: Elliott Roosevelt, *Untold Story*, pp. 220–21.
299 "I just hate to see": Cited in Ward, *First Class*, p. 701n.
299 Eleanor would say she was "ashamed": Nearly twenty years later she wrote, "In the thick of political fights, one always feels that all methods of campaigning are honest and fair, but I now think that this was a rough stunt. . . ." (Eleanor Roosevelt, *This I Remember* [New York, 1949], pp. 31–32.)
299 "Wait!": *Day Before Yesterday*, p. 161.
300 "I wonder who": Matthew and Hannah Josephson, *Al Smith: Hero of the Cities* (Boston, 1969), p. 317.

Chapter 12

302 "The Road to Mandalay": Kermit mentions his discussion with Kipling in a letter to TR Jr., 10/3/32.
303 "I had read": Kermit Roosevelt, "The Land Where the Elephants Are," *Scribner's*, 4/24.
304 "No one can be certain": Kermit Roosevelt, "On Soviet Trans Siberia," *Scribner's*, 9/24.
304 "That was grand": KR to ABR, 7/27/22.
304 Kermit was prodding Nick: KR to Nicholas Longworth, 9/5/22.
304 "like all Japanese": ABR to TR Jr., 3/3/23.
305 "He feels that I": TR Jr. Diary, 7/11/24.
305 "When you see him": TR Jr. to ARL, 7/11/24.
305 "Last evening": TR Jr. Diary, 8/27/24.
306 "three partridges flushed": TR Jr. Diary, 4/26/25.
306 "French photographs": TR Jr. Diary, 5/2/25.
307 "the Roosevelt tradition": "The Roosevelts Go A-Hunting," *Literary Digest*, 9/4/25. Ted and Kermit described their trip in the jointly authored *East of the Sun and West of the Moon* (New York, 1926).
307 Eleanor and Belle see husbands: *Day Before Yesterday*, p. 174.
307 "ten points": EAR to Mother, 11/15/25.

308 "The necklace": EAR to Mother, 12/14/25.

308 "All that I wish": EKR to TR Jr., 1/31/26.

308 Warm Springs: For background see Walker, *Roosevelt and the Warm Springs Story;* see also Ward, *First Class,* p. 705ff.

309 "That air!": *Roosevelt and Warm Springs,* p. 22.

309 "No braces at all?": Ibid., p. 25.

310 "The legs are really": FDR to ER, n.d. [10/24], *FDR Letters,* vol. 2, p. 565.

310 "I feel that a great": FDR to SDR, n.d. [10/24] ibid., vol. 2, p. 564.

310 116 out of 208 weeks: Ward, *First Class,* p. 709.

310 "Jimmy says": FDR to Elliott, 5/21/25, *FDR Letters,* vol. 2, p. 581.

311 "Perhaps his great": Cited in James Roosevelt, *Affectionately,* p. 119.

311 FDR changes James's mind: *Affectionately,* p. 121.

311 "the ability to 'relate' ": Boettiger, *A Love in Shadow,* p. 75.

312 "I think you'd better": *Roosevelt and Warm Springs,* p. 63.

313 "We've got to keep them": Ibid., p. 108.

313 "What about": Ibid., p. 94.

313 Crashing the meeting: See *FDR Letters,* vol. 2, p. 610.

313 "I'm cured!": *Affectionately,* p. 192.

314 "It was as if": Author's interview with Donovan La Rue.

314 "Love is a good thing": *Roosevelt and Warm Springs,* p. 136.

314 "What a contrast": Cited in Ward, *First Class,* p. 742.

316 "As a matter of fact": Frances Perkins Oral History.

316 "Why the injured tone": Davis, *Invincible Summer,* p. 59.

317 "everything else depends": *Good Housekeeping,* August 1930.

317 "get some of the foolishness": Cited in Asbell, p. 39.

317 "not only take": *New York Times,* 5/27/27.

317 "Curt, I think": Dall, p. 98.

317 "the intimacies of marriage": Cited in Asbell, p. 41.

317 "to get out": *My Parents,* p. 67.

318 "Too bad": *Affectionately,* p. 125.

318 "Oh, I do wish": FDR to ARC, 6/29/27, *FDR Letters,* vol. 2, p. 625.

319 "In *here,* Leighton": *Roosevelt and Warm Springs,* p. 140.

319 "Don't look at me": Ibid., p. 149.

320 nurse measures muscles: *Roosevelt and Warm Springs,* p. 154.

320 Edsel Ford gift: See Peter Collier and David Horowitz, *The Fords: An American Epic* (New York, 1987), p. 112.

320 FDR able to discard his right-hand cane: *FDR Letters,* vol. 2, p. 642.

320 FDR dictated a letter: See *Roosevelt and Warm Springs,* p. 161.

321 "Well, if I've got to run": Sara Delano Roosevelt, *My Boy Franklin* (New York, 1933), p. 110.

321 "Well, here he is": *My Parents,* p. 125.

321 "No, I am not": *New York Post,* 11/8/28.

322 "Surgeons always remind": Morgan, p. 284.

322 "Oh, that was nothing": *Affectionately,* p. 214.

323 "Both of them": Author's interview with Nancy Roosevelt Jackson.

323 "ladies, or at least": Vincent Astor to KR, 12/19/27.

323 "For the first time": *New York Times,* 10/1/27.

323 "to skip over": *New York Times,* 1/28/28.

324 "To the vast disgust" ABR to ERD, 12/4/28.

324 "Got some information": TR Jr. Diary, 11/18/28.

325 "very large": Theodore Roosevelt, Jr., and Kermit Roosevelt, *Trailing the Giant Panda* (New York, 1929), p. 225.
325 "You are absolutely right": TR Jr. to EAR, 5/22/29.
325 two of the men had died: EAR to ERD, 8/1/29. According to Roosevelt historian John Gable, some forty years later, U.S. soldiers in Vietnam found shacks in the jungle with puzzling signs proclaiming "Theodore Roosevelt hunted here." The signs referred to Ted's trip of 1929.
326 Ted's sickness: *Day Before Yesterday*, p. 217.
326 "Roosevelt is coming": *New York Times*, 6/16/30.
327 "[He] was getting along": EAR to Mother, 11/14/29.
327 "Jimmy is getting": Cited in Morgan, p. 300.
327 "It's hateful!": Elliott Roosevelt, *A Rendezvous with Destiny: The Roosevelts of the White House* (New York, 1975), p. 43.
328 "Archie's mind": TR Jr. to EKR, n.d.
329 "You have always been": ER to CRR, 1/17/29.
329 "We were *awful*": Author's interview with Edith Derby Williams.
329 "She was like a ship": Mrs. Richard Bissel Oral History, TRC.
330 "You thought I'd die": Corinne Alsop and Mr and Mrs Sheffield Cowles, Jr., Oral History, TRC.
330 Conie's old age: Mrs. Ripley Hitchcock Oral History, TRC.
330 "Well, as far as": TR Jr. to EKR, 11/9/30.
331 Ted gets the Treasury to put up $100,000: *Day Before Yesterday*, p. 250.
331 "She has evidently": TR Jr. to EAR, 12/10/31.
331 "I believe that": TR Jr. to EAR, 11/19/31.
331 "He had pictures": TR Jr. to EKR, 2/22/32.
332 "a Governor General": Cited in *Day Before Yesterday*, p. 278.
332 "I have been": TR Jr. to EKR, 3/28/32.
332 "To nominate him": TR Jr. to EAR, 12/2/32.
333 "Men who have had": *New York Times*, 8/26/32.
333 "Providence does not": Morgan, p. 325.
333 "couldn't live": See Davis, *Invincible Summer*, pp. 107–8.
333 "I resisted": TR Jr. to EKR, 8/26/32.
334 "a man who has shown": Cited in *Day Before Yesterday*, p. 299.
334 "widow's weeds": Author's interview with Edith Derby Williams.
334 "I helped him": EKR to CRR, n.d.
334 Edith supports Hoover: See S. Morris, p. 476ff.
334 "I have a distinctly": TR Jr. to EKR, 9/24/32.
334 "I believe that": TR Jr. to EKR, 9/19/32.
335 "These last few years": TR Jr. to EKR, 10/14/32.
335 "I can say": KR to FDR, 1/12/33, FDRL.
335 "Personally I would rather": KR to TR Jr., 1/33/33. Kermit, it should be noted, compounded his "disloyalty" by showing up at the FDR victory celebration at the Biltmore on election night, 1932.
336 "I do not remember": Memorandum by EAR in Theodore Roosevelt, Jr., Papers.
336 "Rift between": *New York Times*, 1/25/33.
336 "Because his mother": *Day Before Yesterday*, p. 301.
336 "Tony, keep quiet": Morgan, p. 369.
336 "I was shocked": TR Jr. to EKR, 2/16/33.

337 "Sister was here": EKR to TR Jr., 3/8/33.
337 "Well, Eleanor": Felsenthal, p. 180.
337 "Fifth cousin": *Day Before Yesterday,* p. 304. Ted actually *was* a fifth cousin, once removed, so the comment is doubly witty.
338 ER and Charles Scribner: ER to CRR, 9/23/33.
338 Ted and FDR Jr. on *Manhattan: New York Times,* 9/8/33.

Chapter 13

345 "After the President": *Time,* 10/8/45.
345 "I have none": Elliott Roosevelt, *Rendezvous,* p. 196.
345 "had polio": Felsenthal, p. 171.
346 "doing very well": Elliott Roosevelt, *Rendezvous,* p. 153.
348 "Dishonorable Franklin": Elliott Roosevelt, *Mother R* (New York, 1977), p. 53.
349 "like a St. Bernard": Martha Gellhorn Oral History, FDRL.
349 "I realize more": ER to Lorena Hickok, 10/16/36, cited in Faber, p. 221.
350 "What good": Lillian Rogers Parks, *The Roosevelts: A Family in Turmoil* (Englewood Cliffs, N.J., 1981), p. 156.
350 "Betsey just thinks": Asbell, p. 99. Anna also told Bernard Asbell that Eleanor would become upset when Betsey set up FDR's menu. But this reaction, part of a pattern of jealousy, had nothing to do with emotion. It was rather what a later age would call a turf struggle: "She had no feeling personally about—this had nothing to do with Father. But this was her *position.*" (Ibid.)
351 "Good!": Ward, *First Class,* p. 3.
351 "devotion in all classes": *Affectionately,* p. 302.
352 "Infidelity": Lash, p. 568.
352 "a spoil sport": ER to Anna, 11/19/34.
352 it might upset Missy: Asbell, p. 54.
352 a new community called Arthurdale: For details see *This I Remember,* p. 127ff; also Lash, p. 527ff.
353 "My missus": Harold Ickes, *The Secret Diary of Harold Ickes* (New York, 1954), vol. 2, p. 219. FDR's final word on Arthurdale was ambivalent: "These projects represent something new, and because we in America had little or no experience along these lines, there were some failures. . . ." (Elliott Roosevelt, *Rendezvous,* p. 85.)
354 "It was good": Eleanor Roosevelt, *My Day: Her Acclaimed Columns, 1936–45,* ed. Martha Gellhorn (New York, 1989), p. 95.
355 "ugly and boring": Martha Gellhorn Oral History.
355 Hickok background: See Faber, p. 40ff.
355 "That woman": Ibid., p. 85.
356 "I couldn't say": ER to LH, 3/6/33. Cited in Faber, p. 121.
356 "It won't help you": ER to LH, 1/19/38. Cited in Faber, p. 238.
356 "I think you will": ER to LH, 6/28/34. Cited in Faber, p. 170.
356 "Of course": ER to LH, 2/1/35. Cited in Faber, p. 186.
356 Howe suggested ER presidency: Faber, p. 281.
357 "I've just lost": James Halsted Oral History, FDRL; see also Lash, *Eleanor and Franklin,* p. 661.
358 Archie Jr. wrestled to the floor: *Time,* 2/19/40.
358 "I'm not too happy": Author's interview with Archibald Roosevelt Jr.

358 FDR and AYC: For background see Lash, p. 776ff.
358 "I disliked the regimentation": Elliott Roosevelt, *Rendezvous*, p. 250.
358 "How *dare* you": Lash, p. 786. In *Rendezvous* (p. 252), Elliott says that it was his mother and not her secretary who made the response to the students. He also says that while ER paid lip service to independence for Finland, she still had doubts: "She was confused in her own mind about what deserved priority in the United States. . . . The Finns were worthy of financial aid as victims of aggression, but she couldn't rid herself of the suspicion that these youthful objectors might be partially correct in their views about the imperialistic nature of the war" (p. 251).
359 "Many of them": ER to Anna, 2/21/40.
359 "Can't this bill": Mr. and Mrs. William Sheffield Cowles Oral History.
359 "Well, Eleanor": See Asbell, p. 136.
359 "Eleanor, so humorless and weighed down": Asbell, p. 76.
360 "And despite her global milling": The poem, entitled "The Lady of Eleanor," is quoted by Morgan, p. 676.
360 "the damage": Elliott Roosevelt, *Rendezvous*, p. 248.
361 At Harvard, John: *Newsweek*, 3/9/35.
361 "the psychology of making": Morgan, p. 455.
362 "happy, delightful": Dickerman Oral History.
362 Dickerman reprimands FDR Jr.: Ibid.
362 "He's a good egg": *Newsweek*, 11/21/37.
363 "have to rely on Pa": Author's interview with James Roosevelt.
363 FDR Jr.'s female houseguests: Parks, *A Family in Turmoil*, p. 149.
363 Ethel distracted: Ibid.
363 "As soon as": Author's interview with Elliott Roosevelt.
363 "tall, blonde, and graceful": Smith Ms.
363 "*no* affinity": Anna Seagraves Oral History, FDRL.
363 "You certainly know": Dall, p. 49.
364 "Pa seems to": Cited in Asbell, p. 51.
364 Anna ties Buzzie's hands: Boettiger, *Shadow*, p. 53.
365 "It's time Sis": Seagraves Oral History.
365 "A great number of people": Dickerman Oral History.
365 Jimmy and Joe Kennedy: See Collier and Horowitz, *The Kennedys*, pp. 74–75.
365 Jimmy reveals tax returns: Walter Davenport, "I'm So Glad You Asked," *Collier's*, 8/20 and 8/27/38.
366 "Just to be able": *Affectionately*, p. 308.
366 Jimmy goes to William Douglas: William O. Douglas, *Go East, Young Man* (New York, 1974), pp. 301–2.
367 "He said early on": Interview with Richard Simon.
367 Elliott in Wyoming: The details of the trip come from the Smith Ms.
368 "I have never enjoyed": Elliott to FDR, 8/26/26, FDRL.
368 "patting him on the back": *Affectionately*, p. 89.
368 "a fierce player": Ibid., p. 90.
368 Chinese tattoo parlor: Elliott's adventures in the summer of 1928 are related in the Smith MS.
369 "Do you think": Elliott to FDR and ER, n.d. Cited in *Affectionately*, p. 183.
370 "I hope in the future": Elliott to FDR, n.d. [5/29].
370 Elliott and FDR in Paris: *Affectionately*, p. 220.

370 Elliott and Jane Wyatt: Smith Ms.
371 "I saw my life": Author's interview with Elliott Roosevelt.
371 He told Betty: Parks, *A Family in Turmoil*, p. 142.
371 "How are you, Bunny?": There are various versions of Elliott's trip. This
     one comes from the Smith Ms. See also *Rendezvous*, p. 37ff.
372 Elliott in Fort Worth: Ibid.
372 "I was vaguely aware": Elliott Roosevelt, *Rendezvous*, p. 39.
372 "Gosh, but this": Elliott to ER, 3/13/33.
374 Elliott and the *Nourmahal: Affectionately*, p. 280.
374 Elliott and Fokker: *Time*, 10/19/36.
375 "my three oilmen": Smith Ms.
375 "Elliott says Granny": ER to Anna, 11/15/37.
376 Eleanor dictating a memo: Parks, *A Family in Turmoil*, p. 142.
376 "All I ever wanted": Author's interview with Patricia Peabody Roosevelt.
376 "Couldn't you or James": *Affectionately,"* p. 266.
376 Elliott might take his own life: *My Parents*, p. 222.
376 "Mr. Elliott Roosevelt": Steve Early to Walter Kramer, 10/29/39, FDRL.
377 Jesse Jones and John Hartford: *Time*, 10/8/45.
377 "It was clear": Author's interview with Elliott Roosevelt.
377 "To Elliott": Smith Ms.

Chapter 14

378 "Your cousin": TR Jr. to Cornelius, 10/1/40.
378 *"We* don't do": Author's interview with Archibald Roosevelt, Jr.
379 Alice shocked the family: Author's interview with Nancy Roosevelt
     Jackson.
379 "that he seemed to dance": Author's interview with Henry Milton.
379 he always brought them some gift: Interview with Edith Derby Williams.
379 a thumb amputated: Kermit discusses the problems with the graft in his
     Diary, 1/12/21.
379 "Things like that": Cornelius to Quentin [II], 1/9/44.
379 using Belle's inheritance: BWR to Nancy Thayer, n.d. [1950].
380 "As you probably know": KR to Eliz Herbert, 4/8/32.
380 "Don't speak": KR to Willard, 5/24/32.
380 income tax: Kermit's tax data for these years can be found in the Kermit
     Roosevelt Papers.
380 "At the time": KR to Marcus Conrad, 5/7/34.
380 Belle's bracelet: BWR Diary, 2/20/40.
381 "He didn't fit": Author's interview with Goodhue Livingston.
381 "My father always": Author's interview with Willard Roosevelt.
381 Kermit and Admiral Byrd: Author's interview with Goodhue Livingston.
382 "James would certainly": Author's interview with Carla Peters.
382 "If I can't sleep: Ibid.
382 Swiss sanatorium: The episode is alluded to in a letter from TR Jr. to Edith,
     3/24/37.
382 "Oh no": Author's interview with Carla Peters.
382 "I hope you won't": Ibid.
383 "Groton disappoints": Dirck to KR and BWR, n.d. [9/37].
383 "Groton disappoints me still more": Dirck to KR and BWR, n.d. [10/37].
383 "Kehoe returned the blow": *New York Times*, 4/17/38.

384 "Once I get out": KR to Dirck, 6/4/38.
384 he wrote again: KR to Dirck, 6/22/38.
384 "If I don't": Dirck to Catherine Beyer, n.d.
384 "If I am not; Dirck to BWR and KR, n.d.
384 "Why can't you": Author's interview with Carla Peters.
384 "Grandmother knew": Author's interview with Nancy Roosevelt Jackson.
385 "Alfred is just": Ibid.
385 "Franklin is quite right": Ibid.
385 "The most difficult": BWR to KR, 11/4/38.
385 "We who love Kermit": BWR to Richard Derby, n.d. [11/38].
386 "I don't know": TR Jr. to BWR, 11/8/38.
386 to urge a "war": KR to FDR, 12/30/33.
386 "and he told me": TR Jr. to EKR, n.d. [1933].
386 "Our liberties": *New York Times*, 7/11/34.
387 "making false promises": *New York Times*, 2/13/35.
387 "to leave a stench": *New York Times*, 3/24/35.
387 "morally and spiritually": New York *Times*, 4/17/35.
387 "You have been": *New York Times*, 9/15/35.
387 "Where once [liberalism]": George Creel, *Rebel at Large* (New York, 1947),
     p. 371.
387 "reform under the Constitution": *New York Times*, 10/26/37.
388 "Alice, why don't you": Marion Dickerman Oral History.
388 "I could not help": TR Jr. to EKR, n.d. [1935].
388 "It seems to me": ER to Corinne Alsop, 11/11/36.
388 Ted mentioned for governor: *New York Times*, 5/25/36.
388 Ted and Borah: *New York Times*, 10/10/36.
389 Archie's family life: Author's interviews with Archibald Roosevelt, Jr.,
     Nancy Roosevelt Jackson, and Theodora Roosevelt Rauschfuss.
389 Theodora in Rio: Sumner Welles to ER, 9/28/42, FDRL.
390 "Do you think": Author's interview with Polly Roosevelt.
390 Archie Jr. feeling the presence of TR: Archibald Roosevelt, Jr., *For Lust of
     Knowing: Memoirs of an Intelligence Officer* (New York, 1988), p. 7.
390 "As far as he is concerned": EKR to KR, 7/19/36.
391 "I am the only one": TR Jr. to ABR, draft, n.d., Theodore Roosevelt, Jr.,
     Papers.
391 "It looked like a museum": Interview with Howard Nichols.
392 "I have seen war": For FDR's diplomatic maneuvering during this period,
     see James MacGregor Burns, *Roosevelt: The Lion and the Fox* (New York,
     1956, paper), p. 393ff.
392 "Bodies in the street": *Vital Speeches*, 9/3/37.
393 "Our frontiers": *New York Times*, 2/19/39.
393 "The only thing worth": *Vital Speeches*, 8/1/39.
393 "the history of one family": See Theodore Roosevelt, Jr., *Colonial Policies
     of the United States* (New York, 1937), Introduction, p. viii.
393 "I can remember": TR Jr. to Alexander Woollcott, 3/3/41.
393 "I am doing": TR Jr. to Cornelius, 6/29/39.
394 "Like you": TR Jr. to ARL, 9/1/39.
394 "I'd rather vote": Felsenthal, p. 194.
394 "I don't ever want": Ibid., p. 195.
394 "We are working": TR Jr. to Cornelius, 1/20/41.
395 "It's interesting that he": KR to TR Jr., 3/15/39.

395 "Looking at it": KR to TR Jr., 4/14/39.
395 Kermit in England: BWR Diary, entries for spring 1940.
395 "reminiscent of [the] sparkling quality": Ibid., 3/5/40.
395 Churchill and TR: Ibid.
396 Kermit at Buckingham Palace: Ibid., 3/20/40.
396 Kermit watched dive bombers: KR to ERD, 10/16/40.
396 "amazing feats": BWR to Becyan Joy, 1/9/46.
396 "I certainly never": KR to TR Jr., n.d.
397 "Wish absolutely": KR cable, 6/23/40.
397 "shaking like a leaf": BWR to Eliz Herbert, 6/28/41.
397 "I understand": ER to BWR, n.d.
397 "Remind the President": ER to Watson, 7/15/41, FDRL.
397 Vincent Astor and J. Edgar Hoover: See Kermit Roosevelt file, obtained
    from FBI under Freedom of Information Act.
398 "You go!": Author's interview with Carla Peters.
398 "His liver": Kermit Roosevelt FBI file.
398 "[The agent] stated": Ibid.
398 Kermit and Archie: Author's interview with Carla Peters.
399 "I found that": TR Jr. to ABR Jr., 4/9/41.
399 "Ted is very well": EAR to Alexander Woollcott, n.d. [10/41].
399 "emotional homecoming": Interview with Archibald Roosevelt, Jr.

Chapter 15

400 "Well, friends": Felsenthal p. 202.
400 Jimmy asked her apprehensively: Lash, p. 798.
401 "a positive horror": FDR to John Boettiger, 3/3/41.
401 "It will do something": TR Jr. to EKR, 12/15/41.
401 "I couldn't feel": ER to Anna, 9/10/41.
402 "Suppose we collected": Cited in Morgan, p. 674. FDR's witty response
    was to tell Eleanor that her correspondent had "a bee in his bonnet."
402 "Well, you're not": Boettiger, A Love in Shadow, p. 238.
403 "A real old Tory": Elliott Roosevelt, As He Saw It (New York, 1946),
    p. 38.
403 "The Chinese are killing": Ibid., p. 54.
403 Elliott crash-lands: Smith Ms.
404 "And I'm going up": As He Saw It, p. 82.
404 "General de Gaulle": FDR to John, 2/13/43.
406 Flora and Quentin: The prayer is discussed in a letter from Quentin to
    Flora, now Flora Miller, 12/27/41.
406 Ted's family at Ponte Vedra: Day Before Yesterday, p. 422.
406 Quentin profiled: Life, 1/8/40.
406 "Q. thinks": TR Jr. to EAR, 11/5/42.
406 Ted kills a man: TR Jr. to EAR, 11/11/42.
406 "War is an abomination": Kenneth Davis, "The Untold Story About Gen-
    eral Ted" (privately printed pamphlet, 1976), p. 4.
407 "as if he were": TR Jr. to EAR, 2/24/43.
407 "Father would be very": TR Jr. to EAR, 3/1/43.
407 "Do you realize": TR Jr. to EAR, 6/5/43.
407 a single white feather: Author's interview with Carla Peters.
408 "mentally and morally": ABR to FDR, 1/3/42.

408 Watson told him: Watson to FDR, 1/20/42.
408 Archie at Christmas Island: ABR Ms.
408 Archie and MacArthur: Ibid.
409 "I have been trying": ABR to EKR, 4/23/42.
409 "ups and downs": ERD to ABR, 1/2/44.
409 note of apology: ABR to EKR, 7/29/43.
409 Archie explored the jungle: ABR to ERD, 1/20/44.
409 swarms of huge bats: ABR to EKR, 4/2/43.
409 "exhausted by problems": ABR to Grace, 7/29/43.
409 "All of us look": ABR to TR Jr., 2/12/44.
409 "I can't help thinking": ABR to TR Jr., 10/15/43.
410 "While Colonel Roosevelt": AP dispatch, 9/14/43.
410 "I know he's worthless": Watson to J. E. Hoover, 9/9/41; J. E. Hoover to Watson, 9/11/41; Kermit Roosevelt FBI file.
411 "excited and delighted": BWR Diary, 7/15/42.
411 "Because of her infantile": Ibid., n.d.
412 "I heard about Kermit's": ABR to Grace, 4/23/43.
412 Kermit and Peters: Author's interview with Carla Peters.
412 "I seem to feel": EKR to KR, 5/9/43.
413 "due to despondence": telegram to J. Edgar Hoover, 6/6/43, Kermit Roosevelt FBI file.
413 "If feelings": Author's interview with Carla Peters.
413 "I know it is": ABR to EKR, 6/14/43.
414 Jimmy booed in Chicago: *My Parents*, p. 65.
414 "They won't let": BWR Diary, 6/9/42.
414 FDR Jr.'s bravery: Described by journalist Quentin Reynolds, on the scene for *Collier's*, in a letter to ER, 9/29/43, FDRL.
414 "Don't worry": Author's interview with Ruth Chandler Roosevelt Lindsley.
415 "Fundamentally": ER to Anna, 8/1/42.
415 Hughes and Elliott: Charles Higham, *Howard Hughes* (New York, 1993).
415 "Jane, show Elliott": Smith Ms.
416 "Somebody told me": Elliott to ER, 5/29/43.
416 "Any such attitude": *As He Saw It*, p. 188ff.
417 "It takes my breath": ER to Anna, 3/19/44.
417 "a little man": Belle related the conversation and her comment about Ted in a letter to John Winant, n.d.
418 "with the large facility": A. J. Liebling, "Letter from France," *The New Yorker*, 7/29/44.
418 "On the boat from": Memorandum by Clark Lee, International News Service reporter, Theodore Roosevelt, Jr., Papers.
418 Ted and Quentin censored: The charge is made by Ted's wife, Eleanor, in *Day Before Yesterday*.
418 Ted versus Patton: Ted related the foxhole incident in a letter to Eleanor, 10/14/43.
419 "I don't think": TR Jr. to EAR, 11/30/43.
419 Ted's plan with Stilwell: TR Jr. to EAR, n.d.
419 "I'm just back": Cited in *Day Before Yesterday*, p. 448.
419 "in a bad way": TR Jr. to EAR, 12/14/43.
419 "I know one": TR Jr. to EAR, 12/12/43.
420 "She is 26": TR Jr. to EAR, 3/19/44.

420 She detected a peculiar coldness: EAR to TR Jr., 4/8/44.

420 "I feel like": ABR to EKR, 3/8/44.

420 "I don't know enough": ABR to TR Jr., 5/10/44.

421 "I wish Archie": TR Jr. to EKR, n.d. [1944].

421 "Let's hope God": TR Jr. to EAR, 5/28/44.

421 "I asked you over": Davis, "The Untold Story About General Ted," op cit.

422 Ted's request to Eisenhower: *Time,* 7/24/44.

422 "We are starting": TR Jr. to EAR, 6/5/44.

423 French women scatter rose petals: TR Jr. to EAR, 6/26/44.

423 Ted sent in his men to kill them: TR Jr. to EAR, 6/27/44.

423 "I was a pretty sick": TR Jr. to EAR, 7/11/44.

424 "The old lion is dead": *Day Before Yesterday,* p. 457.

424 "a dilettante soldier": Liebling, "Letter from France."

424 "We have all": ABR to EKR, 7/15/44.

424 "You were the first": S. Morris, p. 511.

424 Stimson meeting: F. Trubee Davison Oral History.

426 "She was right": BWR Diary, 6/8/44.

426 "Well, what did you": *As He Saw It,* p. 220.

426 "I will have flown": Elliott to ER, 3/25/44.

427 "What a shocking": ABR to EKR, 1/15/45.

427 "I pray I don't": Boettiger, *A Love in Shadow,* p. 254.

427 "Now Franklin": Asbell, p. 177.

428 "unless he were rescued": Ibid., p. 184.

428 "Over there": Boettiger, *A Love in Shadow,* p. 256.

429 "Vice President Wallace": ABR to Jean Roosevelt, 6/9/44.

429 "desperately unhappy": Grace Roosevelt to FDR, n.d. [9/44].

429 "I have put the case": Watson to FDR, 10/24/44.

430 "I am quite sure": FDR to Grace Roosevelt, 11/27/44.

430 "Since you have taken": ABR to FDR, 3/25/45.

430 "an awfully nice fellow": FDR to General George Marshall, 4/5/45. Also, Marshall to FDR, 4/9/45, FDRL.

431 "He said you had been": The letter is printed in its entirety in Asbell, p. 188.

Chapter 16

432 "Boy, am I": *Mother R,* p. 31.

433 "I should have tried": Ibid., p. 37.

433 "The story is over now": Joseph Lash, *Eleanor: The Years Alone* (New York, 1972), p. 15.

434 "In the sense": Ibid., p. 174.

436 "I still feel": Anna to FDR Jr., 5/20/48.

436 Elliott and Israeli air force: Smith Ms.

437 "about what we could do": Elliott to ER, 3/2/45.

437 "Elliott had": Interview with John Thorne.

437 "Elliott and Faye": ER to Anna, 8/25/45.

438 "Would you consider": *Mother R,* p. 55.

438 "If Elliott were not": ER to Henry Morgenthau, 3/2/51.

438 Elliott and Val-Kill: Author's interview with Jim Brown of National Park Service at Hyde Park.

439 "the original Christmas trees": *The New Yorker,* 12/28/48.
440 Anna immediately wrote asking querulously: Anna to Elliott, 7/27/47.
440 Elliott replied: Elliott to Anna, 7/29/47.
440 "critical and almost hostile": ER to Anna, 7/28/47.
440 Elliott highlighted FDR's differences with Churchill: *As He Saw It,* Introduction, p. xiii.
440 "the current communist line": See Arthur Schlesinger, "Two Years Later," *Life,* 4/4/47.
441 "Few people could": Cited in Smith Ms.
441 "quite horrified": Ibid.
441 information secretly supplied by FDR Jr.: Lash, *Years Alone,* p. 91.
442 Soviet request to examine FDR's body: Ibid.
442 "and I needed": Ibid.
442 "The Russians": See *Time,* 12/9/46.
443 "Here I am": Cited in Lash, *Years Alone,* p. 150.
443 "Mr. Vishinsky": *Mother R,* p. 80.
443 "No matter how much": Lash, *Years Alone,* p. 84.
443 "peculiarly fitted": ER to Henry Wallace, 4/17/45.
444 "nearly always obstructionist": Lash, *Years Alone,* p. 99.
444 "a garrulous, feeble": *Mother R,* p. 109.
445 Dirck arrested in Spain: *New York Times,* 7/3/51.
445 "You know": Author's interview with Edith Derby Roosevelt.
446 "trying to look mysterious": Author's interview with Archibald Roosevelt, Jr.
446 "Owen Lattimore": Ibid.
447 "[The intelligence officer]": *Lust for Knowing,* p. 430.
447 Kim and CIA: Author's interview with Kermit Roosevelt, Jr. See also Kermit Roosevelt, Jr., *Counter Coup* (New York, 1979).
448 Kim versus Philby: *Counter Coup,* p. 109.
448 "a courteous, soft spoken": Ibid., p. 110.
449 "If I had been": Ibid., p. 207.
450 Chinese communists accused of killing Quentin: Author's interview with Frances Webb Roosevelt.
451 [She] is a very ambitious": Elliott to Anna, 10/21/49.
451 "watching Sammie run": John to Anna, 10/1/49.
451 "I want you to agree": Cited in *Mother R,* p. 114.
451 She even threatened to resign: Lash, *Years Alone,* p. 178.
452 "cloud" over annual summer visit: James Roosevelt, Jr., Oral History, FDRL.
453 "Mother would like to knit us": Elliott to Anna, 10/21/49.
453 "a poor excuse": Smith MS.
453 Elliott hires private eye: Ibid.
453 "None of you children": *Mother R,* p. 169.
454 "I have thought": Boettiger, *A Love in Shadow,* p. 119.
454 Boettiger's suicide: *Mother R,* p. 173. Eleanor continued to feel guilty, writing, "Is there nothing I might have done to help poor John? What dreadful things can happen when people *fail* each other. I did try to offer him friendship, but what good did it do?" (Asbell, p. 273.)
454 ER and psychiatrist: Lash, *Years Alone,* pp. 182–83.
456 "I was appalled": Cited in Smith Ms.
456 "We have our 12": ER to Anna, 10/21/50.

456 "bringing Mother's voice": FDR Jr. to Anna, 3/6/51.
457 Elliott courts Minnewa: Author's interview with Rex Ross, son of Minnewa Bell by her first marriage.
458 ER badgers Anne: Nina Roosevelt Gibson Oral History, FDRL.
458 "You just don't know": *Mother R,* p. 200.
458 "She did not think: Minnewa Bell Oral History, FDRL.
458 Elliott had sold a tea set: Author's interview with Haven Roosevelt.
459 Val-Kill holidays: John Boettiger, Jr., Oral History, FDRL.
459 "She was terribly disappointed": Author's interview with Maureen Corr.
459 "disturbed, angry": *Mother R,* p. 202.
459 ER excludes Elliott as executor: Author's interview with James Roosevelt.
459 Elliott and ER never close again: Smith Ms.
460 "The trash man": Felsenthal, p. 231.
460 Jimmy admits affairs: *Newsweek* 4/12/54; *Time,* 5/31/54.
461 "Your obsession": Halsted to James Roosevelt, 3/15/54.
461 "the only thing": James Roosevelt to Halsted, 3/16/54.
461 "He has embedded": *Mother R,* p. 223.
462 "F Jr. was defeated": Lash, *Years Alone,* p. 274.
462 "Don't make a fool': *My Parents,* p. 335.
462 "They did heavy partying": Author's interview with Rex Ross.
463 "He was just": Minnewa Bell Oral History.
463 "Oh, we're doing": Ibid.
463 Elliott's financial problems: Author's interview with Rex Ross.
464 John as entrepreneur: Author's interview with Haven Roosevelt.
464 Payoff from Jimmy Hoffa: In the Smith Ms Elliott says: "John's wife Anne, who was a Boston aristocrat and an avid Republican, had been badgering him to switch parties for years. But it was not until Jimmy Hoffa offered to get him a position with Bache that John buckled under and became a Republican. Hoffa promised him control of a large part of the Teamsters' portfolio to assure his defection."
464 "I've finally done it": Smith Ms.
464 "[He and his brothers]": Minnewa Bell Oral History.
464 "My mother spent": Author's interview with Rex Ross. Ross confirms that Elliott tried for a conservatorship, a charge suggested by Minnewa in her Oral History.
465 "Get the hell out": Author's interview with Patricia Peabody Roosevelt.
465 "There is nothing": *Mother R,* p. 266.
466 "I can see why Eleanor": Author's interview with Patricia Peabody Roosevelt.
466 "I don't remember": The account of this dinner at Eleanor's apartment comes from an author's interview with Patricia Peabody Roosevelt. See also Smith Ms.
466 "Grand-mère!": Nina Roosevelt Gibson Oral History.
466 Eleanor takes off her glasses: Author's interview with Robert Traugott.
467 Eleanor in old age: See Lash, *Years Alone,* p. 302ff; see also Eleanor Seagraves Oral History and Nina Roosevelt Gibson Oral History.
467 "Mr. McNamara": Author's interview with Justin Feldman.
467 ER drives and swims: Nina Roosevelt Gibson Oral History.
467 ER's visit to California: James Roosevelt, Jr., Oral History.
468 ER clothes Chandler and Tony: Author's interview with Ruth Chandler Lindsley and Elliott ("Tony") Roosevelt, Jr.

468 ER puts together dinner for Haven: Author's interview with Haven Roosevelt.
468 ER and FDR III: Franklin D. Roosevelt III Oral History, FDRL.
468 Sistie dragged off: Eleanor Seagraves Oral History.
468 ER and John Boettiger, Jr.: John Boettiger, Jr., Oral History.
469 ER burns herself: Nina Roosevelt Gibson Oral History.
469 ER asks clergyman: Ward, *Before the Trumpet*, p. 287; also, author's interview with Geoffrey Ward.
469 illness dismissed as bad flu: *Mother R*, p. 274.
470 "No, David": Author's interview with Maureen Corr.
470 "All I want": *Mother R*, p. 273.
470 "I do not want": James Halsted Oral History.

Epilogue

471 Kermit's hunting rifles: Author's interview with Carla Peters.
472 Ethel and Theodore Roosevelt Association: Author's interview with John Gable.
473 "There is only one way": See memorandum dated 7/6/57 in Archibald Roosevelt FBI file, obtained under provisions of the Freedom of Information Act.
473 "For years": Memorandum by William Frippinger, TRC.
473 "I realize how little": ABR Ms.
473 "soft on communism": Interview with Archibald Roosevelt, Jr.
474 "Mr. Rockefeller": Ibid.
474 "I worked hard": *For Lust of Knowing*, p. 14.
474 Paulina dies: According to her niece Nancy Roosevelt Jackson, Paulina's unhappiness was accented by Alice's decision to tell her that she was illegitimate.
475 "I look like": Teague, p. xv.
475 "Do let me know": Ibid., p. vii.
476 Alice sticks out tongue: Felsenthal, p. 267.
476 Quarrel at ER's funeral: Author's interview with Patricia Peabody Roosevelt.
476 "Methods of achieving": FDR Jr. memo, 6/21/64, FDRL.
476 "[He] appointed himself": Smith Ms.
476 "there was no trace": *Mother R*, p. 279.
479 "geriatric terrorism": See Crocker Coulson, "Geezer Sleaze," *The New Republic*, 4/20/87.
479 Elliott's jobs: the Smith Ms details the jobs Elliott had in the years after Eleanor's death.
479 Elliott in Portugal: Smith Ms.
480 "He finally made it": Author's interview with Patricia Peabody Roosevelt.
480 "Don't you recognize me?": Ibid.
480 "I want to go home": Ibid.
480 "I'll never forgive": Smith Ms.
482 "It was remarkable": Author's interview with confidential source.

INDEX

ABOUT THE AUTHOR

Peter Collier is the author, along with David Horowitz, of *The Rockefellers: An American Dynasty, The Kennedys: An American Dream, The Fords: An American Epic,* and *Destructive Generation: Second Thoughts About the Sixties.* He also wrote *Downriver: A Novel* and *The Fondas: A Hollywood Dynasty.* He lives in Nevada City, California.